Ch. 9, 10

1040 EZ

N JOURNAL • MULTICOLUMN JOURNAL • MULTICOLUMN JOURNAL • MULTICOLUMN JOURNAL

Century 21

SOUTH-WESTERN

Accounting 8E

INTRODUCTORY COURSE

CLAUDIA BIENIAS GILBERTSON, CPA
Teaching Professor
North Hennepin Community College
Brooklyn Park, Minnesota

MARK W. LEHMAN, CPA
Associate Professor
School of Accountancy
Mississippi State University
Starkville, Mississippi

KENTON E. ROSS, CPA
Professor Emeritus of Accounting
Texas A&M University—Commerce
Commerce, Texas

THOMSON
SOUTH-WESTERN

Australia · Canada · Mexico · Singapore · Spain · United Kingdom · United States

Multicolumn Journal, Introductory Course, Century 21 Accounting 8E
Claudia Bienias Gilbertson, CPA; Mark W. Lehman, CPA; Kenton E. Ross, CPA

VP/Editorial Director:
Jack W. Calhoun

VP/Editor-in-Chief:
Karen Schmohe

Acquisitions Editor:
Marilyn Hornsby

Project Manager:
Carol Sturzenberger

Consulting Editor:
Bill Lee

Verification Editors:
Howard Rankin; Sara Wilson

Editorial Assistant:
Kelly Resch

VP/Director of Marketing:
Carol Volz

Marketing Manager:
Courtney Schulz

Marketing Coordinator:
Angela Russo

Senior Promotions Manager:
Terron Sanders

Production Editor:
Kim Kusnerak

Production Manager:
Patricia Matthews Boies

Manufacturing Buyer:
Kevin Kluck

Manager of Technology-Editorial:
Liz Prigge

Technology Project Editor:
Mike Jackson

Web Coordinator:
Ed Stubenrauch

Art Director:
Tippy McIntosh

Photography/Permissions Editor:
Darren Wright

Production House:
Lachina Publishing Services

Cover/Internal Design:
Ann Small, a small design studio

Cover Illustration:
Philip Brooker

Internal Illustration:
Mark Shaver, The Wiley Group

Printer:
RR Donnelley & Sons
Willard, OH

Printed in the United States of America
3 4 5 6 7 8 9 10
08 07

Text ISBN-13: 978-0-538-97417-2
Text ISBN-10: 0-538-97417-6
Data CD ISBN-13: 978-0-538-97416-5
Data CD ISBN-10: 0-538-97416-8
Package ISBN-13: 978-0-538-97281-9
Package ISBN-10: 0-538-97281-5

For more information contact Thomson Higher Education
5191 Natorp Boulevard
Mason, Ohio 45040
USA
Or you can visit our Internet site at: http://www.swlearning.com

ASIA (including India)
Thomson Learning
5 Shenton Way
#01-01 UIC Building
Singapore 068808

CANADA
Thomson Nelson
1120 Birchmount Road
Toronto, Ontario
Canada M1K 5G4

AUSTRALIA/NEW ZEALAND
Thomson Learning Australia
102 Dodds Street
Southbank, Victoria 3006
Australia

UK/EUROPE/MIDDLE EAST/AFRICA
Thomson Learning
High Holborn House
50-51 Bedford Road
London WC1R 4LR
United Kingdom

LATIN AMERICA
Thomson Learning
Seneca, 53
Colonia Polanco
11560 Mexico
D.F.Mexico

SPAIN (includes Portugal)
Thomson Paraninfo
Calle Magallanes, 25
28015 Madrid, Spain

Century 21 SOUTH-WESTERN Accounting 8E

CENTURY 21 ACCOUNTING • CENTURY 21 ACCOUNTING • CENTURY 21

Give students real-life experience with Century 21 Accounting simulations and working papers!

SIMULATION 1: EDDIE ORTEGA, DJ —

a service business organized as a proprietorship may be completed after Chapter 8

manual simulation: 0-538-97286-6
automated simulation: 0-538-97287-4

SIMULATION 2: ZENITH GLOBAL IMPORTS —

a merchandising business organized as a corporation may be completed after Chapter 16

manual simulation: 0-538-97288-2
automated simulation: 0-538-97289-0

SIMULATION 3: TRONICS, INC. —

a merchandising business organized as a corporation may be completed after Chapter 22

manual simulation: 0-538-97290-4
automated simulation: 0-538-97291-2

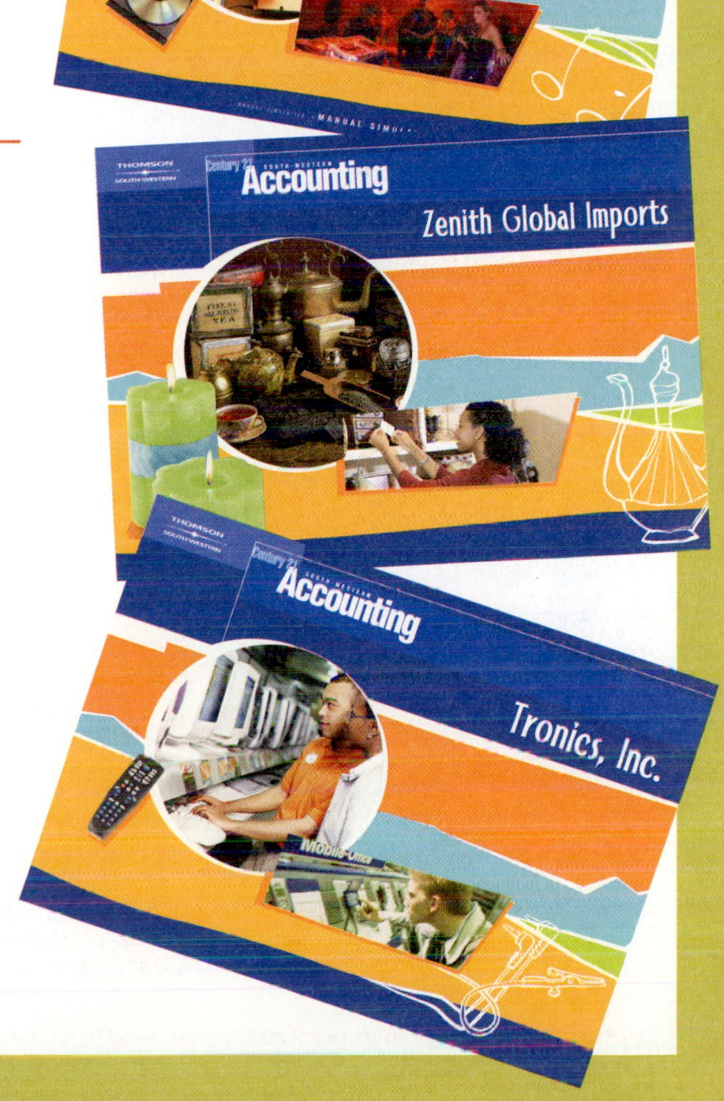

THOMSON SOUTH-WESTERN

Join us on the Internet at www.swlearning.com

How to Use This Book

PART OPENERS focus on a particular business that you'll learn about:

- **A listing of the chapters** covered in each Part helps you focus on what you'll be learning.
- **"The Business"** introduces you to the business you'll be studying throughout the Part.
- The **Chart of Accounts** used in the entire Part is provided for easy reference as you work through the chapters.

PART 1 Accounting for a Service Business Organized as a Proprietorship

CHAPTER
1 Starting a Proprietorship: Changes That Affect the Accounting Equation
2 Analyzing Transactions into Debit and Credit Parts
3 Journalizing Transactions
4 Posting to a General Ledger
5 Cash Control Systems
6 Work Sheet for a Service Business
7 Financial Statements for a Proprietorship
8 Recording Adjusting and Closing Entries for a Service Business

TECHKNOW CONSULTING

TechKnow Consulting is the business that will be used in the chapters in Part 1 to illustrate the accounting concepts and procedures for a service business organized as a proprietorship. TechKnow rents the office space in which the business is located as well as the equipment used. The service provided by the business involves setting up and troubleshooting network problems for a variety of clients.

TECHKNOW CONSULTING
CHART OF ACCOUNTS

General Ledger

Balance Sheet Accounts

(100)	ASSETS
110	Cash
120	Petty Cash
130	Accounts Receivable—Oakdale School
140	Accounts Receivable—Campus Internet Cafe
150	Supplies
160	Prepaid Insurance
(200)	LIABILITIES
210	Accounts Payable—Supply Depot
220	Accounts Payable—Thomas Supply Company
(300)	OWNER'S EQUITY
310	Kim Park, Capital
320	Kim Park, Drawing
330	Income Summary

Income Statement Accounts

(400)	REVENUE
410	Sales
(500)	EXPENSES
510	Advertising Expense
520	Insurance Expense
530	Miscellaneous Expense
540	Rent Expense
550	Supplies Expense
560	Utilities Expense

The chart of accounts for TechKnow Consulting is illustrated above for ready reference as you study the accounting cycle for a proprietorship in this textbook.

CHAPTER 3 Journalizing Transactions

OBJECTIVES & TERMS

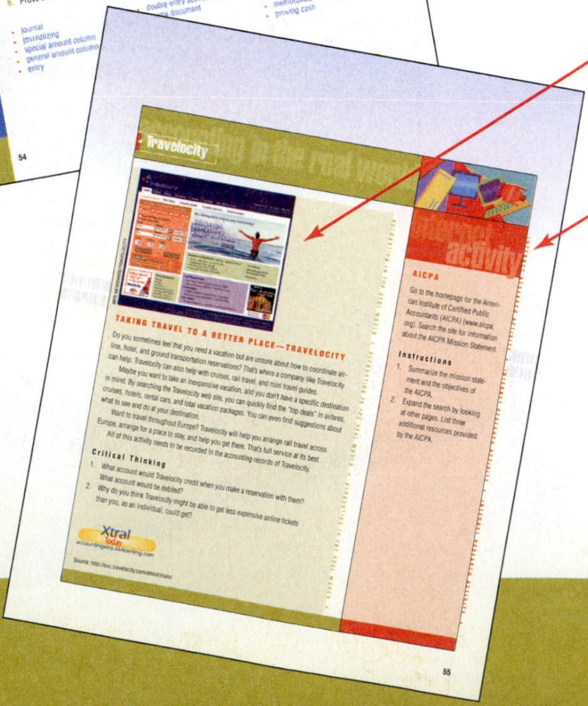

After studying Chapter 3, you will be able to:

1. Define accounting terms related to journalizing transactions.
2. Identify accounting concepts and practices related to journalizing transactions.
3. Record transactions to set up a business in a five-column journal.
4. Record transactions to buy insurance for cash and supplies on account in a five-column journal.
5. Record transactions that affect owner's equity and receiving cash on account in a five-column journal.
6. Prove and rule a five-column journal and prove cash.

- journal
- journalizing
- special amount column
- general amount column
- entry
- double-entry accounting
- sales invoice
- receipt
- memorandum
- proving cash

54

CHAPTER OPENERS introduce the subject matter you'll investigate:

- **Objectives** listed at the beginning of each chapter highlight lesson concepts and preview what you will learn.
- The **Terms Preview** displays all the key words introduced in the chapter. You can also find these terms and their definitions in the Glossary at the back of the text.
- **Accounting in the Real World** features a photo and description of a real company with questions linked to the chapter's content.
- **Internet Research Activity** sends you to the Internet to locate information to answer questions related to the chapter's subject matter.

Travelocity

TAKING TRAVEL TO A BETTER PLACE—TRAVELOCITY

AICPA

55

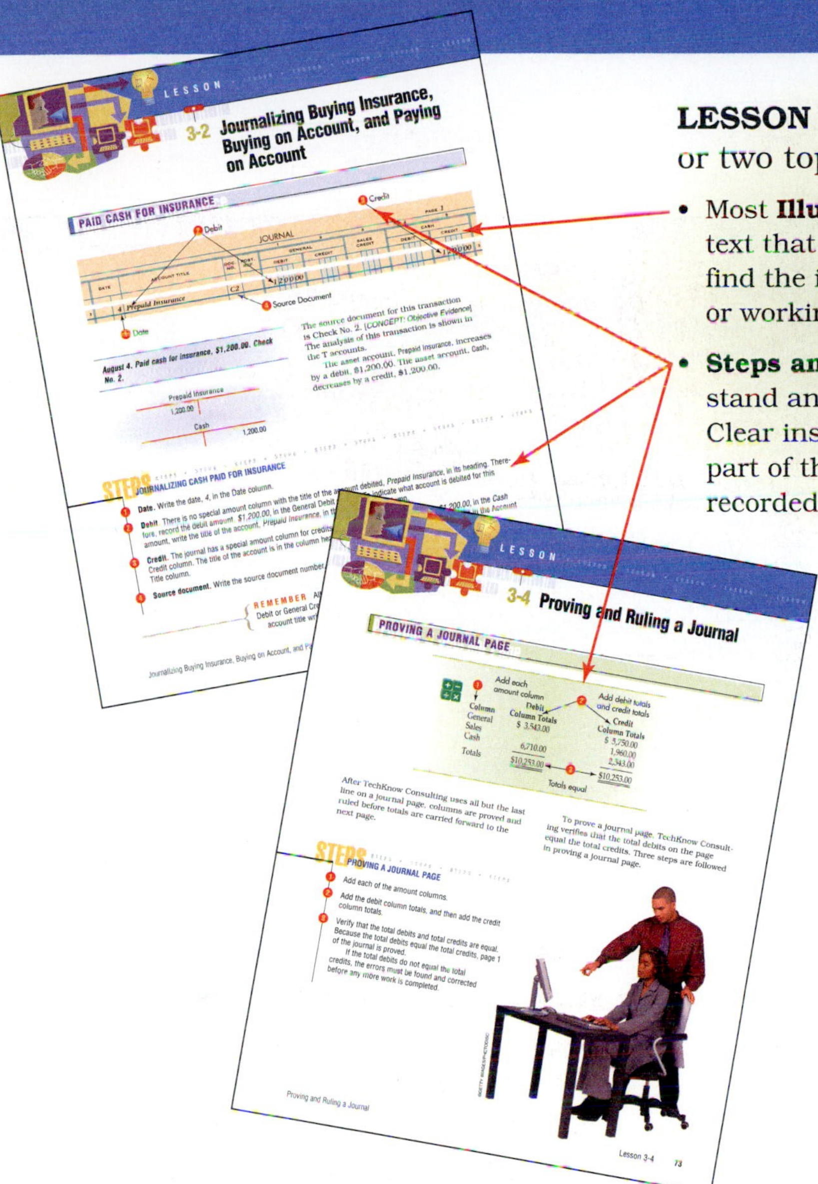

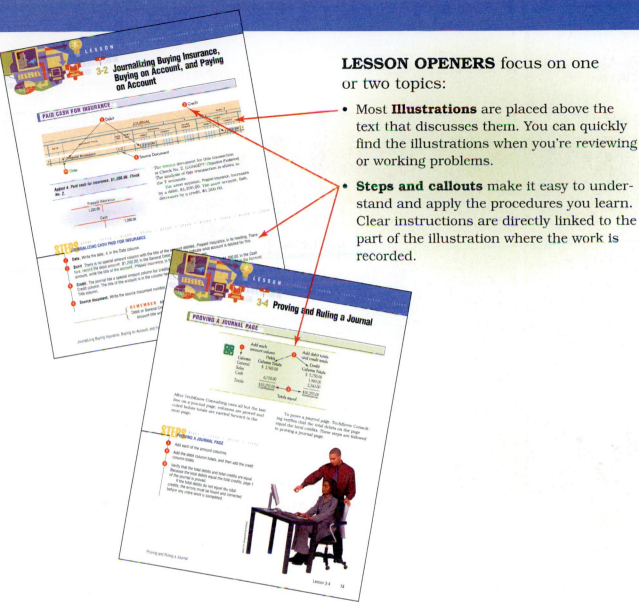

LESSON OPENERS focus on one or two topics:

- Most **Illustrations** are placed above the text that discusses them. You can quickly find the illustrations when you're reviewing or working problems.
- **Steps and callouts** make it easy to understand and apply the procedures you learn. Clear instructions are directly linked to the part of the illustration where the work is recorded.

END-OF-LESSON PAGES help you fully understand all concepts and procedures before moving on to the next lesson:

- **Terms Review** lists all the new words learned in the lesson.
- **Audit Your Understanding** asks two or more questions about the lesson material. You can check your answers in the Appendix.
- **Work Together** gives you guided practice through hands-on application of the lesson's procedures and concepts.
- **On Your Own** challenges you to complete problems by yourself.

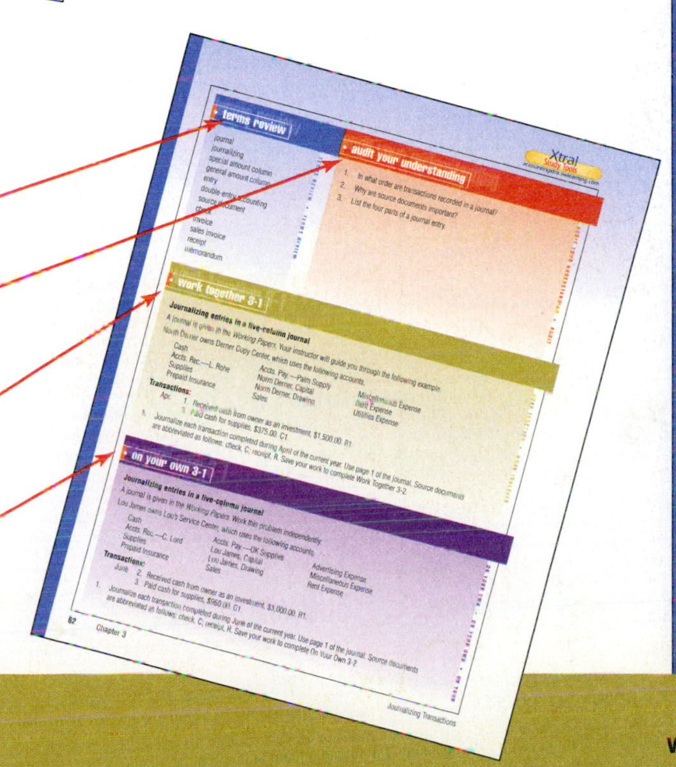

COURTESY OF EVERLYN JOHNSON

By the age of 18, you will have gained experiences that will change your life in ways you might never imagine. These experiences may come from an extracurricular activity, a part-time job, or a hobby, and they may influence the direction of your career or retirement.

For Everlyn Johnson, the youthful experience that would affect her life was learning to sew. Her mother taught her the basics when Everlyn was 11. Advancing from quilts to doll clothes to her prom dress, Everlyn learned that human sciences (formerly home economics) would lead her to a fulfilling career. Earning bachelor's, master's, and doctoral degrees in the area, Dr. Johnson worked with her state's cooperative extension service for over 27 years. In her role as a county agent, she was responsible for educating the public on home living skills—including sewing. Later she advanced to a position where she was responsible for gathering and communicating current knowledge and research with other county agents.

Most people plan to relax in their retirement. But not Dr. Johnson. She says, "I constantly heard people say that they wish they knew how to sew. I saw a niche that needed filling and decided I was the person to fulfill it." So after just three years of retirement, Everlyn decided to open a fabric store.

One of her first tasks to prepare for the store opening was to enroll in an income tax course at th local university. She recalls, "I felt the tax course would help me do a better job of keeping the recor of the business and would ensure that I planned the business to take advantage of tax laws." Then started doing her homework, meeting with a variety of small business owners to learn the reward pitfalls of small business ownership.

Everlyn visited fabric stores outside her market area. "The owners of many stores painted a rosy picture of the prospect of opening a store," she remarks. "I felt they were missing someth main ingredient that would make the store successful. Then I visited two stores that were constantly conducting sewing classes. It was clear to see that these classes were the key to the success of the stores. Perfect!" Having spent most of her career teaching classes, Everlyn now plans sewing classes, teaching some herself, to serve her customers and to promote the sale of fabric and accessories in her store.

Salary: Approximately $70,000, depending on experience.

Qualifications: A master's degree requires one year of university courses beyond the bachelor's degree. Most doctoral programs require another four years of university study and research.

Occupational Outlook: The budgetary constraints of county, state, and federal governments have reduced the financial resources devoted to cooperative education. Thus, the opportunities for individuals in this career have been declining. However, in Dr. Johnson's situation, she was able to use her background to move into a successful business venture.

How often have you said something you later regretted? Chances are you spoke before you thought about how your words might affect others. Had you taken the time to think how your words would hurt someone else, you might have said something different or simply kept quiet.

The first step of the ethical model is to recognize you are facing an ethical dilemma. Few business decisions will require you to act immediately. Take whatever time is required to determine whether your actions could harm someone else. If you have any doubts that your action will violate your morals, stop to evaluate the decision, using the ethical model.

The second step of the ethical model is to identify the action taken or the proposed action. Write down every possible action you think of, even if the idea might seem outrageous at first. Seek the advice of others who may have encountered similar dilemmas or whom you admire for their ethical behavior. Many companies assign a mentor to new employees to encourage them to seek advice.

Instructions

In private, write down the names of at least five individuals from whom you would feel comfortable seeking advice on ethical dilemmas.

SPECIAL FEATURES provide information about real-life issues:

- **Careers in Accounting** introduces you to actual people working in accounting or in positions where accounting knowledge is useful. This feature includes entry-level job requirements, career tracks, and projected trends for the future.
- **Making Ethical Decisions** helps you understand complicated issues in the business world, such as confidentiality and integrity.
- **Business Structures** provides information on characteristics of proprietorships, corporations, and partnerships.

Many businesses need amounts of capital that cannot be easily provided by a proprietorship. These businesses choose to organize using another form of business. An organization with the legal rights of a person and which many persons may own is called a **corporation**. A corporation is formed by receiving approval from a state or federal agency. Each unit of ownership in a corporation is called a **share of stock**. Total shares of ownership in a corporation are called **capital stock**. An owner of one or more shares of a corporation is called a **stockholder**.

A corporation is a business organization that has the legal rights of a person. A corporation can own property, incur liabilities, and enter into contracts in its own name. A corporation may also sell ownership in itself. A person becomes an owner of a corporation by purchasing shares of stock.

The principal difference between the accounting records of proprietorships and corporations is in the capital accounts. Proprietorships have a single capital and drawing account for the owner. A corporation has separate capital accounts for the stock issued and for the earnings kept in the business, which will be explained in more detail in Chapter 16. As in proprietorships, information in a corporation's accounting system is kept separate from the personal records of its owners. [*CONCEPT: Business Entity*] Periodic financial statements must be sent to the stockholders of the corporation to report the financial activities of the business.

Critical Thinking

1. The names of many corporations include the words *Corporation*, *Incorporated*, *Corp.*, or *Inc.* in their names. Based on their names, identify several corporations in your area.
2. Why do you think many very large companies are organized as corporations?

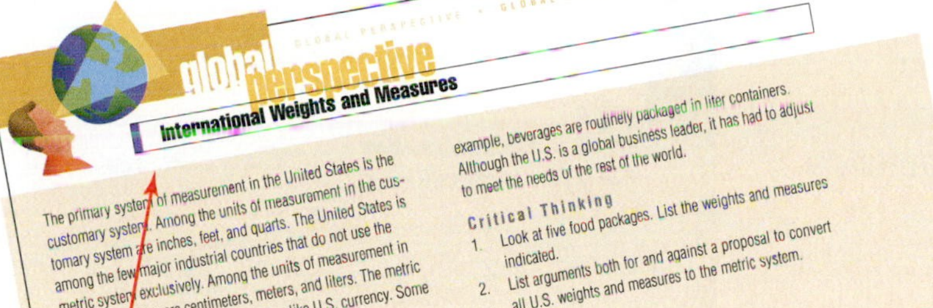

global perspective

International Weights and Measures

The primary system of measurement in the United States is the customary system. Among the units of measurement in the customary system are inches, feet, and quarts. The United States is among the few major industrial countries that do not use the metric system exclusively. Among the units of measurement in the metric system are centimeters, meters, and liters. The metric system is based on a decimal system—like U.S. currency. Some U.S. industries have converted to the metric system. Others specify measurements in both customary and metric systems.

To conduct international business, the U.S. has recognized the need to convert customary units to the metric system. For example, beverages are routinely packaged in liter containers. Although the U.S. is a global business leader, it has had to adjust to meet the needs of the rest of the world.

Critical Thinking

1. Look at five food packages. List the weights and measures indicated.
2. List arguments both for and against a proposal to convert all U.S. weights and measures to the metric system.

technology for business

Computerized Accounting—Not Just for Corporations

For many years, only large corporations could afford to computerize their accounting functions. Today a variety of computer software programs are available to handle the record keeping and accounting needs of small and not-so-small businesses. Examples include Peachtree, Microsoft Small Business Manager, Oracle Small Business Suite, QuickBooks, and MYOB.

Depending on the needs of the business, there is a software program available to complete all or some accounting functions using a personal computer. These functions include the general ledger, accounts payable, accounts receivable, financial statements, and inventory. The software programs can print checks and maintain a check register, as well as reconcile bank statements. Some programs can process payroll, calculate taxes, and prepare tax forms.

Accounting software provides significant benefits. The software allows a business to improve the accuracy and completeness of financial records. Safeguards within the software alert the user to mistakes, problems, and inconsistencies. In addition, the software can create graphs and charts to complement financial reports and statements. The data is organized in a manner that enables management to create a variety of reports to analyze the effectiveness of its operations.

Instructions

1. Use Automated Accounting or some other accounting software to work one of the problems in this chapter. Report on any time that would be saved if this software were used to record the daily transactions of a real business.
2. Does the accounting software you used in question 1 have a graphing feature? If so, explore it to discover what kinds of graphs are available. Report on the usefulness of these graphs.

- **Global Perspective** will expose you to some of the ways in which accounting and business differ in other countries.
- **Technology for Business** focuses on common business applications of technology.
- **Cultural Diversity** explains how different cultures have contributed to the field of accounting.

cultural diversity

Timeless Tools

Throughout history, people of different cultures and civilizations have devised tools for counting, calculating, and recordkeeping.

The Jibaro Indians living in the Amazon rain forest in South America use the most basic counting tools of all—their fingers. Jibaros use phrases to express the numbers five and ten that translate to "I have finished one hand" and "I have finished both hands."

A more complex device of ancient origin is the abacus. The abacus is a calculating device that developed in several different cultures. The Babylonians in Asia Minor had an early form of abacus, as did the Egyptians in northern Africa. The first abacus was known in China as early as the 6th century B.C. This abacus was a flat piece of wood divided into squares. Its use spread to the rest of the Asian world.

The abacus may be used to add, subtract, multiply, and divide. Twelfth-century Chinese mathematicians used the abacus to solve algebraic equations. Today some highly skilled people, particularly of Asian descent, still use the abacus for calculations.

Recordkeepers in the Incan civilization (in present-day Peru) memorized business transactions and recited them when necessary. Incan recordkeepers used small ropes of different colors and sizes and knotted and joined them in different ways to help remember financial data. These ropes, called *quipu*, were one of the earliest means of recording transactions.

Accounting tools have changed over the course of history. They will continue to evolve with future advances in technology.

Critical Thinking

1. What tools do most accounting workers today use for calculations?
2. Discuss whether the use of modern calculating tools results in the creation of more complex accounting transactions.

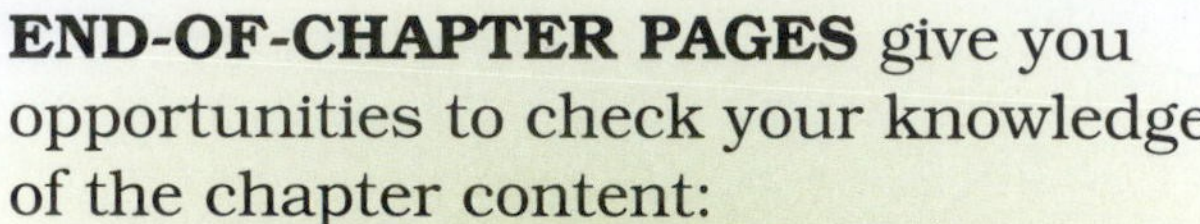

END-OF-CHAPTER PAGES give you opportunities to check your knowledge of the chapter content:

- **Chapter Summary** restates the chapter objectives for your reference.
- **Explore Accounting** includes opportunities for higher-level learning.

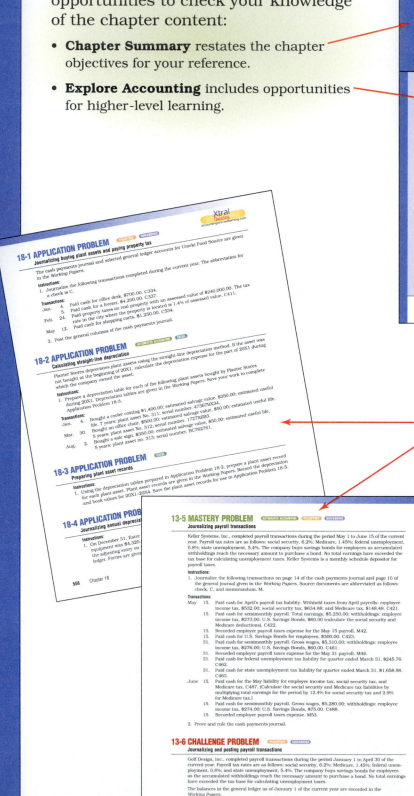

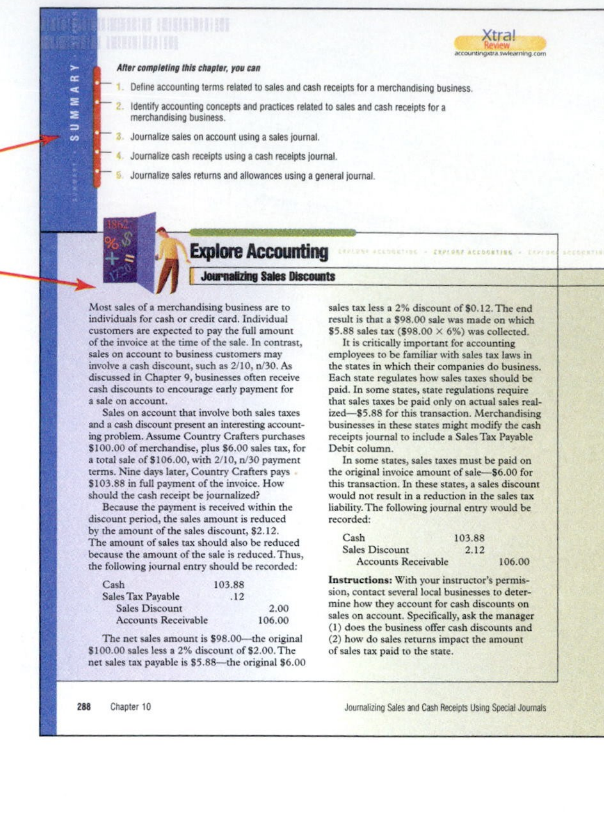

SUMMARY

Xtral Review accountingxtra.swlearning.com

After completing this chapter, you can

1. Define accounting terms related to sales and cash receipts for a merchandising business.
2. Identify accounting concepts and practices related to sales and cash receipts for a merchandising business.
3. Journalize sales on account using a sales journal.
4. Journalize cash receipts using a cash receipts journal.
5. Journalize sales returns and allowances using a general journal.

Explore Accounting

Journalizing Sales Discounts

Most sales of a merchandising business are to individuals for cash or credit card. Individual customers are expected to pay the full amount of the invoice at the time of the sale. In contrast, sales on account to business customers may involve a cash discount, such as 2/10, n/30. As discussed in Chapter 9, businesses often receive cash discounts to encourage early payment for a sale on account.

Sales on account that involve both sales taxes and a cash discount present an interesting accounting problem. Assume Country Crafters purchases $100.00 of merchandise, plus $6.00 sales tax, for a total sale of $106.00, with 2/10, n/30 payment terms. Nine days later, Country Crafters pays $103.88 in full payment of the invoice. How should the cash receipt be journalized?

Because the payment is received within the discount period, the sales amount is reduced by the amount of the sales discount, $2.12. The amount of sales tax should also be reduced because the amount of the sale is reduced. Thus, the following journal entry should be recorded:

Cash	103.88	
Sales Tax Payable	.12	
Sales Discount		2.00
Accounts Receivable		106.00

The net sales amount is $98.00—the original $100.00 sales less a 2% discount of $2.00. The net sales tax payable is $5.88—the original $6.00 sales tax less a 2% discount of $0.12. The end result is that a $98.00 sale was made on which $5.88 sales tax ($98.00 × 6%) was collected.

It is critically important for accounting employees to be familiar with sales tax laws in the states in which their companies do business. Each state regulates how sales taxes should be paid. In some states, state regulations require that sales taxes be paid only on actual sales realized—$5.88 for this transaction. Merchandising businesses in these states might modify the cash receipts journal to include a Sales Tax Payable Debit column.

In some states, sales taxes must be paid on the original invoice amount of sale—$6.00 for this transaction. In these states, a sales discount would not result in a reduction in the sales tax liability. The following journal entry would be recorded:

Cash	103.88	
Sales Discount	2.12	
Accounts Receivable		106.00

Instructions: With your instructor's permission, contact several local businesses to determine how they account for cash discounts on sales on account. Specifically, ask the manager (1) does the business offer cash discounts and (2) how do sales returns impact the amount of sales tax paid to the state.

288 Chapter 10 Journalizing Sales and Cash Receipts Using Special Journals

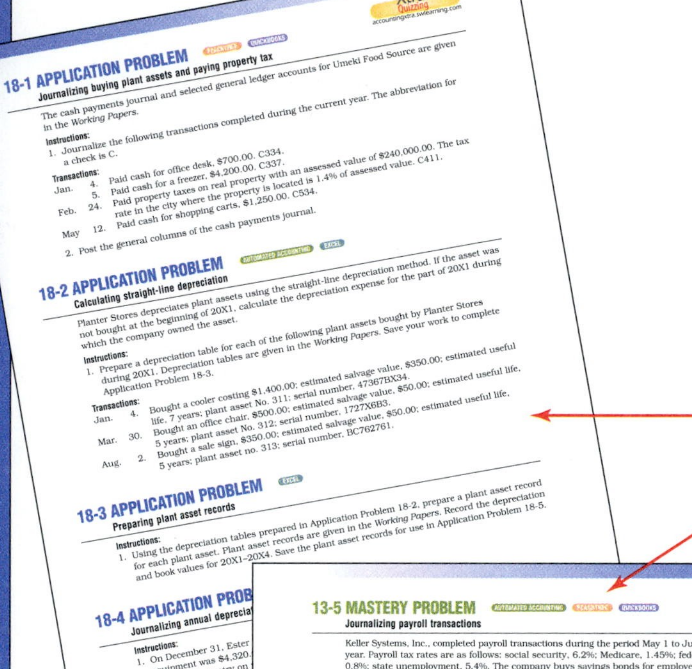

Xtral Quizzing accountingxtra.swlearning.com

18-1 APPLICATION PROBLEM PEACHTREE QUICKBOOKS

Journalizing buying plant assets and paying property tax

The cash payments journal and selected general ledger accounts for Umeki Food Source are given in the *Working Papers*.

Instructions:

1. Journalize the following transactions completed during the current year. The abbreviation for a check is C.

Transactions:

Jan. 4. Paid cash for office desk, $700.00. C334.
5. Paid cash for a freezer, $4,200.00. C337.
Feb. 24. Paid property taxes on real property with an assessed value of $240,000.00. The tax rate in the city where the property is located is 1.4% of assessed value. C411.
May 12. Paid cash for shopping carts, $1,250.00. C534.

2. Post the general columns of the cash payments journal.

18-2 APPLICATION PROBLEM AUTOMATED ACCOUNTING EXCEL

Calculating straight-line depreciation

Planter Stores depreciates plant assets using the straight-line depreciation method. If the asset was not bought at the beginning of 20X1, calculate the depreciation expense for the part of 20X1 during which the company owned the asset.

Instructions:

1. Prepare a depreciation table for each of the following plant assets bought by Planter Stores during 20X1. Depreciation tables are given in the *Working Papers*. Save your work to complete Application Problem 18-3.

Transactions:

Jan. 4. Bought a cooler costing $1,400.00; estimated salvage value, $350.00; estimated useful life, 7 years; plant asset No. 311; serial number, 47367BX34.
Mar. 30. Bought an office chair, $500.00; estimated salvage value, $50.00; estimated useful life, 5 years; plant asset No. 312; serial number, 1727X6B3.
Aug. 2. Bought a sale sign, $350.00; estimated salvage value, $50.00; estimated useful life, 5 years; plant asset no. 313; serial number, BC762761.

18-3 APPLICATION PROBLEM EXCEL

Preparing plant asset records

Instructions:

1. Using the depreciation tables prepared in Application Problem 18-2, prepare a plant asset record for each plant asset. Plant asset records are given in the *Working Papers*. Record the depreciation and book values for 20X1–20X4. Save the plant asset records for use in Application Problem 18-5.

18-4 APPLICATION PROB

Journalizing annual deprecia

Instructions:

1. On December 31, Ester equipment was $4,320. the adjusting entry on ledger. Forms are give

556 Chapter 18

- Exercises contain at least one **Application Problem** for each lesson, plus one **Mastery Problem** and one **Challenge Problem** to test your understanding of the entire chapter. Many of these problems can also be worked using accounting software: **Automated Accounting, Peachtree®, QuickBooks®,** and **Microsoft® Excel!**

13-5 MASTERY PROBLEM AUTOMATED ACCOUNTING PEACHTREE QUICKBOOKS

Journalizing payroll transactions

Keller Systems, Inc., completed payroll transactions during the period May 1 to June 15 of the current year. Payroll tax rates are as follows: social security, 6.2%; Medicare, 1.45%; federal unemployment, 0.8%; state unemployment, 5.4%. The company buys savings bonds for employees as accumulated withholdings reach the necessary amount to purchase a bond. No total earnings have exceeded the tax base for calculating unemployment taxes. Keller Systems is a monthly schedule depositor for payroll taxes.

Instructions:

1. Journalize the following transactions on page 14 of the cash payments journal and page 10 of the general journal given in the *Working Papers*. Source documents are abbreviated as follows: check, C, and memorandum, M.

Transactions:

May 15. Paid cash for April's payroll tax liability. Withheld taxes from April payrolls: employee income tax, $532.00; social security tax, $634.88; and Medicare tax, $148.48. C421.
15. Paid cash for semimonthly payroll. Total earnings, $5,250.00; withholdings: employee income tax, $273.00; U.S. Savings Bonds, $60.00 (calculate the social security and Medicare deductions). C422.
15. Recorded employer payroll taxes expense for the May 15 payroll. M42.
15. Paid cash for U.S. Savings Bonds for employees, $300.00. C423.
31. Paid cash for semimonthly payroll. Gross wages, $5,310.00; withholdings: employee income tax, $276.00; U.S. Savings Bonds, $60.00. C461.
31. Recorded employer payroll taxes expense for the May 31 payroll. M46.
31. Paid cash for federal unemployment tax liability for quarter ended March 31, $245.76. C462.
31. Paid cash for state unemployment tax liability for quarter ended March 31, $1,658.88. C463.
June 15. Paid cash for the May liability for employee income tax, social security tax, and Medicare tax. C487. (Calculate the social security and Medicare tax liabilities by multiplying total earnings for the period by 12.4% for social security tax and 2.9% for Medicare tax.)
15. Paid cash for semimonthly payroll. Gross wages, $5,280.00; withholdings: employee income tax, $274.00; U.S. Savings Bonds, $75.00. C488.
15. Recorded employer payroll taxes expense. M53.

2. Prove and rule the cash payments journal.

13-6 CHALLENGE PROBLEM PEACHTREE QUICKBOOKS

Journalizing and posting payroll transactions

Golf Design, Inc., completed payroll transactions during the period January 1 to April 30 of the current year. Payroll tax rates are as follows: social security, 6.2%; Medicare, 1.45%; federal unemployment, 0.8%; and state unemployment, 5.4%. The company buys savings bonds for employees as the accumulated withholdings reach the necessary amount to purchase a bond. No total earnings have exceeded the tax base for calculating unemployment taxes.

The balances in the general ledger as of January 1 of the current year are recorded in the *Working Papers*.

Payroll Accounting, Taxes, and Reports Chapter 13 393

- Enrichment materials help you take a step further into understanding accounting. **Applied Communication** offers exercises for strengthening your communication skills—a must for future employment! **Cases for Critical Thinking** asks you to consider questions based on accounting scenarios. **SCANS Workplace Competency** helps you learn about skills you'll need in the business world. **Using Source Documents, Graphing Workshop,** and **Auditing for Errors** provide you with specific situations in which you can analyze and investigate accounting tools. **Analyzing Best Buy's Financial Statements** allows you to examine a real business's annual report and financial documents and put your knowledge to work.

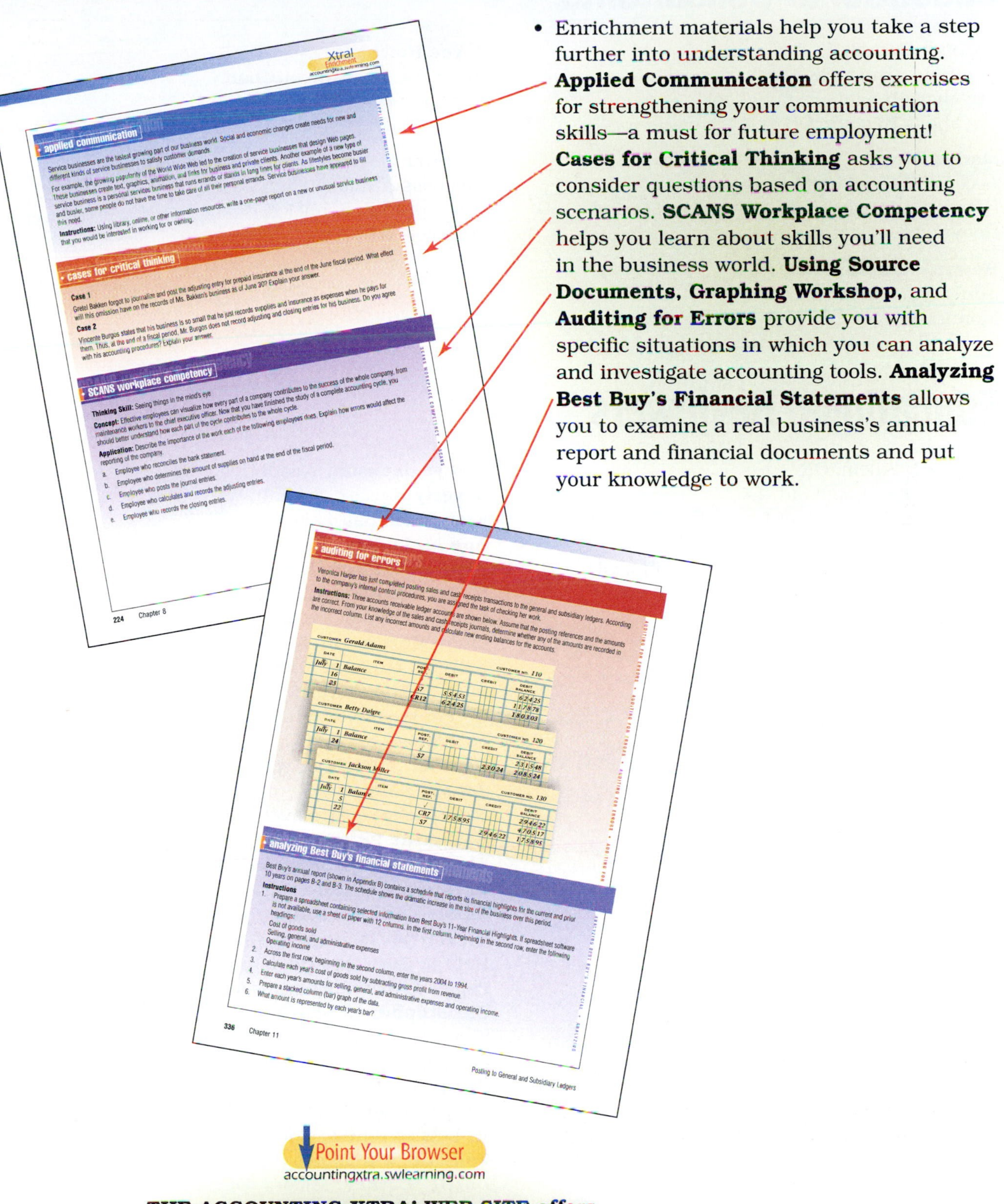

Xtra! Enrichment
accountingxtra.swlearning.com

applied communication

Service businesses are the fastest growing part of our business world. Social and economic changes create needs for new and different kinds of service businesses to satisfy customer demands.

For example, the growing popularity of the World Wide Web led to the creation of service businesses that design Web pages. These businesses create text, graphics, animation, and links for business and private clients. Another example of a new type of service business is a personal services business that runs errands or stands in long lines for clients. As lifestyles become busier and busier, some people do not have the time to take care of all their personal errands. Service businesses have appeared to fill this need.

Instructions: Using library, online, or other information resources, write a one-page report on a new or unusual service business that you would be interested in working for or owning.

cases for critical thinking

Case 1

Gretel Bakken forgot to journalize and post the adjusting entry for prepaid insurance at the end of the June fiscal period. What effect will this omission have on the records of Ms. Bakken's business as of June 30? Explain your answer.

Case 2

Vincente Burgos states that his business is so small that he just records supplies and insurance as expenses when he pays for them. Thus, at the end of a fiscal period, Mr. Burgos does not record adjusting and closing entries for his business. Do you agree with his accounting procedures? Explain your answer.

SCANS workplace competency

Thinking Skill: Seeing things in the mind's eye

Concept: Effective employees can visualize how every part of a company contributes to the success of the whole company, from maintenance workers to the chief executive officer. Now that you have finished the study of a complete accounting cycle, you should better understand how each part of the cycle contributes to the whole cycle.

Application: Describe the importance of the work each of the following employees does. Explain how errors would affect the reporting of the company.

a. Employee who reconciles the bank statement.
b. Employee who determines the amount of supplies on hand at the end of the fiscal period.
c. Employee who posts the journal entries.
d. Employee who calculates and records the adjusting entries.
e. Employee who records the closing entries.

224 Chapter 8

auditing for errors

Veronica Harper has just completed posting sales and cash receipts transactions to the general and subsidiary ledgers. According to the company's internal control procedures, you are assigned the task of checking her work.

Instructions: Three accounts receivable ledger accounts are shown below. Assume that the posting references and the amounts are correct. From your knowledge of the sales and cash receipts journals, determine whether any of the amounts are recorded in the incorrect column. List any incorrect amounts and calculate new ending balances for the accounts.

CUSTOMER Gerald Adams — CUSTOMER NO. 110

DATE		ITEM	POST. REF.	DEBIT	CREDIT	DEBIT BALANCE
July	1	Balance	✓			624 25
	16		S7	554 53		1 178 78
	25		CR12	624 25		1 803 03

CUSTOMER Betty Dalgre — CUSTOMER NO. 120

DATE		ITEM	POST. REF.	DEBIT	CREDIT	DEBIT BALANCE
July	1	Balance	✓			2 315 48
	24		S7		230 24	2 085 24

CUSTOMER Jackson Miller — CUSTOMER NO. 130

DATE		ITEM	POST. REF.	DEBIT	CREDIT	DEBIT BALANCE
July	1	Balance	✓			2 946 22
	5		CR7	1 758 95		4 705 17
	22		S7		2 946 22	1 758 95

analyzing Best Buy's financial statements

Best Buy's annual report (shown in Appendix B) contains a schedule that reports its financial highlights for the current and prior 10 years on pages B-2 and B-3. The schedule shows the dramatic increase in the size of the business over this period.

Instructions

1. Prepare a spreadsheet containing selected information from Best Buy's 11-Year Financial Highlights. If spreadsheet software is not available, use a sheet of paper with 12 columns. In the first column, beginning in the second row, enter the following headings:
   Cost of goods sold
   Selling, general, and administrative expenses
   Operating income
2. Across the first row, beginning in the second column, enter the years 2004 to 1994.
3. Calculate each year's cost of goods sold by subtracting gross profit from revenue.
4. Enter each year's amounts for selling, general, and administrative expenses and operating income.
5. Prepare a stacked column (bar) graph of the data.
6. What amount is represented by each year's bar?

336 Chapter 11

Posting to General and Subsidiary Ledgers

Point Your Browser
accountingxtra.swlearning.com

THE ACCOUNTING XTRA! WEB SITE offers a variety of resources and activities for you to explore. As you use this textbook, watch for the Xtra! Web Site icons that will lead you to your online accounting connection!

Educational Consultants

Carolyn Holt Balis
Computer/Business Teacher
Cuyahoga Heights High School
Cuyahoga Heights, OH

Madge Gregg
Accounting Teacher
Hoover High School
Hoover, AL

Howard Rankin, MBA
Educational Consultant
Monticello, KY

Joyce Rowe
Business Department Chair
Monterey High School
Lubbock, TX

Jennifer Wegner
Business & Information Technology
Mishicot High School
Mishicot, WI

Educational Reviewers

Jon Abel, Salem, OR
Abe Aleman, Levelland, TX
Kathy Andreason, Salt Lake City, UT
Cynthia S. Aycock, Eagle Lake, FL
Carolyn Holt Balis, Cuyahoga Heights, OH
Anne Berten, Portland, OR
Chad E. Bobb, Indianapolis, IN
Ellen Clizbe, Moreno Valley, CA
Tony Composto, Brooklyn, NY
Becky Cornacchia, Naples, FL
Alicia E. Censi Corso, Los Angeles, CA
Donna Davis, Charlotte, NC
Paula Davis, Atlanta, GA
Sylvia Davis, Lakewood, CA
Dana Dingell, Vienna, VA
Kathy Dixon, Richmond, VA
Keith Downs, Dallastown, PA
Dr. Judith A. Drager-McCoy, Lititz, PA
Ann Droptini, Gladewater, TX
Kathy Dunaway, Erlanger, KY
Jean Eckert, Wexford, PA
Julie Eckhart, Salem, WI
Carrie English, Woodbridge, VA
Barbara Erwin, Orlando, FL
K. Skip Fabritius, Olympia, WA
Debbie Fischer, St. Petersburg, FL
Kathleen Ford, Rochester, MI
Lance B. Garvin, Indianapolis, IN
Debbie Gentene, Mason, OH
Wendy Gentry, Garden Grove, CA
Andy Gilley, Hendersonville, TN
Kathy Goos, Moreno Valley, CA
Madge Gregg, Hoover, AL
Tracy Gutierrez, Garden Grove, CA
Jean Harms, Port Orange, FL
Cindy Hiester, Astoria, OR
Beth Hubbard, Virginia Beach, VA
Lisa Huddlestun, Kansas, IL
Steve Ingmire, Indianapolis, IN
Gladys Jackson, Woodbridge, NJ
Beverly Kaesar, Neenah, WI
Fran Loos, Salt Lake City, UT
Ann M. Ludlow, St. Louis, MO
Frances Mallard, Brentwood, TN
H. Jean Malonson, Hayward, CA
Chris Marshall, Denver, CO
Libby Martin, Chattanooga, TN
Sally M. Graham Martin, Nokesville, VA
Barb Mason, Paris, MO
Kelvin Meeks, Memphis, TN
Lori Meseke, CPA, Vandalia, IL
Heather Moraru, Suwanee, GA
Jennifer Mundy, O'Fallon, IL
Barb Nichols, Evansville, IN
Katherine Prange, Breese, IL
Eleanor Rankin, Rio Rico, AZ
Dr. Andrea B. Reiter, Dingman's Falls, PA
Nicole Reitz-Larson, Salt Lake City, UT
Dr. Harriet D. Rogers, Whitewater, WI
George Roth, Prairie du Sac, WI
Peggy J. Scott, Chesapeke, VA
Christopher G. Shaffer, Cincinnati, OH
Janet Shaw, Bailey, NC
Mary Ann Shea, Amherst, MA
Jenny V. Shippy, Naples, FL
Sherri Small, Las Vegas, NV
H. Leland Smith, Racine, WI
Tommie Stanaland, Perry, FL
Dottie Starkey, Milford, DE
Laurel Stein, Wall, NJ
Claire Thoke, Glendale, CA
John Tingley, Bradley, IL
Linda Underwood, Gilcrest, CO
Jennifer Wegner, Mishicot, WI
Linda White, Fayetteville, PA
Parnell Wiggins, Memphis, TN
Lonnie Wilson, Evansville, IN
Vickie Wolfe, Glens Ferry, ID

CONTENTS

©GETTY IMAGES/PHOTODISC

PART 2
Accounting for a Merchandising Business Organized as a Corporation 230

©GETTY IMAGES/PHOTODISC

Additional Features in This Book

Chapter Review and Practice

PART

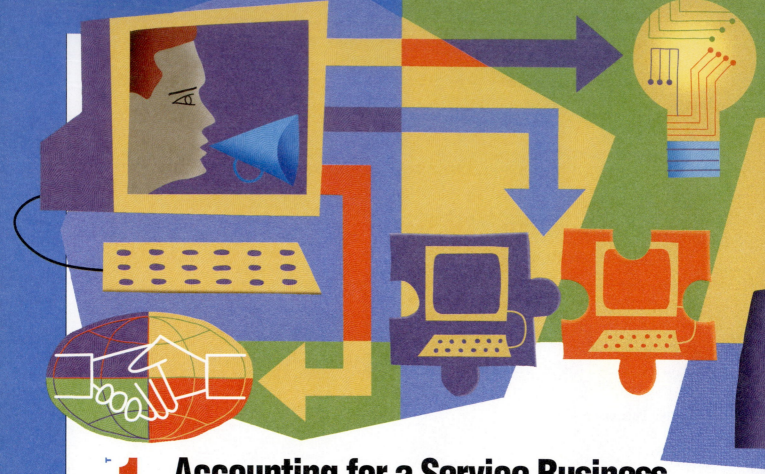

1 Accounting for a Service Business Organized as a Proprietorship

SINESS • THE BUSINESS • THE BUSINESS • THE BUSINESS

TECHKNOW CONSULTING

TechKnow Consulting is the business that will be used in the chapters in Part 1 to illustrate the accounting concepts and procedures for a service business organized as a proprietorship. TechKnow rents the office space in which the business is located as well as the equipment used. The service provided by the business involves setting up and troubleshooting network problems for a variety of clients.

TECHKNOW CONSULTING CHART OF ACCOUNTS

General Ledger

Balance Sheet Accounts

(100)	ASSETS
110	Cash
120	Petty Cash
130	Accounts Receivable—Oakdale School
140	Accounts Receivable—Campus Internet Cafe
150	Supplies
160	Prepaid Insurance
(200)	LIABILITIES
210	Accounts Payable—Supply Depot
220	Accounts Payable—Thomas Supply Company
(300)	OWNER'S EQUITY
310	Kim Park, Capital
320	Kim Park, Drawing
330	Income Summary

Income Statement Accounts

(400)	REVENUE
410	Sales
(500)	EXPENSES
510	Advertising Expense
520	Insurance Expense
530	Miscellaneous Expense
540	Rent Expense
550	Supplies Expense
560	Utilities Expense

The chart of accounts for TechKnow Consulting is illustrated above for ready reference as you study the accounting cycle for a proprietorship in this textbook.

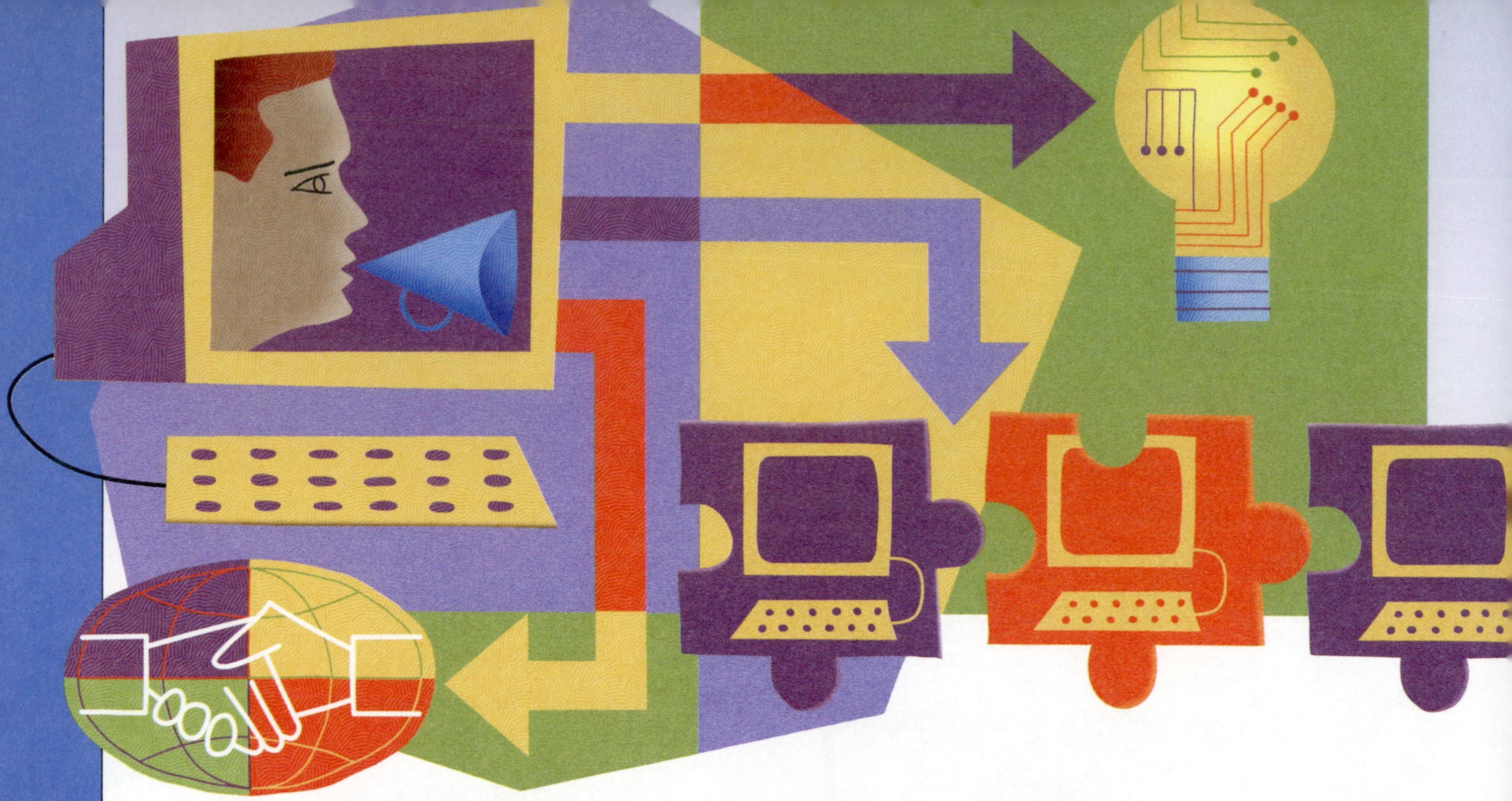

CHAPTER

1 Starting a Proprietorship: Changes That Affect the Accounting Equation

OBJECTIVES & TERMS

After studying Chapter 1, you will be able to:

1. Define accounting terms related to starting a service business organized as a proprietorship and to changes that affect the accounting equation.
2. Identify accounting concepts and practices related to starting a service business organized as a proprietorship and to changes that affect the accounting equation.
3. Classify accounts as assets, liabilities, or owner's equity and demonstrate their relationships in the accounting equation.
4. Analyze how transactions affect accounts in an accounting equation.

- accounting
- accounting system
- accounting records
- financial statements
- service business
- proprietorship
- asset
- equities
- liability
- owner's equity
- accounting equation
- ethics
- business ethics
- transaction
- account
- account title
- account balance
- capital
- revenue
- sale on account
- expense
- withdrawals

Point Your Browser
accountingxtra.swlearning.com

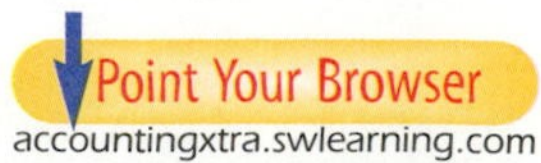

accounting in the real world

Gold's Gym

©GOLD'S GYM INTERNATIONAL

GOLD'S GYM AND THE IMPORTANCE OF LOCATION

Are you ready for a good workout? With so many labor-saving devices available today, many people look to fitness facilities for their daily physical exercise. For a fee, a member can make use of a variety of cardiovascular machines, weightlifting/resistance equipment, free weights, and indoor tracks. Many facilities offer classes and personal trainers. You can even shop for specialty food and workout clothing.

Gold's Gym is a franchise operation, meaning that individuals or groups buy the right to open and operate a Gold's Gym. The first Gold's Gym opened in 1965 in Venice, California. Since then, more than 650 Gold's Gyms have opened in the United States and in 23 countries around the world.

When considering the possibility of opening a new Gold's Gym, there are many decisions that have to be made. These decisions include where to locate the gym, how big the facility should be, what equipment to include, and how to let people know about the new facility.

Critical Thinking

1. Why is the location of a business important to the success of that business?
2. What things would you consider when deciding where to locate a business such as Gold's Gym?

accountingxtra.swlearning.com

Source: www.goldsgym.com

ACCOUNTING IN THE REAL WORLD • ACCOUNTING IN THE REAL WORLD • ACCOUNTING IN THE REAL WORLD •

internet activity

SMALL BUSINESS ADMINISTRATION

Go to the homepage for the Small Business Administration, a government organization designed to help small businesses in the United States. Search the site for advice about starting a business. Use the link www.sba.gov, or do a search for the Small Business Administration if the link is no longer accurate.

Instructions

1. List at least five items that the Small Business Administration site provides to help a person start a business.
2. Briefly explain which aid you feel is most helpful.

INTERNET RESEARCH ACTIVITY • INTERNET RESEARCH ACTIVITY • INTERNET RESEARCH ACTIVITY •

LESSON • LESSON • LESSON • LESSON • LESSON • LESSON

1-1 The Accounting Equation

WHAT IS ACCOUNTING?

Planning, recording, analyzing, and interpreting financial information is called **accounting**. A planned process for providing financial information that will be useful to management is called an **accounting system**. Organized summaries of a business's financial activities are called **accounting records**.

Accounting is the language of business. Many individuals in a business complete accounting forms and prepare accounting reports. Owners, managers, and accounting personnel use their knowledge of accounting to understand the information provided in the accounting reports. Regardless of their responsibilities within an organization, individuals can perform their jobs more efficiently if they know the language of business—accounting.

Suppliers that are considering extending credit to a business and institutions that are considering extending loans to a business are also interested in a business's financial activities. Financial reports that summarize the financial condition and operations of a business are called **financial statements**. Business owners and managers also use financial statements to make business decisions.

Inaccurate accounting records often contribute to business failure and bankruptcy. Failure to understand accounting information can result in poor business decisions for both businesses and nonprofit organizations. Understanding accounting helps managers and owners make better business decisions.

In addition, nearly everyone in the United States earns money and must submit income tax reports to the federal and state governments. Everyone must plan ways to keep spending within available income in both their personal and business lives.

THE BUSINESS—TECHKNOW CONSULTING

A business that performs an activity for a fee is called a **service business**. Kim Park decided to start her own business, helping set up and troubleshoot computer networks. A business owned by one person is called a **proprietorship**. A proprietorship is also referred to as a *sole proprietorship.* Kim named her new proprietorship "TechKnow Consulting." TechKnow Consulting will rent office space and the equipment needed to troubleshoot network problems.

Since TechKnow Consulting is a new business, Kim must design the accounting system that will be used to keep TechKnow Consulting's accounting records. Kim must be careful to keep these accounting records separate from her own personal financial records. For example, Kim owns a house and a personal car. TechKnow Consulting's financial records must not include information about Kim's house, car, or other personal belongings. Kim must use one checking account for her personal expenses and another checking account for TechKnow Consulting. The accounting concept *Business Entity* is applied when a business's financial information is recorded and reported separately from the owner's personal financial information. [*CONCEPT: Business Entity*]

Accounting concepts are described throughout this textbook when an application of a concept first occurs. When additional applications occur, a concept reference, such as [*CONCEPT: Business Entity*], indicates an application of a specific accounting concept. A brief description of each accounting concept used in this text is also provided in Appendix C.

©GETTY IMAGES/PHOTODISC

After completing a computer networking program at a local community college, Kim decided to start her own business so she would have more control over her daily schedule. After only two months, she has made all the arrangements and is ready to begin.

Kim enjoys both helping schools, businesses, and individuals set up a computer network and troubleshooting a network that is not working properly. She also enjoys being her own boss. She gets satisfaction from keeping her own accounting records and seeing that she is making money every month.

Forming and Dissolving a Proprietorship

A proprietorship is a business owned and controlled by one person. The advantages of a proprietorship include:

- *Ease of formation.*
- *Total control by the owner.*
- *Profits that are not shared.*

However, there are some disadvantages of organizing a proprietorship:

- *Limited resources.* The owner is the only person who can invest cash and other assets in the business.
- *Unlimited liability.* The owner is totally responsible for the liabilities of the business. Personal assets, such as a car, can be claimed by creditors to pay the business's liabilities.
- *Limited expertise.* Limited time, energy, and experience can be put into the business by the owner.
- *Limited life.* A proprietorship must be dissolved when the owner dies or decides to stop doing business.
- *Obligation to follow the laws of both the federal government and the state and city in which the business is formed.* Most cities and states have few, if any, legal procedures to follow. Once any legal requirements are met, the proprietorship can begin business. Should the owner decide to dissolve the proprietorship, he or she merely needs to stop doing business. Noncash assets can be sold, with the cash used to pay any outstanding liabilities.

Critical Thinking

1. Why do you think more businesses are organized as proprietorships than any other form of business organization?
2. What kinds of people do you think would be most successful as owners of a proprietorship?

THE ACCOUNTING EQUATION

Assets	=	Liabilities + Owner's Equity
Left side amount		Right side amounts
$0	=	$0 + $0

TechKnow Consulting will own items such as cash and supplies that will be used to conduct daily operations. Anything of value that is owned is called an **asset**. Assets have value because they can be used either to acquire other assets or to operate a business. For example, TechKnow Consulting will use cash to buy supplies for the business. TechKnow Consulting will then use the asset—supplies—in the operation of the computer consulting business.

Financial rights to the assets of a business are called **equities**. A business has two types of equities: (1) *Equity of those to whom money is owed*. For example, TechKnow Consulting may buy some supplies and agree to pay for the supplies at a later date. The business from whom supplies are bought will have a right to some of TechKnow's assets until TechKnow pays for the supplies. An amount owed by a business is called a **liability**. (2) *Equity of the owner*. Ms. Park will own TechKnow Consulting and invest in the assets of the business. Therefore, she will have a right to decide how the assets will be used. The amount remaining after the value of all liabilities is subtracted from the value of all assets is called **owner's equity**.

The relationship among assets, liabilities, and owner's equity can be written as an equation. An equation showing the relationship among assets, liabilities, and owner's equity is called the **accounting equation**. The accounting equation is most often stated as:

Assets = **Liabilities** + **Owner's Equity**

The accounting equation must be in balance. The total of the amounts on the left side must always equal the total of the amounts on the right side. Before a business starts, its accounting equation would show all zeros.

MAKING ETHICAL DECISIONS • MAKING ETHICAL DECISIONS • MAKING ETHICAL DECISIONS

making ethical decisions

Accounting Scandals Rock the Financial World

Entering the 21st century, Enron, WorldCom, and Andersen were three of the most celebrated names in corporate America. But the actions of a few individuals forced financial mammoths Enron and WorldCom into bankruptcy. Andersen, once one of the prestigious "Big 5" accounting firms, was forced out of business. These accounting scandals caused hundreds of thousands of employees to lose their jobs and millions of individuals to lose billions of dollars in investment and retirement accounts. The scandals rocked the public's confidence in the accounting profession and the stock markets.

The principles of right and wrong that guide an individual in making decisions are called **ethics**. The use of ethics in making business decisions is called **business ethics**.

Making ethical business decisions is a skill you can learn. Each chapter of this textbook contains a feature on business ethics. In Part 1, you will explore a model that guides your evaluation of business decisions. In later chapters, you will apply that model to make ethical business decisions. You will also be exposed to sources that will enable you to continue learning about business ethics long after you have completed this accounting course.

Instructions

Obtain an article that describes an accounting scandal such as Enron, WorldCom, Adelphia, Healthcorp South, or Parmalat. Write a one-paragraph summary that describes what happened and the individuals involved.

Xtra! Study Tools
accountingxtra.swlearning.com

terms review

accounting
accounting system
accounting records
financial statements
service business
proprietorship
asset
equities
liability
owner's equity
accounting equation
ethics
business ethics

audit your understanding

1. What is accounting?
2. Give two examples of service businesses.
3. What is a proprietorship?
4. State the accounting equation.

work together 1-1

Completing the accounting equation

Write the answers to the following problem in the *Working Papers.* Your instructor will guide you through the following example.

1. For each line, fill in the missing amount to complete the accounting equation.

Assets	=	Liabilities	+	Owner's Equity
?		3,000		8,000
10,000		?		6,000
63,000		35,000		?

on your own 1-1

Completing the accounting equation

Write the answers to the following problem in the *Working Papers.* Work this problem independently.

1. For each line, fill in the missing amount to complete the accounting equation.

Assets	=	Liabilities	+	Owner's Equity
30,000		?		13,000
?		60,000		20,000
51,000		25,000		?

1-2 How Business Activities Change the Accounting Equation

RECEIVING CASH

	Assets	=	Liabilities	+	Owner's Equity
	Cash	=			Kim Park, Capital
Beginning Balances	$0		$0		$0
Received cash from owner as an investment	+5,000				+5,000
New Balances	$5,000		$0		$5,000

Business activities change the amounts in the accounting equation. A business activity that changes assets, liabilities, or owner's equity is called a **transaction**. For example, a business that pays cash for supplies is engaging in a transaction. After each transaction, the accounting equation must remain in balance.

The accounting concept *Unit of Measurement* is applied when business transactions are stated in numbers that have common values—that is, using a common unit of measurement. [*CONCEPT: Unit of Measurement*] For example, in the United States, business transactions are recorded in dollars. The unit of measurement concept is followed so that the financial reports of businesses can be clearly stated and understood in numbers that have comparable values.

Received Cash Investment from Owner

Ms. Park uses $5,000.00 of her own money to invest in TechKnow Consulting. TechKnow Consulting should be concerned only with the effect of this transaction on TechKnow Consulting's records. The business should not be concerned about Ms. Park's personal records. [*CONCEPT: Business Entity*]

Transaction 1 ***August 1. Received cash from owner as an investment, $5,000.00.***

A record summarizing all the information pertaining to a single item in the accounting equation is called an **account**. The name given to an account is called an **account title**. Each part of the accounting equation consists of one or more accounts.

In the accounting equation shown above, the asset account, Cash, is increased by $5,000.00, the amount of cash received by the business. This increase is on the left side of the accounting equation. The amount in an account is called the **account balance**. Before the owner's investment, the account balance of Cash was zero. After the owner's investment, the account balance of Cash is $5,000.00.

The account used to summarize the owner's equity in a business is called **capital**. The capital account is an owner's equity account. In the accounting equation shown above, the owner's equity account, Kim Park, Capital, is increased by $5,000.00. This increase is on the right side of the accounting equation. Before the owner's investment, the account balance of Kim Park, Capital was zero. After the owner's investment, the account balance of Kim Park, Capital is $5,000.00.

The accounting equation has changed as a result of the receipt of cash. However, both sides of the equation are changed by the same amount: The $5,000.00 increase on the left side of the equation equals the $5,000.00 increase on the right side of the equation. Therefore, the accounting equation is still in balance.

PAYING CASH

	Assets			=	Liabilities +	Owner's Equity
	Cash	+ Supplies	+ Prepaid Insurance	=		Kim Park, Capital
Balances	$5,000	$0	$0		$0	$5,000
Paid cash for supplies	−275	+275				
Balances	$4,725	$275	$0		$0	$5,000
Paid cash for insurance	−1,200		+1,200			
New Balances	$3,525	$275	$1,200		$0	$5,000

TechKnow Consulting pays cash for supplies and insurance.

Paid Cash for Supplies

TechKnow Consulting needs supplies to operate the business. Kim Park uses some of TechKnow Consulting's cash to buy supplies.

Transaction 2 ***August 3. Paid cash for supplies, $275.00.***

In this transaction, two asset accounts are changed. One asset, cash, has been exchanged for another asset, supplies. The asset account, Cash, is decreased by $275.00, the amount of cash paid out. This decrease is on the left side of the accounting equation. The asset account, Supplies, is increased by $275.00, the amount of supplies bought. This increase is also on the left side of the accounting equation.

For this transaction, two assets are changed. Therefore, the two changes are both on the left side of the accounting equation. When changes are made on only one side of the accounting equation, the equation must still be in balance. Therefore, if one account is increased, another account on the same side of the equation must be decreased. After this transaction, the new account balance of Cash is $4,725.00. The new account balance of Supplies is $275.00. The sum of the amounts on the left side is $5,000.00 (Cash, $4,725.00 + Supplies, $275.00). The amount on the right side is also $5,000.00. Therefore, the accounting equation is still in balance.

Paid Cash for Insurance

Insurance premiums must be paid in advance. For example, TechKnow Consulting pays a $1,200.00 insurance premium for future insurance coverage.

Transaction 3 ***August 4. Paid cash for insurance, $1,200.00.***

In return for this payment, TechKnow Consulting is entitled to insurance coverage for the length of the policy. The insurance coverage is something of value owned by TechKnow Consulting. Therefore, the insurance coverage is an asset. Because insurance premiums are paid in advance, or prepaid, the premiums are recorded in an asset account titled Prepaid Insurance.

In this transaction, two assets are changed. One asset, cash, has been exchanged for another asset, prepaid insurance. The asset account, Cash, is decreased by $1,200.00, the amount of cash paid out. The asset account, Prepaid Insurance, is increased by $1,200.00, the amount of insurance bought.

After this transaction, the new account balance of Cash is $3,525.00. The new account balance of Prepaid Insurance is $1,200.00. The sum of the amounts on the left side is $5,000.00 (Cash, $3,525.00 + Supplies, $275.00 + Prepaid Insurance, $1,200.00). The amount on the right side is also $5,000.00. Therefore, the accounting equation is still in balance.

TRANSACTIONS ON ACCOUNT

	Assets			= Liabilities +	Owner's Equity
	Cash	+ Supplies	+ Prepaid Insurance	= Accts. Pay.—Supply Depot	+ Kim Park, Capital
Balances	$3,525	$275	$1,200	$0	$5,000
Bought supplies on account		+500		+500	
New Balances	$3,525	$775	$1,200	$500	$5,000
Paid cash on account	−300			−300	
New Balances	$3,225	$775	$1,200	$200	$5,000

Bought Supplies on Account

TechKnow Consulting needs to buy additional supplies. The supplies are obtained from Supply Depot, and TechKnow arranges to pay for them at the end of the month. It is a common business practice to buy items and pay for them at a future date. Another way to state this activity is to say that these items are bought *on account.*

Transaction 4 ***August 7. Bought supplies on account from Supply Depot, $500.00.***

In this transaction, one asset and one liability are changed. The asset account, Supplies, is increased by $500.00, the amount of supplies bought. Supply Depot will have a claim against some of TechKnow Consulting's assets until TechKnow Consulting pays for the supplies bought. Therefore, Accounts Payable—Supply Depot is a liability account. The liability account, Accounts Payable—Supply Depot, is increased by $500.00, the amount owed for the supplies.

After this transaction, the new account balance of Supplies is $775.00. The new account balance of Accounts Payable—Supply Depot is $500.00. The sum of the amounts on the left side is $5,500.00 (Cash, $3,525.00 + Supplies, $775.00 + Prepaid Insurance, $1,200.00). The sum of the amounts on the right side is also $5,500.00 (Accounts Payable—Supply Depot, $500.00 + Kim Park, Capital, $5,000.00). Therefore, the accounting equation is still in balance.

Paid Cash on Account

Since TechKnow Consulting is a new business, Supply Depot has not done business with TechKnow Consulting before. Supply Depot allows TechKnow Consulting to buy supplies on account but requires TechKnow Consulting to send a check for $300.00 immediately. TechKnow Consulting will pay the remaining portion of this liability at a later date.

Transaction 5 ***August 11. Paid cash on account to Supply Depot, $300.00.***

In this transaction, one asset and one liability are changed. The asset account, Cash, is decreased by $300.00, the amount of cash paid out. After this payment, TechKnow Consulting owes less money to Supply Depot. Therefore, the liability account, Accounts Payable—Supply Depot, is decreased by $300.00, the amount paid on account.

After this transaction, the new account balance of Cash is $3,225.00. The new account balance of Accounts Payable—Supply Depot is $200.00. The sum of the amounts on the left side is $5,200.00 (Cash, $3,225.00 + Supplies, $775.00 + Prepaid Insurance, $1,200.00). The sum of the amounts on the right side is also $5,200.00 (Accounts Payable—Supply Depot, $200.00 + Kim Park, Capital, $5,000.00). Therefore, the accounting equation is still in balance.

REMEMBER The left side of the accounting equation (assets) must always equal the right side (liabilities plus owner's equity).

terms review

transaction
account
account title
account balance
capital

audit your understanding

1. What must be done if a transaction increases the left side of the accounting equation?
2. How can a transaction affect only one side of the accounting equation?
3. To what does the phrase *on account* refer?

work together 1-2

Determining how transactions change an accounting equation

Write the answers to the following problem in the *Working Papers.* Your instructor will guide you through the following example.

Trans. No.	Assets	= Liabilities	+ Owner's Equity
1.			

1. For each transaction, place a plus (+) in the appropriate column if the classification is increased. Place a minus (−) in the appropriate column if the classification is decreased.

Transactions:

1. Bought supplies on account.
2. Received cash from owner as an investment.
3. Paid cash for insurance.
4. Paid cash on account.

on your own 1-2

Determining how transactions change an accounting equation

Write the answers to the following problem in the *Working Papers.* Work this problem independently.

Trans. No.	Assets	= Liabilities	+ Owner's Equity
1.			

1. For each transaction, place a plus (+) in the appropriate column if the classification is increased. Place a minus (−) in the appropriate column if the classification is decreased.

Transactions:

1. Received cash from owner as investment.
2. Bought supplies on account.
3. Paid cash for supplies.
4. Paid cash for insurance.
5. Paid cash on account.

LESSON • LESSON • LESSON • LESSON • LESSON • LESSON

1-3 How Transactions Change Owner's Equity in an Accounting Equation

REVENUE TRANSACTIONS

	Assets				= Liabilities +	Owner's Equity
	Cash +	Accts. Rec.—Oakdale School	+ Supplies +	Prepaid Insurance =	Accts. Pay.—Supply Depot +	Kim Park, Capital
Balances	$3,225	—0—	$775	$1,200	$200	$5,000
Received cash from sales	+295					+295 (revenue)
New Balances	$3,520	—0—	$775	$1,200	$200	$5,295
Sold services on account		+350				+350 (revenue)
New Balances	$3,520	$350	$775	$1,200	$200	$5,645

Total of left side: $3,520 + $350 + $775 + $1,200 = $5,845

Total of right side: $200 + $5,645 = $5,845

Received Cash from Sales

A transaction for the sale of goods or services results in an increase in owner's equity. An increase in owner's equity resulting from the operation of a business is called **revenue**. When cash is received from a sale, the total amount of both assets and owner's equity is increased.

Transaction 6 ***August 12. Received cash from sales, $295.00.***

When TechKnow Consulting receives cash for services performed, the asset account, Cash, is increased by the amount of cash received, $295.00. This increase is on the left side of the equation. The owner's equity account, Kim Park, Capital, is also increased by $295.00. This increase is on the right side of the equation. After this transaction is recorded, the equation is still in balance.

In this chapter, three different kinds of transactions that affect owner's equity are described. Therefore, a description of the transaction is shown in parentheses to the right of the amount in the accounting equation.

Sold Services on Account

A sale for which cash will be received at a later date is called a **sale on account**, or a *charge sale*. TechKnow Consulting contracts with a school and an Internet cafe to provide consulting services for payment at a later date. All other customers must pay cash at the time of the service. Regardless of when payment is made, the revenue should be recorded at the time of a sale. The accounting concept *Realization of Revenue* is applied when revenue is recorded at the time goods or services are sold. [*CONCEPT: Realization of Revenue*]

Transaction 7 ***August 12. Sold services on account to Oakdale School, $350.00.***

When TechKnow Consulting sells services on account, the asset account, Accounts Receivable—Oakdale School, is increased by $350.00, the amount of cash that will be received.

This increase is on the left side of the equation. The owner's equity account, Kim Park, Capital, is also increased by $350.00 on the right side of the equation. The equation is still in balance.

EXPENSE TRANSACTIONS

	Assets				= Liabilities +	Owner's Equity
	Cash +	Accts. Rec.— Oakdale School	+ Supplies +	Prepaid Insurance =	Accts. Pay.— Supply Depot +	Kim Park, Capital
Balances	$3,520	$350	$775	$1,200	$200	$5,645
Paid cash for rent	−300					−300 (expense)
New Balances	$3,220	$350	$775	$1,200	$200	$5,345
Paid cash for telephone bill	−40					−40 (expense)
New Balances	$3,180	$350	$775	$1,200	$200	$5,305

Total of left side:
$3,180 + $350 + $775 + $1,200 = $5,505

Total of right side:
$200 + $5,305 = $5,505

A transaction to pay for goods or services needed to operate a business results in a decrease in owner's equity. A decrease in owner's equity resulting from the operation of a business is called an **expense**. When cash is paid for expenses, the business has less cash. Therefore, the asset account, Cash, is decreased. The owner's equity account, Kim Park, Capital, is also decreased by the same amount.

Paid Cash for Rent

Transaction 8 ***August 12. Paid cash for rent, $300.00.***

The asset account, Cash, is decreased by $300.00, the amount of cash paid out. This decrease is on the left side of the equation. The owner's equity account, Kim Park, Capital, is also decreased by $300.00. This decrease is on the right side of the equation. After this transaction is recorded, the equation is still in balance.

Paid Cash for Telephone Bill

Transaction 9 ***August 12. Paid cash for telephone bill, $40.00.***

The asset account, Cash, is decreased by $40.00, the amount of cash paid out. This decrease is on the left side of the equation. The owner's equity account, Kim Park, Capital, is also decreased by $40.00. This decrease is on the right side of the equation. After this transaction is recorded, the equation is still in balance.

Other expense transactions might be for advertising, equipment rental or repairs, charitable contributions, and other miscellaneous items. All expense transactions affect the accounting equation in the same way as in Transactions 8 and 9.

OTHER CASH TRANSACTIONS

	Assets				= Liabilities +	Owner's Equity
	Cash +	Accts. Rec.— Oakdale School	+ Supplies +	Prepaid Insurance =	Accts. Pay.— Supply Depot +	Kim Park, Capital
Balances	$3,180	$350	$775	$1,200	$200	$5,305
Received cash on account	+200	−200				
New Balances	$3,380	$150	$775	$1,200	$200	$5,305
Paid cash to owner for personal use	−125					−125 (withdrawal)
New Balances	$3,255	$150	$775	$1,200	$200	$5,180

Total of left side:
$3,255 + $150 + $775 + $1,200 = $5,380

Total of right side:
$200 + $5,180 = $5,380

Received Cash on Account

When a company receives cash from a customer for a prior sale, the transaction increases the cash account balance and decreases the accounts receivable balance.

Transaction 10 ***August 12. Received cash on account from Oakdale School, $200.00.***

The asset account, Cash, is increased by $200.00. This increase is on the left side of the equation. The asset account, Accounts Receivable—Oakdale School, is decreased by $200.00. This decrease is also on the left side of the equation. After this transaction is recorded, the equation is still in balance.

Paid Cash to Owner for Personal Use

Assets taken out of a business for the owner's personal use are called **withdrawals**. A withdrawal decreases owner's equity. Although an owner may withdraw any kind of asset, usually an owner withdraws cash. The withdrawal decreases the account balance of the withdrawn asset, such as Cash.

Transaction 11 ***August 12. Paid cash to owner for personal use, $125.00.***

The asset account, Cash, is decreased by $125.00. This decrease is on the left side of the accounting equation. The owner's equity account, Kim Park, Capital, is also decreased by $125.00. This decrease is on the right side of the equation. After this transaction is recorded, the equation is still in balance.

A decrease in owner's equity because of a withdrawal is not a result of the normal operations of a business. Therefore, a withdrawal is not considered an expense.

Summary of Changes in Owner's Equity

Immediately after recording the beginning investment used to start TechKnow Consulting, the total owner's equity was $5,000.00, which represented the investment by the owner, Kim Park. Since that initial investment, five additional transactions that changed owner's equity were recorded in the accounting equation.

These transactions increased owner's equity by $180.00, from $5,000.00 to $5,180.00. Transaction 10, cash received on account, is not listed because it affects two accounts that are both on the left side of the accounting equation.

Transaction Number	Kind of Transaction	Change in Owner's Equity
6	Revenue (cash)	+295.00
7	Revenue (on account)	+350.00
8	Expense (rent)	−300.00
9	Expense (telephone)	− 40.00
11	Withdrawal	−125.00
Net change in owner's equity		+180.00

Xtra! Study Tools
accountingxtra.swlearning.com

terms review

revenue
sale on account
expense
withdrawals

TERMS REVIEW

audit your understanding

1. How is owner's equity affected when cash is received from sales?
2. How is owner's equity affected when services are sold on account?
3. How is owner's equity affected when cash is paid for expenses?

AUDIT YOUR

work together 1-3

Determining how transactions change an accounting equation

Write the answers to the following problem in the *Working Papers*. Your instructor will guide you through the following example.

1. Place a plus (+) in the appropriate column if the account is increased. Place a minus (−) in the appropriate column if the account is decreased.

Trans. No.	Assets				= Liabilities	+ Owner's Equity
	Cash	+ Accts. Rec.— Bowman Co.	+ Supplies	+ Prepaid Insurance	= Accts. Pay.— Maxwell Co.	+ Susan Sanders, Capital
1.						

Transactions:

1. Received cash from sales.
2. Sold services on account to Bowman Company.
3. Paid cash for telephone bill.
4. Received cash on account from Bowman Company.
5. Paid cash to owner for personal use.

WORK TOGETHER • WORK TOGETHER • WORK

on your own 1-3

Determining how transactions change an accounting equation

Write the answers to the following problem in the *Working Papers*. Work this problem independently.

1. Place a plus (+) in the appropriate column if the account is increased. Place a minus (−) in the appropriate column if the account is decreased.

Trans. No.	Assets				= Liabilities	+ Owner's Equity
	Cash	+ Accts. Rec.— Navarro Co.	+ Supplies	+ Prepaid Insurance	= Accts. Pay.— Barrett Co.	+ Vincent Orr, Capital
1.						

Transactions:

1. Sold services on account to Navarro Company.
2. Received cash from sales.
3. Received cash on account from Navarro Company.
4. Paid cash to owner for personal use.
5. Paid cash for rent.

ON YOUR OWN • ON YOUR OWN • ON YOUR OWN

SUMMARY

After completing this chapter, you can

1. Define accounting terms related to starting a service business organized as a proprietorship and to changes that affect the accounting equation.
2. Identify accounting concepts and practices related to starting a service business organized as a proprietorship and to changes that affect the accounting equation.
3. Classify accounts as assets, liabilities, or owner's equity and demonstrate their relationships in the accounting equation.
4. Analyze how transactions affect accounts in an accounting equation.

Explore Accounting

What Is GAAP?

The standards and rules that accountants follow while recording and reporting financial activities are commonly referred to as *generally accepted accounting principles*, or *GAAP*. These rules have not been developed by any one group of rule makers but have instead evolved over time and from many sources.

By law, the Securities and Exchange Commission (SEC) has the authority to establish GAAP. The SEC, however, has allowed a series of private organizations to determine GAAP. Currently, the organization that has the authority to set accounting standards is the Financial Accounting Standards Board (FASB), which was established in 1973.

The standard-setting process includes getting input and feedback from many sources. FASB listens to this feedback and considers all sides of each issue.

Why Is GAAP Necessary?

Users of financial statements rely on the information those statements contain. If the preparers of financial statements were allowed to follow any measurement, recording, and reporting rules, the users of the statements would have no way to determine if the financial statements present fairly the financial position of the business.

By requiring the financial statement preparers to consistently follow certain standards and rules—such as GAAP—the users are able to compare the financial statements of several companies and to track the results of one company over several time periods.

Discussion: Why would a group of people disagree with a proposed accounting standard?

Research: Using your local library or the Internet, find additional information about the FASB. Write a one-page report on your findings.

1-1 APPLICATION PROBLEM

Completing the accounting equation

Instructions:

For each line, fill in the missing amount to complete the accounting equation. Use the form in your *Working Papers* to complete this problem.

Assets	=	Liabilities	+	Owner's Equity
95,000		51,000		?
?		44,000		20,000
4,000		?		2,500
138,000		70,000		?
19,000		?		11,000
?		4,000		12,000
35,000		13,000		?
?		120,000		49,000
8,000		?		3,200
86,000		48,000		?
12,000		?		7,000
?		8,000		22,000
47,000		24,000		?
?		29,000		13,000
57,000		?		36,000
125,000		69,000		?
11,000		?		6,000
?		2,000		3,300

1-2 APPLICATION PROBLEM

Determining how transactions change an accounting equation

Calvin Parish is starting Parish Repair Shop, a small service business. Parish Repair Shop uses the accounts shown in the following accounting equation. Use the form in your *Working Papers* to complete this problem.

Trans. No.	Assets			= Liabilities		+ Owner's Equity
	Cash +	Supplies +	Prepaid Insurance =	Accts. Pay.—Five Star Supply +	Accts. Pay.—Riverland Company +	Calvin Parish, Capital
Beg. Bal. 1.	—0— +3,000	—0—	—0—	—0—	—0—	—0— +3,000
New Bal. 2.	3,000	—0—	—0—	—0—	—0—	3,000

Transactions:

1. Received cash from owner as an investment, $3,000.00.
2. Paid cash for insurance, $1,600.00.
3. Bought supplies on account from Five Star Supply, $700.00.

4. Bought supplies on account from Riverland Company, $300.00.
5. Paid cash on account to Five Star Supply, $700.00.
6. Paid cash on account to Riverland Company, $200.00.
7. Paid cash for supplies, $100.00.
8. Received cash from owner as an investment, $1,500.00.

Instructions:

For each transaction, complete the following. Transaction 1 is given as an example.

a. Analyze the transaction to determine which accounts in the accounting equation are affected.
b. Write the amount in the appropriate columns using a plus (+) if the account increases or a minus (−) if the account decreases.
c. Calculate the new balance for each account in the accounting equation.
d. Before going on to the next transaction, determine that the accounting equation is still in balance.

1-3 APPLICATION PROBLEM

Determining how revenue, expense, and withdrawal transactions change an accounting equation

Peter Smith operates a service business called Peter's Service Company. Peter's Service Company uses the accounts shown in the following accounting equation. Use the form in your *Working Papers* to complete this problem.

Trans. No.	Assets				= Liabilities	+ Owner's Equity
	Cash +	Accts. Rec.—Lisa Lee +	Supplies +	Prepaid Insurance =	Accts. Pay.—Kline Co. +	Peter Smith, Capital
Beg. Bal.	625	—0—	375	300	200	1,100
1.	*−300*					*−300 (expense)*
New Bal.	*325*	*—0—*	*375*	*300*	*200*	*800*
2.						

Transactions:

1. Paid cash for rent, $300.00.
2. Paid cash to owner for personal use, $150.00.
3. Received cash from sales, $800.00.
4. Paid cash for equipment repairs, $100.00.
5. Sold services on account to Lisa Lee, $400.00.
6. Received cash from sales, $650.00.
7. Paid cash for charitable contributions, $35.00.
8. Received cash on account from Lisa Lee, $300.00.

Instructions:

For each transaction, complete the following. Transaction 1 is given as an example.

a. Analyze the transaction to determine which accounts in the accounting equation are affected.
b. Write the amount in the appropriate columns, using a plus (+) if the account increases or a minus (−) if the account decreases.
c. For transactions that change owner's equity, write in parentheses a description of the transaction to the right of the amount.
d. Calculate the new balance for each account in the accounting equation.
e. Before going on to the next transaction, determine that the accounting equation is still in balance.

1-4 MASTERY PROBLEM

Determining how transactions change an accounting equation

Marion Cassidy operates a service business called Cassidy Company. Cassidy Company uses the accounts shown in the following accounting equation. Use the form in your *Working Papers* to complete this problem.

Trans. No.	Assets				= Liabilities	+ Owner's Equity
	Cash +	Accts. Rec.— Ana Santiago +	Supplies +	Prepaid Insurance =	Accts. Pay.— Delta Co. +	Marion Cassidy, Capital
Beg. Bal.	2,300	—0—	200	100	1,800	800
1.	*−400*					*−400 (expense)*
New Bal.	*1,900*	*—0—*	*200*	*100*	*1,800*	*400*
2.						

Transactions:

1. Paid cash for rent, $400.00.
2. Received cash from owner as an investment, $500.00.
3. Paid cash for telephone bill, $50.00.
4. Received cash from sales, $1,025.00.
5. Bought supplies on account from Delta Company, $450.00.
6. Sold services on account to Ana Santiago, $730.00.
7. Paid cash for advertising, $660.00.
8. Paid cash for supplies, $150.00.
9. Received cash on account from Ana Santiago, $400.00.
10. Paid cash on account to Delta Company, $1,500.00.
11. Paid cash for one month of insurance, $100.00.
12. Received cash from sales, $1,230.00.
13. Paid cash to owner for personal use, $1,200.00.

Instructions:

For each transaction, complete the following. Transaction 1 is given as an example.

a. Analyze the transaction to determine which accounts in the accounting equation are affected.
b. Write the amount in the appropriate columns, using a plus (+) if the account increases or a minus (−) if the account decreases.
c. For transactions that change owner's equity, write in parentheses a description of the transaction to the right of the amount.
d. Calculate the new balance for each account in the accounting equation.
e. Before going on to the next transaction, determine that the accounting equation is still in balance.

1-5 CHALLENGE PROBLEM

Determining how transactions change an accounting equation

Zachary Martin owns Zachary's Repair Shop. On February 1, Zachary's Repair Shop's accounting equation indicated the following account balances. Use the form in your *Working Papers* to complete this problem.

	Assets				= Liabilities	+ Owner's Equity
Trans. No.	Cash	+ Accts. Rec.— Mary Lou Pier	+ Supplies	+ Prepaid Insurance	= Accts. Pay.— Kollasch Co.	+ Zachary Martin, Capital
Beg. Bal.	8,552	1,748	1,485	615	3,145	9,255
1.						

Transactions:

1. Took $400.00 of supplies for personal use.
2. Had equipment repaired at Kollasch Company and agreed to pay Kollasch Company at a later date, $250.00.
3. Mr. Martin had some personal property, which he sold for $500.00 cash.
4. Paid Kollasch Company $120.00 on account.

Instructions:

1. For each transaction, complete the following.
   a. Analyze the transaction to determine which accounts in the accounting equation are affected.
   b. Write the amount in the appropriate columns, using a plus (+) if the account increases or a minus (−) if the account decreases.
   c. For transactions that change owner's equity, write in parentheses a description of the transaction to the right of the amount.
   d. Calculate the new balance for each account in the accounting equation.
   e. Before going on to the next transaction, determine that the accounting equation is still in balance.
2. Answer the following questions.
   a. Why can the owner of a business withdraw assets from that business for personal use?
   b. Why would the owner withdraw assets other than cash?

applied communication

A resume provides a statement of your education, experience, and qualifications for a prospective employer. Your resume should be accurate, honest, and perfect in every respect. It should include all work experience along with the companies and dates of employment. Education, activities, and interests are all important items that should be covered.

Instructions:

Research how to prepare an appropriate resume using the library or the Internet. Then prepare a resume that you could send to a prospective employer.

APPLIED COMMUNICATION

cases for critical thinking

Case 1

Akira Shinoda starts a new business. Mr. Shinoda uses his personal car in the business with the expectation that later the business can buy a car. All expenses for operating the car, including license plates, gasoline, oil, tune-ups, and new tires, are paid for out of business funds. Is this an acceptable procedure? Explain.

Case 2

At the end of the first day of business, Quick Clean Laundry has the assets and liabilities shown below.

The owner, Anh Vu, wants to know the amount of her equity in Quick Clean Laundry. Determine this amount and explain what this amount represents.

Assets		Liabilities	
Cash	$3,500.00	A/P—Smith Office Supplies	$ 750.00
Supplies	950.00	A/P—Super Supplies Company	1,500.00
Prepaid Insurance	1,200.00		

CASES FOR CRITICAL THINKING

SCANS workplace competency

Resource Competency: Selects Goal-Relevant Activities

Concept: Employers need workers who can identify job tasks as the first step in completing their jobs. Many people manage their time by creating a to-do list for each day. The to-do list shows everything that must be done in that day, both in work or school and personal activities. As tasks are completed, they are checked off as complete. Tasks left undone are transferred to the next day's to-do list.

Application: Create a to-do list of your activities for tomorrow.

SCANS WORKPLACE

graphing workshop

The assets, liabilities, and owner's equity for three different companies are given in the graph below.

Analyze the graph to answer the following questions.

1. Which category is largest?
2. Why will assets always be 50% of the total?

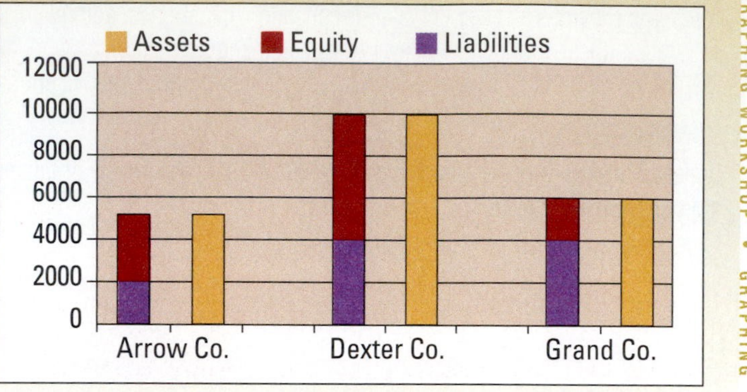

analyzing Best Buy's financial statements

Selected published financial information for Best Buy Co., Inc., is reproduced in Appendix B. Look at pages B-4 through B-8, where you will find Best Buy's financial statements. Under the heading on each page, you will see the phrase "$ in millions." This means that all dollar amounts are rounded to the nearest million. Therefore, an amount such as $174 actually means $174,000,000. Another way to think of this is that you can calculate the actual amount by multiplying the rounded amount by 1,000,000 ($174 × 1,000,000 = $174,000,000).

Not all companies round the amounts in their financial statements to the nearest million. Many companies round to the nearest thousand.

Instructions

1. List the actual amount of Accounts Payable and Revenue for Best Buy for 2004.
2. The financial statements for Barnes & Noble include the phrase "thousands of dollars." In 2003, the financial statements included Accounts Payable, $858,068 and Sales, $5,951,015. List the actual amount of Accounts Payable and Sales.

Automated Accounting

Computer Safety and Health Basics

Electrical Equipment

1. Don't unplug equipment by pulling on the electrical cord. Instead, grasp the plug at the outlet and remove it.
2. Don't stretch electrical cords across an aisle where someone might trip.
3. Avoid food and beverages near equipment where a spill might result in an electrical short.
4. Don't attempt to remove the cover of equipment while the power is on.
5. Don't attempt to repair equipment while it's plugged in. Most repairs should be done by an authorized technician or knowledgeable expert.
6. Always turn the power off when finished using equipment.
7. Don't overload extension cords.
8. Follow manufacturer recommendations for safe use.
9. Replace frayed electrical cords immediately.

Computers

1. To prevent equipment overheating, avoid blocking air vents.
2. Position keyboards to prevent bumping or dropping them off the work surface.
3. Don't spill food or liquid on or in any computer component. If you do, turn off the computer immediately, unplug it, and notify your instructor before cleaning up the spill or turning on the equipment.
4. Avoid jostling the computer if it becomes necessary to move it.
5. Do NOT attempt to open or repair any part of the computer unless directed to do so by your instructor.

Monitors

1. Repairs should be done by authorized service technicians only.
2. Adjust brightness and focus for comfortable viewing.
3. Reposition the monitor to avoid glare on the screen or use glare visors.
4. Don't leave fingerprints on the screen, and keep it clear of dust. Use only a soft cloth for cleaning.

Magnetic Media

1. Store software installation disks and CDs in a safe place.
2. Protect personal data disks and CDs. Make backup copies of critical files.
3. Keep disks and CDs away from extreme hot or cold temperatures. Don't leave disks in a car during very hot or cold weather.
4. Keep magnetic media away from magnetic fields such as transformers and magnets.

Health Concerns

1. Your back should be fully supported when sitting; your feet should be flat on the floor or on a footrest; and your thighs and hips should be parallel to the floor.
4. Your knees should be at the same height as your hips with your feet slightly forward.
5. Elbows should be close to the body and positioned at a 90-degree angle.
6. Your shoulders should be relaxed, and your arms should hang naturally.
7. Your hands, wrists, and forearms should be straight and parallel to the floor.
8. Your head should be level or bent slightly forward.
9. For prolonged sessions at the computer, change your body position frequently. Stand up and walk around for a few minutes. Stretch your hands, fingers, arms, and torso. If possible, make small adjustments to your chair, chair back, or backrest.

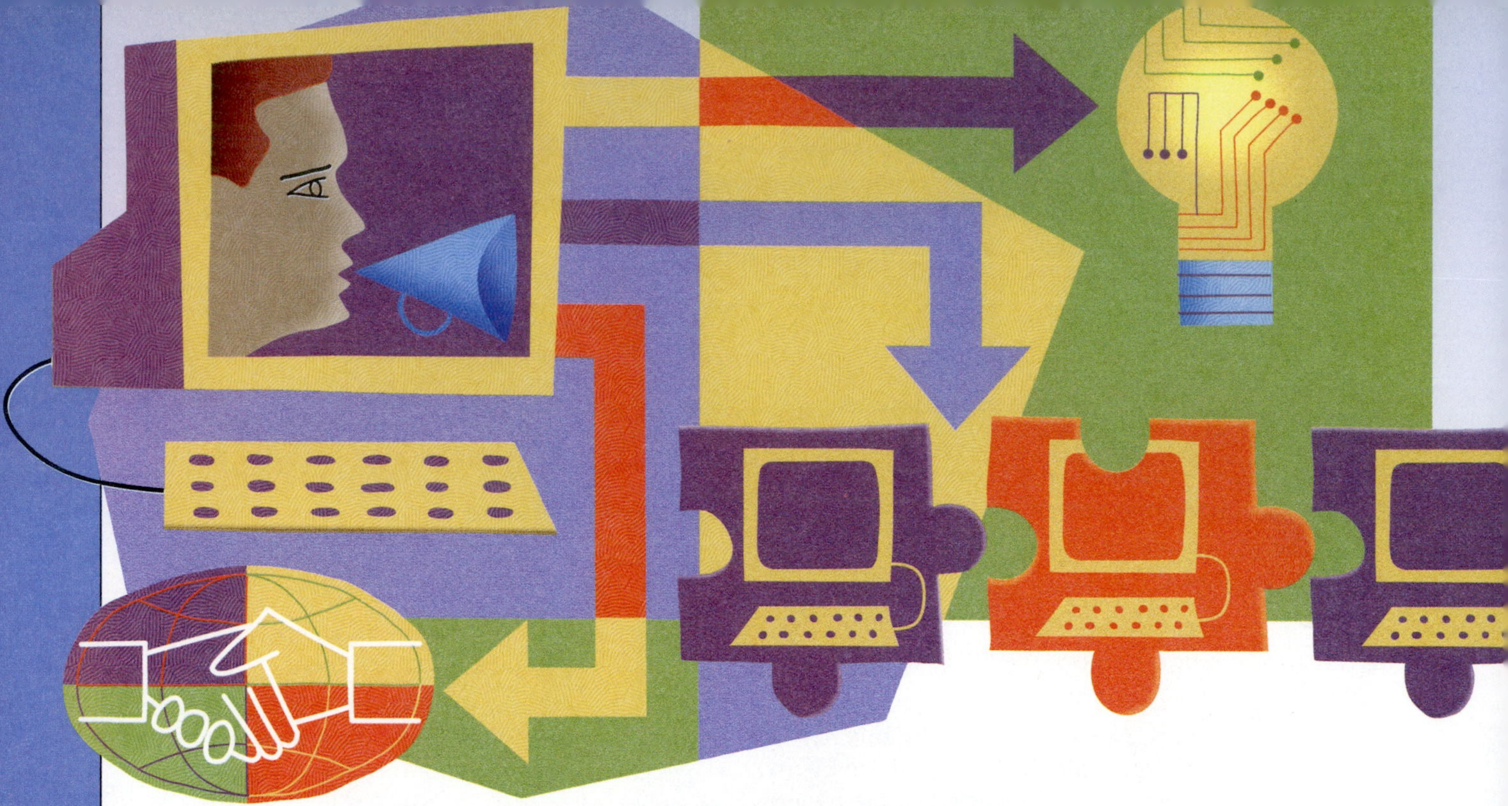

CHAPTER

2 Analyzing Transactions into Debit and Credit Parts

OBJECTIVES & TERMS

After studying Chapter 2, you will be able to:

1. Define accounting terms related to analyzing transactions into debit and credit parts.
2. Identify accounting practices related to analyzing transactions into debit and credit parts.
3. Use T accounts to analyze transactions showing which accounts are debited or credited for each transaction.
4. Analyze how transactions to set up a business affect accounts.
5. Analyze how transactions affect owner's equity accounts.

- T account
- debit
- credit
- normal balance
- chart of accounts

Point Your Browser
accountingxtra.swlearning.com

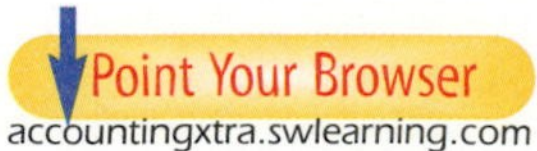

accounting in the real world

American Automobile Association (AAA)

©AAA, WWW.AAANEWSROOM.NET, ABOUT AAA, 2004

TRAVELING WITH THE AMERICAN AUTOMOBILE ASSOCIATION (AAA)

Picture yourself driving on a dark, deserted road. Suddenly your car stalls. You pull over to the side of the road. What do you do next? If you are a member of the American Automobile Association (AAA), you can pick up your cell phone and call for emergency roadside assistance.

Many people realize the benefits of a membership with the AAA. However, not many people know that the AAA was instrumental in starting the nationwide School Safety Patrol program back in 1920. In 1930, the AAA pioneered the driver education program still in existence in many high schools. As early as 1916, the AAA was fighting for federal dollars to be used to construct a national highway system.

The AAA sells memberships to individuals and families. In exchange for the membership fee, the AAA provides an array of benefits including emergency roadside assistance, travel services, insurance services, driver protection services, and even emergency check cashing services.

Critical Thinking

1. What asset and liability accounts might the AAA use to record its transactions?
2. List at least two transactions that the AAA might record.

accountingxtra.swlearning.com

Source: www.aaa.com

internet activity

COMPANY HEADQUARTERS

Go to the homepage of a company of your choice.

Instructions

Search the site to find when the company was started and where its headquarters (or home office) is located. This information is typically found under one of the following headings: "About Us," "Investor Relations," "History," or "Contact Us."

2-1 Using T Accounts

ANALYZING THE ACCOUNTING EQUATION

Even though the effects of transactions can be recorded in an accounting equation, the procedure is not practical in an actual accounting system. The number of accounts used by most businesses would make the accounting equation cumbersome to use as a major financial record. Therefore, a separate record is commonly used for each account. The accounting equation can be represented as a T, as shown below.

Assets =	Liabilities + Owner's Equity
Left side	Right side

The values of all things owned (assets) are on the left side of the accounting equation. The values of all equities or claims against the assets (liabilities and owner's equity) are on the right side of the accounting equation. The total of amounts on the left side of the accounting equation must always equal the total of amounts on the right side. Therefore, the total of all assets on the left side of the accounting equation must always equal the total of all liabilities and owner's equity on the right side.

MAKING ETHICAL DECISIONS • MAKING ETHICAL DECISIONS • MAKING ETHICAL DECISIONS

making ethical decisions

Ethics Versus Morality

Ethics and morality—these words are often used to refer to an individual's ability to "do what is right." These synonymous English words were derived from different languages. "Ethics" is derived from Greek, and "morality" is derived from Latin. Over time, our society has given a slightly different meaning to each word.

Over 100 years ago, C. C. Everett wrote, "Ethics is the science of morality." Morality is the standard of conduct that is acceptable in a society. Ethics is an organized method that relies on our morality to make moral decisions. Science students learn the scientific method—a model that guides how a proper experiment should be conducted. In the same manner, many ethical models have been proposed to guide individuals in applying their morality to business decisions.

The following ethical model will be used in this textbook:

1. Recognize you are facing an ethical dilemma.
2. Identify the action taken or the proposed action.
3. Analyze the action.
   a. Is the action illegal?
   b. Does the action violate company or professional standards?
   c. Who is affected, and how, by the action?
4. Determine if the action is ethical.

Instructions

Prepare a short report that contrasts the ethical model with the scientific method. How are the models similar? How are they different?

ACCOUNTS

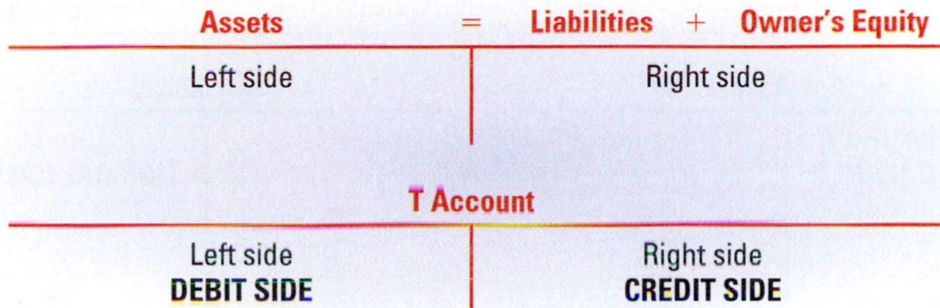

A record summarizing all the information pertaining to a single item in the accounting equation is known as an *account*. Transactions change the balances of accounts in the accounting equation. Accounting transactions must be analyzed to determine how account balances are changed. An accounting device used to analyze transactions is called a **T account**.

There are special names for amounts recorded on the left and right sides of a T account. An amount recorded on the left side is called a **debit**. An amount recorded on the right side is called a **credit**. The words debit and credit come from the Latin and Italian words *debere* and *credere*. Common abbreviations are *dr.* for debit and *cr.* for credit.

ACCOUNT BALANCES

Assets = Liabilities + Owner's Equity

Any Asset

Debit	Credit
NORMAL BALANCE	

Any Liability

Debit	Credit
	NORMAL BALANCE

Owner's Capital Account

Debit	Credit
	NORMAL BALANCE

The side of the account that is increased is called the **normal balance**. The process of increasing or decreasing account balances is discussed on the next page. Assets are on the left side of the accounting equation and have normal debit balances (left side). Liabilities are on the right side of the accounting equation and have normal credit balances (right side). The owner's capital account is on the right side of the accounting equation and has a normal credit balance (right side).

INCREASES AND DECREASES IN ACCOUNTS

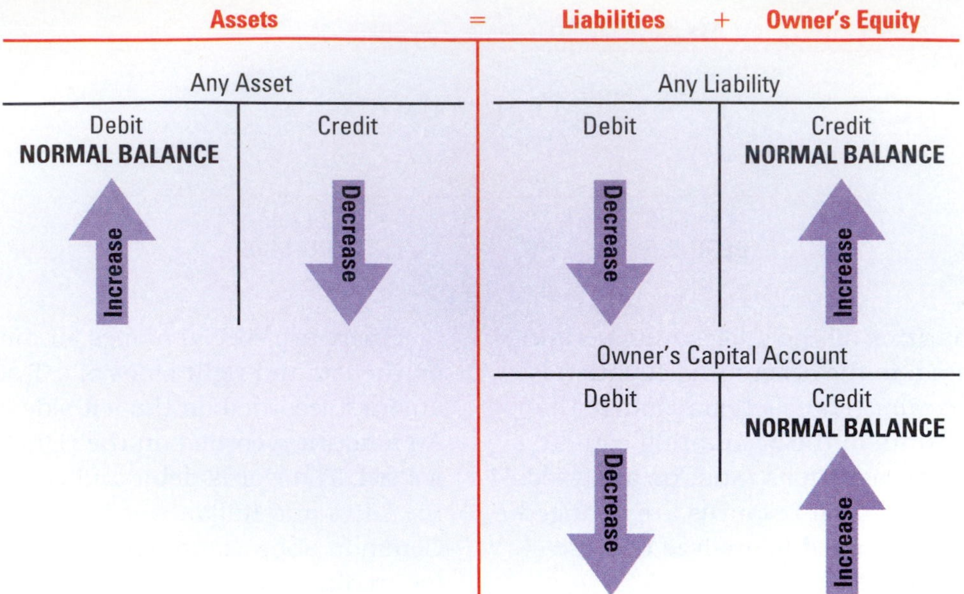

The sides of a T account are used to show increases and decreases in account balances.

Two basic accounting rules regulate increases and decreases of account balances.

1. Account balances increase on the normal balance side of an account.
2. Account balances decrease on the side opposite the normal balance side of an account.

Asset accounts have normal debit balances; therefore, asset accounts increase on the debit side and decrease on the credit side. Liability accounts have normal credit balances; therefore, liability accounts increase on the credit side and decrease on the debit side. The owner's capital account has a normal credit balance; therefore, the capital account increases on the credit side and decreases on the debit side.

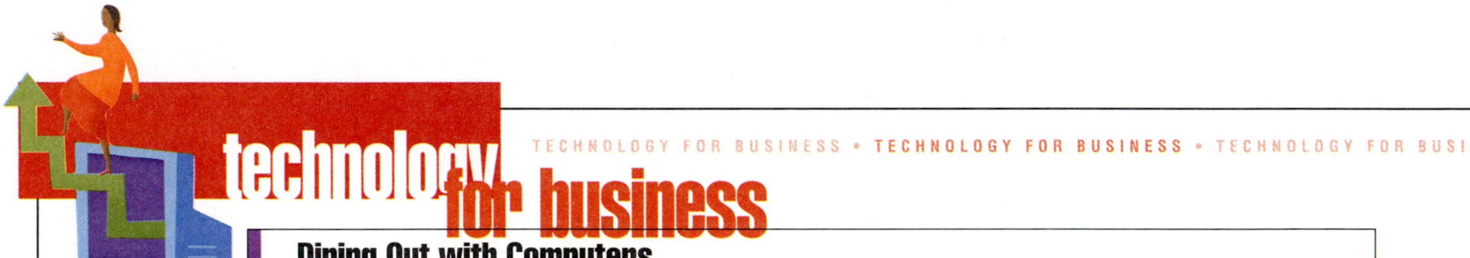

technology for business

Dining Out with Computers

Next time you order a taco—think technology. That's right, technology is changing the way restaurants do business. Computers are widely used to enter orders, generate guest checks, and print receipts. Computers also track the menu items that diners order—how many of each item are served each day, what time of day it is ordered, and what other items are ordered along with it.

The technology makes it possible for restaurant managers to predict how much of each food item to order, how much to prepare on a given day, and when to start cooking. Computer software programs also help managers plan their staffing needs, based on trends developed from historical data.

Hand-held computers are used by servers in some restaurants to transmit information to the kitchen, where it is printed or displayed for the chef. This technology can reduce the time diners sit at a table. That translates into more diners served and more revenue for the restaurant.

Remember, technology is all around, even when you order that taco.

Critical Thinking

Use your imagination to think of possible future uses of technology in restaurants.

terms review

T account
debit
credit
normal balance

audit your understanding

1. Draw the accounting equation on a T account.
2. What are the two accounting rules that regulate increases and decreases of account balances?

work together 2-1

Determining the normal balance and increase and decrease sides for accounts

Write the answers to the following problems in the *Working Papers*. Your instructor will guide you through the following examples.

Cash
Accounts Receivable—Christine Kelly
Supplies
Prepaid Insurance
Accounts Payable—Miller Supplies
Accounts Payable—Wayne Office Supplies
Jeff Dixon, Capital

For each of the accounts, complete the following:

1. Prepare a T account.
2. Label the debit and credit sides.
3. Label each side of the T account using the following labels:
   a. Normal Balance
   b. Increase
   c. Decrease

on your own 2-1

Determining the normal balance and increase and decrease sides for accounts

Write the answers to the following problems in the *Working Papers*. Work this problem independently.

Cash
Accounts Receivable—Lee McCann
Accounts Receivable—Sonya Lopez
Supplies
Prepaid Insurance
Accounts Payable—Topline Supplies
Vickie Monson, Capital

For each of the accounts, complete the following:

1. Prepare a T account.
2. Label the debit and credit sides.
3. Label each side of the T account using the following labels:
   a. Normal Balance
   b. Increase
   c. Decrease

LESSON

2-2 Analyzing How Transactions Affect Accounts

RECEIVED CASH FROM OWNER AS AN INVESTMENT

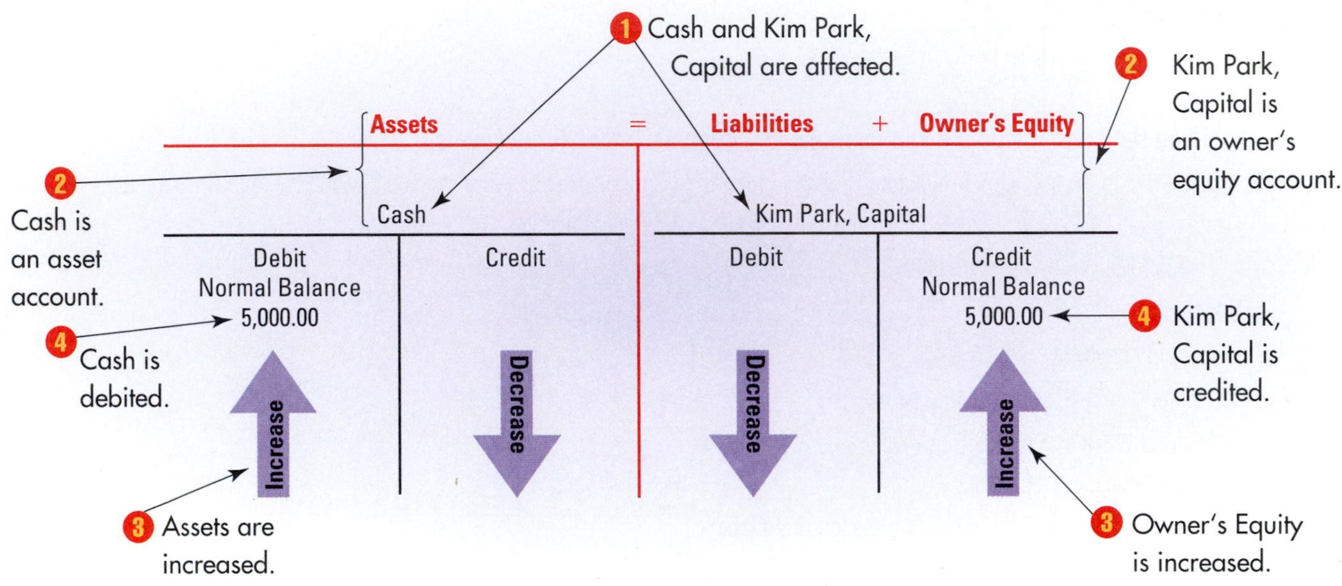

1 Cash and Kim Park, Capital are affected.
2 Kim Park, Capital is an owner's equity account.
Assets
=
Liabilities
+
Owner's Equity
2 Cash is an asset account.
Cash
Kim Park, Capital
Debit
Normal Balance
5,000.00
Credit
Debit
Credit
Normal Balance
5,000.00
4 Cash is debited.
4 Kim Park, Capital is credited.
Increase
Decrease
Decrease
Increase
3 Assets are increased.
3 Owner's Equity is increased.

August 1. Received cash from owner as an investment, $5,000.00.

The effect of this transaction is shown in the illustration. Before a transaction is recorded in the records of a business, the information is analyzed to determine which accounts are changed and how. Each transaction changes the balances of at least two accounts. A list of accounts used by a business is called a **chart of accounts**. The chart of accounts for TechKnow Consulting is found on page 3.

When accounts are analyzed, debits must equal credits for each transaction. In addition, after a transaction is recorded, total debits must equal total credits.

The same four questions are used every time a transaction is analyzed into its debit and credit parts.

STEPS

QUESTIONS FOR ANALYZING A TRANSACTION INTO ITS DEBIT AND CREDIT PARTS

1. Which accounts are affected?
Cash and *Kim Park, Capital*
2. How is each account classified?
Cash is an asset account. *Kim Park, Capital* is an owner's equity account.
3. How is each classification changed?
Assets increase. Owner's equity increases.
4. How is each amount entered in the accounts?
Assets increase on the debit side. Therefore, debit the asset account, *Cash*. Owner's equity accounts increase on the credit side. Therefore, credit the owner's equity account, *Kim Park, Capital*.

PAID CASH FOR SUPPLIES

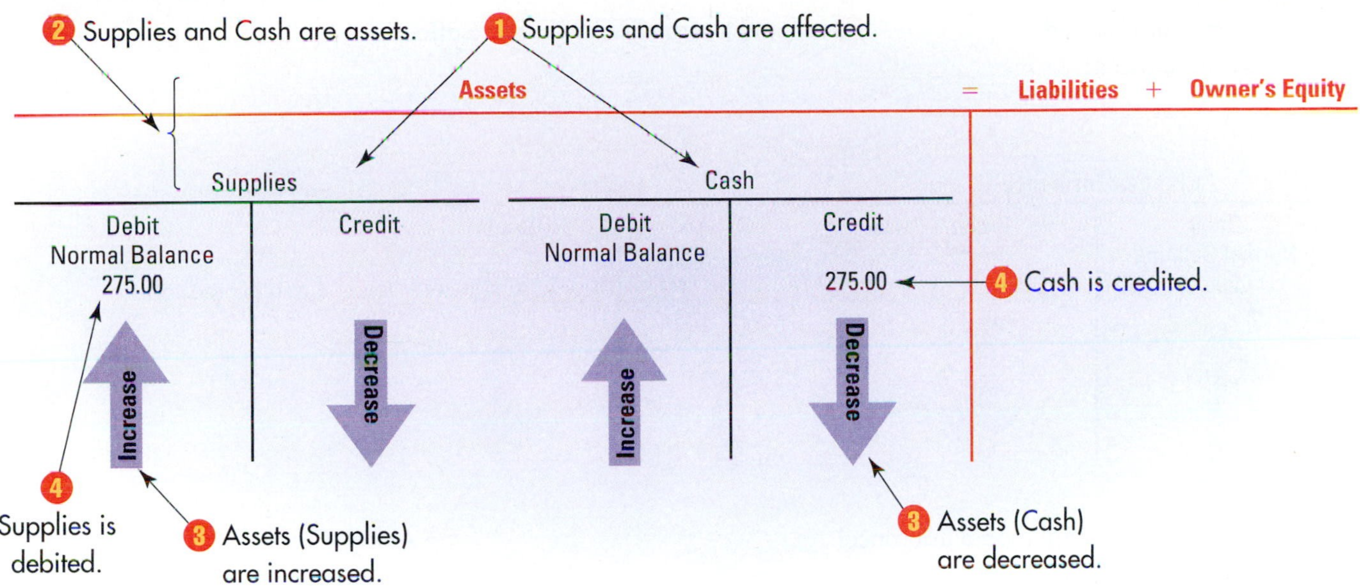

2 Supplies and Cash are assets.
1 Supplies and Cash are affected.
Assets
= Liabilities + Owner's Equity
Supplies
Cash
Debit
Normal Balance
275.00
Credit
Debit
Normal Balance
Credit
275.00
4 Cash is credited.
Increase
Decrease
Increase
Decrease
4 Supplies is debited.
3 Assets (Supplies) are increased.
3 Assets (Cash) are decreased.

August 3. Paid cash for supplies, $275.00.

The effect of this transaction on the accounting equation is shown in the illustration. In this transaction, two asset accounts are changed. One asset, cash, has been exchanged for another asset, supplies. The asset account, Cash, decreases by $275.00, the amount of cash paid out. This decrease is on the left side of the accounting equation. The asset account, Supplies, increases by $275.00, the amount of supplies bought. This increase is also on the left side of the accounting equation.

The two changes are both on the left side of the accounting equation. When changes are made on only one side of the accounting equation, the equation must still be in balance. Therefore, if one account is increased, another account on the same side of the equation must be decreased.

As you have seen, transactions must be carefully analyzed. A transaction may affect accounts from both sides of the accounting equation. Or, a transaction may affect accounts that are on the same side of the accounting equation, as is true in this example. A common error is to assume that every transaction must affect accounts on both sides of the accounting equation.

STEPS • STEPS • STEPS • STEPS • STEPS • STEPS • STEPS • STEPS • STEPS • STEPS

QUESTIONS FOR ANALYZING A TRANSACTION INTO ITS DEBIT AND CREDIT PARTS

1. Which accounts are affected?
   Supplies and *Cash*
2. How is each account classified?
   Supplies is an asset account. *Cash* is an asset account.
3. How is each classification changed?
   One asset (*Supplies*) increases and another asset (*Cash*) decreases.
4. How is each amount entered in the accounts?
   Assets increase on the debit side. Therefore, debit the asset account, *Supplies*. Assets decrease on the credit side. Therefore, credit the asset account, *Cash*.

PAID CASH FOR INSURANCE

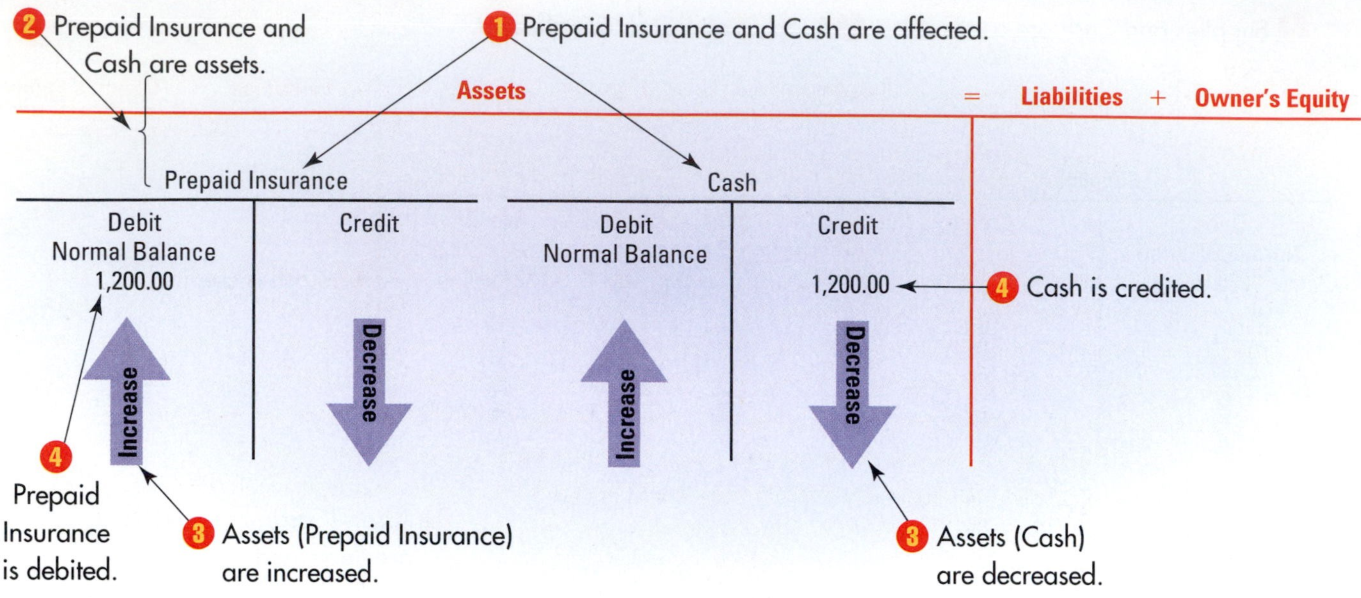

1 Prepaid Insurance and Cash are affected.
2 Prepaid Insurance and Cash are assets.
Assets
= Liabilities + Owner's Equity
Prepaid Insurance
Debit
Normal Balance
1,200.00
Credit
Increase
Decrease
Cash
Debit
Normal Balance
Credit
1,200.00
4 Cash is credited.
4 Prepaid Insurance is debited.
3 Assets (Prepaid Insurance) are increased.
3 Assets (Cash) are decreased.

August 4. Paid cash for insurance, $1,200.00.

Paying cash for insurance is very similar to paying cash for supplies. One asset is increased and one asset is decreased.

The effect of this transaction on the accounting equation is shown in the illustration. In this transaction, two assets are changed. One asset, cash, has been exchanged for another asset, prepaid insurance. The asset account, Cash, decreases by $1,200.00, the amount of cash paid out. This decrease is on the left side of the accounting equation. The asset account, Prepaid Insurance, increases by $1,200.00, the amount of insurance bought. This increase is also on the left side of the accounting equation.

FYI FOR YOUR INFORMATION

T accounts get their name from the arrangement of the lines making up the account. The horizontal line on top of the centered vertical line looks like a capital "T."

FYI FOR YOUR INFORMATION

Paying cash for insurance and buying supplies for cash are examples of transactions that affect only one side of the accounting equation. All the accounts involved in these transactions are assets.

STEPS STEPS • STEPS • STEPS • STEPS • STEPS • STEPS • STEPS • STEPS • STEPS • STEPS •

QUESTIONS FOR ANALYZING A TRANSACTION INTO ITS DEBIT AND CREDIT PARTS

1. Which accounts are affected?
   Prepaid Insurance and *Cash*
2. How is each account classified?
   Prepaid Insurance is an asset account. *Cash* is an asset account.
3. How is each classification changed?
   One asset (*Prepaid Insurance*) increases and another asset (*Cash*) decreases.
4. How is each amount entered in the accounts?
   Assets increase on the debit side. Therefore, debit the asset account, *Prepaid Insurance*. Assets decrease on the credit side. Therefore, credit the asset account, *Cash*.

BOUGHT SUPPLIES ON ACCOUNT

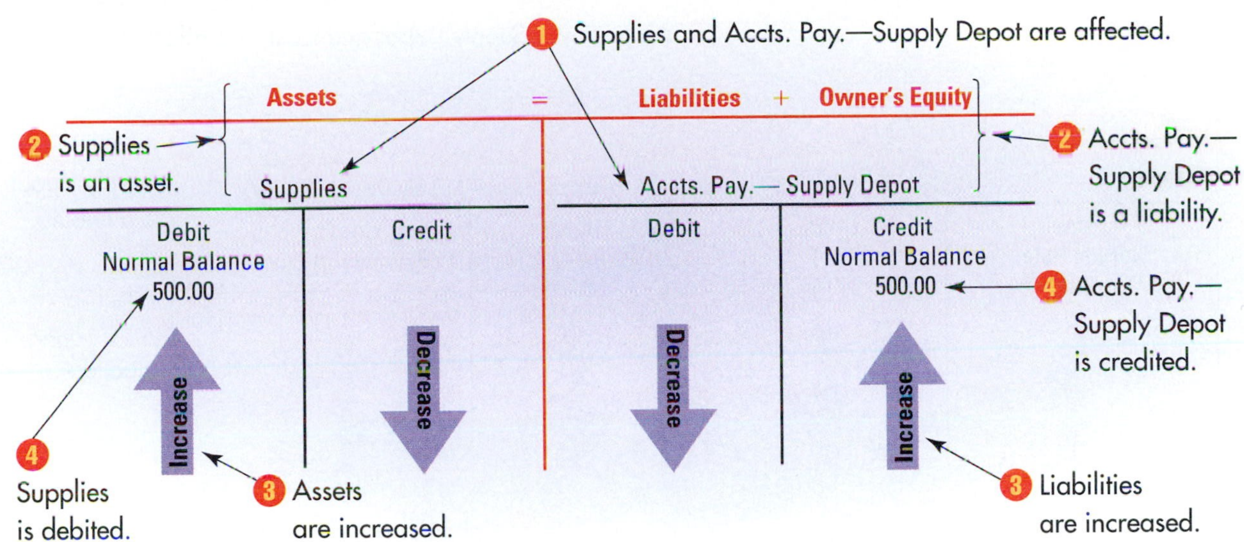

1 Supplies and Accts. Pay.—Supply Depot are affected.
Assets = Liabilities + Owner's Equity
2 Supplies is an asset.
Supplies
Debit
Normal Balance
500.00
Credit
Increase
Decrease
4 Supplies is debited.
3 Assets are increased.
Accts. Pay.—Supply Depot
Debit
Credit
Normal Balance
500.00
Decrease
Increase
2 Accts. Pay.—Supply Depot is a liability.
4 Accts. Pay.—Supply Depot is credited.
3 Liabilities are increased.

August 7 Bought supplies on account from Supply Depot, $500.00.

The effect of this transaction on the accounting equation is shown in the illustration. In this transaction, one asset and one liability are changed. The asset account, Supplies, increases by $500.00, the amount of supplies bought. This increase is on the left side of the accounting equation. Supply Depot will have a claim against some of TechKnow Consulting's assets until TechKnow Consulting pays for the supplies bought. Therefore, Accounts Payable—Supply Depot is a liability account. The liability account, Accounts Payable—Supply Depot, increases by $500.00, the amount owed for the supplies. This increase is on the right side of the accounting equation.

STEPS • STEPS • STEPS • STEPS

QUESTIONS FOR ANALYZING A TRANSACTION INTO ITS DEBIT AND CREDIT PARTS

1. Which accounts are affected?
   Supplies and *Accounts Payable—Supply Depot*
2. How is each account classified?
   Supplies is an asset account. *Accounts Payable—Supply Depot* is a liability account.
3. How is each classification changed?
   Assets increase. Liabilities increase.
4. How is each amount entered in the accounts?
   Assets increase on the debit side. Therefore, debit the asset account, *Supplies*. Liabilities increase on the credit side. Therefore, credit the liability account, *Accounts Payable—Supply Depot*.

©GETTY IMAGES/PHOTODISC

PAID CASH ON ACCOUNT

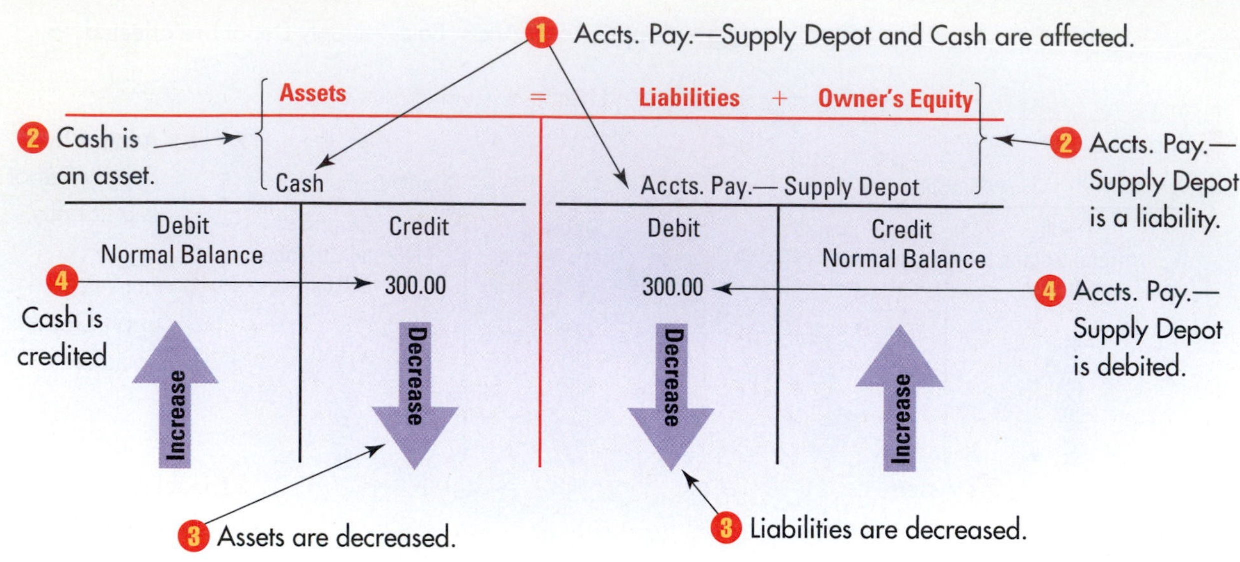

1 Accts. Pay.—Supply Depot and Cash are affected.
Assets
=
Liabilities + Owner's Equity
2 Cash is an asset.
Cash
Accts. Pay.— Supply Depot
2 Accts. Pay.— Supply Depot is a liability.
Debit
Normal Balance
Credit
300.00
Debit
Credit
Normal Balance
300.00
4 Cash is credited
4 Accts. Pay.— Supply Depot is debited.
Increase
Decrease
Decrease
Increase
3 Assets are decreased.
3 Liabilities are decreased.

August 11. Paid cash on account to Supply Depot, $300.00.

The effect of this transaction on the accounting equation is shown in the illustration. In this transaction, one asset and one liability are changed. The asset account, Cash, is decreased by $300.00, the amount of cash paid out. This decrease is on the left side of the accounting equation. After this payment, TechKnow Consulting owes less money to Supply Depot. Therefore, the liability account, Accounts Payable—Supply Depot, is decreased by $300.00, the amount paid on account. The decrease is on the right side of the accounting equation.

STEPS • STEPS • STEPS • STEPS • STEPS • STEPS • STEPS • STEPS • STEPS • STEPS •

QUESTIONS FOR ANALYZING A TRANSACTION INTO ITS DEBIT AND CREDIT PARTS

1. Which accounts are affected?
   Accounts Payable—Supply Depot and *Cash*
2. How is each account classified?
   Accounts Payable—Supply Depot is a liability account. *Cash* is an asset account.
3. How is each classification changed?
   Liabilities decrease. Assets decrease.
4. How is each amount entered in the accounts?
   Liabilities decrease on the debit side. Therefore, debit the liability account, *Accounts Payable—Supply Depot.*
   Assets decrease on the credit side. Therefore, credit the asset account, *Cash.*

REMEMBER When you decrease an account balance, record the decrease on the side opposite the normal balance side of the account. The side opposite the normal balance side can be on the left or the right, depending on the type of account.

Xtra! Study Tools
accountingxtra.swlearning.com

• term review

chart of accounts

• audit your understanding

1. State the four questions used to analyze a transaction.
2. What two accounts are affected when a business pays cash for supplies?

• work together 2-2

Analyzing transactions into debit and credit parts

T accounts are given in the *Working Papers*. Your instructor will guide you through the following examples. Kathy Bergum owns Bergum Services. Bergum Services uses the following accounts. Some of the accounts will be explained in Lesson 2-3.

Cash	Accts. Pay.—Bales Supplies	Sales
Accts. Rec.—Sam Erickson	Kathy Bergum, Capital	Advertising Expense
Supplies	Kathy Bergum, Drawing	Rent Expense
Prepaid Insurance		

Transactions:

Apr. 1. Received cash from owner as an investment, $5,000.00.
2. Paid cash for supplies, $50.00.
5. Paid cash for insurance, $75.00.
6. Bought supplies on account from Bales Supplies, $100.00.
9. Paid cash on account to Bales Supplies, $50.00.

1. Prepare two T accounts for each transaction. On each T account, write the account title of one of the accounts affected by the transaction.
2. Write the debit or credit amount in each T account to show the transaction's effect.

• on your own 2-2

Analyzing transactions into debit and credit parts

T accounts are given in the *Working Papers*. Work this problem independently. Derrick Hoffman owns Hoffman Accounting Service. Hoffman Accounting Service uses the following accounts. Some of the accounts will be explained in Lesson 2-3.

Cash	Accts. Pay.—Nash Supply	Sales
Accts. Rec.—Jon Roe	Derrick Hoffman, Capital	Miscellaneous Expense
Supplies	Derrick Hoffman, Drawing	Utilities Expense
Prepaid Insurance		

Transactions:

Sept. 1. Received cash from owner as an investment, $2,000.00.
4. Paid cash for insurance, $300.00.
5. Paid cash for supplies, $100.00.
6. Bought supplies on account from Nash Supply, $230.00.
11. Paid cash on account to Nash Supply, $115.00.

1. Prepare two T accounts for each transaction. On each T account, write the account title of one of the accounts affected by the transaction.
2. Write the debit or credit amount in each T account to show the transaction's effect.

LESSON • LESSON • LESSON • LESSON • LESSON • LESSON

2-3 Analyzing How Transactions Affect Owner's Equity Accounts

RECEIVED CASH FROM SALES

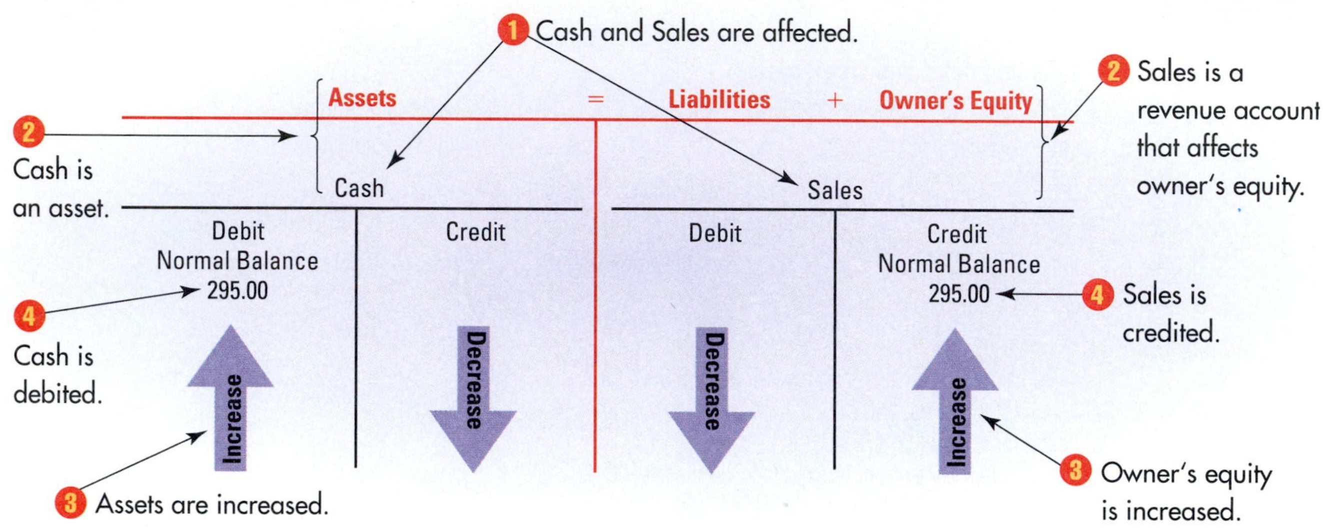

1 Cash and Sales are affected.
Assets = Liabilities + Owner's Equity
2 Cash is an asset.
2 Sales is a revenue account that affects owner's equity.
Cash
Sales
Debit
Normal Balance
295.00
Credit
Debit
Credit
Normal Balance
295.00
4 Cash is debited.
4 Sales is credited.
Increase
Decrease
Decrease
Increase
3 Assets are increased.
3 Owner's equity is increased.

August 12. Received cash from sales, $295.00.

Revenue increases owner's equity. The increases from revenue could be recorded directly in the owner's capital account. However, to avoid a capital account with a large number of entries and to summarize revenue information separately from the other records, TechKnow Consulting uses a separate revenue account titled Sales.

The owner's capital account has a normal credit balance. Increases in the owner's capital account are shown as credits. Because revenue increases owner's equity, increases in revenue are also recorded as credits. Therefore, a revenue account has a normal credit balance.

FYI FOR YOUR INFORMATION

The Small Business Administration (SBA) offers two major types of loans to small businesses. One type of loan is made by private lending institutions. Another type of loan is made directly by the SBA.

STEPS STEPS • STEPS • STEPS • STEPS • STEPS • STEPS • STEPS • STEPS • STEPS • STEPS •

QUESTIONS FOR ANALYZING A TRANSACTION INTO ITS DEBIT AND CREDIT PARTS

1. Which accounts are affected?
   Cash and *Sales*
2. How is each account classified?
   Cash is an asset account. *Sales* is a revenue account that affects owner's equity.
3. How is each classification changed?
   Assets increase. Owner's equity increases.
4. How is each amount entered in the accounts?
   Assets increase on the debit side. Therefore, debit the asset account, *Cash*. Owner's equity accounts increase on the credit side. Revenue increases owner's equity. Therefore, credit the revenue account, *Sales*.

SOLD SERVICES ON ACCOUNT

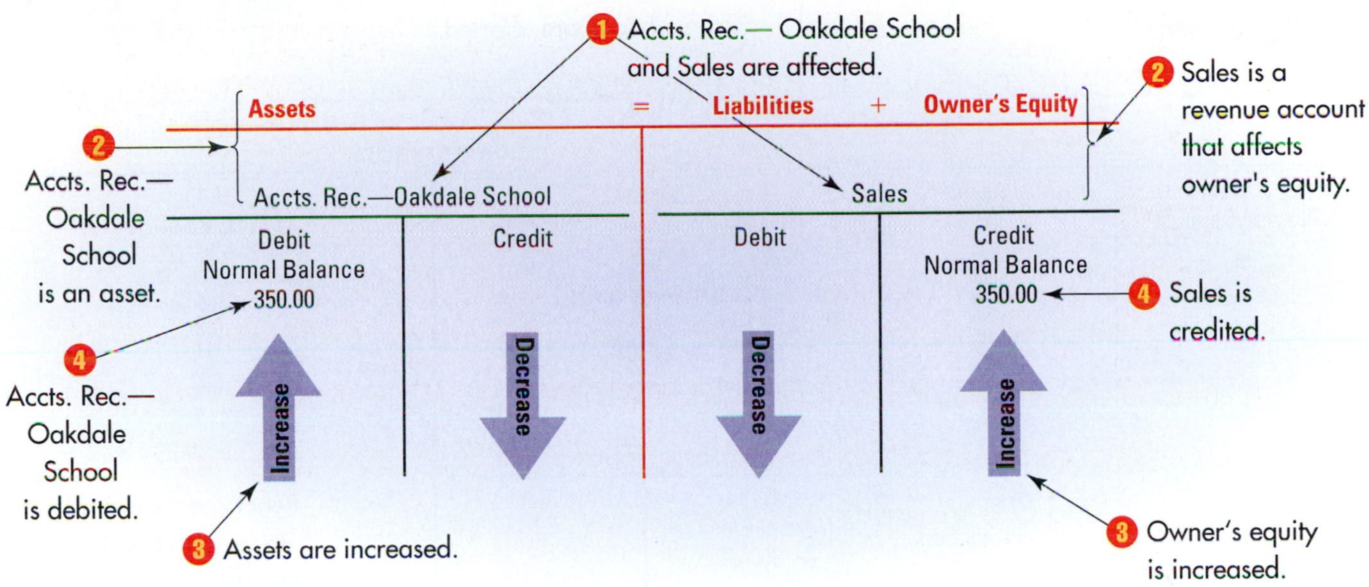

1 Accts. Rec.— Oakdale School and Sales are affected.
Assets
=
Liabilities
+
Owner's Equity
2 Sales is a revenue account that affects owner's equity.
2 Accts. Rec.— Oakdale School is an asset.
Accts. Rec.—Oakdale School
Sales
Debit
Normal Balance
350.00
Credit
Debit
Credit
Normal Balance
350.00
4 Sales is credited.
4 Accts. Rec.— Oakdale School is debited.
Increase
Decrease
Decrease
Increase
3 Assets are increased.
3 Owner's equity is increased.

August 12. Sold services on account to Oakdale School, $350.00.

The analysis for selling services on account is similar to that for selling services for cash. The only difference is that cash is not received at this time; therefore, the cash account is not affected by the transaction. Instead, this transaction increases an accounts receivable account. The same four questions are used to analyze this transaction into its debit and credit parts.

STEPS • STEPS • STEPS • STEPS • STEPS • STEPS • STEPS • STEPS • STEPS • STEPS

QUESTIONS FOR ANALYZING A TRANSACTION INTO ITS DEBIT AND CREDIT PARTS

1. Which accounts are affected?
   Accounts Receivable—Oakdale School and *Sales*
2. How is each account classified?
   Accounts Receivable—Oakdale School is an asset account. *Sales* is a revenue account that affects owner's equity.
3. How is each classification changed?
   Assets increase. Owner's equity increases.
4. How is each amount entered in the accounts?
   Assets increase on the debit side. Therefore, debit the asset account, *Accounts Receivable—Oakdale School.* Owner's equity accounts increase on the credit side. Revenue increases owner's equity. Therefore, credit the revenue account, *Sales.*

REMEMBER Owner's equity is recorded on the right side of the accounting equation. The right side of a T account is the credit side. Therefore, owner's equity has a normal credit balance.

PAID CASH FOR AN EXPENSE

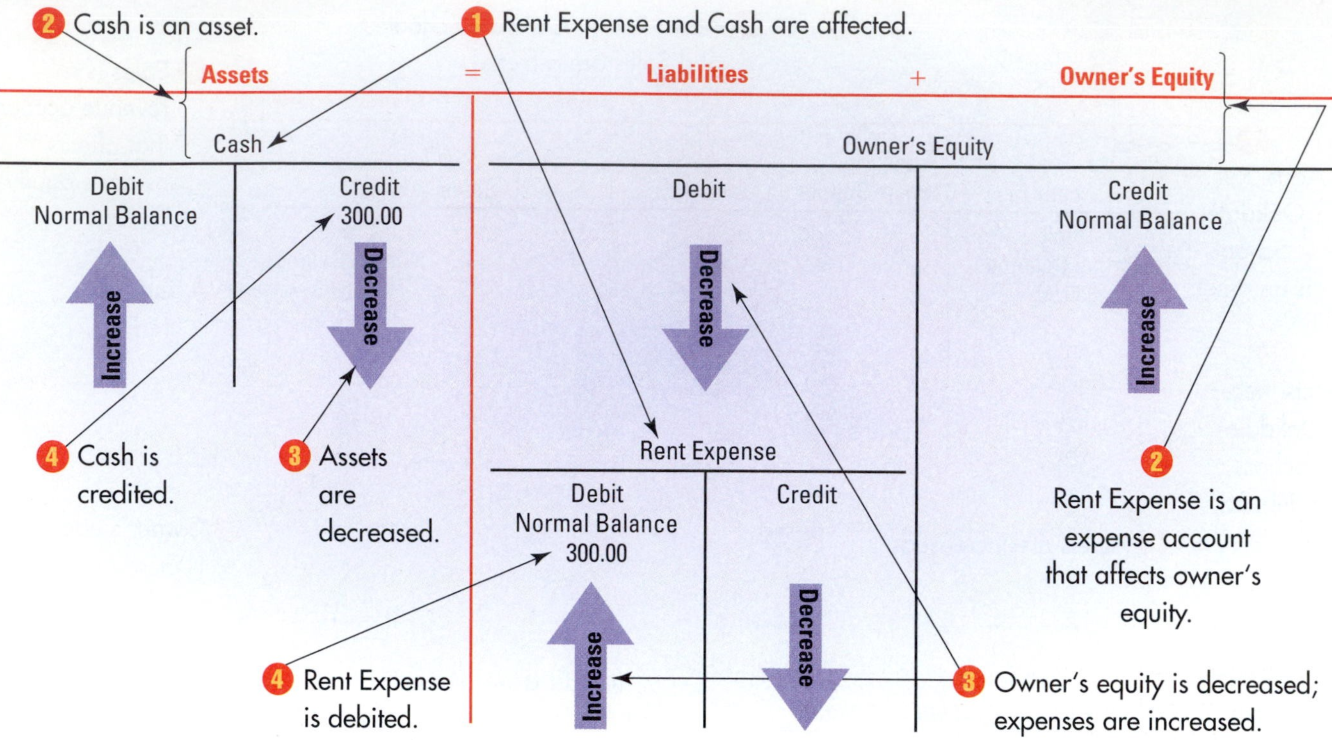

August 12. Paid cash for rent, $300.00.

Expenses decrease owner's equity. The decreases from expenses could be recorded directly in the owner's capital account. However, to avoid a capital account with a large number of entries and to summarize expense information separately from the other records, TechKnow Consulting uses separate expense accounts.

The titles of TechKnow Consulting's expense accounts are shown on its chart of accounts.

The expense account Rent Expense is used to record all payments for rent.

The owner's capital account has a normal credit balance. Decreases in the owner's capital account are shown as debits. Therefore, an expense account has a normal debit balance. Because expenses decrease owner's equity, increases in expenses are recorded as debits.

All expense transactions are recorded in a similar manner.

STEPS STEPS • STEPS • STEPS • STEPS • STEPS • STEPS • STEPS • STEPS • STEPS • STEPS •

QUESTIONS FOR ANALYZING A TRANSACTION INTO ITS DEBIT AND CREDIT PARTS

1. Which accounts are affected?
   Rent Expense and *Cash*
2. How is each account classified?
   Rent Expense is an expense account that affects owner's equity. *Cash* is an asset account.
3. How is each classification changed?
   Owner's equity decreases from an increase in expenses. Assets decrease.
4. How is each amount entered in the accounts?
   Owner's equity accounts decrease on the debit side. An increase in expenses decreases owner's equity. Expense accounts have normal debit balances. Therefore, debit the expense account, *Rent Expense*. Assets decrease on the credit side. Therefore, credit the asset account, *Cash*.

RECEIVED CASH ON ACCOUNT

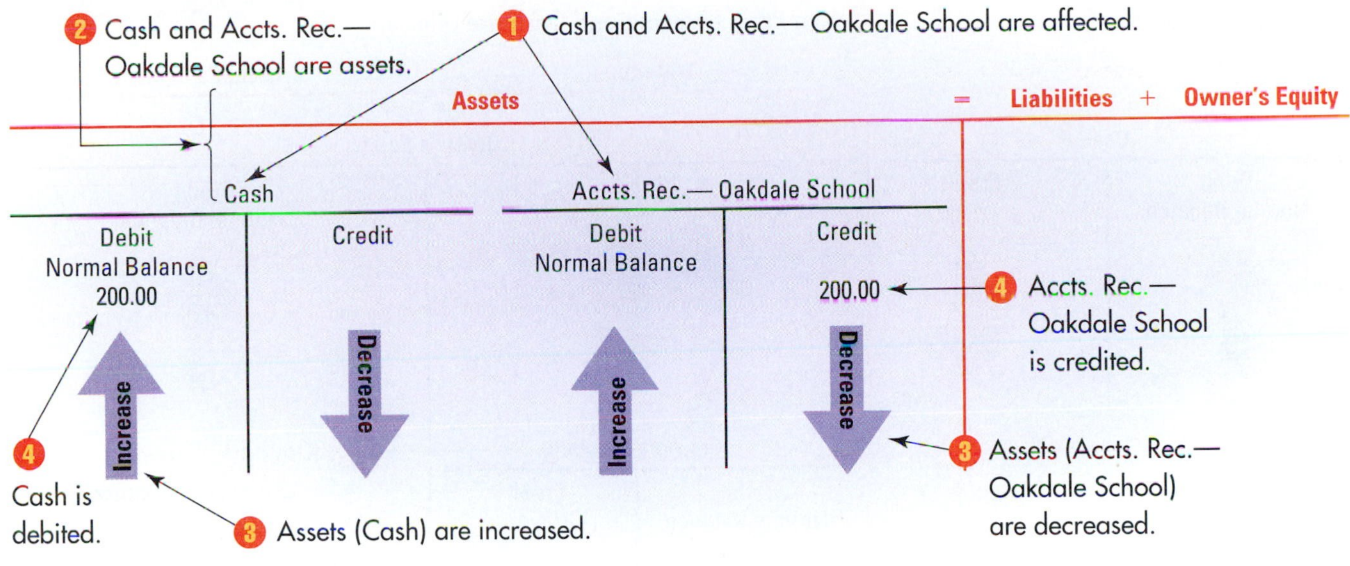

1 Cash and Accts. Rec.— Oakdale School are affected.
2 Cash and Accts. Rec.— Oakdale School are assets.
Assets = Liabilities + Owner's Equity
Cash
Debit
Normal Balance
200.00
Credit
Increase
Decrease
Accts. Rec.— Oakdale School
Debit
Normal Balance
Credit
200.00
Increase
Decrease
4 Accts. Rec.— Oakdale School is credited.
3 Assets (Accts. Rec.— Oakdale School) are decreased.
4 Cash is debited.
3 Assets (Cash) are increased.

August 12. Received cash on account from Oakdale School, $200.00.

STEPS: QUESTIONS FOR ANALYZING A TRANSACTION INTO ITS DEBIT AND CREDIT PARTS

1. Which accounts are affected?
   Cash and *Accounts Receivable—Oakdale School*
2. How is each account classified?
   Cash is an asset account. *Accounts Receivable—Oakdale School* is an asset account.
3. How is each classification changed?
   One asset (*Cash*) increases and another asset (*Accounts Receivable—Oakdale School*) decreases.
4. How is each amount entered in the accounts?
   Assets increase on the debit side. Therefore, debit the asset account, *Cash*. Assets decrease on the credit side. Therefore, credit the asset account, *Accounts Receivable—Oakdale School*.

PAID CASH TO OWNER FOR PERSONAL USE

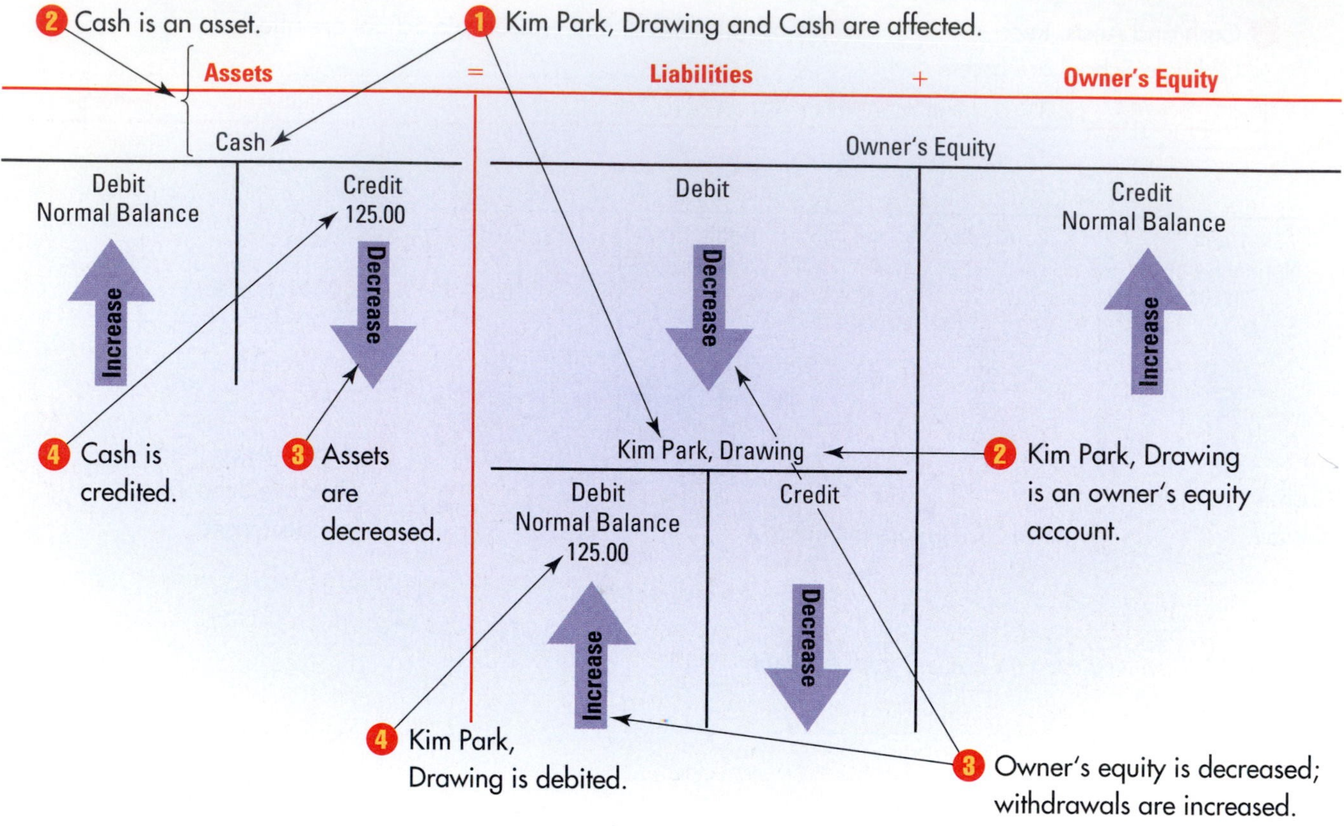

August 12. Paid cash to owner for personal use, $125.00.

Withdrawals decrease owner's equity. Withdrawals could be recorded directly in the owner's capital account. However, to avoid a capital account with a large number of entries and to summarize withdrawal information separately from the other records, TechKnow Consulting uses a separate withdrawal account titled Kim Park, Drawing.

FYI FOR YOUR INFORMATION

When drawing T accounts to analyze transactions, stack the accounts instead of writing them horizontally. Stacking the accounts will make it easier to recognize debits and credits.

STEPS — QUESTIONS FOR ANALYZING A TRANSACTION INTO ITS DEBIT AND CREDIT PARTS

1. Which accounts are affected?
   Kim Park, Drawing and *Cash*
2. How is each account classified?
   Kim Park, Drawing is an owner's equity account. *Cash* is an asset account.
3. How is each classification changed?
   Owner's equity decreases from an increase in withdrawals. Assets decrease.
4. How is each amount entered in the accounts?
   Owner's equity accounts decrease on the debit side. An increase in withdrawals decreases owner's equity. Withdrawal accounts have normal debit balances. Therefore, debit the owner's equity account, *Kim Park, Drawing*. Assets decrease on the credit side. Therefore, credit the asset account, *Cash*.

CAREERS IN ACCOUNTING • CAREERS IN ACCOUNTING • CAREERS IN ACCOUNTI

careers in accounting

Rita J. Cowans, Internal Auditor

COURTESY OF RITA J. COWANS

As a highly respected employee at FedEx Corporation, Rita J. Cowans is a Manager in the Internal Audit Department. During her tenure at FedEx, Rita has held various positions in financial, operational, international, and information systems audit. Presently she is responsible for the financial, information systems, and international audit activities for FedEx Worldwide operations.

Her audit team conducts business process reviews, integrated financial and information system reviews, international entity reviews, fraud examinations, and vendor audits. Rita has been a leader in developing and promoting best practices as an integral part of the Internal Audit Department. "It's my responsibility to ensure that the employees and management of FedEx are effectively safeguarding the assets of the corporation, complying with all laws and regulations, and accomplishing the corporate strategic objectives as established by senior management."

While in high school, Rita developed a love for mathematics and accounting. "I became a very critical and detail-oriented thinker and excelled at analyzing information and solving problems." With her parents' direction and strong support, she continued her education and graduated with a bachelor's degree in accounting. In addition, she successfully earned her Certified Internal Auditor (CIA) and Certified Information Systems Auditor (CISA) professional designations. "Being certified in the area of accounting in which you work is critical to your professional success. Certifications demonstrate that you are committed to your profession and communicate to others that you are an expert in your field."

Certifications also enable you to become active in organizations that provide educational opportunities for their members. Rita is a member of the Institute of Internal Auditors and Information Systems Audit and Control Association.

As a member of the FedEx Services Diversity Council, Rita works to ensure that individuals from every background have the opportunity to excel at FedEx. Ultimately, "having a passion for what you do and setting high standards will determine your level of success."

Salary Range: $30,000-$130,000 and up. Can lead to high-level careers at public accounting firms, private and public corporations, and government agencies, such as the Internal Revenue Service (IRS Auditor).

Qualifications: Bachelor's degree in accounting, finance, and information systems for entry-level position, plus normally five years of auditing experience for senior level or above. Professional Certifications preferred (CPA, CIA, CISA, CFE, etc). Familiarity with business, information technology, and legal concepts and procedures are beneficial.

Occupational Outlook: The Sarbanes-Oxley Act of 2002 requires public corporations to expand the documentation and testing of their accounting systems. Internal auditors are an integral part of corporations' compliance with this law. As a result, the demand for internal auditors will be strong for years to come.

audit your understanding

1. What two accounts are affected when a business receives cash from sales?
2. What two accounts are affected when services are sold on account?
3. What two accounts are affected when a business pays cash to the owner for personal use?
4. Are revenue accounts increased on the debit side or credit side? Explain why.
5. Are expense accounts increased on the debit side or credit side? Explain why.

AUDIT YOUR UNDERSTANDING

work together 2-3

Analyzing revenue, expense, and withdrawal transactions into debit and credit parts

T accounts are given in the *Working Papers*. Your instructor will guide you through the following examples.

Use the chart of accounts for Bergum Services in Work Together 2-2.

Transactions:

Apr. 10. Received cash from sales, $600.00.
11. Sold services on account to Sam Erickson, $850.00.
14. Paid cash for rent, $250.00.
18. Received cash on account from Sam Erickson, $425.00.
20. Paid cash to owner for personal use, $300.00.

1. Prepare two T accounts for each transaction. In each T account, write the account title of one of the accounts affected by the transaction.
2. Write the debit or credit amount in each T account to show the transaction's effect.

WORK TOGETHER • WORK TOGETHER

on your own 2-3

Analyzing revenue, expense, and withdrawal transactions into debit and credit parts

T accounts are given in the *Working Papers*. Work this problem independently.

Use the chart of accounts for Hoffman Accounting Service in On Your Own 2-2.

Transactions:

Sept. 13. Received cash from sales, $1,500.00.
15. Sold services on account to Jon Roe, $500.00.
16. Paid cash for utilities, $450.00.
18. Received cash on account from Jon Roe, $250.00.
21. Paid cash to owner for personal use, $700.00.

1. Prepare two T accounts for each transaction. On each T account, write the account title of one of the accounts affected by the transaction.
2. Write the debit or credit amount in each T account to show the transaction's effect.

ON YOUR OWN • ON YOUR OWN

SUMMARY

After completing this chapter, you can

1. Define accounting terms related to analyzing transactions into debit and credit parts.
2. Identify accounting practices related to analyzing transactions into debit and credit parts.
3. Use T accounts to analyze transactions, showing which accounts are debited or credited for each transaction.
4. Analyze how transactions to set up a business affect accounts.
5. Analyze how transactions affect owner's equity accounts.

Explore Accounting

Owner Withdrawals

Employee salaries are considered an expense that reduces the net income of a company. When the owner withdraws cash from the company, this withdrawal is not considered an expense. The income of a business is calculated by subtracting total expenses from total revenue. Since withdrawals are not considered to be an expense, they do not affect the business's income.

A business owned by one person is called a proprietorship. The Internal Revenue Service does not require the proprietorship, itself, to pay taxes. However, the owner of the proprietorship must include the net income of the proprietorship in his or her own taxable income.

Because the income of a proprietorship is not affected by owner withdrawals, the income tax paid by the owner is not affected by how much cash the owner withdraws from the business. If Wang Accounting Services has revenues of $2,500.00 and expenses of $1,100.00, its income is $1,400.00 ($2,500.00 − $1,100.00). Wang Accounting Services will have income of $1,400.00 regardless of whether the owner withdraws $100.00 or $1,000.00 from the business during that period.

Discussion

1. Hector Moya owns ESW Party Service. He is considering giving his employees a raise that would increase total salaries by $15,000.00 per year. What effect would this raise have on Mr. Moya's income tax?
2. Mr. Moya is also considering withdrawing $5,000.00 from ESW Party Service for his personal use. What effect would this withdrawal have on the income tax Mr. Moya must pay this year?

2-1 APPLICATION PROBLEM

Determining the normal balance and increase and decrease sides for accounts

Write the answers for the following problem in the *Working Papers.*

Cash
Accounts Receivable—Jens Olefson
Accounts Receivable—Toni Nolan
Supplies
Prepaid Insurance
Accounts Payable—United Company
Juan Reo, Capital

1	2	3	4	5	6	7	8
Account	Account Classification	Account's Normal Balance		Increase Side		Decrease Side	
		Debit	Credit	Debit	Credit	Debit	Credit
Cash	*Asset*	✓		✓			✓

Instructions:

Do the following for each account. The cash account is given as an example.

1. Write the account title in Column 1.
2. Write the account classification in Column 2.
3. Place a check mark in either Column 3 or 4 to indicate the normal balance of the account.
4. Place a check mark in either Column 5 or 6 to indicate the increase side of the account.
5. Place a check mark in either Column 7 or 8 to indicate the decrease side of the account.

2-2 APPLICATION PROBLEM

Analyzing transactions into debit and credit parts

Hal Rosen owns Hal's Marketing Services, which uses the following accounts.

Cash
Supplies
Prepaid Insurance
Accounts Receivable—Dominik Field
Accounts Payable—All Star Company
Hal Rosen, Capital
Hal Rosen, Drawing
Sales
Advertising Expense
Rent Expense

Transactions:

Mar. 1. Received cash from owner as an investment, $1,000.00.
1. Paid cash for insurance, $400.00.
3. Bought supplies on account from All Star Company, $600.00
5. Paid cash for supplies, $100.00.
8. Paid cash on account to All Star Company, $400.00.

Instructions:

1. Prepare two T accounts for each transaction. On each T account, write the account title of one of the accounts affected by the transaction. Use the forms in your *Working Papers.*
2. Write the debit or credit amount in each T account to show how the transaction affected that account. T accounts for the first transaction are given as an example.

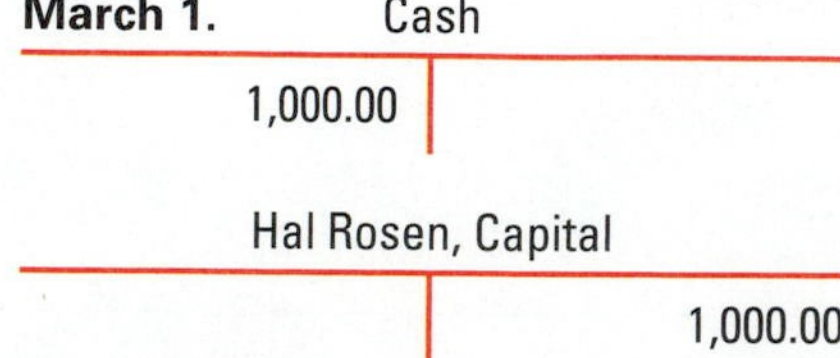

2-3 APPLICATION PROBLEM

Analyzing revenue, expense, and withdrawal transactions into debit and credit parts

Use the chart of accounts for Hal's Marketing Services given in Application Problem 2-2.

Transactions:

Mar. 11. Received cash from sales, $2,200.00.
12. Paid cash for advertising, $150.00.
14. Sold services on account to Dominik Field, $1,700.00.
18. Paid cash to owner for personal use, $500.00.
19. Received cash on account from Dominik Field, $1,000.00.

Instructions:

1. Prepare two T accounts for each transaction. On each T account, write the account title of one of the accounts affected by the transaction. Use the forms in your *Working Papers*.
2. Write the debit or credit amount in each T account to show how the transaction affected that account.

2-4 APPLICATION PROBLEM

Analyzing revenue, expense, and withdrawal transactions into debit and credit parts

Use the chart of accounts for Hal's Marketing Services given in Application Problem 2-2.

Transactions:

Mar. 25. Sold services for cash, $1,100.00.
26. Performed $500.00 of services for Dominik Field on account.
27. Ran an ad in the local newspaper. Paid $125.00 cash.
28. Hal Rosen withdrew $450.00 for his personal use.
29. Received a $250.00 check from Dominik Field on account.

Instructions:

1. Prepare two T accounts for each transaction. On each T account, write the account title of one of the accounts affected by the transaction. Use the forms in your *Working Papers*.
2. Write the debit or credit amount in each T account to show how the transaction affected that account.

2-5 MASTERY PROBLEM

Analyzing transactions into debit and credit parts

Vickie Lands owns a business called LandScape. LandScape uses the following accounts.

Cash
Accounts Receivable—Alston Goff
Accounts Receivable—Josie Leveson
Supplies
Prepaid Insurance
Accounts Payable—North End Supplies
Accounts Payable—Bethany Supplies
Vickie Lands, Capital
Vickie Lands, Drawing
Sales
Advertising Expense
Miscellaneous Expense
Rent Expense
Repair Expense
Utilities Expense

Instructions:

1. Prepare a T account for each account. Use the forms in your *Working Papers*.
2. Analyze each transaction into its debit and credit parts. Write the debit and credit amounts in the proper T accounts to show how each transaction changes account balances. Write the date of the transaction in parentheses before each amount.

Transcriptions:

June 1. Received cash from owner as an investment, $2,700.00.
2. Paid cash for rent, $500.00.
4. Paid cash for supplies, $300.00.
4. Received cash from sales, $850.00.
5. Paid cash for insurance, $275.00.
8. Sold services on account to Alston Goff, $700.00.
9. Bought supplies on account from Bethany Supplies, $200.00.
10. Paid cash for repairs, $75.00.
11. Received cash from owner as an investment, $1,900.00.
11. Received cash from sales, $900.00.
12. Bought supplies on account from North End Supplies, $130.00.
13. Received cash on account from Alston Goff, $500.00.
15. Paid cash for miscellaneous expense, $25.00.
16. Paid cash on account to Bethany Supplies, $50.00.
22. Paid cash for electric bill (utilities expense), $55.00.
23. Paid cash for advertising, $95.00.
25. Sold services on account to Josie Leveson, $450.00.
26. Paid cash to owner for personal use, $400.00.
30. Received cash on account from Josie Leveson, $200.00.

2-6 CHALLENGE PROBLEM

Analyzing transactions recorded in T accounts

Adriana Janek owns a business for which the following T accounts show the current financial situation. Write the answers for the following problem in the *Working Papers*.

Cash

(1)	6,000.00	(2)	100.00
(5)	700.00	(3)	65.00
(8)	400.00	(6)	75.00
(9)	900.00	(7)	900.00
		(10)	600.00
		(11)	550.00
		(12)	500.00

Sales

		(5)	700.00
		(8)	400.00
		(9)	900.00
		(13)	225.00

Accts. Rec.—Ralph Dahl

(13)	225.00		

Advertising Expense

(6)	75.00		

Supplies

(4)	1,100.00		
(10)	600.00		

Miscellaneous Expense

(3)	65.00		

Accts. Pay.—Tri City Supplies

(11)	550.00	(4)	1,100.00

Rent Expense

(7)	900.00		

Adriana Janek, Capital

		(1)	6,000.00

Utilities Expense

(2)	100.00		

Adriana Janek, Drawing

(12)	500.00		

1	2	3	4	5	6
Trans. No.	Accounts Affected	Account Classification	Entered in Account as a		Description of Transaction
			Debit	Credit	
1.	*Cash* *Adriana Janek, Capital*	*Asset* *Owner's Equity*	√	 √	*Received cash from owner as an investment*

Instructions:

1. Analyze each numbered transaction in the T accounts. Write the titles of accounts affected in Column 2. For each account, write the classification of the account in Column 3.
2. For each account, place a check mark in either Column 4 or 5 to indicate if the account is affected by a debit or a credit.
3. For each transaction, write a brief statement in Column 6 describing the transaction. Information for Transaction 1 is given as an example.

©GETTY IMAGES/PHOTODISC

applied communication

An entrepreneur is a person who attempts to earn a profit by taking the risk of operating a business. You have expressed an interest in starting your own business after graduation. Your family has agreed to help finance your new business if you can convince them that you would be successful.

Instructions: Develop a formal plan outlining the details of the business you would operate. Describe the type of business, the equipment or resources needed, and financial information, such as start-up costs and expenses. Write clear and persuasive sentences.

APPLIED COMMUNICATION

cases for critical thinking

Case 1

Aruna Patel records all cash receipts as revenue and all cash payments as expenses. Is Ms. Patel recording her cash receipts and cash payments correctly? Explain your answer.

Case 2

Thomas Bueler records all investments, revenue, expenses, and withdrawals in his capital account. At the end of each month, Mr. Bueler sorts the information to prepare a summary of what has caused the changes in his capital account balance. To help Mr. Bueler prepare this summary in the future, what changes would you suggest he make in his records?

CASES FOR CRITICAL THINKING

SCANS workplace competency

Resource Competency: Ranking Activities

Concept: Employers need workers who can identify tasks to be completed and prioritize them so that time is spent on tasks that are the most productive. It is human nature to do the tasks that are enjoyable or easy to complete first; however, these tasks are not necessarily the ones that contribute most to the success of a business.

Application: Use the planning sheet on the *Student Resource CD* or create your own form for prioritizing tasks. The form should have four narrow columns labeled *A, B, C,* and ✓ and a wider column for tasks that need to be completed. List all the tasks or activities you need to do tomorrow or this week in the wide column. Then place a checkmark in one of the three columns for each item on the list to show whether it is of the highest priority (*A*), medium priority (*B*), or low priority (*C*). Place a checkmark in the column labeled ✓ as each task is completed.

SCANS WORKPLACE COMPETENCY

• auditing for errors

The bookkeeper for Lyons Company used T accounts to analyze three transactions as follows.

Transaction 1:

Cash	
200.00	

Ruth Lyons, Capital	
	200.00

Transaction 2:

Accounts Payable	
	500.00

Supplies	
	500.00

Transaction 3:

Accounts Receivable	
100.00	

Sales	
	100.00

Review the three sets of T accounts and answer the following questions.

1. Which T account analysis is incorrect? How did you determine it was incorrect?
2. What information would you need to determine the correct T account analysis for this transaction?

• analyzing Best Buy's financial statements

The Best Buy financial statement on Appendix B pages B-4 and B-5 lists the assets, liabilities, and shareholder's equity of Best Buy. Shareholder's equity for a corporation is the same as capital for a proprietorship.

Instructions: Find the total assets, total liabilities, and total equity for Best Buy for 2003 and 2004. Put your answer in the form of an accounting equation. You will have to add the total current liabilities, long-term liabilities, and long-term debt to find the total liabilities.

Automated Accounting

Language and Skills

Using computer software to process accounting data can be an efficient and effective way to control the financial information of a business. In order to use the software, it is important to have a general understanding of computer and software terminology. Keyboarding skills are also essential for entering data. The more skilled you are and the greater your understanding, the better able you will be to accurately process financial information.

Automated Accounting Software

Automated Accounting 8.0 or higher software is used to teach students about computerized accounting principles. Accounting software is a set of instructions that operate the computer and enable the user to enter financial information and create reports, spreadsheets, graphs, and documents. Specifically, Automated Accounting can process transactions for:

- The purchase of assets, supplies, services, and the related payments.
- Investments in the business.
- Sales, cash receipts, and noncash transactions.

There are many other types of transactions that can be entered into an automated accounting system. Many of the various types of transactions will be studied in this course.

Automated Accounting versus Manual Accounting

Most students learn accounting by first processing transactions manually (with pencil or pen and paper). It is important to learn the methods of recording transactions manually before entering this information into an automated accounting system. Learning the principles of accounting is necessary because you always need to analyze transactions before recording them in an automated accounting system. Once you learn accounting principles, you will be better able to understand the functions of an automated system.

Understanding automated accounting will help you in the workplace. Many businesses use computers to enter accounting transaction data to process information more efficiently. After learning automated accounting, you will be able to more easily follow trails of information to analyze and correct errors.

Menu Bar and Drop-Down Lists versus Toolbar

The menu bar and drop-down lists enable you to communicate with the software. When a menu title is selected, a drop-down menu list appears. This drop-down list presents additional options to the user to direct the software to perform specific actions. There are also toolbar buttons that can be selected without using the drop-down list. Each toolbar button has a unique function that is similar to an item found on a drop-down list. The illustration shows the menu bar titles and the toolbar.

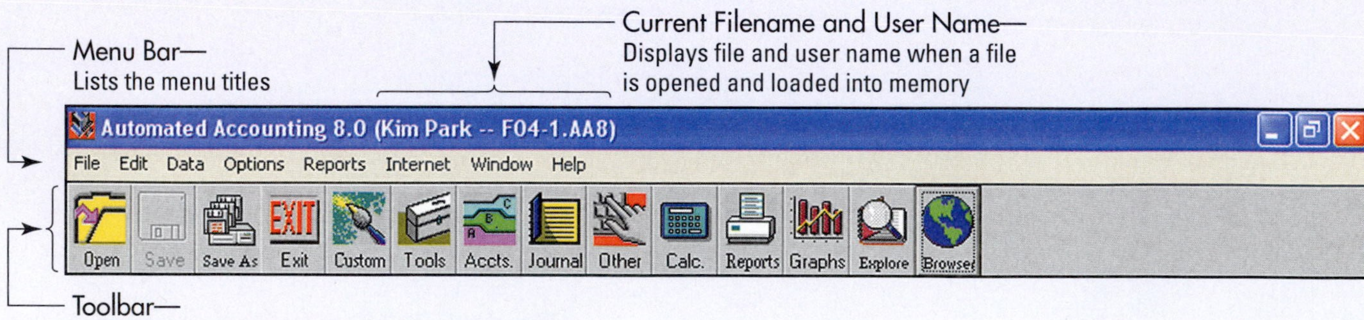

The following terms are elements of the *Automated Accounting 8.0* menu bar. Most of the terms will be studied again in later chapters.

File is a menu title that includes options to create a new document, open an existing document, save new or existing documents, and print. The Exit menu item is also listed under the File menu title.

Edit is a menu title that includes options to cut, copy, and paste text to separate spreadsheet and word processing documents. When you process information in the Journal Entries window, Find and Find Next can be used to locate data you wish to find.

Data is a menu title that includes options to customize accounting elements, select planning tools, maintain accounts, and create journal entries. The Other Activities option leads to special activities such as Bank Reconciliation.

Options is a menu title that includes choices to generate depreciation adjusting entries, current payroll journal entries, employer's payroll taxes, and closing journal entries. Options also includes a calculator.

Reports is a menu title that includes options for report selection and graph selection. The Explore Accounting System option allows a quick look at the chart of accounts, vendor and customer accounts, fixed assets (plant assets), employee list, and inventory items whenever these are part of the data file that has been loaded.

Internet is an option that connects with the default Internet browser on your system.

Window is a menu title that includes an option to close all windows that are open, rather than clicking each one closed individually.

Help includes options to search and view help contents, problem instructions, and information about Automated Accounting. It also provides for turning Tool Tips and Transaction Summary on and off.

Selecting and Opening Files

When selecting and opening files, it is important to open the appropriate directory/folder in order to select the desired file. Also, it is best to save your files promptly upon completion of a problem before properly exiting the Automated Accounting system.

Changing Directories/Folders

When changing directories/folders, choose the disk drive that contains the file you want to open. The desired file may not always be in the default folder shown when the Open command is selected. Your instructor may tell you to change folders. After selecting the directory/folder that includes the file you need, highlight the file you wish to choose and click OK.

Saving Files

Choose the Save menu item from the File menu or click on the Save toolbar button. Before using the Save menu item, be sure to check the upper line of the screen for the filename to which you want to save. The opening balance file, also called a *data file*, includes a database of information about a particular business and can be used more than once.

Specifically, the opening balance file includes general information about the business, a chart of accounts, and account balances. If the filename has not been changed from the original opening balance filename, you must use the Save As menu item first. Automated Accounting will not allow you to save to the opening balance file (data file).

Exit

After you have completed your session and saved your file, click on the Exit toolbar button to exit Automated Accounting.

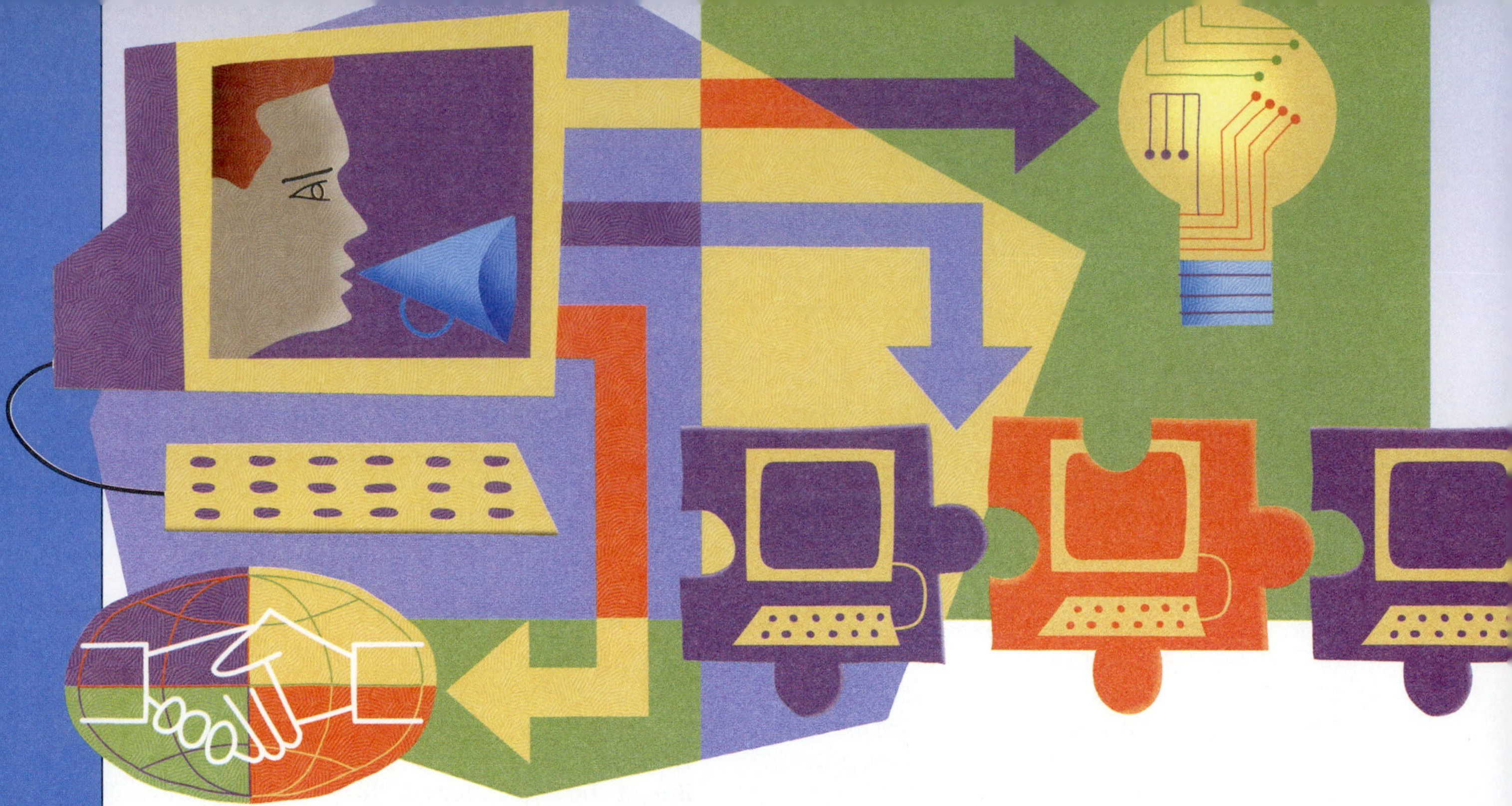

CHAPTER 3

Journalizing Transactions

OBJECTIVES & TERMS

After studying Chapter 3, you will be able to:

1. Define accounting terms related to journalizing transactions.
2. Identify accounting concepts and practices related to journalizing transactions.
3. Record transactions to set up a business in a five-column journal.
4. Record transactions to buy insurance for cash and supplies on account in a five-column journal.
5. Record transactions that affect owner's equity and receiving cash on account in a five-column journal.
6. Prove and rule a five-column journal and prove cash.

- journal
- journalizing
- special amount column
- general amount column
- entry
- double-entry accounting
- source document
- check
- invoice
- sales invoice
- receipt
- memorandum
- proving cash

Point Your Browser
accountingxtra.swlearning.com

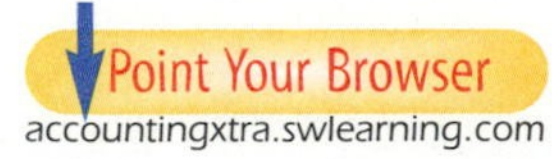

accounting in the real world

Travelocity

internet activity

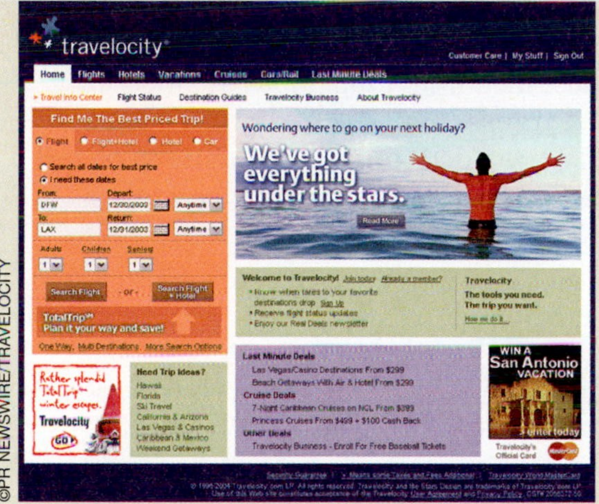
©PR NEWSWIRE/TRAVELOCITY

TAKING TRAVEL TO A BETTER PLACE—TRAVELOCITY

Do you sometimes feel that you need a vacation but are unsure about how to coordinate airline, hotel, and ground transportation reservations? That's where a company like Travelocity can help. Travelocity can also help with cruises, rail travel, and mini travel guides.

Maybe you want to take an inexpensive vacation, and you don't have a specific destination in mind. By searching the Travelocity web site, you can quickly find the "top deals" in airfares, cruises, hotels, rental cars, and total vacation packages. You can even find suggestions about what to see and do at your destination.

Want to travel throughout Europe? Travelocity will help you arrange rail travel across Europe, arrange for a place to stay, and help you get there. That's full service at its best.

All of this activity needs to be recorded in the accounting records of Travelocity.

Critical Thinking

1. What account would Travelocity credit when you make a reservation with them? What account would be debited?
2. Why do you think Travelocity might be able to get less expensive airline tickets than you, as an individual, could get?

accountingxtra.swlearning.com

Source: http://svc.travelocity.com/about/main/

AICPA

Go to the homepage for the American Institute of Certified Public Accountants (AICPA) (www.aicpa.org). Search the site for information about the AICPA Mission Statement.

Instructions

1. Summarize the mission statement and the objectives of the AICPA.
2. Expand the search by looking at other pages. List three additional resources provided by the AICPA.

LESSON • LESSON • LESSON • LESSON • LESSON • LESSON

3-1 Journals, Source Documents, and Recording Entries in a Journal

JOURNALS AND JOURNALIZING

As described in Chapter 2, transactions are analyzed into debit and credit parts before information is recorded. A form for recording transactions in chronological order is called a **journal**. Recording transactions in a journal is called **journalizing**.

Transactions could be recorded in the accounting equation. However, most companies wish to create a more permanent record by recording transactions in a journal.

Each business uses the kind of journal that best fits the needs of that business. The nature of a business and the number of transactions to be recorded determine the kind of journal to be used.

The word journal comes from the Latin *diurnalis*, meaning *daily*. Most businesses conduct transactions every day. To keep from getting overloaded, businesses usually record transactions in their journals every day.

FYI FOR YOUR INFORMATION

The Small Business Administration (SBA) has programs that offer free management and accounting advice to small business owners. The SBA sponsors various workshops and publishes a variety of booklets for small business owners. Visit their Web site at www.sba.gov.

MAKING ETHICAL DECISIONS • MAKING ETHICAL DECISIONS • MAKING ETHICAL DECISIONS

making ethical decisions

Recognizing Ethical Dilemmas and Actions

How often have you said something you later regretted? Chances are you spoke before you thought about how your words might affect others. Had you taken the time to think how your words would hurt someone else, you might have said something different or simply kept quiet.

The first step of the ethical model is to recognize you are facing an ethical dilemma. Few business decisions will require you to act immediately. Take whatever time is required to determine whether your actions could harm someone else. If you have any doubts that your action will violate your morals, stop to evaluate the decision, using the ethical model.

The second step of the ethical model is to identify the action taken or the proposed action. Write down every possible action you think of, even if the idea might seem outrageous at first. Seek the advice of others who may have encountered similar dilemmas or whom you admire for their ethical behavior. Many companies assign a mentor to new employees to encourage them to seek advice.

Instructions

In private, write down the names of at least five individuals from whom you would feel comfortable seeking advice on ethical dilemmas.

A FIVE-COLUMN JOURNAL

JOURNAL PAGE

	DATE		ACCOUNT TITLE	DOC. NO.	POST. REF.	1 GENERAL DEBIT	2 GENERAL CREDIT	3 SALES CREDIT	4 CASH DEBIT	5 CASH CREDIT	
1											1
2											2
3											3

Using a Journal

TechKnow Consulting uses a multicolumn journal that has five amount columns: General Debit, General Credit, Sales Credit, Cash Debit, and Cash Credit. A journal amount column headed with an account title is called a **special amount column**. These columns are used for transactions that occur frequently. For example, most of TechKnow Consulting's transactions involve receipt or payment of cash. A large number of the transactions involve receiving cash from sales. Therefore, TechKnow Consulting uses three special amount columns in its journal: Sales Credit, Cash Debit, and Cash Credit. Using special amount columns eliminates writing an account title in the Account Title column and saves time.

A journal amount column that is not headed with an account title is called a **general amount column**. In TechKnow Consulting's journal, the General Debit and General Credit columns are general amount columns.

Accuracy

Information recorded in a journal includes the debit and credit parts of each transaction recorded in one place. The information can be verified by comparing the data in the journal with the transaction data.

Chronological Record

Transactions are recorded in a journal in order by date. All information about a transaction is recorded in one place, making the information for a specific transaction easy to locate.

Double-Entry Accounting

Information for each transaction recorded in a journal is called an **entry**. The recording of debit and credit parts of a transaction is called **double-entry accounting**. In double-entry accounting, each transaction affects at least two accounts. Both the debit and the credit parts are recorded, reflecting the dual effect of each transaction on the business's records. Double-entry accounting assures that debits equal credits.

Source Documents

A business paper from which information is obtained for a journal entry is called a **source document**. Each transaction is described by a source document that proves that the transaction did occur. For example, TechKnow Consulting prepares a check stub for each cash payment made. The check stub describes information about the cash payment transaction for which the check is prepared. The accounting concept *Objective Evidence* is applied when a source document is prepared for each transaction. [*CONCEPT: Objective Evidence*]

A transaction should be journalized only if it actually occurs. The amounts recorded must be accurate and true. Nearly all transactions result in the preparation of a source document. TechKnow Consulting uses five source documents: checks, sales invoices, receipts, calculator tapes, and memorandums.

CHECKS

NO. 1 $ 275.00
Date August 3, 20 --
To Port City Supply
For Supplies

BAL. BRO'T. FOR'D.	0	00
AMT. DEPOSITED 8 1 -- (Date)	5,000	00
SUBTOTAL	5,000	00
OTHER:		
SUBTOTAL	5,000	00
AMT. THIS CHECK	275	00
BAL. CAR'D. FOR'D.	4,725	00

TechKnow Consulting
7549 Broadway
Portland, OR 97202-2531

NO. 1 24-317/1230

August 3, 20 --

PAY TO THE ORDER OF Port City Supply $ 275.00

Two hundred seventy-five no/100 DOLLARS

For Classroom Use Only

Pacific national bank
Portland, OR

FOR Supplies Kim Park

⑆123003175⑆ 43⑈452119⑈

A business form ordering a bank to pay cash from a bank account is called a **check**. The source document for cash payments is a check. TechKnow Consulting makes all cash payments by check. The checks are prenumbered to help TechKnow Consulting account for all checks.

TechKnow Consulting's record of information on a check is the check stub prepared at the same time as the check.

Procedures for preparing checks and check stubs are described in Chapter 5.

SALES INVOICES

TechKnow Consulting
7549 Broadway
Portland, OR 97202-2531

Sold to: Oakdale School
5211 SE Oak Street
Portland, OR 97208-5392

No. 1
Date 8/12/--
Terms 30 days

Description	Amount
Computer Network Setup	$350.00
Total	$350.00

When services are sold on account, the seller prepares a form showing information about the sale. A form describing the goods or services sold, the quantity, and the price is called an **invoice**. An invoice used as a source document for recording a sale on account is called a **sales invoice**. A sales invoice is also referred to as a *sales ticket* or a *sales slip*.

A sales invoice is prepared in duplicate. The original is given to the customer. The copy is used as the source document for the sale on account transaction. [*CONCEPT: Objective Evidence*] Sales invoices are pre-numbered in sequence to help account for all sales invoices.

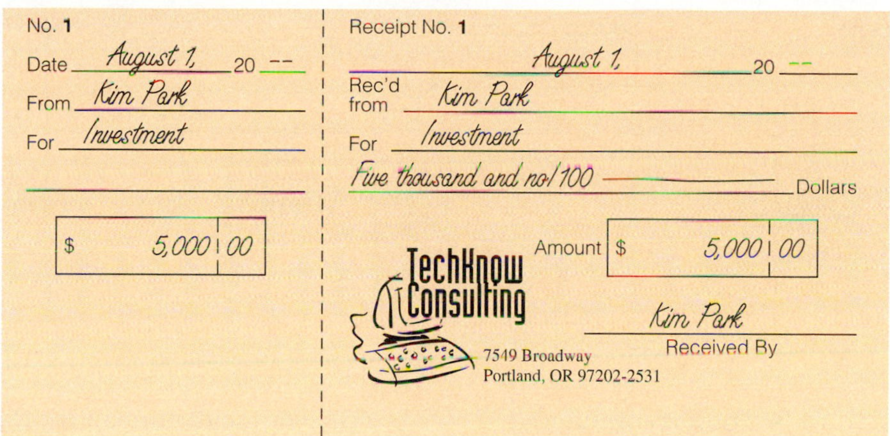

No. 1
Date August 1, 20--
From Kim Park
For Investment

$ 5,000 00

Receipt No. 1
August 1, 20--
Rec'd from Kim Park
For Investment
Five thousand and no/100 Dollars
Amount $ 5,000 00

TechKnow Consulting
7549 Broadway
Portland, OR 97202-2531

Kim Park
Received By

Receipts

A business form giving written acknowledgement for cash received is called a **receipt**. When cash is received from sources other than sales, TechKnow Consulting prepares a receipt. The receipts are prenumbered to help account for all of the receipts. A receipt is the source document for cash received from transactions other than sales. [*CONCEPT: Objective Evidence*]

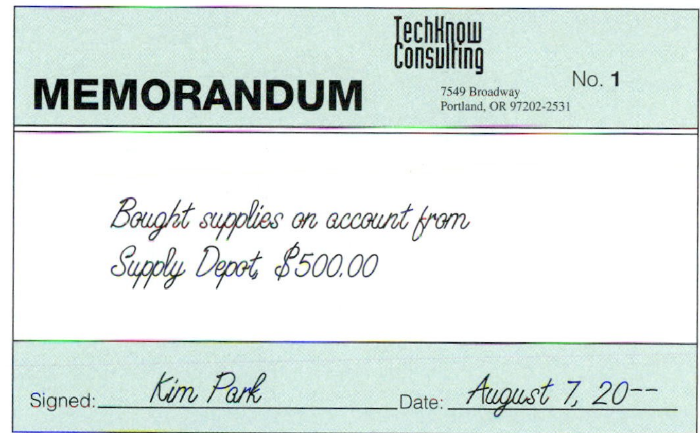

MEMORANDUM

TechKnow Consulting
7549 Broadway
Portland, OR 97202-2531

No. 1

Bought supplies on account from Supply Depot, $500.00

Signed: Kim Park Date: August 7, 20--

Memorandums

A form on which a brief message is written describing a transaction is called a **memorandum**. When no other source document is prepared for a transaction, or when an additional explanation is needed about a transaction, TechKnow Consulting prepares a memorandum. [*CONCEPT: Objective Evidence*] TechKnow Consulting's memorandums are prenumbered to help account for all memorandums. A brief note is written on the memorandum to describe the transaction.

Calculator Tapes

TechKnow Consulting collects cash at the time services are rendered to customers. At the end of each day, TechKnow Consulting uses a printing electronic calculator to total the amount of cash received from sales for that day. By totaling all the individual sales, a single source document is produced for the total sales of the day. Thus, time and space are saved by recording only one entry for all of a day's sales. The calculator tape is the source document for daily sales. [*CONCEPT: Objective Evidence*] A calculator tape used as a source document is shown here.

TechKnow Consulting dates and numbers each calculator tape. For example, in the illustration, the number *T12* indicates that the tape is for the twelfth day of the month.

0·00 *
150·00 +
35·00 +
110·00 +
295·00 *
Aug. 12, 20--
T12

RECEIVED CASH FROM OWNER AS AN INVESTMENT

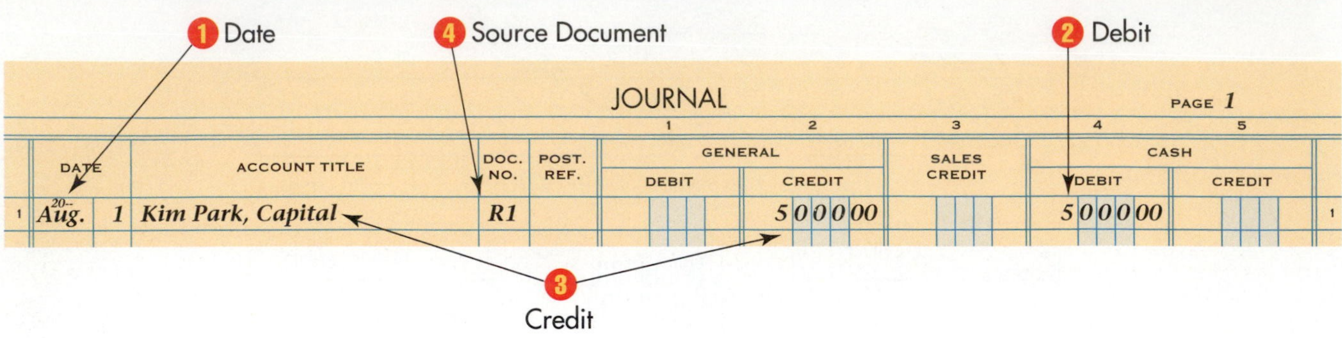

					GENERAL			CASH		
					1	2	3	4	5	
	DATE	ACCOUNT TITLE	DOC. NO.	POST. REF.	DEBIT	CREDIT	SALES CREDIT	DEBIT	CREDIT	
1	20-- Aug. 1	Kim Park, Capital	R1			5 000 00		5 000 00		1

Information for each transaction recorded in a journal is known as an entry. An entry consists of four parts: (1) date, (2) debit, (3) credit, and (4) source document. Before a transaction is recorded in a journal, the transaction is analyzed into its debit and credit parts.

August 1. Received cash from owner as an investment, $5,000.00. Receipt No. 1.

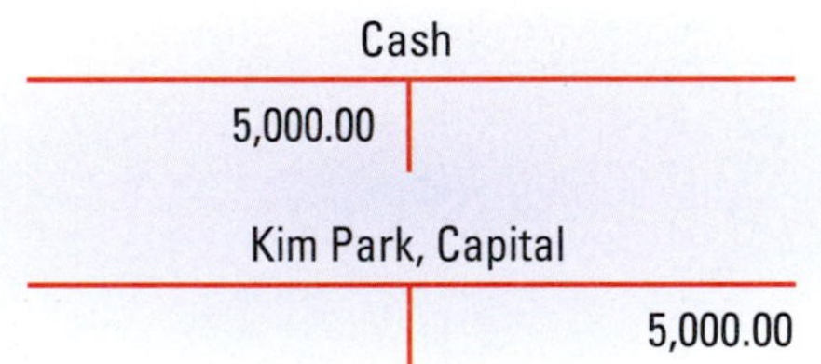

The source document for this transaction is Receipt No. 1. [*CONCEPT: Objective Evidence*] The analysis of this transaction is shown in the T accounts.

The asset account, Cash, increases by a debit, $5,000.00. The owner's capital account, Kim Park, Capital, increases by a credit, $5,000.00.

FYI FOR YOUR INFORMATION

Dollars and cents signs and decimal points are not used when writing amounts on ruled accounting paper. Sometimes a color tint or a heavy vertical rule is used on printed accounting paper to separate the dollars and cents columns.

STEPS • STEPS • STEPS • STEPS • STEPS • STEPS • STEPS • STEPS • STEPS • STEPS •

JOURNALIZING CASH RECEIVED FROM OWNER AS AN INVESTMENT

1. **Date.** Write the date, *20--, Aug. 1*, in the Date column. This entry is the first one on this journal page. Therefore, write both the year and the month for this entry. Do not write either the year or the month again on the same page.
2. **Debit.** The journal has a special amount column for debits to *Cash*. Write the debit amount, *$5,000.00*, in the Cash Debit column. The title of the account is in the column heading. Therefore, you do not need to write the account title in the Account Title column.
3. **Credit.** There is no special amount column with the title of the account credited, *Kim Park, Capital*, in its heading. Therefore, record the credit amount, *$5,000.00*, in the General Credit column. To indicate what account is credited for this amount, write the title of the account, *Kim Park, Capital*, in the Account Title column. (All amounts recorded in the General Debit or General Credit amount columns must have an account title written in the Account Title column.)
4. **Source document.** Write the source document number, *R1*, in the Doc. No. column. The source document number, *R1*, indicates that this is Receipt No. 1. (The source document number is a cross reference from the journal to the source document. Receipt No. 1 is filed in case more details about this transaction are needed.)

PAID CASH FOR SUPPLIES

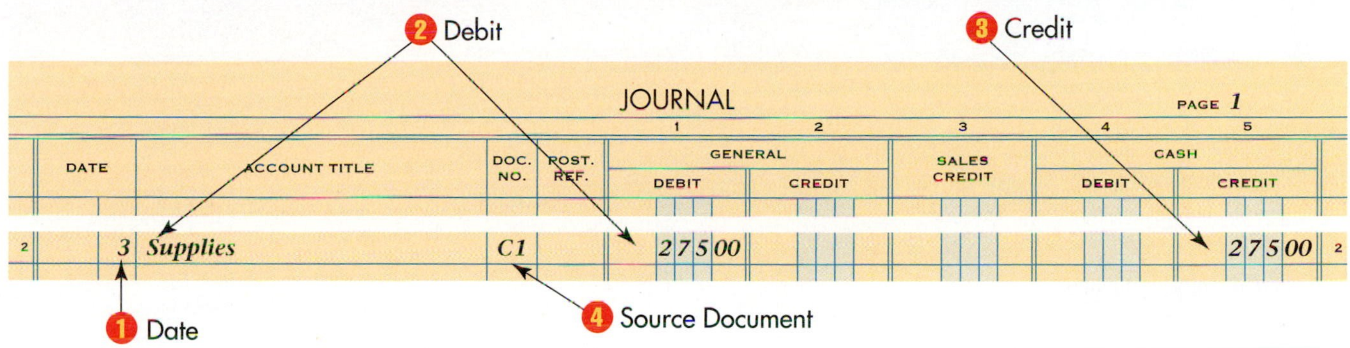

August 3. Paid cash for supplies, $275.00. Check No. 1.

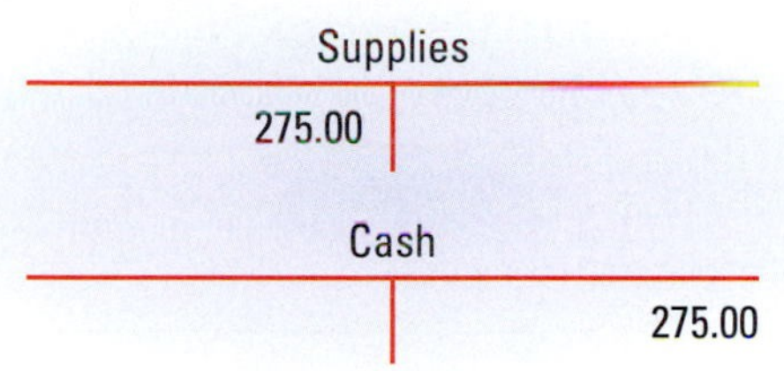

The source document for this transaction is Check No. 1. [*CONCEPT: Objective Evidence*]

The analysis of this transaction is shown in the T accounts.

The asset account, Supplies, increases by a debit, $275.00. The asset account, Cash, decreases by a credit, $275.00.

Drawing T accounts for analyzing transactions will make journalizing easier.

STEPS • STEPS • STEPS • STEPS • STEPS • STEPS • STEPS • STEPS • STEPS • STEPS

JOURNALIZING CASH PAID FOR SUPPLIES

1. **Date.** Write the date, *3*, in the Date column. This is not the first entry on the journal page. Therefore, do not write the year and month for this entry.
2. **Debit.** There is no special amount column with the title of the account debited, *Supplies*, in its heading. Therefore, record the debit amount, *$275.00*, in the General Debit column. In order to indicate what account is debited for this amount, write the title of the account, *Supplies*, in the Account Title column.
3. **Credit.** The journal has a special amount column for credits to *Cash*. Write the credit amount, *$275.00*, in the Cash Credit column. The title of the account is in the column heading. Therefore, do not write the account title in the Account Title column.
4. **Source document.** Write the source document number, *C1*, in the Doc. No. column. The source document number, C1, indicates that this is Check No. 1.

REMEMBER When an account such as *Cash* is used frequently, it can be time-consuming to write the account title over and over. Using a special amount column for a frequently-used account saves time.

terms review

journal
journalizing
special amount column
general amount column
entry
double-entry accounting
source document
check
invoice
sales invoice
receipt
memorandum

TERMS REVIEW • TERMS REVIEW

audit your understanding

1. In what order are transactions recorded in a journal?
2. Why are source documents important?
3. List the four parts of a journal entry.

AUDIT YOUR UNDERSTANDING • AUDIT

work together 3-1

Journalizing entries in a five-column journal

A journal is given in the *Working Papers.* Your instructor will guide you through the following example.

Norm Derner owns Derner Copy Center, which uses the following accounts.

Cash	Accts. Pay.—Palm Supply	Miscellaneous Expense
Accts. Rec.—L. Rohe	Norm Derner, Capital	Rent Expense
Supplies	Norm Derner, Drawing	Utilities Expense
Prepaid Insurance	Sales	

Transactions:

Apr. 1. Received cash from owner as an investment, $1,500.00. R1.
2. Paid cash for supplies, $375.00. C1.

1. Journalize each transaction completed during April of the current year. Use page 1 of the journal. Source documents are abbreviated as follows: check, C; receipt, R. Save your work to complete Work Together 3-2.

WORK TOGETHER • WORK TOGETHER

on your own 3-1

Journalizing entries in a five-column journal

A journal is given in the *Working Papers.* Work this problem independently.

Lou James owns Lou's Service Center, which uses the following accounts.

Cash	Accts. Pay.—OK Supplies	Advertising Expense
Accts. Rec.—C. Lord	Lou James, Capital	Miscellaneous Expense
Supplies	Lou James, Drawing	Rent Expense
Prepaid Insurance	Sales	

Transactions:

June 2. Received cash from owner as an investment, $3,000.00. R1.
3. Paid cash for supplies, $950.00. C1.

1. Journalize each transaction completed during June of the current year. Use page 1 of the journal. Source documents are abbreviated as follows: check, C; receipt, R. Save your work to complete On Your Own 3-2.

ON YOUR OWN • ON YOUR OWN • ON YOUR

3-2 Journalizing Buying Insurance, Buying on Account, and Paying on Account

PAID CASH FOR INSURANCE

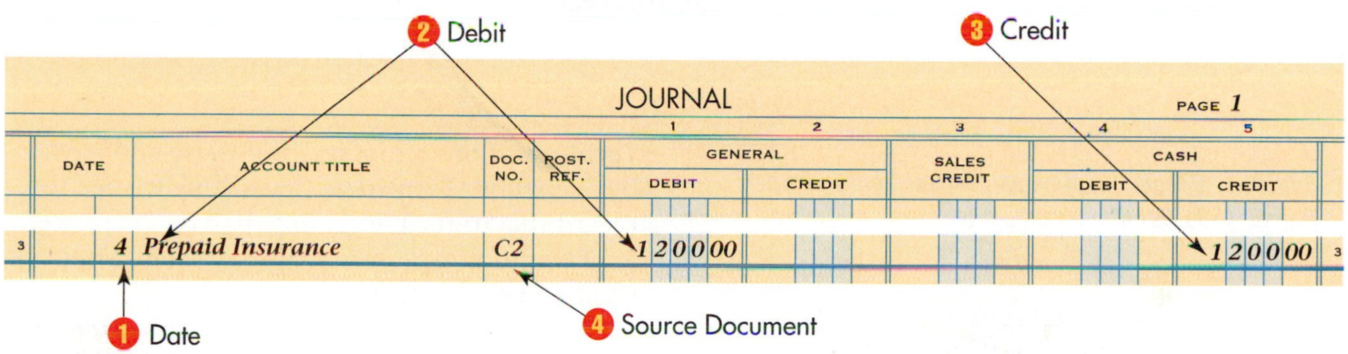

2 Debit
3 Credit
JOURNAL
PAGE 1
DATE
ACCOUNT TITLE
DOC. NO.
POST. REF.
GENERAL
DEBIT
CREDIT
SALES CREDIT
CASH
DEBIT
CREDIT
4 Prepaid Insurance
C2
1 200 00
1 200 00
1 Date
4 Source Document

August 4. Paid cash for insurance, $1,200.00. Check No. 2.

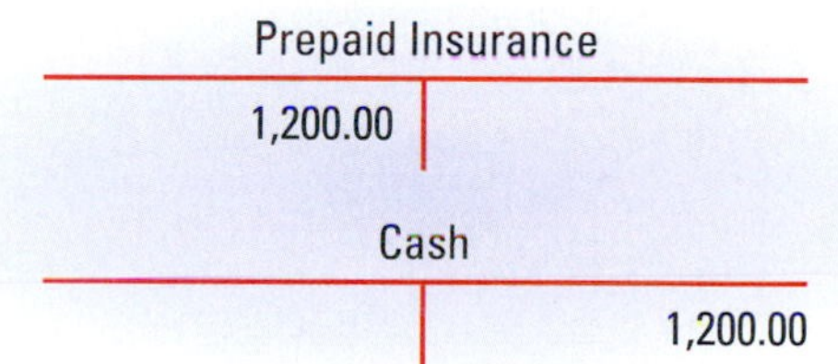

The source document for this transaction is Check No. 2. [*CONCEPT: Objective Evidence*] The analysis of this transaction is shown in the T accounts.

The asset account, Prepaid Insurance, increases by a debit, $1,200.00. The asset account, Cash, decreases by a credit, $1,200.00.

STEPS: JOURNALIZING CASH PAID FOR INSURANCE

1. **Date.** Write the date, *4*, in the Date column.
2. **Debit.** There is no special amount column with the title of the account debited, *Prepaid Insurance*, in its heading. Therefore, record the debit amount, *$1,200.00*, in the General Debit column. To indicate what account is debited for this amount, write the title of the account, *Prepaid Insurance*, in the Account Title column.
3. **Credit.** The journal has a special amount column for credits to *Cash*. Write the credit amount, *$1,200.00*, in the *Cash* Credit column. The title of the account is in the column heading. Therefore, do not write the account title in the Account Title column.
4. **Source document.** Write the source document number, *C2*, in the Doc. No. column.

REMEMBER All amounts recorded in the General Debit or General Credit amount columns must have an account title written in the Account Title column.

BOUGHT SUPPLIES ON ACCOUNT

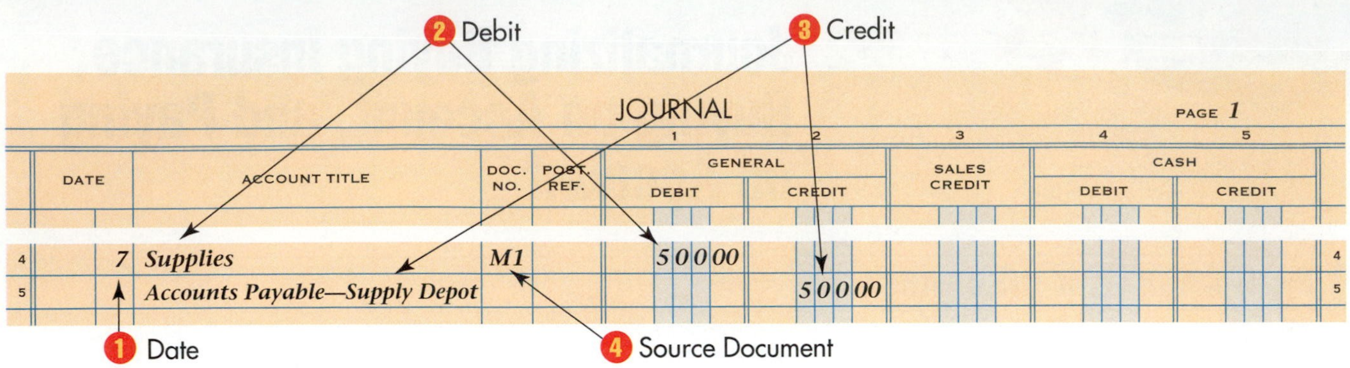

August 7. Bought supplies on account from Supply Depot, $500.00. Memorandum No. 1.

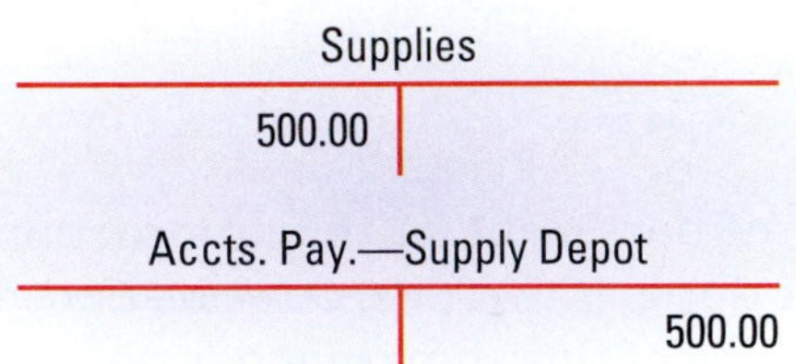

TechKnow Consulting ordered these supplies by telephone. TechKnow Consulting wishes to record this transaction immediately. Therefore, a memorandum is prepared that shows supplies received on account.

The source document for this transaction is Memorandum No. 1. [*CONCEPT: Objective Evidence*] The analysis of this transaction is shown in the T accounts.

The asset account, Supplies, increases by a debit, $500.00. The liability account, Accounts Payable—Supply Depot, increases by a credit, $500.00.

STEPS: JOURNALIZING SUPPLIES BOUGHT ON ACCOUNT

1. **Date.** Write the date, *7*, in the Date column.
2. **Debit.** There is no special amount column with the title of the account debited, *Supplies*, in its heading. Therefore, record the debit amount, *$500.00*, in the General Debit column. In order to indicate what account is to be debited for this amount, write the title of the account, *Supplies*, in the Account Title column.
3. **Credit.** There is no special amount column with the title of the account credited, *Accounts Payable—Supply Depot*, in its heading. Therefore, record the credit amount, *$500.00*, on the next line in the General Credit column. To indicate what account is credited for this amount, write the title of the account, *Accounts Payable—Supply Depot*, in the Account Title column on the same line as the credit amount.

   This entry requires two lines in the journal because account titles for both the debit and credit amounts must be written in the Account Title column.
4. **Source document.** Write the source document number, *M1*, in the Doc. No. column on the first line of the entry.

PAID CASH ON ACCOUNT

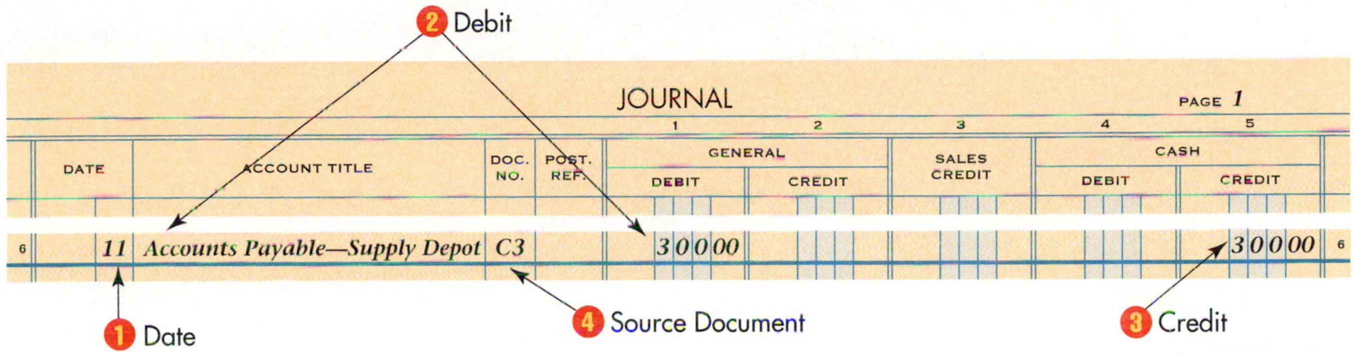

2 Debit
JOURNAL
PAGE 1
DATE
ACCOUNT TITLE
DOC. NO.
POST. REF.
GENERAL DEBIT
GENERAL CREDIT
SALES CREDIT
CASH DEBIT
CASH CREDIT
6 11 Accounts Payable—Supply Depot C3 300 00 300 00 6
1 Date
4 Source Document
3 Credit

August 11. Paid cash on account to Supply Depot, $300.00. Check No. 3.

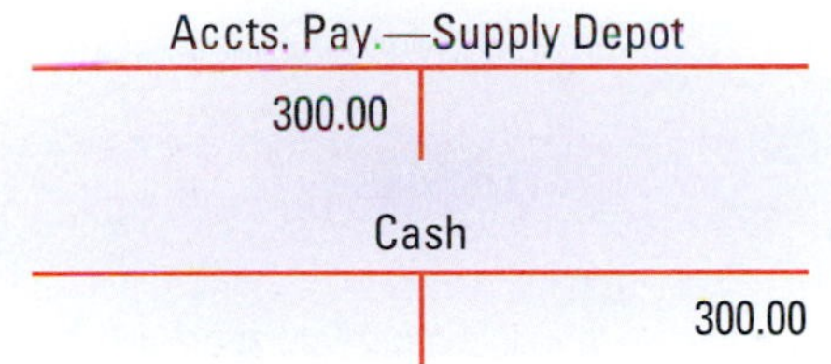

The source document for this transaction is Check No. 3. [*CONCEPT: Objective Evidence*] The analysis of this transaction is shown in the T accounts.

The liability account, Accounts Payable—Supply Depot, decreases by a debit, $300.00. The asset account, Cash, decreases by a credit, $300.00.

STEPS • STEPS • STEPS • STEPS • STEPS
JOURNALIZING CASH PAID ON ACCOUNT

1. **Date.** Write the date, *11*, in the Date column.
2. **Debit.** There is no special amount column with the title of the account debited, *Accounts Payable—Supply Depot*, in its heading. Therefore, record the debit amount, *$300.00*, in the General Debit column. In order to indicate what account is debited for this amount, write the title of the account, *Accounts Payable—Supply Depot*, in the Account Title column.
3. **Credit.** The journal has a special amount column for credits to *Cash*. Write the credit amount, *$300.00*, in the Cash Credit column. The title of the account is in the column heading. Therefore, do not write the account title in the Account Title column.
4. **Source document.** Write the source document number, *C3*, in the Doc. No. column.

©GETTY IMAGES/PHOTODISC

audit your understanding

1. Which journal columns are used to record paying cash for insurance?
2. Which journal columns are used to record buying supplies on account?
3. Which journal columns are used to record paying cash on account?

work together 3-2

Journalizing entries in a five-column journal

Use the journal that you started for Work Together 3-1. Your instructor will guide you through the following example.

Norm Derner owns Derner Copy Center, which uses the following accounts.

Cash	Accts. Pay.—Palm Supply	Miscellaneous Expense
Accts. Rec.—L. Rohe	Norm Derner, Capital	Rent Expense
Supplies	Norm Derner, Drawing	Utilities Expense
Prepaid Insurance	Sales	

Transactions:

Apr. 5. Bought supplies on account from Palm Supply, $500.00. M1.
7. Paid cash for insurance, $300.00. C2.
9. Paid cash on account to Palm Supply, $250.00. C3.

1. Journalize the transactions continuing on the next blank line of page 1 of the journal. Source documents are abbreviated as follows: check, C; memorandum, M. Save your work to complete Work Together 3-3.

on your own 3-2

Journalizing entries in a five-column journal

Use the chart of accounts below and the journal that you started for On Your Own 3-1. Work this problem independently.

Lou James owns Lou's Service Center, which uses the following accounts.

Cash	Accts. Pay.—OK Supplies	Advertising Expense
Accts. Rec.—C. Lord	Lou James, Capital	Miscellaneous Expense
Supplies	Lou James, Drawing	Rent Expense
Prepaid Insurance	Sales	

Transactions:

June 5. Paid cash for insurance, $400.00. C2.
9. Bought supplies on account from OK Supplies, $300.00. M1.
10. Paid cash on account to OK Supplies, $300.00. C3.

1. Journalize the transactions continuing on the next blank line of page 1 of the journal. Source documents are abbreviated as follows: check, C; memorandum, M. Save your work to complete On Your Own 3-3.

3-3 Journalizing Transactions That Affect Owner's Equity and Receiving Cash on Account

RECEIVED CASH FROM SALES

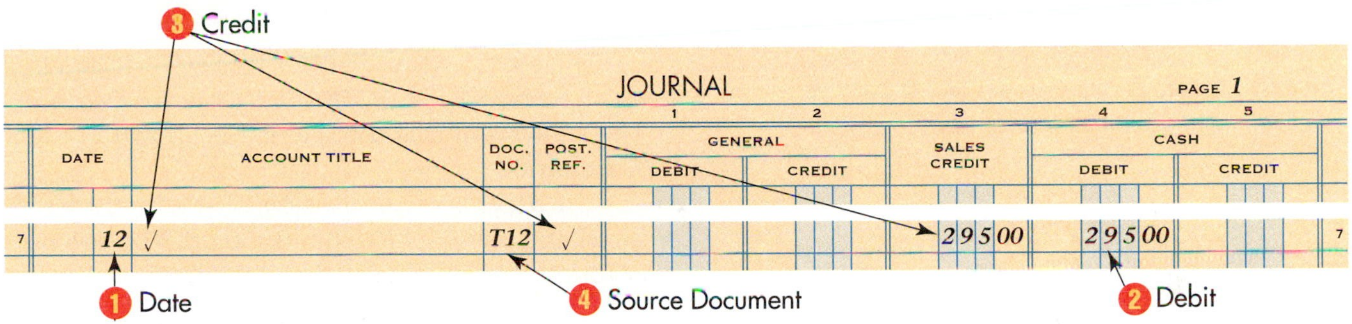

August 12. Received cash from sales, $295.00. Tape No. 12.

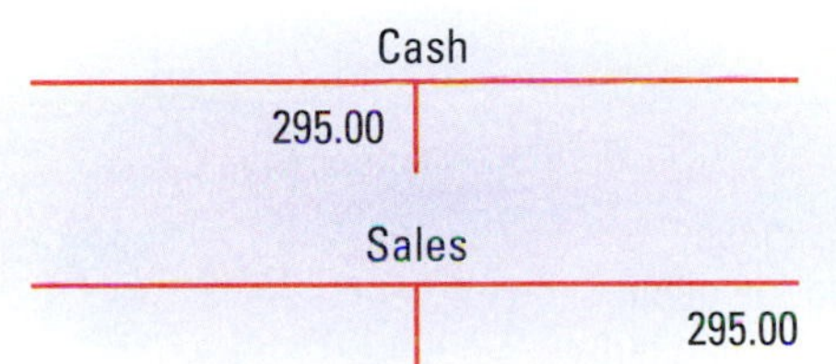

The source document for this transaction is Calculator Tape No. 12. [*CONCEPT: Objective Evidence*] The analysis of this transaction is shown in the T accounts.

The asset account, Cash, is increased by a debit, $295.00. The revenue account, Sales, is increased by a credit, $295.00.

The reason that Sales increases by a credit is discussed in the previous chapter. The owner's capital account has a normal credit balance. Increases in the owner's capital account are shown as credits. Because revenue increases owner's equity, increases in revenue are recorded as credits. A revenue account, therefore, has a normal credit balance.

STEPS • STEPS • STEPS • STEPS • STEPS • STEPS • STEPS • STEPS • STEPS • STEPS • STEPS

JOURNALIZING CASH RECEIVED FROM SALES

1. **Date.** Write the date, *12*, in the Date column.
2. **Debit.** The journal has a special amount column for debits to *Cash*. Write the debit amount, *$295.00*, in the Cash Debit column. The title of the account is in the column heading. Therefore, do not write the account title in the Account Title column.
3. **Credit.** The journal also has a special amount column for credits to *Sales*. Write the credit amount, *$295.00*, in the Sales Credit column. The title of the account is in the column heading. Therefore, do not write the account title in the Account title column.

   Because both amounts for this entry are recorded in special amount columns, no account titles are written in the Account Title column. Therefore, place a check mark in the Account Title column to show that no account titles need to be written for this transaction. A check mark is also placed in the Post. Ref. column.

   The use of the Post. Ref. column is described in Chapter 4.
4. **Source document.** Write the source document number, *T12*, in the Doc. No. column.

SOLD SERVICES ON ACCOUNT

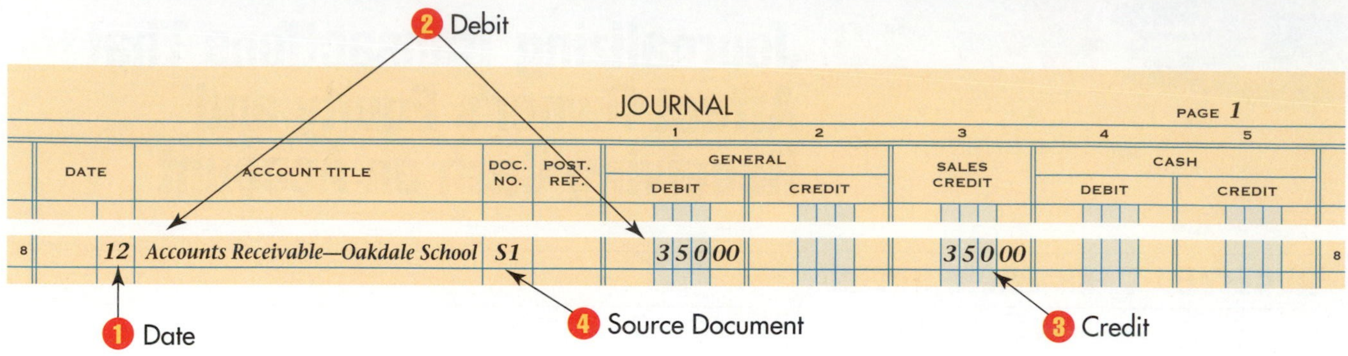

August 12. Sold services on account to Oakdale School, $350.00. Sales Invoice No. 1.

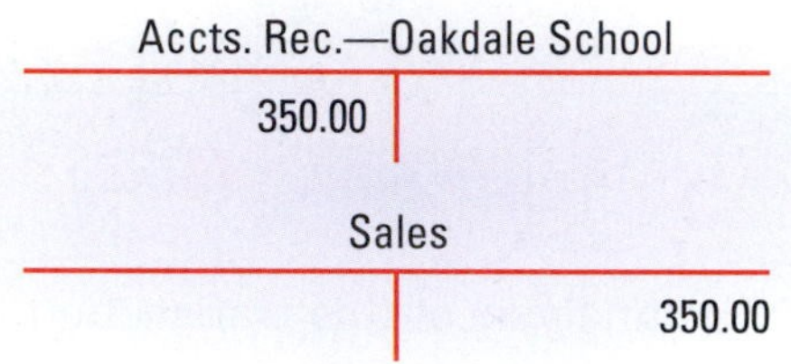

The source document for this transaction is Sales Invoice No. 1. [*CONCEPT: Objective Evidence*] The analysis of this transaction is shown in the T accounts.

The asset account, Accounts Receivable—Oakdale School, increases by a debit, $350.00. The revenue account, Sales, increases by a credit, $350.00.

STEPS • STEPS • STEPS • STEPS • STEPS • STEPS • STEPS • STEPS • STEPS • STEPS •

JOURNALIZING SERVICES SOLD ON ACCOUNT

1. **Date.** Write the date, *12*, in the Date column.
2. **Debit.** There is no special amount column with the title of the account debited, *Accounts Receivable—Oakdale School*, in its heading. Therefore, record the debit amount, *$350.00*, in the General Debit column. To indicate what account is debited for this amount, write the title of the account, *Accounts Receivable—Oakdale School*, in the Account Title column.
3. **Credit.** The journal has a special amount column for credits to *Sales*. Write the credit amount, *$350.00*, in the Sales Credit column. The title of the account is in the column heading. Therefore, do not write the account title in the Account Title column.
4. **Source document.** Write the source document number, *S1*, in the Doc. No. column.

©GETTY IMAGES/PHOTODISC

FYI FOR YOUR INFORMATION

Accounting is not just for accountants. For example, a performing artist earns revenue from providing a service. Financial decisions must be made such as the cost of doing a performance, the percentage of revenue paid to a manager, travel expenses, and the cost of rehearsal space.

PAID CASH FOR AN EXPENSE

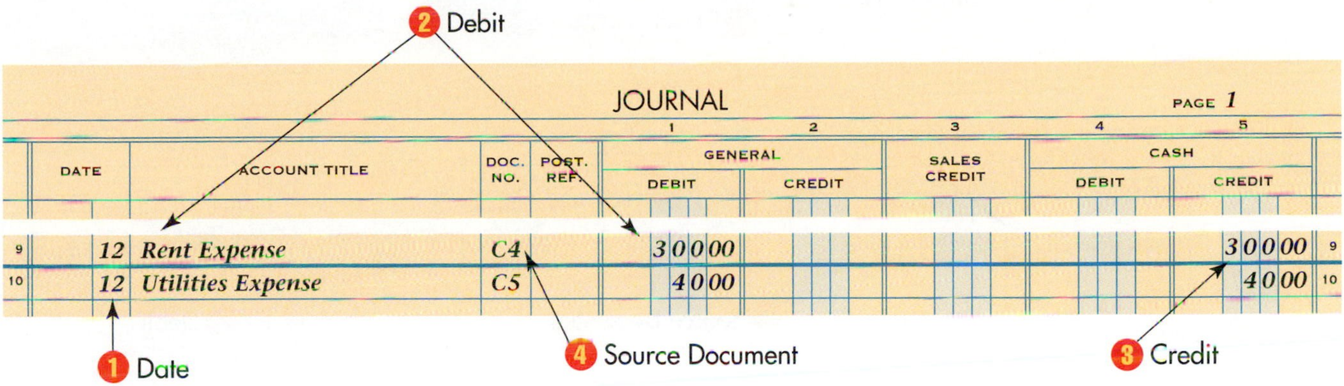

August 12. Paid cash for rent, $300.00. Check No. 4.

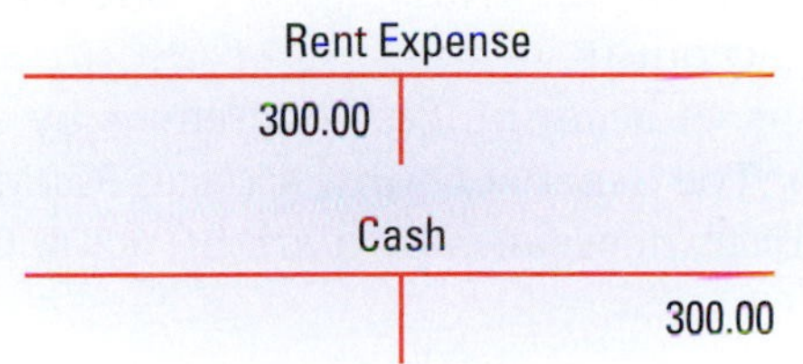

The source document for this transaction is Check No. 4. [*CONCEPT: Objective Evidence*] The analysis of this transaction is shown in the T accounts.

The expense account, Rent Expense, increases by a debit, $300.00. The asset account, Cash, decreases by a credit, $300.00.

The reason that Rent Expense is increased by a debit is discussed in the previous chapter. The owner's capital account has a normal credit balance. Decreases in the owner's capital account are shown as debits.

Because expenses decrease owner's equity, increases in expenses are recorded as debits. An expense account, therefore, has a normal debit balance.

Whenever cash is paid for an expense, the journal entry is similar to the entry discussed above. Therefore, the journal entry to record paying cash for utilities is also illustrated.

FYI FOR YOUR INFORMATION

Source documents can be critically important in tracking down errors. Businesses file their source documents so they can be referred to if it is necessary to verify information entered into their journals.

STEPS

JOURNALIZING CASH PAID FOR AN EXPENSE

1. **Date.** Write the date, *12*, in the Date column.
2. **Debit.** There is no special amount column with the title of the account debited, *Rent Expense*, in its heading. Therefore, write the debit amount, *$300.00*, in the General Debit column. To indicate what account is to be debited for this amount, write the title of the account, *Rent Expense*, in the Account Title column.
3. **Credit.** The journal has a special amount column for credits to *Cash*. Write the credit amount, *$300.00*, in the Cash Credit column. The title of the account is in the column heading. Therefore, do not write the account title in the Account Title column.
4. **Source document.** Write the source document number, *C4*, in the Doc. No. column.

RECEIVED CASH ON ACCOUNT

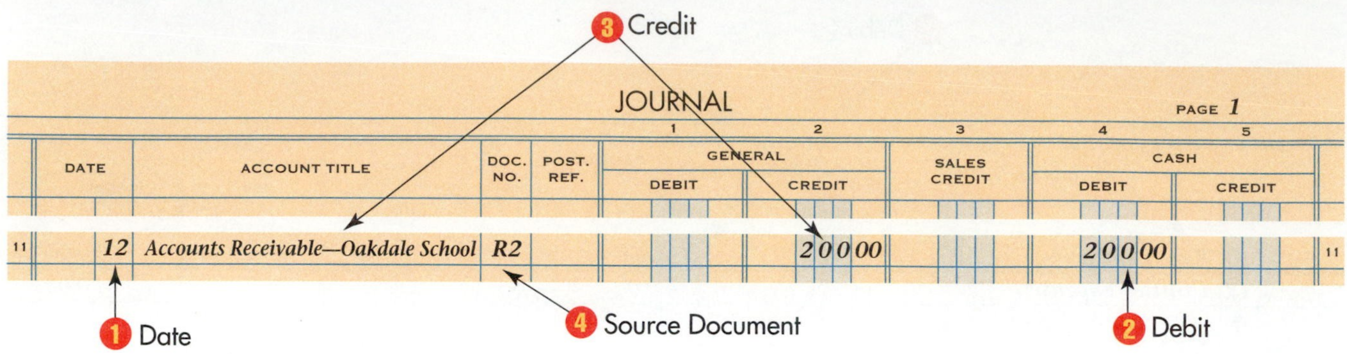

August 12. Received cash on account from Oakdale School, $200.00. Receipt No. 2.

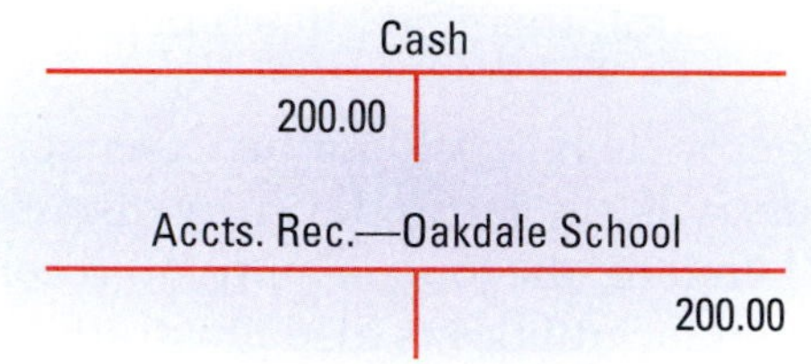

The source document for this transaction is Receipt No. 2. [*CONCEPT: Objective Evidence*] The analysis of this transaction is shown in the T accounts.

The asset account, Cash, increases by a debit, $200.00. The asset account, Accounts Receivable—Oakdale School, decreases by a credit, $200.00.

STEPS: JOURNALIZING CASH RECEIVED ON ACCOUNT

1. **Date.** Write the date, *12*, in the Date column.
2. **Debit.** The journal has a special amount column for debits to Cash. Write the debit amount, *$200.00*, in the Cash Debit column. The title of the account is in the column heading. Therefore, do not write the account title in the Account Title column.
3. **Credit.** There is no special amount column with the title of the account credited, *Accounts Receivable—Oakdale School*, in its heading. Therefore, record the credit amount, *$200.00*, in the General Credit column. To indicate what account is to be credited for this amount, write the title of the account, *Accounts Receivable—Oakdale School*, in the Account Title column.
4. **Source document.** Write the source document number, *R2*, in the Doc. No. column.

REMEMBER If you misspell words in your written communications, people may mistrust the quality of your accounting skills. Note that in the word *receipt*, the "e" comes before the "i" and there is a silent "p" before the "t" at the end of the word.

PAID CASH TO OWNER FOR PERSONAL USE

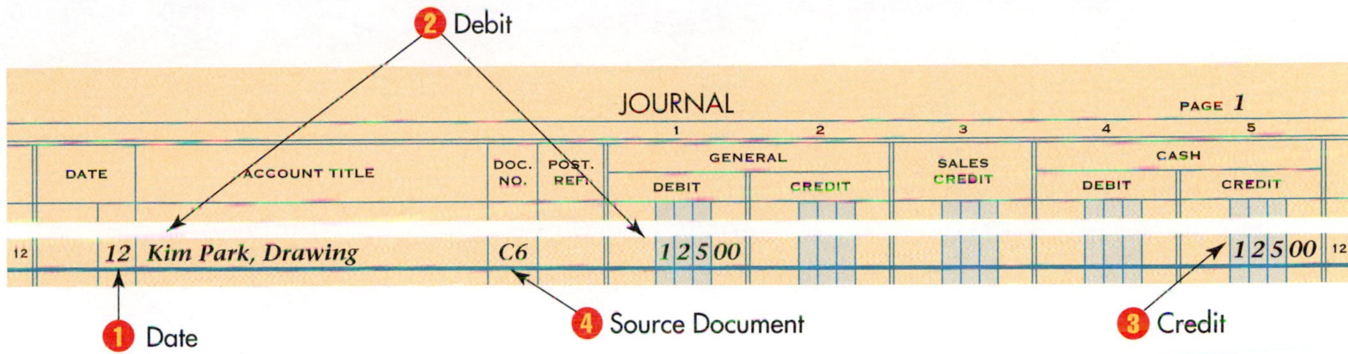

August 12. Paid cash to owner for personal use, $125.00. Check No. 6.

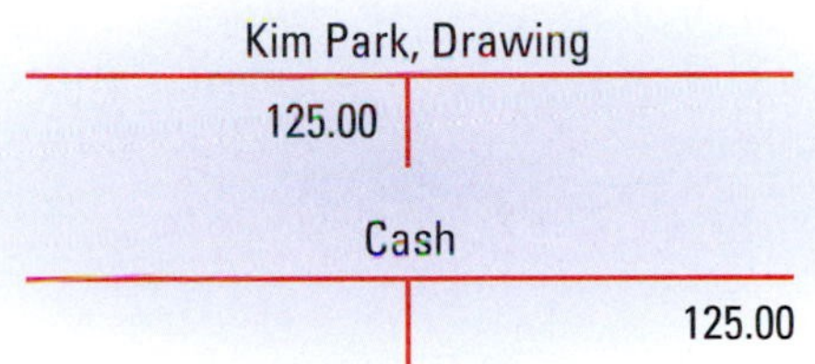

The source document for this transaction is Check No. 6. [*CONCEPT: Objective Evidence*] The analysis of this transaction is shown in the T accounts.

The reason that Kim Park, Drawing increased by a debit is discussed in the previous chapter. Decreases in the owner's capital account are shown as debits. Because withdrawals decrease owner's equity, increases in withdrawals are recorded as debits. A withdrawal account, therefore, has a normal debit balance.

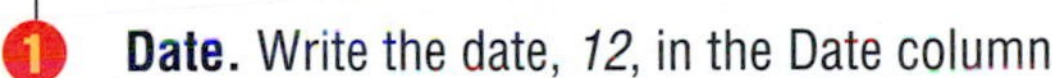

JOURNALIZING CASH PAID TO OWNER FOR PERSONAL USE

1. **Date.** Write the date, *12*, in the Date column.
2. **Debit.** There is no special amount column with the title of the account debited, *Kim Park, Drawing*, in its heading. Therefore, record the debit amount, *$125.00*, in the General Debit column. To indicate what account is debited for this amount, write the title of the account, *Kim Park, Drawing*, in the Account Title column.
3. **Credit.** The journal has a special amount column for credits to *Cash*. Write the credit amount, *$125.00*, in the Cash Credit column. The title of the account is in the column heading. Therefore, do not write the account title in the Account Title column.
4. **Source document.** Write the source document number, *C6*, in the Doc. No. column.

Successful small business owners typically have the following characteristics: confidence to make decisions, determination to keep trying during hard times for the business, willingness to take risks, creativity to surpass the competition, and an inner need to achieve.

audit your understanding

1. Which journal columns are used to record receiving cash from sales?
2. Which journal columns are used to record sales on account?
3. Which journal columns are used to record paying cash for an expense?
4. Which journal columns are used to record receiving cash on account?
5. Which journal columns are used to record paying cash to the owner for personal use?

work together 3-3

Journalizing transactions that affect owner's equity in a five-column journal

Use the chart of accounts and journal from Work Together 3-2. Your instructor will guide you through the following example.

Transactions:

Apr. 12. Paid cash for rent, $1,000.00. C4.
13. Received cash from sales, $2,500.00. T13.
14. Sold services on account to L. Rohe, $510.00. S1.
19. Paid cash for electric bill, $148.00. C5.
20. Received cash on account from L. Rohe, $255.00. R2.
21. Paid cash to owner for personal use, $1,000.00. C6.

1. Journalize the transactions continuing on the next blank line of page 1 of the journal. Source documents are abbreviated as follows: check, C; receipt, R; sales invoice, S; calculator tape, T. Save your work to complete Work Together 3-4.

on your own 3-3

Journalizing transactions that affect owner's equity in a five-column journal

Use the chart of accounts and journal from On Your Own 3-2. Work this problem independently.

Transactions:

June 11. Paid cash for rent, $525.00. C4.
12. Sold services on account to C. Lord, $700.00. S1.
16. Received cash from sales, $2,300.00. T16.
17. Paid cash for postage (Miscellaneous Expense), $37.00. C5.
19. Received cash on account from C. Lord, $350.00. R2.
20. Paid cash to owner for personal use, $850.00. C6.

1. Journalize the transactions continuing on the next blank line of page 1 of the journal. Source documents are abbreviated as follows: check, C; receipt, R; sales invoice, S; calculator tape, T. Save your work to complete On Your Own 3-4.

LESSON

3-4 Proving and Ruling a Journal

PROVING A JOURNAL PAGE

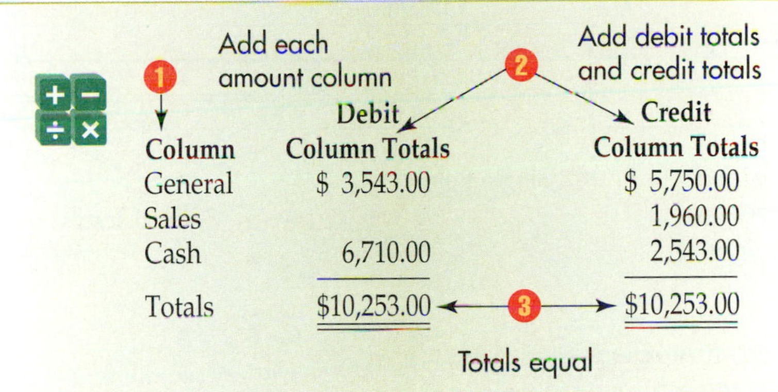

Add each amount column
Add debit totals and credit totals
Column
Debit Column Totals
Credit Column Totals
General $ 3,543.00 $ 5,750.00
Sales 1,960.00
Cash 6,710.00 2,543.00
Totals $10,253.00 $10,253.00
Totals equal

After TechKnow Consulting uses all but the last line on a journal page, columns are proved and ruled before totals are carried forward to the next page.

To prove a journal page, TechKnow Consulting verifies that the total debits on the page equal the total credits. Three steps are followed in proving a journal page.

STEPS PROVING A JOURNAL PAGE

1. Add each of the amount columns.
2. Add the debit column totals, and then add the credit column totals.
3. Verify that the total debits and total credits are equal. Because the total debits equal the total credits, page 1 of the journal is proved.
   If the total debits do not equal the total credits, the errors must be found and corrected before any more work is completed.

RULING A JOURNAL PAGE

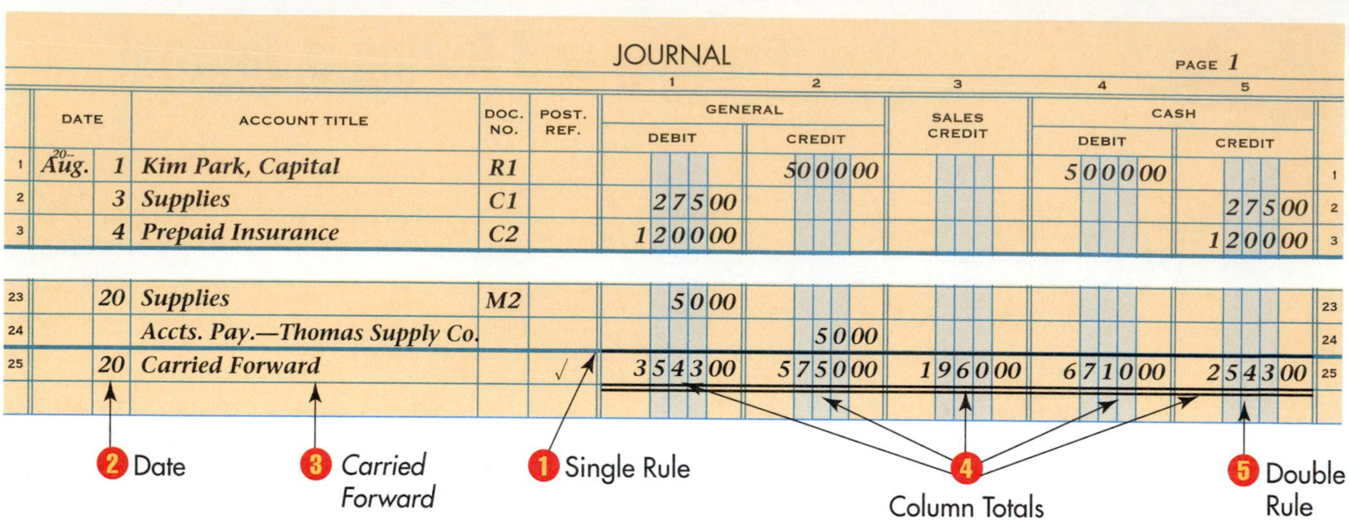

JOURNAL — PAGE 1

	DATE		ACCOUNT TITLE	DOC. NO.	POST. REF.	1 GENERAL DEBIT	2 GENERAL CREDIT	3 SALES CREDIT	4 CASH DEBIT	5 CASH CREDIT	
1	20-- Aug.	1	Kim Park, Capital	R1			5000 00		5000 00		1
2		3	Supplies	C1		275 00				275 00	2
3		4	Prepaid Insurance	C2		1200 00				1200 00	3
23		20	Supplies	M2		50 00					23
24			Accts. Pay.—Thomas Supply Co.				50 00				24
25		20	Carried Forward		✓	3543 00	5750 00	1960 00	6710 00	2543 00	25

After a journal page is proved, it is ruled. Five steps are followed in ruling a journal page.

STEPS RULING A JOURNAL PAGE

1. Rule a single line across all amount columns directly below the last entry to indicate that columns are to be totaled.
2. On the next line, write the date, *20*, in the Date column.
3. Write *Carried Forward* in the Account Title column. Place a check mark in the Post. Ref. column. The use of the Post. Ref. column is described in Chapter 4.
4. Write each column total below the single line.
5. Rule double lines below the column totals across all amount columns. A double rule in a journal indicates that the amounts are totals and that the sum of the debit totals equals the sum of the credit totals.

FYI FOR YOUR INFORMATION

Account titles in accounting records should always be written so that there is no question about the meaning. The usual practice is to write the full account title. If a title is long, however, and the space is short, an account title may sometimes have to be abbreviated.

STARTING A NEW JOURNAL PAGE

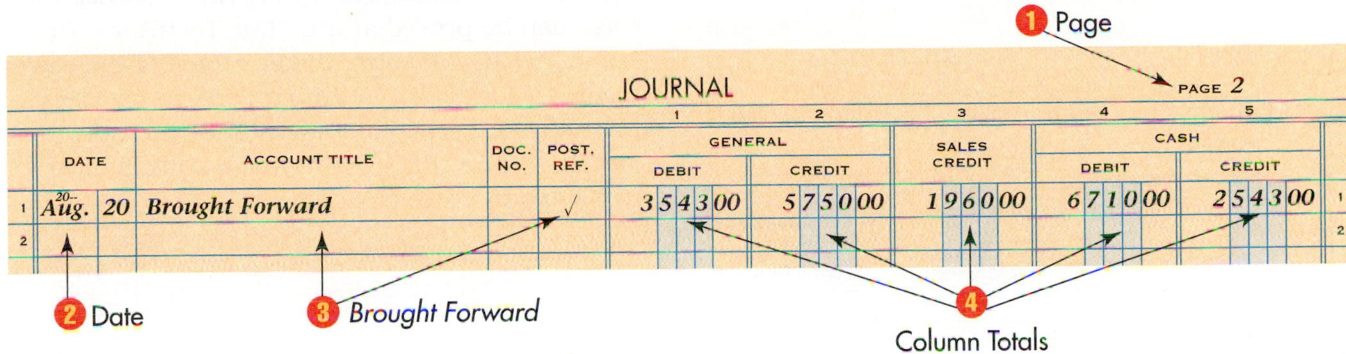

JOURNAL — PAGE 2

	DATE		ACCOUNT TITLE	DOC. NO.	POST. REF.	1 GENERAL DEBIT	2 GENERAL CREDIT	3 SALES CREDIT	4 CASH DEBIT	5 CASH CREDIT	
1	20-- Aug.	20	Brought Forward		✓	3543 00	5750 00	1960 00	6710 00	2543 00	1
2											2

The column totals from the previous page are carried forward to a new page. The totals are recorded on the first line of the new page, using the following four steps.

STEPS: STARTING A NEW JOURNAL PAGE

1. Write the page number, *2*, at the top of the journal.
2. Write the date, *20--, Aug. 20*, in the Date column. Because this is the first time that a date is written on page 2, the year, month, and day are all written in the Date column.
3. Write *Brought Forward* in the Account Title column. A check mark is also placed in the Post. Ref. column.
4. Record the column totals brought forward from the previous page.

PROVING AND RULING A JOURNAL AT THE END OF A MONTH

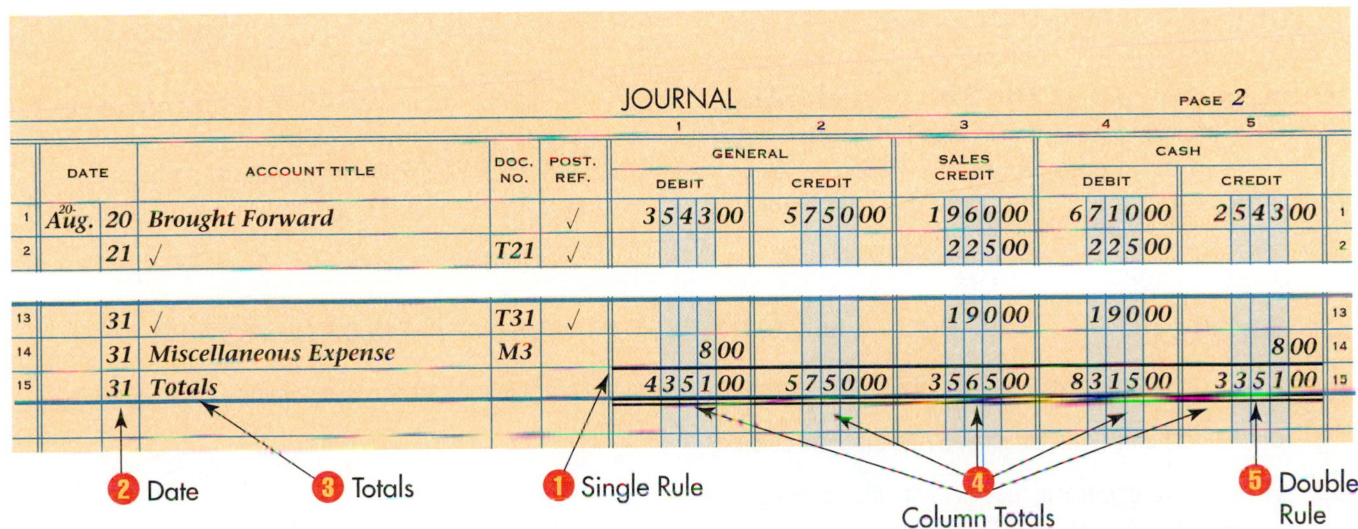

JOURNAL — PAGE 2

	DATE		ACCOUNT TITLE	DOC. NO.	POST. REF.	1 GENERAL DEBIT	2 GENERAL CREDIT	3 SALES CREDIT	4 CASH DEBIT	5 CASH CREDIT	
1	20-- Aug.	20	Brought Forward		✓	3543 00	5750 00	1960 00	6710 00	2543 00	1
2		21	✓	T21	✓			225 00	225 00		2
13		31	✓	T31	✓			190 00	190 00		13
14		31	Miscellaneous Expense	M3		8 00				8 00	14
15		31	Totals			4351 00	5750 00	3565 00	8315 00	3351 00	15

TechKnow Consulting always proves and rules a journal at the end of each month, even if the last page for the month is not full.

The last page of a journal for a month is proved using the same steps previously described. Then, cash is proved and the journal is ruled. The proof of page 2 of TechKnow Consulting's journal is completed as shown on the next page. Proving cash is also discussed on the next page.

Page 2 of TechKnow Consulting's journal is proved because the total debits are equal to the total credits, $12,666.00.

Column	Debit Column Totals	Credit Column Totals
General	$ 4,351.00	$ 5,750.00
Sales		3,565.00
Cash	8,315.00	3,351.00
Totals	$12,666.00	$12,666.00

Proving Cash

Determining that the amount of cash agrees with the accounting records is called **proving cash**. Cash can be proved at any time TechKnow Consulting wishes to verify the accuracy of the cash records. However, TechKnow Consulting always proves cash at the end of a month when the journal is proved. TechKnow Consulting uses two steps to prove cash.

1. Calculate the cash balance.

   Cash on hand at the beginning of the month .... $ 0.00

   TechKnow Consulting began the month with no cash balance. Ms. Park invested the initial cash on August 1.

   Plus total cash received during the month .... +8,315.00

   This amount is the total of the journal's Cash Debit column.

   Equals total .... $ 8,315.00

   Less total cash paid during the month .... −3,351.00

   This amount is the total of the journal's Cash Credit column.

   Equals cash balance at the end of the month .... $ 4,964.00

2. Verify that the cash balance equals the checkbook balance on the next unused check stub in the checkbook. Because the cash balance calculated using the journal and the checkbook balance are the same, $4,964.00, cash is proved.

   Checkbook balance on the next unused check stub .... $ 4,964.00

   The double rules in the calculations above indicate that the amounts are totals and the work is proved.

Ruling a Journal at the End of a Month

A journal is ruled at the end of each month even if the last journal page is not full. The procedures for ruling a journal at the end of a month are similar to those for ruling a journal page to carry the totals forward.

TechKnow Consulting uses five steps in ruling a journal at the end of each month.

STEPS • STEPS • STEPS • STEPS • STEPS • STEPS • STEPS • STEPS • STEPS • STEPS • STEPS •

RULING A JOURNAL AT THE END OF A MONTH (THESE STEPS ARE ILLUSTRATED ON THE PREVIOUS PAGE)

1. Rule a single line across all amount columns directly below the last entry to indicate that the columns are to be added.
2. On the next line, write the date, *31*, in the Date column.
3. Write the word *Totals* in the Account Title column.
   A check mark is not placed in the Post. Ref. column for this line. More information about the Totals line will be provided in Chapter 4.
4. Write each column total below the single line.
5. Rule double lines below the column totals across all amount columns. The double lines mean that the amounts are totals and that the debit totals equal the credit totals.

STANDARD ACCOUNTING PRACTICES

JOURNAL — PAGE 2

	DATE		ACCOUNT TITLE	DOC. NO.	POST. REF.	GENERAL DEBIT (1)	GENERAL CREDIT (2)	SALES CREDIT (3)	CASH DEBIT (4)	CASH CREDIT (5)	
17		28	✓ (4)	T28				350 00	350 00 ~~3 500 00~~ ← (1)		17
18	(2) →	~~29~~	~~Rent Expense~~	~~C22~~		(5) ~~5 00~~				~~5 00~~	18
19		29	Repair Expense	C22		50 00				50 00	19
20	(3) →	29	Supplies ~~Miscellaneous Expense~~	C21		100 00			(7)	100 00	20
21		30	Kim Park, Drawing	C24		500 00 ← (6)				500 00	21
22		30	Totals		(8) →	8 750 00	9 200 00	4 000 00	12 300 00	7 850 00	22
23						(9) →					

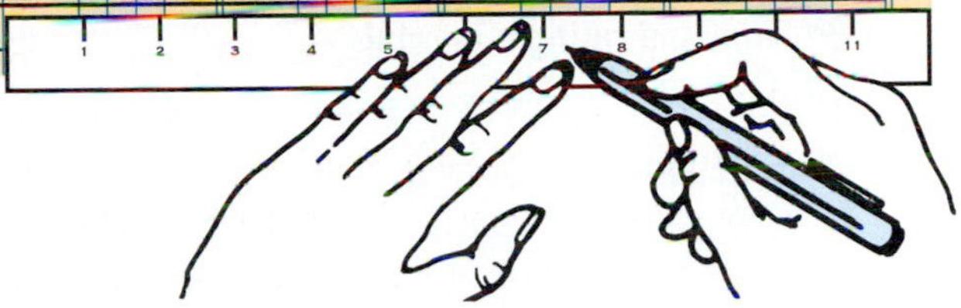

In completing accounting work, TechKnow Consulting follows standard accounting practices. These practices include procedures for error corrections, abbreviating words, writing dollar and cents signs, and ruling columns.

1. Errors are corrected in a way that does not cause doubts about what the correct information is. If an error is recorded, cancel the error by neatly drawing a line through the incorrect item. Write the correct item immediately above the canceled item.
2. Sometimes an entire entry is incorrect and is discovered before the next entry is journalized. Draw neat lines through all parts of the incorrect entry. Journalize the entry correctly on the next blank line.
3. Sometimes several correct entries are recorded after an incorrect entry is made. The next blank lines are several entries later. Draw neat lines through all incorrect parts of the entry. Record the correct items on the same lines as the incorrect items, directly above the canceled parts.
4. Words in accounting records are written in full when space permits. Words may be abbreviated only when space is limited. All items are written legibly.
5. Dollars and cents signs and decimal points are not used when writing amounts on ruled accounting paper. Sometimes a color tint or a heavy vertical rule is used on printed accounting paper to separate the dollars and cents columns.
6. Two zeros are written in the cents column when an amount is in even dollars, such as $500.00. If the cents column is left blank, doubts may arise later about the correct amount.
7. A single line is ruled across amount columns to indicate a calculation such as addition.
8. A double line is ruled across amount columns to indicate that the amounts are totals. In a journal the double rules also indicate that the debit totals equal the credit totals.
9. Neatness is very important in accounting records so that there is never any doubt about what information has been recorded. A ruler is used to make single and double lines.

• term review

proving cash

TERM REVIEW

• audit your understanding

1. List the three steps for proving a journal.
2. State the formula for proving cash.
3. List the five steps to rule a journal at the end of a month.

AUDIT YOUR

• work together 3-4

Proving and ruling a journal

Use the journal from Work Together 3-3. Your instructor will guide you through the following examples.

Transactions:

Apr. 23. Sold services on account to L. Rohe, $375.00. S2.
27. Paid cash to owner for personal use, $500.00. C7.
29. Received cash on account from L. Rohe, $300.00. R3.
30. Received cash from sales, $544.00. T30.

1. Journalize the transactions for April 23 and 27. Source documents are abbreviated as follows: check, C; receipt, R; sales invoice, S; calculator tape, T.
2. Prove and rule page 1 of the journal. Carry the column totals forward to page 2 of the journal.
3. Use page 2 of the journal to journalize the rest of the transactions for April.
4. Prove page 2 of the journal.
5. Prove cash. The beginning cash balance on April 1 is zero. The balance on the next unused check stub is $1,526.00.
6. Rule page 2 of the journal.

WORK TOGETHER • WORK TOGETHER • WORK TOGETHER

• on your own 3-4

Proving and ruling a journal

Use the journal from On Your Own 3-3. Work these problems independently.

Transactions:

June 23. Sold services on account to C. Lord, $400.00. S2.
26. Paid cash for delivery charges (Miscellaneous Expense), $23.00. C7.
27. Received cash on account from C. Lord, $200.00. R3.
30. Received cash from sales, $422.00. T30.

1. Journalize the transactions for June 23 and 26. Source documents are abbreviated as follows: check, C; memorandum, M; receipt, R; sales invoice, S; calculator tape, T.
2. Prove and rule page 1 of the journal. Carry the column totals forward to page 2 of the journal.
3. Use page 2 of the journal to journalize the rest of the transactions for June.
4. Prove page 2 of the journal.
5. Prove cash. The beginning cash balance on June 1 is zero. The balance on the next unused check stub is $3,187.00.
6. Rule page 2 of the journal.

ON YOUR OWN • ON YOUR OWN • ON YOUR OWN

SUMMARY

After completing this chapter, you can

1. Define accounting terms related to journalizing transactions.
2. Identify accounting concepts and practices related to journalizing transactions.
3. Record transactions to set up a business in a five-column journal.
4. Record transactions to buy insurance for cash and supplies on account in a five-column journal.
5. Record transactions that affect owner's equity and receiving cash on account in a five-column journal.
6. Prove and rule a five-column journal and prove cash.

Explore Accounting

Prenumbered Documents

As one way to control the operations of the business, a company often will use prenumbered documents. Such a document is one that has the form number printed on it in advance. The most common example in everyday life is the personal check.

Businesses use several prenumbered documents. Examples include business checks, sales invoices, receipts, and memorandums.

The use of prenumbered documents allows a simple way to ensure that all documents are recorded. For example, when a business records the checks written during a period of time, all check numbers should be accounted for in numeric order. The person recording the checks must watch to see that no numbers are skipped. In this way, the business is more confident that all checks are recorded.

By using several types of prenumbered documents, the business helps ensure that all transactions are properly recorded.

Another way a business tries to control operations is through the use of batch totals. When many (sometimes hundreds) of documents are being recorded, the total amount can be used to help ensure that all documents are recorded.

For example, when sales invoices are recorded, the total of all the invoices is calculated prior to the invoices being recorded. Once all invoices are recorded, another total can be calculated. If the two totals are equal, it is assumed that all invoices have been recorded. If the totals do not equal, it may indicate that a document was skipped.

Research: With your instructor's permission, contact a local business and ask what prenumbered documents are used there. Determine how the business uses the documents to ensure that all documents are recorded properly.

3-1 APPLICATION PROBLEM

Journalizing transactions in a five-column journal

Dennis Gilbert owns a service business called D & G Company, which uses the following accounts.

Cash
Accts. Rec.—Covey Company
Supplies
Prepaid Insurance
Accts. Pay.—Scott Supplies
Dennis Gilbert, Capital
Dennis Gilbert, Drawing
Sales
Miscellaneous Expense
Rent Expense
Utilities Expense

Transactions:

Feb. 1. Received cash from owner as an investment, $10,000.00. R1.
4. Paid cash for supplies, $3,000.00. C1.
5. Paid cash for supplies, $250.00. C2.

Instructions:

Journalize the transactions completed during February of the current year. Use page 1 of the journal given in the *Working Papers*. Source documents are abbreviated as follows: check, C; receipt, R.

Save your work to complete Application Problem 3-2.

3-2 APPLICATION PROBLEM

Journalizing buying insurance, buying on account, and paying on account in a five-column journal

Use the chart of accounts and journal from Application Problem 3-1.

Transactions:

Feb. 6. Paid cash for insurance, $600.00. C3.
7. Bought supplies on account from Scott Supplies, $2,000.00. M1.
8. Paid cash on account to Scott Supplies, $1,000.00. C4.
12. Paid cash on account to Scott Supplies, $1,000.00. C5.

Instructions:

Journalize the transactions. Source documents are abbreviated as follows: check, C; memorandum, M. Save your work to complete Application Problem 3-3.

3-3 APPLICATION PROBLEM

Journalizing transactions that affect owner's equity and receiving cash on account in a five-column journal

Use the chart of accounts given in Application Problem 3-1 and the journal from Application Problem 3-2.

Transactions:

Feb. 12. Paid cash for rent, $800.00. C6.
13. Received cash from sales, $500.00. T13.
14. Sold services on account to Covey Company, $450.00. S1.
15. Paid cash for telephone bill, $380.00. C7.
15. Paid cash to owner for personal use, $2,800.00. C8.
18. Received cash from sales, $278.00. T18.
19. Paid cash for postage (Miscellaneous Expense), $64.00. C9.
21. Received cash on account from Covey Company, $250.00. R2.
22. Received cash from sales, $700.00. T22.
22. Paid cash for heating bill, $329.00. C10.
25. Bought supplies on account from Scott Supplies, $340.00. M2.

Instructions:

Journalize the transactions. Source documents are abbreviated as follows: check, C; memorandum, M; receipt, R; sales invoice, S; calculator tape, T. Save your work to complete Application Problem 3-4.

3-4 APPLICATION PROBLEM

Proving and ruling a journal

Use the chart of accounts given in Application Problem 3-1 and the journal from Application Problem 3-3.

Transactions:

Feb. 25. Received cash on account from Covey Company, $200.00. R3.
25. Paid cash for a delivery (Miscellaneous Expense), $25.00. C11.
26. Sold services on account to Covey Company, $800.00. S2.
26. Paid cash for supplies, $44.00. C12.
27. Paid cash for rent, $200.00. C13.
27. Paid cash for postage (Miscellaneous Expense), $37.00. C14.
28. Received cash from sales, $1,365.00. T28.
28. Paid cash to owner for personal use, $800.00. C15.

Instructions:

1. Journalize the transactions for February 25 and 26. Source documents are abbreviated as follows: check, C; receipt, R; sales invoice, S; calculator tape, T.
2. Prove and rule page 1 of the journal. Carry the column totals forward to page 2 of the journal.
3. Use page 2 of the journal to journalize the transactions for February 27 and 28.
4. Prove page 2 of the journal.
5. Prove cash. The beginning cash balance on February 1 is zero. The balance on the next unused check stub is $1,964.00.
6. Rule page 2 of the journal.

3-5 APPLICATION PROBLEM AUTOMATED ACCOUNTING

Journalizing transactions and proving and ruling a five-column journal

Hans Schultz owns a service business called YardCare, which uses the following accounts.

Cash
Accts. Rec.—Frank Morris
Supplies
Prepaid Insurance
Accts. Pay.—Midwest Supplies
Hans Schultz, Capital
Hans Schultz, Drawing
Sales
Advertising Expense
Utilities Expense

Transactions:

Apr. 1. Hans Schultz invested $2,500.00 of his own money in the business. Receipt No. 1.
3. Used business cash to purchase supplies costing $105.00. Wrote Check No. 1.
4. Wrote Check No. 2 for insurance, $240.00.
5. Purchased supplies for $75.00 over the phone from Midwest Supplies, promising to send the check next week. Memo. No. 1.
11. Sent Check No. 3 to Midwest Supplies, $75.00.
12. Sent a check for the electricity bill, $65.00. Check No. 4.
15. Wrote a $700.00 check to Mr. Schultz for personal use. Used Check No. 5.
16. Sold services for $358.00 to Frank Morris, who agreed to pay for them within 10 days. Sales Invoice No. 1.
17. Recorded cash sales of $1,287.00.
18. Paid $90.00 for advertising. Wrote Check No. 6.
25. Received $358.00 from Frank Morris for the services performed last week. Wrote Receipt No. 2.

Instructions:

1. Journalize the transactions completed during April of the current year. Use page 1 of the journal given in the *Working Papers*. Remember to record appropriate source document numbers.
2. Prove and rule the journal.
3. Prove cash. The beginning cash balance on April 1 is zero. The balance on the next unused check stub is $2,870.00.

3-6 MASTERY PROBLEM

AUTOMATED ACCOUNTING

Journalizing transactions and proving and ruling a five-column journal

Jane Fernandez owns a service business called Jane's Car Wash, which uses the following accounts.

Cash
Accts. Rec.—Tony's Limos
Supplies
Prepaid Insurance
Accts. Pay.—Atkin Supplies
Accts. Pay.—Pine Supplies
Jane Fernandez, Capital
Jane Fernandez, Drawing
Sales
Advertising Expense
Miscellaneous Expense
Rent Expense
Repair Expense
Utilities Expense

Transactions:

June 1. Received cash from owner as an investment, $16,000.00. R1.
2. Paid cash for supplies, $300.00. C1.
3. Paid cash for rent, $900.00. C2.
4. Bought supplies on account from Atkin Supplies, $1,700.00. M1.
5. Paid cash for electric bill, $146.00. C3.
8. Paid cash on account to Atkin Supplies, $1,000.00. C4.
8. Received cash from sales, $980.00. T8.
8. Sold services on account to Tony's Limos, $450.00. S1.
9. Paid cash for insurance, $1,200.00. C5.
10. Paid cash for repairs, $388.00. C6.
10. Received cash from sales, $476.00. T10.
11. Paid cash for miscellaneous expense, $15.00. C7.
11. Received cash from sales, $630.00. T11.
12. Received cash from sales, $900.00. T12.
15. Paid cash to owner for personal use, $400.00. C8.
15. Received cash from sales, $850.00. T15.
16. Paid cash for supplies, $1,100.00. C9.
17. Received cash on account from Tony's Limos, $225.00. R2.
17. Bought supplies on account from Pine Supplies, $600.00. M2.
17. Received cash from sales, $500.00. T17.
18. Received cash from sales, $800.00. T18.
19. Received cash from sales, $650.00. T19.
22. Bought supplies on account from Pine Supplies, $60.00. M3.
22. Received cash from sales, $610.00. T22.
23. Paid cash for telephone bill, $85.00. C10.
23. Sold services on account to Tony's Limos, $582.00. S2.
24. Paid cash for advertising, $125.00. C11.
24. Received cash from sales, $300.00. T24.
25. Received cash from sales, $770.00. T25.
26. Paid cash for supplies, $90.00. C12.
26. Received cash from sales, $300.00. T26.
29. Received cash on account from Tony's Limos, $350.00. R3.
30. Paid cash to owner for personal use, $450.00. C13.
30. Received cash from sales, $500.00. T30.

Instructions:

1. The journals for Jane's Car Wash are given in the *Working Papers*. Use page 1 of the journal to journalize the transactions for June 1 through June 19. Source documents are abbreviated as follows: check, C; memorandum, M; receipt, R; sales invoice, S; calculator tape, T.
2. Prove and rule page 1 of the journal. Carry the column totals forward to page 2 of the journal.
3. Use page 2 of the journal to journalize the transactions for the remainder of June.
4. Prove page 2 of the journal.
5. Prove cash. The beginning cash balance on June 1 is zero. The balance on the next unused check stub is $18,642.00.
6. Rule page 2 of the journal.

3-7 CHALLENGE PROBLEM

Journalizing transactions using a variation of the five-column journal

Tony Wirth owns a service business called Wirth's Tailors, which uses the following accounts.

Cash	Accts. Pay.—Marker Supplies	Rent Expense
Accts. Rec.—Amy's Uniforms	Tony Wirth, Capital	Utilities Expense
Supplies	Tony Wirth, Drawing	
Prepaid Insurance	Sales	

Transactions:

June	1.	Received cash from owner as an investment, $17,000.00. R1.
	2.	Paid cash for insurance, $3,000.00. C1.
	3.	Bought supplies on account from Marker Supplies, $2,500.00. M1.
	4.	Paid cash for supplies, $1,400.00. C2.
	8.	Paid cash on account to Marker Supplies, $1,300.00. C3.
	9.	Paid cash for rent, $800.00. C4.
	12.	Received cash from sales, $550.00. T12.
	15.	Sold services on account to Amy's Uniforms, $300.00. S1.
	16.	Paid cash for telephone bill, $70.00. C5.
	22.	Received cash on account from Amy's Uniforms, $300.00. R2.
	25.	Paid cash to owner for personal use, $900.00. C6.

Instructions:

The journal for Wirth's Tailors is given in the *Working Papers*. Wirth's Tailors uses a journal with a column arrangement slightly different from the journal used in this chapter, as shown below.

JOURNAL — PAGE *1*

CASH		DATE	ACCOUNT TITLE	DOC. NO.	POST. REF.	GENERAL		SALES CREDIT
DEBIT	CREDIT					DEBIT	CREDIT	

1. Use page 1 of the journal to journalize the transactions. Source documents are abbreviated as follows: check, C; memorandum, M; receipt, R; sales invoice, S; calculator tape, T.
2. Prove and rule the journal.
3. Prove cash. The beginning cash balance on June 1 is zero. The balance on the next unused check stub is $10,380.00.

applied communication

Careful research about careers will help prepare you for making career choices. There are several U.S. government publications that provide detailed descriptions of many job titles. Two that are available in most public libraries are the *Dictionary of Occupational Titles* (*DOT*) and the *Occupational Outlook Handbook*.

Instructions: Go to the library and, using one of the two publications listed or any other appropriate resource, find the description for any accounting-related job. Record information you find, such as qualifications needed, job outlook, and earnings. Write one paragraph describing the pros and cons of working in such a job. Be sure to write a topic sentence and a conclusion.

APPLIED COMMUNICATION

cases for critical thinking

Case 1

During the summer, Willard Kelly does a variety of small jobs for many different people in the community to earn money. Mr. Kelly keeps all his money in a single checking account. He writes checks to pay for personal items and for business expenses. These payments include personal clothing, school supplies, gasoline for his car, and recreation. Mr. Kelly uses his check stubs as his accounting records. Are Mr. Kelly's accounting procedures and records correct? Explain your answer.

Case 2

In her business, Monica Zapata uses a journal with the following columns: Date, Account Title, Check No., Cash Debit, and Cash Credit. Ms. Zapata's husband, Rodrigo, suggests that she needs three additional amount columns: General Debit, General Credit, and Sales Credit. Ms. Zapata states that all her business transactions are for cash, and she never buys on account. Therefore, she doesn't see the need for more than the Cash Debit and Cash Credit special amount columns. Who is correct, Ms. or Mr. Zapata? Explain your answer.

CASES FOR CRITICAL THINKING • CASES

SCANS workplace competency

Basic Skill: Writing

Concept: Employers frequently cite the ability to communicate as one of the most important skills they require in employees. When communicating thoughts, ideas, and information, it is important to be clear and concise so that the intended receiver of the communication understands the message.

Application: Proprietorships are the most common form of business organization in the United States with over 17 million proprietorships filing tax returns. Review the advantages and disadvantages of proprietorships in Chapter 1 and write a paragraph describing why you think proprietorships are the most common form of business organization.

SCANS WORKPLACE COMPETENCY

using source documents

Journalizing transactions and proving and ruling a journal

Cy Sawyer owns a service business called Cy's Repair Service, which uses the following accounts.

Cash	Accts. Pay.–Atlas Supplies	Miscellaneous Expense
Accts. Rec.–J. Hutton	Cy Sawyer, Capital	Rent Expense
Supplies	Cy Sawyer, Drawing	Utilities Expense
Prepaid Insurance	Sales	

Source documents related to the transactions for Cy's Repair Service for May are provided in the *Working Papers*.

Instructions

1. The journal for Cy's Repair Service is given in the *Working Papers*. Use page 1 of the journal to journalize the transactions for May. Source documents are abbreviated as follows: check, C; memorandum, M; receipt, R; sales invoice, S; calculator tape, T.
2. Prove the journal.
3. Prove cash. The beginning cash balance on May 1 is zero. The balance on the next unused check stub is $5,223.00.
4. Rule the journal.

analyzing Best Buy's financial statements

To calculate what percentage one amount is of another amount, you divide the smaller amount by the total that contains the amount. Using Best Buy as an example, Cash for 2004 = 2,600,000,000. Total assets for 2004 = 8,652,000,000. To calculate what percentage cash is of total assets, use the following formula: Cash, 2,600,000,000 ÷ total assets, 8,652,000,000. The answer is .3005, or 30.05%.

Instructions

1. Use the information on page B-4 in Appendix B. Find the amount of Receivables and Total Assets for Best Buy for 2003 and 2004. Calculate what percentage Receivables are of Total Assets for 2003 and 2004.
2. Did the percentage increase or decrease over this period of time?
3. If this percentage would increase rapidly, what could be happening?

Automated Accounting

Recording Transactions

General Journal

A journal with two amount columns in which all kinds of entries can be recorded is called a *general journal*. General journal entries are entered in the automated accounting system through the General Journal tab. In a later chapter, special journals will be discussed to instruct you on how to use the other journals on the Journal Entries screen for specific types of transactions. The other tabs on the Journal Entries screen are used for entering purchases, cash payments, cash receipts, and sales.

In an automated accounting system, the transactions that are entered and posted in the general journal update ledger account balances immediately. For verification purposes, a general ledger report can be displayed or printed to prove account balances.

Recording Transactions in the General Journal Screen

Entering general journal entries can be done in five steps:

1. Enter the date of the transaction; then press the Tab key. The format for the date is mm/dd/yy. You may key a new date, use the + or − keys to increase or decrease the default date one day at a time, or click the calendar icon to select a date.
2. Enter the source document number in the Reference column; then press the Tab key.
3. Enter the number of the account to be debited; then press the Tab key. If the account number is not known, use the Chart of Accounts button to find the account number. The account title will be displayed next to the account number after you tab to the next column.
4. Enter the debit amount; then press the Tab key twice. The cursor will automatically position itself in the Account Number field on the next line of the journal. Enter the number of the account to be credited, press the Tab key twice, and then enter the credit amount.
5. When the transaction is complete, click the Post button or press the Enter key to post the transaction. Posting will be discussed in Chapter 4.

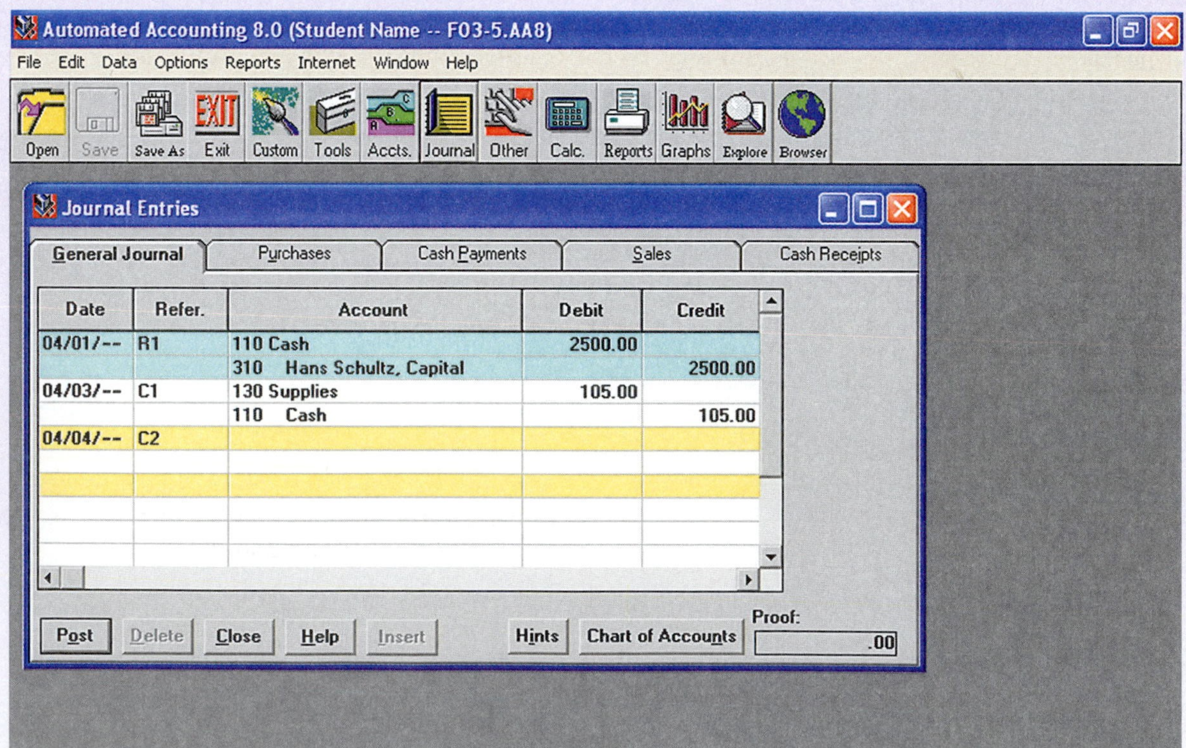

Adding, Changing, and Deleting General Journal Transactions

If you wish to add a part of a transaction, select the journal entry to which you want to add a debit or credit. Click on the Insert button. When the blank line appears, enter the additional debit or credit and click the Post button.

If you wish to change a general journal transaction, position the cursor in the field you wish to change and key the change; then click the Post button.

If you wish to delete a transaction, position the cursor in any field in the transaction and click the Delete button.

General Journal Report

The general journal report will display or print the general journal entries that were posted for a specified period. Reports are useful for detecting errors and verifying that debits and credits are equal.

A general journal report can be generated in four steps:

1. Choose the Report Selection menu item from the Reports menu or click the Reports toolbar button.
2. When the Report Selection window appears, choose the Journals option. To change the run date, shown in the upper right corner of the screen, enter the desired date or use the + key to increase and the − key to decrease the date. You may also click on the calendar.
3. Select the General Journal report; then click the OK button. You can choose to include all general journal entries or to customize your report.
4. You may display the report or click Print to print a copy of the report. You may also click Copy if you wish to paste the report into a word processing document or spreadsheet for further use.

AUTOMATING APPLICATION PROBLEM 3-5: Journalizing transactions and proving and ruling a five-column journal

Instructions:

1. Load *Automated Accounting 8.0* or higher software.
2. Select data file F03-5 from the appropriate directory/folder. The "F" in the filename indicates a data file for the *F*irst-year textbook. Template files that begin with "A" are for problems in the *A*dvanced textbook. Filenames that begin with AA8 are for problems in the *A*utomated *A*ccounting *8*.0 textbook. The software will ask you for your name. The name you provide will be printed at the top of all reports you print.
3. Select File from the menu bar and choose the Save As menu command. Key the path to the drive and directory that contains your data files. Save the file with a filename of F03-5 XXX XXX (where the X's are your first and last name). (Your instructor may direct you to use your initials instead of your full name when saving your files.)
4. Read the Problem Instructions screen by clicking the Browser toolbar button.
5. Key the transactions listed in Application Problem 3-5.
6. Save your file periodically as you work and always when you finish the problem.
7. Complete the problem instructions.
8. Save your file and exit the Automated Accounting software.

AUTOMATING MASTERY PROBLEM 3-6: Journalizing transactions and proving and ruling a five-column journal

Instructions:

1. Load *Automated Accounting 8.0* or higher software.
2. Select data file F03-6 from the appropriate directory/folder. The software will ask you for your name. The name you provide will be printed at the top of all reports you print.
3. Select File from the menu bar and choose the Save As menu command. Key the path to the drive and directory that contains your data files. Save the file with a filename of F03-6 XXX XXX (where the X's are your first and last name). (Your instructor may direct you to use your initials instead of your full name when saving your files.)
4. Read the Problem Instructions screen by clicking the Browser toolbar button.
5. Key the transactions listed in Mastery Problem 3-6.
6. Save your file periodically as you work and always when you finish the problem.
7. Complete the problem instructions.
8. Save your file and exit the Automated Accounting software.

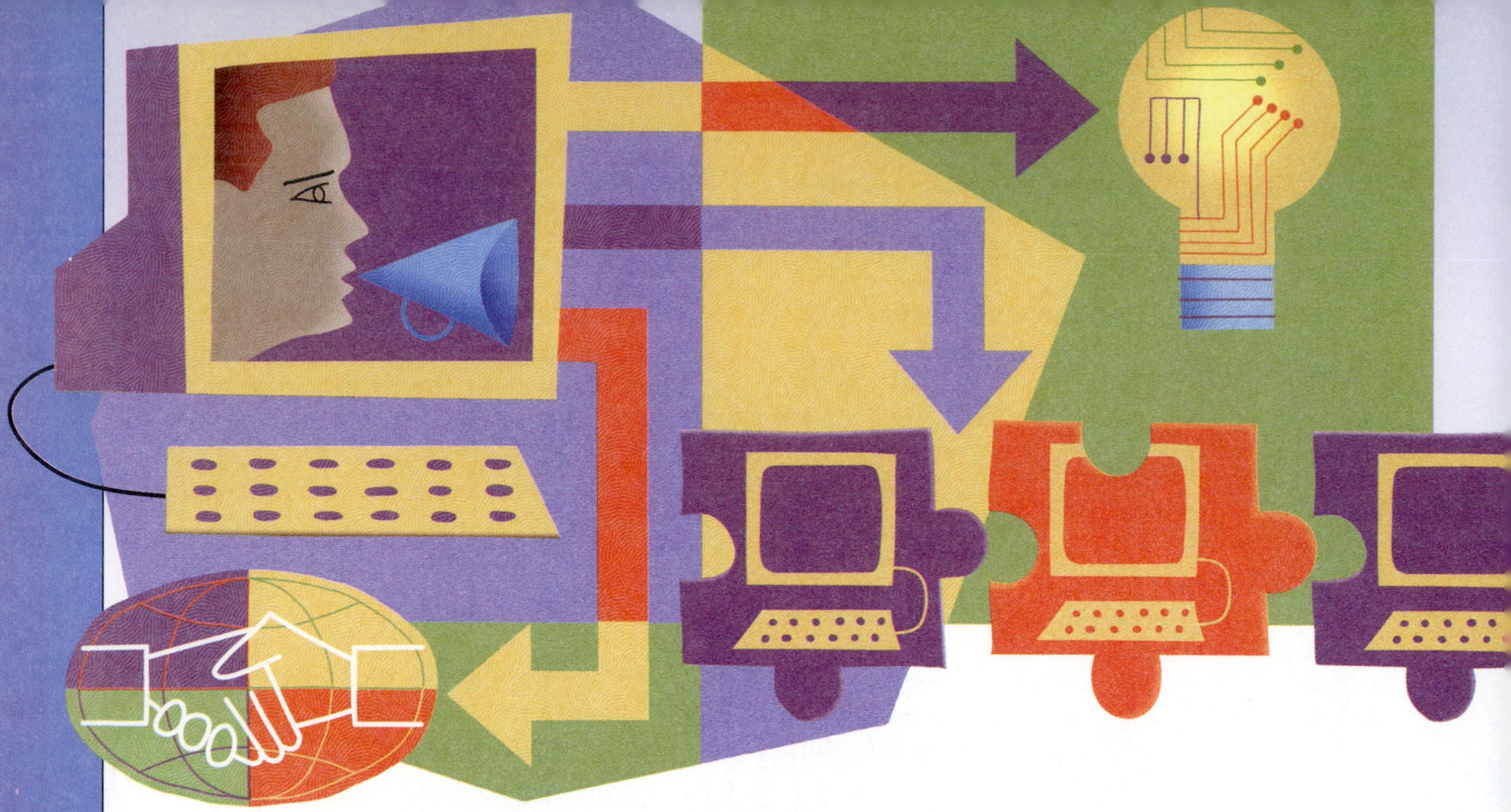

CHAPTER 4 Posting to a General Ledger

OBJECTIVES & TERMS

After studying Chapter 4, you will be able to:

1. Define accounting terms related to posting from a journal to a general ledger.
2. Identify accounting concepts and practices related to posting from a journal to a general ledger.
3. Prepare a chart of accounts for a service business organized as a proprietorship.
4. Post separate amounts from a journal to a general ledger.
5. Post column totals from a journal to a general ledger.
6. Analyze and journalize correcting entries.

- ledger
- general ledger
- account number
- file maintenance
- opening an account
- posting
- correcting entry

Point Your Browser
accountingxtra.swlearning.com

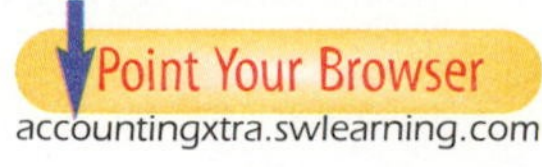

accounting in the real world

AMAZON.COM

©AP PHOTO/SCOTT SADY

RECORD SALES VOLUME AT AMAZON.COM

Have you ever realized the day before a special occasion that you forgot to purchase a gift for someone? Have you ever thought of going online, purchasing a gift, and getting it delivered the very next day?

On December 24 of a recent year, more than 70,000 gift certificates were ordered on Amazon.com. These certificates were delivered, via e-mail, on December 25. Recently Amazon.com, headquartered in Seattle, experienced its busiest holiday season and set a single-day record for items ordered—averaging 24 items per second!

In a letter to stockholders, Jeffrey P. Bezos, the founder and CEO of Amazon.com, explained about a Customer Review feature that had been established. This feature allows customers to rate both products and vendors. Mr. Bezos noted that "negative reviews cost us some sales in the short run." Also, an Instant Order Update feature reminds customers that they have already ordered an item if they order the same item again. Mr. Bezos stated that this feature "slightly reduced sales."

Critical Thinking

1. If the Customer Review feature and the Instant Order Update feature both reduce sales, why would Amazon.com continue to make these features available to its customers?
2. What problems might occur when Amazon.com receives orders at the rate of 24 items per second?

accountingxtra.swlearning.com

Source: www.amazon.com and Letter to Shareholders in 2003 Annual Report

ACCOUNTING IN THE REAL WORLD • ACCOUNTING IN THE REAL WORLD • ACCOUNTING IN THE REAL WORLD •

internet activity

SECURITIES AND EXCHANGE COMMISSION

Go to the homepage for the Securities and Exchange Commission (SEC) at www.sec.gov. The SEC was created through two Acts of Congress. Search the site to find out more about these two Acts. This information is usually found under the headings such as "About the SEC" and/or "What We Do."

Instructions

1. List the names of the two Acts of Congress that created the SEC.
2. Briefly summarize the purposes of these two Acts.

INTERNET RESEARCH ACTIVITY • INTERNET RESEARCH ACTIVITY • INTERNET RESEARCH ACTIVITY •

LESSON

4-1 Preparing a Chart of Accounts

ACCOUNT FORM

TechKnow Consulting records transactions in a journal, as described in Chapter 3. A journal is a permanent record of the debit and credit parts of each transaction with transactions recorded in chronological order. However, a journal does not show, in one place, all the changes in a single account.

If only a journal is used, a business must search through all journal pages to find items affecting a single account balance. For this reason, a form is used to summarize in one place all the changes to a single account. A separate form is used for each account.

making ethical decisions

Are Your Actions Legal?

"A man should be upright, not be kept upright." This famous statement by Marcus Aurelius suggests that, in a perfect world, everyone would always do the right thing. In the real world, however, governments have been forced to create complex systems of laws to force individuals to adhere to the social norm of right and wrong. We rely on these laws for our protection as well as the orderly operation of our society. For example, think about the chaos that might result if individuals could choose which side of the road to drive on!

Many laws are common knowledge for individuals working in business:

- Employers may not discriminate on the basis of national origin.
- Customers may not be charged different prices for the same item.
- Taxes must be paid to the government.

Whether an action is legal is not always so obvious. Did you know:

- It may be illegal to sell certain items, such as computers and oil, to countries that violate global norms of conduct.
- An interviewer may not ask a prospective employee if he or she has children.
- Companies with more than $10 million in assets having more than 500 owners must file annual and other periodic reports with the government.

No one can be expected to know every law that might affect the operation of a business. To assist its managers, businesses hire lawyers to provide their managers with legal advice. Most large businesses have their own legal departments staffed with lawyers. Smaller businesses typically pay a retainer fee to an independent lawyer to provide legal advice when needed. All businesses should provide their managers with regular training on legal issues. Managers should be encouraged to consult the lawyers if there is any question whether an action might be illegal.

Instructions

Use an Internet or library source to prepare a list of questions that are illegal for an employer to ask during a job interview.

RELATIONSHIP OF A T ACCOUNT TO AN ACCOUNT FORM

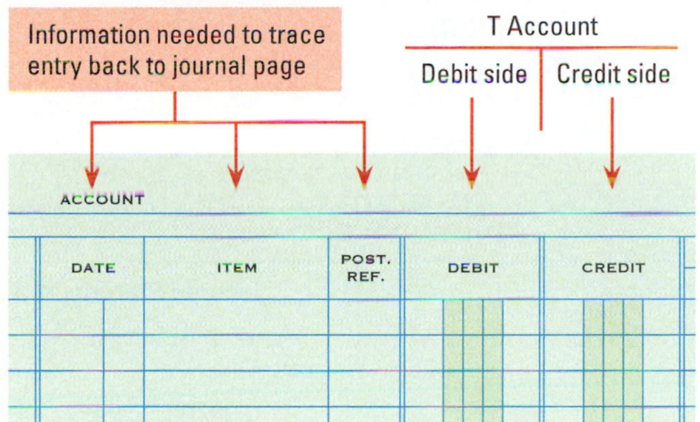

An account form is based on and includes the debit and credit sides of a T account. In addition to debit and credit columns, space is provided in the account form for recording the transaction date and journal page number. This information can be used to trace a specific entry back to where a transaction is recorded in a journal.

The major disadvantage of the account form illustrated above is that no current, up-to-date account balance is shown. If this form is used, an up-to-date balance must be calculated each time the account is examined. When an account has a large number of entries, the balance is difficult and time consuming to calculate. Therefore, a more commonly used account form has Debit and Credit Balance columns, as shown below.

ACCOUNT ACCOUNT NO.

DATE	ITEM	POST. REF.	DEBIT	CREDIT	BALANCE	
					DEBIT	CREDIT

Balance columns

Because the form has columns for the debit and credit balance, it is often referred to as the *balance-ruled account form.*

The account balance is calculated and recorded as each entry is recorded in the account. Recording information in an account is described later in this chapter. The T account is a useful device for analyzing transactions into debit and credit parts. However, the balance-ruled account form is more useful than the T account as a permanent record of changes to account balances. TechKnow Consulting uses the balance-ruled account form.

©GETTY IMAGES/PHOTODISC

CHART OF ACCOUNTS

7549 Broadway
Portland, OR 97202-2531

CHART OF ACCOUNTS

Balance Sheet Accounts		Income Statement Accounts	
	(100) ASSETS		(400) REVENUE
110	Cash	410	Sales
120	Petty Cash		(500) EXPENSES
130	Accounts Receivable—Oakdale School	510	Advertising Expense
140	Accounts Receivable—Campus Internet Cafe	520	Insurance Expense
150	Supplies	530	Miscellaneous Expense
160	Prepaid Insurance	540	Rent Expense
	(200) LIABILITIES	550	Supplies Expense
210	Accounts Payable—Supply Depot	560	Utilities Expense
220	Accounts Payable—Thomas Supply Co.		
	(300) OWNER'S EQUITY		
310	Kim Park, Capital		
320	Kim Park, Drawing		
330	Income Summary		

A group of accounts is called a **ledger**. A ledger that contains all accounts needed to prepare financial statements is called a **general ledger**. The name given to an account is known as an *account title*. The number assigned to an account is called an **account number**.

Preparing a Chart of Accounts

A list of account titles and numbers showing the location of each account in a ledger is known as a *chart of accounts*. TechKnow Consulting's chart of accounts is shown above. For ease of use while studying the chapters in Part 1, TechKnow Consulting's chart of accounts is also shown on page 3.

Accounts in a general ledger are arranged in the same order as they appear on financial statements. TechKnow Consulting's chart of accounts shows five general ledger divisions: (1) Assets, (2) Liabilities, (3) Owner's Equity, (4) Revenue, and (5) Expenses.

ACCOUNT NUMBERS

TechKnow Consulting assigns a three-digit account number to each account. For example, Supplies is assigned the number 150, as shown.

The first digit of each account number shows the general ledger division in which the account is located. For example, the asset division accounts are numbered in the 100s. Therefore, the number for the asset account, Supplies, begins with a 1.

The second two digits indicate the location of each account within a general ledger division. The 50 in the account number for Supplies indicates that the account is located between account number 140 and account number 160.

Assigning Account Numbers

TechKnow Consulting initially assigns account numbers by 10s so that new accounts can be added easily. Nine numbers are unused between each account on TechKnow Consulting's chart of accounts. For example, numbers 111 to 119 are unused between accounts numbered 110 and 120. New numbers can be assigned between existing account numbers without renumbering all existing accounts. The procedure for arranging accounts in a general ledger, assigning account numbers, and keeping records current is called **file maintenance.**

Unused account numbers are assigned to new accounts. TechKnow Consulting records payments for gasoline in Miscellaneous Expense. If Ms. Park found that the amount paid each month for gasoline had become a major expense, she might decide to use a separate account. The account might be titled Gasoline Expense. TechKnow Consulting arranges expense accounts in alphabetic order in its general ledger. Therefore, the new account would be inserted between Advertising Expense and Insurance Expense.

510	Advertising Expense	(Existing account)
	Gasoline Expense	***(New Account)***
520	Insurance Expense	(Existing account)

The number selected for the new account should leave some unused numbers on either side of it for other accounts that might need to be added. The middle, unused account number between existing numbers 510 and 520 is 515. Therefore, 515 is assigned as the account number for the new account.

510	Advertising Expense	(Existing account)
515	***Gasoline Expense***	***(New Account)***
520	Insurance Expense	(Existing account)

When an account is no longer needed, it is removed from the general ledger and the chart of accounts. For example, if TechKnow Consulting were to buy its own equipment and building, there would be no need for the rent expense account. The account numbered 540 would be removed, and that number would become unused and available to assign to another account if the need should arise.

When a new account is added at the end of a ledger division, the next number in a sequence of 10s is used. For example, suppose TechKnow Consulting needs to add another expense account, Water Expense, to show more detail about one of the utility expenses. The expense accounts are arranged in alphabetic order. Therefore, the new account would be added at the end of the expense section of the chart of accounts. The last used expense account number is 560, as shown on the chart of accounts. The next number in the sequence of 10s is 570, which is assigned as the number of the new account.

550	Supplies Expense	(Existing account)
560	Utilities Expense	(Existing account)
570	***Water Expense***	***(New Account)***

TechKnow Consulting has relatively few accounts in its general ledger and does not anticipate adding many new accounts in the future. Therefore, a three-digit account number adequately provides for the few account numbers that might be added. However, as the number of general ledger accounts increases, a business may change to four or more digits.

Charts of accounts with more than three digits are described in later chapters.

OPENING AN ACCOUNT IN A GENERAL LEDGER

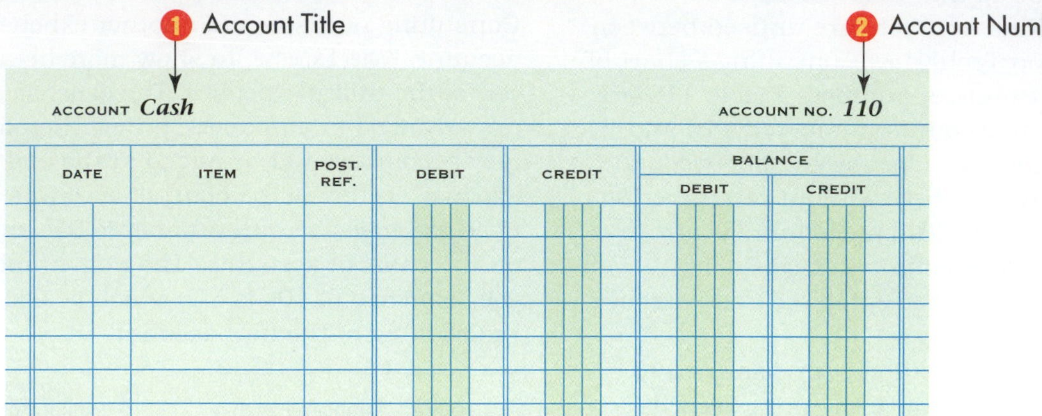

Writing an account title and number on the heading of an account is called **opening an account.** A general ledger account is opened for each account listed on a chart of accounts. Accounts are opened and arranged in a general ledger in the same order as on the chart of accounts.

Cash, account number 110, is the first account on TechKnow Consulting's chart of accounts. The cash account is opened using the steps shown below. The same procedure is used to open all accounts listed on TechKnow Consulting's chart of accounts.

STEPS: OPENING AN ACCOUNT IN A GENERAL LEDGER

1. Write the account title, *Cash*, after the word *Account* in the heading.
2. Write the account number, *110*, after the words *Account No.* in the heading.

Cultural Diversity: Accounting in Ancient Civilizations

In the ancient civilizations of Asia Minor and northern Africa, most citizens were illiterate. The scribe, who could read and write, became a very important person in the society. Of ancient Hebrew origin, the scribe has been called the forerunner of today's accountant.

Public scribes often recorded transactions as citizens arrived to do business. Most scribes recorded transactions on moist clay tablets that were then dried in the sun. Therefore, permanent records of transactions were not possible until scribes could write them down on clay tablets.

The Greeks invented coined money around 630 B.C., which facilitated assigning values to transactions.

The Babylonians in Asia Minor used an early form of banking. They transferred funds with a system resembling our modern-day checking accounts, one of the first uses of business documents.

These early practices provided the foundation for today's financial system and recordkeeping methods.

Critical Thinking

1. Estimate how many transactions might occur in a single day in a modern grocery store with which you are familiar.
2. List the number of different methods of payments that are accepted by modern grocery stores.

terms review

ledger
general ledger
account number
file maintenance
opening an account

audit your understanding

1. Describe the two parts of an account number.
2. List the two steps for opening an account.

work together 4-1

Preparing a chart of accounts and opening an account

Forms are given in the *Working Papers.* Your instructor will guide you through the following examples.

Clara Ross owns a service business called Ross Company, which uses these accounts.

Accts. Pay.—Sherer Supplies	Miscellaneous Expense	Cash	Automobile Expense
Accts. Rec.—Tyler Link	Insurance Expense	Sales	Clara Ross, Capital
Accts. Pay.—Mid City Supplies	Prepaid Insurance	Supplies	Rent Expense
Accts. Rec.—Megan Alvarez	Clara Ross, Drawing	Supplies Expense	

1. Prepare a chart of accounts. Arrange expense accounts in alphabetical order. Use 3-digit account numbers and number the accounts within a division by 10s.
2. Two new accounts, Postage Expense and Utilities Expense, are to be added to the chart of accounts prepared in Instruction 1. Assign account numbers to the two new accounts.
3. Using the account form in the *Working Papers*, open Cash.

on your own 4-1

Preparing a chart of accounts and opening an account

Forms are given in the *Working Papers.* Work this problem independently.

Eric Roen owns a service business called Roen's Hair Care, which uses these accounts.

Accts. Pay.—Milton Company	Supplies Expense	Cash	Delivery Expense
Accts. Rec.—Superior Supplies	Insurance Expense	Sales	Accts. Pay.—North Star
Prepaid Insurance	Telephone Expense	Supplies	Accts. Rec.—M. Waller
Eric Roen, Drawing	Eric Roen, Capital		

1. Prepare a chart of accounts. Arrange expense accounts in alphabetical order. Use 3-digit account numbers and number the accounts within a division by 10s.
2. Two new accounts, Gasoline Expense and Water Expense, are to be added to the chart of accounts prepared in Instruction 1. Assign account numbers to the two new accounts.
3. Using the account form in the *Working Papers*, open Delivery Expense.

LESSON

4-2 Posting Separate Amounts from a Journal to a General Ledger

POSTING AN AMOUNT FROM A GENERAL DEBIT COLUMN

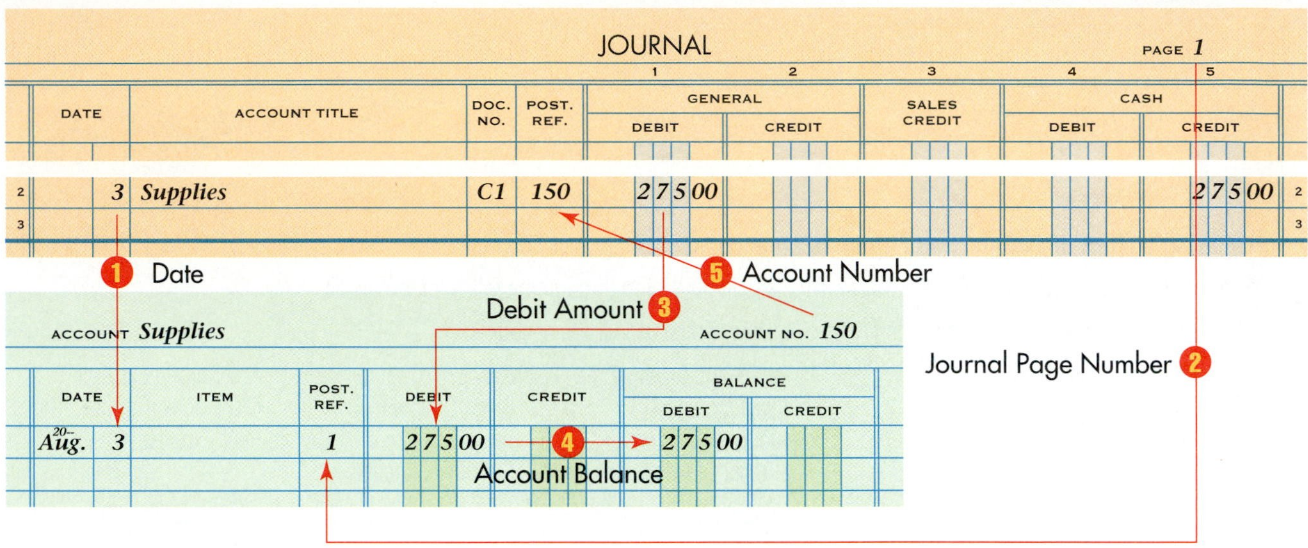

Transferring information from a journal entry to a ledger account is called **posting**. Posting sorts journal entries so that all debits and credits affecting each account are brought together. For example, all changes to Cash are brought together in the cash account.

Amounts in journal entries are recorded in either general amount columns or special amount columns. There are two rules for posting amounts from a journal: (1) Separate amounts in a journal's general amount columns are posted individually to the account written in the Account Title column. (2) Separate amounts in a journal's special amount columns are not posted individually. Instead, the special amount column totals are posted to the account named in the heading of the special amount column.

Posting a Separate Amount from a General Debit Column

For most journal entries, at least one separate amount is posted individually to a general ledger account. When an entry in a journal includes an amount in a general amount column, the amount is posted individually.

Each separate amount in the General Debit and General Credit columns of a journal is posted to the account written in the Account Title column.

STEPS

POSTING AN AMOUNT FROM A GENERAL DEBIT COLUMN

1. Write the date, *20--, Aug. 3*, in the Date column of the account *Supplies*.
2. Write the journal page number, *1*, in the Post. Ref. column of the account. *Post. Ref.* is an abbreviation for Posting Reference.
3. Write the debit amount, *$275.00*, in the Debit amount column.
4. Write the new account balance, *$275.00*, in the Balance Debit column. Because this entry is the first in the *Supplies* account, the previous balance is zero.

Previous Balance	+	Debit Column Amount	=	New Debit Balance
$0.00	+	$275.00	=	$275.00

5. Return to the journal and write the account number, *150*, in the Post. Ref. column of the journal.

POSTING A SECOND AMOUNT TO AN ACCOUNT

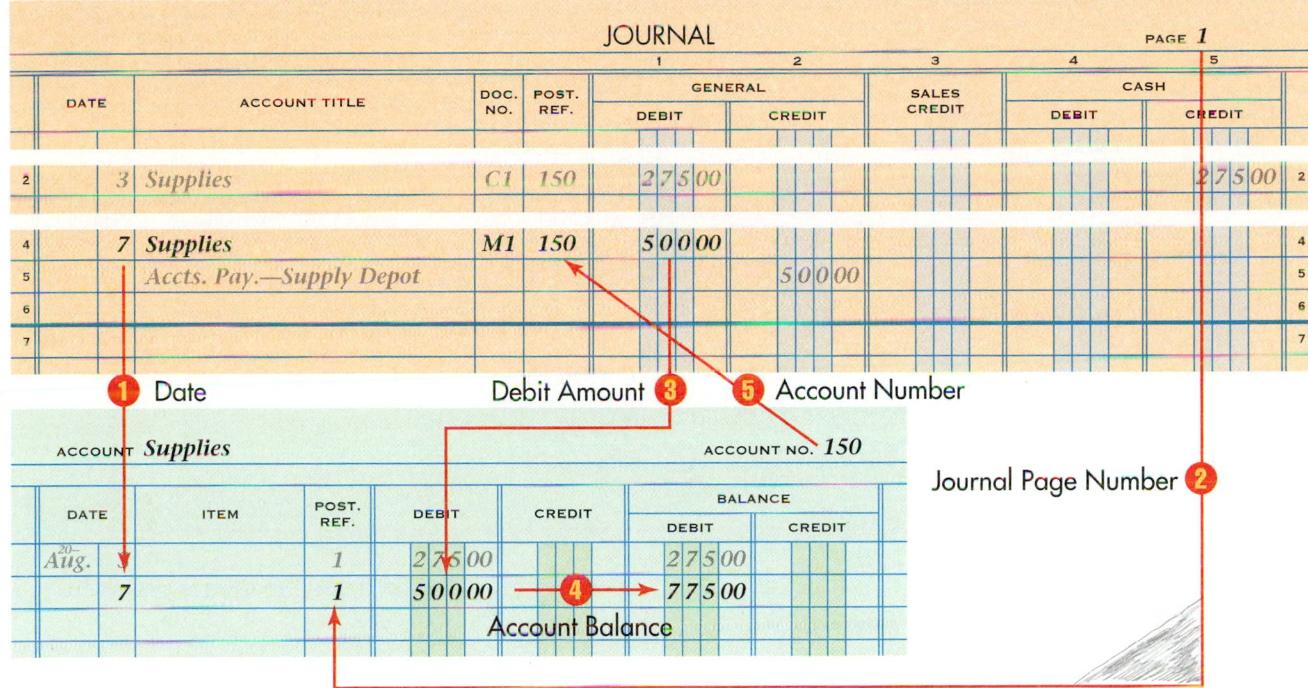

The numbers in the Post. Ref. columns of the general ledger account and the journal serve three purposes: (1) An entry in an account can be traced to its source in a journal. (2) An entry in a journal can be traced to where it was posted in an account. (3) If posting is interrupted, the accounting personnel can easily see which entries in the journal still need to be posted. A blank in the Post. Ref. column of the journal indicates that posting for that line still needs to be completed. Therefore, the posting reference is always recorded in the journal as the last step in the posting procedure.

The same five steps are followed when a second amount is posted to an account.

STEPS: POSTING A SECOND AMOUNT TO AN ACCOUNT

1. Write the date, *7*, in the Date column of the account. The month and year are written only once on a page of a ledger account, unless the month or year changes.
2. Write the journal page number, *1*, in the Post. Ref. column of the account.
3. Write the debit amount, *$500.00*, in the Debit amount column.
4. Write the new account balance, *$775.00*, in the Balance Debit column.
5. Return to the journal and write the account number, *150*, in the Post. Ref. column of the journal.

Previous Debit Balance	+	Debit Column Amount	=	New Debit Balance
$275.00	+	$500.00	=	$775.00

REMEMBER Each separate amount in the General Debit and Credit columns of a journal is posted individually. Therefore, the totals of these columns are not posted.

POSTING AN AMOUNT FROM A GENERAL CREDIT COLUMN

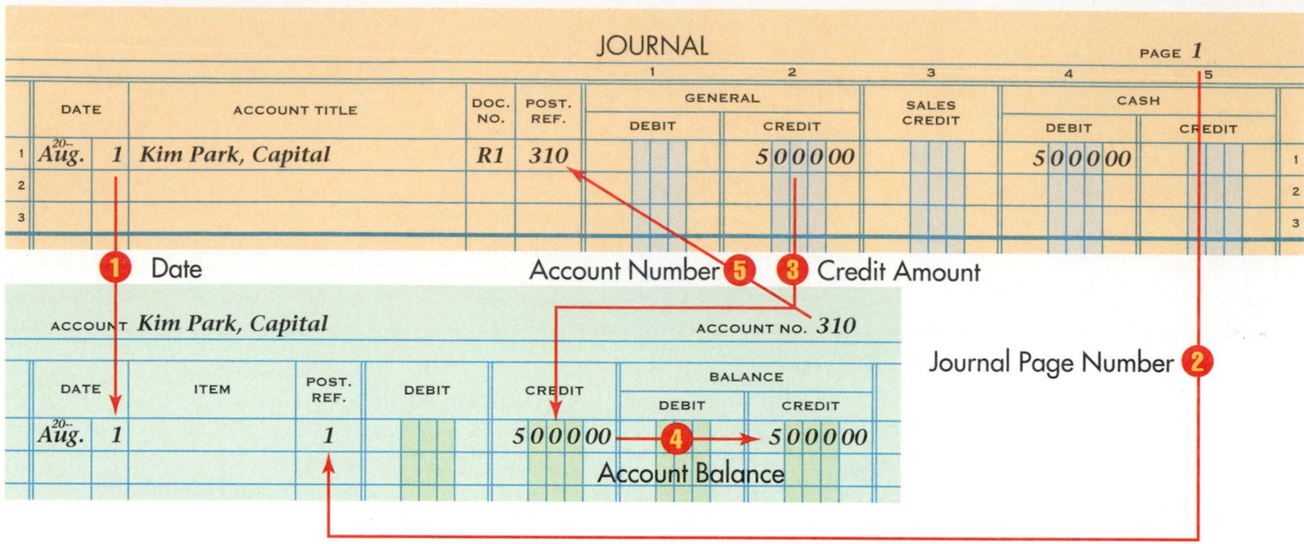

JOURNAL
PAGE 1
DATE
ACCOUNT TITLE
DOC. NO.
POST. REF.
GENERAL
DEBIT
CREDIT
SALES CREDIT
CASH
DEBIT
CREDIT
20-- Aug. 1 Kim Park, Capital
R1
310
5 000 00
5 000 00
1 Date
Account Number 5
3 Credit Amount
Journal Page Number 2
ACCOUNT Kim Park, Capital
ACCOUNT NO. 310
DATE
ITEM
POST. REF.
DEBIT
CREDIT
BALANCE
DEBIT
CREDIT
20-- Aug. 1
1
5 000 00
4
5 000 00
Account Balance

An amount in the General Credit column is posted separately. Five steps are followed when posting an amount from the General Credit column.

STEPS: POSTING AN AMOUNT FROM A GENERAL CREDIT COLUMN

1. Write the date, *20--, Aug. 1*, in the Date column of the account.
2. Write the journal page number, *1*, in the Post. Ref. column of the account.
3. Write the credit amount, *$5,000.00*, in the Credit amount column.
4. Write the new account balance, *$5,000.00*, in the Balance Credit column.
5. Return to the journal and write the account number, *310*, in the Post. Ref. column of the journal.

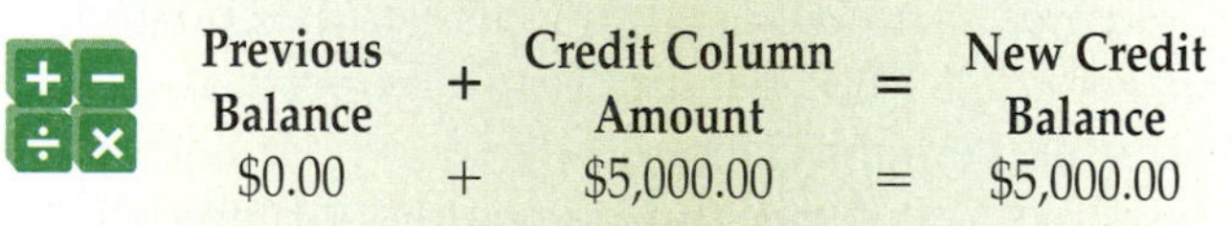

Previous Balance	+	Credit Column Amount	=	New Credit Balance
$0.00	+	$5,000.00	=	$5,000.00

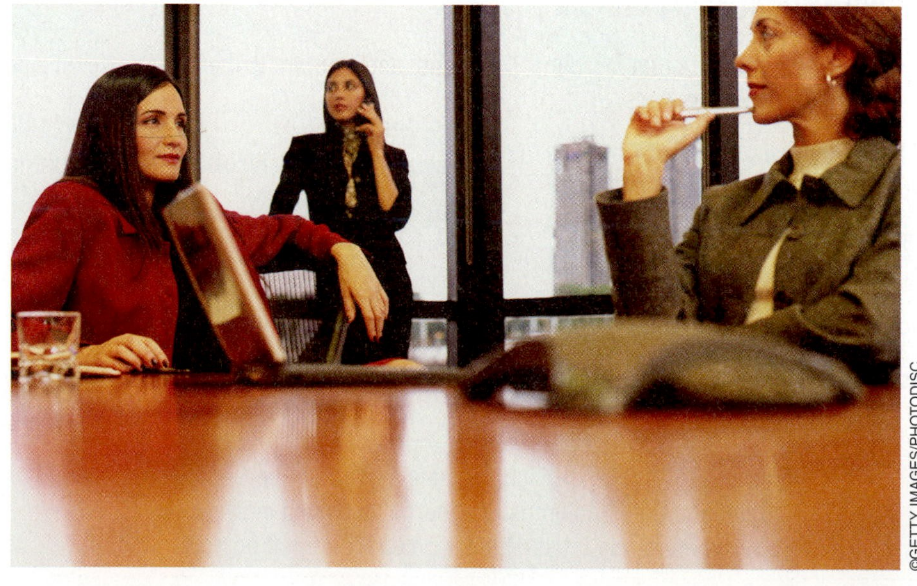

©GETTY IMAGES/PHOTODISC

term review

posting

audit your understanding

1. List the five steps of posting from the general columns of a journal to the general ledger.
2. Are the totals of the General Debit and Credit columns posted? Why or why not?

work together 4-2

Posting separate amounts to a general ledger

A completed journal and general ledger accounts are given in the *Working Papers*. Your instructor will guide you through the following example.

Leonard Witkowski owns a service business that uses the following accounts.

Assets
110 Cash
120 Accounts Receivable—Danielle Braastad
130 Supplies
140 Prepaid Insurance

Liabilities
210 Accounts Payable—Joshua's Supplies

Owner's Equity
310 Leonard Witkowski, Capital
320 Leonard Witkowski, Drawing

Revenue
410 Sales

Expenses
510 Rent Expense

1. Post the separate amounts (on each line of the journal) that need to be posted individually. Save your work to complete Work Together 4-3.

on your own 4-2

Posting separate amounts to a general ledger

A completed journal and general ledger accounts are given in the *Working Papers*. Work this problem independently.

Heather Hasley owns a service business, which uses the following accounts.

Assets
110 Cash
120 Accounts Receivable—Ken Garlie
130 Supplies
140 Prepaid Insurance

Liabilities
210 Accounts Payable—Bodden Company

Owner's Equity
310 Heather Hasley, Capital
320 Heather Hasley, Drawing

Revenue
410 Sales

Expenses
510 Advertising Expense

1. Post the separate amounts (on each line of the journal) that need to be posted individually. Save your work to complete On Your Own 4-3.

LESSON

4-3 Posting Column Totals from a Journal to a General Ledger

CHECK MARKS SHOW THAT AMOUNTS ARE NOT POSTED

JOURNAL — PAGE 2

	DATE		ACCOUNT TITLE	DOC. NO.	POST. REF.	1 GENERAL DEBIT	2 GENERAL CREDIT	3 SALES CREDIT	4 CASH DEBIT	5 CASH CREDIT	
1	20-- Aug.	20	Brought Forward		√	3 543 00	5 750 00	1 960 00	6 710 00	2 543 00	1
13		31	√	T31	√			190 00	190 00		13
14		31	Miscellaneous Expense	M3		8 00				8 00	14
15		31	Totals			4 351 00	5 750 00	3 565 00	8 315 00	3 351 00	15
16						(√)	(√)				16
17											17

Check mark indicates that amounts ARE NOT posted individually.

Check marks indicate that general amount column totals ARE NOT posted.

Journal Entries That Are Not Posted Individually

Several lines in TechKnow Consulting's journal contain amounts that are not to be posted individually. These include forwarding totals and amounts recorded in special amount columns. The totals brought forward from page 1 are shown on line 1 of the journal. None of these separate total amounts on line 1 are posted individually to general ledger accounts. To assure that no postings are overlooked, no blank posting reference spaces should be left in the Post. Ref. column of the journal. Therefore, when the totals were forwarded to page 2 of the journal, a check mark was placed in the Post. Ref. column of line 1 to show that no separate amounts are posted individually.

Separate amounts in the special amount columns—Sales Credit, Cash Debit, and Cash Credit—are not posted individually. For example, on line 13 of the journal, two separate $190.00 amounts are recorded in two special amount columns, Sales Credit and Cash Debit.

A check mark was placed in the Post. Ref. column on line 13 when the entry was journalized. The check mark indicates that no separate amounts are posted individually from this line. Instead, the totals of the special amount columns are posted.

Totals of General Debit and General Credit Amount Columns

The General Debit and General Credit columns are not special amount columns because the column headings do not contain the name of an account. All of the separate amounts in the General Debit and General Credit amount columns are posted individually.

Therefore, the column totals are not posted. A check mark in parentheses is placed below each general amount column total as shown. The check mark indicates that the total of the General Debit column is not posted.

A check mark in the Post. Ref. column indicates that no amounts on that line are posted individually. On the totals line, the amounts in the special amount columns are posted. Therefore, a check mark is not placed in the Post. Ref. column for the totals line.

POSTING THE TOTAL OF THE SALES CREDIT COLUMN

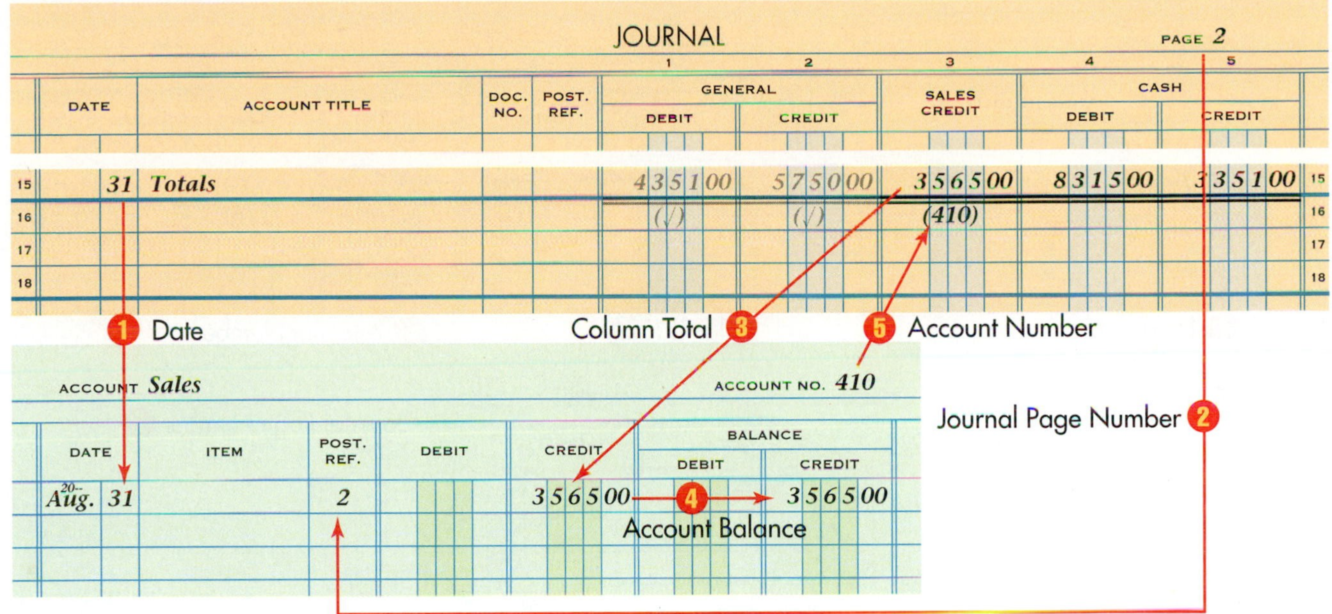

JOURNAL
PAGE 2
DATE
ACCOUNT TITLE
DOC. NO.
POST. REF.
GENERAL
DEBIT
CREDIT
SALES CREDIT
CASH
DEBIT
CREDIT
31 Totals
4 3 5 1 00
5 7 5 0 00
3 5 6 5 00
8 3 1 5 00
3 3 5 1 00
(✓)
(✓)
(410)
1 Date
Column Total 3
5 Account Number
ACCOUNT Sales
ACCOUNT NO. 410
Journal Page Number 2
DATE
ITEM
POST. REF.
DEBIT
CREDIT
BALANCE
DEBIT
CREDIT
20--
Aug. 31
2
3 5 6 5 00
4
3 5 6 5 00
Account Balance

Separate amounts in special amount columns are not posted individually. The separate amounts are part of the special amount column totals. Only the totals of special amount columns are posted.

TechKnow Consulting's journal has three special amount columns for which only totals are posted: Sales Credit, Cash Debit, and Cash Credit.

The Sales Credit column of a journal is a special amount column with the account title Sales in the heading. Each separate amount in a special amount column could be posted individually. However, all of the separate amounts are debits or credits to the same account. Therefore, an advantage of a special amount column is that only the column total needs to be posted. For example, 16 separate sales transactions are recorded in the Sales Credit column of TechKnow Consulting's August journal. Instead of making 16 separate credit postings to Sales, only the column total is posted. As a result, only one posting is needed, which saves 15 postings. The smaller number of postings means 15 fewer opportunities to make a posting error. Posting special amount column totals saves time and results in greater accuracy.

STEPS — POSTING THE TOTAL OF THE SALES CREDIT COLUMN

1. Write the date, *20--, Aug. 31*, in the Date column of the account, Sales.
2. Write the journal page number, *2*, in the Post. Ref. column of the account.
3. Write the column total, *$3,565.00*, in the Credit amount column.
4. Write the new account balance, *$3,565.00*, in the Balance Credit column.
5. Return to the journal and write the account number in parentheses, *(410)*, below the Sales Credit column total.

Previous Balance	+	Credit Column Amount	=	New Credit Balance
$0.00	+	$3,565.00	=	$3,565.00

POSTING THE TOTAL OF THE CASH DEBIT COLUMN

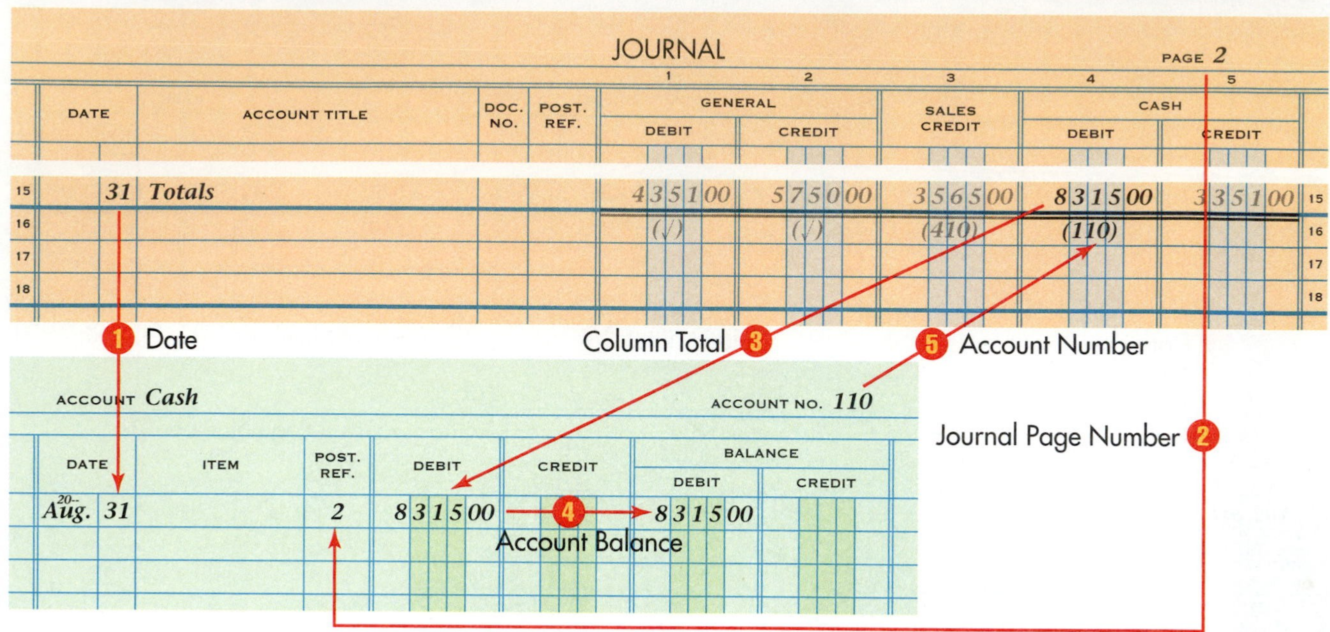

The Cash Debit column of a journal is a special amount column with the account title Cash in the heading.

The Cash Debit column is posted using the following steps.

STEPS POSTING THE TOTAL OF THE CASH DEBIT COLUMN

1. Write the date, *20--, Aug. 31*, in the Date column of the account, Cash.
2. Write the journal page number, *2*, in the Post. Ref. column of the account.
3. Write the column total, *$8,315.00*, in the Debit amount column.
4. Write the new account balance, *$8,315.00*, in the Balance Debit column.
5. Return to the journal and write the account number in parentheses, *(110)*, below the Cash Debit column total.

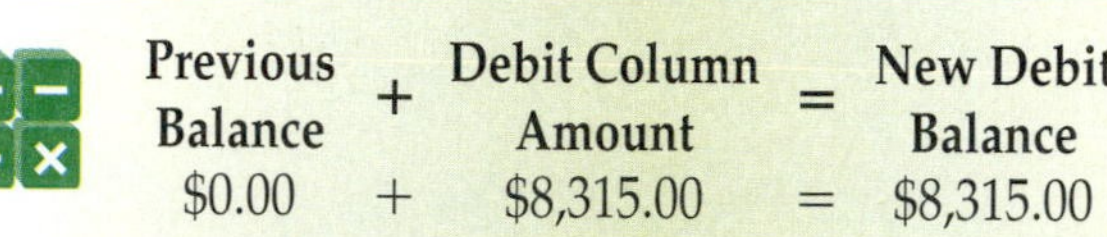

Previous Balance	+	Debit Column Amount	=	New Debit Balance
$0.00	+	$8,315.00	=	$8,315.00

REMEMBER Errors are corrected in a way that does not cause doubts about what the correct information is. If an error is recorded, cancel the error by neatly drawing a line through the incorrect item. Write the correct items immediately above the canceled item.

POSTING THE TOTAL OF THE CASH CREDIT COLUMN

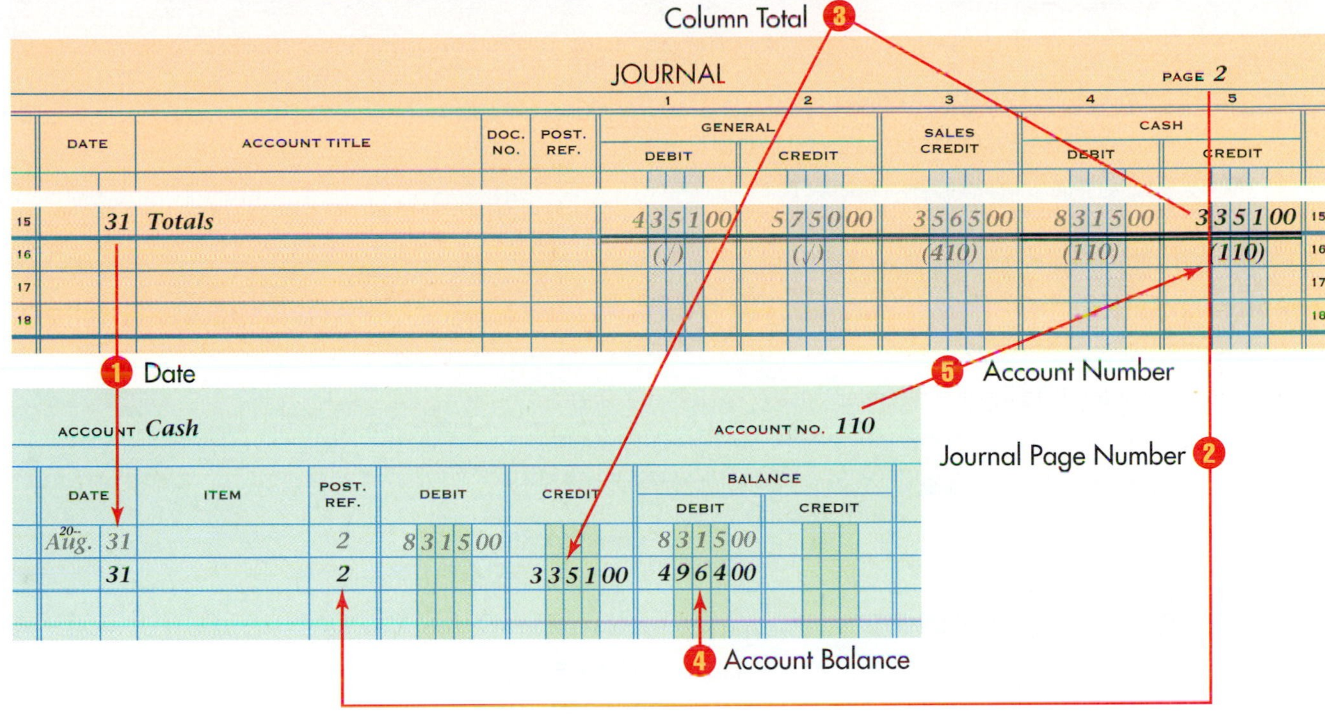

The Cash Credit column of a journal is a special amount column with the account title Cash in the heading. The Cash Credit column is posted using the following steps.

STEPS: POSTING THE TOTAL OF THE CASH CREDIT COLUMN

1. Write the date, *31*, in the Date column of the account, Cash.
2. Write the journal page number, *2*, in the Post. Ref. column of the account.
3. Write the column total, *$3,351.00*, in the credit amount column.
4. Write the new account balance, *$4,964.00*, in the Balance Debit column.
5. Return to the journal and write the account number in parentheses, *(110)*, below the Cash Credit column total.

Previous Debit Balance	−	Credit Column Amount	=	New Debit Balance
$8,315.00	−	$3,351.00	=	$4,964.00

REMEMBER Whenever the debits in an account exceed the credits, the account balance is a debit. Whenever the credits in an account exceed the debits, the account balance is a credit.

• audit your understanding

1. Which column totals of a journal are posted?
2. Under what conditions will an account balance be a debit?
3. Under what conditions will an account balance be a credit?

• work together 4-3

Posting column totals to a general ledger

Use the journal and general ledger accounts from Work Together 4-2. Your instructor will guide you through the following example.

Leonard Witkowski owns a service business that uses the following accounts.

Assets
110 Cash
120 Accounts Receivable—Danielle Braastad
130 Supplies
140 Prepaid Insurance

Liabilities
210 Accounts Payable—Joshua's Supplies

Owner's Equity
310 Leonard Witkowski, Capital
320 Leonard Witkowski, Drawing

Revenue
410 Sales

Expenses
510 Rent Expense

1. Post the journal's special amount column totals.

• on your own 4-3

Posting column totals to a general ledger

Use the journal and general ledger accounts from On Your Own 4-2. Work this problem independently.

Heather Hasley owns a service business that uses the following accounts.

Assets
110 Cash
120 Accounts Receivable—Ken Garlie
130 Supplies
140 Prepaid Insurance

Liabilities
210 Accounts Payable—Bodden Company

Owner's Equity
310 Heather Hasley, Capital
320 Heather Hasley, Drawing

Revenue
410 Sales

Expenses
510 Advertising Expense

1. Post the journal's special amount column totals.

LESSON · LESSON · LESSON · LESSON · LESSON · LESSON

4-4 Completed Accounting Forms and Making Correcting Entries

JOURNAL PAGE WITH POSTING COMPLETED

JOURNAL PAGE 2

	DATE		ACCOUNT TITLE	DOC. NO.	POST. REF.	1 GENERAL DEBIT	2 GENERAL CREDIT	3 SALES CREDIT	4 CASH DEBIT	5 CASH CREDIT	
1	20-- Aug.	20	Brought Forward		√	3543 00	5750 00	1960 00	6710 00	2543 00	1
2		21	√	T21	√			225 00	225 00		2
3		24	√	T24	√			205 00	205 00		3
4		25	√	T25	√			275 00	275 00		4
5		26	√	T26	√			290 00	290 00		5
6		27	Utilities Expense	C10	560	70 00				70 00	6
7		27	√	T27	√			205 00	205 00		7
8		28	Supplies	C11	150	200 00				200 00	8
9		28	√	T28	√			215 00	215 00		9
10		31	Miscellaneous Expense	C12	530	20 00				30 00	10
11			Advertising Expense		510	10 00					11
12		31	Kim Park, Drawing	C13	320	500 00				500 00	12
13		31	√	T31	√			190 00	190 00		13
14		31	Miscellaneous Expense	M3	530	8 00				8 00	14
15		31	Totals			4351 00	5750 00	3565 00	8315 00	3351 00	15
16						(√)	(√)	(410)	(110)	(110)	16

Page 2 of TechKnow Consulting's August journal is shown after all posting has been completed. With the exception of the Totals line, notice that the Post. Ref. Column is completely filled in with either an account number or a check mark.

GENERAL LEDGER WITH POSTING COMPLETED

ACCOUNT *Cash* ACCOUNT NO. *110*

DATE		ITEM	POST. REF.	DEBIT	CREDIT	BALANCE DEBIT	BALANCE CREDIT
20-- Aug.	31		2	8315 00		8315 00	
	31		2		3351 00	4964 00	

ACCOUNT *Petty Cash* ACCOUNT NO. *120*

DATE		ITEM	POST. REF.	DEBIT	CREDIT	BALANCE DEBIT	BALANCE CREDIT
20-- Aug.	17		1	100 00		100 00	

After all posting from the August journal is completed, TechKnow Consulting's general ledger is shown here and on the next several pages.

The use of the accounts Income Summary, Insurance Expense, and Supplies Expense is described in Chapter 6.

ACCOUNT *Accounts Receivable—Oakdale School* ACCOUNT NO. *130*

DATE		ITEM	POST. REF.	DEBIT	CREDIT	BALANCE DEBIT	BALANCE CREDIT
20-- Aug.	12		1	350 00		350 00	
	12		1		200 00	150 00	

ACCOUNT *Accounts Receivable—Campus Internet Cafe* ACCOUNT NO. *140*

DATE		ITEM	POST. REF.	DEBIT	CREDIT	BALANCE DEBIT	BALANCE CREDIT
20-- Aug.	13		1	100 00		100 00	

ACCOUNT *Supplies* ACCOUNT NO. *150*

DATE		ITEM	POST. REF.	DEBIT	CREDIT	BALANCE DEBIT	BALANCE CREDIT
20-- Aug.	3		1	275 00		275 00	
	7		1	500 00		775 00	
	20		1	50 00		825 00	
	28		2	200 00		1 025 00	

ACCOUNT *Prepaid Insurance* ACCOUNT NO. *160*

DATE		ITEM	POST. REF.	DEBIT	CREDIT	BALANCE DEBIT	BALANCE CREDIT
20-- Aug.	4		1	1 200 00		1 200 00	

ACCOUNT *Accounts Payable—Supply Depot* ACCOUNT NO. *210*

DATE		ITEM	POST. REF.	DEBIT	CREDIT	BALANCE DEBIT	BALANCE CREDIT
20-- Aug.	7		1		500 00		500 00
	11		1	300 00			200 00

ACCOUNT *Accounts Payable—Thomas Supply Co.* ACCOUNT NO. *220*

DATE		ITEM	POST. REF.	DEBIT	CREDIT	BALANCE DEBIT	BALANCE CREDIT
20-- Aug.	20		1		50 00		50 00

ACCOUNT *Kim Park, Capital* ACCOUNT NO. *310*

DATE		ITEM	POST. REF.	DEBIT	CREDIT	BALANCE DEBIT	BALANCE CREDIT
20-- Aug.	1		1		5 000 00		5 000 00

ACCOUNT *Kim Park, Drawing* ACCOUNT NO. *320*

DATE		ITEM	POST. REF.	DEBIT	CREDIT	BALANCE DEBIT	BALANCE CREDIT
20-- Aug.	12		1	125 00		125 00	
	31		2	500 00		625 00	

A General Ledger after Posting Has Been Completed (continued)

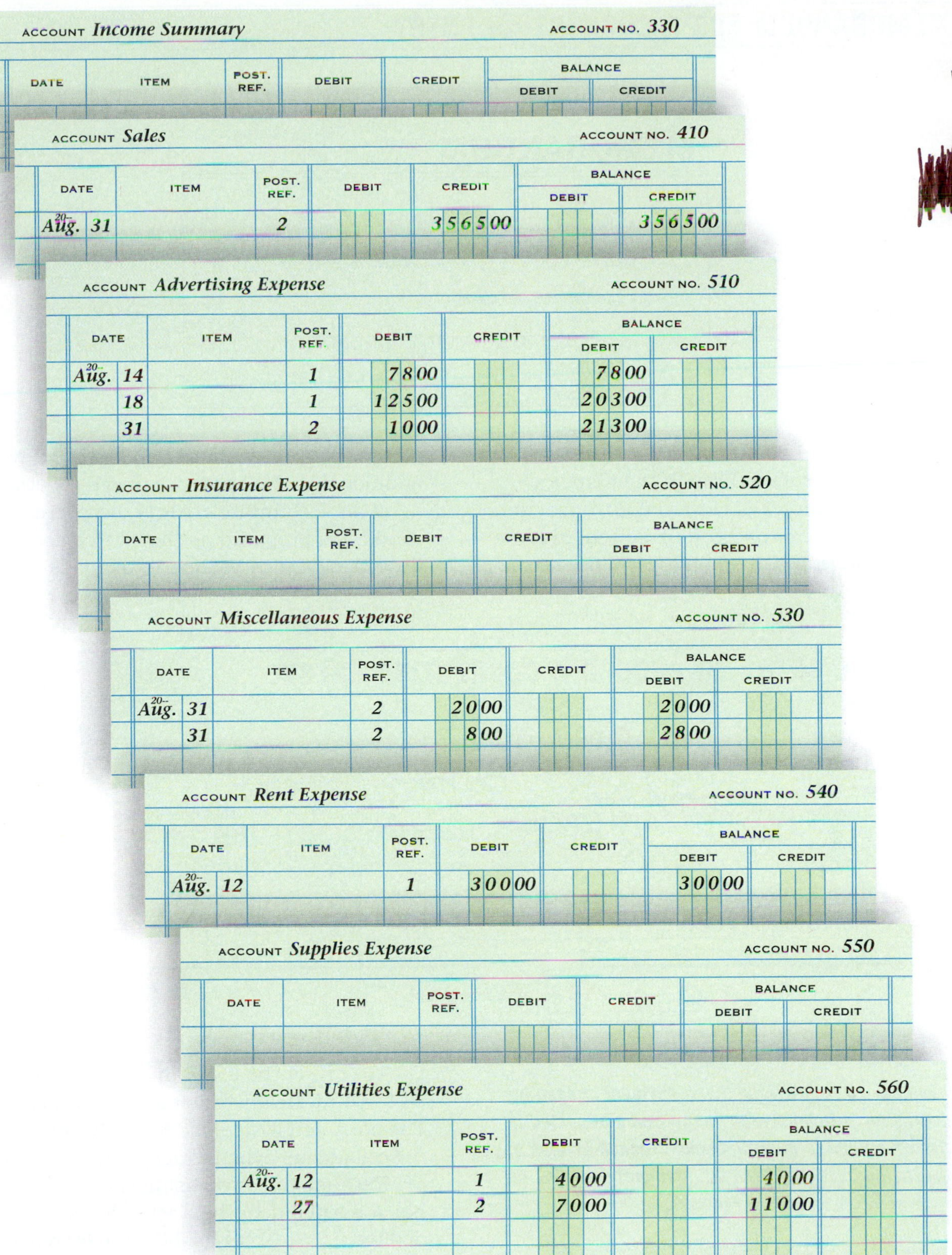

ACCOUNT *Income Summary* ACCOUNT NO. *330*

DATE		ITEM	POST. REF.	DEBIT	CREDIT	BALANCE DEBIT	BALANCE CREDIT

ACCOUNT *Sales* ACCOUNT NO. *410*

DATE		ITEM	POST. REF.	DEBIT	CREDIT	BALANCE DEBIT	BALANCE CREDIT
20-- Aug.	31		2		3,565.00		3,565.00

ACCOUNT *Advertising Expense* ACCOUNT NO. *510*

DATE		ITEM	POST. REF.	DEBIT	CREDIT	BALANCE DEBIT	BALANCE CREDIT
20-- Aug.	14		1	78.00		78.00	
	18		1	125.00		203.00	
	31		2	10.00		213.00	

ACCOUNT *Insurance Expense* ACCOUNT NO. *520*

DATE		ITEM	POST. REF.	DEBIT	CREDIT	BALANCE DEBIT	BALANCE CREDIT

ACCOUNT *Miscellaneous Expense* ACCOUNT NO. *530*

DATE		ITEM	POST. REF.	DEBIT	CREDIT	BALANCE DEBIT	BALANCE CREDIT
20-- Aug.	31		2	20.00		20.00	
	31		2	8.00		28.00	

ACCOUNT *Rent Expense* ACCOUNT NO. *540*

DATE		ITEM	POST. REF.	DEBIT	CREDIT	BALANCE DEBIT	BALANCE CREDIT
20-- Aug.	12		1	300.00		300.00	

ACCOUNT *Supplies Expense* ACCOUNT NO. *550*

DATE		ITEM	POST. REF.	DEBIT	CREDIT	BALANCE DEBIT	BALANCE CREDIT

ACCOUNT *Utilities Expense* ACCOUNT NO. *560*

DATE		ITEM	POST. REF.	DEBIT	CREDIT	BALANCE DEBIT	BALANCE CREDIT
20-- Aug.	12		1	40.00		40.00	
	27		2	70.00		110.00	

A General Ledger after Posting Has Been Completed (concluded)

MEMORANDUM FOR A CORRECTING ENTRY

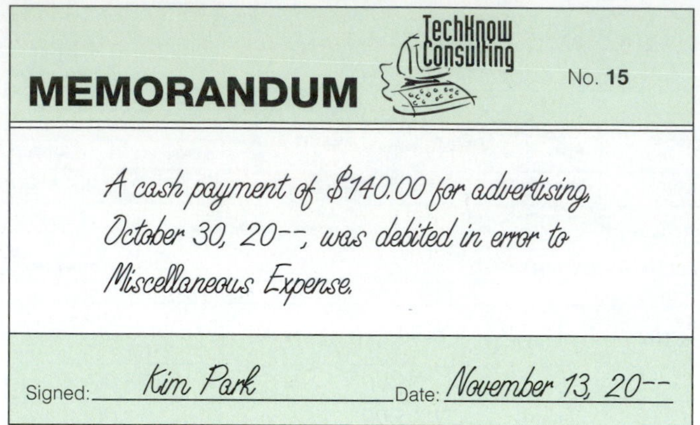
MEMORANDUM

TechKnow Consulting

No. 15

A cash payment of $140.00 for advertising, October 30, 20--, was debited in error to Miscellaneous Expense.

Signed: Kim Park Date: November 13, 20--

Errors discovered before entries are posted may be corrected by ruling through the item, as described in Chapter 3. However, a transaction may have been improperly journalized and posted to the ledger. In such a case, the incorrect journal entry should be corrected with an additional journal entry, called a **correcting entry**.

If an accounting error is discovered, a memorandum is prepared as the source document describing the correction to be made.

JOURNAL ENTRY TO RECORD A CORRECTING ENTRY

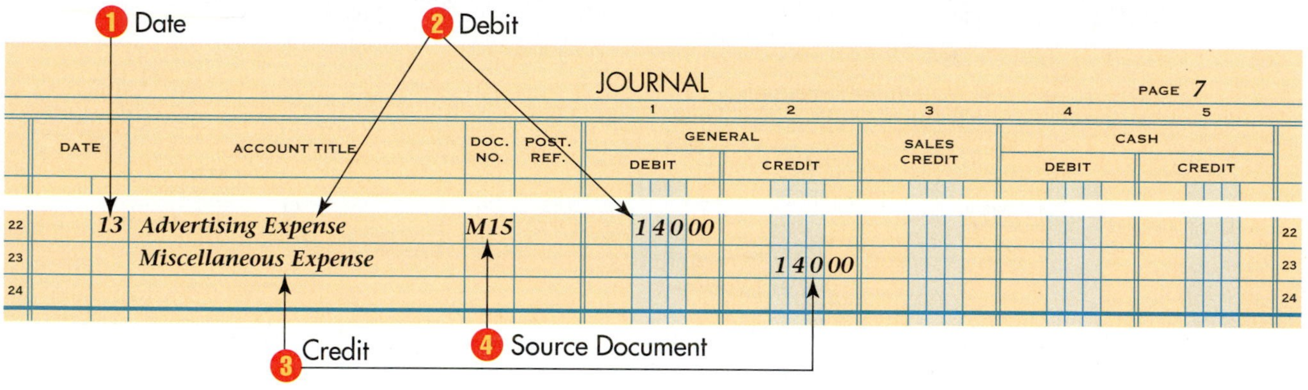

JOURNAL PAGE 7

	DATE		ACCOUNT TITLE	DOC. NO.	POST. REF.	1 GENERAL DEBIT	2 GENERAL CREDIT	3 SALES CREDIT	4 CASH DEBIT	5 CASH CREDIT	
22		13	Advertising Expense	M15		140 00					22
23			Miscellaneous Expense				140 00				23
24											24

November 13. Discovered that a payment of cash for advertising in October was journalized and posted in error as a debit to Miscellaneous Expense instead of Advertising Expense, $140.00. Memorandum No. 15.

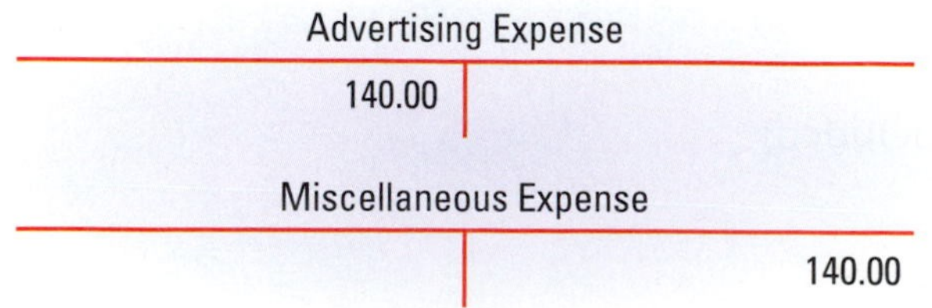

To correct the error, an entry is made to add $140.00 to the advertising expense account. The entry must also deduct $140.00 from the miscellaneous expense account.

Because the advertising expense account has a normal debit balance, Advertising Expense is debited for $140.00 to show the increase in this expense account. The miscellaneous expense account also has a normal debit balance. Therefore, Miscellaneous Expense is credited for $140.00 to show the decrease in this expense account.

term review

correcting entry

audit your understanding

1. What is a correcting entry?
2. When is a correcting entry necessary?
3. When an amount is journalized and posted as a debit to an incorrect expense account, why is the amount of the correcting entry debited to the correct expense account?
4. When an amount is journalized and posted as a debit to an incorrect expense account, why is the amount of the correcting entry credited to the incorrect expense account?

work together 4-4

Journalizing correcting entries

A journal is given in the *Working Papers.* Your instructor will guide you through the following example.

Transactions:

Nov. 1. Discovered that a transaction for supplies bought last month was journalized and posted in error as a debit to Prepaid Insurance instead of Supplies, $60.00. M15.

1. Discovered that a transaction for rent expense for last month was journalized and posted in error as a debit to Repair Expense instead of Rent Expense, $550.00. M16.

1. Journalize each correcting entry discovered during November of the current year. Use page 21 of the journal.

on your own 4-4

Journalizing correcting entries

A journal is given in the *Working Papers.* Work this problem independently.

Transactions:

June 1. Discovered that a transaction for supplies bought last month was journalized and posted in error as a debit to Prepaid Insurance instead of Supplies, $150.00. M23.

1. Discovered that a transaction for utilities expense for last month was journalized and posted in error as a debit to Miscellaneous Expense instead of Utilities Expense, $850.00. M24.

1. Journalize each correcting entry discovered during June of the current year. Use page 11 of the journal.

SUMMARY

After completing this chapter, you can

1. Define accounting terms related to posting from a journal to a general ledger.
2. Identify accounting concepts and practices related to posting from a journal to a general ledger.
3. Prepare a chart of accounts for a service business organized as a proprietorship.
4. Post separate amounts from a journal to a general ledger.
5. Post column totals from a journal to a general ledger.
6. Analyze and journalize correcting entries.

Explore Accounting

Chart of Accounts

Each company designs its chart of accounts to meet the needs of that company. TechKnow Consulting, the company described in this section of the textbook, has a relatively simple chart of accounts, with a small number of accounts. Therefore, TechKnow Consulting can use a three-digit account number for each account. A company with more accounts may need to use a four- or five-digit account number for each account. The numbering system used by the company should ensure that each account can be assigned a unique number.

When setting up a chart of accounts, a company does not have to use a straight series of numbers. If a company has several departments, it may choose to use account numbers such as 12-150. The first two digits (12) can be used to designate a specific department. The last three digits (150) identify a unique account within that department. If this company has many departments or many accounts within each department, it may have to increase the number of digits in the account, such as 123-4567.

A large corporation made up of smaller companies may have one chart of accounts for the entire corporation. If the managers of the corporation also want to be able to separate out the accounts for each company, they may choose to set up the account numbers in an xx-yyy-zzzz format. The first two digits (xx) would be a unique number for each company, the second set of numbers (yyy) refer to a department number, and the third set of numbers (zzzz) is a unique account.

Another example would be a company that manufactures goods for its customers. Such a company may want to include the job order number in each account number, so that it can easily trace the cost of each job.

As you can see, there is an infinite number of possible systems that can be followed when assigning account numbers. A company should consider future growth when first setting up a system so that it can avoid having to renumber accounts at a later date.

Group Activity: Develop a chart of accounts for an imaginary business. Write a detailed description of the company and a rationale for the account numbering system you have developed.

4-1 APPLICATION PROBLEM

AUTOMATED ACCOUNTING

Preparing a chart of accounts and opening an account

Lillian Deters owns a service business called Deters Duplicating, which uses the following accounts.

Accounts Receivable—Teegan Walters	Lillian Deters, Capital	Postage Expense	Supplies
Accounts Receivable—Austin Kirnyczuk	Lillian Deters, Drawing	Charitable Expense	Sales
Accounts Payable—Dakota Company	Prepaid Insurance	Rent Expense	Cash
Accounts Payable—Falls Supply	Advertising Expense		

Instructions:

1. Prepare a chart of accounts similar to the one described in this chapter. Arrange expense accounts in alphabetical order. Use 3-digit account numbers and number the accounts within a division by 10s.
2. Two new accounts, Delivery Expense and Telephone Expense, are to be added to the chart of accounts prepared in Instruction 1. Assign account numbers to the two new accounts.
3. Using the forms in the *Working Papers*, open the Prepaid Insurance and the Postage Expense accounts.

4-2 APPLICATION PROBLEM

Posting separate amounts to a general ledger

A completed journal and general ledger accounts are given in the *Working Papers*.

Alto Komoko owns a service business that uses the accounts given in the *Working Papers*.

Instructions:

Post the separate amounts (on each line of the journal) that need to be posted individually. Save your work to complete Application Problem 4-3.

4-3 APPLICATION PROBLEM

Posting column totals to a general ledger

Use the journal and general ledger from Application Problem 4-2.

Instructions:

Post the journal's special amount column totals.

4-4 APPLICATION PROBLEM

Journalizing correcting entries

The following errors were discovered after the incorrect entries were already journalized and posted.

Transactions:

Apr. 1. Discovered that a transaction for utilities expense was journalized and posted in error as a debit to Repairs Expense instead of Utilities Expense, $265.00. M66.

5. Discovered that a cash investment by Manuel Ricardo, owner, was journalized and posted in error as a credit to Sales instead of Manuel Ricardo, Capital, $600.00. M67.

Instructions:

Journalize each correcting entry discovered during April of the current year. Use page 7 of the journal given in the *Working Papers*.

4-5 MASTERY PROBLEM

Journalizing transactions and posting to a general ledger

Patrick O'Kalla owns a service business called O'Kalla Lawn and Garden. O'Kalla Lawn and Garden's general ledger accounts are given in the *Working Papers*.

Transactions:

Nov. 1. Received cash from owner as an investment, $5,500.00. R1.
3. Paid cash for supplies, $400.00. C1.
5. Received cash from sales, $900.00. T5.
6. Sold services on account to Merilda Domingo, $280.00. S1.
9. Paid cash for rent, $600.00. C2.
11. Paid cash for miscellaneous expense, $50.00. C3.
13. Bought supplies on account from Park Supplies, $240.00. M1.
13. Received cash from sales, $430.00. T13.
16. Paid cash for advertising, $143.00. C4.
18. Paid cash on account to Park Supplies, $140.00. C5.
20. Paid cash for electric bill, $230.00. C6.
20. Received cash on account from Merilda Domingo, $150.00. R2.
25. Paid cash for supplies, $150.00. C7.
27. Paid cash for supplies, $80.00. C8.
27. Received cash from sales, $2,100.00. T27.
30. Paid cash to owner for personal use, $500.00. C9.
30. Received cash from sales, $110.00. T30.

Instructions:

1. Open an account for Utilities Expense. Use the 3-digit numbering system described in the chapter.
2. Journalize the transactions completed during November of the current year. Use page 1 of a journal. Source documents are abbreviated as follows: check, C; memorandum, M; receipt, R; sales invoice, S; calculator tape, T.
3. Prove the journal.
4. Prove cash. The beginning cash balance on November 1 is zero. The balance on the next unused check stub is $6,897.00.
5. Rule the journal.
6. Post from the journal to the general ledger.

4-6 CHALLENGE PROBLEM

Posting using a variation of the five-column journal

Frances Fessler owns a service business called HouseCare. HouseCare uses a five-column journal that is different from the journal used in this chapter. HouseCare's March journal and general ledger accounts (before posting) are given in the *Working Papers*.

Instructions:

1. Post the separate amounts (on each line of the journal) that need to be posted individually.
2. Post the journal's special amount column totals.

applied communication

A fax machine allows a business to send or receive documents anywhere using a telephone line. Today, most documents can also be transmitted by e-mail if they are in an electronic format.

Instructions: Write a memorandum responding to the following scenario: Kim Park is at the bank, applying for a business loan. Ms. Park has just called you and asked that you fax her with the following information: TechKnow Consulting's asset, liability, owner's equity, sales, and expense accounts, and their current balances. In your memorandum, include an introductory sentence or paragraph and end with a concluding statement.

APPLIED COMMUNICATION

cases for critical thinking

Case 1

Janna Sturm does not use a journal in her business records. She records the debits and credits for each transaction directly in the general ledger accounts. Is Ms. Sturm using the correct procedure? Explain your answer.

Case 2

Trent Marvets does the accounting work for his business. When posting, he first transfers all of the information to the general ledger accounts. Then he returns to the journal and, all at one time, writes the account numbers in the Post. Ref. column of the journal. Eiko Harada also does the accounting work for her business. When posting, she writes all the account numbers in the Post. Ref. column of the journal before she transfers any information to the accounts. Is Mr. Marvets or Ms. Harada following the correct procedure? Explain your answer.

CASES FOR CRITICAL THINKING

SCANS workplace competency

Resource Competency: Organizing and Maintaining Information

Concept: Businesses collect information about customers, competitors, resources, and economic conditions, as well as information about their own organization. To be useful, however, information must be organized in such a way that information can be accessed when needed. Spreadsheet or database software is often used to organize and maintain information.

Application: Examine the accounting employment advertisements in the Sunday edition of a major metropolitan newspaper. Use software to organize the data about job responsibilities, educational and experience requirements, and personal and software skills for each position. Include at least ten different advertisements and add ten more the following week. Describe any trends you discover.

SCANS WORKPLACE COMPETENCY

using source documents

Journalizing transactions and posting to a general ledger

The journal, ledger, and source documents for July of the current year for Darcia's School of Dance are given in the *Working Papers.*

Instructions

1. The journal for Darcia's School of Dance is given in the *Working Papers.* Use page 1 of the journal to journalize the transactions for July.
2. Prove the journal.
3. Prove cash. The beginning cash balance on July 1 is zero. The balance on the next unused check stub is $6,576.00.
4. Rule the journal.
5. Post from the journal to the general ledger.

USING SOURCE DOCUMENTS • USING

analyzing Best Buy's financial statements

In order to move into smaller markets, Best Buy has intentionally planned smaller stores, with 20,000 to 30,000 square feet as compared to the standard Best Buy showroom, which is 45,000 square feet. In order to calculate the average total retail square footage per U.S. Best Buy store, divide the total retail square footage by the number of stores. You will find this data in the 11-Year Financial Highlights on Appendix page B-2.

Instructions

1. Calculate the average total retail square footage per store for U.S. Best Buy stores for 2001 through 2004.
2. Is Best Buy succeeding on the goal of smaller stores?

ANALYZING BEST BUY'S FINANCIAL

Automated Accounting

Automated General Ledger Accounting

The automated accounting system includes a chart of accounts, which is a list of account titles and numbers. The chart of accounts can be created or changed by clicking the Accts. toolbar button. Next, click on the Accounts tab to access the Chart of Accounts maintenance screen. Accounts can be added or deleted on this screen. Adding a new account would be considered opening an account, just as deleting an account would be considered removing an account.

Chart of Accounts Maintenance

Accounts can be added, deleted, or changed. The Account Maintenance screen will appear when you choose the Maintain Accounts menu item from the Data drop-down list or click on the Accts. toolbar button.

Adding a New Account

1. Enter the account number in the Account column at the end of the list; then hit the Tab key.
2. Enter the title for the new account.
3. For a departmentalized business, enter the department number.
4. Click the Add Account button.
5. Click the Close button to exit the Accounts window.

Changing an Account Title

1. Select the account that you wish to change.
2. Enter the correct account title or department number.
3. Click the Change button when the account title has been changed.

The account number cannot be changed. If an account number needs to be changed because of an incorrect account number, the account must be deleted and then added as a new account number.

Deleting an Account

1. Select the account that you wish to delete.
2. Click the Delete button. General ledger accounts cannot be deleted unless the account has a zero balance.
3. Click the OK button.

Posting Amounts to the General Ledger

In automated accounting, journal entries are automatically posted by clicking the Post button or pressing the Enter key after a transaction is entered in a journal. The debit and credit amounts are automatically transferred to the general ledger accounts.

Every entry that is made to the journal includes the date, reference, account number, and the debit or credit entry. This is the information that is transferred to the general and subsidiary ledgers, updating the accounts immediately.

AUTOMATING APPLICATION PROBLEM 4-1: Preparing a chart of accounts and opening an account

Instructions:

1. Load the *Automated Accounting 8.0* or higher software.
2. Select data file F04-1 from the appropriate directory/folder.
3. Select File from the menu bar and choose the Save As menu command. Key the path to the drive and directory that contains your data files. Save the data file with a filename of F04-1 XXX XXX (where the X's are your first and last name).
4. Access Problem Instructions through the Help menu. Read the Problem Instructions screen by clicking the Browser toolbar button.
5. Refer to Application Problem 4-1 for the data used in this problem. Create the chart of accounts.
6. Add the two new accounts in instruction 2 of the problem.
7. Display or print the chart of accounts.
8. Save your file and exit the Automated Accounting software.

AUTOMATING MASTERY PROBLEM 4-5: Journalizing transactions and posting to a general ledger

Instructions:

1. Load the *Automated Accounting 8.0* or higher software.
2. Select data file F04-5 from the appropriate directory/folder.
3. Save your file with a filename of F04-5 XXX XXX (where the X's are your first and last name).
4. Access Problem Instructions through the Help menu. Read the Problem Instructions screen by clicking the Browser toolbar button.
5. Perform the file maintenance described in Mastery Problem 4-5.
6. Key the transactions listed in Mastery Problem 4-5.
7. Display or print a journal entries report.
8. Save your file and exit the Automated Accounting software.

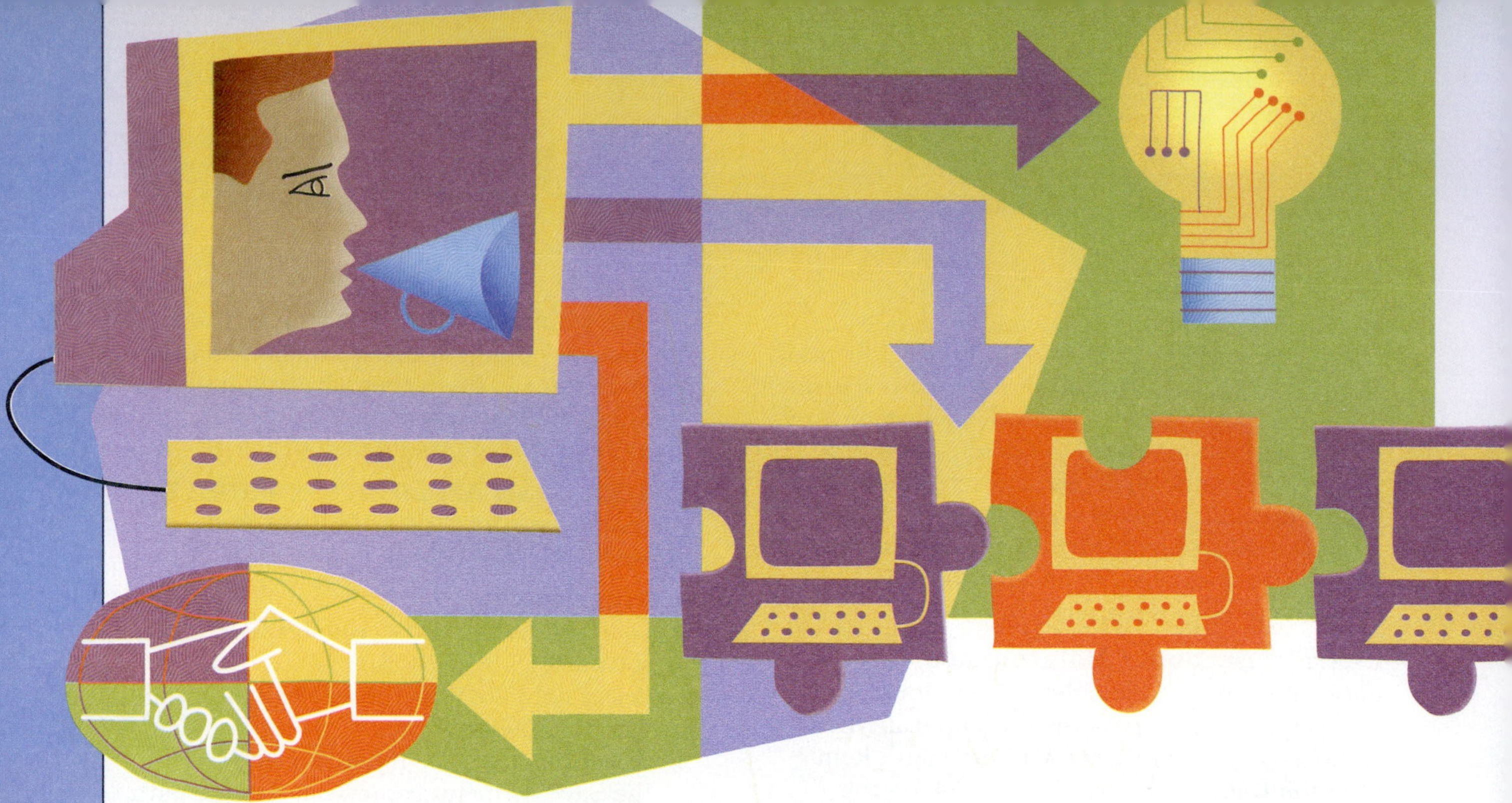

CHAPTER 5

Cash Control Systems

OBJECTIVES & TERMS

After studying Chapter 5, you will be able to:

1. Define accounting terms related to using a checking account and a petty cash fund.
2. Identify accounting concepts and practices related to using a checking account.
3. Prepare business papers related to using a checking account.
4. Reconcile a bank statement.
5. Journalize dishonored checks and electronic banking transactions.
6. Establish and replenish a petty cash fund.

- code of conduct
- checking account
- endorsement
- blank endorsement
- special endorsement
- restrictive endorsement
- postdated check
- bank statement
- dishonored check
- electronic funds transfer
- debit card
- petty cash
- petty cash slip

accounting in the real world

Books-A-Million

COURTESY OF BOOKS-A-MILLION, INC.

GRAB A BOOK AND A CAPPUCCINO—BOOKS-A-MILLION

You expect a library to have tables, chairs, and maybe even more comfortable furniture such as a couch or armchair. It's acceptable to spend an extended period of time in a library, reading the materials instead of checking them out and bringing them home.

Until a few years ago, bookstores didn't encourage you to sit around and read the material before buying it. However, each Books-A-Million superstore also features a Joe Muggs Café, which offers a delicious selection of items including coffees, teas, and desserts.

In addition to its Internet bookstore (BAMM.COM), Books-A-Million operates stores using two other concepts. Bookland is a smaller, more traditional bookstore designed primarily for mall environments. Joe Muggs Newsstands combine an expanded Joe Muggs Café with an exhaustive newsstand selection of magazines, newspapers, and best sellers.

Critical Thinking

1. At Books-A-Million, customers use cash or credit cards to make purchases. What control problems may occur when employees accept cash for a sale?
2. Can you suggest another store concept that would enable Books-A-Million to further expand its sales?

accountingxtra.swlearning.com

Source: www.bamminc.com/profile/index.html

ACCOUNTING IN THE REAL WORLD • ACCOUNTING IN THE REAL WORLD • ACCOUNTING IN THE REAL WORLD •

internet activity

INTEREST RATES

Banks offer many services, including savings accounts and loans. If you have a savings account with a bank, the bank pays you interest on the money in the account. If you take out a loan, you pay interest to the bank on the money you owe.

Go to the homepage for a bank of your choice.

Instructions

1. Find the range of interest the bank offers for its savings accounts.
2. Find the range of interest charged by the bank on an auto loan.
3. Compare the two rates. Why does the bank charge more interest on loans than it pays on savings accounts?

INTERNET RESEARCH ACTIVITY • INTERNET RESEARCH ACTIVITY • INTERNET RESEARCH ACTIVITY •

LESSON

5-1 Checking Accounts

HOW BUSINESSES USE CASH

In accounting, money is usually referred to as cash. Most businesses make major cash payments by check. However, small cash payments for items such as postage and some supplies may be made from a cash fund kept at the place of business.

Because cash transactions occur more frequently than other types of transactions, more chances occur to make recording errors affecting cash. Cash can be transferred from one person to another without any question about ownership. Also, cash may be lost as it is moved from one place to another.

As a safety measure, TechKnow Consulting keeps most of its cash in a bank. Because all cash receipts are placed in a bank, TechKnow Consulting has written evidence to support its accounting records. TechKnow Consulting can compare its record of checks written with the bank's record of checks paid. Greater control of TechKnow Consulting's cash and greater accuracy of its cash records result from these procedures.

making ethical decisions

Business Codes of Conduct

A statement that guides the ethical behavior of a company and its employees is called a **code of conduct**. Merck & Co., Inc., a leading pharmaceutical company, makes its code of conduct available to its employees, consultants, and the public. The document, titled "Our Values and Standards," begins by stating:

> *At Merck, our values and standards have always formed the basis of our success. They inspire trust and confidence on the part of the medical community, government officials, regulatory agencies, financial markets, our customers and patients—all who are essential to our success.*

The code of conduct contains sections that focus on Merck's relationship with customers, employees, shareholders, suppliers, and communities/society. Each section contains specific guidance on Merck policies. Common questions and answers are provided to expand on these policies. Throughout the document, individuals are encouraged to seek the guidance of upper-level managers, the Legal Department, and the Office of Ethics if they are unsure whether their actions comply with the code of conduct.

Instructions

Obtain access to Merck's code of conduct at www.merck.com. Assuming you are a Merck employee, may you:

1. Give a physician a gift consisting of a medical textbook?
2. Use your cellular phone to discuss new research methods with another Merck employee?
3. Accept a supplier's invitation to attend the Super Bowl?

DEPOSITING CASH

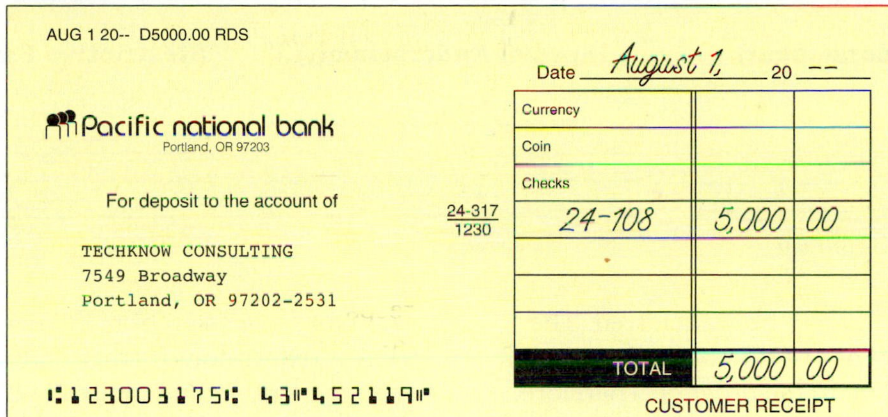

AUG 1 20-- D5000.00 RDS

Pacific national bank
Portland, OR 97203

For deposit to the account of

TECHKNOW CONSULTING
7549 Broadway
Portland, OR 97202-2531

24-317
1230

Date August 1, 20 --

Currency		
Coin		
Checks		
24-108	5,000	00
TOTAL	5,000	00

CUSTOMER RECEIPT

⑆123003175⑆ 43⑈452119⑈

A business form ordering a bank to pay cash from a bank account is known as a check. A bank account from which payments can be ordered by a depositor is called a **checking account**.

When a checking account is opened, the bank customer must provide a signature on a signature card for the bank records. If several persons are authorized to sign checks, each person's signature must be on the signature card.

A bank customer prepares a deposit slip each time cash or checks are placed in a bank account. Deposit slips may differ slightly from one bank to another. Each bank designs its own deposit slips to fit the bank's recording machines. However, all deposit slips contain the same basic information.

Checks are listed on a deposit slip according to the bank routing number on each check. For example, the routing number 24-108 identifies the bank on which the $5,000.00 check is written.

When a deposit is made, a bank gives the depositor a receipt. Many banks use a copy of the deposit slip with a printed or stamped verification as the receipt. The printed verification, *Aug 1, 20-- D5000.00 RDS*, is printed along the top left edge of the deposit slip. This printed verification means that a total of $5,000.00 was deposited on August 1. The initials *RDS* next to the amount are those of the bank employee who accepted the deposit.

DEPOSIT RECORDED ON A CHECK STUB

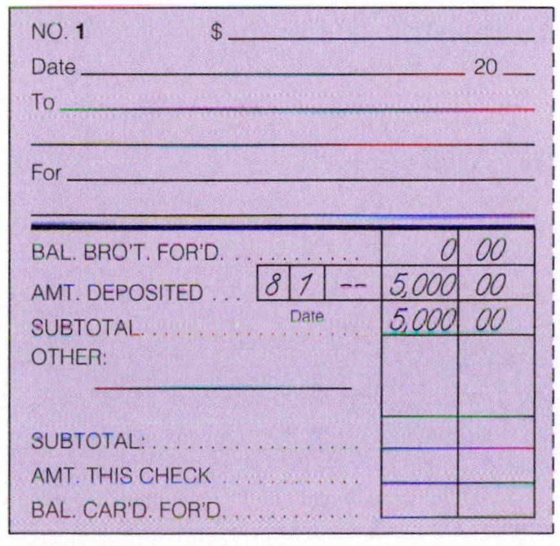

NO. 1 $
Date 20
To

For

BAL. BRO'T. FOR'D.	0	00
AMT. DEPOSITED 8 1 -- (Date)	5,000	00
SUBTOTAL	5,000	00
OTHER:		
SUBTOTAL:		
AMT. THIS CHECK		
BAL. CAR'D. FOR'D.		

After the deposit is recorded on the check stub, a checkbook subtotal is calculated. The balance brought forward on Check Stub No. 1 is zero. The previous balance, $0.00, plus the deposit, $5,000.00, equals the subtotal, $5,000.00.

Cash receipts are journalized at the time cash is received. Later, the cash receipts are deposited in the checking account. Therefore, no journal entry is needed for deposits because the cash receipts have already been journalized.

BLANK ENDORSEMENT, SPECIAL ENDORSEMENT, AND RESTRICTIVE ENDORSEMENT

[Blank Endorsement]

Endorse here
X Kim Park

DO NOT WRITE, STAMP, OR SIGN BELOW THIS LINE
Reserved for Financial Institution Use

[Special Endorsement]

Endorse here
X Pay to the order of
Eleanor Johnson
Kim Park

DO NOT WRITE, STAMP, OR SIGN BELOW THIS LINE
Reserved for Financial Institution Use

[Restrictive Endorsement]

Endorse here
X For deposit only to
the account of
TECHKNOW CONSULTING
Kim Park

DO NOT WRITE, STAMP, OR SIGN BELOW THIS LINE
Reserved for Financial Institution Use

Ownership of a check can be transferred. The name of the first owner is stated on a check following the words *Pay to the order of*. Therefore, the person to whom payment is to be made must indicate that ownership of the check is being transferred. One person transfers ownership to another person by signing on the back of a check. A signature or stamp on the back of a check transferring ownership is called an **endorsement**. Federal regulations require that an endorsement be confined to a limited amount of space that is indicated on the back of a check.

An endorsement should be signed exactly as the person's name appears on the front of the check. For example, a check made payable to K. A. Park is endorsed on the back as *K. A. Park*. Immediately below that endorsement, Ms. Park would write her official signature, *Kim Park*.

Ownership of a check might be transferred several times, resulting in several endorsements. Each endorser guarantees payment of the check. If a bank does not receive payment from the person who signed the check, each endorser is individually liable for payment.

Three types of endorsements are commonly used, each having a specific use in transferring ownership.

Blank Endorsement

An endorsement consisting only of the endorser's signature is called a **blank endorsement**. A blank endorsement indicates that the subsequent owner is whoever has the check.

If a check with a blank endorsement is lost or stolen, the check can be cashed by anyone who has possession of it. Ownership may be transferred without further endorsement. A blank endorsement should be used only when a person is at the bank ready to cash or deposit a check.

Special Endorsement

An endorsement indicating a new owner of a check is called a **special endorsement**. Special endorsements are sometimes known as *endorsements in full*.

Special endorsements include the words *Pay to the order of* and the name of the new check owner. Only the person or business named in a special endorsement can cash, deposit, or further transfer ownership of the check.

Restrictive Endorsement

An endorsement restricting further transfer of a check's ownership is called a **restrictive endorsement**. A restrictive endorsement limits use of the check to whatever purpose is stated in the endorsement.

Many businesses have a stamp prepared with a restrictive endorsement. When a check is received, it is immediately stamped with the restrictive endorsement. This prevents unauthorized persons from cashing the check if it is lost or stolen.

FYI FOR YOUR INFORMATION

The Federal Deposit Insurance Corporation (FDIC) protects depositors from banks that fail. Bank deposits are generally covered up to $100,000 per depositor.

COMPLETED CHECK STUB AND CHECK

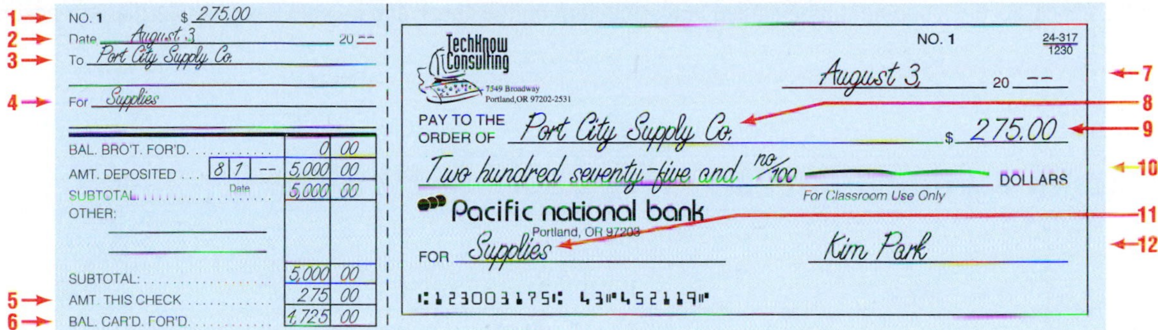

1 NO. 1 $ 275.00
2 Date August 3 20 --
3 To Port City Supply Co.
4 For Supplies

BAL. BRO'T. FOR'D.	0	00
AMT. DEPOSITED 8/1 --	5,000	00
SUBTOTAL	5,000	00
OTHER:		
SUBTOTAL	5,000	00
5 AMT. THIS CHECK	275	00
6 BAL. CAR'D. FOR'D.	4,725	00

TechKnow Consulting
7549 Broadway
Portland, OR 97202-2531
NO. 1
24-317
1230
August 3 20 -- 7
PAY TO THE ORDER OF Port City Supply Co. 8 $ 275.00 9
Two hundred seventy-five and no/100 DOLLARS 10
For Classroom Use Only
Pacific national bank 11
Portland, OR 97208
FOR Supplies Kim Park 12
⑆123003175⑆ 43⑈452119⑈

TechKnow Consulting uses printed checks with check stubs attached. Consecutive numbers are preprinted on TechKnow Consulting's checks. Consecutive numbers on checks provide an easy way of identifying each check. Also, the numbers help keep track of all checks to assure that none are lost or misplaced.

A check stub is a business's record of each check written for a cash payment transaction. [*CONCEPT: Objective Evidence*] To avoid forgetting to prepare a check stub, the check stub is prepared before the check is written.

After the check stub is completed, the check is written.

STEPS

PREPARING CHECK STUBS

1. Write the amount of the check, *$275.00*, in the space after the dollar sign at the top of the stub.
2. Write the date of the check, *August 3, 20--*, on the Date line at the top of the stub.
3. Write to whom the check is to be paid, *Port City Supply Co.*, on the To line at the top of the stub.
4. Record the purpose of the check, *Supplies*, on the For line.
5. Write the amount of the check, *$275.00*, in the amount column at the bottom of the stub on the line with the words "Amt. This Check."
6. Calculate the new checking account balance, *$4,725.00*, and record the new balance in the amount column on the last line of the stub. The new balance is calculated as shown.

Subtotal	−	Amount of This Check	=	New Balance
$5,000.00	−	$275.00	=	$4,725.00

PREPARING CHECKS

7. Write the date, *August 3, 20--*, in the space provided. The date should be the month, day, and year on which the check is issued. A check with a future date on it is called a **postdated check**. Most banks will not accept postdated checks because money cannot be withdrawn from a depositor's account until the date on the check.
8. Write to whom the check is to be paid, *Port City Supply Co.*, following the words "Pay to the order of." If the person to whom a check is to be paid is a business, use the business's name rather than the owner's name. [*CONCEPT: Business Entity*] If the person to whom the check is to be paid is an individual, use that person's name.
9. Write the amount in figures, *$275.00*, following the dollar sign. Write the figures close to the printed dollar sign. This practice prevents anyone from writing another digit in front of the amount to change the amount of the check.
10. Write the amount in words, *Two hundred seventy-five and no/100*, on the line with the word "Dollars." This written amount verifies the amount written in figures after the dollar sign. Begin the words at the extreme left. Draw a line through the unused space up to the word "Dollars." This line prevents anyone from writing in additional words to change the amount. If the amounts in words and in figures are not the same, a bank may pay only the amount in words. Often, when the amounts do not agree, a bank will refuse to pay the check. *(continued on next page)*

11. Write the purpose of the check, *Supplies*, on the line labeled "For." (On some checks this space is labeled "Memo.") Some checks do not have a line for writing the purpose of the check.
12. Sign the check. A check should not be signed until each item on the check and its stub has been verified for accuracy.

RECORDING A VOIDED CHECK

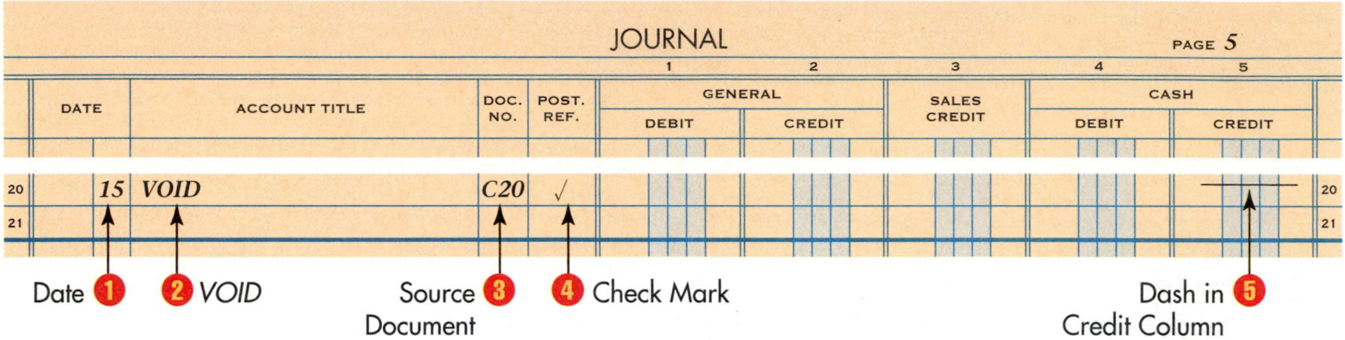

JOURNAL — PAGE 5

	DATE	ACCOUNT TITLE	DOC. NO.	POST. REF.	GENERAL DEBIT (1)	GENERAL CREDIT (2)	SALES CREDIT (3)	CASH DEBIT (4)	CASH CREDIT (5)	
20	15	VOID	C20	√					—	20
21										21

Banks usually refuse to accept altered checks. If any kind of error is made in preparing a check, a new check should be prepared. Because checks are prenumbered, all checks not used should be retained for the records. This practice helps account for all checks and assures that no checks have been lost or stolen.

A check that contains errors must be marked so that others will know that it is not to be used. The word *VOID* is written in large letters across both the check and its stub.

When TechKnow Consulting records a check in its journal, the check number is placed in the journal's Doc. No. column. If a check number is missing from the Doc. No. column, there is a question whether all checks have been journalized. To assure that all check numbers are listed in the journal, TechKnow Consulting records voided checks in the journal.

STEPS — RECORDING A VOIDED CHECK IN THE JOURNAL

1. Record the date, *15*, in the Date column.
2. Write the word *VOID* in the Account Title column.
3. Write the check number, *C20*, in the Doc. No. column.
4. Place a check mark in the Post. Ref. column.
5. Place a dash in the Cash Credit column.

©GETTY IMAGES/PHOTODISC

REMEMBER Always complete the check stub before writing the check. Otherwise you may forget to record the amount of the check on the check stub.

terms review

code of conduct
checking account
endorsement
blank endorsement
special endorsement
restrictive endorsement
postdated check

audit your understanding

1. List the three types of endorsements.
2. List the steps for preparing a check stub.
3. List the steps for preparing a check.

work together 5-1

Endorsing and writing checks

Write the answers to the following problems in the *Working Papers*. Your instructor will guide you through the following examples. You are authorized to sign checks for Balsam Lake Accounting.

1. For each of these situations, prepare the appropriate endorsement.
   a. Write a blank endorsement.
   b. Write a special endorsement to transfer a check to Kelsey Sather.
   c. Write a restrictive endorsement to deposit a check in the account of Balsam Lake Accounting.
2. Record the balance brought forward on Check Stub No. 78, $1,805.75.
3. Record a deposit of $489.00 made on October 30 of the current year on Check Stub No. 78.
4. Prepare check stubs and write the following checks. Use October 30 of the current year as the date.
   a. Check No. 78 to Corner Garage for repairs, $162.00.
   b. Check No. 79 to St. Croix Supply for supplies, $92.00.

on your own 5-1

Endorsing and writing checks

Write the answers to the following problems in the *Working Papers*. Work these problems independently. You are authorized to sign checks for Centuria Hair Care.

1. For each of these situations, prepare the appropriate endorsement.
   a. Write a special endorsement to transfer a check to Kenneth Burleson.
   b. Write a restrictive endorsement to deposit a check in the account of Centuria Hair Care.
2. Record the balance brought forward on Check Stub No. 345, $2,106.53.
3. Record a deposit of $456.25 made on May 31 of the current year on Check Stub No. 345.
4. Prepare check stubs and write the following checks. Use May 31 of the current year as the date.
   a. Check No. 345 to Uniforms Plus for uniform rental, $355.00.
   b. Check No. 346 to HairWorld for supplies, $412.00.

LESSON • LESSON • LESSON • LESSON • LESSON • LESSON

5-2 Bank Reconciliation

BANK STATEMENT

Pacific national bank
Portland, OR 97203

STATEMENT OF ACCOUNT FOR
TECHKNOW CONSULTING
7549 Broadway
Portland, OR 97202-2531

ACCOUNT NUMBER: 43-452-119

STATEMENT DATE: August 30, 20--

BALANCE FROM PREVIOUS STATEMENT	NO. OF CHECKS	AMOUNT OF CHECKS	NO. OF DEPOSITS	AMOUNT OF DEPOSITS	SERVICE CHARGES	STATEMENT BALANCE
0.00	11	2,821.00	14	8,125.00	8.00	5,304.00

DATE	CHECK	AMOUNT	CHECK	AMOUNT	DEPOSIT	BALANCE
08/01/--						0.00
08/01/--					5,000.00	5,000.00
08/04/--	1	275.00				4,725.00
08/07/--	2	1,200.00				3,525.00
08/12/--					495.00	4,020.00
08/13/--	4	300.00	6	125.00		3,595.00
08/14/--	3	300.00				3,295.00
08/15/--					250.00	3,545.00
08/16/--					195.00	3,740.00
08/17/--	5	40.00			175.00	3,875.00
08/18/--	7	78.00			205.00	4,002.00
08/19/--	8	100.00			180.00	4,082.00
08/20/--	9	125.00			210.00	4,167.00
08/21/--					225.00	4,392.00
08/24/--					205.00	4,597.00
08/25/--					275.00	4,872.00
08/26/--					290.00	5,162.00
08/27/--					205.00	5,367.00
08/28/--					215.00	5,582.00
08/29/--	10	70.00				5,512.00
08/30/--	11	200.00				5,312.00
	SC	8.00				5,304.00

PLEASE EXAMINE AT ONCE - IF NO ERRORS ARE REPORTED WITHIN 10 DAYS THE ACCOUNT WILL BE CONSIDERED CORRECT. REFER ANY DISCREPANCY TO OUR ACCOUNTING DEPARTMENT IMMEDIATELY.

A report of deposits, withdrawals, and bank balances sent to a depositor by a bank is called a **bank statement**.

When a bank receives checks, the amount of each check is deducted from the depositor's account. The bank stamps the checks to indicate that the checks are canceled and are not to be transferred further. Canceled checks may be returned to a depositor with a bank statement or may be kept on record by the bank. Account service charges are also listed on a bank statement.

Although banks seldom make mistakes, occasionally a check or deposit might be recorded in a wrong account. If errors are discovered, the bank should be notified at once. However, a bank's records and a depositor's records may differ for several reasons:

1. A service charge may not have been recorded in the depositor's business records.
2. Outstanding deposits may be recorded in the depositor's records but not on a bank statement.
3. Outstanding checks may be recorded in the depositor's records but not on a bank statement.
4. A depositor may have made math or recording errors.

BANK STATEMENT RECONCILIATION

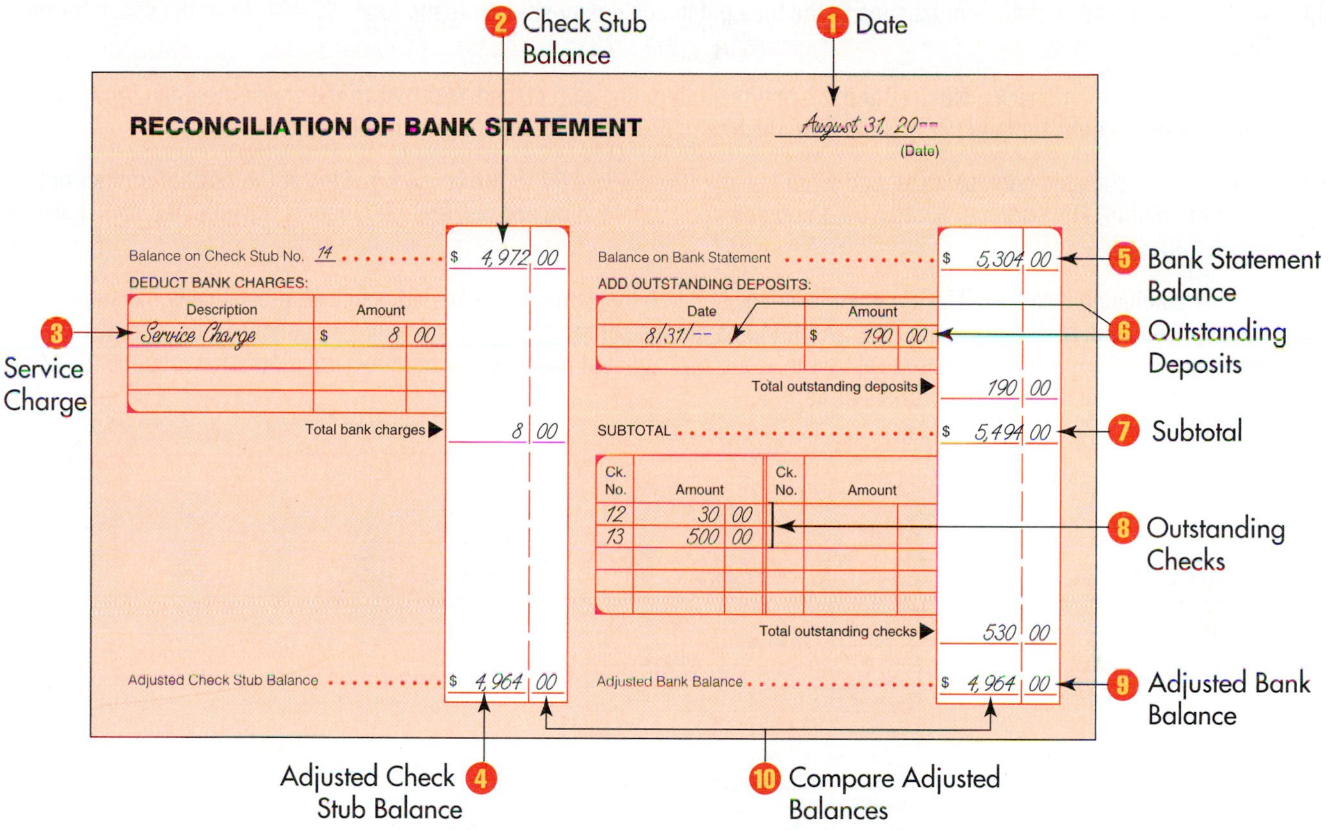

A bank statement is reconciled by verifying that information on a bank statement and a checkbook are in agreement. Reconciling immediately is an important aspect of cash control.

TechKnow Consulting's canceled checks are kept on record at the bank. The bank statement is used to determine the canceled checks. For each canceled check listed on the bank statement, a check mark is placed on the corresponding check stub. A check stub with no check mark indicates an outstanding check. Outstanding checks are those checks issued by a depositor but not yet reported on a bank statement. Outstanding deposits are those deposits made at a bank but not yet shown on a bank statement.

TechKnow Consulting receives a bank statement dated August 30 on August 31. TechKnow Consulting uses a reconciliation form printed on the back of the bank statement.

STEPS
RECONCILING A BANK STATEMENT

1. Write the date on which the reconciliation is prepared, *August 31, 20--*.
2. In the left amount column, list the balance brought forward on Check Stub No. 14, the next unused check stub, *$4,972.00*.
3. In the space for bank charges, list any charges. The only such charge for TechKnow Consulting is the bank service charge, *$8.00*. The bank service charge is labeled "SC" on the bank statement.
4. Write the adjusted check stub balance, *$4,964.00*, in the space provided at the bottom of the left amount column. The balance on the check stub, $4,972.00, minus the bank's service charge, $8.00, equals the adjusted check stub balance, $4,964.00.
5. Write the ending balance shown on the bank statement, *$5,304.00*, in the right amount column. *(continued on next page)*

6 Write the date, *8/31/--*, and the amount, *$190.00*, of any outstanding deposits in the space provided. Add the outstanding deposits. Write the total outstanding deposits, *$190.00*, in the right amount column.

7 Add the ending bank statement balance to the total outstanding deposits. Write the total, *$5,494.00*, in the space for the Subtotal.

8 List the outstanding checks, Nos. *12* and *13*, and their amounts, *$30.00* and *$500.00*, in the space provided. Add the amounts of the outstanding checks, and write the total, *$530.00*, in the right amount column.

9 Calculate the adjusted bank balance, and write the amount, *$4,964.00*, in the space provided at the bottom of the right amount column. The subtotal, $5,494.00, minus the total outstanding checks, $530.00, equals the adjusted bank balance, $4,964.00.

10 Compare adjusted balances. The adjusted balances must be the same. The adjusted check stub balance is the same as the adjusted bank balance. Because the two amounts are the same, the bank statement is reconciled. The completed reconciliation form is filed for future reference. If the two adjusted balances are not the same, the error must be found and corrected before any more work is done.

RECORDING A BANK SERVICE CHARGE ON A CHECK STUB

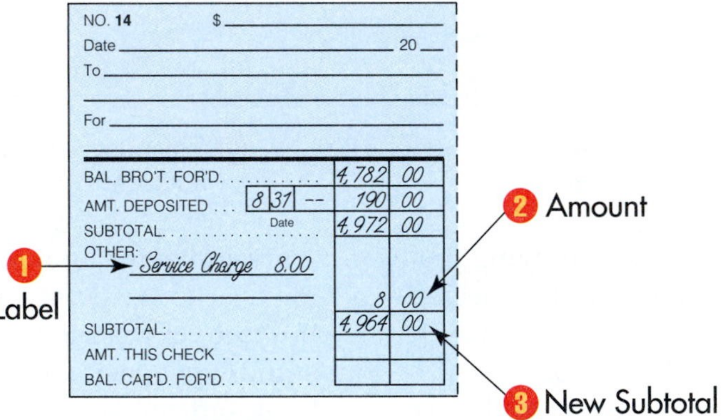

The bank deducts the service charge from TechKnow Consulting's checking account each month. Although TechKnow Consulting did not write a check for the bank service charge, this cash payment must be recorded in TechKnow Consulting's accounting records as a cash payment. TechKnow Consulting makes a record of a bank service charge on a check stub.

STEPS • STEPS • STEPS • STEPS • STEPS • STEPS • STEPS • STEPS • STEPS • STEPS •

RECORDING A BANK SERVICE CHARGE ON A CHECK STUB

1 Write *Service Charge $8.00* on the check stub under the heading "Other."

2 Write the amount of the service charge, *$8.00*, in the amount column.

3 Calculate and record the new subtotal, *$4,964.00*, on the Subtotal line. A new Balance Carried Forward is not calculated until after Check No. 14 is written.

JOURNALIZING A BANK SERVICE CHARGE

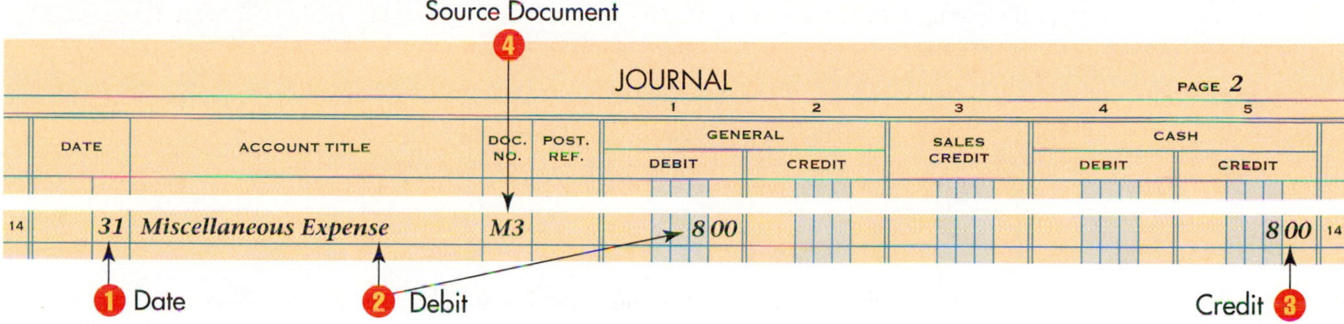

Source Document
JOURNAL
PAGE 2
DATE
ACCOUNT TITLE
DOC. NO.
POST. REF.
GENERAL
DEBIT
CREDIT
SALES CREDIT
CASH
DEBIT
CREDIT
14
31
Miscellaneous Expense
M3
8 00
8 00
14
Date
Debit
Credit

Because the bank service charge is a cash payment for which no check is written, TechKnow Consulting prepares a memorandum as the source document. TechKnow Consulting's bank service charges are relatively small and occur only once a month. Therefore, a separate ledger account for the expense is not used. Instead, TechKnow Consulting records the bank service charge as a miscellaneous expense.

August 31. Received bank statement showing August bank service charge, $8.00. Memorandum No. 3.

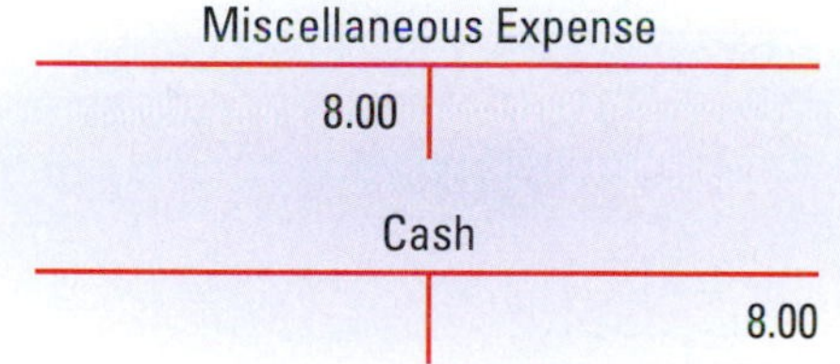

A memorandum is the source document for a bank service charge transaction. [*CONCEPT: Objective Evidence*] The analysis of this transaction is shown in the T accounts.

The expense account, Miscellaneous Expense, is debited for $8.00 to show the decrease in owner's equity. The asset account, Cash, is credited for $8.00 to show the decrease in assets.

STEPS: JOURNALIZING A BANK SERVICE CHARGE

1. **Date.** Write the date, *31*, in the Date column.
2. **Debit.** Write the title of the account to be debited, *Miscellaneous Expense*, in the Account Title column. Record the amount debited, $8.00, in the General Debit column.
3. **Credit.** Record the amount credited, *$8.00*, in the Cash Credit column.
4. **Source document.** Write the source document number, *M3*, in the Doc. No. column.

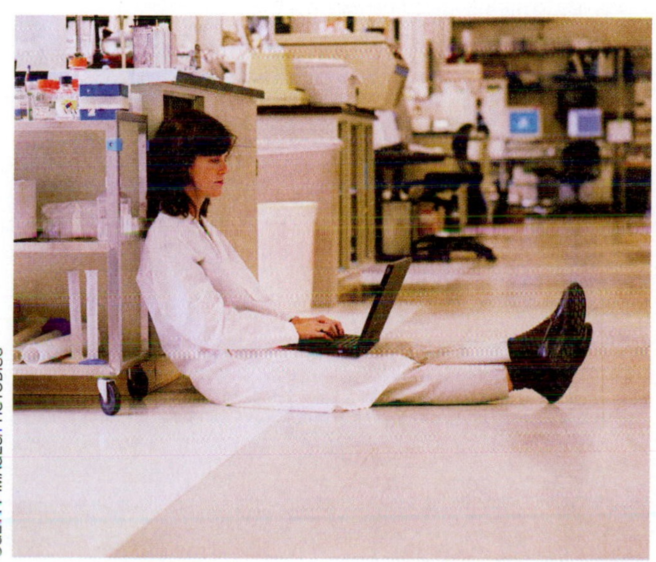

©GETTY IMAGES/PHOTODISC

Three factors generally motivate people to start a new business: the desire to control their own destinies, the desire to work more closely with customers, and the desire to achieve substantial profits.

term review

bank statement

audit your understanding

1. List four reasons why a depositor's records and a bank's records may differ.
2. If a check mark is placed on the check stub of each canceled check, what does a check stub with no check mark indicate?

work together 5-2

Reconciling a bank statement and recording a bank service charge

Forms are given in the *Working Papers*. Your instructor will guide you through the following examples.

On July 29 of the current year, DeepClean received a bank statement dated July 28. The following information is obtained from the bank statement and from the records of the business.

Bank statement balance	$1,528.00	Outstanding checks:	
Bank service charge	2.00	No. 103	$ 70.00
Outstanding deposit, July 28	150.00	No. 105	35.00
		Checkbook balance on Check Stub No. 106	1,575.00

1. Prepare a bank statement reconciliation. Use July 29 of the current year as the date.
2. Record the service charge on check stub No. 106.
3. Record the service charge on journal page 14. Use Memorandum No. 44 as the source document.

on your own 5-2

Reconciling a bank statement and recording a bank service charge

Forms are given in the *Working Papers*. Work these problems independently.

On April 30 of the current year, Able Service Co. received a bank statement dated April 29. The following information is obtained from the bank statement and from the records of the business.

Bank statement balance	$3,184.00	Outstanding checks:	
Bank service charge	15.00	No. 115	$ 70.00
Outstanding deposits:		No. 117	313.00
April 29	360.00	No. 118	80.00
April 30	510.00		
		Checkbook balance on Check Stub No. 119	3,606.00

1. Prepare a bank statement reconciliation. Use April 30 of the current year as the date.
2. Record the service charge on check stub No. 119.
3. Record the service charge on journal page 8. Use Memorandum No. M84 as the source document.

5-3 Dishonored Checks and Electronic Banking

RECORDING A DISHONORED CHECK ON A CHECK STUB

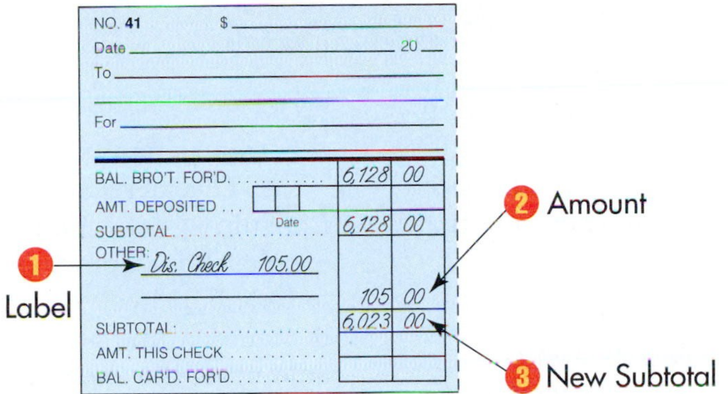

A check that a bank refuses to pay is called a **dishonored check**. Banks dishonor a check when the account of the person who wrote the check has insufficient funds to pay the check. Banks may also dishonor a check for other reasons: (1) The check appears to be altered. (2) The signature of the person who signed the check does not match the one on the signature card at the bank. (3) The amounts written in figures and in words do not agree. (4) The check is postdated. (5) The person who wrote the check has stopped payment on the check.

Issuing a check on an account with insufficient funds is illegal. Altering or forging a check is also illegal. A dishonored check may affect the credit rating of the person or business that issued the check.

Sometimes money for a dishonored check can be collected directly from the person or business that wrote the check. Often, however, the value of a dishonored check cannot be recovered and becomes an expense to the business.

Most banks charge a fee for handling dishonored checks that have been previously accepted for deposit. This fee is an expense of the business receiving a dishonored check. TechKnow Consulting's bank charges a $35.00 fee for handling dishonored checks. TechKnow Consulting attempts to collect the $35.00 fee in addition to the amount of the dishonored check from the person or business that wrote the check.

When TechKnow Consulting receives a check, it records the check as a debit to Cash and deposits the check in the bank. When a check is dishonored, the bank deducts the amount of the check plus the fee, $35.00, from TechKnow Consulting's checking account. Therefore, TechKnow Consulting records a dishonored check as a cash payment transaction.

STEPS: RECORDING A DISHONORED CHECK ON A CHECK STUB

1. Write *Dishonored check $105.00* on the line under the heading "Other." The amount is the amount of the dishonored check, $70.00, plus the service fee of $35.00.
2. Write the total of the dishonored check, *$105.00*, in the amount column.
3. Calculate and record the new subtotal, *$6,023.00*, on the Subtotal line. A new Balance Carried Forward is not calculated until after Check No. 41 is written.

JOURNALIZING A DISHONORED CHECK

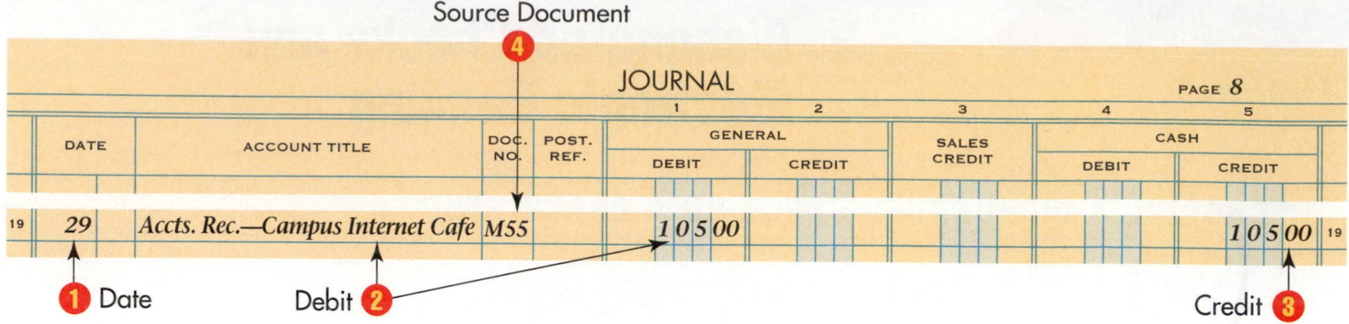

Source Document
JOURNAL
PAGE 8
DATE
ACCOUNT TITLE
DOC. NO.
POST. REF.
GENERAL
DEBIT
CREDIT
SALES CREDIT
CASH
DEBIT
CREDIT
29
Accts. Rec.—Campus Internet Cafe
M55
105 00
105 00
Date
Debit
Credit

During August, TechKnow Consulting received no checks that were subsequently dishonored. However, in November TechKnow Consulting did receive a check from Campus Internet Cafe that was eventually dishonored.

November 29. Received notice from the bank of a dishonored check from Campus Internet Cafe, $70.00, plus $35.00 fee; total, $105.00. Memorandum No. 55.

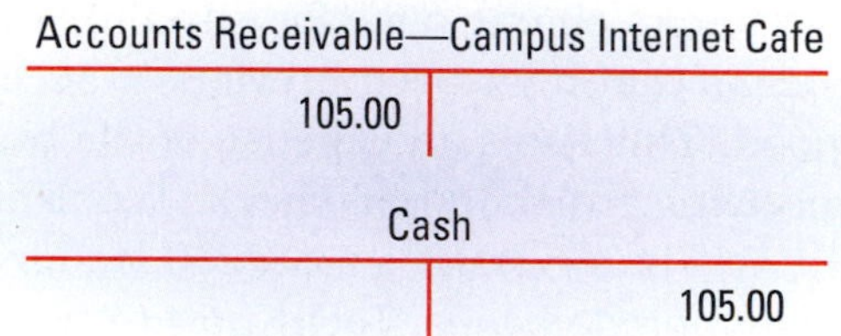

TechKnow Consulting receives a notice of the dishonored check and the fee from the bank. TechKnow attaches the notice to a memorandum, which is used as the source document. [*CONCEPT: Objective Evidence*] The analysis of this transaction is shown in the T accounts.

All checks received are deposited in TechKnow Consulting's checking account. The entry for each cash receipts transaction includes a debit to Cash. If a check is subsequently returned as dishonored, the previous cash debit for the amount of the check must be offset by a cash credit. The asset account, Cash, is credited for $105.00 to show the decrease in assets.

When TechKnow Consulting originally received the check from Campus Internet Cafe, Accounts Receivable—Campus Internet Cafe was credited to reduce the balance of the account. When TechKnow Consulting finds out that the check was not accepted by the bank, the account, Accounts Receivable—Campus Internet Cafe, must be increased to show that this amount, plus the bank charge, is still owed to TechKnow Consulting. The asset account, Accounts Receivable—Campus Internet Cafe, is debited for $105.00 to show the increase in assets.

STEPS: JOURNALIZING A DISHONORED CHECK

1. **Date.** Write the date, *29*, in the Date column.
2. **Debit.** Write the title of the account to be debited, *Accounts Receivable—Campus Internet Cafe,* in the Account Title column. Record the amount debited, $105.00, in the General Debit column.
3. **Credit.** Write the amount credited, *$105.00*, in the Cash Credit column.
4. **Source document.** Write the source document number, *M55*, in the Doc. No. column.

REMEMBER Checking accounts and records should be maintained in such a way that all checks will be honored when presented to the bank.

JOURNALIZING AN ELECTRONIC FUNDS TRANSFER

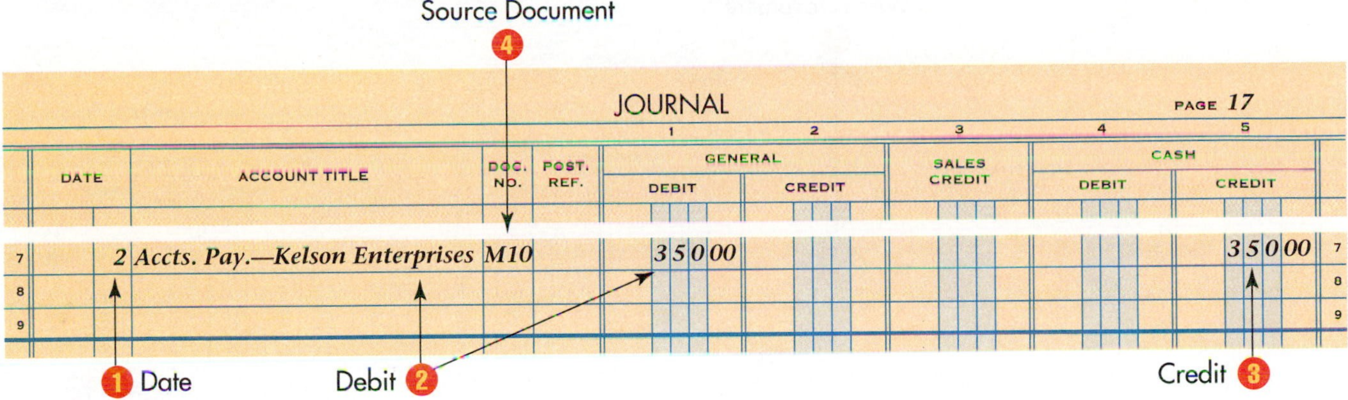

A computerized cash payments system that transfers funds without the use of checks, currency, or other paper documents is called **electronic funds transfer.** Many businesses use electronic funds transfer (EFT) to pay vendors. To use EFT, a business makes arrangements with its bank to process EFT transactions. Arrangements are also made with vendors to accept EFT payments on account. Then a transfer of funds from the business's account to the vendor's account can be completed via the Internet or a telephone call.

To control cash payments through EFT, the person responsible for requesting transfers should be given a password. The bank should not accept EFT requests from any person unable to provide an established password.

Superior Cleaning Service uses electronic funds transfer to make payments on account to vendors. The journal entry for making payments on account through EFT is the same as when a check is written. The only change is the source document used for the transaction. Superior Cleaning Service uses a memorandum as the source document for an EFT. A note is written on the memorandum to describe the transaction.

September 2. Paid cash on account to Kelson Enterprises, $350.00, using EFT. Memorandum No. 10.

Accounts Payable—Kelson Enterprises	
350.00	

Cash	
	350.00

The source document for this transaction is Memorandum No. 10. [*CONCEPT: Objective Evidence*] The analysis of this transaction is shown in the T accounts.

The liability account, Accounts Payable—Kelson Enterprises, is decreased by a debit, $350.00. The asset account, Cash, is decreased by a credit, $350.00.

A cash payment made by EFT is recorded on the check stub as "Other." This procedure keeps the checkbook in balance during the time lag from when the EFT is made until receipt of the bank statement. The EFT payments are verified as part of the regular bank statement reconciliation process. EFT payments are identified in the Check column of the bank statement by the notation "EFT," rather than by a check number.

STEPS: JOURNALIZING AN ELECTRONIC FUNDS TRANSFER

1. **Date.** Write the date, *2,* in the Date column.
2. **Debit.** Write the title of the account to be debited, *Accounts Payable—Kelson Enterprises,* in the Account Title column. Record the amount debited, *$350.00,* in the General Debit column.
3. **Credit.** Record the amount credited, *$350.00,* in the Cash Credit column.
4. **Source document.** Write the source document number, *M10,* in the Doc. No. column.

JOURNALIZING A DEBIT CARD TRANSACTION

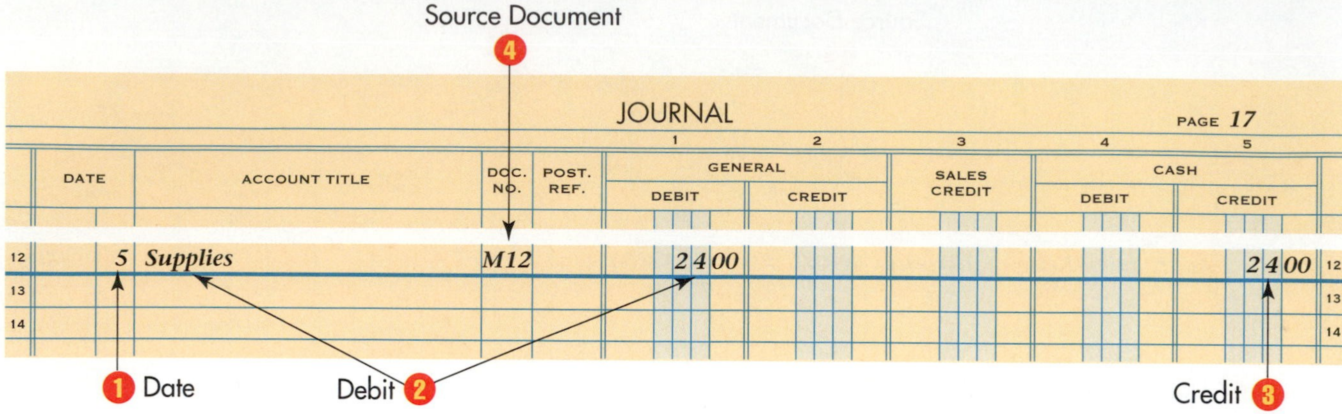

A bank card that automatically deducts the amount of a purchase from the checking account of the cardholder is called a **debit card**. There is one major difference between a debit card and a credit card. When a purchase is made with a debit card, the amount of the purchase is automatically deducted from the checking account of the cardholder. A debit card eliminates the need to write a check for the purchase. However, the effect is the same. The checking account balance is reduced by the amount of the purchase. A debit card also eliminates the need to carry a checkbook.

When using a debit card, it is important to remember to record all purchases to avoid errors in the checking account.

Superior Cleaning Service uses a debit card to make some purchases. Recording a cash payment made by a debit card is similar to recording a cash payment made by electronic funds transfer.

Superior Cleaning Service uses a memorandum as the source document for a debit card purchase. A note is written on the memorandum to describe the transaction.

September 5. Purchased supplies, $24.00, using debit card. Memorandum No. 12.

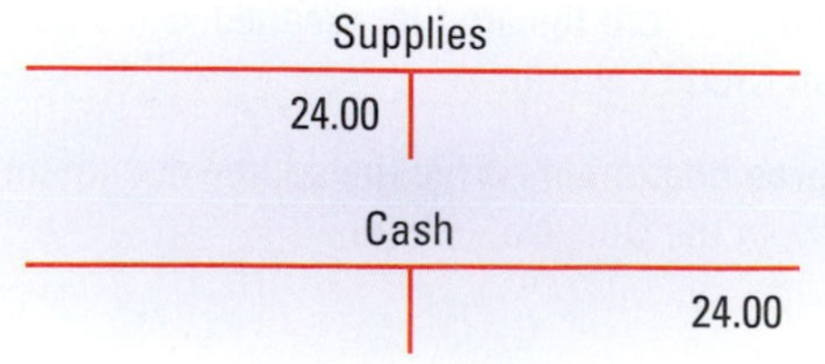

The source document for this transaction is Memorandum No. 12. [*CONCEPT: Objective Evidence*] The analysis of this transaction is shown in the T accounts.

The asset account, Supplies, is increased by a debit, $24.00. The asset account, Cash, is decreased by a credit, $24.00.

A cash payment made with a debit card is recorded on the check stub as "Other." This procedure keeps the checkbook in balance during the time lag from when the debit card payment is made until receipt of the bank statement. The debit card payments are verified as part of the regular bank statement reconciliation process. Debit card payments are identified as a Purchase on the bank statement, with the date, time, location, and the amount of the debit card transaction stated.

STEPS • STEPS • STEPS • STEPS • STEPS

JOURNALIZING A DEBIT CARD PURCHASE

1. **Date.** Write the date, *5*, in the Date column.
2. **Debit.** Write the title of the account to be debited, *Supplies*, in the Account Title column. Record the amount debited, *$24.00*, in the General Debit column.
3. **Credit.** Record the amount credited, *$24.00*, in the Cash Credit column.
4. **Source document.** Write the source document number, *M12*, in the Doc. No. column.

terms review

dishonored check
electronic funds transfer
debit card

TERMS REVIEW

audit your understanding

1. List six reasons why a bank may dishonor a check.
2. What account is credited when electronic funds transfer is used to pay cash on account?
3. What account is credited when a debit card is used to purchase supplies?

AUDIT YOUR

work together 5-3

Recording dishonored checks, electronic funds transfers, and debit card purchases

Write the answers to this problem in the *Working Papers*. Your instructor will guide you through the following example.

1. Enter the following transactions on page 6 of a journal.

Transactions:

March 15. Received notice from the bank of a dishonored check from Christopher Ikola, $63.00, plus $10.00 fee; total, $73.00. Memorandum No. 121.

16. Paid cash on account to Spinoza Enterprises, $135.00, using EFT. Memorandum No. 122.

17. Purchased supplies, $31.00, using a debit card. Memorandum No. 123.

WORK TOGETHER • WORK

on your own 5-3

Recording dishonored checks, electronic funds transfers, and debit card purchases

Write the answers to this problem in the *Working Papers*. Work this problem independently.

1. Enter the following transactions on page 12 of a journal.

Transactions:

June 12. Received notice from the bank of a dishonored check from Thomas Hofski, $65.00, plus $30.00 fee; total, $95.00. Memorandum No. 54.

13. Paid cash on account to Alfonso Company, $243.00, using EFT. Memorandum No. 55.

14. Purchased supplies, $65.00, using a debit card. Memorandum No. 56.

ON YOUR OWN • ON YOUR OWN

LESSON • LESSON • LESSON • LESSON • LESSON • LESSON

5-4 Petty Cash

ESTABLISHING A PETTY CASH FUND

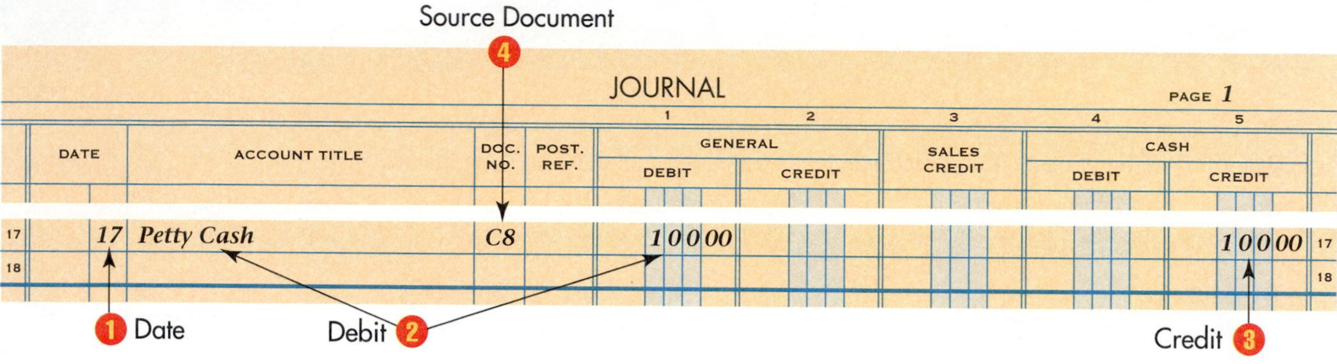

Source Document
4
JOURNAL
PAGE 1
DATE
ACCOUNT TITLE
DOC. NO.
POST. REF.
GENERAL
DEBIT
CREDIT
SALES CREDIT
CASH
DEBIT
CREDIT
17 Petty Cash
C8
100 00
100 00
1 Date
Debit 2
Credit 3

An amount of cash kept on hand and used for making small payments is called **petty cash**. A business usually has some small payments for which writing a check is not time or cost effective. Therefore, a business may maintain a separate cash fund for making small cash payments. The actual dollar amount considered to be a small payment differs from one business to another. Ms. Park has set $20.00 as the maximum amount to be paid at any one time from the petty cash fund.

The petty cash account is an asset with a normal debit balance. The balance of the petty cash account increases on the debit side and decreases on the credit side.

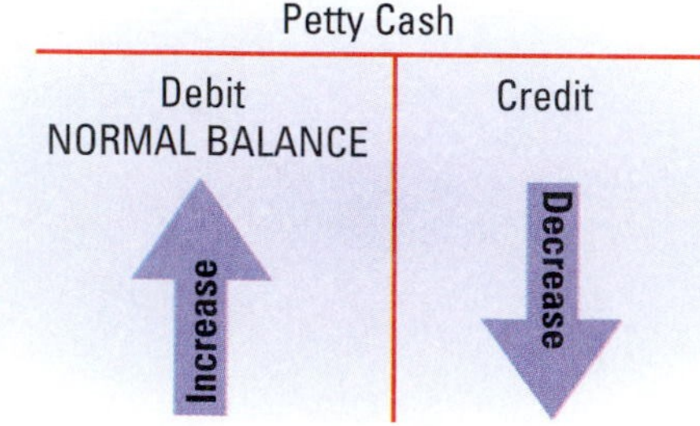

On August 17, Ms. Park decided that TechKnow Consulting needed a petty cash fund of $100.00. This amount should provide for small cash payments during a month.

August 17. Paid cash to establish a petty cash fund, $100.00. Check No. 8.

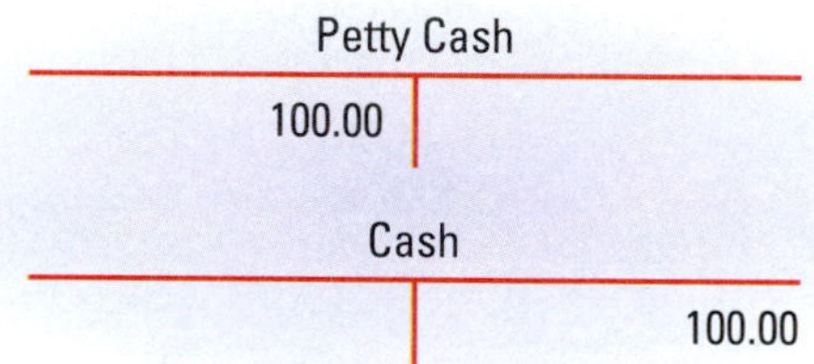

The source document for this transaction is Check No. 8. [*CONCEPT: Objective Evidence*] The analysis is shown in the T accounts. Petty Cash is debited for $100.00 to show the increase in this asset account balance. Cash is credited for $100.00 to show the decrease in this asset account balance.

Ms. Park cashed the check and placed the $100.00 in a locked petty cash box at her place of business. Only she is authorized to make payments from the petty cash fund.

STEPS • STEPS • STEPS • STEPS • STEPS
ESTABLISHING A PETTY CASH FUND

1. **Date.** Write the date, *17*, in the Date column.
2. **Debit.** Write the title of the account to be debited, *Petty Cash,* in the Account Title column. Record the amount debited, *$100.00*, in the General Debit column.
3. **Credit.** Record the amount credited, *$100.00*, in the Cash Credit column.
4. **Source document.** Write the source document number, *C8*, in the Doc. No. column.

MAKING PAYMENTS FROM A PETTY CASH FUND WITH A PETTY CASH SLIP

PETTY CASH SLIP No. 1

Date: *August 18, 20--*

Paid to: *Tribune*

For: *Newspaper Ad* $ *10.00*

Account: *Advertising Expense*

Approved: *Kim Park*

Each time a small payment is made from the petty cash fund, Ms. Park prepares a form showing the purpose and amount of the payment. A form showing proof of a petty cash payment is called a **petty cash slip**.

A petty cash slip shows the following information: (1) petty cash slip number; (2) date of petty cash payment; (3) to whom paid; (4) reason for the payment; (5) amount paid; (6) account in which amount is to be recorded; and (7) signature of person approving the petty cash payment.

The petty cash slips are kept in the petty cash box until the fund is replenished. No entries are made in the journal for the individual petty cash payments.

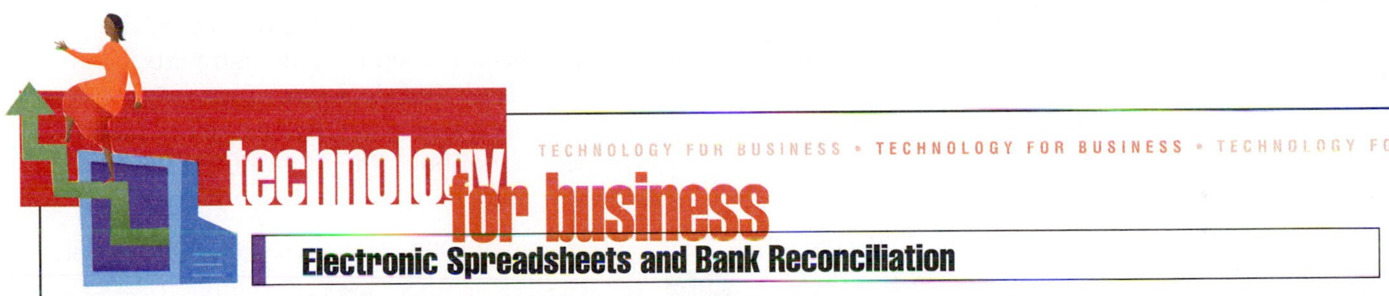

Electronic Spreadsheets and Bank Reconciliation

Businesses often use forms to prepare accounting reports. Electronic spreadsheet software is a useful tool for preparing such accounting reports. Unlike paper forms, however, electronic spreadsheets contain formulas that automatically perform calculations.

An electronic spreadsheet displayed on a computer monitor consists of a group of rows and columns. Such spreadsheets can be extremely large, having hundreds of columns and thousands of rows. The space where a column intersects with a row is a cell. For example, cell A17 is located at the intersection of column A and row 17. This is known as the cell address.

The power of an electronic spreadsheet comes from the ability to let the software make calculations. This is accomplished by attaching formulas to different cells.

A bank reconciliation form increases the efficiency of verifying a bank statement. A spreadsheet can be created with all the formulas necessary to complete a bank reconciliation. For example, a formula attached to a certain cell can calculate the total outstanding deposits.

After the bank reconciliation is printed, the same spreadsheet can be used to reconcile other bank statements. Preparing a bank reconciliation using an electronic spreadsheet can help assure that the calculations are accurate.

REPLENISHING PETTY CASH

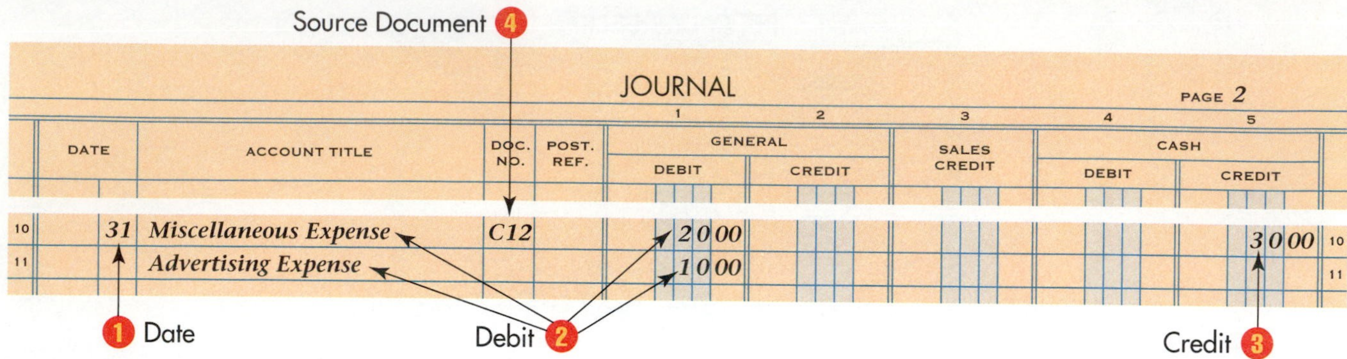

Source Document 4
JOURNAL
PAGE 2
DATE
ACCOUNT TITLE
DOC. NO.
POST. REF.
GENERAL DEBIT
GENERAL CREDIT
SALES CREDIT
CASH DEBIT
CASH CREDIT
31 Miscellaneous Expense C12 20 00 30 00
Advertising Expense 10 00
1 Date
Debit 2
Credit 3

As petty cash is paid out, the amount in the petty cash box decreases. Eventually, the petty cash fund must be replenished and the petty cash payments recorded. TechKnow Consulting replenishes its petty cash fund whenever the amount on hand is reduced to $25.00. Also, the petty cash fund is always replenished at the end of each month so that all of the expenses are recorded in the month they are incurred.

Before petty cash is replenished, a proof of the fund must be completed.

Petty cash remaining in the petty cash fund	$ 70.00
Plus total of petty cash slips	+ 30.00
Equals petty cash fund	$100.00

The last line of the proof must show the same total as the original balance of the petty cash fund, $100.00. If petty cash does not prove, the errors must be found and corrected before any more work is done.

The proof shows that a total of $30.00 has been paid out of petty cash. An inspection of the petty cash slips shows that $20.00 has been paid for miscellaneous expenses and $10.00 has been paid for advertising. Therefore, an additional $30.00 must be placed in the fund. TechKnow Consulting will write a check to replenish the fund.

August 31. Paid cash to replenish the petty cash fund, $30.00: miscellaneous expense, $20.00; advertising, $10.00. Check No. 12.

Unless the petty cash fund is permanently increased or decreased, the balance of the account is always the original amount of the fund. The check issued to replenish petty cash is a credit to Cash and does not affect Petty Cash. When the check is cashed, the money is placed in the petty cash box. The amount in the petty cash box changes, as shown below.

Amount in petty cash box before fund is replenished	$ 70.00
Amount from check issued to replenish petty cash	+ 30.00
Amount in petty cash box after fund is replenished	$100.00

The total amount in the petty cash box, $100.00, is again the same as the balance of the petty cash account.

STEPS: JOURNALIZING THE ENTRY TO REPLENISH PETTY CASH

1. **Date.** Write the date, *31*, in the Date column.
2. **Debit.** Write the title of the first account to be debited, *Miscellaneous Expense,* in the Account Title column. Write the amount to be debited to *Miscellaneous Expense, $20.00,* in the General Debit column on the same line as the account title. Write the title of the second account to be debited, *Advertising Expense,* on the next line in the Account Title column. Record the amount to be debited to *Advertising Expense, $10.00,* in the General Debit column on the same line as the account title.
3. **Credit.** Record the amount to be credited, *$30.00,* in the Cash Credit column on the first line of this entry.
4. **Source document.** Write the source document number, *C12,* in the Doc. No. column on the first line of the entry.

CAREERS IN ACCOUNTING • CAREERS IN ACCOUNTING • CAREERS IN ACCOUNTI

careers in accounting

Tim DuFrene, Sole Proprietor

COURTESY OF TIM DUFRENE

The average person will make at least three career changes over the course of his or her working life. Tim DuFrene fits that average precisely. He has found that accounting is a transferable skill that has served him well throughout his multiple careers.

When Tim took accounting courses in high school and college, he saw himself preparing for a career in banking. His first full-time job was, in fact, in a bank. Working first as a teller, he used his accounting skills to balance cash and reconcile accounts. Advancing to the position of loan officer, Tim relied on his accounting knowledge to review business plans of loan applicants.

After a few years in banking, Tim was drawn into his second professional field—industrial construction. After several years of learning and applying a craft, Tim began working his way into management. Once again, accounting was an important aspect of his work responsibilities. As a project superintendent, he oversaw the construction of various industrial projects throughout the United States. Important accounting aspects of that job included bidding for projects, assessing estimated costs, and setting project budgets.

After 25 years in his second career of industrial construction, Tim became tired of the extensive travel associated with his job and decided to pursue a lifelong dream of owning his own business—career #3. In 2001, he launched Han-D-Man, a home maintenance and repair business that he runs from his home office. As a sole proprietor, he found his accounting skills to be especially important in setting up his business and tracking billing and income, managing expenses, and satisfying tax requirements. Tim says, "Owning my own business has allowed me to interact with many people and improve their quality of life through providing them with more pleasant, functional surroundings. I enjoy having more freedom now to pursue my hobbies, travel, and spend more time with my wife and children. My knowledge of accounting enabled me to change careers and be successful."

Salary Range: Self-employed individuals in a service industry set their desired hourly rate based on their expertise and geographic area. The time required to bid jobs, collect fees, and travel between jobs means that a service provider does not bill all of his or her work time. Thus, a service provider may bill about 1,600 hours during a year. Hourly billing rates between $25.00 and $50.00 per hour and a 1,600-hour work year yield an annual salary of $40,000 to $80,000, less expenses.

Qualifications: Self-employed individuals need three types of skills: (1) communication skills to interact with clients, (2) organizational skills to schedule jobs and manage the business, and (3) a specific skill to sell in the marketplace.

Occupational Outlook: In a career such as Tim's, the sustained growth of the housing market will cause individual homeowners to need more home repairs.

terms review

petty cash
petty cash slip

TERMS REVIEW

audit your understanding

1. Why do businesses use petty cash funds?
2. Why is Cash and not Petty Cash credited when a petty cash fund is replenished?

AUDIT YOUR

work together 5-4

Establishing and replenishing a petty cash fund

Write the answers to this problem in the *Working Papers*. Your instructor will guide you through the following example.

1. Journalize the following transactions completed during July of the current year. Use page 13 of a journal. The abbreviation for check is C.

Transactions:

July 3. Paid cash to establish a petty cash fund, $250.00. C57.
31. Paid cash to replenish the petty cash fund, $78.00: supplies, $25.00; miscellaneous expense, $8.00; repairs, $45.00. C97.

WORK TOGETHER • WORK

on your own 5-4

Establishing and replenishing a petty cash fund

Write the answers to this problem in the *Working Papers*. Work this problem independently.

1. Journalize the following transactions completed during August of the current year. Use page 15 of a journal. The abbreviation for check is C.

Transactions:

Aug. 1. Paid cash to establish a petty cash fund, $200.00. C114.
31. Paid cash to replenish the petty cash fund, $145.00: supplies, $72.00; advertising, $40.00; miscellaneous expense, $33.00. C157.

ON YOUR OWN • ON YOUR OWN

SUMMARY

After completing this chapter, you can

1. Define accounting terms related to using a checking account and a petty cash fund.
2. Identify accounting concepts and practices related to using a checking account.
3. Prepare business papers related to using a checking account.
4. Reconcile a bank statement.
5. Journalize dishonored checks and electronic banking transactions.
6. Establish and replenish a petty cash fund.

Explore Accounting

Cash Controls

Cash transactions occur more frequently than other types of transactions. Because cash is easily transferred from one person to another, a business must try to safeguard its cash to protect it and other assets from errors.

An unintentional error occurs when someone mistakenly records an incorrect amount or forgets to record a transaction. An intentional error occurs when someone intentionally records an incorrect amount or does not record a transaction in order to cover up fraud or theft. Good cash control procedures should guard against both types of errors.

One common method of controlling cash is to insist that all cash payments over a certain amount be paid by check. In addition, checks should be prenumbered so that it is easy to account for each check. The document number column of a journal can be used to ensure that all checks issued are recorded in the journal. Other cash controls are to have one person responsible for authorizing all checks, and requiring a source document in support of each cash payment.

One of the best ways to safeguard assets is to separate duties so that one employee does not have total control of an entire set of processes. For example, one employee could receive and record the receipt of cash on account; a second employee could make and record deposits; and a third employee could reconcile the bank statement. By separating the duties, it is less likely that errors will be made.

A company that does not have enough employees to institute the separation of duties concept may hire a certified public accountant (CPA) to perform some of these duties on a regular basis.

Research Assignment: Talk to a businessperson to determine what kinds of controls are in place in his or her business to safeguard cash. Schools, hospitals, charitable organizations, and government offices as well as retail, wholesale, and service businesses should have established controls that are being followed. Summarize and present your findings to your class.

5-1 APPLICATION PROBLEM

Endorsing and writing checks

You are authorized to sign checks for Accounting Tutors. Forms are given in the *Working Papers*.

Instructions:

1. For each of the following situations, prepare the appropriate endorsement.
   a. Write a blank endorsement.
   b. Write a special endorsement to transfer a check to Vu Kim.
   c. Write a restrictive endorsement to deposit a check in the account of Accounting Tutors.
2. Record the balance brought forward on Check Stub No. 390, $6,711.62.
3. Record a deposit of $1,244.25 made on September 30 of the current year on Check Stub No. 390.
4. Prepare check stubs and write the following checks. Use September 30 of the current year as the date.
   a. Check No. 390 to Williamson Street Supplies for supplies, $945.00.
   b. Check No. 391 to Spring Park Tribune for advertising, $112.00.
   c. Check No. 392 to Bryce Wilton for rent, $250.00.

5-2 APPLICATION PROBLEM  

Reconciling a bank statement and recording a bank service charge

Forms are given in the *Working Papers*. On May 31 of the current year, Parties Plus received a bank statement dated May 30. The following information is obtained from the bank statement and from the records of the business.

Bank statement balance	$1,927.00
Bank service charge	20.00
Outstanding deposit, May 30	756.25
Outstanding checks:	
No. 310	421.76
No. 311	150.50
Checkbook balance on Check Stub No. 312	2,130.99

Instructions:

1. Prepare a bank statement reconciliation. Use May 31 of the current year as the date.
2. Record the service charge on check stub No. 312.
3. Record the service charge on journal page 10. Use Memorandum No. 58 as the source document.

5-3 APPLICATION PROBLEM

Recording dishonored checks, electronic funds transfers, and debit card purchases

Enter the following transactions on page 8 of the journal given in the *Working Papers*.

Transactions:

Jan.	25.	Received notice from the bank of a dishonored check from Ralston Eubanks, $125.00, plus $30.00 fee; total, $155.00. Memorandum No. 333.
	26.	Paid cash on account to Reed Rosman, $289.00, using EFT. Memorandum No. 334.
	27.	Purchased supplies, $54.00, using a debit card. Memorandum No. 335.

5-4 APPLICATION PROBLEM

Establishing and replenishing a petty cash fund

Journalize the following transactions completed during November of the current year. Use page 22 of the journal given in the *Working Papers*. The abbreviation for check is C.

Transactions:

Nov. 5. Paid cash to establish a petty cash fund, $300.00. C527.

30. Paid cash to replenish the petty cash fund, $165.00: supplies, $57.00; miscellaneous expense, $58.00; repairs, $40.00; postage (Postage Expense), $10.00. C555.

5-5 MASTERY PROBLEM

AUTOMATED ACCOUNTING PEACHTREE QUICKBOOKS

Reconciling a bank statement; journalizing a bank service charge, a dishonored check, and petty cash transactions

James Astrup owns a business called LawnMow. Selected general ledger accounts are given below.

110 Cash
115 Petty Cash
120 Accts. Rec.—Bruce Kassola
130 Supplies
140 Prepaid Insurance
320 James Astrup, Drawing
520 Miscellaneous Expense
530 Rent Expense
535 Repair Expense
540 Supplies Expense
550 Utilities Expense

Instructions:

1. Journalize the following transactions completed during August of the current year. Use page 20 of the journal given in the *Working Papers*. Source documents are abbreviated as follows: check, C; memorandum, M.

Transactions:

Aug. 21. Paid cash to establish a petty cash fund, $300.00. C110.

24. Paid cash for repairs, $165.00. C111.

26. Paid cash for supplies, $60.00. C112.

27. Received notice from the bank of a dishonored check from Bruce Kassola, $140.00, plus $35.00 fee; total, $175.00. M33.

28. Paid cash for miscellaneous expense, $31.00. C113.

31. Paid cash to owner for personal use, $400.00. C114.

31. Paid cash to replenish the petty cash fund, $255.00: supplies, $125.00; miscellaneous expense, $130.00. C115.

31. Received cash from sales, $350.00. T31.

2. On August 31 of the current year, LawnMow received a bank statement dated August 30. Prepare a bank statement reconciliation. Use August 31 of the current year as the date. The following information is obtained from the August 30 bank statement and from the records of the business.

Bank statement balance	$2,721.00
Bank service charge	15.00
Outstanding deposit, August 31	350.00
Outstanding checks, Nos. 114 and 115	
Checkbook balance on Check Stub No. 116	2,431.00

3. Continue using the journal and journalize the following transaction:

Transaction:

Aug. 31. Received bank statement showing August bank service charge, $15.00. M34.

5-6 CHALLENGE PROBLEM

Reconciling a bank statement and recording a bank service charge

Use the bank statement, canceled checks, and check stubs for GolfPro given in the *Working Papers*.

Instructions:

1. Compare the canceled checks with the check stubs. For each canceled check, place a check mark next to the appropriate check stub number. For each deposit shown on the bank statement, place a check mark next to the deposit amount on the appropriate check stub.
2. Prepare a bank statement reconciliation. Use August 29 of the current year as the date.
3. Record the following transactions on page 8 of a journal. The abbreviation for memorandum is M.

Transactions:

Sept. 1. Received bank statement showing August bank service charge, $5.00. M25.

1. Received notice from the bank of a dishonored check from Sheldon Martindale, $170.00, plus $5.00 fee; total, $175.00. M26.

4. Record the bank service charge and dishonored check on Check Stub No. 165.

©GETTY IMAGES/PHOTODISC

applied communication

All businesses are affected to some degree by issues and events that occur in the areas in which the businesses are located. For example, a city may gain an industry that will employ many people for a long time. Or, a town might build new roads or schools.

Instructions: Collect three to five newspaper or magazine articles about issues in your area that you think will affect local businesses. For each article, prepare a written list of consequences that a business might encounter.

APPLIED COMMUNICATION

cases for critical thinking

Case 1

Iris Velez and Suanne Merker have personal checking accounts for which they receive a bank statement every month. Ms. Merker does not prepare a reconciliation; instead she records the balance on the bank statement as her new checkbook balance. Ms. Velez prepares a bank statement reconciliation for each bank statement received. Is Ms. Velez or Ms. Merker following the better procedure? Explain.

Case 2

Dorset Company decides to establish a petty cash fund. The owner, Edna Dorset, wants to establish a $100.00 petty cash fund and limit payments to $20.00 or less. The manager, Roy Evans, suggests a petty cash fund of $3,000.00 limited to payments of $50.00 or less. Mr. Evans claims this limit will help him avoid writing so many checks. Do you agree with Ms. Dorset or Mr. Evans? Explain.

CASES FOR CRITICAL THINKING

SCANS workplace competency

Personal Qualities: Responsibility

Concept: Employers seek individuals who exert a high level of effort and persevere toward goal attainment.

Application: Make a list of your responsibilities in this accounting course; then assess whether you meet these responsibilities with a low, medium, or high level of effort. Make a plan for how you can improve your performance on those responsibilities that you are not already fulfilling at a high level of effort.

SCANS WORKPLACE

graphing workshop

A bar chart of the assets, liabilities, and owner's equity of Moua Company is shown here. Analyze the chart to answer the following questions.

1. What was the amount of total assets in May?
2. In what month were liabilities the lowest?

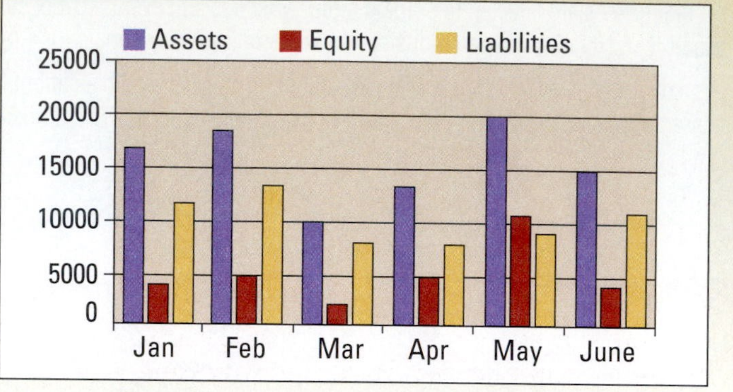

analyzing Best Buy's financial statements

On a financial statement, the term "Cash and cash equivalents" includes more than just cash on hand. Checking accounts, savings accounts, and even some very short-term investments are also included in this total. Best Buy's financial statement on Appendix B page B-4 shows the total "Cash and cash equivalents" for Best Buy for each year.

Published financial statements include notes that explain some of the titles and amounts used in the statements. Note 1 for Best Buy's financial statements begins on page B-9. Read the first page of Note 1.

Instructions: List the amount of Best Buy's cash and cash equivalents for 2003 and 2004. Look at Note 1 and list what Best Buy considers to be "cash and cash equivalents."

Automated Accounting

Automated Cash Control Systems

Cash transactions include those involving both cash in the bank and cash on hand. Because cash transactions occur so frequently, there are more chances to make recording errors. In each accounting period, cash account balances should be verified.

Cash kept on hand and used for making small payments is called *petty cash*. Each business must decide the appropriate dollar limit for payments from the petty cash fund. A check is written and cashed to transfer money to the petty cash account. Each time a payment is made from the petty cash fund, a form called a petty cash slip is prepared. A petty cash report is prepared, summarizing the petty cash slips, whenever the petty cash fund needs to be replenished. At that time, the petty cash fund balance is verified, and journal entries are made to record the expenses paid from the fund.

In addition, completing a bank reconciliation verifies that the cash account balance in the bank equals the checkbook balance. Checkbook transactions should be reconciled to the bank statement each month. At that time, bank charges such as service charges and dishonored checks should be recorded.

The automated accounting system may be used to prepare the monthly bank reconciliation. Information maintained by the software, such as the checkbook balance and checks that were written during the period, will be automatically provided to make the reconciliation process simpler and more accurate.

While the *Automated Accounting 8.0* Help system contains detailed instructions, the bank statement can be reconciled to the checkbook balance in the following steps:

1. Choose the Other Activities menu item from the Data menu, or click on the Other toolbar button.
2. When the Reconciliation window appears, click on the Clear button to erase any previous data.
3. Enter the bank credits, bank charges, bank statement balance, and outstanding deposit amounts.
4. Checks written during the period are displayed in the Checks from the Journals list box. Select the outstanding checks by pointing and double-clicking. Each selected check will appear in the Outstanding Checks list, and the Adjusted Bank Balance will automatically be updated.
5. Click the Report command button in the Reconciliation window to see the completed reconciliation.
6. Click the Close command button to dismiss the report window.
7. When the Bank Reconciliation reappears, click the OK command button to record your data and end the Bank Reconciliation process.

AUTOMATING APPLICATION PROBLEM 5-2: Reconciling a bank statement and recording a bank service charge

Instructions:

1. Load the *Automated Accounting 8.0* or higher software.
2. Select data file F05-2 from the appropriate directory/folder.
3. Select File from the menu bar and choose the Save As menu command. Key the path to the drive and directory that contains your data files. Save your file with a filename of F05-2 XXX XXX (where the X's are your first and last name).
4. Access Problem Instructions through the Browser tool. Read the Problem Instructions screen.
5. Refer to Application Problem 5-2 for the data used in this problem.
6. Save your file and exit the Automated Accounting software.

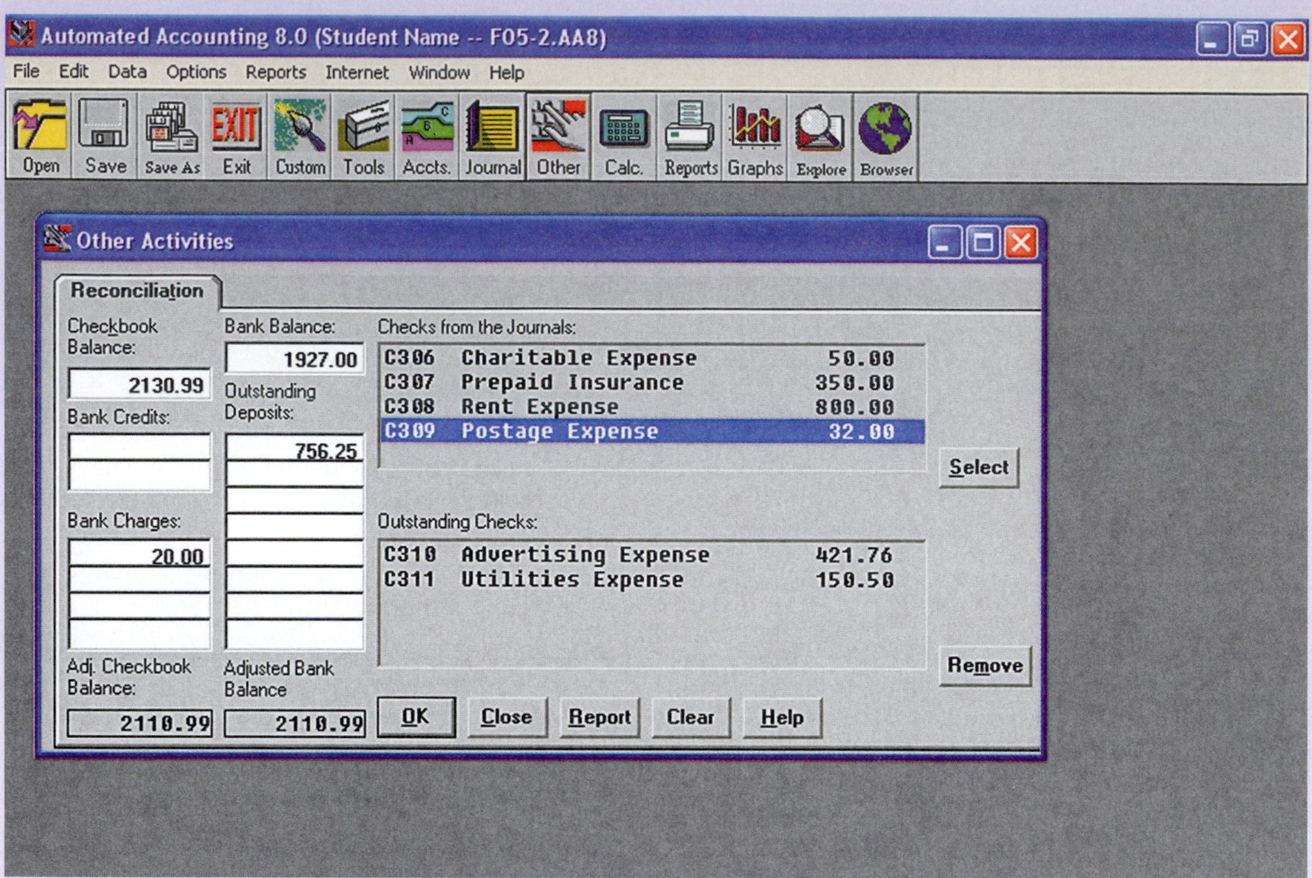

AUTOMATING MASTERY PROBLEM 5-5: Reconciling a bank statement; journalizing a bank service charge, a dishonored check, and petty cash transactions

Instructions:

1. Load the *Automated Accounting 8.0* or higher software.
2. Select data file F05-5 from the appropriate directory/folder.
3. Select File from the menu bar and choose the Save As menu command. Key the path to the drive and directory that contains your data files. Save your file with a filename of F05-5 XXX XXX (where the X's are your first and last name).
4. Access Problem Instructions through the Browser tool. Read the Problem Instructions screen.
5. Key the data listed in Mastery Problem 5-5.
6. Save your file and exit the Automated Accounting software.

An Accounting Cycle for a Proprietorship: Journalizing and Posting Transactions

AUTOMATED ACCOUNTING
PEACHTREE
QUICKBOOKS

Reinforcement activities strengthen the learning of accounting concepts and procedures. Reinforcement Activity 1 is a single problem divided into two parts. Part A includes learning from Chapters 1 through 5. Part B includes learning from Chapters 6 through 8. An accounting cycle is completed in Parts A and B for a single business—Extreme Adventures.

EXTREME ADVENTURES

In May of the current year, Brian Dawson starts a service business called Extreme Adventures. The business provides adventure trips throughout the world, such as trekking in the Himalayas and helo skiing in Colorado. The business rents the facilities in which it operates, pays the utilities, and is responsible for maintenance. Extreme Adventures charges clients for each visit. Most of Extreme Adventures' sales are for cash. However, two private schools use Extreme Adventures for some physical education classes. These schools have an account with Extreme Adventures.

CHART OF ACCOUNTS

Extreme Adventures uses the following chart of accounts.

CHART OF ACCOUNTS

Balance Sheet Accounts

(100) ASSETS
110 Cash
120 Petty Cash
130 Accts. Rec.—Matterhorn University
140 Accts. Rec.—Midwest College
150 Supplies
160 Prepaid Insurance

(200) LIABILITIES
210 Accts. Pay.—Dunn Supplies
220 Accts. Pay.—Greenway Supplies

(300) OWNER'S EQUITY
310 Brian Dawson, Capital
320 Brian Dawson, Drawing
330 Income Summary

Income Statement Accounts

(400) REVENUE
410 Sales

(500) EXPENSES
510 Advertising Expense
520 Insurance Expense
530 Miscellaneous Expense
540 Rent Expense
550 Repair Expense
560 Supplies Expense
570 Utilities Expense

RECORDING TRANSACTIONS

Instructions:

1. Journalize the following transactions completed during May of the current year. Use page 1 of the journal given in the *Working Papers.* Source documents are abbreviated as follows: check stub, C; memorandum, M; receipt, R; sales invoice, S; calculator tape, T.

   May 1. Received cash from owner as an investment, $15,000.00. R1.
   1. Paid cash for rent, $1,800.00. C1.
   2. Paid cash for electric bill, $105.00. C2.
   4. Paid cash for supplies, $450.00. C3.
   4. Paid cash for insurance, $1,200.00. C4.
   7. Bought supplies on account from Dunn Supplies, $900.00. M1.
   11. Paid cash to establish a petty cash fund, $250.00. C5.
   12. Received cash from sales, $475.00. T12.
   13. Paid cash for repairs, $250.00. C6.
   13. Paid cash for miscellaneous expense, $40.00. C7.
   13. Received cash from sales, $235.00. T13.
   13. Sold services on account to Midwest College, $225.00. S1.
   14. Paid cash for advertising, $300.00. C8.
   15. Paid cash to owner for personal use, $200.00. C9.
   15. Paid cash on account to Dunn Supplies, $500.00. C10.
   15. Received cash from sales, $305.00. T15.
   15. Sold services on account to Matterhorn University, $425.00. S2.
   18. Paid cash for miscellaneous expense, $95.00. C11.
   18. Received cash on account from Midwest College, $125.00. R2.
   19. Received cash from sales, $480.00. T19.
   20. Paid cash for repairs, $160.00. C12.
   20. Bought supplies on account from Greenway Supplies, $120.00. M2.

2. Prove and rule page 1 of the journal. Carry the column totals forward to page 2 of the journal.

3. Post the separate amounts on each line of page 1 of the journal that need to be posted individually.

4. Use page 2 of the journal. Journalize the following transactions.

   May 21. Paid cash for water bill, $265.00. C13.
   21. Received cash from sales, $620.00. T21.
   25. Paid cash for supplies, $25.00. C14.
   25. Received cash from sales, $605.00. T25.
   26. Paid cash for miscellaneous expense, $37.00. C15.
   26. Received cash on account from Matterhorn University, $250.00. R3.
   27. Received cash from sales, $715.00. T27.
   28. Paid cash for telephone bill, $245.00. C16.
   28. Received cash from sales, $650.00. T28.

5. Extreme Adventures received a bank statement dated May 27. The following information is obtained from the bank statement and from the records of the business. Prepare a bank statement reconciliation. Use May 29 as the date.

Bank statement balance	$13,180.00
Bank service charge	15.00
Outstanding deposit, May 28	650.00
Outstanding checks:	
No. 14	25.00
No. 15	37.00
No. 16	245.00
Checkbook balance on Check Stub No. 17	$13,538.00

6. Continue using page 2 of the journal, and journalize the following transactions.

May 29. Received bank statement showing May bank service charge, $15.00. M3.
29. Paid cash for supplies, $30.00. C17.
29. Received cash from sales, $695.00. T29.
31. Paid cash to replenish the petty cash fund, $165.00: miscellaneous expense, $120.00; repairs, $45.00. C18.
31. Paid cash to owner for personal use, $1,000.00. C19.
31. Received cash from sales, $660.00. T31.

7. Prove page 2 of the journal.

8. Prove cash. The beginning cash balance on May 1 is zero. The balance on the next unused check stub is $13,683.00.

9. Rule page 2 of the journal.

10. Post the separate amounts on each line of page 2 of the journal that need to be posted individually.

11. Post the column totals on page 2 of the journal.

The general ledger prepared in Reinforcement Activity 1—Part A is needed to complete Reinforcement Activity 1—Part B.

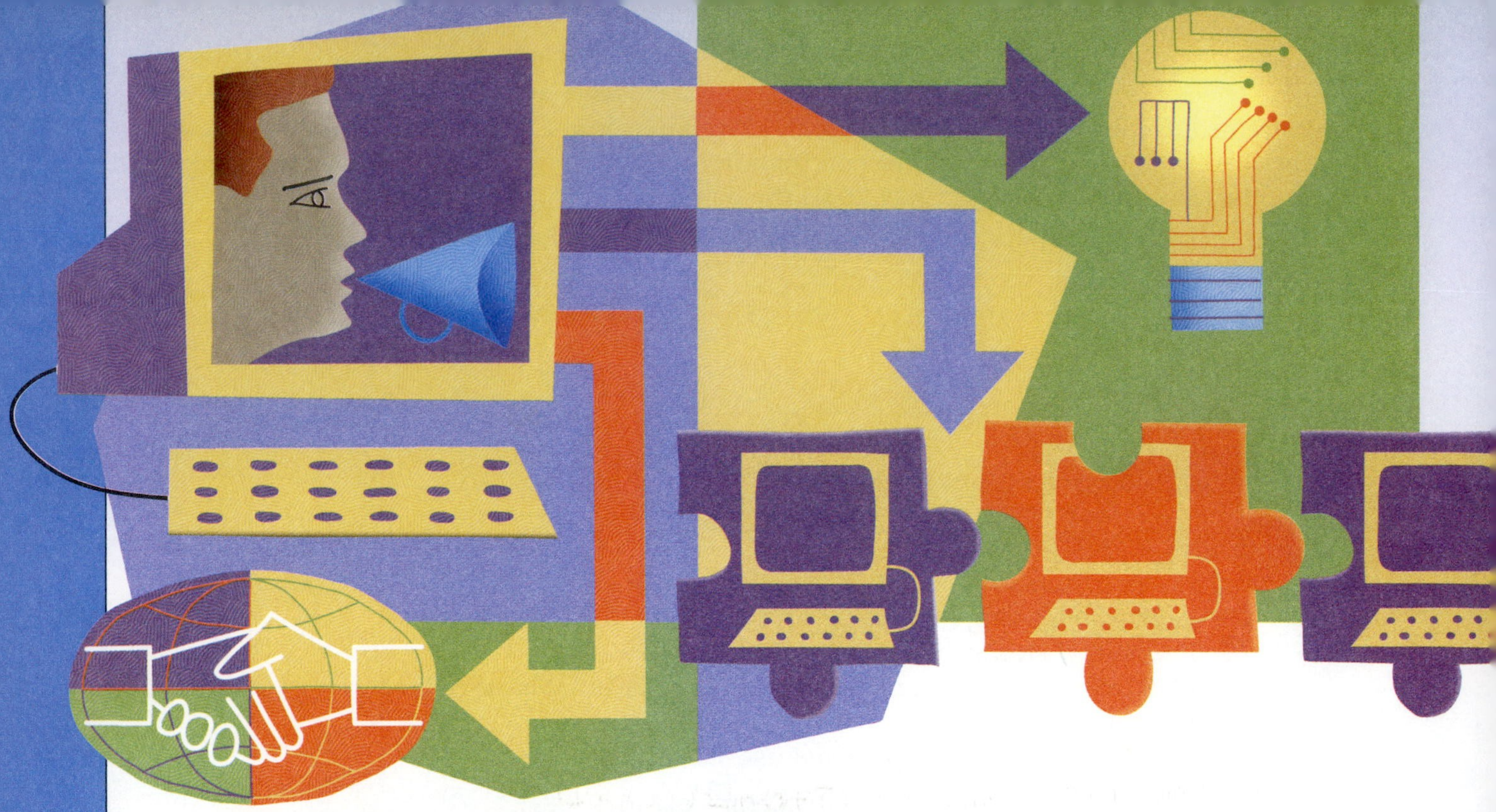

CHAPTER 6

Work Sheet for a Service Business

OBJECTIVES & TERMS

After studying Chapter 6, you will be able to:

1. Define accounting terms related to a work sheet for a service business organized as a proprietorship.
2. Identify accounting concepts and practices related to a work sheet for a service business organized as a proprietorship.
3. Prepare a heading and a trial balance on a work sheet.
4. Plan adjustments for supplies and prepaid insurance.
5. Complete a work sheet for a service business organized as a proprietorship.
6. Identify selected procedures for finding and correcting errors in accounting records.

- fiscal period
- work sheet
- trial balance
- adjustments
- balance sheet
- income statement
- net income
- net loss

Point Your Browser
accountingxtra.swlearning.com

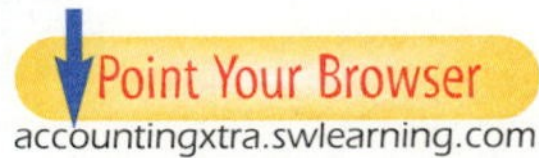

accounting in the real world

The AICPA

PROFESSIONALISM AND THE AICPA

The American Institute of Certified Public Accountants (AICPA) is America's leading professional CPA organization, with more than 340,000 members who work for public accounting firms, multinational corporations, small businesses, not-for-profit organizations, governmental agencies, and educational institutions.

Certified Public Accountants—CPAs—who work for public accounting firms provide many services to their clients, such as auditing financial statements, forensic accounting (sometimes called fraud auditing), consulting services, information technology services, evaluating operating performance, international accounting, and tax and financial planning services.

CPAs who are employed by corporations and businesses often work in finance and accounting departments as financial analysts and have the opportunity to rise up the ranks to positions such as controller and Chief Financial Officer (CFO), and even Chief Executive Officer (CEO). Others work in the areas of international finance, treasury, or internal auditing.

To find out more about CPA career opportunities, salary information, and the accounting profession, visit www.StartHereGoPlaces.com or www.aicpa.org, or e-mail the AICPA at educat@aicpa.org. In addition, each state has a CPA society or association that can provide you with more information. You can contact a state CPA society or association through the "CPA links" section of the AICPA web site.

Critical Thinking

1. If you were going to hire an accountant, why might you choose to hire a CPA?
2. If you were a CPA, why might you choose to join a professional association like the AICPA?

Source: www.aicpa.org

ACCOUNTING IN THE REAL WORLD • ACCOUNTING IN THE REAL WORLD • ACCOUNTING IN THE REAL WORLD •

internet activity

AICPA CAREER RESOURCES

Go to the homepage for the American Institute of Certified Public Accountants (AICPA) (www.aicpa.org). Search the site for information about career resources for students.

Instructions

1. List two resources provided by the AICPA designed to help students with career choices in the field of accounting.
2. Pick one of these two resources and examine it in more detail. List two interesting pieces of information you learned from this resource.

INTERNET RESEARCH ACTIVITY • INTERNET RESEARCH ACTIVITY • INTERNET RESEARCH ACTIVITY •

LESSON

6-1 Creating a Work Sheet

CONSISTENT REPORTING

General ledger accounts contain information needed by managers and owners. Before the information can be used, however, it must be analyzed, summarized, and reported in a meaningful way. The accounting concept *Consistent Reporting* is applied when the same accounting procedures are followed in the same way in each accounting period. [*CONCEPT: Consistent Reporting*] For example, in one year a delivery business might report the number of deliveries made. The next year, the same business reports the amount of revenue received for the deliveries made. The information for the two years cannot be compared because the business has not been consistent in reporting information about deliveries.

A summary of preparing a work sheet is shown on the Work Sheet Overlay within this chapter.

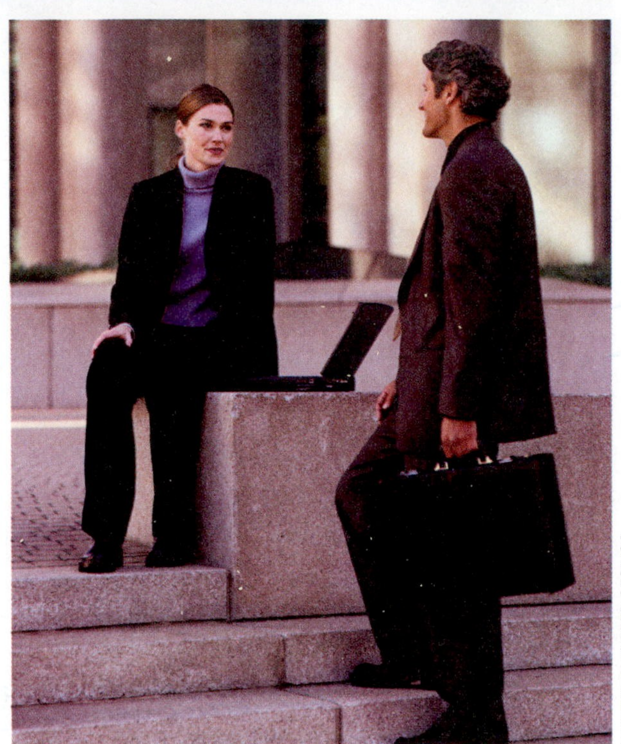

©GETTY IMAGES/PHOTODISC

FISCAL PERIODS

The length of time for which a business summarizes and reports financial information is called a **fiscal period** (also known as an accounting period). Businesses usually select a period of time for which to summarize and report financial information. The accounting concept *Accounting Period Cycle* is applied when changes in financial information are reported for a specific period of time in the form of financial statements. [*CONCEPT: Accounting Period Cycle*] Each business chooses a fiscal period length that meets its needs. Because federal and state tax reports are based on one year, most businesses use a one-year fiscal period. However, because TechKnow Consulting is a new business, Ms. Park wishes to have financial information reported frequently to help her make decisions. For this reason, TechKnow Consulting uses a one-month fiscal period.

A fiscal period can begin on any date. However, most businesses begin their fiscal periods on the first day of a month. TechKnow Consulting started business on August 1. Therefore, TechKnow Consulting's monthly fiscal period is for the period from August 1 through August 31, inclusive. Businesses often choose a one-year fiscal period that ends during a period of low business activity. In this way, the end-of-year accounting work comes at a time when other business activities are the lightest.

Financial information may be analyzed, summarized, and reported on any date a business needs the information. However, financial information is always summarized and reported at the end of a fiscal period.

WORK SHEET

A columnar accounting form used to summarize the general ledger information needed to prepare financial statements is called a **work sheet**.

Accountants use a work sheet for four reasons: (1) to summarize general ledger account balances to prove that debits equal credits; (2) to plan needed changes to general ledger accounts to bring account balances up to date; (3) to separate general ledger account balances according to the financial statements to be prepared; and (4) to calculate the amount of net income or net loss for a fiscal period.

Journals and ledgers are permanent records of a business and are usually prepared in ink or printed by a computer. However, a work sheet is a planning tool and is not considered a permanent accounting record. Therefore, a work sheet is prepared in pencil.

PREPARING THE HEADING OF A WORK SHEET

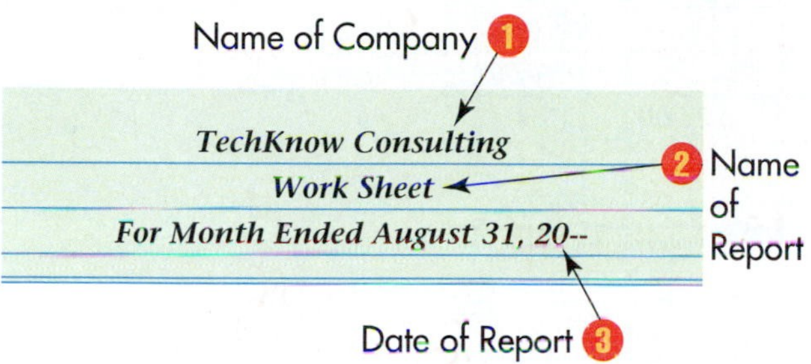

The heading on a work sheet consists of three lines and contains the name of the business, the name of the report, and the date of the report.

The date on TechKnow Consulting's work sheet indicates that the work sheet covers the 31 days from August 1 through and including August 31. If a work sheet were for a calendar year fiscal period, it might have a date stated as *For Year Ended December 31, 20--*.

MAKING ETHICAL DECISIONS • MAKING ETHICAL DECISIONS • MAKING ETHICAL DECISIONS

making ethical decisions

Professional Codes of Conduct

Most professional organizations have a code of professional conduct to guide the actions of their members. One of the best-known codes of professional conduct is that of the American Institute of Certified Public Accountants (AICPA). A national organization of over 340,000 certified public accountants, the AICPA seeks to help its members provide professional services that benefit their employees, clients, and society. An important component of this mission is the AICPA Code of Professional Conduct.

The Code contains Rules of Conduct that its members must follow in their performance of professional services. The Rules address the topics of independence, integrity, objectivity, client relations, and colleague relations. Some Rules have Interpretations that provide further insight into the Rules. The Code is also supported by Ethics Rulings, a series of questions and answers that the AICPA elects to share with its members.

AICPA members who fail to adhere to the Code can be disciplined or expelled from the membership. Losing membership in the AICPA can result in serious consequences for a certified public accountant working in the profession.

Instructions

Access the AICPA's Code of Professional Conduct at www.aicpa.org. Citing the exact source of each answer, determine whether a member of the AICPA may:

1. Accept a gift from a client. (*Hint:* Search Independence Ethics Rulings)
2. Charge a client a fee based on the net income reported on the audited income statement. (*Hint:* Search Contingent Fees)
3. Advertise professional services in television commercials. (*Hint:* Search Other Professional Responsibilities and Practices, Advertising Interpretations)

PREPARING A TRIAL BALANCE ON A WORK SHEET

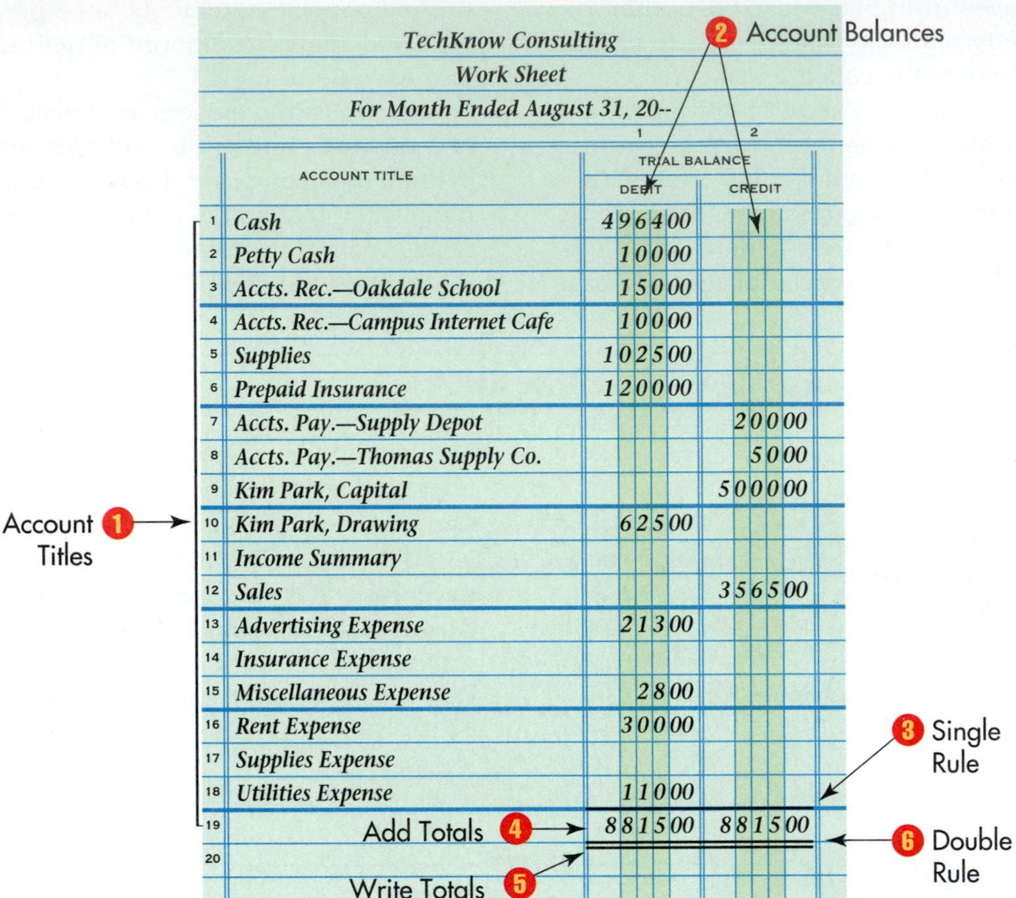

TechKnow Consulting
Work Sheet
For Month Ended August 31, 20--

	ACCOUNT TITLE	1 TRIAL BALANCE DEBIT	2 TRIAL BALANCE CREDIT
1	Cash	4964 00	
2	Petty Cash	100 00	
3	Accts. Rec.—Oakdale School	150 00	
4	Accts. Rec.—Campus Internet Cafe	100 00	
5	Supplies	1025 00	
6	Prepaid Insurance	1200 00	
7	Accts. Pay.—Supply Depot		200 00
8	Accts. Pay.—Thomas Supply Co.		50 00
9	Kim Park, Capital		5000 00
10	Kim Park, Drawing	625 00	
11	Income Summary		
12	Sales		3565 00
13	Advertising Expense	213 00	
14	Insurance Expense		
15	Miscellaneous Expense	28 00	
16	Rent Expense	300 00	
17	Supplies Expense		
18	Utilities Expense	110 00	
19		8815 00	8815 00
20			

The total of all debit account balances must equal the total of all credit account balances. A proof of the equality of debits and credits in a general ledger is called a **trial balance**.

Information for the trial balance is taken from the general ledger. General ledger account titles are listed on a trial balance in the same order as they are listed on the chart of accounts. All the account titles are listed, even if some accounts do not have balances.

STEPS • STEPS • STEPS • STEPS • STEPS • STEPS • STEPS • STEPS • STEPS • STEPS

PREPARING A TRIAL BALANCE ON A WORK SHEET

1. Write the general ledger account titles in the work sheet's Account Title column.
2. Write the general ledger debit account balances in the Trial Balance Debit column. Write the general ledger credit account balances in the Trial Balance Credit column. If an account does not have a balance, the space in the Trial Balance columns is left blank.
3. Rule a single line across the two Trial Balance columns below the last line on which an account title is written. This single line shows that each column is to be added.
4. Add both the Trial Balance Debit and Credit columns. If the two column totals are the same, then debits equal credits in the general ledger accounts. If the two column totals are not the same, recheck the Trial Balance columns to find the error. Other parts of a work sheet are not completed until the Trial Balance columns are proved. Suggestions for locating errors are described later in this chapter.
5. Write each column's total below the single line.
6. Rule double lines across both Trial Balance columns. The double lines mean that the Trial Balance column totals have been verified as correct.

• terms review

fiscal period
work sheet
trial balance

TERMS REVIEW

• audit your understanding

1. What is written on the three-line heading on a work sheet?
2. What general ledger accounts are listed in the Trial Balance columns of a work sheet?

AUDIT YOUR

• work together 6-1

Recording the trial balance on a work sheet

Use the work sheet given in the *Working Papers*. Your instructor will guide you through the following example.

On February 28 of the current year, Golden Tan has the following general ledger accounts and balances. The business uses a monthly fiscal period.

Account Titles	Account Balances	
	Debit	**Credit**
Cash	$9,800.00	
Petty Cash	150.00	
Accounts Receivable—Ruby Prince	2,795.00	
Supplies	456.00	
Prepaid Insurance	750.00	
Accounts Payable—Richard Navarro		$ 555.00
Gary Baldwin, Capital		14,885.00
Gary Baldwin, Drawing	3,400.00	
Income Summary		
Sales		4,320.00
Advertising Expense	931.00	
Insurance Expense		
Miscellaneous Expense	378.00	
Supplies Expense		
Utilities Expense	1,100.00	

1. Prepare the heading and trial balance on a work sheet. Total and rule the Trial Balance columns. Save your work to complete Work Together 6-2.

WORK TOGETHER • WORK TOGETHER • WORK TOGETHER • WORK TOGETHER

on your own 6-1

Recording the trial balance on a work sheet

Use the work sheet given in the *Working Papers*. Work this problem independently.

On December 31 of the current year, Copa's Copies has the following general ledger accounts and balances. The business uses a monthly fiscal period.

Account Titles	Account Balances	
	Debit	Credit
Cash	$6,800.00	
Petty Cash	75.00	
Accounts Receivable—Burt Strog	1,498.00	
Supplies	238.00	
Prepaid Insurance	325.00	
Accounts Payable—Janet Dao		$ 298.00
Jabbo West, Capital		7,443.00
Jabbo West, Drawing	1,700.00	
Income Summary		
Sales		4,140.00
Advertising Expense	456.00	
Insurance Expense		
Miscellaneous Expense	189.00	
Supplies Expense		
Utilities Expense	600.00	

1. Prepare the heading and trial balance on a work sheet. Total and rule the Trial Balance columns. Save your work to complete On Your Own 6-2.

ON YOUR OWN • ON YOUR OWN • ON YOUR OWN • ON YOUR OWN • ON YOUR OWN

6-2 Planning Adjusting Entries on a Work Sheet

PLANNING ADJUSTMENTS ON A WORK SHEET

Sometimes a business will pay cash for an expense in one fiscal period, but the expense is not used until a later period. The expense should be reported in the same fiscal period that it is used to produce revenue. The accounting concept *Matching Expenses with Revenue* is applied when revenue from business activities and expenses associated with earning that revenue are recorded in the same accounting period. For example, TechKnow Consulting buys supplies in quantity in August, but some of the supplies are not used until September. Only the value of the supplies used in August should be reported as expenses in August. In this way, August revenue and the supplies expense associated with earning the August revenue are recorded in the same accounting period. [*CONCEPT: Matching Expenses with Revenue*]

In order to give accurate information on financial statements, some general ledger accounts must be brought up to date at the end of a fiscal period. For example, TechKnow Consulting debits an asset account, Supplies, each time supplies are bought. Supplies on hand are items of value owned by a business until the supplies are used. The value of supplies that are used becomes an expense to the business. However, recording an expense each time an individual supply, such as a pencil, is used would be impractical. Therefore, on August 31 the balance of the asset account, Supplies, is the value of all supplies bought rather than the value of only the supplies that have not yet been used. The amount of supplies that have been used must be deducted from the asset account, Supplies, and recorded in the expense account, Supplies Expense.

Likewise, the amount of insurance that has been used during the fiscal period is also an expense of the business. When the insurance premium for a year of insurance coverage is paid, the entire amount is debited to an asset account, Prepaid Insurance. Recording each day's amount of insurance used during August is impractical. Therefore, at the end of a fiscal period, the amount of the insurance coverage used must be deducted from the asset account, Prepaid Insurance, and recorded in the expense account, Insurance Expense.

Changes recorded on a work sheet to update general ledger accounts at the end of a fiscal period are called **adjustments**. The assets of a business, such as supplies and prepaid insurance, are used to earn revenue. The portions of the assets consumed in order to earn revenue become expenses of the business. The portions consumed are no longer assets but are now expenses. Therefore, adjustments must be made to both the asset and expense accounts for supplies and insurance. After the adjustments are made, the expenses incurred to earn revenue are reported in the same fiscal period as the revenue is earned and reported. [*CONCEPT: Matching Expenses with Revenue*]

A work sheet is used to plan adjustments. Changes are not made in general ledger accounts until adjustments are journalized and posted. The accuracy of the planning for adjustments is checked on a work sheet before adjustments are actually journalized.

Procedures for journalizing TechKnow Consulting's adjustments are described in Chapter 8.

REMEMBER The ending balance of the asset account, *Supplies*, should represent the amount of supplies remaining on hand at the end of the fiscal period. The amount of supplies used during the period should be recorded in the expense account, *Supplies Expense*.

SUPPLIES ADJUSTMENT ON A WORK SHEET

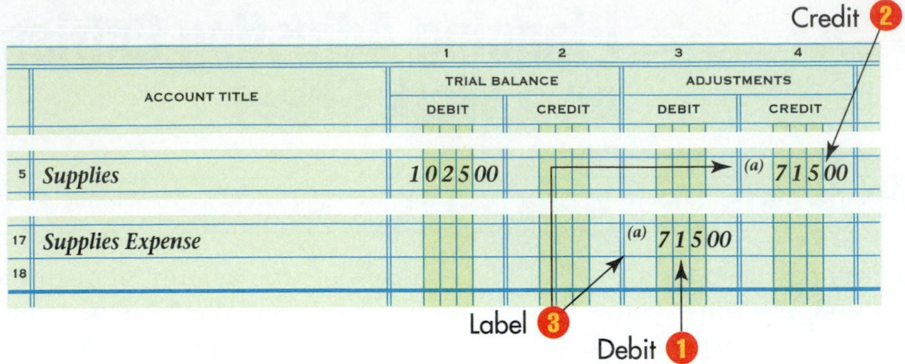

On August 31, before adjustments, the balance of Supplies is $1,025.00, and the balance of Supplies Expense is zero, as shown in the T accounts.

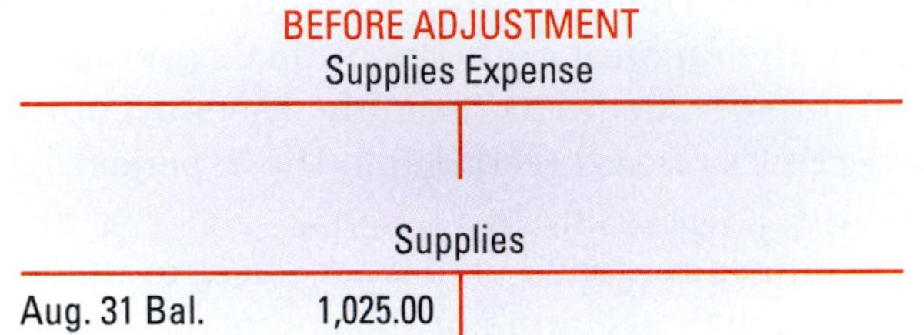

BEFORE ADJUSTMENT
Supplies Expense
Supplies
Aug. 31 Bal. 1,025.00

On August 31, Ms. Park counted the supplies on hand and found that the value of supplies still unused on that date was $310.00. The value of the supplies used is calculated as follows.

Supplies Account Balance, August 31	–	Supplies on Hand, August 31	=	Supplies Used During August
$1,025.00	–	$310.00	=	$715.00

Four questions are asked in analyzing the adjustment for the asset account, Supplies.

1. **What is the balance of Supplies?** *$1,025.00*
2. **What should the balance be for this account?** *$310.00*
3. **What must be done to correct the account balance?** *Decrease $715.00*
4. **What adjustment is made?**
   Debit Supplies Expense, *$715.00*
   Credit Supplies, *$715.00*

The expense account, Supplies Expense, is increased by a debit, $715.00, the value of supplies used. The balance of Supplies Expense, $715.00, is the value of supplies used during the fiscal period from August 1 to August 31. [*CONCEPT: Matching Expenses with Revenue*]

AFTER ADJUSTMENT

Supplies Expense

Debit		Credit	
Adj. (a)	715.00		

Supplies

Debit		Credit	
Aug. 31 Bal.	1,025.00	Adj. (a)	715.00
(New Bal.	*310.00)*		

The asset account, Supplies, is decreased by a credit, $715.00, the value of supplies used. The debit balance, $1,025.00, less the credit adjustment, $715.00, equals the new balance, $310.00. The new balance of Supplies is the same as the value of supplies on hand on August 31.

STEPS • STEPS • STEPS • STEPS • STEPS • STEPS • STEPS • STEPS • STEPS • STEPS

RECORDING THE SUPPLIES ADJUSTMENT ON A WORK SHEET

1. Write the debit amount, *$715.00*, in the work sheet's Adjustments Debit column on the line with the account title *Supplies Expense.*
2. Write the credit amount, *$715.00*, in the Adjustments Credit column on the line with the account title *Supplies.*
3. Label the two parts of this adjustment with a small letter *a* in parentheses, *(a)*. The letter *a* identifies the debit and credit amounts as part of the same adjustment.

PREPAID INSURANCE ADJUSTMENT ON A WORK SHEET

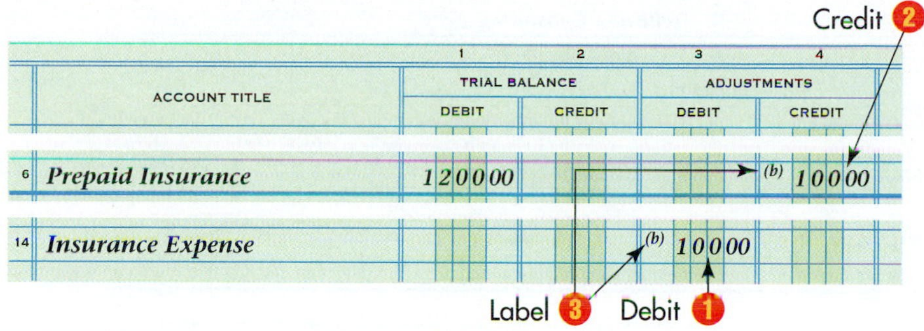

On August 31, before adjustments, the balance of Prepaid Insurance is $1,200.00 and the balance of Insurance Expense is zero.

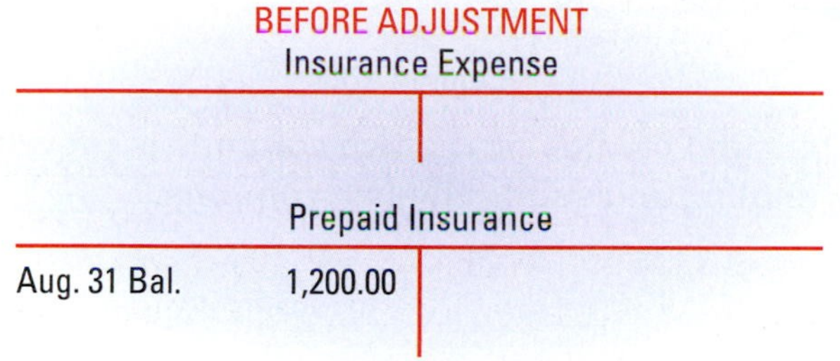

On August 31, Ms. Park checked the insurance records and found that the value of insurance coverage remaining was $1,100.00. The value of the insurance coverage used during the fiscal period is calculated as follows.

Prepaid Insurance Balance, August 31	−	Insurance Coverage Remaining Unused, August 31	=	Insurance Coverage Used During August
$1,200.00	−	$1,100.00	=	$100.00

Four questions are asked in analyzing the adjustment for the asset account, Prepaid Insurance.

1. **What is the balance of Prepaid Insurance?** *$1,200.00*
2. **What should the balance be for this account?** *$1,100.00*
3. **What must be done to correct the account balance?** *Decrease $100.00*
4. **What adjustment is made?**
   Debit Insurance Expense, *$100.00*
   Credit Prepaid Insurance, *$100.00*

The expense account, Insurance Expense, is increased by a debit, $100.00, the value of insurance used. The balance of Insurance Expense, $100.00, is the value of insurance coverage used from August 1 to August 31. [*CONCEPT: Matching Expenses with Revenue*]

AFTER ADJUSTMENT

Insurance Expense

Adj. (b) 100.00	

Prepaid Insurance

Aug. 31 Bal. 1,200.00 *(New Bal. 1,100.00)*	Adj. (b) 100.00

The asset account, Prepaid Insurance, is decreased by a credit, $100.00, the value of insurance used. The debit balance, $1,200.00, less the credit adjustment, $100.00, equals the new balance, $1,100.00. The new balance of Prepaid Insurance is the same as the amount of insurance coverage unused on August 31.

STEPS: RECORDING THE PREPAID INSURANCE ADJUSTMENT ON A WORK SHEET

1. Write the debit amount, *$100.00*, in the work sheet's Adjustments Debit column on the line with the account title *Insurance Expense*.
2. Write the credit amount, *$100.00*, in the Adjustments Credit column on the line with the account title *Prepaid Insurance*.
3. Label the two parts of this adjustment with a small letter *b* in parentheses, *(b)*. The letter *b* identifies the debit and credit amounts as part of the same adjustment.

PROVING THE ADJUSTMENTS COLUMNS OF A WORK SHEET

TechKnow Consulting
Work Sheet
For Month Ended August 31, 20--

	ACCOUNT TITLE	TRIAL BALANCE DEBIT (1)	TRIAL BALANCE CREDIT (2)	ADJUSTMENTS DEBIT (3)	ADJUSTMENTS CREDIT (4)
5	Supplies	1025 00			(a) 715 00
6	Prepaid Insurance	1200 00			(b) 100 00
14	Insurance Expense			(b) 100 00	
15	Miscellaneous Expense	28 00			
16	Rent Expense	300 00			
17	Supplies Expense			(a) 715 00	
18	Utilities Expense	110 00			
19		8815 00	8815 00	815 00	815 00

1. Single Rule
2. Totals
3. Double Rule

After all adjustments are recorded in a work sheet's Adjustments columns, the equality of debits and credits for the two columns is proved by totaling and ruling the two columns.

STEPS: PROVING THE ADJUSTMENTS COLUMNS OF A WORK SHEET

1. Rule a single line across the two Adjustments columns on the same line as the single line for the Trial Balance columns.
2. Add both the Adjustments Debit and Credit columns. If the two column totals are the same, then debits equal credits for these two columns, and the work sheet's Adjustments columns are in balance. Write each column's total below the single line. If the two Adjustments column totals are not the same, the Adjustments columns are rechecked and errors corrected before the work sheet is completed.
3. Rule double lines across both Adjustments columns. The double lines mean that the totals have been verified as correct.

global perspective

International Weights and Measures

The primary system of measurement in the United States is the customary system. Among the units of measurement in the customary system are inches, feet, and quarts. The United States is among the few major industrial countries that do not use the metric system exclusively. Among the units of measurement in the metric system are centimeters, meters, and liters. The metric system is based on a decimal system—like U.S. currency. Some U.S. industries have converted to the metric system. Others specify measurements in both customary and metric systems.

To conduct international business, the U.S. has recognized the need to convert customary units to the metric system. For example, beverages are routinely packaged in liter containers. Although the U.S. is a global business leader, it has had to adjust to meet the needs of the rest of the world.

Critical Thinking

1. Look at five food packages. List the weights and measures indicated.
2. List arguments both for and against a proposal to convert all U.S. weights and measures to the metric system.

SUMMARY OF PREPARATION OF A WORK SHEET FOR A SERVICE BUSINESS

The following overlay summarizes the preparation of a work sheet. Follow the directions below in using the overlay.

1. Before using the overlay, be sure the pages and transparent overlays are arranged correctly. The correct arrangement is shown below.

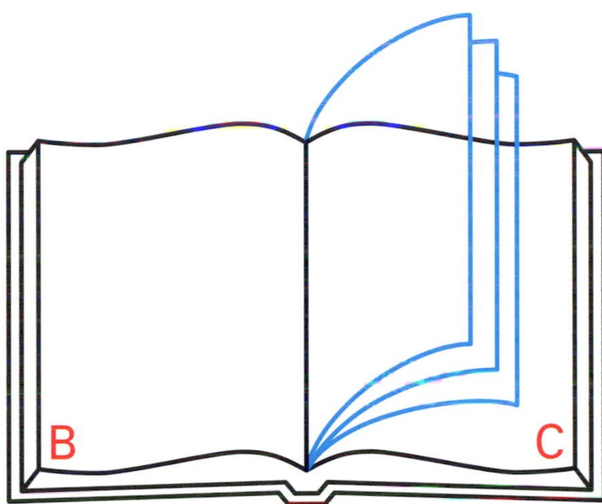

2. Place your book in a horizontal position. Study the steps on page C in preparing the work sheet. You will be able to read the text through the transparent overlays. When directed, carefully lift the transparent overlays and lay them over the work sheet as shown below.

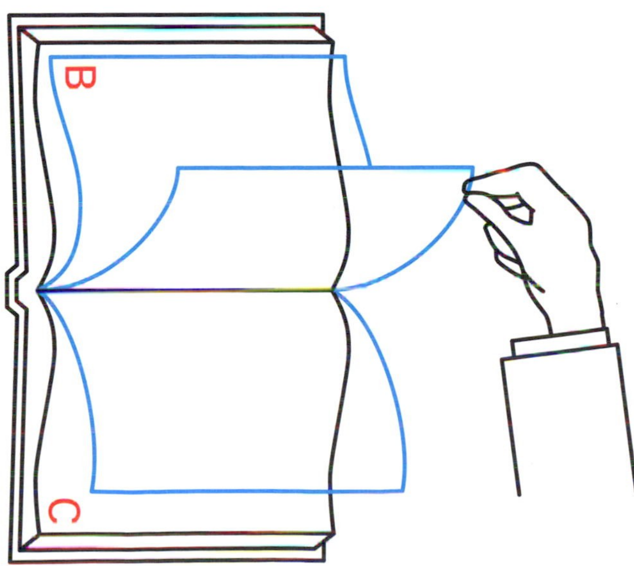

PREPARING A WORK SHEET

To correctly use the insert, read the steps on page C. Apply the transparent overlays when directed to do so in the steps.

TechKnow Consulting
Work Sheet
For Month Ended August 31, 20--

1

2

	ACCOUNT TITLE	TRIAL BALANCE (1)		ADJUSTMENTS (3)	(4)	INCOME STATEMENT (5)	(6)	BALANCE SHEET (7)	(8)	
		DEBIT	CREDIT	DEBIT	CREDIT	DEBIT	CREDIT	DEBIT	CREDIT	
1	Cash	4964 00								1
2	Petty Cash	100 00								2
3	Accts. Rec.—Oakdale School	150 00								3
4	Accts. Rec.—Campus Internet Cafe	100 00								4
5	Supplies	1025 00								5
6	Prepaid Insurance	1200 00								6
7	Accts. Pay.—Supply Depot		200 00							7
8	Accts. Pay.—Thomas Supply Co.		50 00							8
9	Kim Park, Capital		5000 00							9
10	Kim Park, Drawing	625 00								10
11	Income Summary									11
12	Sales		3565 00							12
13	Advertising Expense	213 00								13
14	Insurance Expense									14
15	Miscellaneous Expense	28 00								15
16	Rent Expense	300 00								16
17	Supplies Expense									17
18	Utilities Expense	110 00								18
19		8815 00	8815 00							19
20										20
21										21

making ethical decisions

Malpractice Liability of Accountants

Accountants are subject to the legal consequences of malpractice. They can be held financially liable for misconduct or improper practice in their profession.

Most lawsuits against public accountants involve audits of financial statements. Consider the following example. Best & Farrish, CPAs, audited the financial statements of Richmond, Inc. Relying on these statements, American Bank loaned $1,000,000 to Richmond. Unknown to the accountants, however, Richmond's president was involved in a scheme to steal cash. Richmond experienced financial difficulties and was unable to repay the loan to American Bank. The bank sued Best & Farrish for $1,000,000, claiming it was negligent for not detecting the president's fraud.

Should Best & Farrish be required to pay $1,000,000 to American Bank? Over many years, the courts have established four guidelines for determining whether accountants are liable for the financial losses of third parties.

1. *Financial loss.* Did the third party incur a financial loss? Answering this question is typically an easy task. American Bank lost $1,000,000 when Richmond did not repay its loan.
2. *Reliance on financial statements.* Did the third party actually rely on the financial statements for making its decision? Accountants should not be held liable unless the third party used the financial statements in making its decision. If American Bank received a copy of the financial statements but relied solely on other information obtained from Richmond's managers, then Best & Farrish should not be held liable for American Bank's loss.
3. *Level of negligence.* Accountants who fail to exhibit a reasonable level of care are guilty of ordinary negligence. Gross negligence occurs when an accountant's actions represent a flagrant violation of professional standards.

   Professional standards recognize that accountants are not able to detect all frauds. Whether Best & Farrish were negligent in not detecting the president's fraud would depend on the facts of the case.
4. *Accountant-third party relationship.* Accountants have a contract with their clients; a client can sue the accountant for breach of contract. However, third parties do not have a contract with the accountant. Whether a third party can sue the accountant depends on whether the accountant specifically knew the third party intended to use the financial statements.

   If Best & Farrish knew American Bank would use the audited financial statements to grant a loan, then American Bank could sue Best & Farrish for ordinary negligence. However, if Best & Farrish did not know Richmond even intended to obtain a bank loan, then gross negligence or fraud would need to be proven for American Bank to win its case.

Accountants must take great care in performing their professional services. Accountants who can prove the audit was performed in accordance with professional accounting standards will prevail against negligence lawsuits.

Instructions

Using your local library or online resources, locate an article describing a malpractice lawsuit against a public accounting firm. What were the main facts of this case? What is your opinion of the firm's liability?

PREPARING A WORK SHEET

1. Write the heading.
2. Record the trial balance.
   - Write the general ledger account titles in the Account Title column.
   - Write the account balances in either the Trial Balance Debit or Credit column.
   - Rule a single line across the Trial Balance columns.
   - Add the Trial Balance columns and compare the totals.
   - Rule double lines across both Trial Balance columns.
   - *Carefully apply the first overlay.*
3. Record the supplies adjustment.
   - Write the debit amount in the Adjustments Debit column on the line with the account title Supplies Expense.
   - Write the credit amount in the Adjustments Credit column on the line with the account title Supplies.
   - Label this adjustment *(a)*.
4. Record the prepaid insurance adjustment.
   - Write the debit amount in the Adjustments Debit column on the line with the account title Insurance Expense.
   - Write the credit amount in the Adjustments Credit column on the line with the account title Prepaid Insurance.
   - Label this adjustment *(b)*.
5. Prove the Adjustments columns.
   - Rule a single line across the Adjustments columns.
   - Add the Adjustments columns and compare the totals to ensure that they are equal.
   - Write the proving totals below the single line.
   - Rule double lines across both Adjustments columns.
   - *Carefully apply the second overlay.*
6. Extend all balance sheet account balances.
   - Extend the up-to-date asset account balances to the Balance Sheet Debit column.
   - Extend the up-to-date liability account balances to the Balance Sheet Credit column.
   - Extend the owner's capital and drawing account balances to the Balance Sheet columns.
7. Extend all income statement account balances.
   - Extend the up-to-date revenue account balance to the Income Statement Credit column.
   - Extend the up-to-date expense account balances to the Income Statement Debit column.
   - *Carefully apply the third overlay.*
8. Calculate and record the net income (or net loss).
   - Rule a single line across the Income Statement and Balance Sheet columns.
   - Add the columns and write the totals below the single line.
   - Calculate the net income or net loss amount.
   - Write the amount of net income (or net loss) below the smaller of the two Income Statement column totals. Write the words *Net Income* or *Net Loss* in the Account Title column.
   - Extend the amount of net income (or net loss) to the Balance Sheet columns. Write the amount under the smaller of the two column totals. Write the amount on the same line as the words *Net Income* (or *Net Loss*).
9. Total and rule the Income Statement and Balance Sheet columns.
   - Rule a single line across the Income Statement and Balance Sheet columns immediately below the net income (or net loss) amounts.
   - Add the net income (or net loss) to the previous column totals. Compare the column totals to ensure that totals for each pair of columns are in balance.
   - Write the proving totals for each column below the single line.
   - Rule double lines across the Income Statement and Balance Sheet columns immediately below the proving totals.

1150
1938

C

term review

adjustments

audit your understanding

1. Explain how the concept of Matching Expenses with Revenue relates to adjustments.
2. List the four questions asked in analyzing an adjustment on a work sheet.

work together 6-2

Planning adjustments on a work sheet

Use the work sheet from Work Together 6-1. Your instructor will guide you through the following examples.

1. Analyze the following adjustment information into debit and credit parts. Record the adjustments on the work sheet.

Adjustment Information, February 28	
Supplies on hand	$325.00
Value of prepaid insurance	500.00

2. Total and rule the Adjustments columns. Save your work sheet to complete Work Together 6-3.

on your own 6-2

Planning adjustments on a work sheet

Use the work sheet from On Your Own 6-1. Work these problems independently.

1. Analyze the following adjustment information into debit and credit parts. Record the adjustments on the work sheet.

Adjustment Information, December 31	
Supplies on hand	$120.00
Value of prepaid insurance	225.00

2. Total and rule the Adjustments columns. Save your work sheet to complete On Your Own 6-3.

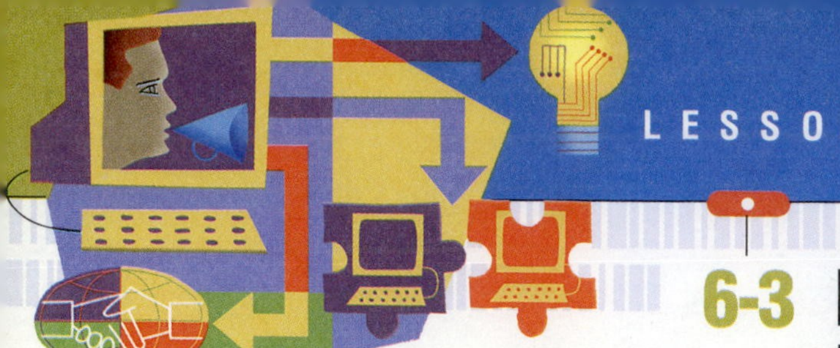

LESSON

6-3 Extending Financial Statement Information on a Work Sheet

EXTENDING BALANCE SHEET ACCOUNT BALANCES ON A WORK SHEET

TechKnow Consulting
Work Sheet
For Month Ended August 31, 20--

		1	2	3	4	5	6	7	8	
	ACCOUNT TITLE	TRIAL BALANCE		ADJUSTMENTS		INCOME STATEMENT		BALANCE SHEET		
		DEBIT	CREDIT	DEBIT	CREDIT	DEBIT	CREDIT	DEBIT	CREDIT	
1	*Cash*	4964 00						4964 00		1
2	*Petty Cash*	100 00						100 00		2
3	*Accts. Rec.—Oakdale School*	150 00						150 00		3
4	*Accts. Rec.—Campus Internet Cafe*	100 00						100 00		4
5	*Supplies*	1025 00			(a) 715 00			310 00		5
6	*Prepaid Insurance*	1200 00			(b) 100 00			1100 00		6
7	*Accts. Pay.—Supply Depot*		200 00						200 00	7
8	*Accts. Pay.—Thomas Supply Co.*		50 00						50 00	8
9	*Kim Park, Capital*		5000 00						5000 00	9
10	*Kim Park, Drawing*	625 00						625 00		10

1

Debit Balances with Adjustments 2

Credit Balances without Adjustments 3

At the end of each fiscal period, TechKnow Consulting prepares two financial statements from information on a work sheet. [*CONCEPT: Accounting Period Cycle*] The up-to-date account balances on a work sheet are extended to columns for the two financial statements.

A financial statement that reports assets, liabilities, and owner's equity on a specific date is called a **balance sheet**. The balance sheet accounts are the asset, liability, and owner's equity accounts. Up-to-date balance sheet account balances are extended to the Balance Sheet Debit and Credit columns of the work sheet.

STEPS

EXTENDING BALANCE SHEET ACCOUNT BALANCES ON A WORK SHEET

1. Extend the balance of *Cash, $4,964.00,* to the Balance Sheet Debit column. The balance of *Cash* in the Trial Balance Debit column is up-to-date because no adjustment affects this account. Extend to the Balance Sheet Debit column the balances of all accounts with debit balances that are not affected by adjustments.

2. Calculate the up-to-date adjusted balance of *Supplies*. The balance of *Supplies* in the Trial Balance Debit column is not up-to-date because it is affected by an adjustment. The debit balance, $1,025.00, minus the credit adjustment, $715.00, equals the up-to-date adjusted balance, $310.00. Extend the up-to-date balance, *$310.00,* to the Balance Sheet Debit column. Using the same procedure, calculate and extend the up-to-date adjusted balance of the other asset account affected by an adjustment, *Prepaid Insurance*.

3. Extend the up-to-date balance of *Accounts Payable—Supply Depot, $200.00,* to the Balance Sheet Credit column. The balance of *Accounts Payable—Supply Depot* in the Trial Balance Credit column is up-to-date because no adjustment affects this account. Extend to the Balance Sheet Credit column the balances of all accounts with credit balances that are not affected by adjustments.

EXTENDING INCOME STATEMENT ACCOUNT BALANCES ON A WORK SHEET

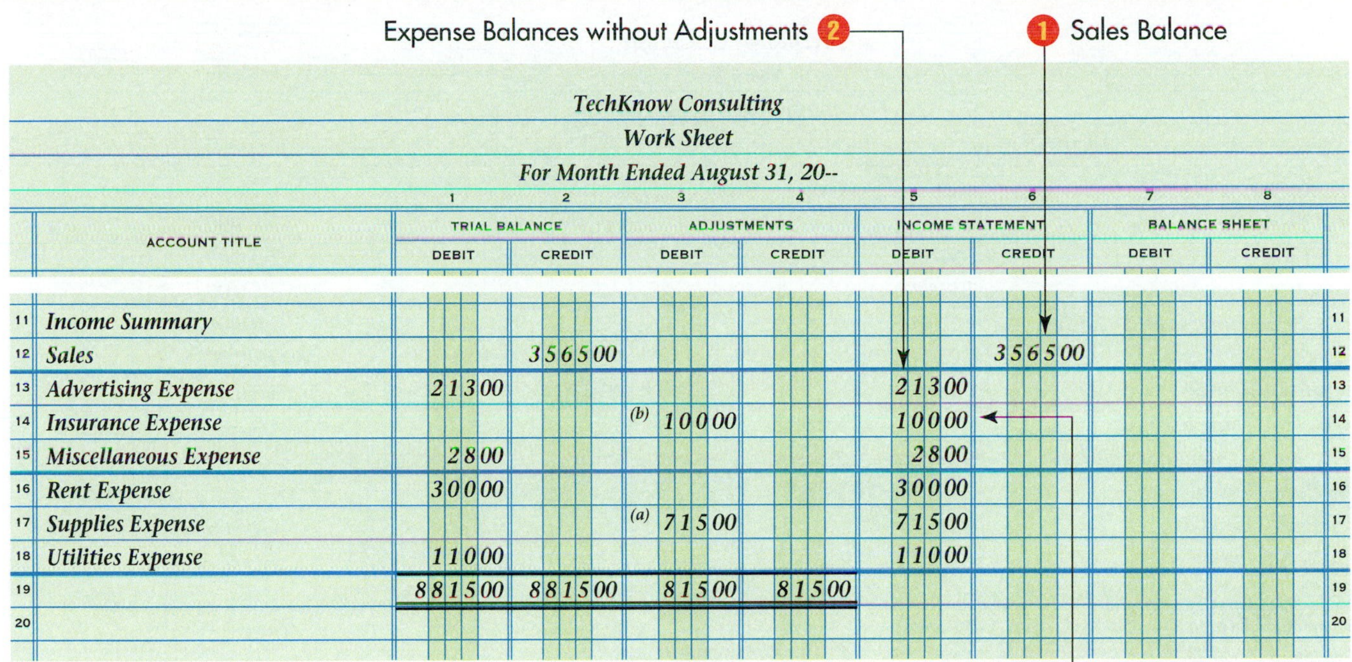

TechKnow Consulting
Work Sheet
For Month Ended August 31, 20--

	ACCOUNT TITLE	1 TRIAL BALANCE DEBIT	2 TRIAL BALANCE CREDIT	3 ADJUSTMENTS DEBIT	4 ADJUSTMENTS CREDIT	5 INCOME STATEMENT DEBIT	6 INCOME STATEMENT CREDIT	7 BALANCE SHEET DEBIT	8 BALANCE SHEET CREDIT	
11	Income Summary									11
12	Sales		3565 00				3565 00			12
13	Advertising Expense	213 00				213 00				13
14	Insurance Expense			(b) 100 00		100 00				14
15	Miscellaneous Expense	28 00				28 00				15
16	Rent Expense	300 00				300 00				16
17	Supplies Expense			(a) 715 00		715 00				17
18	Utilities Expense	110 00				110 00				18
19		8815 00	8815 00	815 00	815 00					19
20										20

Expense Balances with Adjustments 3

A financial statement showing the revenue and expenses for a fiscal period is called an **income statement**. TechKnow Consulting's income statement accounts are the revenue and expense accounts. Up-to-date income statement account balances are extended to the Income Statement Debit and Credit columns of the work sheet.

Use a ruler when extending amounts on a work sheet to keep track of the line you are on.

STEPS
EXTENDING INCOME STATEMENT ACCOUNT BALANCES ON A WORK SHEET

1. Extend the balance of *Sales*, *$3,565.00*, to the Income Statement Credit column. The balance of *Sales* in the Trial Balance Credit column is up-to-date because no adjustment affects this account.
2. Extend the balance of *Advertising Expense*, *$213.00*, to the Income Statement Debit column. The balance of *Advertising Expense* is up-to-date because no adjustment affects this account. Extend the balances of all expense accounts not affected by adjustments to the Income Statement Debit column.
3. Calculate the up-to-date adjusted balance of *Insurance Expense*. The balance of *Insurance Expense* in the Trial Balance Debit column is zero. This zero balance is not up-to-date because this account is affected by an adjustment. The debit balance, $0.00, plus the debit adjustment, $100.00, equals the adjusted balance, $100.00. Extend the up-to-date adjusted debit balance, *$100.00*, to the Income Statement Debit column. Using the same procedure, calculate and extend the up-to-date adjusted balance of each expense account affected by an adjustment.

FYI FOR YOUR INFORMATION

A work sheet is prepared in manual accounting to adjust the accounts and sort amounts needed to prepare financial statements. However, in automated accounting, adjustments are prepared from the trial balance, and the software automatically generates the financial statements with no need for a work sheet.

RECORDING NET INCOME, AND TOTALING AND RULING A WORK SHEET

TechKnow Consulting
Work Sheet
For Month Ended August 31, 20--

	ACCOUNT TITLE	1 TRIAL BALANCE DEBIT	2 TRIAL BALANCE CREDIT	3 ADJUSTMENTS DEBIT	4 ADJUSTMENTS CREDIT	5 INCOME STATEMENT DEBIT	6 INCOME STATEMENT CREDIT	7 BALANCE SHEET DEBIT	8 BALANCE SHEET CREDIT	
1	Cash	4964 00						4964 00		1
2	Petty Cash	100 00						100 00		2
3	Accts. Rec.—Oakdale School	150 00						150 00		3
4	Accts. Rec.—Campus Internet Cafe	100 00						100 00		4
5	Supplies	1025 00			(a) 715 00			310 00		5
6	Prepaid Insurance	1200 00			(b) 100 00			1100 00		6
7	Accts. Pay.—Supply Depot		200 00						200 00	7
8	Accts. Pay.—Thomas Supply Co.		50 00						50 00	8
9	Kim Park, Capital		5000 00						5000 00	9
10	Kim Park, Drawing	625 00						625 00		10
11	Income Summary									11
12	Sales		3565 00				3565 00			12
13	Advertising Expense	213 00				213 00				13
14	Insurance Expense			(b) 100 00		100 00				14
15	Miscellaneous Expense	28 00				28 00				15
16	Rent Expense	300 00				300 00				16
17	Supplies Expense			(a) 715 00		715 00				17
18	Utilities Expense	110 00				110 00				18
19		8815 00	8815 00	815 00	815 00	1466 00	3565 00	7349 00	5250 00	19
20	Net Income					2099 00			2099 00	20
21						3565 00	3565 00	7349 00	7349 00	21

Single Rule 1
Totals 2
Net Income 3
Extend Net Income 4
Single Rule 5
Totals 6
Double Rule 7

The difference between total revenue and total expenses when total revenue is greater is called **net income**. Before the work sheet is complete, net income must be calculated and the work sheet must be totaled and ruled. A summary of preparing a work sheet is shown on the Work Sheet Overlay.

STEPS • STEPS • STEPS • STEPS • STEPS • STEPS • STEPS • STEPS • STEPS • STEPS •

CALCULATING AND RECORDING NET INCOME ON A WORK SHEET; TOTALING AND RULING A WORK SHEET

1. Rule a single line across the four income statement and balance sheet columns.
2. Add both the Income Statement and Balance Sheet columns. Write the totals below the single line.
3. Calculate the net income. The Income Statement Credit column total, \$3,565.00, minus the Income Statement Debit column total, \$1,466.00, equals net income, \$2,099.00. Write the amount of net income, *\$2,099.00*, below the Income Statement Debit column total. Write the words *Net Income* on the same line in the Account Title column.
4. Extend the amount of net income, *\$2,099.00*, to the Balance Sheet Credit column. Since the owner's equity account, *Kim Park, Capital*, increases by a credit, extend the net income amount to the Balance Sheet Credit column.
5. Rule a single line across the four Income Statement and Balance Sheet columns just below the net income amounts.
6. Add the subtotal and net income amount for each column to get proving totals for the Income Statement and Balance Sheet columns. Write the totals below the single line. Check the equality for each pair of columns.
7. Rule double lines across the Income Statement and Balance Sheet columns.

CALCULATING AND RECORDING A NET LOSS ON A WORK SHEET

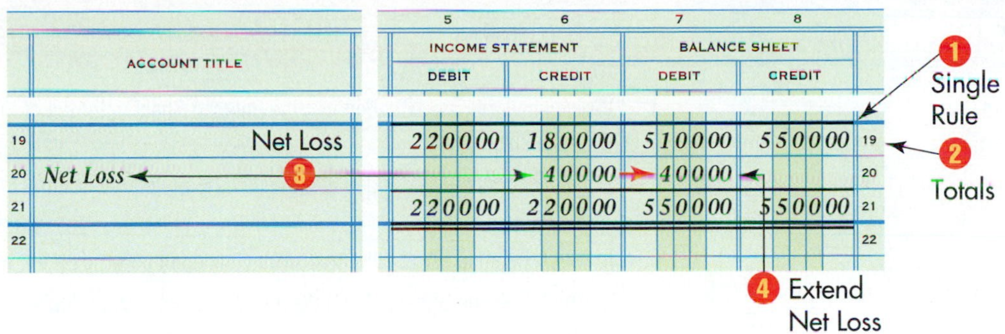

	ACCOUNT TITLE	5 INCOME STATEMENT DEBIT	6 INCOME STATEMENT CREDIT	7 BALANCE SHEET DEBIT	8 BALANCE SHEET CREDIT	
19	Net Loss	220000	180000	510000	550000	19
20	*Net Loss*		40000	40000		20
21		220000	220000	550000	550000	21
22						22

TechKnow Consulting's completed work sheet shows a net income. However, a business might have a net loss to report. The difference between total revenue and total expenses when total expenses are greater is called a **net loss**.

STEPS: CALCULATING AND RECORDING A NET LOSS ON A WORK SHEET

1. Rule a single line across the four Income Statement and Balance Sheet columns.
2. Add both the Income Statement and Balance Sheet columns. Write the totals below the single line.
3. Calculate the net loss. The Income Statement Debit column total, $2,200.00, minus the Income Statement Credit column total, $1,800.00, equals net loss, $400.00. The Income Statement Debit column total (expenses) is greater than the Income Statement Credit column total (revenue). Therefore, because expenses exceed revenue, there is a net loss. Write the amount of net loss, *$400.00*, below the Income Statement Credit column total. Write the words *Net Loss* on the same line in the Account Title column.
4. Extend the amount of net loss, *$400.00*, to the Balance Sheet Debit column on the same line as the words *Net Loss*. The owner's equity account, *Kim Park, Capital*, is decreased by a debit. Therefore, a net loss is extended to the Balance Sheet Debit column.

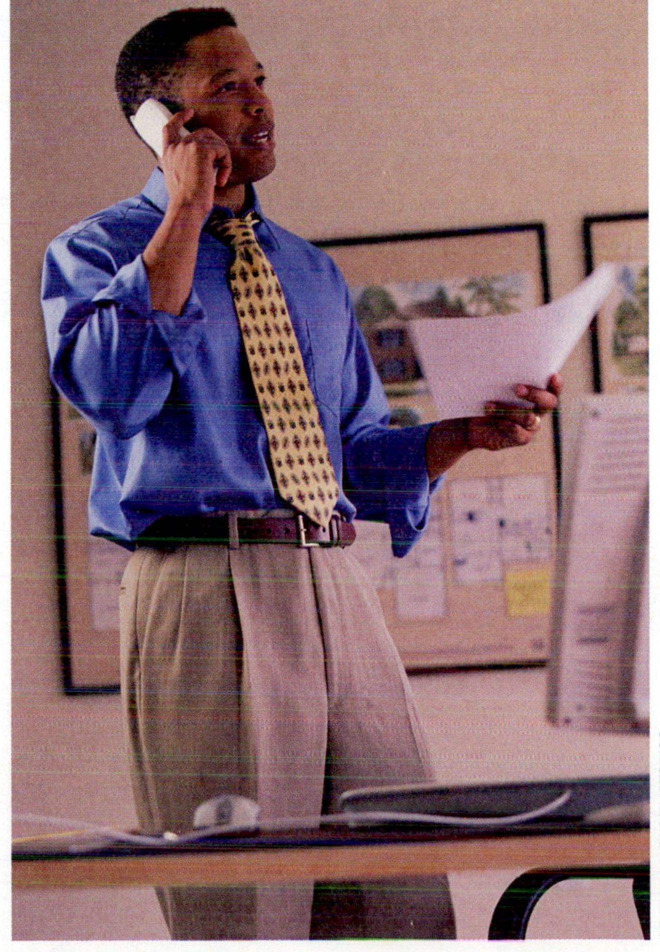

©GETTY IMAGES/PHOTODISC

terms review

balance sheet
income statement
net income
net loss

TERMS REVIEW • TERMS

audit your understanding

1. Which accounts are extended into the Balance Sheet columns of the work sheet?
2. Which accounts are extended into the Income Statement columns of the work sheet?
3. In which Balance Sheet column do you record net income on the work sheet?
4. In which Balance Sheet column do you record net loss on the work sheet?

AUDIT YOUR UNDERSTANDING

work together 6-3

Completing a work sheet

Use the work sheet from Work Together 6-2. Your instructor will guide you through the following examples.

1. Extend the up-to-date balances to the Balance Sheet and Income Statement columns.
2. Rule a single line across the Income Statement and Balance Sheet columns. Total each column. Calculate and record the net income or net loss. Label the amount in the Account Title column.
3. Total and rule the Income Statement and Balance Sheet columns.

WORK TOGETHER • WORK

on your own 6-3

Completing a work sheet

Use the work sheet from On Your Own 6-2. Work these problems independently.

1. Extend the up-to-date balances to the Balance Sheet or Income Statement columns.
2. Rule a single line across the Income Statement and Balance Sheet columns. Total each column. Calculate and record the net income or net loss. Label the amount in the Account Title column.
3. Total and rule the Income Statement and Balance Sheet columns.

ON YOUR OWN • ON YOUR OWN

LESSON • LESSON • LESSON • LESSON • LESSON • LESSON

6-4 Finding and Correcting Errors on the Work Sheet

CORRECTING ACCOUNTING ERRORS ON THE WORK SHEET

Some errors in accounting records are not discovered until a work sheet is prepared. For example, a debit to supplies may not have been posted from a journal to the general ledger supplies account. The omission may not be discovered until the work sheet's trial balance does not balance. Also, information may be transferred incorrectly from general ledger accounts to the work sheet's trial balance. Additional errors may be made, such as recording adjustment information incorrectly or adding columns incorrectly. In addition, errors may be made in extending amounts to the Income Statement and Balance Sheet columns.

Any errors found on a work sheet must be corrected before any further work is completed. If an incorrect amount is found on a work sheet, erase the error and replace it with the correct amount. If an amount is written in an incorrect column, erase the amount and record it in the correct column.

CHECKING FOR TYPICAL CALCULATION ERRORS

When two column totals are not in balance, subtract the smaller total from the larger total to find the difference. Check the difference between the two amounts against the following guides.

1. **The difference is 1, such as $.01, $.10, $1.00, or $10.00.** For example, if the totals of the two columns are Debit, $14,657.00, and Credit, $14,658.00, the difference between the two columns is $1.00. The error is most likely in addition. Add the columns again.
2. **The difference can be divided evenly by 2.** For example, the difference between two column totals is $48.00, which can be divided by 2 with no remainder. Look for a $24.00 amount in the Trial Balance columns of the work sheet. If the amount is found, check to make sure it has been recorded in the correct Debit or Credit column. A $24.00 debit amount recorded in a credit column results in a difference between column totals of $48.00. If the error is not found on the work sheet, check the general ledger accounts and journal entries. An entry for $24.00 may have been recorded in an incorrect column in the journal or in an account.
3. **The difference can be divided evenly by 9.** For example, the difference between two columns is $45.00, which can be divided by 9 with no remainder. When the difference can be divided equally by 9, look for transposed numbers such as 54 written as 45 or 19 written as 91. Also, check for a "slide." A "slide" occurs when numbers are moved to the right or left in an amount column. For example, $12.00 is recorded as $120.00 or $350.00 is recorded as $35.00.
4. **The difference is an omitted amount.** Look for an amount equal to the difference. If the difference is $50.00, look for an account balance of $50.00 that has not been extended. Look for any $50.00 amount on the work sheet and determine if it has been handled correctly. Look in the accounts and journals for a $50.00 amount, and check if that amount has been handled correctly. Failure to record a $50.00 account balance will make a work sheet's column totals differ by $50.00.

CHECKING FOR ERRORS IN THE WORK SHEET

Check for Errors in the Trial Balance Column

1. Have all general ledger account balances been copied in the trial balance column correctly?
2. Have all general ledger account balances been recorded in the correct Trial Balance column?

Check for Errors in the Adjustments Columns

1. Do the debits equal the credits for each adjustment? Use the small letters that label each part of an adjustment to help check accuracy and equality of debits and credits.
2. Is the amount for each adjustment correct?

Check for Errors in the Income Statement and Balance Sheet Columns

1. Has each amount been copied correctly when extended to the Income Statement or Balance Sheet column?
2. Has each account balance been extended to the correct Income Statement or Balance Sheet column?
3. Has the net income or net loss been calculated correctly?
4. Has the net income or net loss been recorded in the correct Income Statement or Balance Sheet column?

For all three of these cases, correct any errors found and add the columns again.

CORRECTING AN ERROR IN POSTING TO THE WRONG ACCOUNT

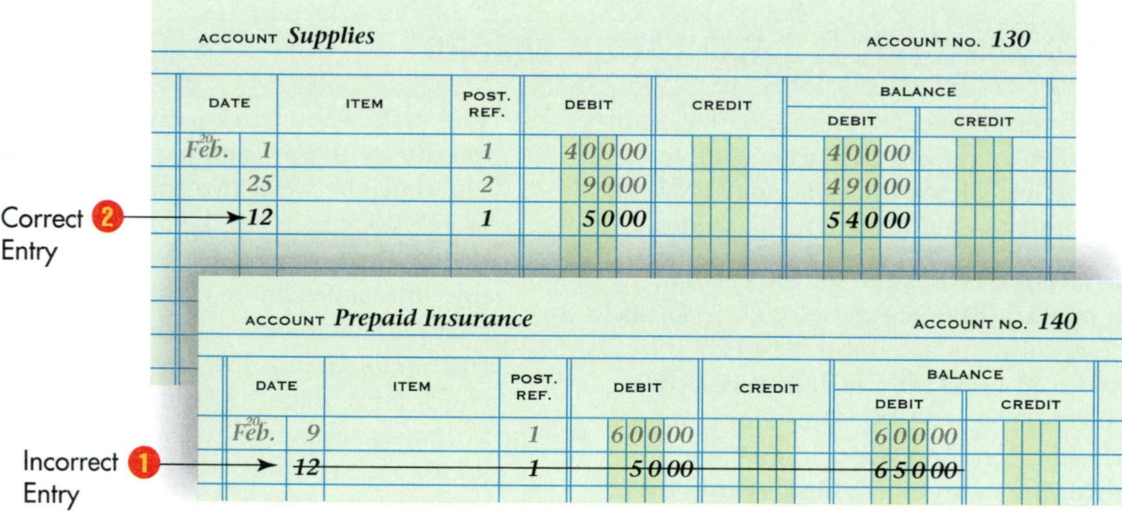

ACCOUNT *Supplies* ACCOUNT NO. *130*

DATE		ITEM	POST. REF.	DEBIT	CREDIT	BALANCE DEBIT	BALANCE CREDIT
20-- Feb.	1		1	400 00		400 00	
	25		2	90 00		490 00	
	12		1	50 00		540 00	

ACCOUNT *Prepaid Insurance* ACCOUNT NO. *140*

DATE		ITEM	POST. REF.	DEBIT	CREDIT	BALANCE DEBIT	BALANCE CREDIT
20-- Feb.	9		1	600 00		600 00	
	~~12~~		~~1~~	~~50 00~~		~~650 00~~	

If a pair of work sheet columns does not balance and an error cannot be found on the work sheet, look for an error in posting from the journal to the general ledger accounts.

As each item in an account or a journal entry is verified, a check mark should be placed next to it. The check mark indicates that the item has been checked for accuracy.

1. Have all amounts that need to be posted actually been posted from the journal? To correct, complete the posting to the correct account. When posting is corrected, recalculate the account balance and correct it on the work sheet.
2. Have all amounts been posted to the correct accounts? To correct, follow these steps.

STEPS STEPS • STEPS • STEPS • STEPS

CORRECTING AN ERROR IN POSTING TO THE WRONG ACCOUNT

1. Draw a line through the entire incorrect entry. Recalculate the account balance and correct the work sheet.
2. Record the posting in the correct account. Recalculate the account balance, and correct the work sheet.

CORRECTING AN INCORRECT AMOUNT AND AN AMOUNT POSTED TO THE WRONG COLUMN

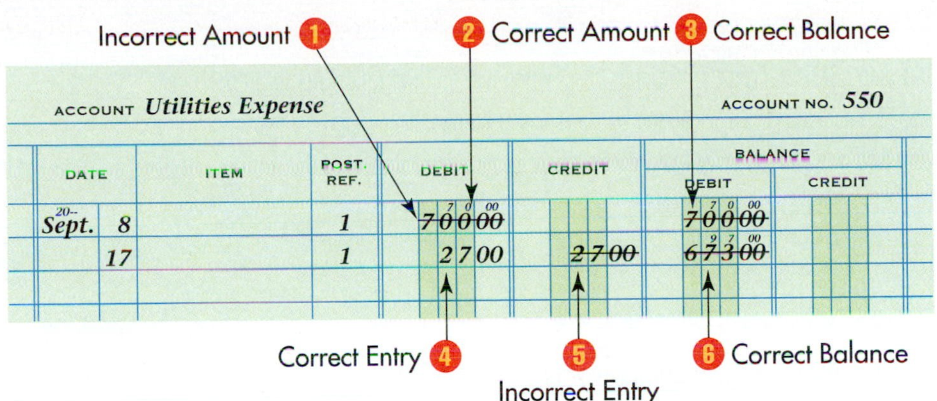

Errors can be made in writing amounts in general ledger accounts. Errors in permanent records should never be erased. Erasures in permanent records raise questions about whether important financial information has been altered.

STEPS

CORRECTING AN INCORRECT AMOUNT

1. Draw a line through the incorrect amount.
2. Write the correct amount just above the correction in the same space.
3. Recalculate the account balance, and correct the account balance on the work sheet.

CORRECTING AN AMOUNT POSTED TO THE WRONG COLUMN

4. Draw a line through the incorrect item in the account.
5. Record the posting in the correct amount column.
6. Recalculate the account balance, and correct the work sheet.

CHECKING FOR ERRORS IN JOURNAL ENTRIES

1. Do debits equal credits in each journal entry?
2. Is each journal entry amount recorded in the correct journal column?
3. Is information in the Account Title column correct for each journal entry?
4. Are all of the journal amount column totals correct?
5. Does the sum of debit column totals equal the sum of credit column totals in the journal?
6. Have all transactions been recorded?

Some suggestions for correcting errors in journal entries are described in Chapter 3.

PREVENTING ERRORS

The best way to prevent errors is to work carefully. Check the work at each step in an accounting procedure. Most errors occur in doing arithmetic, especially in adding columns. When possible, use a calculator. When an error is discovered, do no more work until the cause of the error is found and corrections are made.

Xtra! Study Tools
accountingxtra.swlearning.com

• audit your understanding

1. What is the first step in checking for arithmetic errors when two column totals are not in balance?
2. What is one way to check for an error caused by transposed numbers?
3. What term is used to describe an error that occurs when numbers are moved to the right or left in an amount column?

AUDIT YOUR

• work together 6-4

Finding and correcting errors in accounting records

Paul Coty has completed the September monthly work sheet for his business, LeafyLift. The work sheet and general ledger accounts are given in the *Working Papers.* Mr. Coty believes that he has made one or more errors in preparing the work sheet. He asks you to help him verify the work sheet. Your instructor will guide you through the following examples.

1. Examine the work sheet and the general ledger accounts. Make a list of the errors you find.
2. Correct any errors you find in the general ledger accounts.
3. Prepare a corrected work sheet.

WORK TOGETHER • WORK

• on your own 6-4

Finding and correcting errors in accounting records

Nadine Fritz has completed the November monthly work sheet for her business, Your Personal Trainer. The work sheet and general ledger accounts are given in the *Working Papers.* Ms. Fritz believes that she has made one or more errors in preparing the work sheet. She asks you to help her verify the work sheet. Work these problems independently.

1. Examine the work sheet and the general ledger accounts. Make a list of the errors you find.
2. Correct any errors you find in the general ledger accounts.
3. Prepare a corrected work sheet.

ON YOUR OWN • ON YOUR OWN

SUMMARY

After completing this chapter, you can

1. Define important accounting terms related to a work sheet for a service business organized as a proprietorship.
2. Identify accounting concepts and practices related to a work sheet for a service business organized as a proprietorship.
3. Prepare a heading and a trial balance on a work sheet.
4. Plan adjustments for supplies and prepaid insurance.
5. Complete a work sheet for a service business organized as a proprietorship.
6. Identify selected procedures for finding and correcting errors in accounting records.

Explore Accounting

Fiscal Periods

A fiscal period is the length of time for which a business summarizes and reports financial information. Since many companies are required to publish yearly annual reports, these companies choose a year for the fiscal period. In such a case, a company will prepare financial statements every year.

A fiscal year can be any consecutive 12-month period. The Internal Revenue Service (IRS) requires many companies to report taxable income for the fiscal year January 1 through December 31. A fiscal year beginning January 1 can also be called a calendar year. Because they use a calendar year for reporting taxable income, many companies choose to use the calendar year for issuing financial statements also.

However, there is no requirement to begin a fiscal year on January 1. Companies often choose a fiscal year that ends during a period of low business activity. Twelve consecutive months which end when business activities have reached the lowest point in their annual cycle are called a natural business year.

The following survey conducted on 600 businesses shows the number of companies that chose a fiscal year ending at the end of a specific month.

Fiscal Year End	No. of Companies
January	32
February	10
March	16
April	8
May	18
June	48
July	8
August	15
September	38
October	19
November	15
December	373

Activity: Assume you work for a company that makes snowmobiles. You must determine what fiscal year should be used. Make a written recommendation to the owner. Explain why your recommendation is preferable.

Source: *Accounting Trends and Techniques*, 2002, published by the American Institute of Certified Public Accountants.

6-1 APPLICATION PROBLEM EXCEL

Recording the trial balance on a work sheet

Use the work sheet given in the *Working Papers*. On June 30 of the current year, Roseville Rental has the following general ledger accounts and balances. The business uses a monthly fiscal period.

Account Titles	Account Balances	
	Debit	Credit
Cash	$11,620.00	
Petty Cash	100.00	
Accounts Receivable—Leslie Naples	855.00	
Supplies	690.00	
Prepaid Insurance	900.00	
Accounts Payable—Russell Goodland		$ 355.00
Sunthi Ling, Capital		12,926.00
Sunthi Ling, Drawing	500.00	
Income Summary		
Sales		2,270.00
Advertising Expense	340.00	
Insurance Expense		
Miscellaneous Expense	184.00	
Supplies Expense		
Utilities Expense	362.00	

Instructions:

Prepare the heading and trial balance on a work sheet. Total and rule the Trial Balance columns. Save your work to complete Application Problem 6-2.

6-2 APPLICATION PROBLEM AUTOMATED ACCOUNTING

Planning adjustments on a work sheet

Use the work sheet from Application Problem 6-1.

Instructions:

1. Analyze the following adjustment information into debit and credit parts. Record the adjustments on the work sheet.

   Adjustment Information, June 30

Supplies on hand	$250.00
Value of prepaid insurance	750.00

2. Total and rule the Adjustments columns. Save your work to complete Application Problem 6-3.

6-3 APPLICATION PROBLEM

Completing a work sheet

Use the work sheet from Application Problem 6-2.

Instructions:

1. Extend the up-to-date balances to the Balance Sheet or Income Statement columns.
2. Rule a single line across the Income Statement and Balance Sheet columns. Total each column. Calculate and record the net income or net loss. Label the amount in the Account Title column.
3. Total and rule the Income Statement and Balance Sheet columns.

6-4 APPLICATION PROBLEM

Finding and correcting errors in accounting records

Ervin Watkins has completed the April monthly work sheet for his business, EverClean. The work sheet and general ledger accounts are given in the *Working Papers*. Mr. Watkins believes that he has made one or more errors in preparing the work sheet. He asks you to help him verify the work sheet.

Instructions:

1. Examine the work sheet and the general ledger accounts. Make a list of the errors you find.
2. Correct any errors you find in the general ledger accounts.
3. Prepare a corrected work sheet.

6-5 MASTERY PROBLEM

AUTOMATED ACCOUNTING PEACHTREE QUICKBOOKS EXCEL

Completing a work sheet

On April 30 of the current year, Bonita Bubbles has the following general ledger accounts and balances. The business uses a monthly fiscal period. A work sheet is given in the *Working Papers*.

Account Titles	Account Balances	
	Debit	Credit
Cash	$2,829.00	
Petty Cash	150.00	
Accounts Receivable—Bernard Corbett	511.00	
Supplies	855.00	
Prepaid Insurance	1,100.00	
Accounts Payable—Spooner Supplies		$ 500.00
Paulo Gutierrez, Capital		4,500.00
Paulo Gutierrez, Drawing	440.00	
Income Summary		
Sales		2,400.00
Advertising Expense	450.00	
Insurance Expense		
Miscellaneous Expense	190.00	
Rent Expense	375.00	
Supplies Expense		
Utilities Expense	500.00	

Instructions:

1. Prepare the heading and trial balance on a work sheet. Total and rule the Trial Balance columns.
2. Analyze the following adjustment information into debit and credit parts. Record the adjustments on the work sheet.

Adjustment Information, April 30

Supplies inventory	$220.00
Value of prepaid insurance	800.00

3. Total and rule the Adjustments columns.
4. Extend the up-to-date balances to the Balance Sheet or Income Statement columns.
5. Rule a single line across the Income Statement and Balance Sheet columns. Total each column. Calculate and record the net income or net loss. Label the amount in the Account Title column.
6. Total and rule the Income Statement and Balance Sheet columns.

6-6 CHALLENGE PROBLEM

Completing a work sheet

LawnPro Company had a small fire in its office. The fire destroyed some of the accounting records. On November 30 of the current year, the end of a monthly fiscal period, the following information was constructed from the remaining records and other sources. A work sheet is given in the *Working Papers*.

Remains of the general ledger:

Account Titles	Account Balances
Accounts Receivable—C. Gabriel	$ 825.00
Supplies	700.00
Don Arnodt, Drawing	300.00
Sales	3,800.00
Advertising Expense	200.00
Rent Expense	600.00
Utilities Expense	390.00

Information from the business's checkbook:	
Cash balance on last unused check stub	$3,119.00
Total payments for miscellaneous expense	50.00
Total payments for insurance	400.00
Information obtained through inquiries to other businesses:	
Owed to St. Croix Supplies	$1,500.00
Value of prepaid insurance, November 30	250.00
Information obtained by counting supplies on hand after the fire:	
Supplies on hand	$200.00

Instructions:

1. From the information given, prepare a heading and reconstruct a trial balance on a work sheet. The owner's capital account balance is the difference between the total of all debit account balances minus the total of all credit account balances.
2. Complete the work sheet.

applied communication

Accounting information is used by managers to make business decisions. But exactly what kind of decisions does the owner of a local business make? How does accounting information enable the manager to make better decisions?

Instructions: Identify a local business of personal interest to you. Write five questions you would ask the manager to learn how that person uses accounting information to make decisions. Interview the manager and write a one- or two-page summary of the interview.

APPLIED COMMUNICATION

cases for critical thinking

Case 1

Peter Dowther owns a small business. At the end of a fiscal period, he does not make an adjustment for supplies. Are Mr. Dowther's accounting procedures correct? What effect will Mr. Dowther's procedures have on the business's financial reporting? Explain your answer.

Case 2

When posting amounts from a journal to general ledger accounts, a $10.00 debit to Supplies is mistakenly posted as a credit to Utilities Expense. Will this error be discovered when the work sheet is prepared? Explain.

CASES FOR CRITICAL THINKING

SCANS workplace competency

Basic Skill: Arithmetic/Mathematics

Concept: Accuracy is of critical importance in accounting. Most employees who are responsible for maintaining accounting records value accuracy and completeness. Accounting employees work very hard to avoid errors and to correct any errors that do get made. Other employees within a business and other people who have contact with a business also value accurate accounting records.

Application: Other than accounting employees, who are some of the other people who expect and require accurate accounting records? Why is accounting accuracy important to these people? How tolerant should people be of mistakes? Are a small number of mistakes acceptable? Are mistakes involving small amounts—for example, just a few cents—acceptable? Or should it be expected that accounting records are completely accurate?

SCANS WORKPLACE COMPETENCY

• auditing for errors

The trial balance for Enfield Company is given below.

Account Titles	Account Balances	
	Debit	Credit
Cash	4,391.00	
Petty Cash	300.00	
Accounts Receivable—Harned Co.		2,950.00
Supplies	327.00	
Accounts Payable—Esby Inc.		1,250.00
Ervin Enfield, Capital	6,500.00	
Ervin Enfield, Drawing	600.00	
Income Summary		
Sales	2,500.00	
Advertising Expense	1,432.00	
Supplies Expense		
Rent Expense	250.00	
Totals	16,300.00	4,200.00

The debit column does not equal the credit column. The new bookkeeper knows that the amounts are correct but is not sure if the amounts are in the correct columns.

Instructions

1. Using what you know about the normal balance side of each account, find which amount(s) are in the wrong column.
2. On a separate piece of paper, copy the balances, putting them in the correct columns.
3. Total the columns to prove that debits now equal credits.

• analyzing Best Buy's financial statements

The length of time for which a business summarizes and reports financial information is known as a *fiscal period.* Annual statements use a fiscal period equal to one year. However, the fiscal year does not necessarily have to begin on January 1 and end on December 31 (a calendar year). A company's fiscal year can begin on any date. Most companies choose a fiscal year that ends during a period of low business activity, often after a period of high activity, when inventories are low. Look at the first page of Note 1 to Best Buy's financial statements on Appendix B page B-9.

Instructions

1. When does Best Buy's fiscal year end?
2. Why do you think Best Buy's management feels that this is a good time for a fiscal year end?

Manual Accounting Cycle vs. Automated Accounting Cycle

The series of accounting activities included in recording financial information for a fiscal period is called an *accounting cycle*. Regardless of the size of the business, the steps in the accounting cycle are generally the same:

1. Source documents are checked for accuracy, and transactions are analyzed into debit and credit parts.
2. Transactions are recorded in a journal.
3. Journal entries are posted to the general ledger, and a trial balance is prepared.
4. Adjusting entries are journalized and posted.
5. Financial statements are prepared.
6. Closing entries are journalized and posted, and a post-closing trial balance is prepared.

Manual Accounting

In a manual accounting system, all the steps are completed by hand, and a work sheet may be used to summarize information about the adjusting and closing entries and to complete the trial balance. Many of the steps are repetitive and time-consuming. However, all of the steps are important to ensure that accurate financial statements are available to management at the end of each period. Managers use these financial statements to make decisions, and must be able to rely on them.

Automated Accounting

In automated accounting, the emphasis is on the analysis of the source documents and the preparation of timely and accurate journal entries and adjusting entries. The automated accounting system is programmed to post journal entries and to prepare trial balances, closing entries, and financial statements as needed. The accounting staff can concentrate on the analysis functions.

Automated accounting software may include additional features to integrate applications within the accounting cycle. Options within the software may aid in the reconciliation of bank accounts and in the processing of accounts payable and accounts receivable. Automated accounting may be used to track inventory and plant assets, and to process sales orders and payroll. Budgeting, graphing, and printing capabilities are also included in automated accounting systems.

Planning Adjustments

Work sheets are not used in automated accounting. However, it is still necessary to plan and journalize adjusting entries at the end of the fiscal period.

A trial balance is printed or displayed to show the current account balances. Adjustments are then planned and journalized and posted to bring general ledger accounts up to date.

AUTOMATING APPLICATION PROBLEM 6-2: Planning adjustments on a work sheet

Instructions:

1. Load the *Automated Accounting 8.0* or higher software.
2. Select data file F06-2 from the appropriate directory/folder.
3. Select File from the menu bar and choose the Save As menu command. Key the path to the drive and directory that contains your data files. Save your file with a filename of F06-2 XXX XXX (where the X's are your first and last name).
4. Access Problem Instructions through the Browser tool. Read the Problem Instructions screen.
5. Display or print a trial balance to plan the adjusting entries.
6. Refer to Application Problem 6-2 for the adjustment data needed to complete this problem.
7. Save your file and exit the Automated Accounting software.

AUTOMATING MASTERY PROBLEM 6-5: Completing a work sheet

Instructions:

1. Load the *Automated Accounting 8.0* or higher software.
2. Select data file F06-5 from the appropriate directory/folder.
3. Select File from the menu bar and choose the Save As menu command. Key the path to the drive and directory that contains your data files. Save your file with a filename of F06-5 XXX XXX (where the X's are your first and last name).
4. Access Problem Instructions through the Browser tool. Read the Problem Instructions screen.
5. Refer to Mastery Problem 6-5 for the adjustment data used in this problem.
6. Save your file and exit the Automated Accounting software.

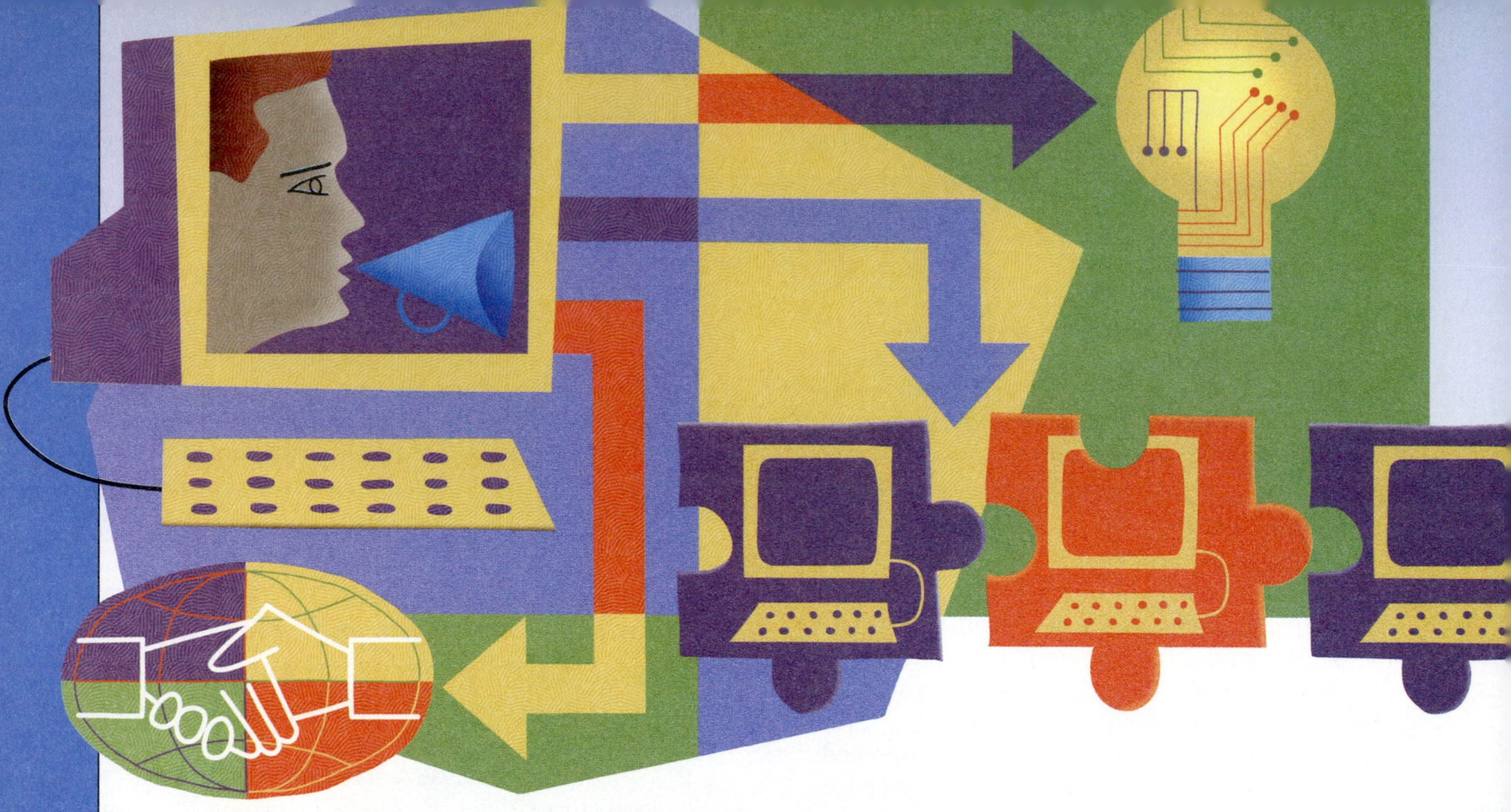

CHAPTER 7 Financial Statements for a Proprietorship

OBJECTIVES & TERMS

After studying Chapter 7, you will be able to:

1. Define accounting terms related to financial statements for a service business organized as a proprietorship.
2. Identify accounting concepts and practices related to preparation of financial statements for a service business organized as a proprietorship.
3. Prepare an income statement for a service business organized as a proprietorship and analyze an income statement using component percentages.
4. Prepare a balance sheet for a service business organized as a proprietorship.

- stakeholders
- component percentage

Point Your Browser
accountingxtra.swlearning.com

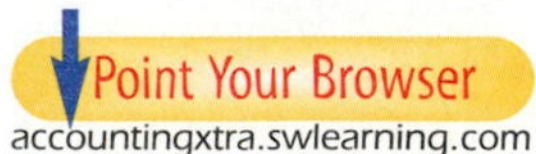

accounting in the real world

Tommy Hilfiger

©MIKE SEGAR/REUTERS/LANDOV

TOMMY HILFIGER AND GLOBAL LABOR POLICIES

If you're talking about clothing, most people under the age of 30 in the United States will recognize the single word "Tommy." Tommy Hilfiger apparel is easily recognized by its Tommy label throughout the country.

Did you know, however, that "Tommy" is made and sold in many corners of the world? In 2004, the Tommy Hilfiger brand was introduced into India. Tommy apparel can be found in stores throughout Canada, Europe, Mexico, Central and South America, Japan, Hong Kong, Australia, Kuwait, Saudi Arabia, Korea, and Taiwan.

Tommy Hilfiger's Web site addresses global labor practices and refers to its "Code of Conduct," which is printed in 35 languages and incorporates internationally recognized labor standards. It outlines the company's expectations concerning the conditions under which its products should be made. The Code of Conduct is enforced by a monitoring program conducted worldwide by an independent social audit organization.

Critical Thinking

1. What account titles might you find on a balance sheet for Tommy Hilfiger?
2. Why should companies like Tommy Hilfiger, who make products throughout the world, be concerned with working conditions?

accountingxtra.swlearning.com

Source: www.tommy.com

ACCOUNTING IN THE REAL WORLD • ACCOUNTING IN THE REAL WORLD • ACCOUNTING IN THE REAL WORLD •

internet activity

FINANCIAL STATEMENT ANALYSIS

Choose two companies in the same industry. Go to the homepage for each company. Search each site for its most current financial statements.

Instructions

1. List the "Total Revenue," "Total Expenses," and "Net Income" or "Net Loss" for each company.
2. For each company, calculate and record the component percentages for total expenses and net income by dividing each item by the amount of net sales. Round percentage calculations to the nearest 0.1%.
3. Compare the component percentages for net income for each company. Which company has the better component percentage?

INTERNET RESEARCH ACTIVITY • INTERNET RESEARCH ACTIVITY • INTERNET RESEARCH ACTIVITY •

LESSON

7-1 Preparing an Income Statement

REPORTING FINANCIAL INFORMATION

The financial information needed by managers and owners to make good business decisions can be found in the general ledger accounts. However, the information in the general ledger is very detailed. Therefore, to make this general ledger information more usable, the information is summarized, organized, and reported to the owners and managers.

Also, all financial information must be reported if good business decisions are to be made. A financial statement with incomplete information is similar to a book with missing pages. The complete story is not told. If a business has both rent and utilities expenses but reports only the rent expense, managers will have incomplete information on which to base decisions. The accounting concept *Adequate Disclosure* is applied when financial statements contain all information necessary to understand a business's financial condition. [*CONCEPT: Adequate Disclosure*]

TechKnow Consulting prepares two financial statements: an income statement and a balance sheet. TechKnow Consulting always prepares financial statements at the end of each monthly fiscal period. [*CONCEPT: Accounting Period Cycle*]

When a business is started, it is expected that the business will continue to operate indefinitely. For example, Kim Park assumes that she will own and operate TechKnow Consulting for many years. When she retires, she expects to sell TechKnow Consulting to someone else, who will continue its operation. The accounting concept *Going Concern* is applied when financial statements are prepared with the expectation that a business will remain in operation indefinitely. [*CONCEPT: Going Concern*]

making ethical decisions

Identifying Stakeholders

Many states now require motorcyclists to wear helmets—a law unpopular with individuals who believe they should have the freedom of choice. Most people recognize that wearing a helmet provides the rider with extra protection in a crash. But why not allow a rider to accept the extra risk of riding without a helmet?

A well-known ethical model, the utilitarian theory, states that an ethical action is one that provides the greatest balance of good over harm. Any persons or groups who will be affected by an action are called **stakeholders**. The impact of the action on all stakeholders should be analyzed. Major stakeholders include owners, employees, customers, local communities, and society. Not every type of stakeholder will apply in each decision. However, the list of stakeholders provides a useful guide for individuals to search beyond themselves for the impact of their actions.

Examine the table below, which analyzes the impact on stakeholders involved in a motorcyclist's decision to ride without a helmet.

This analysis clearly demonstrates how a seemingly personal decision—wearing a helmet—can affect many people. Individuals must make their own conclusions from this analysis. State legislators who have voted for helmet laws believed that benefits to the motorcyclist failed to offset the negative impact on so many stakeholders. Individuals who opposed helmet laws believe the benefits to the individual offset the negative impact on all other stakeholders.

Instructions

Most colleges and universities have minimum academic standards for admission. Create a table that analyzes the positive and negative impact of admission standards. Are admission standards ethical?

Impact on Stakeholders of a Motorcyclist's Decision to Ride Without a Helmet

Stakeholders	Negative Impact	Positive Impact
Motorcyclist	• Likely to have to pay higher insurance premiums. • May incur more serious injuries or death.	• Enjoys the freedom of riding without the confinement of a helmet.
Automobile drivers	• May suffer higher mental anguish if motorcyclist incurs more serious injuries.	• May drive more cautiously when near motorcyclists without helmets.
Relatives	• Personal lives and careers may be negatively affected if accident disables motorcyclist.	
Emergency personnel	• Risks to emergency personnel are greater because they are more aggressive when responding to serious accidents.	
Insurance companies	• Higher medical bills resulting from more serious injuries will hopefully be offset by charging higher insurance premiums.	
State	• May be subject to lawsuits by individuals who believe state was negligent in not passing a helmet law. • More serious accidents require more emergency personnel and equipment, thus spending limited resources.	
Society	• Government programs will pay for medical bills and disability payments not provided by the motorcyclist's insurance.	

INCOME STATEMENT INFORMATION ON A WORK SHEET

		5	6	7	8	
	ACCOUNT TITLE	INCOME STATEMENT		BALANCE SHEET		
		DEBIT	CREDIT	DEBIT	CREDIT	
12	*Sales*		3565 00			12
13	*Advertising Expense*	213 00				13
14	*Insurance Expense*	100 00				14
15	*Miscellaneous Expense*	28 00				15
16	*Rent Expense*	300 00				16
17	*Supplies Expense*	715 00				17
18	*Utilities Expense*	110 00				18
19		1466 00	3565 00			19
20	*Net Income*	2099 00				20
21		3565 00	3565 00			21
22						22

An income statement reports financial information over a specific period of time, indicating the financial progress of a business in earning a net income or a net loss. Expenses are the amounts a business pays to operate the business and earn the revenue. The revenue earned and the expenses incurred to earn that revenue are reported in the same fiscal period. [*CONCEPT: Matching Expenses with Revenue*]

Information needed to prepare TechKnow Consulting's income statement is obtained from two places on the work sheet. Account titles are obtained from the work sheet's Account Title column. Account balances are obtained from the work sheet's Income Statement columns. The income statement for a service business has four sections: (1) heading, (2) revenue, (3) expenses, and (4) net income or net loss.

HEADING OF AN INCOME STATEMENT

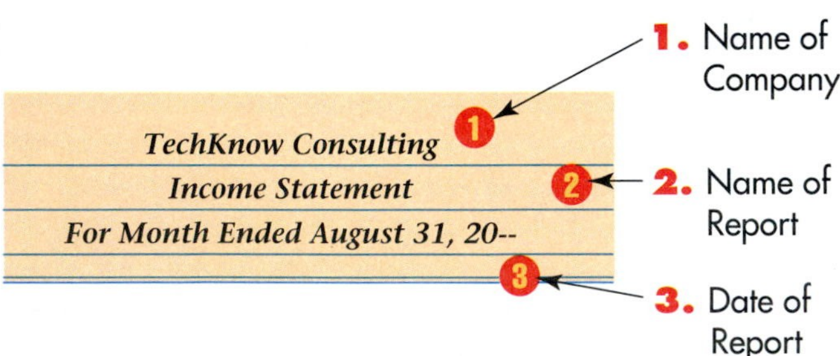

The income statement's date shows that this income statement reports information for the one-month period from August 1 through August 31.

STEPS STEPS • STEPS • STEPS •

PREPARING THE HEADING OF AN INCOME STATEMENT

1. Center the name of the company, *TechKnow Consulting*, on the first line.
2. Center the name of the report, *Income Statement*, on the second line.
3. Center the date of the report, *For Month Ended August 31, 20--*, on the third line.

REVENUE, EXPENSES, AND NET INCOME SECTIONS OF AN INCOME STATEMENT

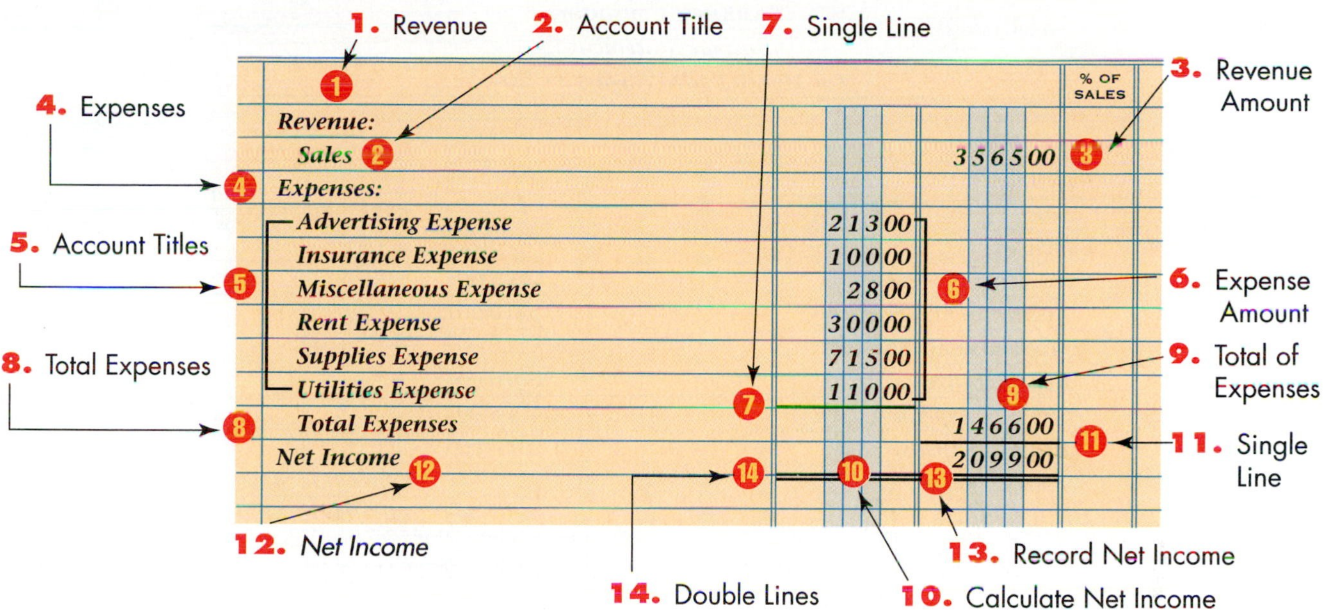

STEPS

PREPARING THE REVENUE, EXPENSES, AND NET INCOME SECTIONS OF AN INCOME STATEMENT

1. Write the name of the first section, *Revenue:*, at the extreme left of the wide column on the first line.
2. Write the title of the revenue account, *Sales*, on the next line, indented about one centimeter.
3. Record the balance of the account, *$3,565.00*, on the same line in the second amount column.
4. Write the name of the second section, *Expenses:*, on the next line at the extreme left of the wide column.
5. Write the title of each expense account in the wide column, indented about one centimeter.
6. Record the balance of each expense account in the first amount column on the same line as the account title.
7. Rule a single line across the first amount column under the last expense account balance to indicate addition.
8. Write the words *Total Expenses* on the next blank line in the wide column, indented about one centimeter.
9. Record the amount of total expenses, *$1,466.00*, on the same line in the second amount column.
10. Calculate and verify the amount of net income.
    a. Calculate net income from information on the income statement, as shown.
    b. Compare the amount of net income, $2,099.00, with the net income on the work sheet. If the two amounts are not the same, an error has been made.

Total Revenue	–	Total Expenses	=	Net Income
$3,565.00	–	$1,466.00	=	$2,099.00

11. Rule a single line across the second amount column just below the amount of total expenses.
12. Write the words *Net Income* on the next line at the extreme left of the wide column.
13. On the same line, record the amount of net income, *$2,099.00*, in the second amount column.
14. Rule double lines across both amount columns below the amount of net income to show that the amount has been verified as correct.

COMPONENT PERCENTAGE ANALYSIS OF AN INCOME STATEMENT

TechKnow Consulting			
Income Statement			
For Month Ended August 31, 20--			
			% OF SALES
Revenue:			
Sales		3 565 00	100.0
Expenses:			
Advertising Expense	213 00		
Insurance Expense	100 00		
Miscellaneous Expense	28 00		
Rent Expense	300 00		
Supplies Expense	715 00		
Utilities Expense	110 00		
Total Expenses		1 466 00	41.1
Net Income		2 099 00	58.9

For a service business, the revenue reported on an income statement includes two components: (1) total expenses and (2) net income. To make decisions about future operations, a manager analyzes relationships between these two income statement components and the total sales. The percentage relationship between one financial statement item and the total that includes that item is called a **component percentage**. On an income statement, component percentages are calculated by dividing the amount of each component by the total amount of sales. TechKnow Consulting calculates a component percentage for total expenses and net income. The relationship between each component and total sales is shown in a separate column on the income statement at the right of the amount columns.

Acceptable Component Percentages

For a component percentage to be useful, Ms. Park needs to know what component percentages are acceptable for businesses similar to TechKnow Consulting. Various industry organizations publish average percentages for similar businesses. In the future, Ms. Park could also compare TechKnow Consulting's component percentages from one fiscal period with the percentages of previous fiscal periods.

Total Expenses Component Percentage

The total expenses component percentage, based on information from the August income statement, is calculated as shown. For businesses similar to TechKnow Consulting, an acceptable total expenses component percentage is not more than 55.0%. Therefore, TechKnow Consulting's percentage, 41.1%, is less than 55.0% and is acceptable.

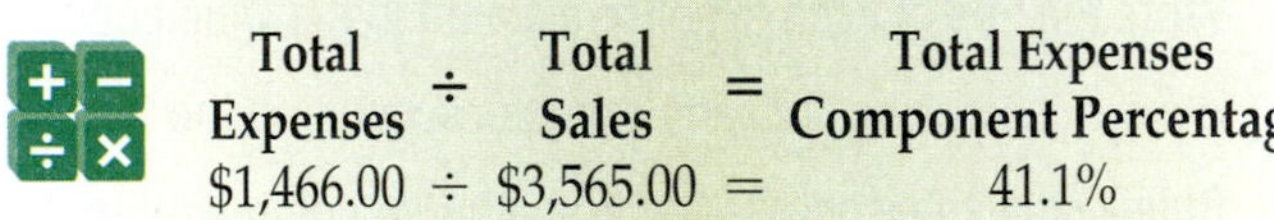

Total Expenses	÷	Total Sales	=	Total Expenses Component Percentage
$1,466.00	÷	$3,565.00	=	41.1%

Net Income Component Percentage

The net income component percentage, based on information from the August income statement, is calculated as shown. For businesses similar to TechKnow Consulting, an acceptable net income component percentage is not less than 45.0%. Therefore TechKnow Consulting's percentage, 58.9%, is greater than 45.0% and is acceptable.

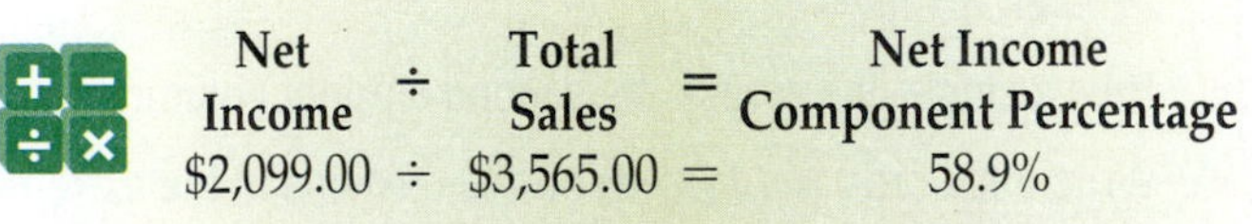

Net Income	÷	Total Sales	=	Net Income Component Percentage
$2,099.00	÷	$3,565.00	=	58.9%

INCOME STATEMENT WITH TWO SOURCES OF REVENUE AND A NET LOSS

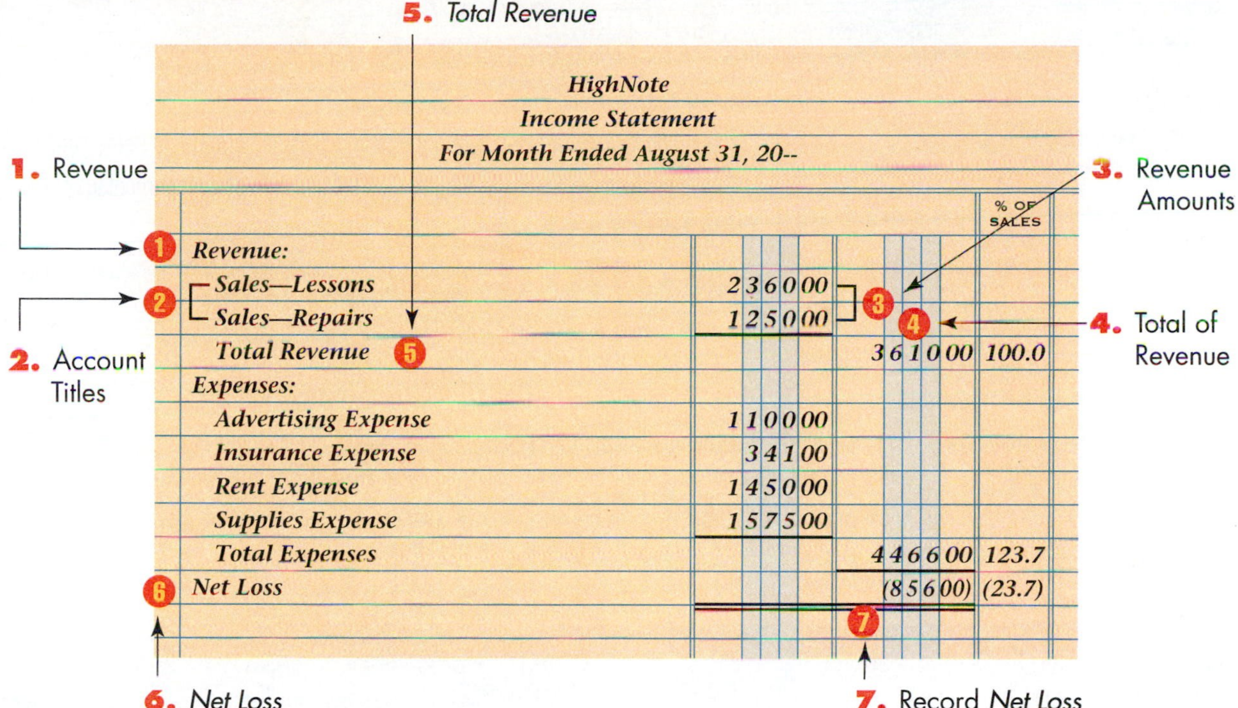

HighNote			
Income Statement			
For Month Ended August 31, 20--			
			% OF SALES
Revenue:			
Sales—Lessons	2,360.00		
Sales—Repairs	1,250.00		
Total Revenue		3,610.00	100.0
Expenses:			
Advertising Expense	1,100.00		
Insurance Expense	341.00		
Rent Expense	1,450.00		
Supplies Expense	1,575.00		
Total Expenses		4,466.00	123.7
Net Loss		(856.00)	(23.7)

TechKnow Consulting receives revenue from only one source, the sale of services for setting up and troubleshooting computer networks. HighNote receives revenue from two sources, the sale of services for music lessons and the sale of services to repair musical instruments. The business's owner wants to know how much revenue is earned from each source. Therefore, the business uses two revenue accounts: *Sales—Lessons* and *Sales—Repairs*.

When an income statement is prepared for HighNote, both revenue accounts are listed. The revenue section of HighNote differs from the income statement prepared by TechKnow Consulting.

If total expenses exceed total revenue, a net loss is reported on an income statement. HighNote reported a net loss on its August income statement.

STEPS • STEPS • STEPS • STEPS • STEPS • STEPS • STEPS • STEPS • STEPS • STEPS •

PREPARING THE REVENUE SECTION OF AN INCOME STATEMENT WITH TWO SOURCES OF REVENUE

1. Write the section heading, *Revenue:*, at the left of the wide column.
2. Write the titles of both revenue accounts in the wide column, indented about one centimeter.
3. Record the balance of each account in the first amount column on the same line as the account title.
4. Total the two revenue account balances. Write the total amount on the next line in the second amount column.
5. Write the words *Total Revenue* in the wide column, indented about one centimeter on the same line as the total revenue amount.

PREPARING THE NET LOSS SECTION OF AN INCOME STATEMENT

6. Write the words *Net Loss* at the extreme left of the wide column.
7. Subtract the total expenses from the revenue to calculate the net loss. Record the amount of net loss in the second amount column in parentheses. An amount written in parentheses on a financial statement indicates a negative amount.

Xtra! Study Tools
accountingxtra.swlearning.com

terms review

stakeholders
component percentage

TERMS REVIEW

audit your understanding

1. List the four sections of an income statement.
2. What is the formula for calculating the total expenses component percentage?
3. What is the formula for calculating the net income component percentage?

AUDIT YOUR

work together 7-1

Preparing an income statement

A partial work sheet of Darlene's Delivery Service for the month ended July 31 of the current year is given in the *Working Papers*. Also given is a blank form for completing an income statement. Your instructor will guide you through the following example.

1. Prepare an income statement for the month ended July 31 of the current year. Calculate and record the component percentages for total expenses and net income. Round percentage calculations to the nearest 0.1%.

WORK TOGETHER

on your own 7-1

Preparing an income statement

A partial work sheet of Cuts by Kelley for the month ended February 28 of the current year is given in the *Working Papers*. Also given is a blank form for completing an income statement. Work this problem independently.

1. Prepare an income statement for the month ended February 28 of the current year. Calculate and record the component percentages for total expenses and net income. Round percentage calculations to the nearest 0.1%.

ON YOUR OWN

LESSON

7-2 Balance Sheet Information on a Work Sheet

BALANCE SHEET

	ACCOUNT TITLE	7 BALANCE SHEET DEBIT	8 BALANCE SHEET CREDIT	
1	*Cash*	4964 00		1
2	*Petty Cash*	100 00		2
3	*Accounts Receivable—Oakdale School*	150 00		3
4	*Accounts Receivable—Campus Internet Cafe*	100 00		4
5	*Supplies*	310 00		5
6	*Prepaid Insurance*	1100 00		6
7	*Accounts Payable—Supply Depot*		200 00	7
8	*Accounts Payable—Thomas Supply Co.*		50 00	8
9	*Kim Park, Capital*		5000 00	9
10	*Kim Park, Drawing*	625 00		10
19		7349 00	5250 00	19
20	*Net Income*		2099 00	20
21		7349 00	7349 00	21

A balance sheet reports financial information on a specific date, indicating the financial condition of a business. The financial condition of a business refers to its financial strength. If a business has adequate available assets and few liabilities, that business is financially strong. If the business's financial condition is not strong, adverse changes in the economy might cause the business to fail.

Information about assets, liabilities, and owner's equity might be obtained from the general ledger accounts or from a work sheet. However, the information is easier to use if reported in an organized manner such as on a balance sheet.

Information needed to prepare TechKnow Consulting's balance sheet is obtained from two places on the work sheet. Account titles are obtained from the work sheet's Account Title column. Account balances are obtained from the work sheet's Balance Sheet columns.

A balance sheet has four sections: (1) heading, (2) assets, (3) liabilities, and (4) owner's equity.

HEADING OF A BALANCE SHEET

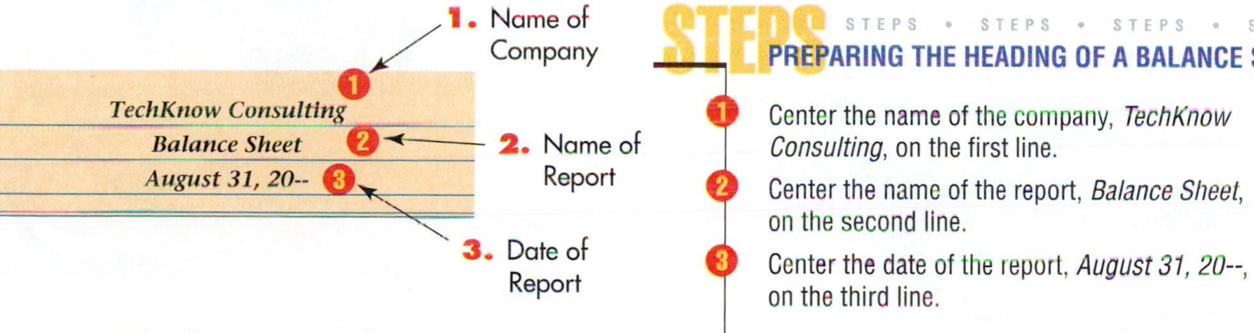

STEPS

PREPARING THE HEADING OF A BALANCE SHEET

1. Center the name of the company, *TechKnow Consulting*, on the first line.
2. Center the name of the report, *Balance Sheet*, on the second line.
3. Center the date of the report, *August 31, 20--*, on the third line.

ASSETS AND LIABILITIES SECTIONS OF A BALANCE SHEET

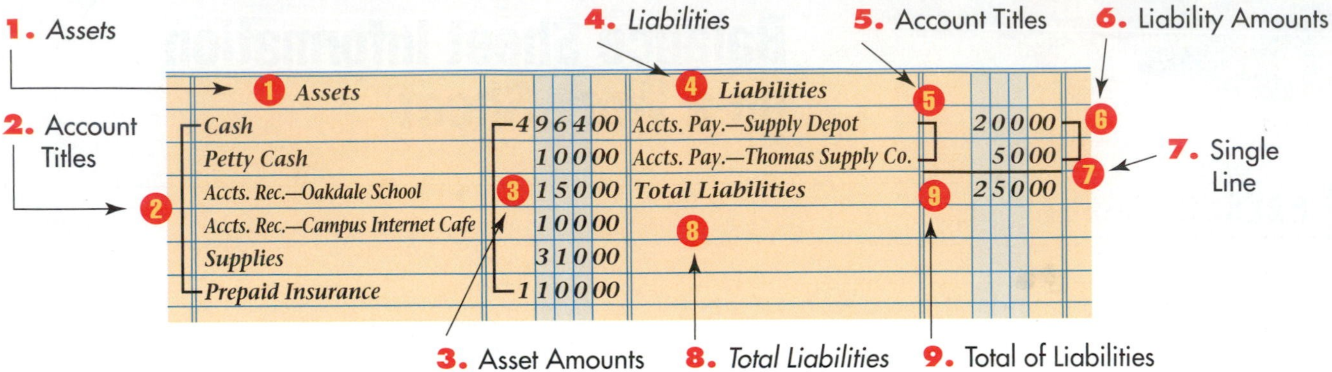

1 Assets		4 Liabilities	
Cash	4 964 00	Accts. Pay.—Supply Depot	200 00
Petty Cash	100 00	Accts. Pay.—Thomas Supply Co.	50 00
Accts. Rec.—Oakdale School	150 00	Total Liabilities	250 00
Accts. Rec.—Campus Internet Cafe	100 00		
Supplies	310 00		
Prepaid Insurance	1 100 00		

A balance sheet reports information about the elements of the accounting equation.

Assets = Liabilities + Owner's Equity

The assets are on the LEFT side of the accounting equation and on the LEFT side of TechKnow Consulting's balance sheet.

Two kinds of equities are reported on a balance sheet: (1) liabilities and (2) owner's equity. Liabilities and owner's equity are on the RIGHT side of the accounting equation and on the RIGHT side of TechKnow Consulting's balance sheet.

The information needed to prepare the assets section is obtained from the work sheet's Account Title column and the Balance Sheet Debit column. The information needed to prepare the liabilities section is obtained from the work sheet's Account Title column and the Balance Sheet Credit column.

STEPS • STEPS • STEPS • STEPS • STEPS

PREPARING THE ASSETS AND LIABILITIES SECTIONS OF A BALANCE SHEET

1. Write the title of the first section, *Assets*, in the middle of the left wide column.
2. Write the titles of all asset accounts under the heading.
3. Record the balance of each asset account in the left amount column on the same line as the account title.
4. Write the title of the next section, *Liabilities*, in the middle of the right wide column.
5. Write the titles of all liability accounts under the heading.
6. Record the balance of each liability account in the right amount column on the same line as the account title.
7. Rule a single line across the right amount column under the last amount, to indicate addition.
8. Write the words *Total Liabilities* in the right wide column on the next blank line.
9. Record the total of all liabilities, *$250.00*, in the right amount column.

©GETTY IMAGES/PHOTODISC

OWNER'S EQUITY SECTION OF A BALANCE SHEET

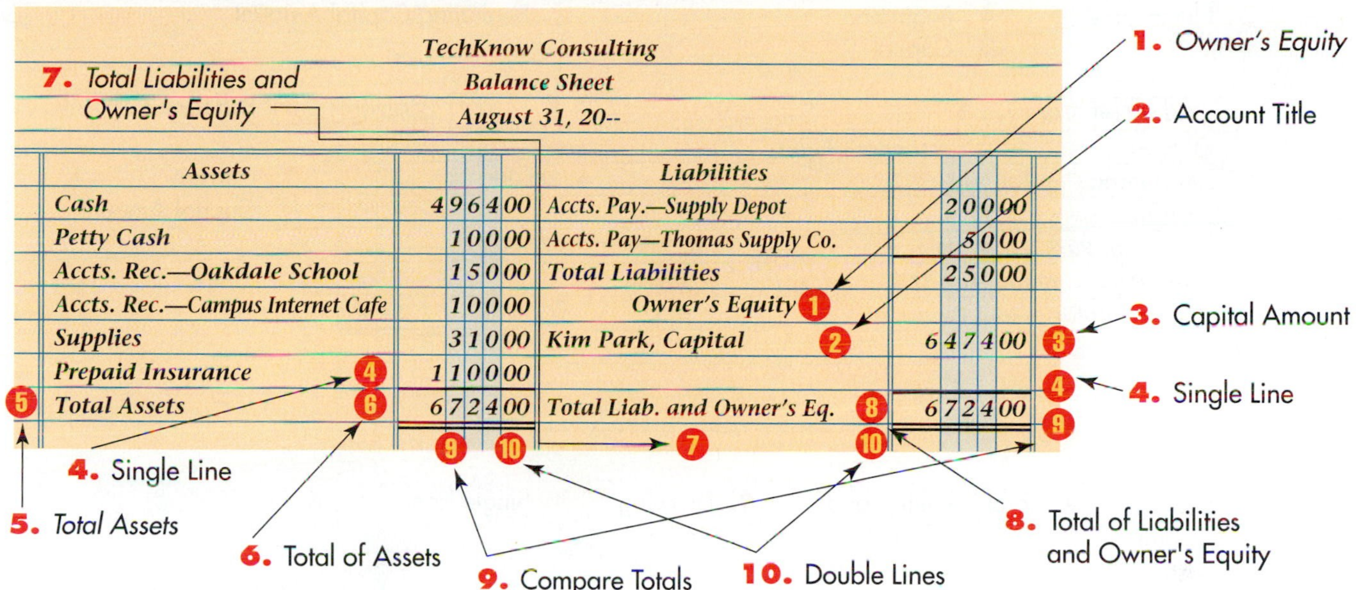

TechKnow Consulting
Balance Sheet
August 31, 20--

Assets		Liabilities	
Cash	4 964 00	Accts. Pay.—Supply Depot	200 00
Petty Cash	100 00	Accts. Pay—Thomas Supply Co.	50 00
Accts. Rec.—Oakdale School	150 00	Total Liabilities	250 00
Accts. Rec.—Campus Internet Cafe	100 00	Owner's Equity	
Supplies	310 00	Kim Park, Capital	6 474 00
Prepaid Insurance	1 100 00		
Total Assets	6 724 00	Total Liab. and Owner's Eq.	6 724 00

Only the amount of current capital is reported on TechKnow Consulting's balance sheet. The amounts needed to calculate the current capital are found in the work sheet's Balance Sheet columns. The amount of current capital is calculated as shown.

Capital Account Balance	+	Net Income	–	Drawing Account Balance	=	Current Capital
$5,000.00	+	$2,099.00	–	$625.00	=	$6,474.00

When a business has a net loss, current capital is calculated as shown. The current capital is reported on the balance sheet in the same way as when the business has a net income.

Capital Account Balance	–	Net Loss	–	Drawing Account Balance	=	Current Capital
$12,000.00	–	$200.00	–	$500.00	=	$11,300.00

STEPS

PREPARING THE OWNER'S EQUITY SECTION OF A BALANCE SHEET

1. Write the title of the section, *Owner's Equity*, in the middle of the right wide column on the next line below "Total Liabilities."
2. Write the title of the owner's capital account, *Kim Park, Capital*, on the next line.
3. Record the current amount of owner's equity, *$6,474.00*, in the right amount column.
4. Rule a single line under the last amount in the longer left amount column. Rule a single line in the right amount column on the same line.
5. Write the words *Total Assets* on the next line, in the left wide column.
6. Record the amount of total assets, *$6,724.00*, in the left amount column.
7. Write the words *Total Liab. and Owner's Eq.* in the right wide column on the same line as Total Assets.
8. Record the amount of total liabilities and owner's equity, *$6,724.00*, in the right amount column.
9. Compare the totals of the two amount columns. The totals are the same, so the balance sheet is in balance.
10. Rule double lines across both the left and right amount columns just below the column totals to show that the totals have been verified as correct.

OWNER'S EQUITY REPORTED IN DETAIL ON A BALANCE SHEET

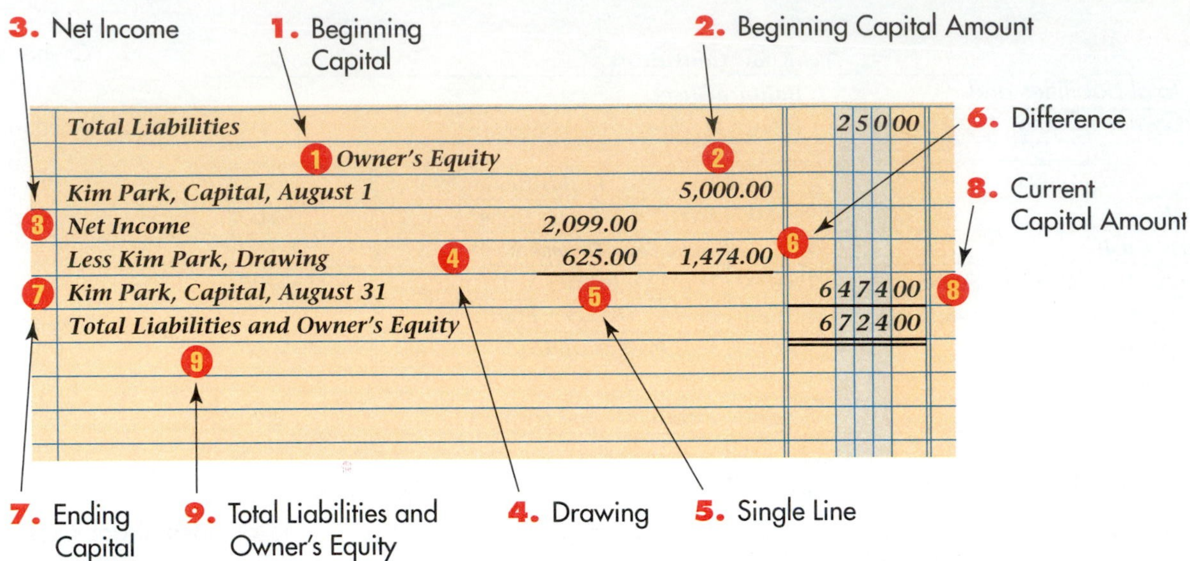

TechKnow Consulting's balance sheet reports the current capital on August 31 but does not show how this amount was calculated. TechKnow Consulting is a small business with relatively few changes in owner's equity to report. Therefore, Kim Park decided that the business does not need to report all the details in the owner's equity section. However, some businesses prefer to report the details about how owner's equity is calculated.

If TechKnow Consulting were to report details about owner's equity, the owner's equity section of the balance sheet would be prepared as shown in the illustration.

STEPS

PREPARING THE OWNER'S EQUITY SECTION REPORTED IN DETAIL ON A BALANCE SHEET

1. Write the words *Kim Park, Capital, August 1* on the first line under the words "Owner's Equity."
2. Record the owner's capital account balance on August 1, *$5,000.00*, in the wide column.
3. Write the words *Net Income* on the next line. Record the net income, *$2,099.00*, in the wide column to the left of the capital account balance.
4. Write the words *Less Kim Park, Drawing* on the next line. Record the balance of the drawing account, *$625.00*, in the wide column.
5. Rule a single line under the amount.
6. Subtract the balance of the drawing account from the net income. Record the difference, *$1,474.00*, in the wide column to the right of the drawing account balance.
7. Write the words *Kim Park, Capital, August 31* on the next line.
8. Add the August 1 capital amount, *$5,000.00*, and the difference between the net income and the drawing account, *$1,474.00*. Record the sum, *$6,474.00*, in the right amount column.
9. Write the words *Total Liabilities and Owner's Equity* on the next line. Record the amount of total liabilities and owner's equity, *$6,724.00*, in the right amount column.

REMEMBER Capital is not copied from the work sheet to the balance sheet. Capital is calculated using beginning capital, plus net income or minus net loss, minus drawing.

CAREERS IN ACCOUNTING • CAREERS IN ACCOUNTING • CAREERS IN ACCOUNTI

careers in accounting

Eric Feng, Entrepreneur/Franchisee

COURTESY OF ERIC FENG

Entrepreneurial spirit is the foundation of our economy. From Henry Ford to Sam Walton to Bill Gates, individuals have dreamed of controlling their destiny by starting their own business. These entrepreneurs identified a need in the marketplace and developed a product to fill that need. Through vision and determination, they created three of the best-known corporations in the world.

Eric Feng is an example of how an entrepreneurial spirit can launch a successful business. He says, "I wanted to be my own boss—a dream for many people—and we were no exception." Eric and his wife, Candy, came to the United States as foreign students to pursue advanced college degrees. Eric finished a master's degree in computer science, and Candy earned a degree in accounting. After several years of working for the local university, they decided it was time to turn their dream into reality.

"We took our first step when we decided to purchase a franchise for a quick-serve restaurant," Eric recalls. After researching numerous opportunities, they decided to pursue the purchase of an Arby's franchise. "We did not have any experience managing a company, much less a restaurant business, nor did we have any significant capital to invest in the business. What we did have, however, was our knowledge of accounting."

The Fengs prepared an extensive business plan that outlined in detail the amount of capital that would be required. The business plan included budgets of sales, expenses, and net income under several different sets of assumptions. They then submitted the business plan to the commercial loan officers of several local banks. "The loan officers at the National Bank of Commerce were confident enough in our business plan to provide us the financing we needed to make our dream come true. The reason, we were told later, was that we had a well-thought-out business plan that made good business sense. All business ventures involve risk. Thanks to the accounting and computer backgrounds we had, we were able to evaluate the business venture in financial accounting terms and demonstrate to the bank that it was a risk worth taking."

Like many entrepreneurs, the Fengs have expanded their operations beyond their initial restaurant. Now the owners of three Arby's units, Eric and Candy credit their success to their knowledge of accounting. "Business success is not a matter of luck. We owe what we have today to our knowledge of accounting and our insistence on quality in all we do."

Salary Range: Virtually unlimited, although the net income from a single unit of a franchise is limited by its physical size and location. However, like the Fengs, an entrepreneur can acquire many units of the same franchise.

Qualifications: Franchisors provide potential franchisees with information on qualifications, which may include specific levels of financial net worth, access to operating capital, and personal experience in the industry.

Occupational Outlook: On its web site (www.franchise.org), the International Franchise Association lists over 800 corporations that offer franchises. Each of these franchisors is actively seeking entrepreneurs to expand the number of company units in operation.

Xtra! Study Tools
accountingxtra.swlearning.com

audit your understanding

1. List the four sections on a balance sheet.
2. What is the formula for calculating current capital?

AUDIT YOUR

work together 7-2

Preparing a balance sheet

A partial work sheet of Ken's Carpet Cleaning for the month ended April 30 of the current year is given in the *Working Papers*. Also given is a blank form for completing a balance sheet. Your instructor will guide you through the following example.

1. Prepare a balance sheet for April 30 of the current year.

WORK TOGETHER

on your own 7-2

Preparing a balance sheet

A partial work sheet of Anne's Alterations for the month ended October 31 of the current year is given in the *Working Papers*. Also given is a blank form for completing a balance sheet. Work this problem independently.

1. Prepare a balance sheet for October 31 of the current year.

ON YOUR OWN

SUMMARY

After completing this chapter, you can

1. Define accounting terms related to financial statements for a service business organized as a proprietorship.
2. Identify accounting concepts and practices related to preparation of financial statements for a service business organized as a proprietorship.
3. Prepare an income statement for a service business organized as a proprietorship and analyze an income statement using component percentages.
4. Prepare a balance sheet for a service business organized as a proprietorship.

Explore Accounting

Comparative and Interim Financial Statements

A corporation that trades its stock on a U.S. stock exchange must submit an annual report to the Securities and Exchange Commission (SEC). The SEC has specific requirements as to what must be included in the financial statements.

One requirement is that the financial statements included in the annual report must show amounts for more than one year. The balance sheet must show ending balances for the current and the previous year. The income statement and statement of stockholder's equity must show amounts for the current year and the two previous years. Financial statements providing information for multiple fiscal periods are called *comparative financial statements*.

These statements make it possible for a user to compare performance from year to year. For example, the net income for the current year can be compared to the net income for the two previous years. In this way, the user can determine if there is a positive or negative trend occurring in net income. On the balance sheet, the ending cash balance for the current year can be compared to the ending cash balance from the previous year to determine if the amount of cash on hand is increasing or decreasing.

Businesses that are required to submit an annual report to the SEC must also submit a quarterly report. This report is not as detailed as the annual report, but it must include the financial statements for the quarter. Financial statements providing information for a time period shorter than the fiscal year are called *interim financial statements*. Users of financial information are able to evaluate the progress of the firm every three months rather than waiting an entire year. The importance of interim financial statements can be verified by the fact that the results reported in these statements are often summarized and reported in financial news sources, such as *The Wall Street Journal* and CNBC.

Activity: Contact a corporation near you. Ask if the business prepares interim financial statements and, if it does, find out how often these statements are prepared.

7-1 APPLICATION PROBLEM

AUTOMATED ACCOUNTING

Preparing an income statement

A form is given in the *Working Papers*. The following information is obtained from the work sheet of Len's Laundry for the month ended August 31 of the current year.

	ACCOUNT TITLE	5 INCOME STATEMENT DEBIT	6 INCOME STATEMENT CREDIT	7 BALANCE SHEET DEBIT	8 BALANCE SHEET CREDIT	
11	*Sales*		6233 00			11
12	*Advertising Expense*	800 00				12
13	*Insurance Expense*	200 00				13
14	*Miscellaneous Expense*	315 00				14
15	*Supplies Expense*	450 00				15
16	*Utilities Expense*	1495 00				16
17		3260 00	6233 00	10436 00	7463 00	17
18	*Net Income*	2973 00			2973 00	18
19		6233 00	6233 00	10436 00	10436 00	19
20						20
21						21

Instructions:

1. Prepare an income statement for the month ended August 31 of the current year.
2. Calculate and record the component percentages for total expenses and net income. Round percentage calculations to the nearest 0.1%.

7-2 APPLICATION PROBLEM

AUTOMATED ACCOUNTING

Preparing a balance sheet

A form is given in the *Working Papers*. The following information is obtained from the work sheet of Len's Laundry for the month ended August 31 of the current year.

	ACCOUNT TITLE	7 BALANCE SHEET DEBIT	8 BALANCE SHEET CREDIT	
1	*Cash*	7607 00		1
2	*Accts. Rec.—Natasha Goodlad*	700 00		2
3	*Accts. Rec.—R. Henry*	498 00		3
4	*Supplies*	431 00		4
5	*Prepaid Insurance*	200 00		5
6	*Accts. Pay.—Tri-County Supplies*		381 00	6
7	*Accts. Pay.—West End Supply Co.*		555 00	7
8	*Leonard Long, Capital*		6527 00	8
9	*Leonard Long, Drawing*	1000 00		9
10	*Income Summary*			10
17		10436 00	7463 00	17
18	*Net Income*		2973 00	18
19		10436 00	10436 00	19
20				20

Instructions:

Prepare a balance sheet for August 31 of the current year.

7-3 MASTERY PROBLEM   

Preparing financial statements with a net loss

Forms are given in the *Working Papers*. The following information is obtained from the work sheet of Rolstad Repair Service for the month ended September 30 of the current year.

	ACCOUNT TITLE	5 INCOME STATEMENT DEBIT	6 INCOME STATEMENT CREDIT	7 BALANCE SHEET DEBIT	8 BALANCE SHEET CREDIT	
1	*Cash*			6958 00		1
2	*Petty Cash*			150 00		2
3	*Accts. Rec.—M. Hollerud*			197 00		3
4	*Supplies*			780 00		4
5	*Prepaid Insurance*			800 00		5
6	*Accts. Pay.—Tampa Supply*				612 00	6
7	*Ron Rolstad, Capital*				9337 00	7
8	*Ron Rolstad, Drawing*			600 00		8
9	*Income Summary*					9
10	*Sales*		3269 00			10
11	*Advertising Expense*	450 00				11
12	*Insurance Expense*	157 00				12
13	*Miscellaneous Expense*	85 00				13
14	*Supplies Expense*	1400 00				14
15	*Utilities Expense*	1641 00				15
16		3733 00	3269 00	9485 00	9949 00	16
17	*Net Loss*		464 00	464 00		17
18		3733 00	3733 00	9949 00	9949 00	18
19						19
20						20

Instructions:

1. Prepare an income statement for the month ended September 30 of the current year.
2. Calculate and record the component percentages for total expenses and net loss. Place the percentage for net loss in parentheses to show that it is for a net loss. Round percentage calculations to the nearest 0.1%.
3. Prepare a balance sheet for September 30 of the current year.

7-4 CHALLENGE PROBLEM

Preparing financial statements with two sources of revenue and a net loss

Forms are given in the *Working Papers*. The information below is obtained from the work sheet of LawnMow for the month ended October 31 of the current year.

Instructions:

1. Prepare an income statement for the month ended October 31 of the current year.
2. Calculate and record the component percentages for total expenses and net loss. Place the percentage for net loss in parentheses to show that it is for a net loss. Round percentage calculations to the nearest 0.1%.
3. Prepare a balance sheet for October 31 of the current year.

	ACCOUNT TITLE	5 INCOME STATEMENT DEBIT	6 INCOME STATEMENT CREDIT	7 BALANCE SHEET DEBIT	8 BALANCE SHEET CREDIT	
1	*Cash*			1898 00		1
2	*Accts. Rec.—Sandra Rohe*			95 00		2
3	*Supplies*			650 00		3
4	*Prepaid Insurance*			1200 00		4
5	*Accts. Pay.—Corner Garage*				58 00	5
6	*Accts. Pay.—Broadway Gas*				110 00	6
7	*Accts. Pay.—Esko Repair*				215 00	7
8	*Ryo Morrison, Capital*				4000 00	8
9	*Ryo Morrison, Drawing*			100 00		9
10	*Income Summary*					10
11	*Sales—Lawn Care*		4900 00			11
12	*Sales—Shrub Care*		2500 00			12
13	*Advertising Expense*	390 00				13
14	*Insurance Expense*	400 00				14
15	*Miscellaneous Expense*	550 00				15
16	*Rent Expense*	3300 00				16
17	*Supplies Expense*	3200 00				17
18		7840 00	7400 00	3943 00	4383 00	18
19	*Net Loss*		440 00	440 00		19
20		7840 00	7840 00	4383 00	4383 00	20
21						21

applied communication

Assume that you are the owner of a proprietorship, and you have just hired a new assistant. In the past, your assistants have had difficulty understanding the importance of financial statements to your business.

Instructions: Write down what you would say to your assistant about the importance of income statements and balance sheets in making financial decisions. Your statements should be no longer than one or two paragraphs.

case for critical thinking

Romelle Woods and Ahti Indihar each own small businesses. Ms. Woods prepares an income statement and balance sheet at the end of each day for her business, in order to make business decisions. Mr. Indihar prepares an income statement and balance sheet for his business only at the end of each one-year fiscal period, when preparing tax reports. Which owner is using the better procedure? Explain your answer.

SCANS workplace competency

Personal Qualities: Self-Esteem

Concept: Individuals with self-esteem believe in their own self-worth and maintain a positive view of self. Other people notice this positive attitude. Employers seek employees with self-esteem because they tend to also be assets in the workplace. One technique for achieving self-esteem is to set goals and then meet the goals.

Application: Set goals for your performance in this accounting course. You might describe the goals in terms of the final grade in the course, your performance on daily assignments, your completion time for assignments, or some combination of these and other activities. Make the goals specific. Then monitor how well you meet the goals through the current term. Consider whether you feel better about yourself after having achieved your goals.

graphing workshop

The net income figures for three companies for three years are given below.

	2005	2006	2007
Atlas Company	15,000	17,000	14,000
Mertzel Company	13,000	15,000	17,000
Tampeau Company	16,000	14,000	13,000

Develop a graph that will best illustrate the difference in the net income for each company each year. Decide for yourself which type of graph to use.

analyzing Best Buy's financial statements

Best Buy's financial reports include a consolidated statement of earnings, which is shown on Appendix B page B-6. This statement reports revenue, expenses, and operating income similar to an income statement for a proprietorship. Best Buy's statement of earnings is more complex than the income statement described in this chapter. Besides reporting net income (called *net earnings*), it also reports "Earnings from continuing operations." The difference between these two amounts is caused by discontinuing or selling a portion of the company or because of changes in accounting procedures. In 2003, Best Buy sold its Musicland stores.

Instructions

1. What are Best Buy's net earnings for each of the three years?
2. What are Best Buy's earnings from continuing operations for each of the three years?
3. What caused the significant difference between these two amounts in 2003?

Automated Accounting

Financial Statements Generated from Automated Accounting

One of the advantages of using accounting software is that once transaction data are entered, the software prepares financial statements automatically.

To display financial statements:

1. Click the Reports toolbar button, or choose the Report Selection menu item from the Report menu.
2. When the Report Selection dialog appears, choose the Financial Statements option from the Select a Report Group list.
3. Choose the financial statement report you would like to display from the Choose a Report to Display list.
4. Click the OK button.
5. The up-to-date account balances stored by the software are used to calculate and display the current financial statements.

Income Statement

The software will display an income statement in one of two formats. The format is controlled by clicking the Custom toolbar button and then selecting either Report by Fiscal Period or Report by Month and Year in the Income Statement selection area.

1. *Report by Fiscal Period:* This format shows the profitability of the business from the beginning of the fiscal year to the date the income statement is displayed.
2. *Report by Month and Year:* This format includes columns for the current month and for the year to date. If there is only one month of transaction data, both columns will be the same.

A component percentage is included for each dollar amount. Component percentages calculated on the income statement show the relationship of items to total sales.

Balance Sheet

The balance sheet reports information about assets, liabilities, and owner's equity on a specific date. Additional information about owner's equity can be obtained by selecting the Statement of Owner's Equity. This statement shows changes to the capital account during the period.

AUTOMATING APPLICATION PROBLEM 7-1: Preparing an income statement and APPLICATION PROBLEM 7-2: Preparing a balance sheet

Instructions:

1. Load the *Automated Accounting 8.0* or higher software.
2. Select data file F07-1 from the appropriate directory/folder.
3. Select File from the menu bar and choose the Save As menu command. Key the path to the drive and directory that contains your data files. Save the data file with a filename of F07-1 XXX XXX (where the X's are your first and last names).
4. Access Problem Instructions through the Browser tool. Read the Problem Instructions screen.
5. Save your file and exit the Automated Accounting software.

AUTOMATING CHALLENGE PROBLEM 7-4: Preparing financial statements with two sources of revenue and a net loss

Instructions:

1. Load the *Automated Accounting 8.0* or higher software.
2. Select data file F07-4 from the appropriate directory/folder.
3. Select File from the menu bar and choose the Save As menu command. Key the path to the drive and directory that contains your data files. Save the data file with a filename of F07-4 XXX XXX (where the X's are your first and last names).
4. Access Problem Instructions through the Browser tool. Read the Problem Instructions screen.
5. Save your file and exit the Automated Accounting software.

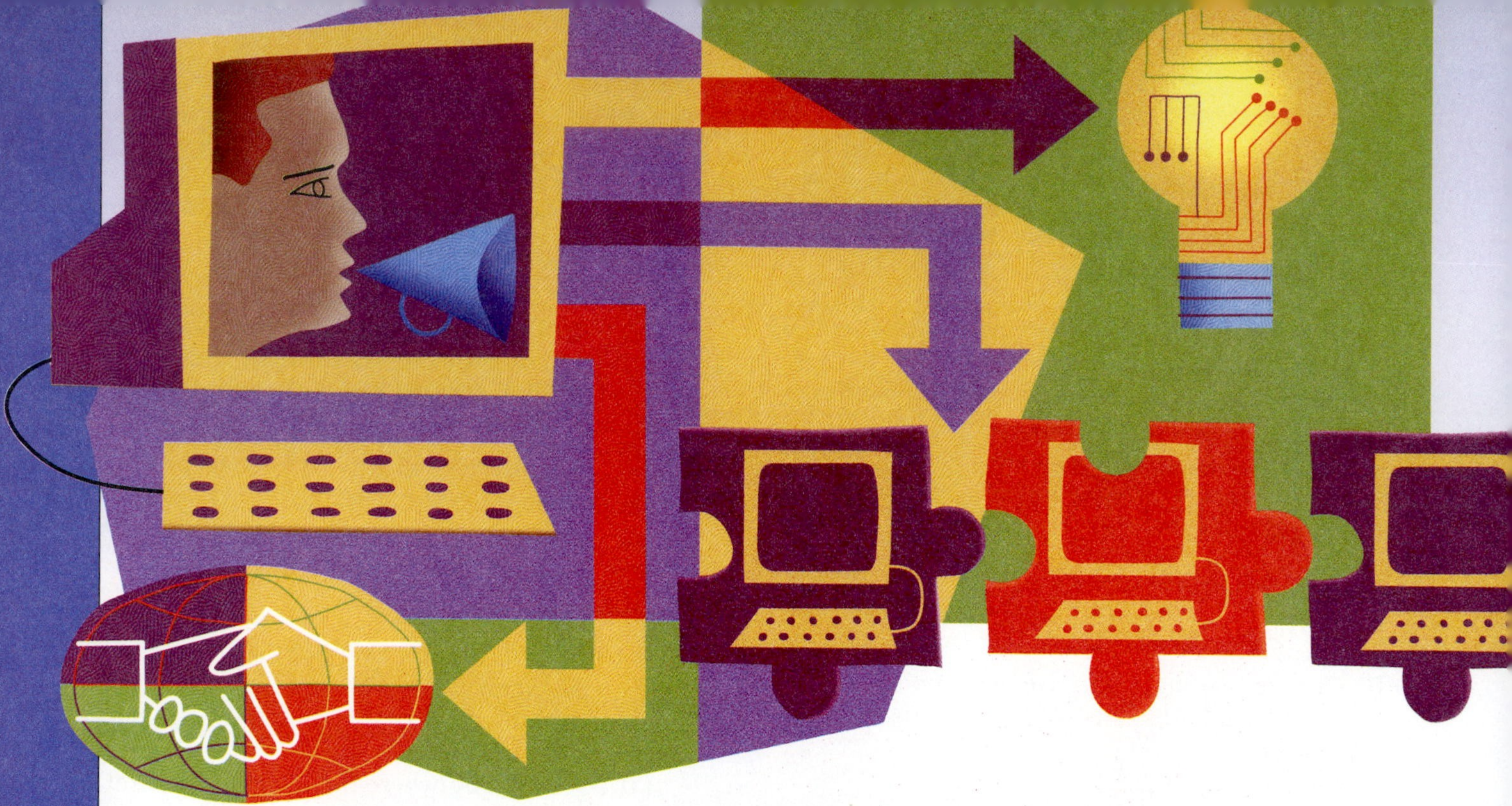

CHAPTER 8

Recording Adjusting and Closing Entries for a Service Business

OBJECTIVES & TERMS

After studying Chapter 8, you will be able to:

1. Define accounting terms related to adjusting and closing entries for a service business organized as a proprietorship.
2. Identify accounting concepts and practices related to adjusting and closing entries for a service business organized as a proprietorship.
3. Record adjusting entries for a service business organized as a proprietorship.
4. Record closing entries for a service business organized as a proprietorship.
5. Prepare a post-closing trial balance for a service business organized as a proprietorship.

- adjusting entries
- permanent accounts
- temporary accounts
- closing entries
- post-closing trial balance
- accounting cycle

Point Your Browser
accountingxtra.swlearning.com

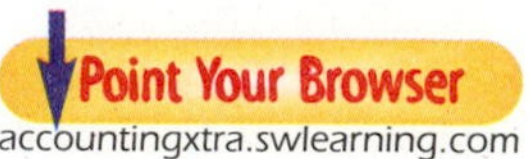

accounting in the real world

The Walt Disney Company

©GREG E. MATHIESON/MAI/LANDOV

CONSERVATION IS GOOD BUSINESS AT THE WALT DISNEY COMPANY

Say the word "Disney" and you may think of any one of hundreds of movies produced by Walt Disney Studios. You may think of a wild, exciting ride in one of the Disney theme parks around the world. You may even think of a fun-filled resort area within Walt Disney World in Orlando.

How many of you, however, would think of the environment when you hear the word "Disney"? In 1990, The Walt Disney Company introduced an initiative called "Environmentality." Disney Online describes Environmentality as "a fundamental ethic that blends business growth with the conservation of natural resources. Attention to the environment drives new business initiatives, demonstrating how environmental stewardship goes hand-in-hand with bottom-line cost savings." Environmentality goes beyond just complying with laws. It includes "purchasing recycled products, waste minimization, resource conservation, research and development, community involvement, and education" to make the program successful.

A 2003 report designed to highlight environmental accomplishments describes many examples of waste reductions and resource conservation. One example is a water-monitoring program in Disney's Animal Kingdom. The monitoring results identified areas where water usage could be reduced, saving an estimated 145,000,000 gallons of water each year.

Critical Thinking

1. List at least two reasons why The Walt Disney Company would be interested in such environmental measures.
2. If The Walt Disney Company purchased equipment to help measure water usage, would that equipment be classified as an asset, liability, or owner's equity on the balance sheet? Why?

Source: www.disney.go.com

accountingxtra.swlearning.com

ACCOUNTING IN THE REAL WORLD • ACCOUNTING IN THE REAL WORLD • ACCOUNTING IN THE REAL WORLD •

internet activity

CLOSING ENTRIES

Go to the homepage for a company or corporation of your choice. Search the site for the most recent annual report. Go to the income statement.

Instructions

1. Looking at the categories of revenues on the income statement, list the accounts that may be included in the company's entry to close the revenue accounts.
2. Looking at the categories of expenses on the income statement, list the accounts that may be included in the company's entry to close the expense accounts.

INTERNET RESEARCH ACTIVITY • INTERNET RESEARCH ACTIVITY • INTERNET RESEARCH ACTIVITY •

LESSON

8-1 Recording Adjusting Entries

ADJUSTING ENTRIES

TechKnow Consulting prepares a work sheet at the end of each fiscal period to summarize the general ledger information needed to prepare financial statements. [*CONCEPT: Accounting Period Cycle*] Financial statements are prepared from information on the work sheet. [*CONCEPT: Adequate Disclosure*]

TechKnow Consulting's adjustments are analyzed and planned on a work sheet. However, these adjustments must be journalized so they can be posted to the general ledger accounts. Journal entries recorded to update general ledger accounts at the end of a fiscal period are called **adjusting entries**.

Adjusting entries are recorded on the next journal page following the page on which the last daily transactions for the month are recorded.

ADJUSTING ENTRY FOR SUPPLIES

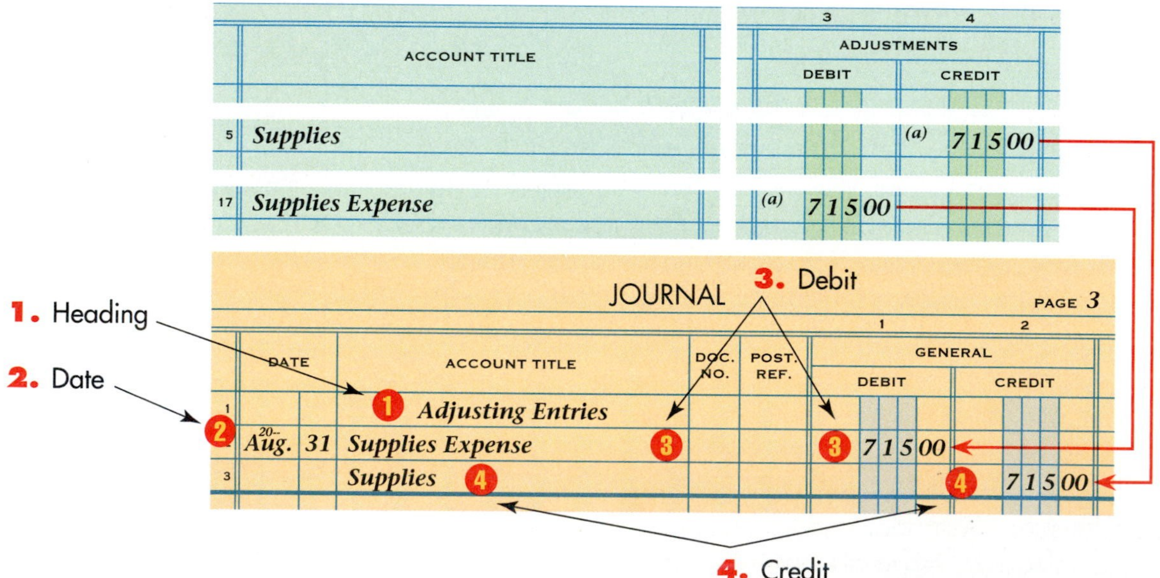

The information needed to journalize the adjusting entry for Supplies is obtained from lines 5 and 17 of the work sheet, as shown in the illustration. The entry must be recorded in a journal and posted to the general ledger accounts affected by the entry.

The effect of posting the adjusting entry for supplies to the general ledger accounts is shown in the T accounts.

Supplies Expense has an up-to-date balance of $715.00, which is the value of the supplies used during the fiscal period. [*CONCEPT: Matching Expenses with Revenue*] Supplies has a new balance of $310.00, which is the cost of the supplies on hand at the end of the fiscal period.

Supplies Expense

Adj. (a)	715.00		

Supplies

Bal.	1,025.00	Adj. (a)	715.00
(New Bal.	*310.00)*		

STEPS ADJUSTING ENTRY FOR SUPPLIES

1. Write the heading, *Adjusting Entries*, in the middle of the Account Title column of the journal. Because no source document is prepared for adjusting entries, the entries are identified with a heading in the journal. The heading is written only once for all adjusting entries.
2. Write the date, *20--, Aug. 31*, in the Date column.
3. Write the title of the account debited, *Supplies Expense*, in the Account Title column. Record the debit amount, *$715.00*, in the General Debit column on the same line as the account title.
4. Write the title of the account credited, *Supplies*, on the next line in the Account Title column. Record the credit amount, *$715.00*, in the General Credit column on the same line as the account title.

MAKING ETHICAL DECISIONS • MAKING ETHICAL DECISIONS • MAKING ETHICAL DECISION

making ethical decisions

Can I Say This on My Resume?

Kendra Wheeler applied for a payroll clerk job with Hampton Group. She slightly exaggerated her work experience on her resume. She felt uncomfortable with this decision, but she was desperate to get a job.

Based on the resume, Kendra was hired. After one year, she received above-average ratings during her annual review. Then, her boss met Kendra's former supervisor and learned the truth.

Was Kendra's action unethical? Let's apply the ethical model to this situation.

1. *Recognize you are facing an ethical dilemma.* Kendra should have realized that her uncomfortable feelings were a sign that her actions might not be ethical.
2. *Identify the action taken or the proposed action.* Kendra could have stated her qualifications honestly. However, she elected to exaggerate her work experience. That action will be evaluated in the following steps.
3. *Analyze the action.*
   a. *Is the action illegal?* No. Overstating qualifications is not illegal, but the employer could terminate her employment.
   b. *Does the action violate company or professional standards?* No. Kendra was neither an employee of the company nor a member of any profession at the time she was hired.
   c. *Who is affected, and how, by the action?*

Impact on Stakeholders of Exaggerating Work Experience on a Resume

Stakeholders	**Negative**	**Positive**
Kendra	• She might be terminated. • If retained, she could have difficulty being promoted.	• She obtained employment.
Other applicants	• More highly qualified applicants lost an employment opportunity	
Hampton Group	• The company lost the opportunity of receiving the benefits of a more qualified employee. • If Kendra is terminated, the company must train another employee. • If Kendra is retained, managers may hesitate to give Kendra responsibilities necessary for the efficient operation of the company.	

4. *Determine if the action is ethical.* Kendra's action was not ethical. Exaggerating her resume provided her with a short-term benefit. However, this benefit does not outweigh the negative impact on other applicants and the Hampton Group. In fact, Kendra's action could possibly cause her more harm in the long run.

ADJUSTING ENTRY FOR PREPAID INSURANCE

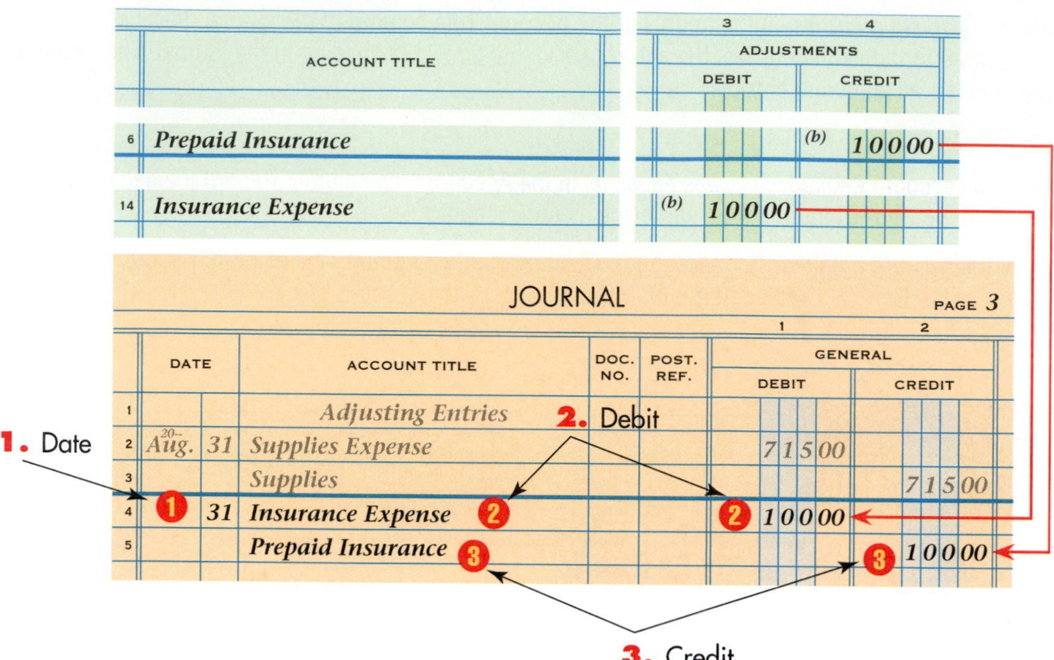

ACCOUNT TITLE
ADJUSTMENTS
DEBIT
CREDIT
Prepaid Insurance
(b) 100 00
Insurance Expense
(b) 100 00
JOURNAL
PAGE 3
DATE
ACCOUNT TITLE
DOC. NO.
POST. REF.
GENERAL
DEBIT
CREDIT
Adjusting Entries
20-- Aug. 31 Supplies Expense 715 00
Supplies 715 00
31 Insurance Expense 100 00
Prepaid Insurance 100 00
1. Date
2. Debit
3. Credit

The information needed to journalize the adjusting entry for Prepaid Insurance is obtained from lines 6 and 14 of the work sheet. The entry must be recorded in a journal and posted to the general ledger accounts affected by the entry.

The effect of posting the adjusting entry for Prepaid Insurance to the general ledger accounts is shown in the T accounts.

Insurance Expense

Adj. (b)	100.00		

Prepaid Insurance

Bal.	1,200.00	Adj. (b)	100.00
(New Bal.	*1,100.00)*		

STEPS: ADJUSTING ENTRY FOR PREPAID INSURANCE

1. Write the date, *31*, in the Date column.
2. Write the title of the account debited, *Insurance Expense*, in the Account Title column. Record the debit amount, *$100.00*, in the General Debit column on the same line as the account title.
3. Write the title of the account credited, *Prepaid Insurance*, on the next line in the Account Title column. Record the credit amount, *$100.00*, in the General Credit column on the same line as the account title.

term review

adjusting entries

TERM REVIEW

audit your understanding

1. Why are adjustments journalized?
2. Where is the information obtained to journalize adjusting entries?
3. What accounts are increased from zero balances after adjusting entries for supplies and prepaid insurance are journalized and posted?

AUDIT YOUR UNDERSTANDING

work together 8-1

Journalizing and posting adjusting entries

A partial work sheet of Darlene's Delivery Service for the month ended July 31 of the current year is given in the *Working Papers*. Also given are a journal and general ledger accounts. The general ledger accounts do not show all details for the fiscal period. The balance shown in each account is the account's balance before adjusting entries are posted. Your instructor will guide you through the following example.

1. Use page 4 of a journal. Journalize and post the adjusting entries. Save your work to complete Work Together 8-2.

WORK TOGETHER

on your own 8-1

Journalizing and posting adjusting entries

A partial work sheet of Cuts by Kelley for the month ended February 28 of the current year is given in the *Working Papers*. Also given are a journal and general ledger accounts. The general ledger accounts do not show all details for the fiscal period. The balance shown in each account is the account's balance before adjusting entries are posted. Work this problem independently.

1. Use page 8 of a journal. Journalize and post the adjusting entries. Save your work to complete On Your Own 8-2.

ON YOUR OWN

workbook p. 163

LESSON • LESSON • LESSON • LESSON • LESSON • LESSON

8-2 Recording Closing Entries

NEED FOR PERMANENT AND TEMPORARY ACCOUNTS

Accounts used to accumulate information from one fiscal period to the next are called **permanent accounts**. Permanent accounts are also referred to as *real accounts*. Permanent accounts include the asset and liability accounts and the owner's capital account. The ending account balances of permanent accounts for one fiscal period are the beginning account balances for the next fiscal period.

Accounts used to accumulate information until it is transferred to the owner's capital account are called **temporary accounts**. Temporary accounts are also referred to as *nominal accounts*. Temporary accounts include the revenue, expense, and owner's drawing accounts plus the income summary account. Temporary accounts show changes in the owner's capital for a single fiscal period. Therefore, at the end of a fiscal period, the balances of temporary accounts are summarized and transferred to the owner's capital account. The temporary accounts begin a new fiscal period with zero balances.

NEED FOR CLOSING TEMPORARY ACCOUNTS

Journal entries used to prepare temporary accounts for a new fiscal period are called **closing entries**. The temporary account balances must be reduced to zero at the end of each fiscal period. This procedure prepares the temporary accounts for recording information about the next fiscal period. Otherwise, the amounts for the next fiscal period would be added to amounts for previous fiscal periods. [*CONCEPT: Matching Expenses with Revenue*] The net income for the next fiscal period would be difficult to calculate because amounts from several fiscal periods remain in the accounts. Therefore, the temporary accounts must start each new fiscal period with zero balances.

To close a temporary account, an amount equal to its balance is recorded in the account on the side opposite to its balance. For example, if an account has a credit balance of $3,565.00, a debit of $3,565.00 is recorded to close the account.

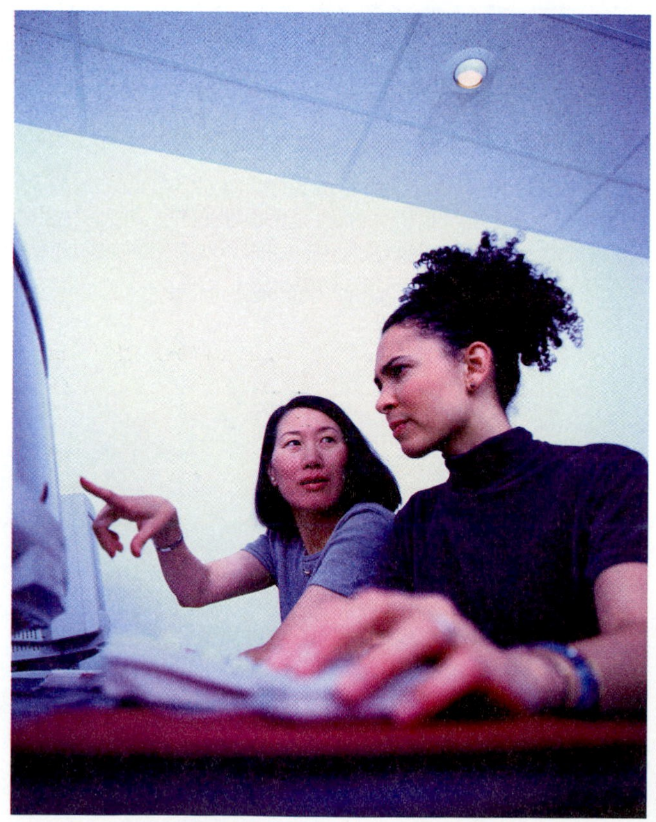

NEED FOR THE INCOME SUMMARY ACCOUNT

Whenever a temporary account is closed, the closing entry must have equal debits and credits. If an account is debited for $3,000.00 to close the account, some other account must be credited for the same amount. A temporary account titled Income Summary is used to summarize the closing entries for the revenue and expense accounts.

The income summary account is unique because it does not have a normal balance side. The balance of this account is determined by the amounts posted to the account at the end of a fiscal period. When revenue is greater than total expenses, resulting in a net income, the income summary account has a credit balance, as shown in the T account.

Income Summary

Debit	Credit
Total expenses	Revenue (greater than expenses) (Credit balance is the net income.)

When total expenses are greater than revenue, resulting in a net loss, the income summary account has a debit balance, as shown in the T account.

Income Summary

Debit	Credit
Total expenses (greater than revenue) (Debit balance is the net loss.)	Revenue

Thus, whether the balance of the income summary account is a credit or a debit depends upon whether the business earns a net income or incurs a net loss. Because Income Summary is a temporary account, the account is also closed at the end of a fiscal period when the net income or net loss is recorded.

TechKnow Consulting records four closing entries: (1) an entry to close income statement accounts with credit balances; (2) an entry to close income statement accounts with debit balances; (3) an entry to record net income or net loss and close Income Summary; and (4) an entry to close the owner's drawing account.

Information needed to record the four closing entries is found in the Income Statement and Balance Sheet columns of the work sheet.

Most small businesses use the calendar year as their fiscal year because it matches the way in which the owners have to file their personal income tax returns.

REMEMBER TechKnow Consulting makes four closing entries: (1) Close income statement accounts with credit balances. (2) Close income statement accounts with debit balances. (3) Record net income or loss in the owner's capital account and close *Income Summary*. (4) Close the owner's drawing account.

CLOSING ENTRY FOR AN INCOME STATEMENT ACCOUNT WITH A CREDIT BALANCE

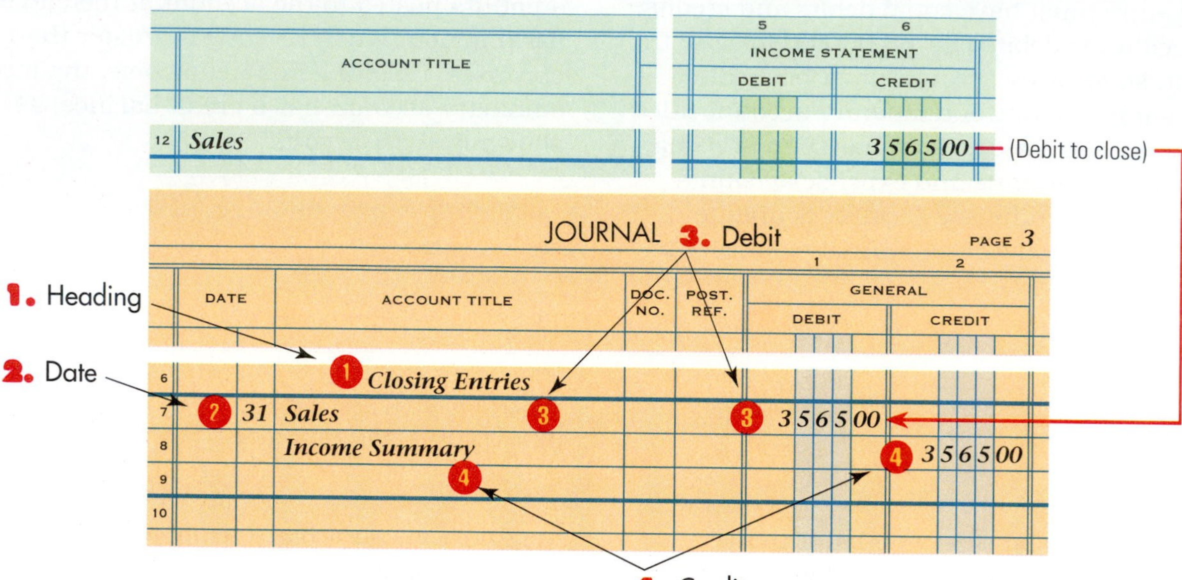

TechKnow Consulting has one income statement account with a credit balance, Sales. This credit balance must be reduced to zero to prepare the account for the next fiscal period. To reduce the balance to zero, Sales is debited for the amount of the balance. Because debits must equal credits for each journal entry, some other account must be credited. The account used for the credit part of this closing entry is Income Summary.

The effect of this closing entry on the general ledger accounts is shown in the T accounts.

Sales			
Closing	3,565.00	Bal.	3,565.00
		(New Bal. zero)	

Income Summary			
		Closing (revenue)	3,565.00

The balance of Sales is now zero, and the account is ready for the next fiscal period. The credit balance of Sales is transferred to Income Summary.

FYI FOR YOUR INFORMATION

The reasons for recording closing entries can be compared to a trip odometer. Closing entries are recorded to prepare the temporary accounts for the next fiscal period by reducing their balances to zero. Likewise, a trip odometer must be reset to zero to begin recording the miles for the next trip.

STEPS • STEPS • STEPS • STEPS • STEPS • STEPS • STEPS • STEPS • STEPS • STEPS •

CLOSING ENTRY FOR AN INCOME STATEMENT ACCOUNT WITH A CREDIT BALANCE

1. Write the heading, *Closing Entries*, in the middle of the Account Title column of the journal. For TechKnow Consulting, this heading is placed in the journal on the first blank line after the last adjusting entry.
2. Write the date, *31*, on the next line in the Date column.
3. Write the title of the account debited, *Sales*, in the Account Title column. Record the debit amount, *$3,565.00*, in the General Debit column on the same line as the account title.
4. Write the title of the account credited, *Income Summary*, on the next line in the Account Title column. Record the credit amount, *$3,565.00*, in the General Credit column on the same line as the account title.

CLOSING ENTRY FOR INCOME STATEMENT ACCOUNTS WITH DEBIT BALANCES

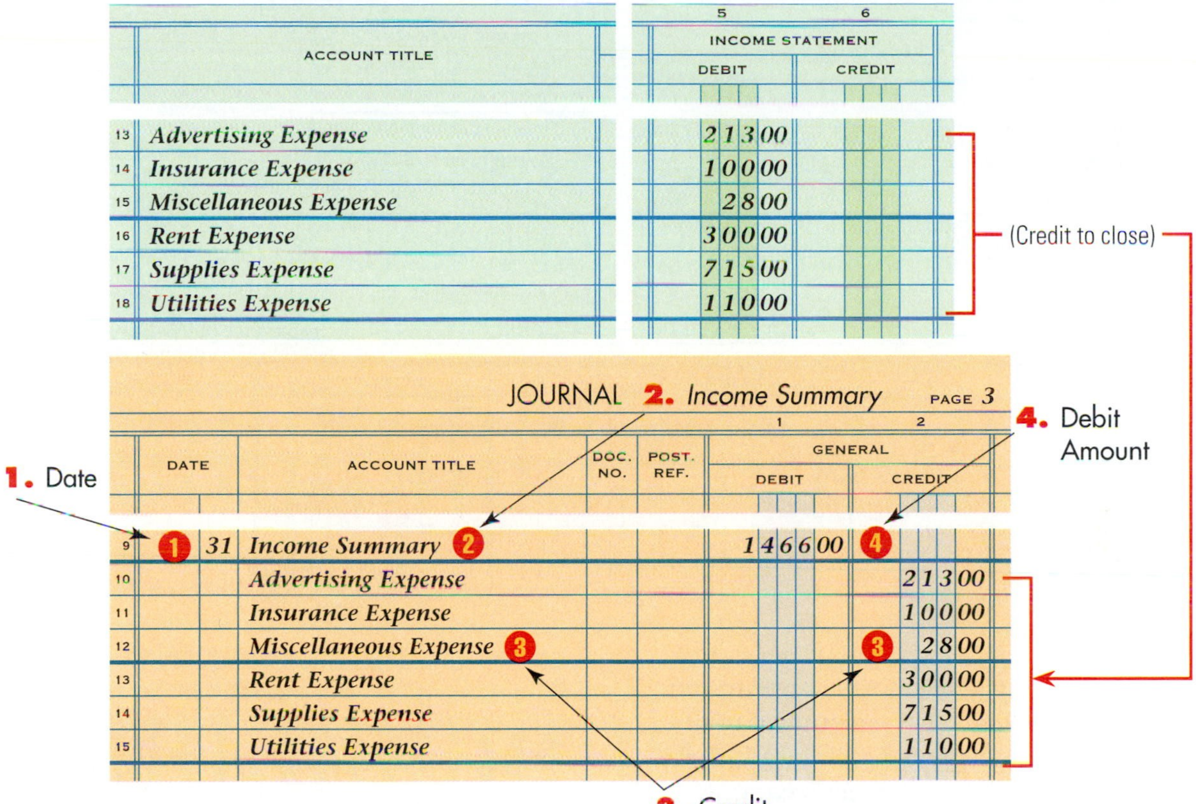

TechKnow Consulting has six income statement accounts with debit balances. The six expense accounts have normal debit balances at the end of a fiscal period. The balances of the expense accounts must be reduced to zero to prepare the accounts for the next fiscal period. Each expense account is credited for an amount equal to its balance. Income Summary is debited for the total of all the expense account balances. The amount debited to Income Summary is not entered in the amount column until all expenses have been journalized and the total amount calculated.

The effect of this closing entry on the general ledger accounts is shown in the T accounts. The balance of each expense account is returned to zero, and the accounts are ready for the next fiscal period. The balance of Income Summary is the net income for the fiscal period, $2,099.00.

Income Summary

Debit		Credit	
Closing (expenses)	1,466.00	Closing (revenue)	3,565.00
		(New Bal.	*2,099.00)*

Advertising Expense

Debit		Credit	
Bal.	213.00	Closing	213.00
(New Bal. zero)			

Rent Expense

Debit		Credit	
Bal.	300.00	Closing	300.00
(New Bal. zero)			

Insurance Expense

Debit		Credit	
Bal.	100.00	Closing	100.00
(New Bal. zero)			

Supplies Expense

Debit		Credit	
Bal.	715.00	Closing	715.00
(New Bal. zero)			

Miscellaneous Expense

Debit		Credit	
Bal.	28.00	Closing	28.00
(New Bal. zero)			

Utilities Expense

Debit		Credit	
Bal.	110.00	Closing	110.00
(New Bal. zero)			

CLOSING ENTRY TO RECORD NET INCOME OR LOSS AND CLOSE THE INCOME SUMMARY ACCOUNT

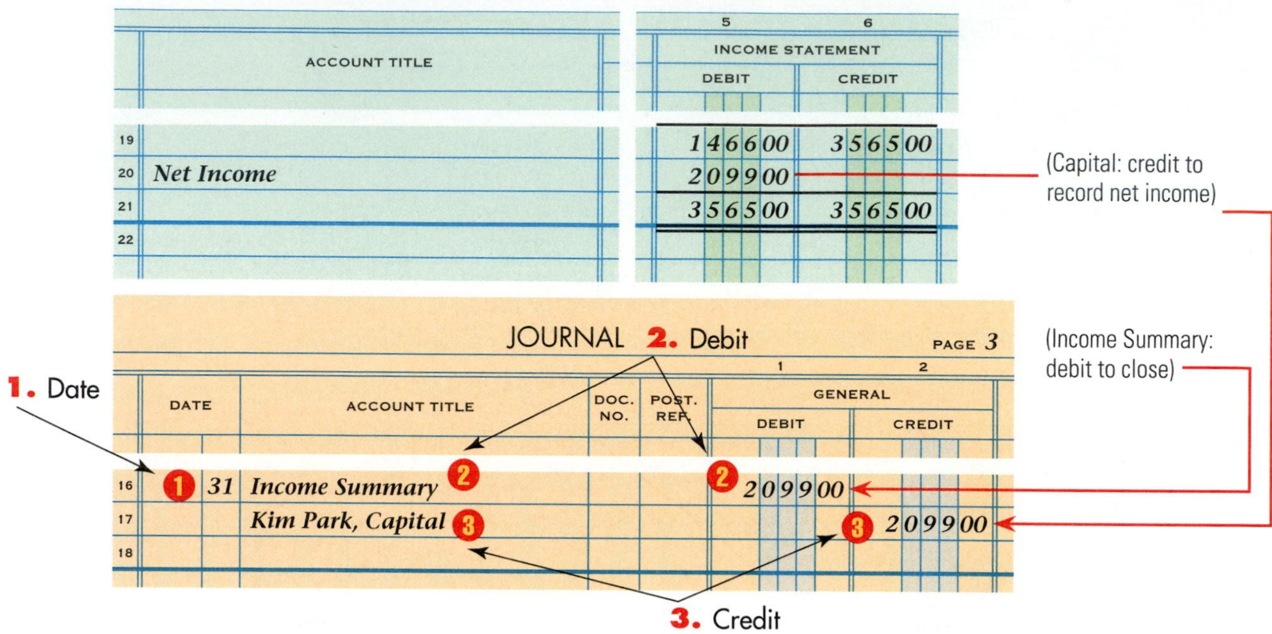

TechKnow Consulting's net income appears on line 20 of the work sheet. The amount of net income increases the owner's capital and, therefore, must be credited to the owner's capital account. The balance of the temporary account, Income Summary, must be reduced to zero to prepare the account for the next fiscal period.

The effect of this closing entry on the general ledger accounts is shown in the T accounts. The debit to the income summary account, $2,099.00, reduces the account balance to zero and prepares the account for the next fiscal period. The credit, $2,099.00, increases the balance of the owner's capital account, Kim Park, Capital.

Income Summary

Debit		Credit	
Closing (expenses)	1,466.00	Closing (revenue)	3,565.00
Closing	2,099.00	*(New Bal. zero)*	

Kim Park, Capital

Debit		Credit	
		Bal.	5,000.00
		Closing (net inc.)	2,099.00
		(New Bal.	*7,099.00)*

If a business incurs a net loss, the closing entry is a debit to the owner's capital account and a credit to the income summary account.

STEPS • STEPS • STEPS • STEPS • STEPS • STEPS • STEPS • STEPS • STEPS • STEPS •

STEPS: CLOSING ENTRY TO RECORD NET INCOME OR LOSS AND CLOSE THE INCOME SUMMARY ACCOUNT

1. Write the date, *31*, on the next line in the Date column.
2. Write the title of the account debited, *Income Summary*, in the Account Title column. Record the debit amount, *$2,099.00*, in the General Debit column on the same line as the account title.
3. Write the title of the account credited, *Kim Park, Capital*, on the next line in the Account Title column. Record the credit amount, *$2,099.00*, in the General Credit column on the same line as the account title.

REMEMBER Amounts for closing entries are taken from the Income Statement and Balance Sheet columns of the work sheet.

CLOSING ENTRY FOR THE OWNER'S DRAWING ACCOUNT

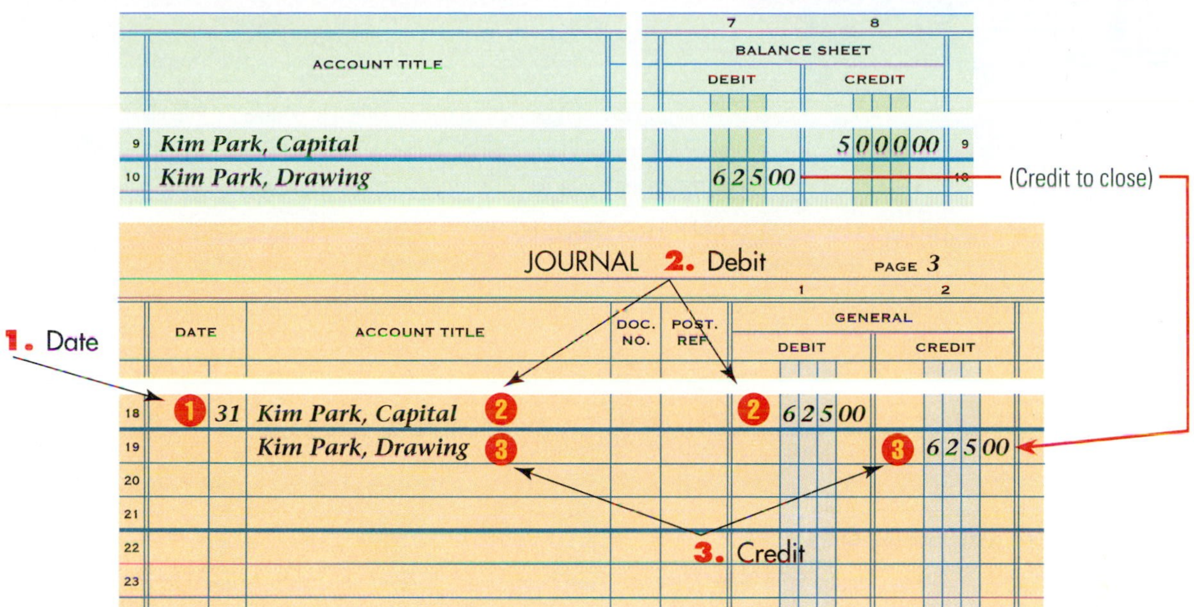

Withdrawals are assets that the owner takes out of a business and which decrease the amount of the owner's equity. The drawing account is a temporary account that accumulates information separately for each fiscal period. Therefore, the drawing account balance is reduced to zero at the end of one fiscal period to prepare the account for the next fiscal period.

The drawing account is neither a revenue nor an expense account. Therefore, the drawing account is not closed through Income Summary. The drawing account balance is closed directly to the owner's capital account.

The effect of the entry to close the drawing account is shown in the T accounts.

The drawing account has a zero balance and is ready for the next fiscal period. The capital account's new balance, $6,474.00, is verified by comparing the balance to the amount of capital shown on the balance sheet prepared at the end of the fiscal period. The capital account balance shown on TechKnow Consulting's balance sheet in Chapter 8 is $6,474.00. The two amounts are the same, and the capital account balance is verified.

Kim Park, Capital			
Closing (drawing)	625.00	Bal.	5,000.00
		Net Income	2,099.00
		(New Bal.	*6,474.00)*

Kim Park, Drawing			
Bal.	625.00	Closing	625.00
(New Bal. zero)			

STEPS • STEPS • STEPS • STEPS • STEPS • STEPS • STEPS • STEPS • STEPS • STEPS

CLOSING ENTRY FOR THE OWNER'S DRAWING ACCOUNT

1. Write the date, *31*, in the Date column.
2. Write the title of the account debited, *Kim Park, Capital*, in the Account Title column. Record the debit amount, *$625.00*, in the General Debit column on the same line as the account title.
3. Write the title of the account credited, *Kim Park, Drawing*, in the Account Title column. Record the credit amount, *$625.00*, in the General Credit column on the same line as the account title.

terms review

permanent accounts
temporary accounts
closing entries

TERMS REVIEW

audit your understanding

1. What do the ending balances of permanent accounts for one fiscal period represent at the beginning of the next fiscal period?
2. What do the balances of temporary accounts show?
3. List the four closing entries.

AUDIT YOUR UNDERSTANDING

work together 8-2

Journalizing and posting closing entries

Use the journal and general ledger accounts from Work Together 8-1. A partial work sheet for the month ended July 31 of the current year is given in the *Working Papers*. Your instructor will guide you through the following example.

1. Continue on the same journal page. Journalize and post the closing entries. Save your work to complete Work Together 8-3.

WORK TOGETHER

on your own 8-2

Journalizing and posting closing entries

Use the journal and general ledger accounts from On Your Own 8-1. A partial work sheet for the month ended February 28 of the current year is given in the *Working Papers*. Work this problem independently.

1. Continue on the same journal page. Journalize and post the closing entries. Save your work to complete On Your Own 8-3.

ON YOUR OWN

LESSON • LESSON • LESSON • LESSON • LESSON • LESSON

8-3 Preparing a Post-Closing Trial Balance

GENERAL LEDGER ACCOUNTS AFTER ADJUSTING AND CLOSING ENTRIES ARE POSTED

ACCOUNT *Cash* ACCOUNT NO. *110*

DATE		ITEM	POST. REF.	DEBIT	CREDIT	BALANCE DEBIT	BALANCE CREDIT
20-- Aug.	31		2	8,315.00		8,315.00	
	31		2		3,351.00	4,964.00	

ACCOUNT *Petty Cash* ACCOUNT NO. *120*

DATE		ITEM	POST. REF.	DEBIT	CREDIT	BALANCE DEBIT	BALANCE CREDIT
20-- Aug.	17		1	100.00		100.00	

ACCOUNT *Accounts Receivable—Oakdale School* ACCOUNT NO. *130*

DATE		ITEM	POST. REF.	DEBIT	CREDIT	BALANCE DEBIT	BALANCE CREDIT
20-- Aug.	12		1	350.00		350.00	
	12		1		200.00	150.00	

ACCOUNT *Accounts Receivable—Campus Internet Cafe* ACCOUNT NO. *140*

DATE		ITEM	POST. REF.	DEBIT	CREDIT	BALANCE DEBIT	BALANCE CREDIT
20-- Aug.	13		1	100.00		100.00	

ACCOUNT *Supplies* ACCOUNT NO. *150*

DATE		ITEM	POST. REF.	DEBIT	CREDIT	BALANCE DEBIT	BALANCE CREDIT
20-- Aug.	3		1	275.00		275.00	
	7		1	500.00		775.00	
	20		1	50.00		825.00	
	28		2	200.00		1,025.00	
	31		3		715.00	310.00	

TechKnow Consulting's general ledger, after the adjusting and closing entries are posted, is shown here and on the next several pages. When an account has a zero balance, lines are drawn in both the Balance Debit and Balance Credit columns. The lines assure a reader that a balance has not been omitted.

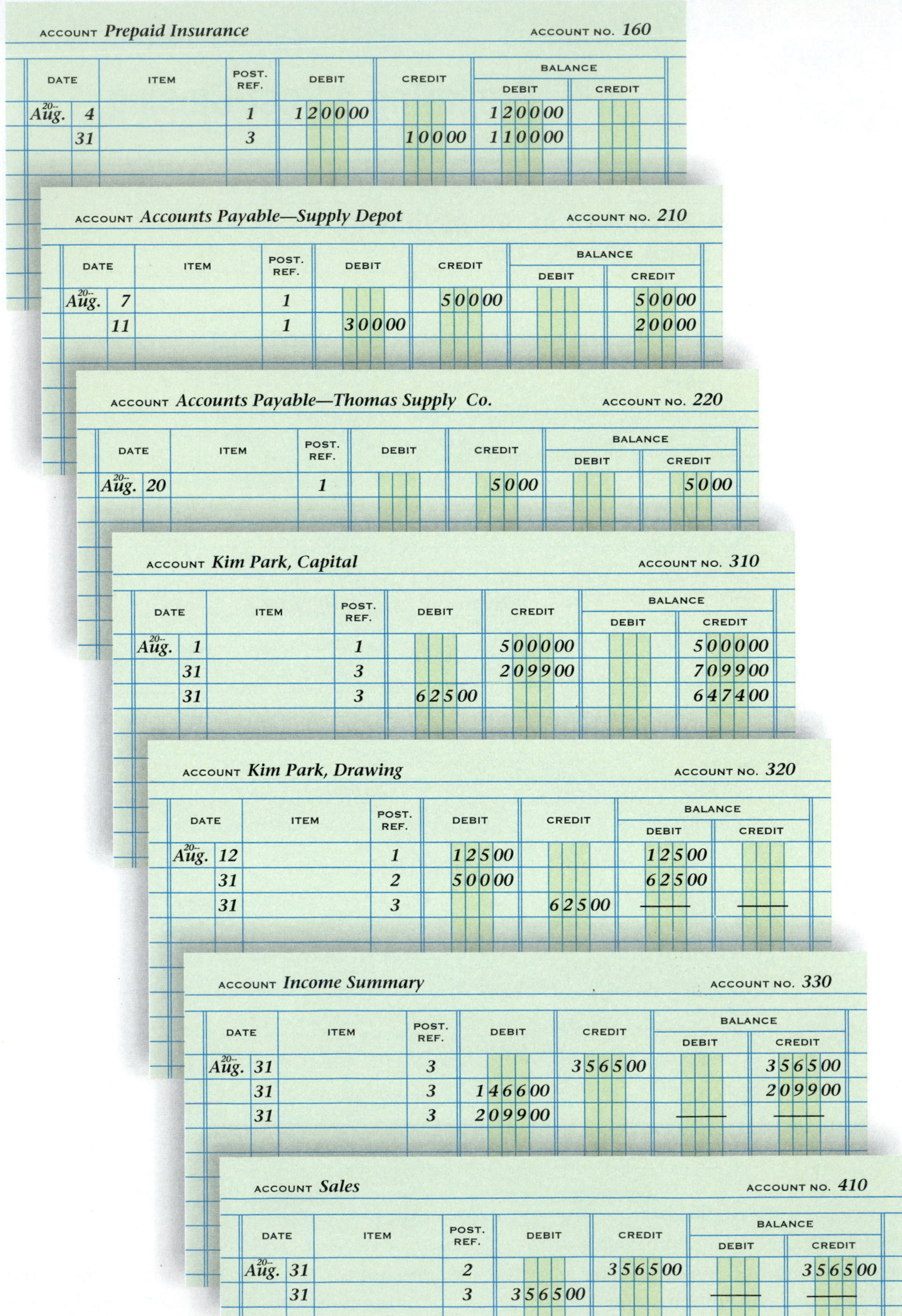

ACCOUNT *Prepaid Insurance* ACCOUNT NO. *160*

DATE		ITEM	POST. REF.	DEBIT	CREDIT	BALANCE DEBIT	BALANCE CREDIT
20-- Aug.	4		1	1200 00		1200 00	
	31		3		100 00	1100 00	

ACCOUNT *Accounts Payable—Supply Depot* ACCOUNT NO. *210*

DATE		ITEM	POST. REF.	DEBIT	CREDIT	BALANCE DEBIT	BALANCE CREDIT
20-- Aug.	7		1		500 00		500 00
	11		1	300 00			200 00

ACCOUNT *Accounts Payable—Thomas Supply Co.* ACCOUNT NO. *220*

DATE		ITEM	POST. REF.	DEBIT	CREDIT	BALANCE DEBIT	BALANCE CREDIT
20-- Aug.	20		1		50 00		50 00

ACCOUNT *Kim Park, Capital* ACCOUNT NO. *310*

DATE		ITEM	POST. REF.	DEBIT	CREDIT	BALANCE DEBIT	BALANCE CREDIT
20-- Aug.	1		1		5000 00		5000 00
	31		3		2099 00		7099 00
	31		3	625 00			6474 00

ACCOUNT *Kim Park, Drawing* ACCOUNT NO. *320*

DATE		ITEM	POST. REF.	DEBIT	CREDIT	BALANCE DEBIT	BALANCE CREDIT
20-- Aug.	12		1	125 00		125 00	
	31		2	500 00		625 00	
	31		3		625 00	—	—

ACCOUNT *Income Summary* ACCOUNT NO. *330*

DATE		ITEM	POST. REF.	DEBIT	CREDIT	BALANCE DEBIT	BALANCE CREDIT
20-- Aug.	31		3		3565 00		3565 00
	31		3	1466 00			2099 00
	31		3	2099 00		—	—

ACCOUNT *Sales* ACCOUNT NO. *410*

DATE		ITEM	POST. REF.	DEBIT	CREDIT	BALANCE DEBIT	BALANCE CREDIT
20-- Aug.	31		2		3565 00		3565 00
	31		3	3565 00		—	—

A General Ledger after Adjusting and Closing Entries Are Posted (continued)

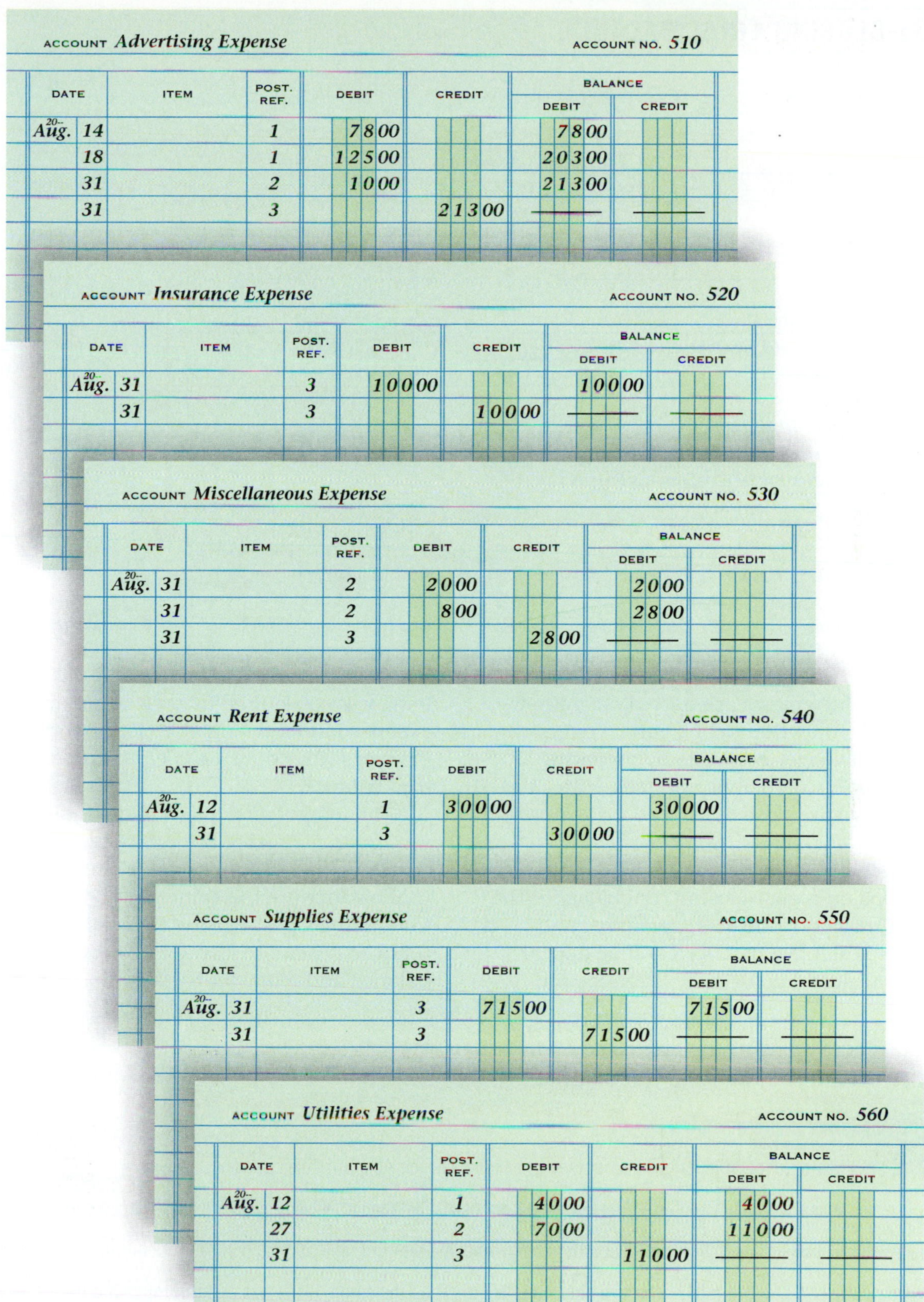

ACCOUNT *Advertising Expense* ACCOUNT NO. *510*

DATE		ITEM	POST. REF.	DEBIT	CREDIT	BALANCE DEBIT	BALANCE CREDIT
20-- Aug.	14		1	78 00		78 00	
	18		1	125 00		203 00	
	31		2	10 00		213 00	
	31		3		213 00	—	—

ACCOUNT *Insurance Expense* ACCOUNT NO. *520*

DATE		ITEM	POST. REF.	DEBIT	CREDIT	BALANCE DEBIT	BALANCE CREDIT
20-- Aug.	31		3	100 00		100 00	
	31		3		100 00	—	—

ACCOUNT *Miscellaneous Expense* ACCOUNT NO. *530*

DATE		ITEM	POST. REF.	DEBIT	CREDIT	BALANCE DEBIT	BALANCE CREDIT
20-- Aug.	31		2	20 00		20 00	
	31		2	8 00		28 00	
	31		3		28 00	—	—

ACCOUNT *Rent Expense* ACCOUNT NO. *540*

DATE		ITEM	POST. REF.	DEBIT	CREDIT	BALANCE DEBIT	BALANCE CREDIT
20-- Aug.	12		1	300 00		300 00	
	31		3		300 00	—	—

ACCOUNT *Supplies Expense* ACCOUNT NO. *550*

DATE		ITEM	POST. REF.	DEBIT	CREDIT	BALANCE DEBIT	BALANCE CREDIT
20-- Aug.	31		3	715 00		715 00	
	31		3		715 00	—	—

ACCOUNT *Utilities Expense* ACCOUNT NO. *560*

DATE		ITEM	POST. REF.	DEBIT	CREDIT	BALANCE DEBIT	BALANCE CREDIT
20-- Aug.	12		1	40 00		40 00	
	27		2	70 00		110 00	
	31		3		110 00	—	—

A General Ledger after Adjusting and Closing Entries Are Posted (concluded)

POST-CLOSING TRIAL BALANCE

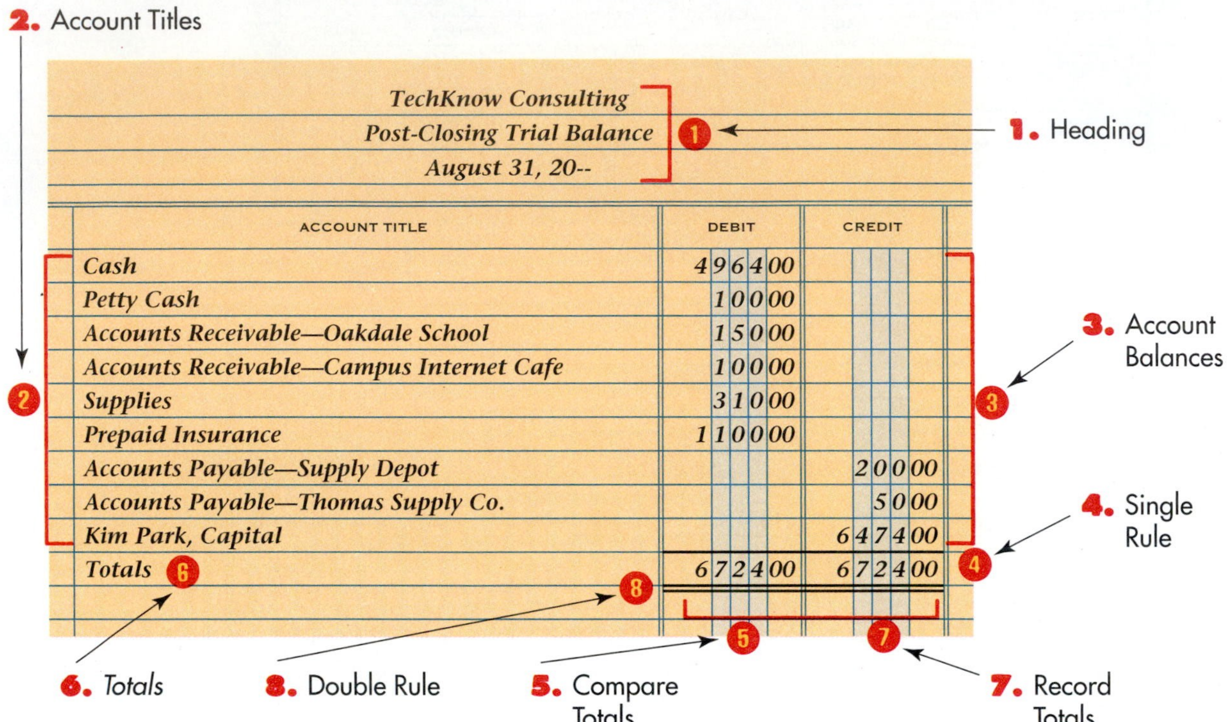

After the closing entries are posted, TechKnow Consulting verifies that debits equal credits in the general ledger accounts by preparing a trial balance. A trial balance prepared after the closing entries are posted is called a **post-closing trial balance**.

Only general ledger accounts with balances are included on a post-closing trial balance. The permanent accounts (assets, liabilities, and owner's capital) have balances and do appear on a post-closing trial balance. Because the temporary accounts (income summary, revenue, expense, and drawing) are closed and have zero balances, they do not appear on a post-closing trial balance.

The total of all debits must equal the total of all credits in a general ledger. The totals of both columns on TechKnow Consulting's post-closing trial balance are the same, $6,724.00. TechKnow Consulting's post-closing trial balance shows that the general ledger account balances are in balance and ready for the new fiscal period.

STEPS • STEPS • STEPS • STEPS • STEPS • STEPS • STEPS • STEPS • STEPS • STEPS •

PREPARING A POST-CLOSING TRIAL BALANCE

1. Write the heading on three lines.
2. Write the titles of all general ledger accounts with balances in the Account Title column.
3. On the same line with each account title, write each account's balance in either the Debit or Credit column.
4. Rule a single line across both amount columns below the last amount, and add each amount column.
5. Compare the two column totals. The two column totals must be the same. If the two column totals are not the same, the errors must be found and corrected before any more work is completed.
6. Write the word *Totals* on the line below the last account title.
7. Write the column totals, *$6,724.00*, below the single line.
8. Rule double lines across both amount columns to show that the totals have been verified as correct.

ACCOUNTING CYCLE FOR A SERVICE BUSINESS

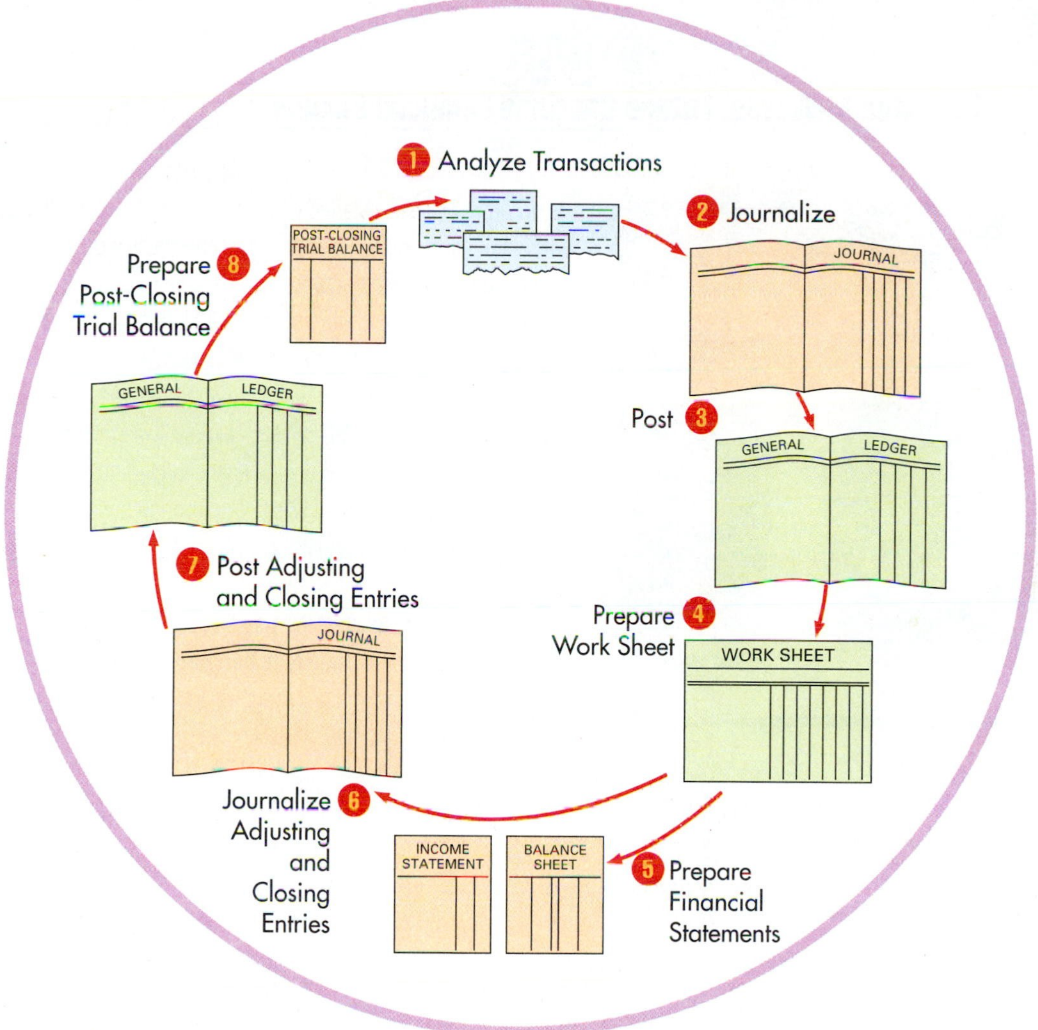

Chapters 1 through 8 describe TechKnow Consulting's accounting activities for a one-month fiscal period. The series of accounting activities included in recording financial information for a fiscal period is called an **accounting cycle**. [*CONCEPT: Accounting Period Cycle*]

For the next fiscal period, the cycle begins again at Step 1.

FYI FOR YOUR INFORMATION

The word *post* means *after*. The Post-Closing Trial Balance is prepared *after* closing entries.

STEPS • STEPS • STEPS • STEPS • STEPS • STEPS

STEPS IN AN ACCOUNTING CYCLE

1. Source documents are checked for accuracy, and transactions are analyzed into debit and credit parts.
2. Transactions, from information on source documents, are recorded in a journal.
3. Journal entries are posted to the general ledger.
4. A work sheet, including a trial balance, is prepared from the general ledger.
5. Financial statements are prepared from the work sheet.
6. Adjusting and closing entries are journalized from the work sheet.
7. Adjusting and closing entries are posted to the general ledger.
8. A post-closing trial balance of the general ledger is prepared.

CAREERS IN ACCOUNTING • CAREERS IN ACCOUNTING • CAREERS IN ACCOUNTI

careers in accounting

Anna McNeese, Future Certified Financial Planner

COURTESY OF ANNA MCNEESE

When Anna McNeese started college, entering the field of accounting wasn't part of her career plan. Through high school she worked at a mental health facility and enjoyed the personal contact she had with the clients in the physical therapy department. But an interest in business (and a sudden lack of interest in biology) led her to change majors as a college sophomore.

After considering the different business degrees offered, she decided to go into accounting. Anna recalls, "I knew I was interested in business, and I thought accounting would be the most challenging. I also heard about the great job market, and since I was going through school during the height of the WorldCom/Enron scandals, any degree that could guarantee job placement was attractive."

But her desire to affect lives personally didn't seem to mix with the large corporate jobs that recruiters from the "Big Four" firms were offering. So when one of her professors told her about a part-time job working for Ernie George, a certified financial planner, Anna saw an opportunity to experience a different type of career.

By working closely with Mr. George and his assistant, Anna has been able use her accounting background to better understand the stock market and what it takes to advise people on how to invest their money. She has found that as a certified financial planner, Mr. George has a close personal relationship with his clients and is able to make the impact that she dreamed of in her early college career.

"I will finish my bachelor's of accountancy next year and immediately enroll in the Master of Taxation program," Anna explains. "Within five years of graduation, I hope to have obtained my certified public accountant (CPA) and certified financial planner (CFP) certifications and go into private practice as a certified financial planner with professional tax expertise."

Salary Range: Median annual earnings of financial planners were $56,680 in 2002, according to the *Occupational Outlook Handbook*. Over 25% of financial planners earn more than $100,000. (Source: Bureau of Labor Statistics, U.S. Department of Labor, *Occupational Outlook Handbook, 2004–05 Edition*; Financial Analysts and Personal Financial Advisors, on the Internet at www.bls.gov/oco/ocos259.htm [visited October 11, 2004].)

Qualifications: A college degree is required, and professional certification is recommended. Financial planners must have good communication skills. Because many financial planners are self-employed, they must also possess the skills necessary to manage a business.

Occupational Outlook: More and more people are choosing alternative ways to plan for retirement. The complexity of the stock market and the tax laws (which can limit how much you can save) have increased the need for professionals who can give sound advice to individuals interested in investing.

terms review

post-closing trial balance
accounting cycle

TERMS REVIEW

audit your understanding

1. Why are lines drawn in both the Balance Debit and Balance Credit columns when an account has a zero balance?
2. Which accounts go on the post-closing trial balance?
3. Why are temporary accounts omitted from a post-closing trial balance?

AUDIT YOUR UNDERSTANDING

work together 8-3

Preparing a post-closing trial balance

Use the general ledger accounts from Work Together 8-2. Your instructor will guide you through the following example. A form to complete a post-closing trial balance is given in the *Working Papers.*

1. Prepare a post-closing trial balance for Darlene's Delivery Service on July 31 of the current year.

WORK TOGETHER

on your own 8-3

Preparing a post-closing trial balance

Use the general ledger accounts from On Your Own 8-2. Work this problem independently. A form to complete a post-closing trial balance is given in the *Working Papers.*

1. Prepare a post-closing trial balance for Cuts by Kelley on February 28 of the current year.

ON YOUR OWN

SUMMARY

After completing this chapter, you can

1. Define accounting terms related to adjusting and closing entries for a service business organized as a proprietorship.
2. Identify accounting concepts and practices related to adjusting and closing entries for a service business organized as a proprietorship.
3. Record adjusting entries for a service business organized as a proprietorship.
4. Record closing entries for a service business organized as a proprietorship.
5. Prepare a post-closing trial balance for a service business organized as a proprietorship.

Explore Accounting

Public Accounting Firms

One type of business that helps other businesses with accounting issues is known as a *public accounting firm*.

The independent reviewing and issuing of an opinion on the reliability of accounting records is known as *auditing*.

When performing an audit for a client, the accounting firm looks closely at the client's financial statements and the way the client records transactions. The auditor's job is to determine if the financial statements fairly present the financial position of the client. The auditor issues an opinion, which is a statement as to whether the financial statements follow standard accounting rules (GAAP). (GAAP stands for *G*enerally *A*ccepted *A*ccounting *P*rinciples.) This "opinion" is used by bankers deciding to lend money to the company. It is also used by investors when making investment decisions.

Auditing, however, is just one of many services provided by public accounting firms. Other services include tax preparation, tax advice, payroll services, bookkeeping services, financial statement preparation, and consulting services. These other services often make up a higher percentage of business for the accounting firm than performing audits.

Many accounting firms report that they are getting more requests for consulting services than for other services they can provide. In many cases, consulting is also the area that produces the largest profit margin for the public accounting firm. Therefore, some firms are actively advertising their ability to provide management consulting services for clients.

Activity: Contact a public accounting firm in your area. Research what services the firm provides and which service area (if any) is growing. Present your findings to your class.

8-1 APPLICATION PROBLEM

Journalizing and posting adjusting entries

A journal and general ledger accounts for Len's Laundry are given in the *Working Papers*. A partial work sheet for the month ended April 30 of the current year is shown below.

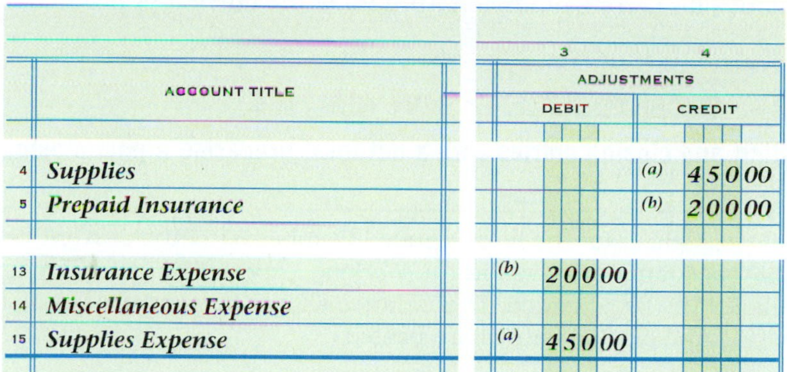

	ACCOUNT TITLE	3 ADJUSTMENTS DEBIT	4 ADJUSTMENTS CREDIT
4	*Supplies*		(a) 450 00
5	*Prepaid Insurance*		(b) 200 00
13	*Insurance Expense*	(b) 200 00	
14	*Miscellaneous Expense*		
15	*Supplies Expense*	(a) 450 00	

Use page 12 of a journal. Journalize and post the adjusting entries. Save your work to complete Application Problem 8-2.

8-2 APPLICATION PROBLEM

Journalizing and posting closing entries

Use the journal and general ledger accounts for Len's Laundry from Application Problem 8-1. A partial work sheet for the month ended April 30 of the current year is shown below.

	ACCOUNT TITLE	5 INCOME STATEMENT DEBIT	6 INCOME STATEMENT CREDIT	7 BALANCE SHEET DEBIT	8 BALANCE SHEET CREDIT	
1	*Cash*			7607 00		1
2	*Accounts Receivable—Natasha Goodlad*			700 00		2
3	*Accounts Receivable—R. Henry*			498 00		3
4	*Supplies*			431 00		4
5	*Prepaid Insurance*			200 00		5
6	*Accounts Payable—Tri-County Supplies*				381 00	6
7	*Accounts Payable—West End Supply Co.*				555 00	7
8	*Leonard Long, Capital*				6527 00	8
9	*Leonard Long, Drawing*			1000 00		9
10	*Income Summary*					10
11	*Sales*		6233 00			11
12	*Advertising Expense*	800 00				12
13	*Insurance Expense*	200 00				13
14	*Miscellaneous Expense*	315 00				14
15	*Supplies Expense*	450 00				15
16	*Utilities Expense*	1495 00				16
17		3260 00	6233 00	10436 00	7463 00	17
18	*Net Income*	2973 00			2973 00	18
19		6233 00	6233 00	10436 00	10436 00	19
20						20

Continue on the same journal page. Journalize and post the closing entries. Save your work to complete Application Problem 8-3.

8-3 APPLICATION PROBLEM

Preparing a post-closing trial balance

Use the general ledger accounts for Len's Laundry from Application Problem 8-2. A form to complete a post-closing trial balance is given in the *Working Papers*.

Prepare a post-closing trial balance for Len's Laundry on April 30 of the current year.

8-4 MASTERY PROBLEM

AUTOMATED ACCOUNTING PEACHTREE QUICKBOOKS

Journalizing and posting adjusting and closing entries with a net loss; preparing a post-closing trial balance

Rolstad Repair Service's partial work sheet for the month ended October 31 of the current year is given below. The general ledger accounts are given in the *Working Papers*. The general ledger accounts do not show all details for the fiscal period. The Balance shown in each account is the account's balance before adjusting and closing entries are posted.

		3	4	5	6	7	8	
	ACCOUNT TITLE	ADJUSTMENTS		INCOME STATEMENT		BALANCE SHEET		
		DEBIT	CREDIT	DEBIT	CREDIT	DEBIT	CREDIT	
1	*Cash*					6958 00		1
2	*Petty Cash*					150 00		2
3	*Accts. Rec.—M. Hollerud*					197 00		3
4	*Supplies*		(a) 1400 00			780 00		4
5	*Prepaid Insurance*		(b) 157 00			800 00		5
6	*Accts. Pay.—Tampa Supply*						612 00	6
7	*Ron Rolstad, Capital*						9337 00	7
8	*Ron Rolstad, Drawing*					600 00		8
9	*Income Summary*							9
10	*Sales*				3269 00			10
11	*Advertising Expense*			450 00				11
12	*Insurance Expense*	(b) 157 00		157 00				12
13	*Miscellaneous Expense*			85 00				13
14	*Supplies Expense*	(a) 1400 00		1400 00				14
15	*Utilities Expense*			1641 00				15
16		1557 00	1557 00	3733 00	3269 00	9485 00	9949 00	16
17	*Net Loss*				464 00	464 00		17
18				3733 00	3733 00	9949 00	9949 00	18
19								19

Instructions:

1. Use page 20 of a journal. Journalize and post the adjusting entries.
2. Continue to use page 20 of the journal. Journalize and post the closing entries.
3. Prepare a post-closing trial balance.

8-5 CHALLENGE PROBLEM

AUTOMATED ACCOUNTING | PEACHTREE | QUICKBOOKS

Journalizing and posting adjusting and closing entries with two revenue accounts and a net loss; preparing a post-closing trial balance

LawnMow's partial work sheet for the month ended September 30 of the current year is given below. The general ledger accounts are given in the *Working Papers.* The general ledger accounts do not show all details for the fiscal period. The Balance shown in each account is the account's balance before adjusting and closing entries are posted.

		3	4	5	6	7	8	
	ACCOUNT TITLE	ADJUSTMENTS		INCOME STATEMENT		BALANCE SHEET		
		DEBIT	CREDIT	DEBIT	CREDIT	DEBIT	CREDIT	
1	*Cash*					1898 00		1
2	*Accts. Rec.—Sandra Rohe*					95 00		2
3	*Supplies*		(a) 3200 00			650 00		3
4	*Prepaid Insurance*		(b) 400 00			1200 00		4
5	*Accts. Pay.—Corner Garage*						58 00	5
6	*Accts. Pay.—Broadway Gas*						110 00	6
7	*Accts. Pay.—Esko Repair*						215 00	7
8	*Ryo Morrison, Capital*						4000 00	8
9	*Ryo Morrison, Drawing*					100 00		9
10	*Income Summary*							10
11	*Sales—Lawn Care*				4900 00			11
12	*Sales—Shrub Care*				2500 00			12
13	*Advertising Expense*			390 00				13
14	*Insurance Expense*	(b) 400 00		400 00				14
15	*Miscellaneous Expense*			550 00				15
16	*Rent Expense*			3300 00				16
17	*Supplies Expense*	(a) 3200 00		3200 00				17
18		3600 00	3600 00	7840 00	7400 00	3943 00	4383 00	18
19	*Net Loss*				440 00	440 00		19
20		3600 00	3600 00	7840 00	7840 00	4383 00	4383 00	20
21								21

Instructions:

1. Use page 18 of a journal. Journalize and post the adjusting entries.
2. Continue to use page 18 of the journal. Journalize and post the closing entries.
3. Prepare a post-closing trial balance.
4. Ryo Morrison, owner of LawnMow, is disappointed that his business incurred a net loss for September of the current year. Mr. Morrison would have preferred not to have to reduce his capital by $440.00. He knows that you are studying accounting, so Mr. Morrison asks you to analyze his work sheet for September. Based on your analysis of the work sheet, what would you suggest might have caused the net loss for LawnMow? What steps would you suggest so that Mr. Morrison can avoid a net loss in future months?

applied communication

Service businesses are the fastest growing part of our business world. Social and economic changes create needs for new and different kinds of service businesses to satisfy customer demands.

For example, the growing popularity of the World Wide Web led to the creation of service businesses that design Web pages. These businesses create text, graphics, animation, and links for business and private clients. Another example of a new type of service business is a personal services business that runs errands or stands in long lines for clients. As lifestyles become busier and busier, some people do not have the time to take care of all their personal errands. Service businesses have appeared to fill this need.

Instructions: Using library, online, or other information resources, write a one-page report on a new or unusual service business that you would be interested in working for or owning.

cases for critical thinking

Case 1

Gretel Bakken forgot to journalize and post the adjusting entry for prepaid insurance at the end of the June fiscal period. What effect will this omission have on the records of Ms. Bakken's business as of June 30? Explain your answer.

Case 2

Vincente Burgos states that his business is so small that he just records supplies and insurance as expenses when he pays for them. Thus, at the end of a fiscal period, Mr. Burgos does not record adjusting and closing entries for his business. Do you agree with his accounting procedures? Explain your answer.

SCANS workplace competency

Thinking Skill: Seeing things in the mind's eye

Concept: Effective employees can visualize how every part of a company contributes to the success of the whole company, from maintenance workers to the chief executive officer. Now that you have finished the study of a complete accounting cycle, you should better understand how each part of the cycle contributes to the whole cycle.

Application: Describe the importance of the work each of the following employees does. Explain how errors would affect the reporting of the company.

a. Employee who reconciles the bank statement.
b. Employee who determines the amount of supplies on hand at the end of the fiscal period.
c. Employee who posts the journal entries.
d. Employee who calculates and records the adjusting entries.
e. Employee who records the closing entries.

• auditing for errors

The closing entries for Greenlund Enterprises are given below. Assuming all account balances are correct, review the entries. List any errors you find.

Date	Account Title	Doc No.	Post Ref.	General	
				Debit	Credit
20-- May 31	Income Summary			32,000	
	Sales				32,000
31	Income Summary			6,200	
	Insurance Expense			900	
	Rent Expense				2,500
	Supplies Expense				1,200
	Utilities Expense				3,400
31	Lionel Greenlund, Capital			38,200	
	Income Summary				38,200
31	Lionel Greenlund, Capital			4,500	
	Lionel Greenlund, Drawing				4,500

AUDITING FOR ERRORS • AUDITING FOR ERRORS • AUDITING

• analyzing Best Buy's financial statements

Refer to Best Buy's consolidated statements of earnings on Appendix B page B-6. To calculate what percentage an item increased or decreased from one year to another, calculate the difference between the two amounts and divide this difference by the amount for the earlier year. For example, the percentage of increase in revenue from 2002 to 2003 would be calculated as follows: (\$20,946,000,000 − \$17,711,000,000) ÷ \$17,711,000,000 = 18.27%.

Instructions

1. What is Best Buy's revenue (sales) for each of the three years? Is this a favorable or unfavorable trend?
2. Calculate the percentage of increase in revenue from 2003 to 2004.
3. How does the increase from 2003 to 2004 compare to the increase from 2002 to 2003?

ANALYZING BEST BUY'S FINANCIAL

Automated Adjusting and Closing Entries for Proprietorships

During the fiscal period, numerous transactions are analyzed, journalized, and posted. When a transaction affects more than one accounting period, an adjusting entry may be needed to match revenues and expenses with the appropriate accounting period. To complete the accounting cycle, adjusting entries are entered into the computer and verified for accuracy. The financial statements are generated, and then closing entries are generated and posted by the software.

Adjusting Entries

After all the usual transactions of the business are entered as journal entries, a preliminary trial balance is generated. This trial balance and period-end adjustment data are used as the basis for the adjusting entries. Usually this will include entries for assets that have been consumed or sold during the period and have become expenses, such as supplies and insurance policies. For most asset accounts, such as Supplies and Prepaid Insurance, the adjustment is made to the related expense account. The General Journal tab within the Journal Entries window is used to enter and post the adjusting entries. All of the adjusting entries are dated the last day of the fiscal period, and use *Adj. Ent.* as the reference. Using a consistent reference for adjusting entries means that you can customize a journal report to include only these entries.

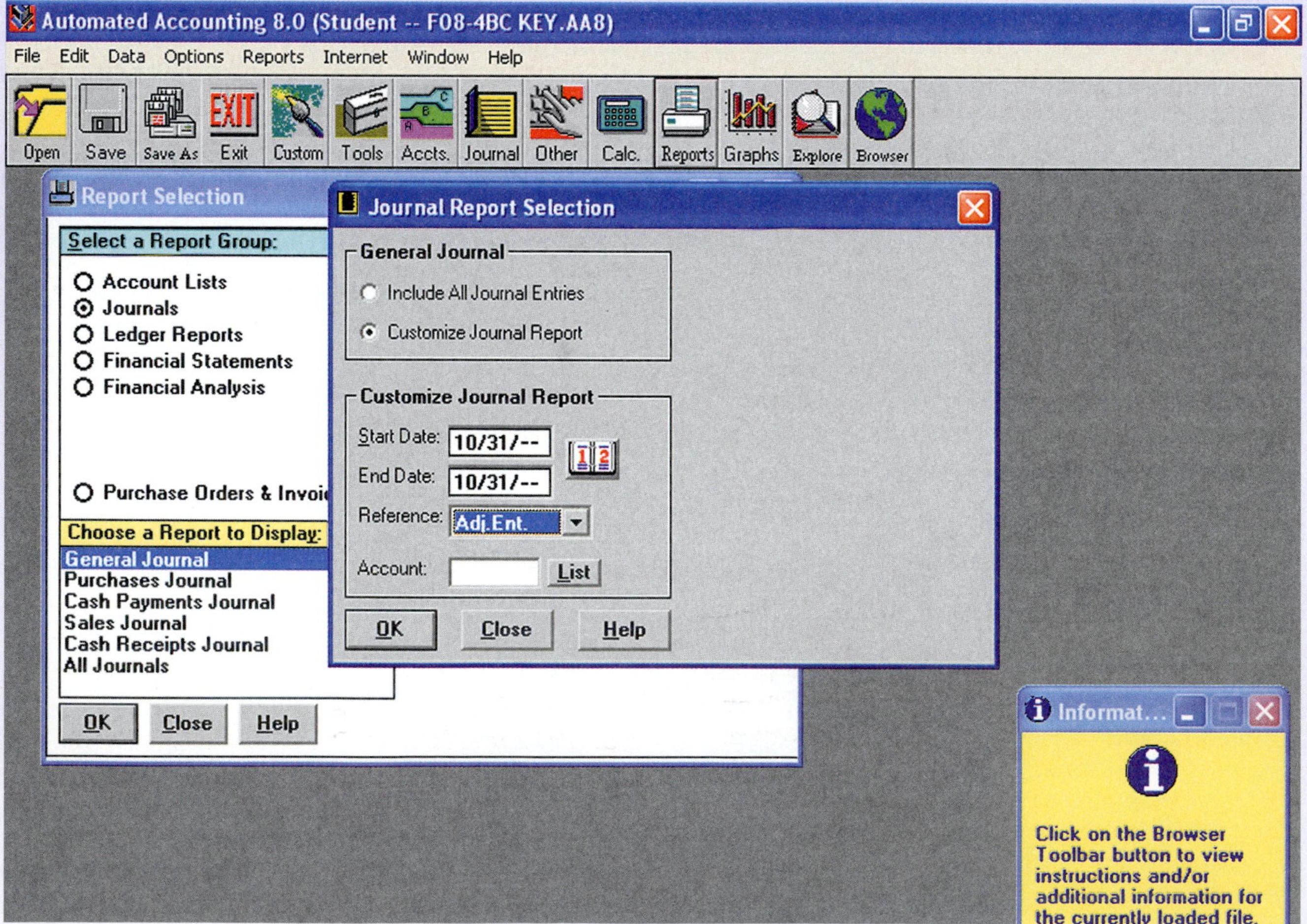

Sequence of the Automated Accounting Cycle

The accounting cycle for an automated system differs somewhat from a manual accounting cycle. In a manual accounting cycle, a work sheet is prepared with adjustments so that financial statements can be prepared from the work sheet's adjusted Income Statement and Balance Sheet columns. The adjusting entries are journalized and posted, closing entries are journalized and posted, and a post-closing trial balance is prepared to prove the general ledger.

In an automated accounting cycle, a work sheet is not prepared. Instead, a trial balance is displayed or printed so that adjustments can be planned. The adjusting entries are then journalized in the automated accounting software, and the financial statements are displayed or printed. Then the software can be used to generate the closing entries, which are checked for accuracy and then posted automatically. An additional trial balance is displayed or printed as a proof of the general ledger.

Period-End Closing for a Proprietorship

In an automated accounting system, closing entries are generated and posted by the software. The software automatically closes net income to the owner's capital account after closing the revenue and expense accounts. The drawing account is closed as well.

To perform a period-end closing:

1. Choose Generate Closing Journal Entries from the Options menu.
2. Click Yes to generate the closing entries.
3. The general journal will appear, containing the journal entries.
4. Click the Post button.

Precautions for Closing Entries

In *Automated Accounting 8.0*, once closing entries are posted, the journal entries of the period cannot be accessed to make corrections if errors are found later. Therefore it is always a good practice to save your file before closing entries are generated; an addition of the letters BC (for *Before Closing*) can be added to the filename. Then the file is saved again after the closing entries are generated, with the letters AC (for *After Closing*) added to the filename. When this procedure is followed, if it is necessary to correct a journal entry, the file with "BC" in its name can be opened and corrected, and closing entries can be generated again.

AUTOMATING MASTERY PROBLEM 8-4: Journalizing and posting adjusting and closing entries with a net loss; preparing a post-closing trial balance

Instructions:

1. Load the *Automated Accounting 8.0* or higher software.
2. Select data file F08-4 from the appropriate directory/folder.
3. Select File from the menu bar and choose the Save As menu command. Key the path to the drive and directory that contains your data files. Save the data file with a filename of F08-4 XXX XXX (where the X's are your first and last name).
4. Access Problem Instructions through the Browser tool. Read the Problem Instructions screen.
5. Refer to Mastery Problem 8-4 in this textbook for data used in this problem.
6. Save your file and exit the Automated Accounting software.

AUTOMATING CHALLENGE PROBLEM 8-5: Journalizing and posting adjusting and closing entries with two revenue accounts and a net loss; preparing a post-closing trial balance

Instructions:

1. Load the *Automated Accounting 8.0* or higher software.
2. Select data file F08-5 from the appropriate directory/folder.
3. Select File from the menu bar and choose the Save As menu command. Key the path to the drive and directory that contains your data files. Save the data file with a filename of F08-5 XXX XXX (where the X's are your first and last name).
4. Access Problem Instructions through the Browser tool. Read the Problem Instructions screen.
5. Refer to Challenge Problem 8-5 for data used in this problem.
6. Save your file and exit the Automated Accounting software.

An Accounting Cycle for a Proprietorship: End-of-Fiscal-Period Work

The general ledger prepared in Reinforcement Activity 1—Part A is needed to complete Reinforcement Activity 1—Part B.

Reinforcement Activity 1—Part B includes end-of-fiscal-period activities studied in Chapters 6 through 8.

WORK SHEET

Instructions:

12. Prepare a trial balance on the work sheet given in the *Working Papers*. Use a one-month fiscal period ended May 31 of the current year.
13. Analyze the following adjustment information into debit and credit parts. Record the adjustments on the work sheet.

Adjustment Information, May 31

Supplies on hand	$ 625.00
Value of prepaid insurance	1,100.00

14. Total and rule the Adjustments columns.
15. Extend the up-to-date account balances to the Balance Sheet and Income Statement columns.
16. Complete the work sheet.

FINANCIAL STATEMENTS

Instructions:

17. Prepare an income statement. Figure and record the component percentages for sales, total expenses, and net income. Round percentage calculations to the nearest 0.1%.
18. Prepare a balance sheet.

ADJUSTING ENTRIES

Instructions:

19. Use page 3 of the journal. Journalize and post the adjusting entries.

CLOSING ENTRIES

Instructions:

20. Continue using page 3 of the journal. Journalize and post the closing entries.

POST-CLOSING TRIAL BALANCE

Instructions:

21. Prepare a post-closing trial balance.

E. T. T

The following activities are included in this simulation:

1. Journalizing transactions in a 5-column journal.
2. Preparing a bank statement reconciliation and recording a bank service charge.
3. Proving cash.
4. Posting from a journal to a general ledger.
5. Preparing a trial balance on a work sheet.
6. Recording adjustments on a work sheet.
7. Completing a work sheet.
8. Preparing financial statements (income statement and balance sheet).
9. Journalizing and posting adjusting entries.
10. Journalizing and posting closing entries.
11. Preparing a post-closing trial balance.

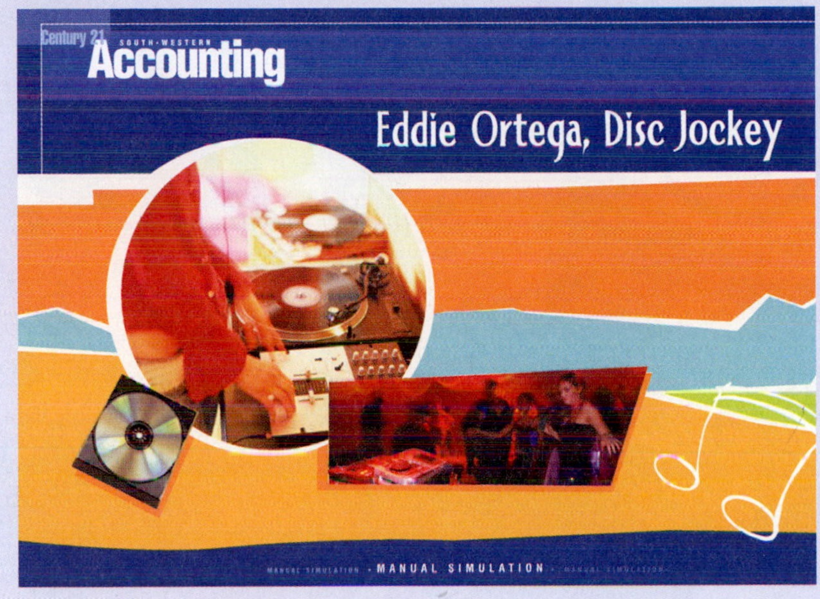

Eddie Ortega, Disc Jockey

This simulation covers the transactions completed by Eddie Ortega, Disc Jockey, a service business organized as a proprietorship. On September 1 of the current year, Eddie Ortega, Disc Jockey, begins business. The owner, Eddie Ortega, performs as a disc jockey at clubs and private parties. He also specializes in karaoke when requested.

The activities included in the accounting cycle for Eddie Ortega, Disc Jockey, are listed at the left. The company uses a 5-column journal and a general ledger similar to those described for TechKnow in Cycle 1.

This simulation is available in manual and in automated versions, for use with *Automated Accounting* software.

PART 2 Accounting for a Merchandising Business Organized as a Corporation

THE BUSINESS • THE BUSINESS • THE BUSINESS

THE BUSINESS—HOBBY SHACK, INC.

Hobby Shack, Inc., the business described in Part 2, is a retail merchandising business organized as a corporation. The business purchases and sells a wide variety of craft and hobby items such as silk flowers, ceramics, paints, and jewelry. Hobby Shack purchases its merchandise directly from businesses that manufacture the items. Hobby Shack rents the building in which the business is located.

HOBBY SHACK, INC., CHART OF ACCOUNTS

General Ledger

Balance Sheet Accounts

(1000) ASSETS
1100 Current Assets
1110 Cash
1120 Petty Cash
1130 Accounts Receivable
1135 Allowance for Uncollectible Accounts
1140 Merchandise Inventory
1145 Supplies—Office
1150 Supplies—Store
1160 Prepaid Insurance
1200 Plant Assets
1205 Office Equipment
1210 Accumulated Depreciation—Office Equipment
1215 Store Equipment
1220 Accumulated Depreciation—Store Equipment

(2000) LIABILITIES
2100 Current Liabilities
2110 Accounts Payable
2120 Federal Income Tax Payable
2130 Employee Income Tax Payable
2135 Social Security Tax Payable
2140 Medicare Tax Payable
2145 Sales Tax Payable
2150 Unemployment Tax Payable—Federal
2155 Unemployment Tax Payable—State
2160 Health Insurance Premiums Payable
2165 U.S. Savings Bonds Payable
2170 United Way Donations Payable
2180 Dividends Payable

(3000) STOCKHOLDERS' EQUITY
3110 Capital Stock
3120 Retained Earnings
3130 Dividends
3140 Income Summary

Income Statement Accounts

(4000) OPERATING REVENUE
4110 Sales
4120 Sales Discount
4130 Sales Returns and Allowances

(5000) COST OF MERCHANDISE
5110 Purchases
5120 Purchases Discount
5130 Purchases Returns and Allowances

(6000) OPERATING EXPENSES
6105 Advertising Expense
6110 Cash Short and Over
6115 Credit Card Fee Expense
6120 Depreciation Expense—Office Equipment
6125 Depreciation Expense—Store Equipment
6130 Insurance Expense
6135 Miscellaneous Expense
6140 Payroll Taxes Expense
6145 Rent Expense
6150 Salary Expense
6155 Supplies Expense—Office
6160 Supplies Expense—Store
6165 Uncollectible Accounts Expense
6170 Utilities Expense
6200 Income Tax Expense
6205 Federal Income Tax Expense

Subsidiary Ledgers

Accounts Receivable Ledger

110 Country Crafters
120 Cumberland Center
130 Fairview Church
140 Playtime Childcare
150 Village Crafts
160 Washington Schools

Accounts Payable Ledger

210 American Paint
220 Ceramic Supply
230 Crown Distributing
240 Floral Designs
250 Gulf Craft Supply
260 Synthetic Arts

The charts of accounts for Hobby Shack, Inc., are illustrated here for ready reference as you study Part 2 of this textbook.

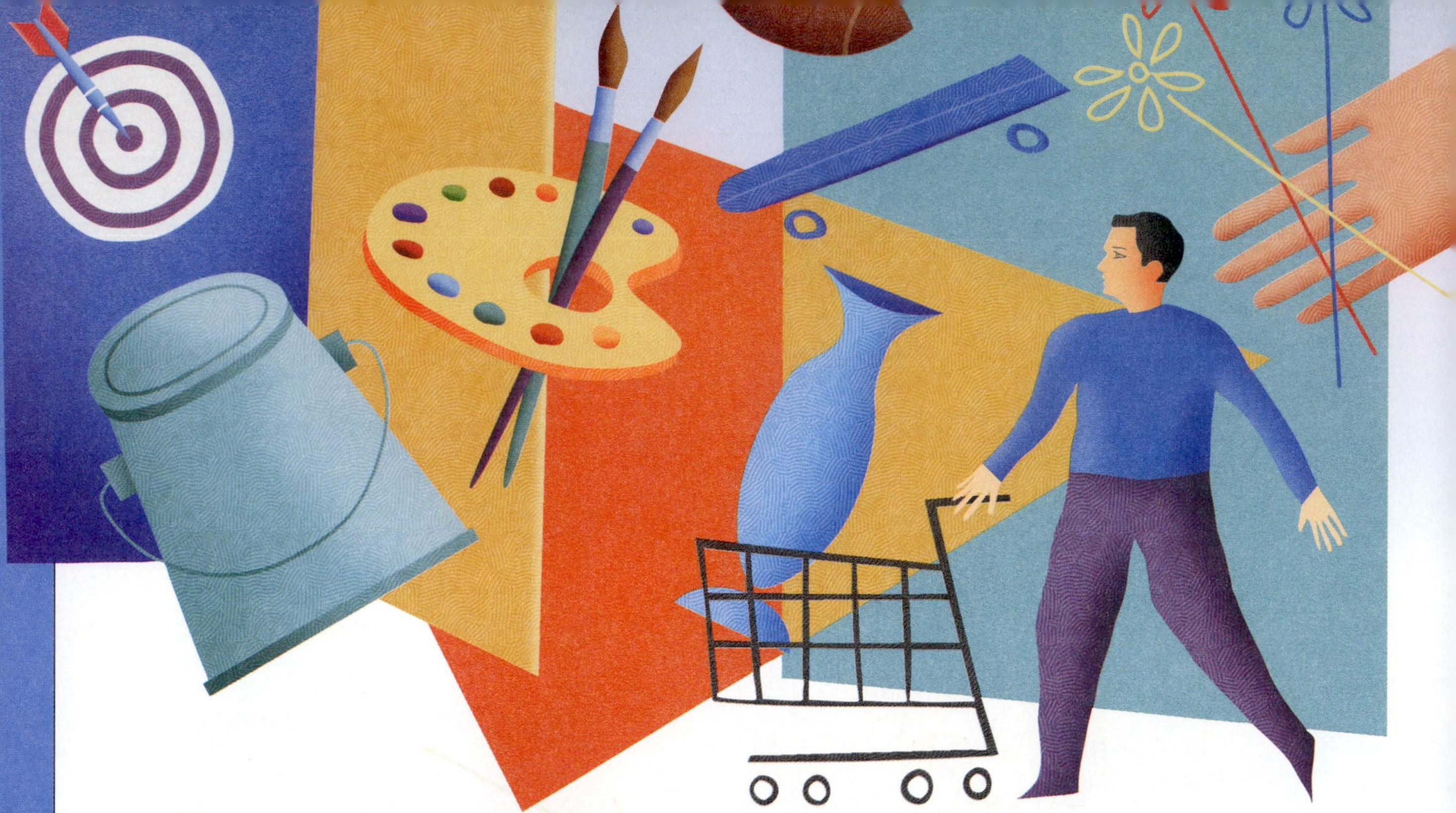

CHAPTER 9

Journalizing Purchases and Cash Payments

OBJECTIVES & TERMS

After studying Chapter 9, you will be able to:

1. Define accounting terms related to purchases and cash payments for a merchandising business.
2. Identify accounting concepts and practices related to purchases and cash payments for a merchandising business.
3. Journalize purchases of merchandise using a purchases journal.
4. Journalize cash payments and cash discounts using a cash payments journal.
5. Prepare a petty cash report and journalize the reimbursement of the petty cash fund.
6. Total, prove, and rule a cash payments journal and start a new cash payments journal page.
7. Journalize purchases returns and allowances and other transactions using a general journal.

- merchandise
- merchandising business
- retail merchandising business
- wholesale merchandising business
- corporation
- share of stock
- capital stock
- stockholder
- special journal
- cost of merchandise
- markup
- vendor
- purchase on account
- purchases journal
- special amount column
- purchase invoice
- terms of sale
- cash payments journal
- cash discount
- purchases discount
- general amount column
- list price
- trade discount
- contra account
- cash short
- cash over
- purchases return
- purchases allowance
- debit memorandum

Point Your Browser
accountingxtra.swlearning.com

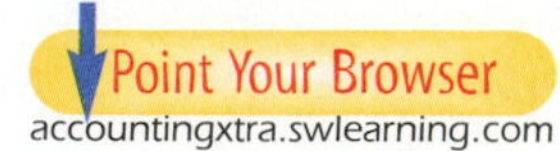

accounting in the real world

OfficeMax

©BLOOMBERG NEWS/LANDOV

PURCHASING SYNERGIES BENEFIT OFFICEMAX AND BOISE OFFICE SOLUTIONS

Like the trees it manages, Boise Cascade Corporation has grown and evolved from its roots as a wood products company in Boise, Idaho. Building on its strength as a manufacturer of wood building products and paper, Boise established Boise Office Solutions to provide office supplies and furniture directly to businesses, government offices, and educational institutions.

In its 2002 annual report, Boise stated, "Boise Office Solutions' primary goal is profitable growth. This means winning new customers, selling more products to existing customers, and controlling operating costs."

Boise took a bold step to achieve that goal through the 2003 acquisition of OfficeMax, an office products company with nearly 1,000 retail outlets. The acquisition more than doubled sales in Boise's office products distribution business.

The company expects to use its combined purchasing power to lower the cost of the office products purchased from other manufacturers and to eliminate duplicate distribution facilities and marketing efforts. Boise expects the combined companies to achieve synergy benefits of $160 million a year.

Critical Thinking

1. How can purchasing more units of an item enable a company to purchase that item at a reduced cost?
2. Can you think of any two other companies that could reduce their operating costs by combining their businesses?

Source: 2002 and 2003 Annual Reports for Boise Cascade Corporation

accountingxtra.swlearning.com

ACCOUNTING IN THE REAL WORLD • ACCOUNTING IN THE REAL WORLD • ACCOUNTING IN THE REAL WORLD •

internet activity

C CORPORATIONS, S CORPORATIONS, AND LLCs

There are several factors to consider when organizing a corporation. One of these is to determine what type of corporation you want to organize. Search the Internet for an explanation of each of the following types of corporations: C Corporation, S Corporation, and a Limited Liability Company (LLC).

Instructions

1. List the benefits and disadvantages of a C Corporation.
2. List the benefits and disadvantages of an S Corporation.
3. List the benefits and disadvantages of a Limited Liability Company.

INTERNET RESEARCH ACTIVITY • INTERNET RESEARCH ACTIVITY • INTERNET RESEARCH ACTIVITY •

LESSON • LESSON • LESSON • LESSON • LESSON • LESSON

9-1 Journalizing Purchases Using a Purchases Journal

MERCHANDISING BUSINESSES

TechKnow Consulting, the business described in Part 1, is a service business; it sells services for a fee. However, many other businesses purchase goods to sell. Goods that a business purchases to sell are called **merchandise**. A business that purchases and sells goods is called a **merchandising business**. A merchandising business that sells to those who use or consume the goods is called a **retail merchandising business**. A business that buys and resells merchandise to retail merchandising businesses is called a **wholesale merchandising business**. Service and merchandising businesses use many of the same accounts. A merchandising business has additional accounts on the balance sheet and income statement to account for the purchase and sale of merchandise.

©GETTY IMAGES/PHOTODISC

business structures • BUSINESS STRUCTURES • BUSINESS STRUCTURES • BUSINESS STRUCTURES

Forming a Corporation

Many businesses need amounts of capital that cannot be easily provided by a proprietorship. These businesses choose to organize using another form of business. An organization with the legal rights of a person and which many persons may own is called a **corporation**. A corporation is formed by receiving approval from a state or federal agency. Each unit of ownership in a corporation is called a **share of stock**. Total shares of ownership in a corporation are called **capital stock**. An owner of one or more shares of a corporation is called a **stockholder**.

A corporation is a business organization that has the legal rights of a person. A corporation can own property, incur liabilities, and enter into contracts in its own name. A corporation may also sell ownership in itself. A person becomes an owner of a corporation by purchasing shares of stock.

The principal difference between the accounting records of proprietorships and corporations is in the capital accounts. Proprietorships have a single capital and drawing account for the owner. A corporation has separate capital accounts for the stock issued and for the earnings kept in the business, which will be explained in more detail in Chapter 16. As in proprietorships, information in a corporation's accounting system is kept separate from the personal records of its owners. [*CONCEPT: Business Entity*] Periodic financial statements must be sent to the stockholders of the corporation to report the financial activities of the business.

Critical Thinking

1. The names of many corporations include the words *Corporation*, *Incorporated*, *Corp.*, or *Inc.* in their names. Based on their names, identify several corporations in your area.
2. Why do you think many very large companies are organized as corporations?

THE BUSINESS—HOBBY SHACK, INC.

Janice Kellogg decided to quit her full-time job and turn her ceramic hobby into a retail hobby business. She developed a plan to rent space in a shopping center and operate Hobby Shack six days a week. Hobby Shack would sell a wide variety of art and hobby supplies to individuals, schools, and businesses. Janice planned to expand the merchandise she offers, rent store and office equipment, and employ other individuals to work in the store. However, Janice did not personally have the capital to implement her plan. But with the help of a small group of investors, Janice formed a corporation called Hobby Shack, Inc. Each stockholder received a number of shares of stock based on the amount invested.

Unlike a proprietorship, a corporation exists independent of its owners. Janice expects the Hobby Shack to continue beyond her lifetime and plans to give her shares of stock to her children. [*CONCEPT: Going Concern*]

USING SPECIAL JOURNALS

A business with a limited number of daily transactions may record all entries in one journal. A business with many daily transactions may choose to use a separate journal for each kind of transaction. A journal used to record only one kind of transaction is called a **special journal**. Hobby Shack uses five journals to record daily transactions:

1. Purchases journal—for all purchases of merchandise on account
2. Cash payments journal—for all cash payments
3. Sales journal—for all sales of merchandise on account
4. Cash receipts journal—for all cash receipts
5. General journal—for all other transactions

Recording transactions in a sales journal and a cash receipts journal is described in Chapter 10.

MAKING ETHICAL DECISIONS • MAKING ETHICAL DECISIONS • MAKING ETHICAL DECISIONS

making ethical decisions

Walking on Ethical Ice

Lockheed Martin is an international corporation engaged in the production of advanced technology systems. The company's largest customers are the U.S. Department of Defense and other U.S. federal government agencies.

Lockheed Martin is working to be a leader in ethical conduct. In its code of conduct, "Setting the Standard," the company provides its employees with detailed guidance on making ethical decisions. One method of assisting its employees to make ethical decisions is to provide a list of statements that are warning signs of unethical behavior, such as the following:

"Well, maybe just this once."
"No one will ever know."
"It doesn't matter how it gets done as long as it gets done."
"It sounds too good to be true."
"Everyone does it."
"Shred that document."
"We can hide it."
"No one will get hurt."
"What's in it for me?"
"This will destroy the competition."
"We didn't have this conversation."

Instructions

Think of statements you hear that are warning signs of unethical behavior.

Source: www.lockheedmartin.com

PURCHASING MERCHANDISE

The price a business pays for goods it purchases to sell is called **cost of merchandise**. The selling price of merchandise must be greater than the cost of merchandise for a business to make a profit. The amount added to the cost of merchandise to establish the selling price is called **markup**. Revenue earned from the sale of merchandise includes both the cost of merchandise and markup. Only the markup increases capital. Accounts for the cost of merchandise are kept in a separate division of the general ledger. The cost of merchandise division is shown in Hobby Shack's chart of accounts on page 231.

In addition to purchasing merchandise to sell, a merchandising business also buys supplies and other assets for use in the business. A business from which merchandise is purchased or supplies or other assets are bought is called a **vendor**.

The account used for recording the cost of merchandise is titled Purchases. Purchases is classified as a cost account because it is in the cost of merchandise division in the chart of accounts. Purchases is a temporary account. Because the cost of merchandise reduces capital when the merchandise is purchased, Purchases has a normal debit balance. Therefore, the purchases account increases by a debit and decreases by a credit, as shown in the T account.

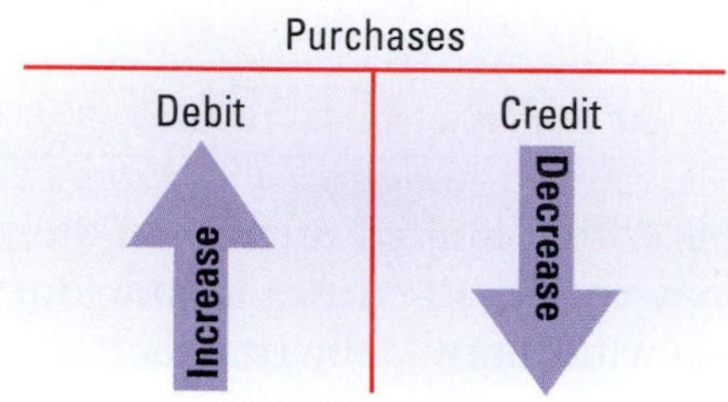

PURCHASES ON ACCOUNT

The cost account, Purchases, is used only to record the cost of merchandise purchased. No other items bought, such as supplies, are recorded in the purchases account. These items are recorded in other accounts, such as Supplies. Merchandise and other items bought are recorded and reported at the price agreed upon at the time the transactions occur. The accounting concept *Historical Cost* is applied when the actual amount paid for merchandise or other items bought is recorded. [*CONCEPT: Historical Cost*]

A transaction in which the merchandise purchased is to be paid for later is called a **purchase on account**. Some businesses that purchase on account from only a few vendors keep a separate general ledger account for each vendor. Businesses that purchase on account from many vendors will have many accounts for vendors. To avoid a bulky general ledger, the total amount owed to all vendors can be summarized in a single general ledger account. A liability account that summarizes the amounts owed to all vendors is titled Accounts Payable. Hobby Shack uses an accounts payable account. The liability account, Accounts Payable, has a normal credit balance. Therefore, the accounts payable account increases by a credit and decreases by a debit, as shown in the T account.

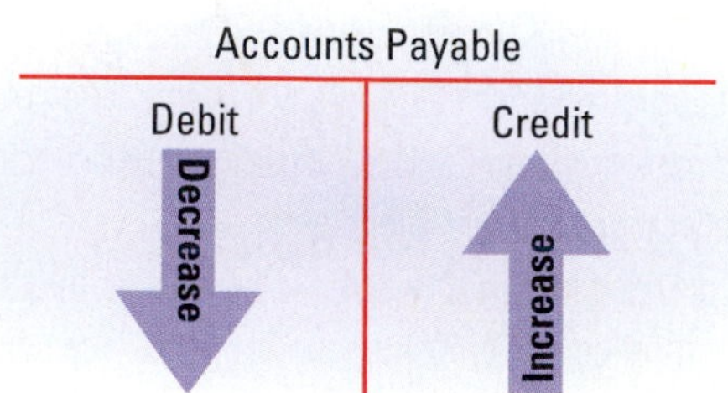

PURCHASES JOURNAL

PURCHASES JOURNAL PAGE

	DATE		ACCOUNT CREDITED	PURCH. NO.	POST. REF.	PURCHASES DR. ACCTS. PAY. CR.	
1							1
2							2

A special journal used to record only purchases of merchandise on account is called a **purchases journal**. A purchase on account transaction is recorded on only one line of Hobby Shack's purchases journal. The amount column has two account titles in its heading: *Purchases Dr.* and *Accts. Pay. Cr.* A journal amount column headed with an account title is called a **special amount column**. Special amount columns are used for frequently occurring transactions. All of Hobby Shack's purchase on account transactions involve a debit to Purchases and a credit to Accounts Payable. Therefore, Hobby Shack's special amount column in the purchases journal includes those accounts in the heading.

Using special amount columns eliminates writing general ledger account titles in the Account Title column. Recording entries in a journal with special amount columns saves time.

REMEMBER All purchase on account transactions are recorded in the purchases journal. If a purchase is made for cash, the transaction is NOT recorded in the purchases journal.

©GETTY IMAGES/PHOTODISC

PURCHASE INVOICE

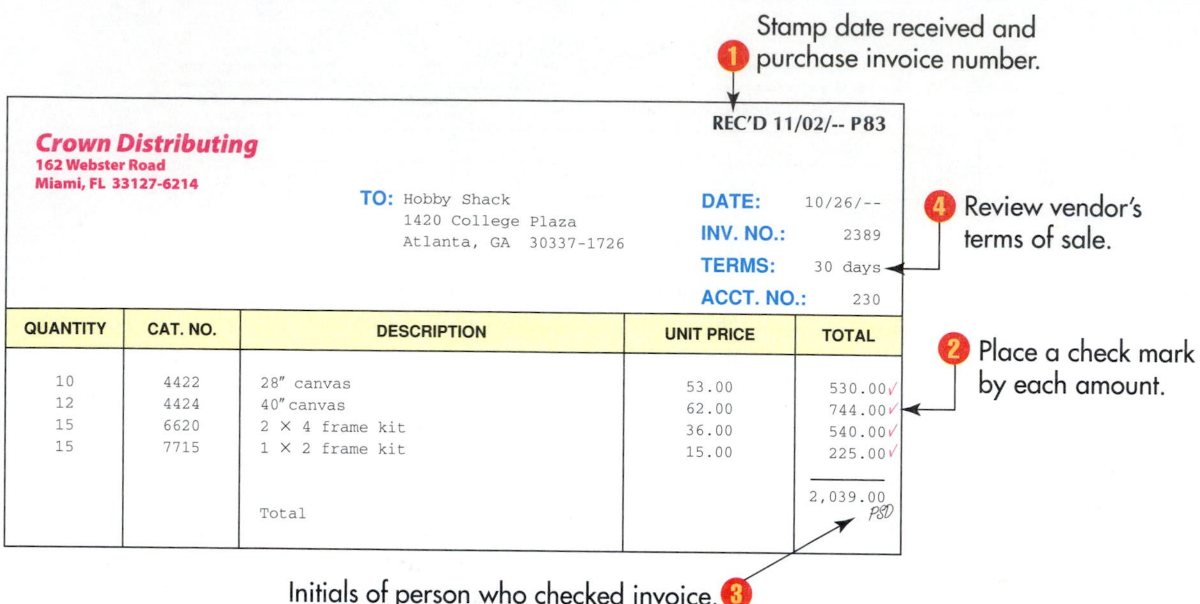

1 Stamp date received and purchase invoice number.
4 Review vendor's terms of sale.
2 Place a check mark by each amount.
Initials of person who checked invoice. 3

REC'D 11/02/-- P83

Crown Distributing
162 Webster Road
Miami, FL 33127-6214

TO: Hobby Shack
1420 College Plaza
Atlanta, GA 30337-1726

DATE: 10/26/--
INV. NO.: 2389
TERMS: 30 days
ACCT. NO.: 230

QUANTITY	CAT. NO.	DESCRIPTION	UNIT PRICE	TOTAL
10	4422	28″ canvas	53.00	530.00✓
12	4424	40″ canvas	62.00	744.00✓
15	6620	2 × 4 frame kit	36.00	540.00✓
15	7715	1 × 2 frame kit	15.00	225.00✓
		Total		2,039.00 PSD

When a vendor sells merchandise to a buyer, the vendor prepares a form showing what has been sold. A form describing the goods sold, the quantity, and the price is known as an invoice. An invoice used as a source document for recording a purchase on account transaction is called a **purchase invoice**. [*CONCEPT: Objective Evidence*]

A purchase invoice lists the quantity, the description, the price of each item, and the total amount of the invoice. A purchase invoice provides the information needed for recording a purchase on account.

Hobby Shack takes the following actions when a purchase invoice is received.

STEPS • STEPS • STEPS • STEPS • STEPS • STEPS • STEPS • STEPS • STEPS • STEPS •

RECEIVING A PURCHASE INVOICE

1. Stamp the date received, *11/02/--*, and Hobby Shack's purchase invoice number, *P83*, in the upper right corner.
   This date should not be confused with the vendor's date on the invoice, *10/26*. Hobby Shack assigns numbers in sequence to easily identify all purchase invoices. The number stamped on the invoice, *P83*, is the number assigned by Hobby Shack to this purchase invoice. This number should not be confused with the invoice number, *2389*, assigned by the vendor. Each vendor uses a different numbering system. Therefore, vendor invoice numbers could not be recorded in sequence, which would make it impossible to detect a missing invoice.
2. Place a check mark by each of the amounts in the Total column to show that the items have been received and that amounts have been checked and are correct.
3. The person who checked the invoice should initial below the total amount in the Total column.
4. Review the vendor's terms. An agreement between a buyer and a seller about payment for merchandise is called the **terms of sale**. The terms of sale on the invoice are 30 days. These terms mean that payment is due within 30 days from the vendor's date of the invoice. The invoice is dated October 26. Therefore, payment must be made by November 25.

PURCHASING MERCHANDISE ON ACCOUNT

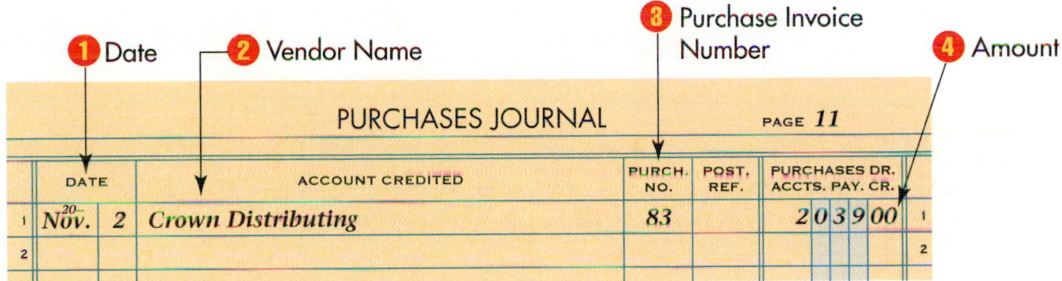

November 2. Purchased merchandise on account from Crown Distributing, $2,039.00. Purchase Invoice No. 83.

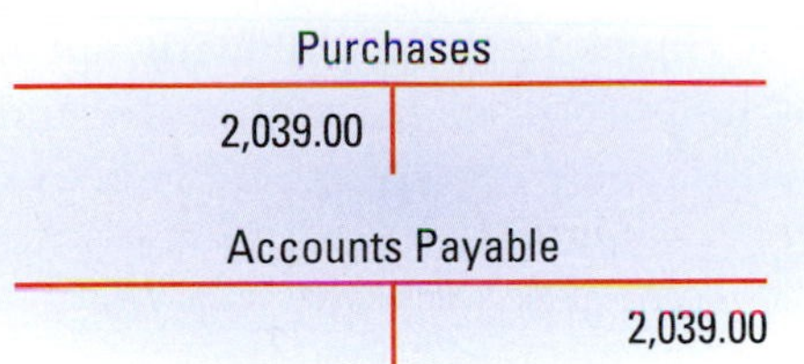

A purchase on account transaction increases the amount owed to a vendor. This transaction increases the purchases account balance and increases the accounts payable account balance. Because the purchases account has a normal debit balance, Purchases is debited for $2,039.00 to show the increase in this cost account. The accounts payable account has a normal credit balance. Therefore, Accounts Payable is credited for $2,039.00 to show the increase in this liability account.

STEPS JOURNALIZING A PURCHASE OF MERCHANDISE ON ACCOUNT

1. Write the date, *20--, Nov. 2*, in the Date column.
2. Write the vendor name, *Crown Distributing,* in the Account Credited column.
3. Write the purchase invoice number, *83*, in the Purch. No. column.
4. Write the amount of the invoice, *$2,039.00*, in the special amount column. This single amount is both a debit to *Purchases* and a credit to *Accounts Payable.* Therefore, it is not necessary to write the title of either general ledger account.

The way Hobby Shack keeps a record of the amount owed to each vendor is described in Chapter 11.

FYI FOR YOUR INFORMATION

Gross Domestic Product (GDP) is the total dollar value of all final goods and services produced by resources located in the United States (regardless of who owns the resources) during one year's time.

TOTALING AND RULING A PURCHASES JOURNAL

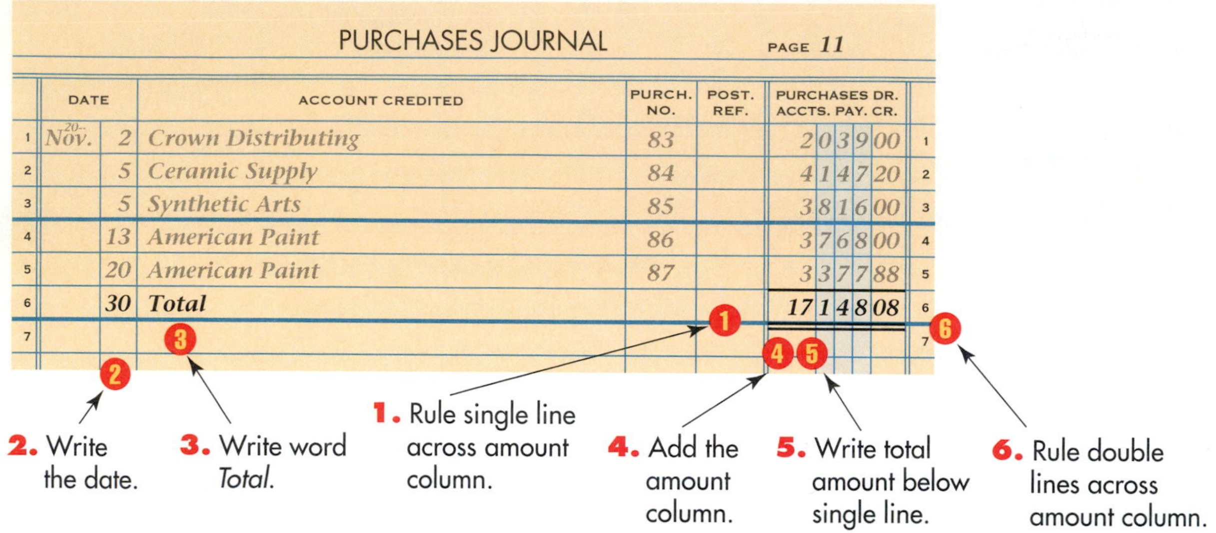

PURCHASES JOURNAL PAGE 11

	DATE		ACCOUNT CREDITED	PURCH. NO.	POST. REF.	PURCHASES DR. ACCTS. PAY. CR.	
1	20-- Nov.	2	Crown Distributing	83		2,039.00	1
2		5	Ceramic Supply	84		4,147.20	2
3		5	Synthetic Arts	85		3,816.00	3
4		13	American Paint	86		3,768.00	4
5		20	American Paint	87		3,377.88	5
6		30	Total			17,148.08	6
7							7

Hobby Shack always rules its purchases journal at the end of each month, even if the page for the month is not full.

Hobby Shack uses the following six steps in ruling its purchases journal at the end of each month.

STEPS

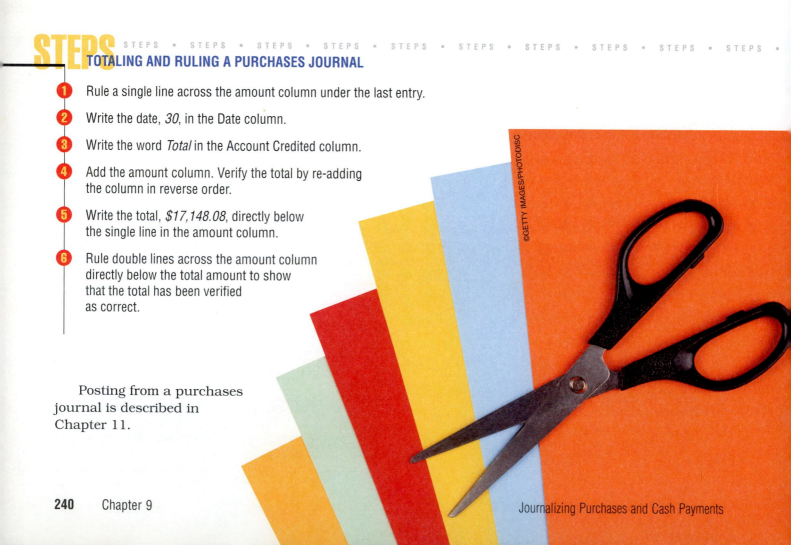

STEPS • STEPS • STEPS • STEPS • STEPS • STEPS • STEPS • STEPS • STEPS • STEPS •

TOTALING AND RULING A PURCHASES JOURNAL

1. Rule a single line across the amount column under the last entry.
2. Write the date, *30*, in the Date column.
3. Write the word *Total* in the Account Credited column.
4. Add the amount column. Verify the total by re-adding the column in reverse order.
5. Write the total, *$17,148.08*, directly below the single line in the amount column.
6. Rule double lines across the amount column directly below the total amount to show that the total has been verified as correct.

©GETTY IMAGES/PHOTODISC

Posting from a purchases journal is described in Chapter 11.

terms review

merchandise
merchandising business
retail merchandising business
wholesale merchandising business
corporation
share of stock
capital stock
stockholder
special journal
cost of merchandise
markup
vendor
purchase on account
purchases journal
special amount column
purchase invoice
terms of sale

audit your understanding

1. What kinds of transactions are recorded in a purchases journal?
2. For what are special amount columns in a journal used?
3. Why are there two account titles in the amount column of the purchases journal?
4. What is the advantage of having special amount columns in a journal?

work together 9-1

Journalizing purchases using a purchases journal

The purchases journal for Lambert Hardware is given in the *Working Papers.* Your instructor will guide you through the following examples.

1. Using the current year, journalize these transactions on page 10 of the purchases journal. Purchase invoices are abbreviated as P.

Transactions:

Oct. 2. Purchased merchandise on account from American Tools, $1,230.00. P116.
7. Purchased merchandise on account from Harris Manufacturing, Inc., $480.00. P117.
11. Purchased merchandise on account from Keasler Supply, $780.00. P118.

2. Total and rule the purchases journal.

on your own 9-1

Journalizing purchases using a purchases journal

The purchases journal for Classic Gifts, Inc., is given in the *Working Papers.* Work this problem independently.

1. Using the current year, journalize these transactions on page 11 of the purchases journal. Purchase invoices are abbreviated as P.

Transactions:

Nov. 4. Purchased merchandise on account from Ulman Supply, Inc., $670.00. P149.
9. Purchased merchandise on account from Else Silver Co., $2,345.00. P150.
18. Purchased merchandise on account from Pratt Paints, $1,150.00. P151.

2. Total and rule the purchases journal.

LESSON

9-2 Journalizing Cash Payments Using a Cash Payments Journal

CASH PAYMENTS JOURNAL

CASH PAYMENTS JOURNAL									PAGE
					1	2	3	4	5
DATE		ACCOUNT TITLE	CK. NO.	POST. REF.	GENERAL DEBIT	GENERAL CREDIT	ACCOUNTS PAYABLE DEBIT	PURCHASES DISCOUNT CREDIT	CASH CREDIT
1									

A special journal used to record only cash payment transactions is called a **cash payments journal**. Only those columns needed to record cash payment transactions are included in Hobby Shack's cash payments journal. A cash payments journal may be designed to accommodate a business's frequent cash payment transactions. Since all cash payment transactions affect the cash account, a special amount column is provided for this general ledger account. In addition, Hobby Shack has many cash payment transactions affecting the accounts payable account. Therefore, a special amount column is provided in the cash payments journal for this general ledger account.

Normally, the total amount shown on a purchase invoice is the amount that a customer is expected to pay. To encourage early payment, however, a vendor may allow a deduction from the invoice amount. A deduction that a vendor allows on the invoice amount to encourage prompt payment is called a **cash discount**. A cash discount on purchases taken by a customer is called a **purchases discount**. When a purchases discount is taken, the customer pays less than the invoice amount previously recorded in the purchases account. Taking purchases discounts reduces the customer's cost of merchandise purchased. Because it often takes purchase discounts, Hobby Shack uses a cash payments journal with a Purchases Discount Credit column.

A journal amount column that is not headed with an account title is called a **general amount column**. Hobby Shack's cash payments journal has General Debit and General Credit columns for cash payment transactions that do not occur often, such as monthly rent.

All cash payments made by Hobby Shack are recorded in a cash payments journal. The source document for most cash payments is the check issued. A few payments, such as bank service charges, are made as direct withdrawals from the company's bank account. For payments not using a check, the source document is a memorandum. Most of Hobby Shack's cash payments are to vendors and for expenses that are paid by check.

REMEMBER Only cash payment transactions are recorded in the cash payments journal.

CASH PAYMENT OF AN EXPENSE

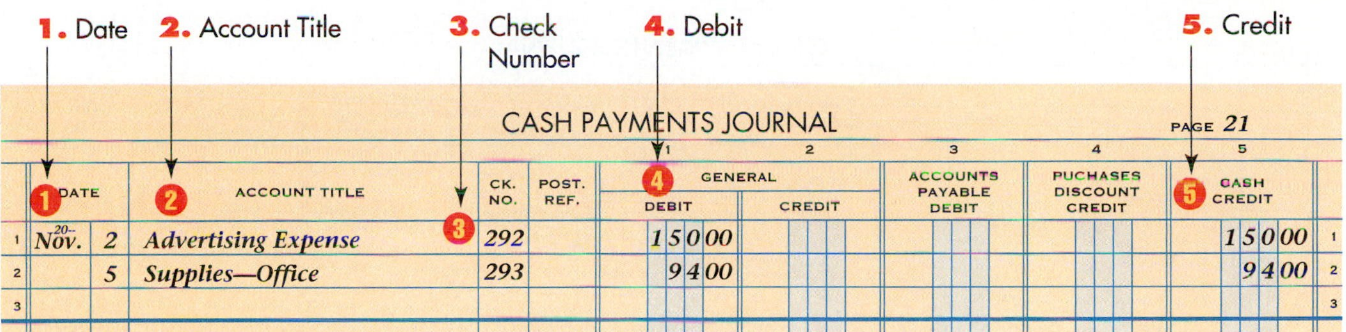

1. Date
2. Account Title
3. Check Number
4. Debit
5. Credit
CASH PAYMENTS JOURNAL
PAGE 21
DATE
ACCOUNT TITLE
CK. NO.
POST. REF.
GENERAL
DEBIT
CREDIT
ACCOUNTS PAYABLE DEBIT
PURCHASES DISCOUNT CREDIT
CASH CREDIT
20-- Nov. 2 Advertising Expense 292 150 00 150 00
5 Supplies—Office 293 94 00 94 00

November 2. Paid cash for advertising, $150.00. Check No. 292.

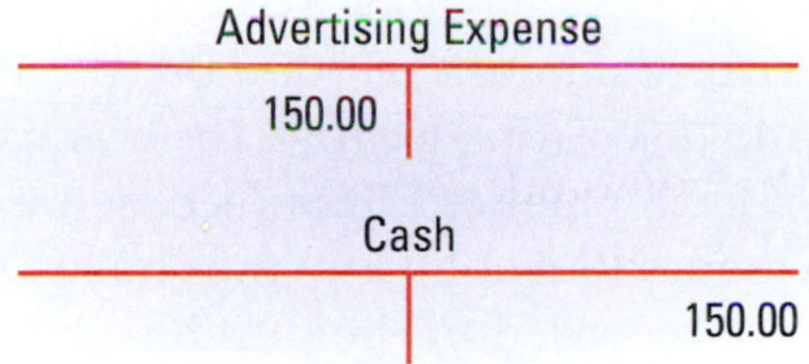

Hobby Shack usually pays for an expense at the time the transaction occurs.

This cash payment increases the advertising expense account balance and decreases the cash account balance. The expense account Advertising Expense has a normal debit balance and increases by a debit of $150.00. The asset account Cash also has a normal debit balance and decreases by a credit of $150.00.

STEPS: JOURNALIZING A CASH PAYMENT OF AN EXPENSE

1. Write the date, *20--, Nov. 2*, in the Date column.
2. Write the account title, *Advertising Expense*, in the Account Title column.
3. Write the check number, *292*, in the Ck. No. column.
4. Write the debit amount to *Advertising Expense, $150.00*, in the General Debit column.
5. Write the credit amount, *$150.00*, in the Cash Credit column.

BUYING SUPPLIES FOR CASH

November 5. Paid cash for office supplies, $94.00. Check No. 293.

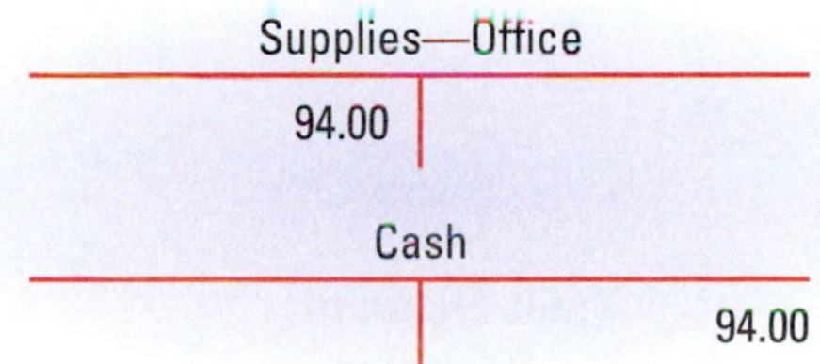

Hobby Shack buys supplies for use in the business. Supplies are not recorded in the purchases account because supplies are not intended for sale. Cash register tapes and price tags are examples of supplies used in a business.

This transaction increases the office supplies account balance and decreases the cash account balance. The steps for journalizing buying supplies for cash are the same as for journalizing purchasing merchandise for cash.

CASH PAYMENTS FOR PURCHASES

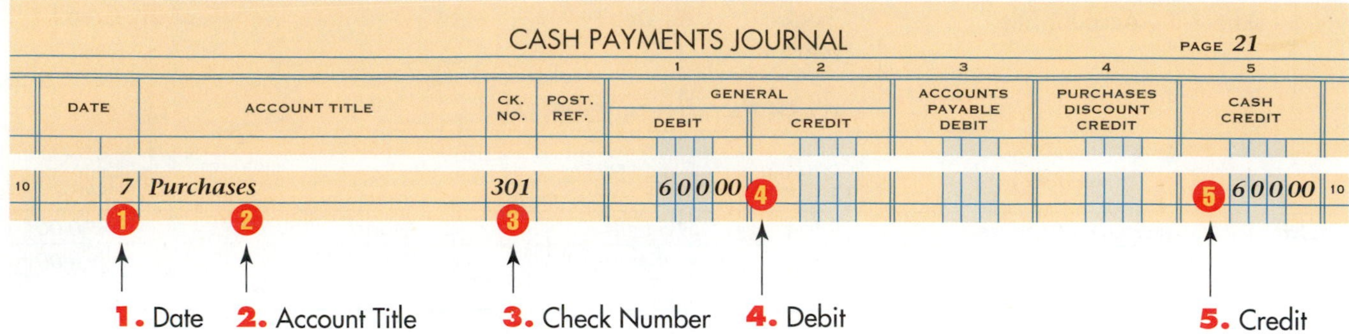

Businesses usually purchase merchandise on account. However, vendors may not extend credit to all of their customers. Thus, these businesses must pay the vendor with a check before the merchandise is either shipped or delivered.

Trade Discount

Most manufacturers and wholesalers print catalogs and maintain Internet sites that describe their products. Generally, the prices listed are the manufacturers' suggested retail prices. The retail price listed in a catalog or on an Internet site is called a **list price**. When a merchandising business purchases a number of products from a manufacturer, the price frequently is quoted as "list price less trade discount." A reduction in the list price granted to customers is called a **trade discount**. Trade discounts are also used to quote different prices for different quantities purchased without changing catalog or list prices.

When a trade discount is granted, the seller's invoice shows the actual amount charged. This amount after the trade discount has been deducted from the list price is referred to as the *invoice amount*. Only the invoice amount is used in a journal entry. [*CONCEPT: Historical Cost*]

No journal entry is made to show the amount of a trade discount.

Cash Purchases

Hobby Shack pays cash for 10 ceramic molds with an invoice amount of $600.00, the list price less a trade discount. Because the transaction involves a cash payment, it is recorded in the cash payments journal. Only purchases on account are recorded in the purchases journal.

November 7. Purchased merchandise for cash, $600.00. Check No. 301.

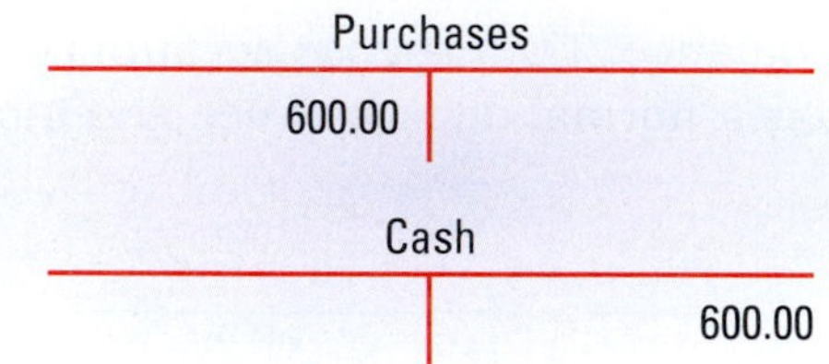

The list price for the 10 ceramic molds is $1,500.00. The invoice price is the list price, less a 60% trade discount. The total invoice amount is calculated in two steps, as follows.

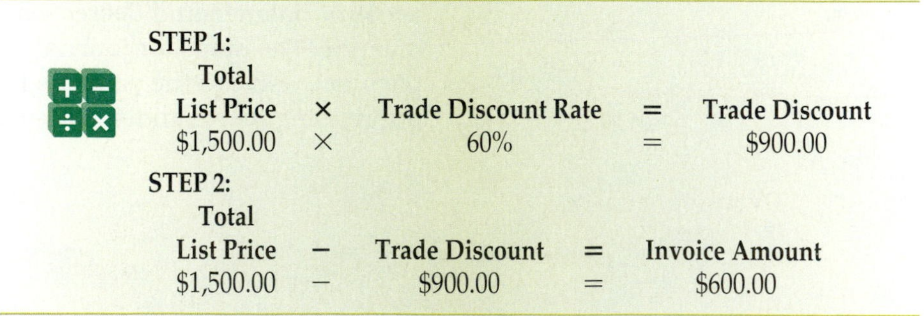

STEP 1:
Total List Price × Trade Discount Rate = Trade Discount
$1,500.00 × 60% = $900.00
STEP 2:
Total List Price − Trade Discount = Invoice Amount
$1,500.00 − $900.00 = $600.00

CASH PAYMENTS ON ACCOUNT WITH PURCHASES DISCOUNTS

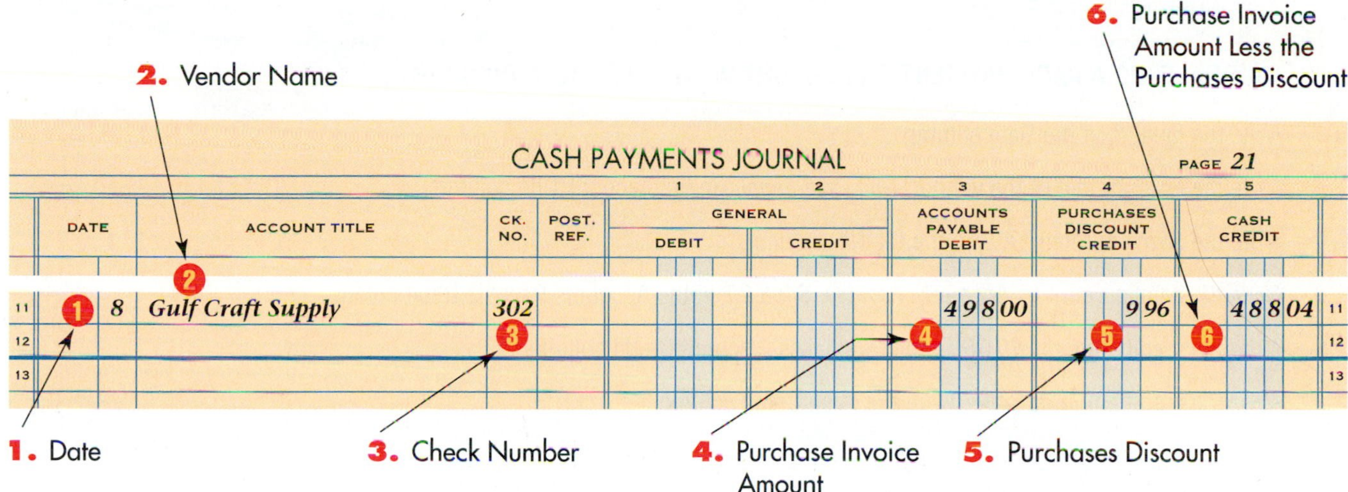

A cash discount is stated as a percentage deducted from the invoice amount. For example, *2/10, n/30* is a common term of sale, which is read *two ten, net thirty*. *Two ten* means that 2% of the invoice amount may be deducted if the invoice is paid within 10 days of the invoice date. *Net thirty* means that the total invoice amount must be paid within 30 days.

Purchases discounts are recorded in a general ledger account titled Purchases Discount. An account that reduces a related account on a financial statement is called a **contra account**. Purchases Discount is a contra account to Purchases and is included in the cost of merchandise division of the general ledger. On an income statement, Purchases Discount is deducted from the balance of its related account, Purchases.

Since contra accounts are deductions from their related accounts, contra account normal balances are opposite the normal balances of their related accounts. The normal balance for Purchases is a debit. Therefore, the normal balance for Purchases Discount, a contra account to Purchases, is a credit. Trade discounts are not recorded; however, cash discounts are recorded as purchases discounts because they decrease the recorded invoice amount.

November 8. Paid cash on account to Gulf Craft Supply, $488.04, covering Purchase Invoice No. 82 for $498.00, less 2% discount, $9.96. Check No. 302.

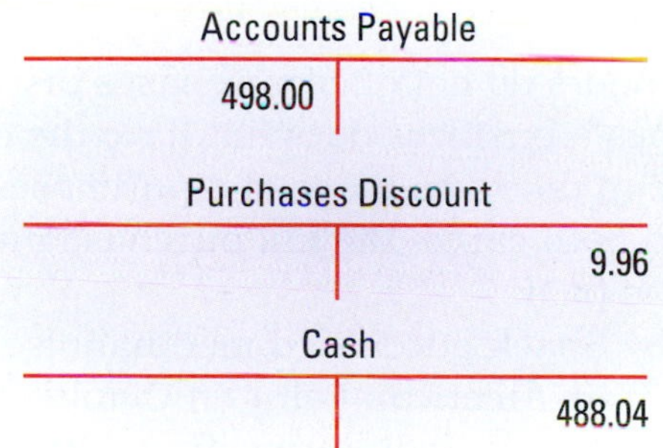

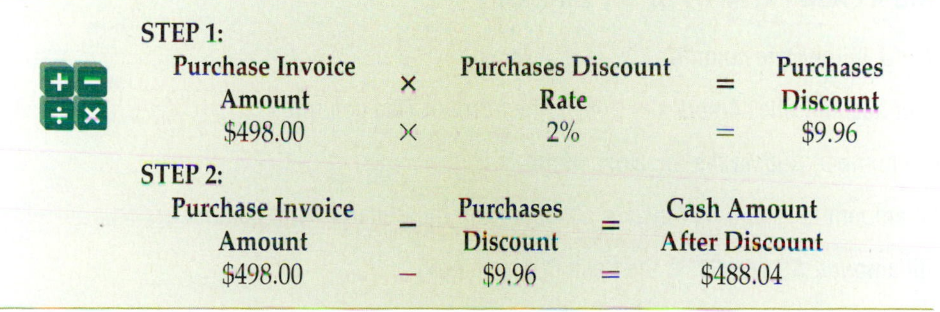

STEP 1:
Purchase Invoice Amount × Purchases Discount Rate = Purchases Discount
$498.00 × 2% = $9.96
STEP 2:
Purchase Invoice Amount − Purchases Discount = Cash Amount After Discount
$498.00 − $9.96 = $488.04

The way Hobby Shack keeps a record of the amount paid to each vendor is described in Chapter 11.

STEPS: JOURNALIZING A CASH PAYMENT ON ACCOUNT WITH PURCHASES DISCOUNT

1. Write the date, *8*, in the Date column.
2. Write the account title of the vendor, *Gulf Craft Supply*, in the Account Title column.
3. Write the check number, *302*, in the Ck. No. column.
4. Write the debit amount to *Accounts Payable*, *$498.00*, in the Accounts Payable Debit column.
5. Write the credit amount, *$9.86*, in the Purchases Discount Credit column.
6. Write the credit amount, *$488.04*, in the Cash Credit column.

CASH PAYMENTS ON ACCOUNT WITHOUT PURCHASES DISCOUNTS

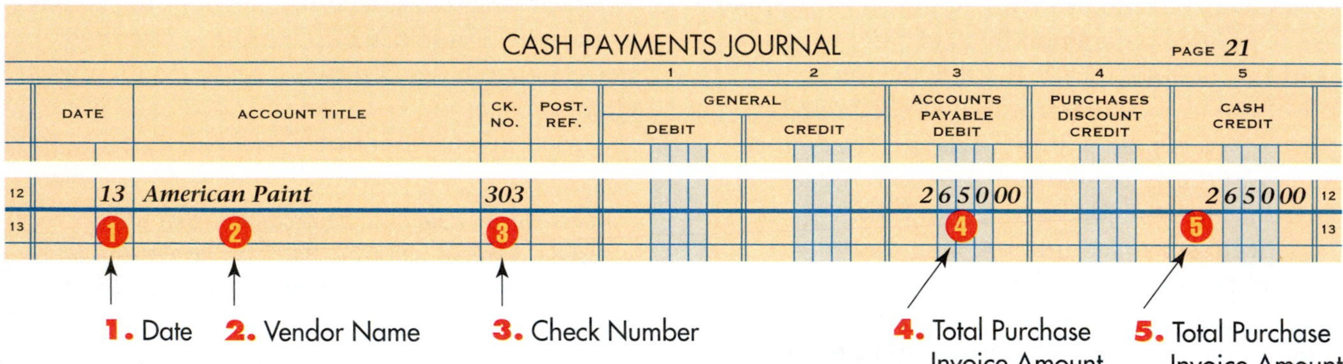

CASH PAYMENTS JOURNAL — PAGE 21

	DATE	ACCOUNT TITLE	CK. NO.	POST. REF.	1 GENERAL DEBIT	2 GENERAL CREDIT	3 ACCOUNTS PAYABLE DEBIT	4 PURCHASES DISCOUNT CREDIT	5 CASH CREDIT	
12	13	American Paint	303				2 650 00		2 650 00	12
13										13

Some vendors do not offer purchases discounts. Sometimes a business does not have the cash available to take advantage of a purchases discount. In both cases, the full purchase invoice amount is paid.

Hobby Shack purchased merchandise on account from American Paint on October 25. American Paint's credit terms are n/30. Therefore, Hobby Shack will pay the full amount of the purchase invoice, $2,650.00, within 30 days of the invoice date, October 25.

November 13. Paid cash on account to American Paint, $2,650.00, covering Purchase Invoice No. 77. Check No. 303.

STEPS: JOURNALIZING A CASH PAYMENT OF AN EXPENSE

1. Write the date, *13*, in the Date column.
2. Write the vendor account title, *American Paint*, in the Account Title column.
3. Write the check number, *303*, in the Ck. No. column.
4. Write the debit amount to *Accounts Payable*, *$2,650.00*, in the General Debit column.
5. Write the credit amount, *$2,650.00*, in the Cash Credit column.

Xtra! Study Tools
accountingxtra.swlearning.com

terms review

cash payments journal
cash discount
purchases discount
general amount column
list price
trade discount
contra account

TERMS REVIEW • TERMS

audit your understanding

1. Why would a vendor offer a cash discount to a customer?
2. What is recorded in the general amount columns of the cash payments journal?
3. What is the difference between purchasing merchandise and buying supplies?
4. What is meant by terms of sale 2/10, n/30?

AUDIT YOUR UNDERSTANDING

work together 9-2

Journalizing cash payments using a cash payments journal

The cash payments journal for Franklin Lumber is given in the *Working Papers*. Your instructor will guide you through the following example.

1. Using the current year, journalize these transactions on page 10 of a cash payments journal. The checks used as source documents are abbreviated as C.

Transactions:

Oct. 1. Paid cash for telephone bill, $85.00. C321.
7. Paid cash for office supplies, $52.00. C322.
11. Paid cash to GMT Hardware for merchandise with a list price of $800.00, less a 60% trade discount. C323.
17. Paid cash on account to West Supply covering Purchase Invoice No. 199 for $3,420.00, less 2% discount. C324.
19. Paid cash on account to Quill Forest Products covering Purchase Invoice No. 182 for $4,380.00. No cash discount was offered. C325.

WORK TOGETHER • WORK TOGETHER

on your own 9-2

Journalizing cash payments using a cash payments journal

The cash payments journal for Rapid Auto Supply is given in the *Working Papers*. Work this problem independently.

1. Using the current year, journalize these transactions on page 11 of the cash payments journal. The checks used as source documents are abbreviated as C.

Transactions:

Nov. 2. Paid cash for the electric bill, $248.00. C432.
6. Paid cash for office supplies, $142.00. C433.
9. Paid cash to Zebra Metals for merchandise with a list price of $3,400.00, less a 40% trade discount. C434.
12. Paid cash on account to Racing Images covering Purchase Invoice No. 543 for $4,230.00, less 2% discount. C435.
14. Paid cash on account to SPL Renovations covering Purchase Invoice No. 182 for $2,573.00. No cash discount was offered. C436.

ON YOUR OWN • ON YOUR OWN • ON YOUR

LESSON • LESSON • LESSON • LESSON • LESSON • LESSON

9-3 Performing Additional Cash Payments Journal Operations

PETTY CASH REPORT

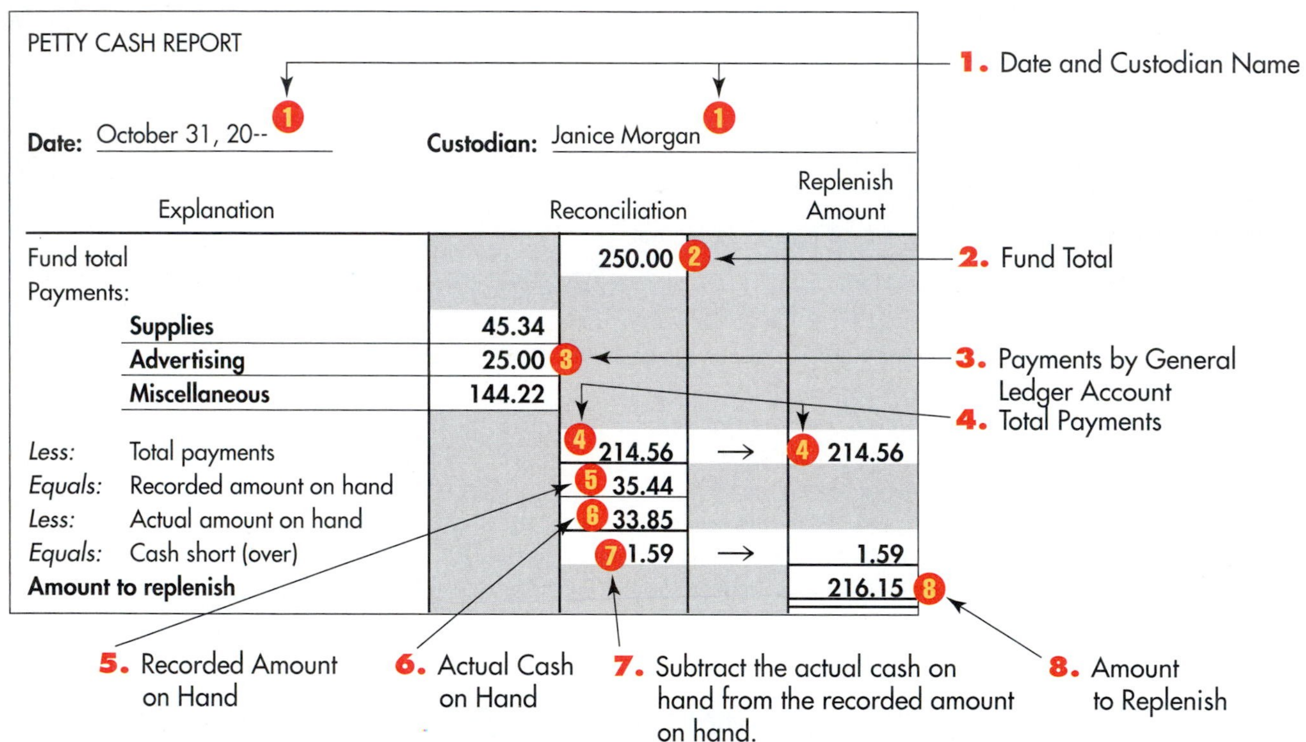

PETTY CASH REPORT

Date: October 31, 20-- (1) **Custodian:** Janice Morgan (1)

Explanation		Reconciliation		Replenish Amount
Fund total		250.00 (2)		
Payments:				
Supplies	45.34			
Advertising	25.00 (3)			
Miscellaneous	144.22			
Less: Total payments		(4) 214.56	→	(4) 214.56
Equals: Recorded amount on hand		(5) 35.44		
Less: Actual amount on hand		(6) 33.85		
Equals: Cash short (over)		(7) 1.59	→	1.59
Amount to replenish				216.15 (8)

A petty cash fund enables a business to pay cash for small expenses without writing a check, as described in Chapter 5.

Errors may be made when making payments from a petty cash fund. These errors cause a difference between actual cash on hand and the record of the amount of cash that should be on hand. A petty cash on hand amount that is less than a recorded amount is called **cash short**. A petty cash on hand amount that is more than a recorded amount is called **cash over**.

The custodian prepares a petty cash report when the petty cash fund is to be replenished.

STEPS • STEPS • STEPS • STEPS • STEPS

PREPARING A PETTY CASH REPORT

1. Write the date, *October 31, 20--*, and custodian name, *Janice Morgan*, in the report heading.
2. Write the fund total, *$250.00*, from the general ledger account.
3. Summarize petty cash payments by totals for each general ledger account.
4. Calculate and write the total payments, *$214.56*, in the Reconciliation and Replenish Amount columns.
5. Calculate and write the recorded amount on hand, *$35.44* ($250.00 – $214.56).
6. Write the actual amount of cash on hand, *$33.85*, in the Reconciliation column.
7. Subtract the actual amount on hand, *$33.85*, from the recorded amount on hand, $35.44, and write the amount, *$1.59*, in the Reconciliation and Replenish Amount columns. Note that petty cash is short by $1.59. The actual amount of petty cash on hand is $1.59 less than the recorded amount.
8. Write the total of the replenish amount, *$216.15*.

REPLENISHING A PETTY CASH FUND

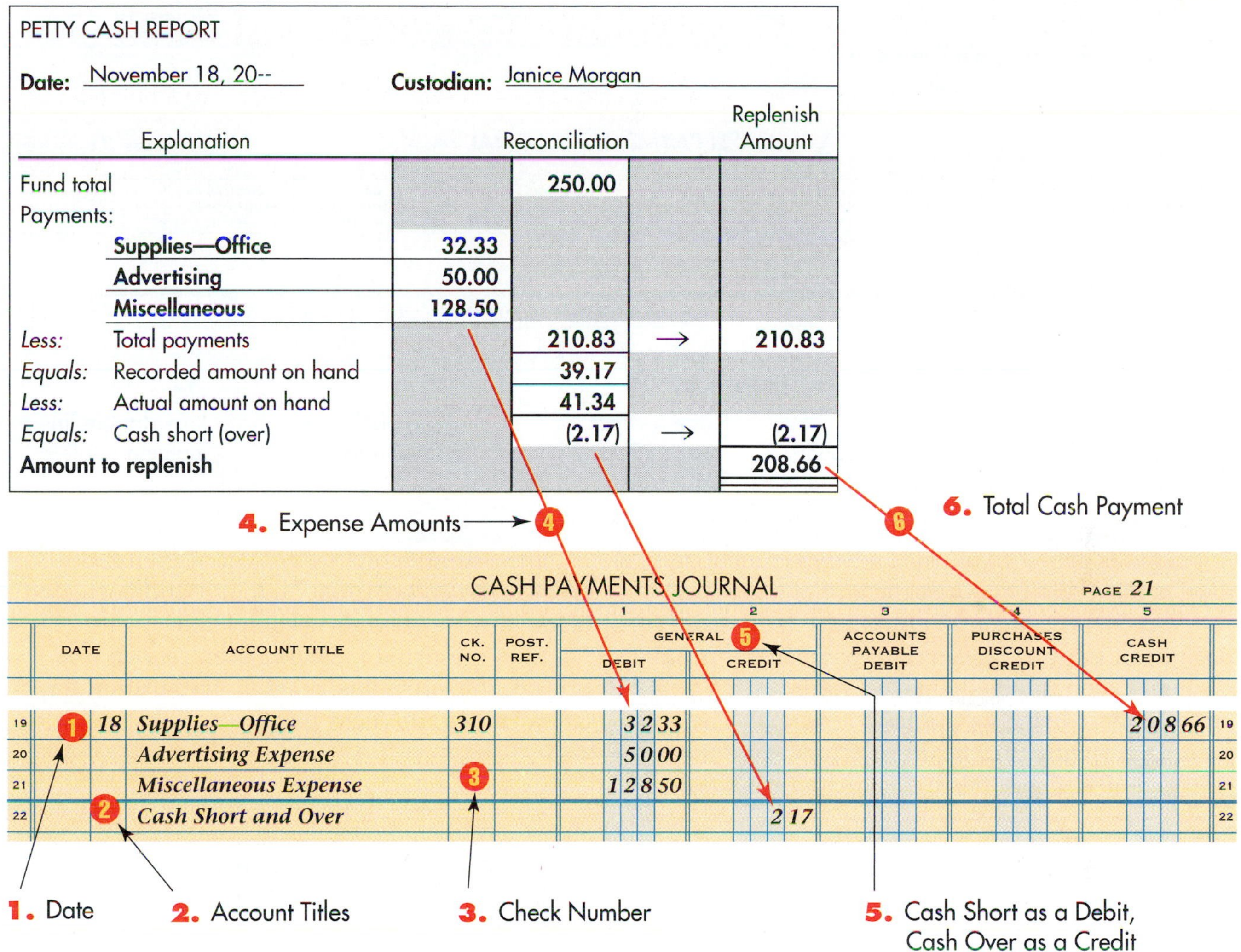

PETTY CASH REPORT

Date: November 18, 20-- Custodian: Janice Morgan

Explanation			Reconciliation		Replenish Amount
Fund total			250.00		
Payments:					
	Supplies—Office	32.33			
	Advertising	50.00			
	Miscellaneous	128.50			
Less:	Total payments		210.83	→	210.83
Equals:	Recorded amount on hand		39.17		
Less:	Actual amount on hand		41.34		
Equals:	Cash short (over)		(2.17)	→	(2.17)
Amount to replenish					208.66

CASH PAYMENTS JOURNAL PAGE 21

	DATE		ACCOUNT TITLE	CK. NO.	POST. REF.	1 GENERAL DEBIT	2 GENERAL CREDIT	3 ACCOUNTS PAYABLE DEBIT	4 PURCHASES DISCOUNT CREDIT	5 CASH CREDIT	
19		18	*Supplies—Office*	310		32 33				208 66	19
20			*Advertising Expense*			50 00					20
21			*Miscellaneous Expense*			128 50					21
22			*Cash Short and Over*				2 17				22

Petty cash short and petty cash over are recorded in an account titled Cash Short and Over. The account is a temporary account. At the end of the fiscal year, the cash short and over account is closed to Income Summary.

The balance of Cash Short and Over can be either a debit or credit. However, the balance is usually a debit because the petty cash fund is more likely to be short than over. A cash shortage adds to the cost of operating a business. Thus, the account is classified as an operating expense. Note that in Step 5, the amount of petty cash over is recorded in the General Credit column. If petty cash were short, the amount would be recorded in the General Debit column.

Cash Short and Over	
Debit Cash short	Credit Cash over

November 18. Paid cash to replenish the petty cash fund, $208.66: office supplies, $32.33; advertising, $50.00; miscellaneous, $128.50; cash over, $2.17. Check No. 310.

The petty cash fund is replenished for the amount paid out, $210.83, less cash over, $2.17. This total amount, $208.66, restores the fund's cash balance to its original amount, $250.00 ($210.83 − $2.17 + $41.34 cash on hand.)

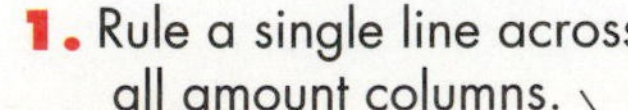

TOTALING, PROVING, AND RULING A CASH PAYMENTS JOURNAL PAGE TO CARRY TOTALS FORWARD

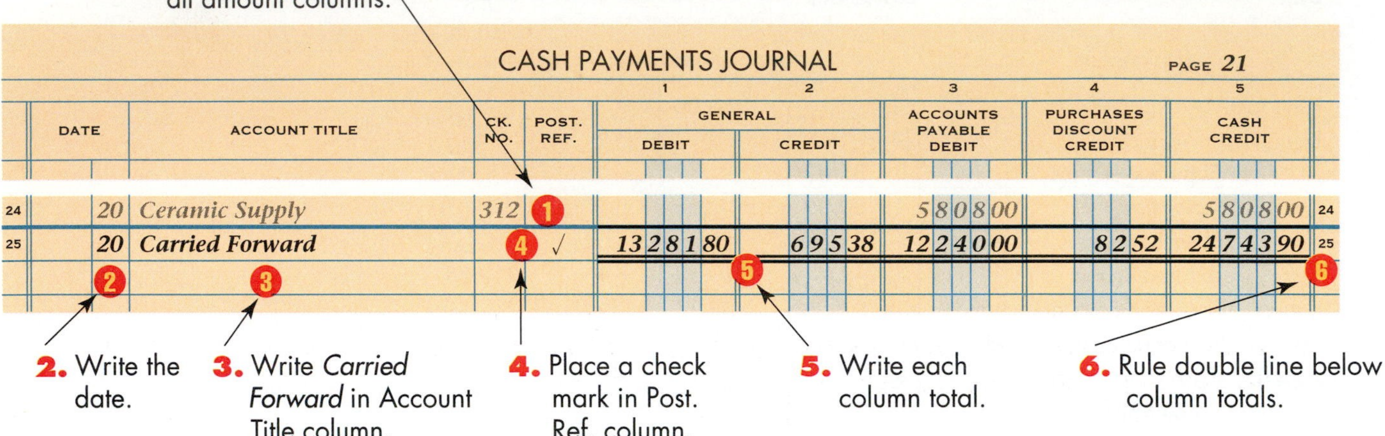

1. Rule a single line across all amount columns.
CASH PAYMENTS JOURNAL
PAGE 21
DATE
ACCOUNT TITLE
CK. NO.
POST. REF.
GENERAL
DEBIT
CREDIT
ACCOUNTS PAYABLE DEBIT
PURCHASES DISCOUNT CREDIT
CASH CREDIT
24 20 Ceramic Supply 312 5 808 00 5 808 00 24
25 20 Carried Forward ✓ 13 281 80 695 38 12 240 00 82 52 24 743 90 25
2. Write the date.
3. Write *Carried Forward* in Account Title column.
4. Place a check mark in Post. Ref. column.
5. Write each column total.
6. Rule double line below column totals.

A journal is proved and ruled whenever a journal page is filled and always at the end of a month.

After all November 20 entries are recorded, page 21 of Hobby Shack's cash payments journal is filled. Column totals of page 21 are totaled and proved before being forwarded to page 22. The proof that Hobby Shack's debit totals equal the credit totals on page 21 of the journal is shown.

If the total debits do not equal the total credits, the errors must be found and corrected before any more work is completed.

After a journal page has been totaled and proved, the journal is ruled in preparation for forwarding to the next page.

Column Title	Debit Column Totals	Credit Column Totals
General Debit	$13,281.80	
General Credit		$ 695.38
Accounts Payable Debit	12,240.00	
Purchases Discount Credit		82.52
Cash Credit		24,743.90
Totals	$25,521.80	$25,521.80

STEPS • STEPS • STEPS • STEPS • STEPS • STEPS • STEPS • STEPS • STEPS • STEPS •

STEPS FOR RULING A CASH PAYMENTS JOURNAL

1. Rule a single line across all amount columns directly below the last entry to indicate that all the columns are to be added.
2. On the next line, write the date, *20*, in the Date column.
3. Write the words *Carried Forward* in the Account Title column.
4. Place a check mark in the Post. Ref. column to show that nothing on this line needs to be posted.
5. Write each column total below the single line.
6. Rule double lines below the column totals across all amount columns to show that the totals have been verified as correct.

STARTING A NEW CASH PAYMENTS JOURNAL PAGE

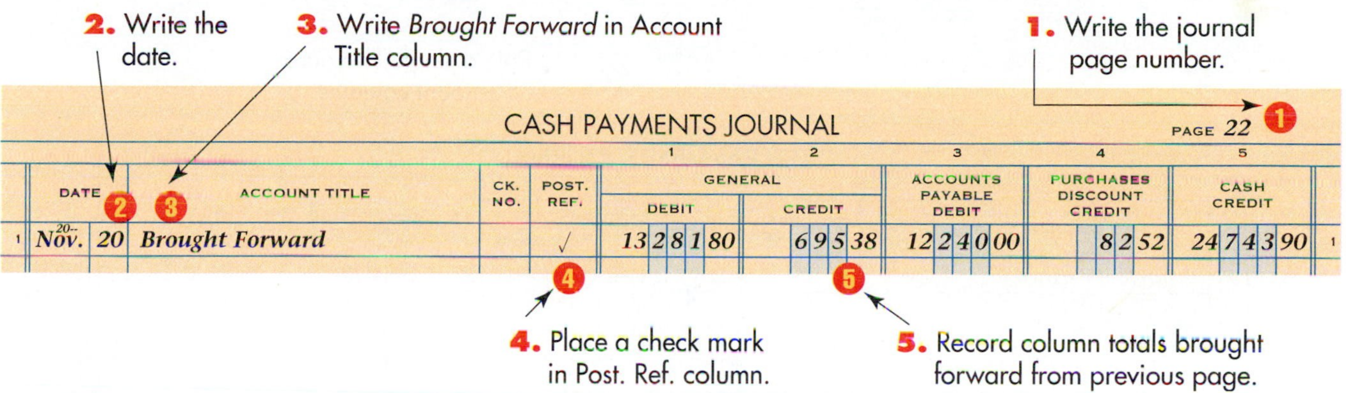

2. Write the date.
3. Write Brought Forward in Account Title column.
1. Write the journal page number.
4. Place a check mark in Post. Ref. column.
5. Record column totals brought forward from previous page.

CASH PAYMENTS JOURNAL — PAGE 22

	DATE		ACCOUNT TITLE	CK. NO.	POST. REF.	1 GENERAL DEBIT	2 GENERAL CREDIT	3 ACCOUNTS PAYABLE DEBIT	4 PURCHASES DISCOUNT CREDIT	5 CASH CREDIT	
1	20-- Nov.	20	Brought Forward		✓	13 281 80	695 38	12 240 00	82 52	24 743 90	1

The totals from the previous journal page are carried forward to the next journal page.

The totals are recorded on the first line of the new page.

STEPS FOR FORWARDING TOTALS TO A NEW JOURNAL PAGE

1. Write the journal page number, *22*, at the top of the journal.
2. Write the date, *20--, Nov. 20*, in the Date column.
3. Write the words *Brought Forward* in the Account Title column.
4. Place a check mark in the Post. Ref. column to show that nothing on this line needs to be posted.
5. Record the column totals brought forward from page 21 of the journal.

global perspective

Accountancy in Africa

The accounting profession in Africa has been influenced by the European colonial powers that formerly governed there. Most African nations gained independence in the mid-twentieth century.

In Nigeria, Kenya, Ghana, and Zimbabwe (formerly under British rule), accounting is seen as a tool for financial management and is oriented toward the needs of the enterprise. Tax authorities are concerned with account items that can be valued in different ways, such as fixed assets, inventories, and depreciation.

In Togo, Rwanda, and Gambia (formerly ruled by France), accountancy is regulated by charts of accounts that standardize financial transactions and annual financial statements.

In Angola, Cape Verde, and São Tomé and Principe (formerly ruled by Portugal), the accounting system also is based on charts of accounts that provide rules and regulations for companies.

There are no professional accounting organizations in many African countries.

In the expanding economies of many developing African countries, the belief is that it is important to have well-qualified and experienced accountants and a sound accounting framework to sustain economic growth.

Critical Thinking

1. What should an investor consider when comparing financial statements of companies in Kenya and Gambia?
2. What would be the advantages of having a professional accounting organization in a country that does not currently have one?

TOTALING, PROVING, AND RULING A CASH PAYMENTS JOURNAL AT THE END OF A MONTH

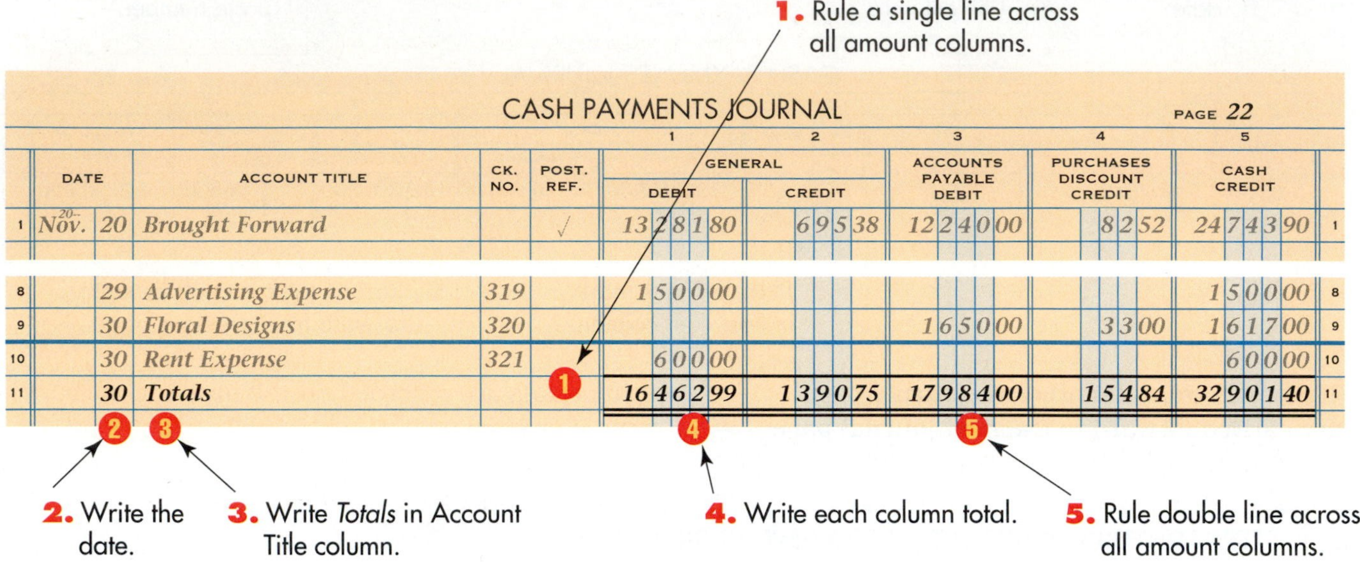

CASH PAYMENTS JOURNAL — PAGE 22

	DATE		ACCOUNT TITLE	CK. NO.	POST. REF.	1 GENERAL DEBIT	2 GENERAL CREDIT	3 ACCOUNTS PAYABLE DEBIT	4 PURCHASES DISCOUNT CREDIT	5 CASH CREDIT	
1	20-- Nov.	20	Brought Forward		✓	13281 80	695 38	12240 00	82 52	24743 90	1
8		29	Advertising Expense	319		150 00				150 00	8
9		30	Floral Designs	320				1650 00	33 00	1617 00	9
10		30	Rent Expense	321		600 00				600 00	10
11		30	Totals			16462 99	1390 75	17984 00	154 84	32901 40	11

1. Rule a single line across all amount columns.
2. Write the date.
3. Write *Totals* in Account Title column.
4. Write each column total.
5. Rule double line across all amount columns.

Equality of debits and credits in a journal is proved at the end of each month. Proof for Hobby Shack's cash payments journal for November is shown.

Column Title	Debit Column Totals	Credit Column Totals
General Debit	$16,462.99	
General Credit		$ 1,390.75
Accounts Payable Debit	17,984.00	
Purchases Discount Credit		154.84
Cash Credit		32,901.40
Totals	$34,446.99	$34,446.99

The two totals, $34,446.99, are equal. Equality of debits and credits in Hobby Shack's cash payments journal for November is proved.

After a cash payments journal has been totaled and proved at the end of the month, the journal is ruled.

STEPS • STEPS • STEPS • STEPS • STEPS • STEPS • STEPS • STEPS • STEPS • STEPS

STEPS FOR RULING A CASH PAYMENTS JOURNAL AT THE END OF THE MONTH

1. Rule a single line across all amount columns directly below the last entry to indicate that all the columns are to be added.
2. On the next line write the date, *30*, in the date column.
3. Write the word *Totals* in the Account Title column.
4. Write each column total below the single line.
5. Rule double lines across all amount columns to show that the totals have been verified as correct.

Posting from a cash payments journal is described in Chapter 11.

Xtra! Study Tools
accountingxtra.swlearning.com

terms review

cash short
cash over

TERMS REVIEW • TERMS

audit your understanding

1. When journalizing a cash payment to replenish petty cash, what is entered in the Account Title column of the cash payments journal?
2. What is the usual balance of the account Cash Short and Over?
3. List the five steps for ruling a cash payments journal at the end of the month.

AUDIT YOUR UNDERSTANDING

work together 9-3

Performing other cash payments journal operations

The cash payments journals and petty cash report for Keller Lighting are given in the *Working Papers*. Your instructor will guide you through the following examples. The abbreviation for a check is C.

1. Rule page 5 of the cash payments journal using March 27 of the current year.
2. Begin page 6 of a cash payments journal.
3. Kevin Tomlinson is the custodian of a $200.00 petty cash account. On March 31, he had receipts for the following total payments: supplies—office, $45.23; supplies—store, $66.18; and miscellaneous, $49.25. A cash count shows $40.59 in the petty cash box. Prepare the petty cash report.
4. Record the replenishment of the fund on March 31. C536.
5. Total, prove, and rule the cash payments journal.

WORK TOGETHER • WORK TOGETHER

on your own 9-3

Performing other cash payments journal operations

The cash payments journals and petty cash report for Magic Music are given in the *Working Papers*. Work these problems independently. The abbreviation for a check is C.

1. Rule page 11 of the cash payments journal using June 28 of the current year.
2. Begin page 12 of a cash payments journal.
3. Jerri Harris is the custodian of a $250.00 petty cash account. On June 30, she had receipts for the following total payments: supplies—office, $56.21; supplies—store, $48.27; repairs, $82.25; and miscellaneous, $36.17. A cash count shows $26.48 in the petty cash box. Prepare the petty cash report.
4. Record the replenishment of the fund on June 30. C627.
5. Total, prove, and rule the cash payments journal.

ON YOUR OWN • ON YOUR OWN

LESSON

9-4 Journalizing Other Transactions Using a General Journal

GENERAL JOURNAL

Not all transactions can be recorded in special journals. Those transactions that cannot be recorded in a special journal are recorded in a general journal. For example, when Hobby Shack buys supplies on account, the transaction cannot be recorded in any of the special journals. Because the transaction is not a cash payment, it cannot be recorded in the cash payments journal. Since the transaction is not a purchase of merchandise on account, it cannot be recorded in the purchases journal.

REMEMBER If a transaction cannot be recorded in one of the special journals, it must be recorded in the general journal.

MEMORANDUM FOR BUYING SUPPLIES ON ACCOUNT

HOBBY SHACK, INC.

MEMORANDUM

NO. 52

DATE November 6, 20--

Attached invoice is for store supplies bought on account.

When Hobby Shack buys store supplies on account, an invoice is received from the vendor. This invoice is similar to the purchase invoice received when merchandise is purchased. To assure that no mistake is made, a memorandum is attached to the invoice, noting that the invoice is for store supplies and not for purchases.

FYI FOR YOUR INFORMATION

Office supplies purchased by an office supplies company to sell to its customers should be recorded as a merchandise purchase. However, office supplies bought by the company for use by employees in its store or office should be recorded as store supplies or office supplies.

BUYING SUPPLIES ON ACCOUNT

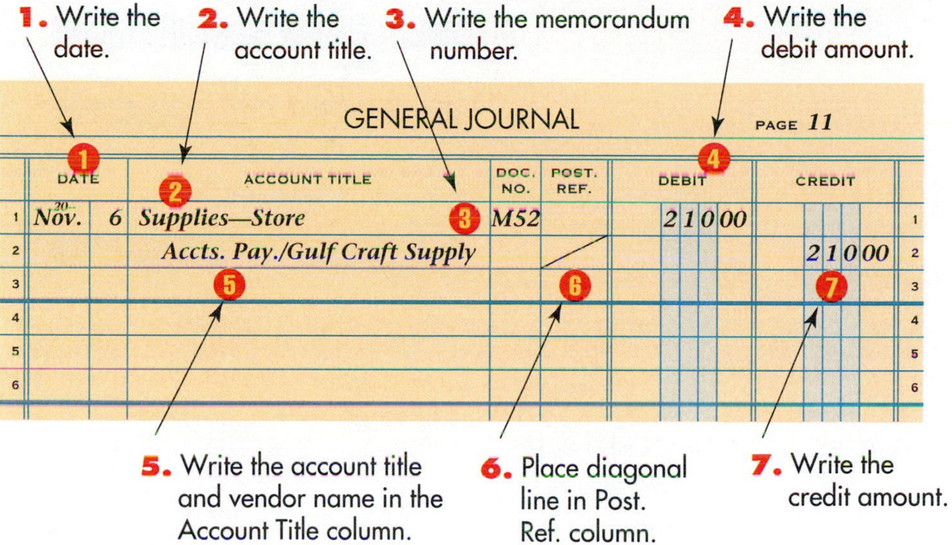

1. Write the date.
2. Write the account title.
3. Write the memorandum number.
4. Write the debit amount.
GENERAL JOURNAL
PAGE 11
DATE
ACCOUNT TITLE
DOC. NO.
POST. REF.
DEBIT
CREDIT
20-- Nov. 6 Supplies—Store M52 210 00
Accts. Pay./Gulf Craft Supply 210 00
5. Write the account title and vendor name in the Account Title column.
6. Place diagonal line in Post. Ref. column.
7. Write the credit amount.

November 6. Bought store supplies on account from Gulf Craft Supply, $210.00. Memorandum No. 52.

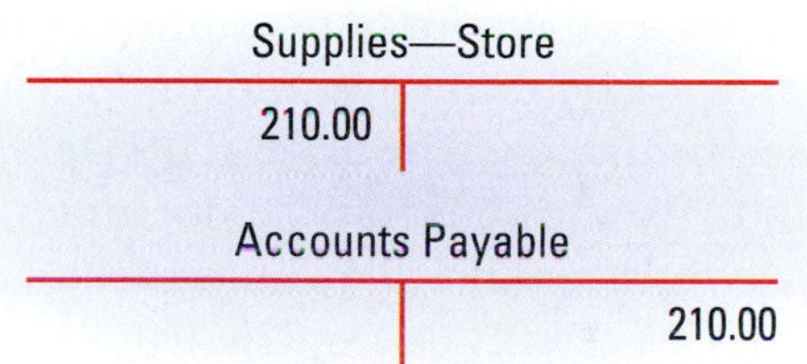

Supplies—Store
210.00
Accounts Payable
210.00

Hobby Shack usually buys supplies for cash. Occasionally, however, Hobby Shack buys some supplies on account.

This transaction increases the store supplies account balance and increases the accounts payable account balance. The asset account Supplies—Store has a normal debit balance and increases by a $210.00 debit. The liability account Accounts Payable has a normal credit balance and increases by a $210.00 credit.

The equality of debits and credits for each general journal entry is checked after each entry is recorded. For this entry, the amount of the debit entry, $210.00, is the same as the amount of the credit entry, $210.00. Therefore, debits equal credits for this entry.

STEPS • STEPS • STEPS • STEPS • STEPS • STEPS • STEPS • STEPS • STEPS • STEPS •

JOURNALIZING BUYING SUPPLIES ON ACCOUNT

1. Write the date, *20--, Nov. 6*, in the Date column.
2. Write the account title, *Supplies—Store*, in the Account Title column.
3. Write the memorandum number, *M52*, in the Doc. No. column.
4. Write the debit amount to *Supplies—Store*, *$210.00*, in the Debit column on the same line as the account title.
5. On the next line indented about one centimeter, write the account title and vendor name, *Accts. Pay./Gulf Craft Supply*, in the Account title column. Place a diagonal line between the two account titles.
6. Place a diagonal line in the Post. Ref. column on the same line to show that the single credit amount is posted to two accounts. Posting of a single amount in the general journal to two accounts is described in Chapter 11.
7. Write the credit amount to *Accts. Pay./Gulf Craft Supply, $210.00*, in the Credit column on the same line as the account titles.

DEBIT MEMORANDUM FOR PURCHASES RETURNS AND ALLOWANCES

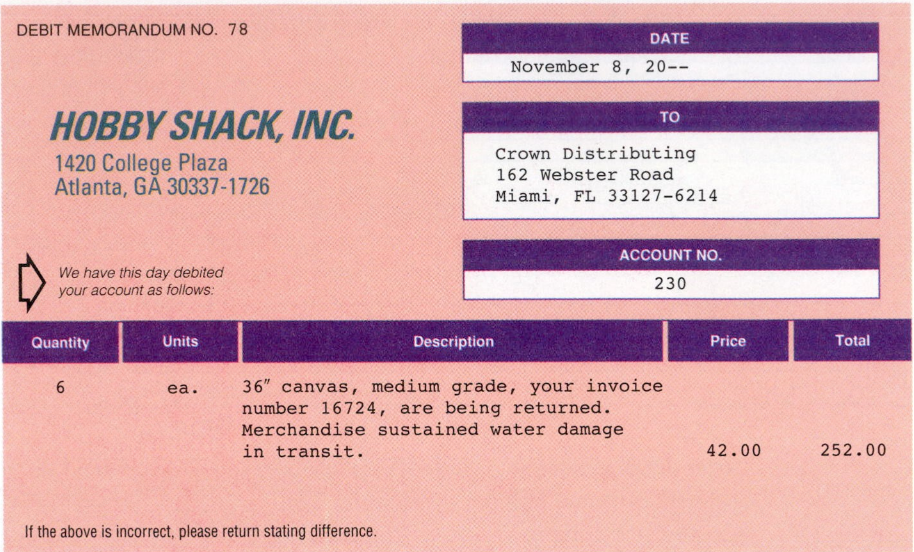

DEBIT MEMORANDUM NO. 78

HOBBY SHACK, INC.
1420 College Plaza
Atlanta, GA 30337-1726

DATE: November 8, 20--

TO: Crown Distributing
162 Webster Road
Miami, FL 33127-6214

We have this day debited your account as follows:

ACCOUNT NO. 230

Quantity	Units	Description	Price	Total
6	ea.	36″ canvas, medium grade, your invoice number 16724, are being returned. Merchandise sustained water damage in transit.	42.00	252.00

If the above is incorrect, please return stating difference.

A customer may not want to keep merchandise that is inferior in quality or is damaged when received. A customer may be allowed to return part or all of the merchandise purchased. Credit allowed for the purchase price of returned merchandise, resulting in a decrease in the customer's accounts payable, is called a **purchases return**.

When merchandise is damaged but still usable or is of a different quality than that ordered, the vendor may let the customer keep the merchandise at a reduced price. Credit allowed for part of the purchase price of merchandise that is not returned, resulting in a decrease in the customer's accounts payable, is called a **purchases allowance**.

A purchases return or allowance should be confirmed in writing. A form prepared by the customer showing the price deduction taken by the customer for returns and allowances is called a **debit memorandum**. The form is called a debit memorandum because the customer records the amount as a debit (deduction) to the vendor account to show the decrease in the amount owed.

The customer may use a copy of the debit memorandum as the source document for journalizing purchases returns and allowances. However, the customer may wait for written confirmation from the vendor and use that confirmation as the source document. Hobby Shack issues a debit memorandum for each purchases return or allowance. This debit memorandum is used as the source document for purchases returns and allowances transactions. [*CONCEPT: Objective Evidence*] The transaction can be recorded immediately without waiting for written confirmation from the vendor. The original of the debit memorandum is sent to the vendor. A copy is kept by Hobby Shack.

Some businesses credit the purchases account for the amount of a purchases return or allowance. However, better information is provided if these amounts are credited to a separate account titled Purchases Returns and Allowances. A business can track the amount of purchases returns and allowances in a fiscal period if a separate account is used for recording them. The account enables a business to evaluate the effectiveness of its merchandise purchasing activities.

JOURNALIZING PURCHASES RETURNS AND ALLOWANCES

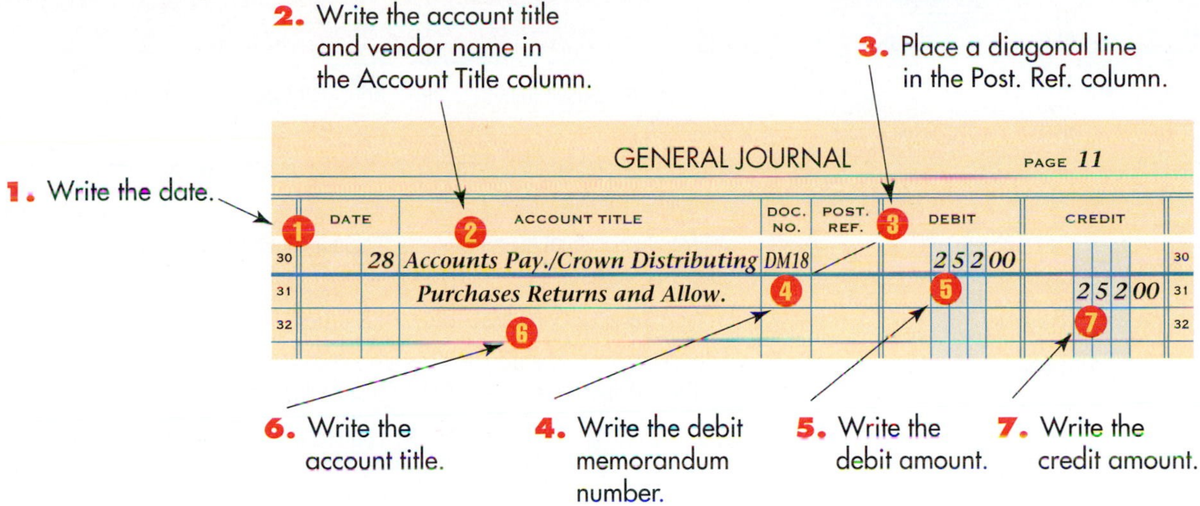

1. Write the date.
2. Write the account title and vendor name in the Account Title column.
3. Place a diagonal line in the Post. Ref. column.
GENERAL JOURNAL
PAGE 11
DATE
ACCOUNT TITLE
DOC. NO.
POST. REF.
DEBIT
CREDIT
28 Accounts Pay./Crown Distributing DM18
252 00
Purchases Returns and Allow.
252 00
6. Write the account title.
4. Write the debit memorandum number.
5. Write the debit amount.
7. Write the credit amount.

Purchases returns and allowances decrease the amount of purchases. Therefore, Purchases Returns and Allowances is a contra account to Purchases. Thus, the normal account balance of Purchases Returns and Allowances is a credit, the opposite of the normal account balance of Purchases, a debit.

The account is in the cost of merchandise division of Hobby Shack's chart of accounts.

Accounts Payable	
252.00	

Purchases Returns and Allowances	
	252.00

November 28. Returned merchandise to Crown Distributing, $252.00, covering Purchase Invoice No. 80. Debit Memorandum No. 78.

FYI FOR YOUR INFORMATION

Using the debit memorandum as a source document is a proper accounting procedure only if the business is confident that the vendor will honor the request for the purchases return or allowance.

STEPS • STEPS • STEPS • STEPS • STEPS • STEPS • STEPS • STEPS • STEPS • STEPS

JOURNALIZING PURCHASES RETURNS AND ALLOWANCES

1. Write the date, *28*, in the Date column.
2. Write the account title and vendor name, *Accounts Pay./Crown Distributing*, in the Account Title column. A diagonal line is placed between the two accounts.
3. Place a diagonal line in the Post. Ref. column to show that the single debit amount is posted to two accounts.
4. Write the debit memorandum number, *DM18*, in the Doc. No. column.
5. Write the amount, *$252.00*, in the Debit column of the first line.
6. On the next line indented about 1 centimeter, write *Purchases Returns and Allow.* in the Account Title column.
7. Write the amount, *$252.00*, in the Credit column of the second line.

terms review

purchases return
purchases allowance
debit memorandum

audit your understanding

1. What journal is used to record transactions that cannot be recorded in special journals?
2. Why is a memorandum used as the source document when supplies are bought on account?
3. Why are two account titles written for the credit amount when supplies are bought on account?
4. When is the equality of debits and credits proved for a general journal?
5. If purchases returns and allowances are a decrease in purchases, why are returns and allowances credited to a separate account?
6. What is a primary difference between a purchases return and a purchases allowance?
7. When is a debit memorandum a proper source document for a purchases return or allowance?

work together 9-4

Journalizing other transactions using a general journal

A general journal for Rood Electric is given in the *Working Papers*. Your instructor will guide you through the following example.

1. Using the current year, journalize the following transactions on page 8 of the general journal. Source documents are abbreviated as follows: memorandum, M; debit memorandum, DM. Save your work to complete On Your Own 9-4.

Transactions:

Oct. 5. Bought store supplies on account from Designer Supplies, $180.00. M35.
7. Returned merchandise to Hendrix Products, $540.00. DM65.

on your own 9-4

Journalizing other transactions using a general journal

Use the general journal that you started for Work Together 9-4. Work this problem independently.

1. Using the current year, journalize the following transactions, continuing on the next blank line of page 8 of the general journal. Source documents are abbreviated as follows: memorandum, M; debit memorandum, DM.

Transactions:

Oct. 11. Bought office supplies on account from Office Express, $240.00. M36.
14. Returned merchandise to Fretz Industries, $1,239.00. DM66.

SUMMARY

After completing this chapter, you can

1. Define accounting terms related to purchases and cash payments for a merchandising business.
2. Identify accounting concepts and practices related to purchases and cash payments for a merchandising business.
3. Journalize purchases of merchandise using a purchases journal.
4. Journalize cash payments and cash discounts using a cash payments journal.
5. Prepare a petty cash report and journalize the reimbursement of the petty cash fund.
6. Total, prove, and rule a cash payments journal and start a new cash payments journal page.
7. Journalize purchases returns and allowances and other transactions using a general journal.

Explore Accounting

Can Accounting Change the Course of History?

According to accounting historians, the start of the Industrial Revolution was delayed by nearly a century by restrictions on the use of the corporate form of organization. Events in Britain had a profound impact on the development of global commerce.

The scientific knowledge that was required to spur the Industrial Revolution began to emerge in the eighteenth century. The massive financial resources necessary to develop new industries could not be generated using partnerships, the traditional form of business organization. The British Parliament developed laws permitting the corporate form of organization, including limited liability for stockholders, as a means to enable these new industries to generate financial resources.

The financial collapse of one corporation caused Parliament to reverse the corporation laws. Financial losses, mismanagement, and improper accounting caused the financial collapse of the South Sea Company. The ensuing personal financial losses of investors generated a public outcry against the corporation laws. The South Sea Bubble Act of 1720 eliminated limited liability, effectively restricting the formation of corporations. Only a limited number of businesses, granted special charters by the British Parliament, were able to form as corporations during the remainder of the century.

During the early nineteenth century, a series of court cases and law changes gradually loosened the rules governing the granting of limited liability. Finally, the 1862 Companies Act completely removed all restrictions, permitting the corporate form of organization used today. Accounting historians believe that the spread of the Industrial Revolution was helped by the growing acceptance of the corporate form of organization.

Instructions: Research the start and growth of a major corporation in your state or region. Prepare a short report that discusses how the company generated the capital required to begin and expand the business. Would the company have been successful had it not been able to form as a corporation?

9-1 APPLICATION PROBLEM

Journalizing purchases using a purchases journal

Eupora Electric is a small appliance store.

Instructions:

1. Journalize the following transactions completed during September of the current year. Use page 9 of the purchases journal given in the *Working Papers*. The purchase invoices used as source documents are abbreviated as P.

Transactions:

Sept. 2. Purchased merchandise on account from Woodland Appliances, $2,600.00. P54.
6. Purchased merchandise on account from Quality Wholesalers, $1,460.00. P55.
12. Purchased merchandise on account from East Gate Appliances, $1,850.00. P56.
18. Purchased merchandise on account from Winston, Inc., $2,300.00. P57.
26. Purchased merchandise on account from Woodland Appliances, $3,800.00. P58.

2. Total and rule the purchases journal at the end of the month.

9-2 APPLICATION PROBLEM

AUTOMATED ACCOUNTING

Journalizing cash payments using a cash payments journal

Second Base is a sports equipment store that sells discontinued and damaged items.

Instructions:

Journalize the following transactions completed during November of the current year. Use page 22 of the cash payments journal given in the *Working Papers*. Source documents are abbreviated as follows: check, C; purchase invoice, P. Save your work to complete Application Problem 9-4.

Transactions:

Nov. 1. Paid cash for telephone bill, $96.00. C241.
4. Paid cash on account to The Pro Shop, $1,250.00, covering P367, less 2% discount. C242.
6. Paid cash for advertising, $75.00. C243.
9. Paid cash on account to Athletic Center, $925.00, covering P362. No cash discount was offered. C244.
11. Paid cash for office supplies, $50.00. C245.
13. Paid cash to Tennis City for merchandise with a list price of $1,850.00, less a 50% trade discount. C246.
18. Paid cash for store supplies, $125.00. C247.
21. Purchased merchandise for cash from Trevor Industries, $250.00. C248.
23. Purchased merchandise for cash from Paris Mfg. Co., $750.00, less a 60% trade discount. C249.
25. Paid cash on account to Best Clothing, $925.00, covering P363. No cash discount was offered. C250.
27. Paid cash on account to Trophy Sports, $2,100.00, covering P373, less 2% discount. C251.

9-3 APPLICATION PROBLEM 

Preparing a petty cash report

Kevin Tomlinson is the custodian of a $200.00 petty cash fund. On January 31 he had receipts for the following payments.

Payee	Description	Amount
City Office Supply	Computer disks	$ 5.95
KEWQ Radio	Voice fee for radio advertisement	50.00
Rocket Computers	Fix laser printer	45.95
Hooksville PTA	Advertisement in monthly newsletter	10.00
John Simmons	Pick up recyclable materials	8.00
Myers Hardware	Nails to repair outdoor sign	2.50
Books and More	Mouse pad	6.15

Instructions:

1. Classify each expense into one of the general ledger accounts used by Hobby Shack in this chapter.
2. Calculate the total of expenses by account.
3. Prepare the petty cash report given in the Working Papers. A cash count shows $70.67 in the petty cash box.

9-4 APPLICATION PROBLEM

Performing additional cash payments journal operations

Second Base is a sports equipment store that sells discontinued and damaged items. The cash payments journal used in Application Problem 9-2 is needed to complete this problem.

Instructions:

1. Total the cash payments journal from Application Problem 9-2. Prove the equality of debits and credits.
2. Rule the cash payments journal.
3. Begin page 23 of a cash payments journal.
4. Wendy Morris is the custodian of a $250.00 petty cash account. On November 30, she had receipts for the following total payments: supplies—office, $45.31; supplies—store, $54.62; repairs, $75.82; and miscellaneous, $41.67. A cash count shows $31.05 in the petty cash box. Prepare the petty cash report.
5. Record the replenishment of the fund on November 30. C252.
6. Total, prove, and rule the cash payments journal.
7. Total the amount columns of the cash payments journal. Prove the equality of debits and credits.
8. Rule the cash payments journal.

9-5 APPLICATION PROBLEM

Journalizing other transactions using a general journal

Jenny's Designs is a bridal shop.

Instructions:

Journalize the following transactions completed during October of the current year. Use page 10 of the general journal given in the *Working Papers*. Source documents are abbreviated as follows: memorandum, M; debit memorandum, DM.

Transactions:

Oct. 5. Bought store supplies on account from Displays Warehouse, $275.00. M39.
9. Returned merchandise to Hendrix Products, $640.00. DM25.
13. Bought office supplies on account from Office Express, $215.00. M40.
18. Returned merchandise to T-J Designs, $390.00. DM26.
25. Bought store supplies on account from Classic Fixtures, $180.00. M41.

9-6 MASTERY PROBLEM   

Journalizing purchases, cash payments, and other transactions

Mercury Computers sells computer parts and accessories.

Instructions:

1. Using the journals given in the *Working Papers*, journalize the following transactions completed during July of the current year. Use page 7 of a purchases journal, page 13 of a cash payments journal, and page 11 of a general journal. Source documents are abbreviated as follows: check, C; memorandum, M; purchase invoice, P; debit memorandum, DM.

Transactions:

Jul. 2. Purchased merchandise on account from Woodland Computers, $2,600.00. P354.
4. Paid cash on account to Pacific Industries, $1,400.00, covering P367, less 2% discount. C242.
6. Purchased merchandise on account from NewWave Electronics, $2,560.00. P355.
8. Paid cash to WCKF Radio for advertising, $750.00. C243.
8. Bought store supplies on account from Willcut & Bishop, $125.00. M39.
9. Paid cash on account to American Semiconductor, $2,690.00, covering P352. No cash discount was offered. C244.
10. Paid cash to Southern Bell for telephone bill, $136.00. C245.
11. Paid cash on account to Woodland Computers, $2,600.00, covering P354, less 2% discount. C246.
12. Returned merchandise to NewWave Electronics, $1,640.00. DM25.
12. Purchased merchandise on account from Helms Supply, $550.00. P356.
13. Paid cash to Edmondson Supply for office supplies, $126.00. C247.
14. Paid cash to Deanes Electronics for merchandise with a list price of $3,480.00, less a 60% trade discount. C248.
15. Bought office supplies on account from Office Express, $106.00. M40.
15. Purchased merchandise on account from Keel, Inc., $3,480.00. P357.
16. Paid cash on account to Farris Cable, $329.00, covering P353. No cash discount was offered. C249.
18. Purchased merchandise for cash from Columbus Industries, $429.00. C250.
20. Purchased merchandise for cash from Mena Mfg. Co., $260.00, less a 40% trade discount. C251.
22. Paid cash on account to Keel, Inc., $3,480.00, covering P357, less 2% discount. C252.
24. Paid cash to Williams Stores for store supplies, $94.00. C253.
25. Paid cash on account to NewWave Electronics, $920.00, covering P355 less DM25. C254.
27. Purchased merchandise on account from Woodland Computers, $3,200.00. P358.
30. Returned merchandise to Woodland Computers, $120.00. DM26.

2. Total the amount columns of cash payments journal page 13. Prove the equality of debits and credits and rule the cash payments journal to carry the totals forward.
3. Record the totals brought forward from cash payments journal page 13 to line 1 of page 14 of the cash payments journal.
4. Journalize the following transactions.

Transactions:

Jul.	31.	Paid cash on account to Helms Supply, $550.00, covering P356. No discount was offered. C255.
	31.	Paid cash to reimburse the petty cash fund, $181.75: supplies—office, $23.45; supplies—store, $84.32; miscellaneous, $74.34; and cash over, $0.36. C256.

5. Total and rule page 7 of the purchases journal.
6. Total the amount columns of cash payments journal page 14. Prove the equality of debits and credits of cash payments journal page 14.
7. Rule page 14 of the cash payments journal.

9-7 CHALLENGE PROBLEM

Journalizing purchases, cash payments, and other transactions

Fitness Connection is an exercise equipment store.

Instructions:

1. Using the journals given in the *Working Papers*, journalize the following transactions completed during November of the current year. Use page 12 of a purchases journal, page 26 of a cash payments journal, and page 11 of a general journal. Record the appropriate source documents in the journals.

Transactions:

Nov.	1.	Wrote Check No. 363 for the monthly rent of $1,300.00.
	2.	Bought $120.00 worth of store supplies on account from Meda Store Supplies, recorded on Memo 43, with 2/10, n/30 payment terms.
	3.	Received an invoice, stamped Purchase Invoice 84, for merchandise on account from Central Fitness for $2,150.00, less a 60% trade discount.
	4.	Paid $150.00 to Pitman Industries with Check No. 364 for merchandise.
	6.	Wrote Check No. 365 for $1,020.00 to Pacer Equipment for Purchase Invoice 82's payment on account.
	8.	Returned $260.00 of the merchandise purchased on Purchase Invoice 84 to Central Fitness, recorded on Debit Memorandum 54.
	9.	Purchased $2,900.00 of merchandise on account from Trackmaster on Purchase Invoice 85, with 2/10, n/30 payment terms.
	10.	Paid $52.00 to myOffice for office supplies with Check No. 366.
	11.	Paid the balance of Purchase Invoice 84 less Debit Memorandum 54, to Central Fitness with Check No. 367, taking advantage of the 2/10, n/30 payment terms.
	12.	Wrote Check No. 368 for $290.00 to pay the monthly insurance premium.
	16.	Paid Trackmaster the amount owed on Purchase Invoice 85, writing Check No. 369.
	29.	Paid Meda Store Supplies for the Nov. 2 purchase of store supplies with Check No. 370.
	30.	Replenished the petty cash fund by writing Check No. 371 to the custodian for $207.00. Receipts were submitted for the following: office supplies, $48.00; store supplies, $24.00; advertising, $68.00; and miscellaneous, $66.00.

2. Evaluate and then write a response to the following questions.
   a. The cash payments journal used in this problem has only three special amount columns. Under what circumstances would you recommend that additional special amount columns be added to a cash payments journal?
   b. When insurance premiums are paid, should the debit entry be to the asset account, Prepaid Insurance, or to the expense account, Insurance Expense? Are there circumstances where either entry could be correct? Explain.

applied communication

When you purchase merchandise for your business, you are considered a customer. Sometimes a customer might have a problem or complaint about the product. There are several ways to go about resolving the problem. One suggestion is to write to the person or company selling the product.

Instructions: Assume that you bought stereo speakers using the Internet site of a consumer electronics company. Unfortunately, the speakers make a strange static noise. Write a persuasive e-mail message to the company requesting a refund or a new set of speakers. Identify (1) information related to the purchase, such as invoice number and date, (2) the problem with the speakers, and (3) a request for a refund or a new set of speakers.

cases for critical thinking

Case 1

Trent Mercer owns and operates a music store in a mature shopping mall. When the largest store in the mall (often referred to as the *anchor*) moved two years ago, the traffic in the shopping center dramatically decreased. Mr. Mercer has an opportunity to move the business to a popular new shopping mall. Additional capital, however, is required to move and operate the business in a new location. The local bank has agreed to lend the money needed. His CPA has suggested that he consider forming a corporation and raise the necessary capital by selling capital stock to a small group of local investors. Should Mr. Mercer (1) borrow the money from the bank or (2) raise capital by creating a corporation? Explain your answer.

Case 2

Sophia Perez is a high school student who works part time in a local sports equipment store. As part of her duties, she records daily transactions in a journal. One day she asks the owner, "You use the purchase invoice as your source document for recording purchases of merchandise on account. You use a memorandum as your source document for recording the entry when supplies are bought on account. Why don't you use the invoice for both entries?" How would you respond to this question?

SCANS workplace competency

Thinking Skill: Creative Thinking

Concept: Every business encounters problems that require new solutions. Methods of cutting costs, new promotions to increase sales, and changes in merchandising and product mix all require creative solutions. Employees who can "think outside the box" and generate new creative ideas are important resources to any company.

Application: Choose a retail merchandising business with which you are familiar. Study as much of the business as is visible to you. Generate new ideas that you think could increase sales for the company.

using source documents

Journalizing purchases, cash payments, and other transactions from source documents

Messler Sailing sells sailboats, parts, and accessories. Source documents related to the purchases and cash payments of Messler Sailing for October are provided in the *Working Papers*.

Instructions

1. Using journals given in the *Working Papers*, journalize the transactions for October of the current year. Use page 10 of a purchases journal, page 15 of a cash payments journal, and page 14 of a general journal. Source documents are abbreviated as follows: check, C; memorandum, M; purchase invoice, P; debit memorandum, DM.
2. Total and rule the purchases journal.
3. Total and rule the cash payments journal.

USING SOURCE DOCUMENTS

analyzing Best Buy's financial statements

Best Buy has two types of stock—preferred and common. The company's Board of Directors must first authorize the issuance of each stock. The company then sells (issues) its stock on stock exchanges and can distribute shares to employees. On occasion, the company may repurchase shares, reducing the number of shares outstanding.

Instructions

1. Using Appendix B in this text, refer to Best Buy's balance sheet to determine the number of shares of preferred stock authorized, issued, and outstanding.
2. Identify the number of shares of common stock authorized, issued, and outstanding.

ANALYZING BEST BUY'S FINANCIAL

Automated Accounting

Automated Entries for Purchases and Cash Payments Using Special Journals

A merchandising business has many frequently occurring transactions that would require numerous entries in the general journal. Therefore, special journals are used to simplify the recording of these repetitive transactions. All transactions involving the payment of cash are recorded in the cash payments journal. The purchase of merchandise on account is recorded in the purchases journal.

A business from which merchandise, supplies, or other assets are bought is called a *vendor*. The total owed to all vendors maintained in a vendor file is summarized in a single general ledger liability account called Accounts Payable. Vendor accounts may be added, changed, or deleted from the accounting system in the same way as general ledger account maintenance. Other transactions related to the purchase of merchandise, such as purchases returns and allowances, are recorded in the general journal.

To maintain the Vendors list:

1. Click the Accounts toolbar button.
2. Select the Vendors tab.
3. To add a vendor, key in the new vendor name. Press Enter or click the Add Vendor command button. The new vendor will be arranged alphabetically with existing vendors.
4. To change a vendor, highlight the vendor name. Key the correct vendor name. Press Enter or click the Add Vendor command button.
5. To delete a vendor, highlight the vendor name. Click the Delete command button. A vendor must have a zero balance to be deleted.
6. Click the Close command button.

Purchases

Only merchandise that is purchased on account is recorded in the purchases journal. Purchase transactions may be entered directly into the computer from the invoice (source document). When the debit portion of a purchase transaction is entered, the computer will automatically make the credit to Accounts Payable.

To record transactions in the purchases journal:

1. Choose the Journal Entries menu item from the Data menu or click the Journal toolbar button.
2. Click the Purchases tab.
3. Enter the transaction date and press Tab.
4. Enter the invoice number in the Refer. column and press Tab.
5. Enter the amount of the invoice in the Purchases Debit column and press Tab. The Accounts Payable credit amount is calculated and displayed automatically.
6. Choose a vendor name from the drop-down list.
7. Click the Post button.

Cash Payments

The cash payments journal is used to enter all cash payments transactions. The credit to cash is automatically calculated and displayed by the computer. There are two types of cash payments:

1. Direct payments that are made for assets or expenses that do not affect Accounts Payable.
2. Payments on account that are made for cash transactions that do affect Accounts Payable.

To record transactions in the cash payments journal:

1. Choose the Journal Entries menu item from the Data menu or click the Journal toolbar button.
2. Click the Cash Payments tab.
3. Enter the transaction date and press Tab. (Remember that the date can be increased and decreased by the + and – keys.)
4. Enter the check number in the Refer. column and press Tab.
5. If making a direct payment, enter the account number (key the account number if you know it, or select the account by clicking the Chart of Accounts button and double-clicking the account) and amount to debit or credit and press Tab. If more than one account is debited or credited in the transaction, enter the first account number and the corresponding debit or credit. Press Tab until the cursor appears in the Acct. No. column on the next line. Then enter the next account number and its corresponding debit or credit. Continue this procedure for all accounts involved in the transaction. The cash credit is automatically calculated and displayed by the computer.

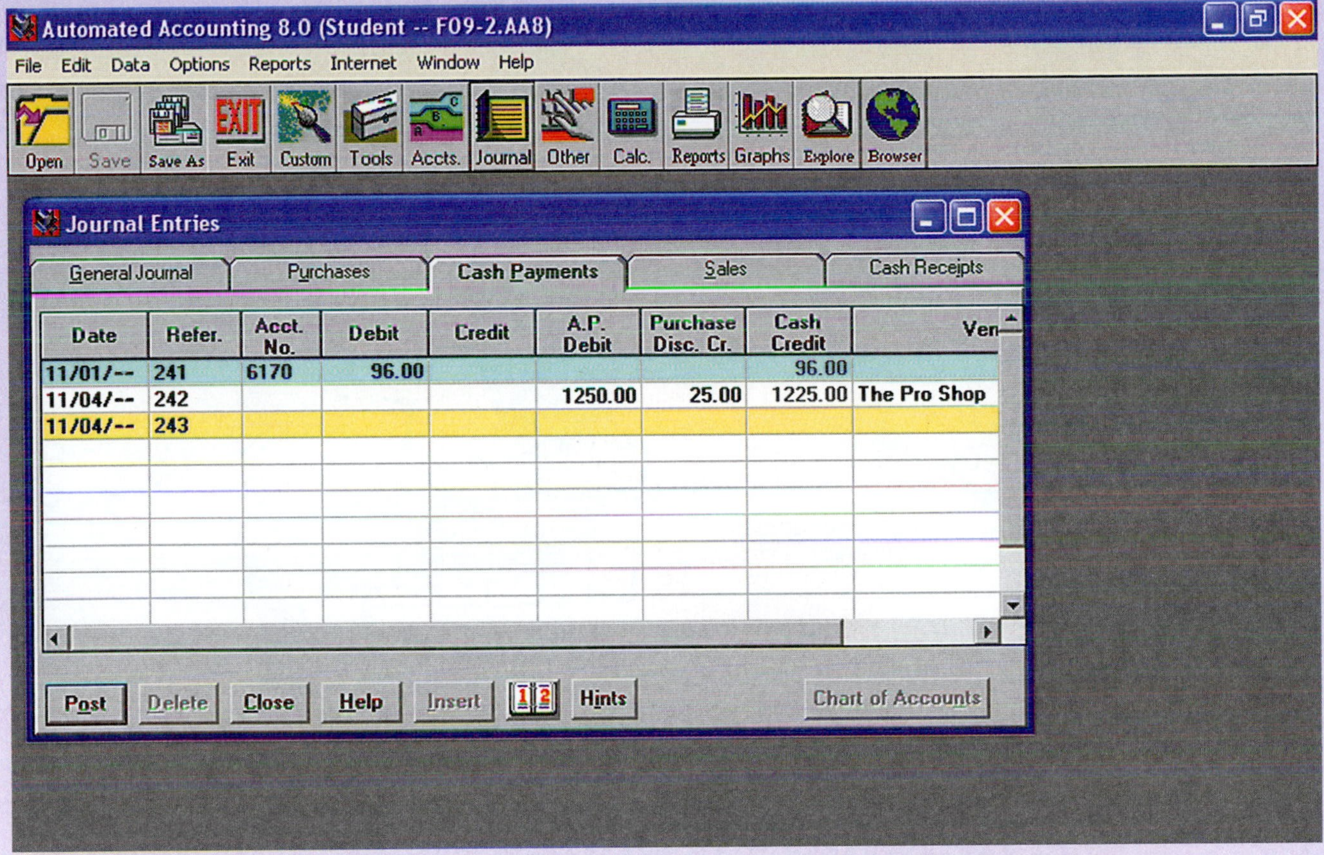

6. If making a payment on account, enter the accounts payable debit amount and choose the vendor from the drop-down vendor list. The cash credit is automatically calculated and displayed by the computer. (An alternative to clicking the drop-down vendor list is to press the key for the first letter of the vendor account title, such as T for The Pro Shop. If more than one account begins with that letter, press the key again. Press Enter when the correct vendor account title appears or click Post.)
7. If the transaction is correct, click the Post button.

AUTOMATING APPLICATION PROBLEM 9-2: Journalizing cash payments using a cash payments journal

Instructions:

1. Load the *Automated Accounting 8.0* or higher software.
2. Select data file F09-2 from the appropriate directory/folder.
3. Select File from the menu bar and choose the Save As menu command. Key the path to the drive and directory that contains your data files. Save the data file with a filename of F09-2 XXX XXX (where the X's are your first and last name).
4. Access Problem Instructions through the Browser tool. Read the Problem Instructions screen.
5. Key the data listed in Application Problem 9-2.
6. Save your file and exit the Automated Accounting software.

AUTOMATING MASTERY PROBLEM 9-6: Journalizing purchases, cash payments, and other transactions

Instructions:

1. Load the *Automated Accounting 8.0* or higher software.
2. Select data file F09-6 from the appropriate directory/folder.
3. Select File from the menu bar and choose the Save As menu command. Key the path to the drive and directory that contains your data files. Save the data file with a filename of F09-6 XXX XXX (where the X's are your first and last name).
4. Access Problem Instructions through the Browser tool. Read the Problem Instructions screen.
5. Key the data listed in Mastery Problem 9-6.
6. Save your file and exit the Automated Accounting software.

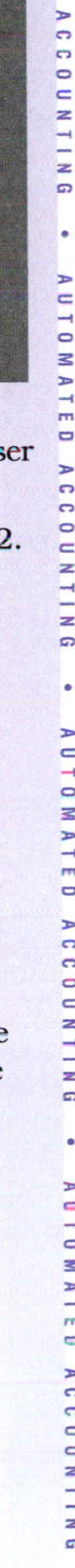

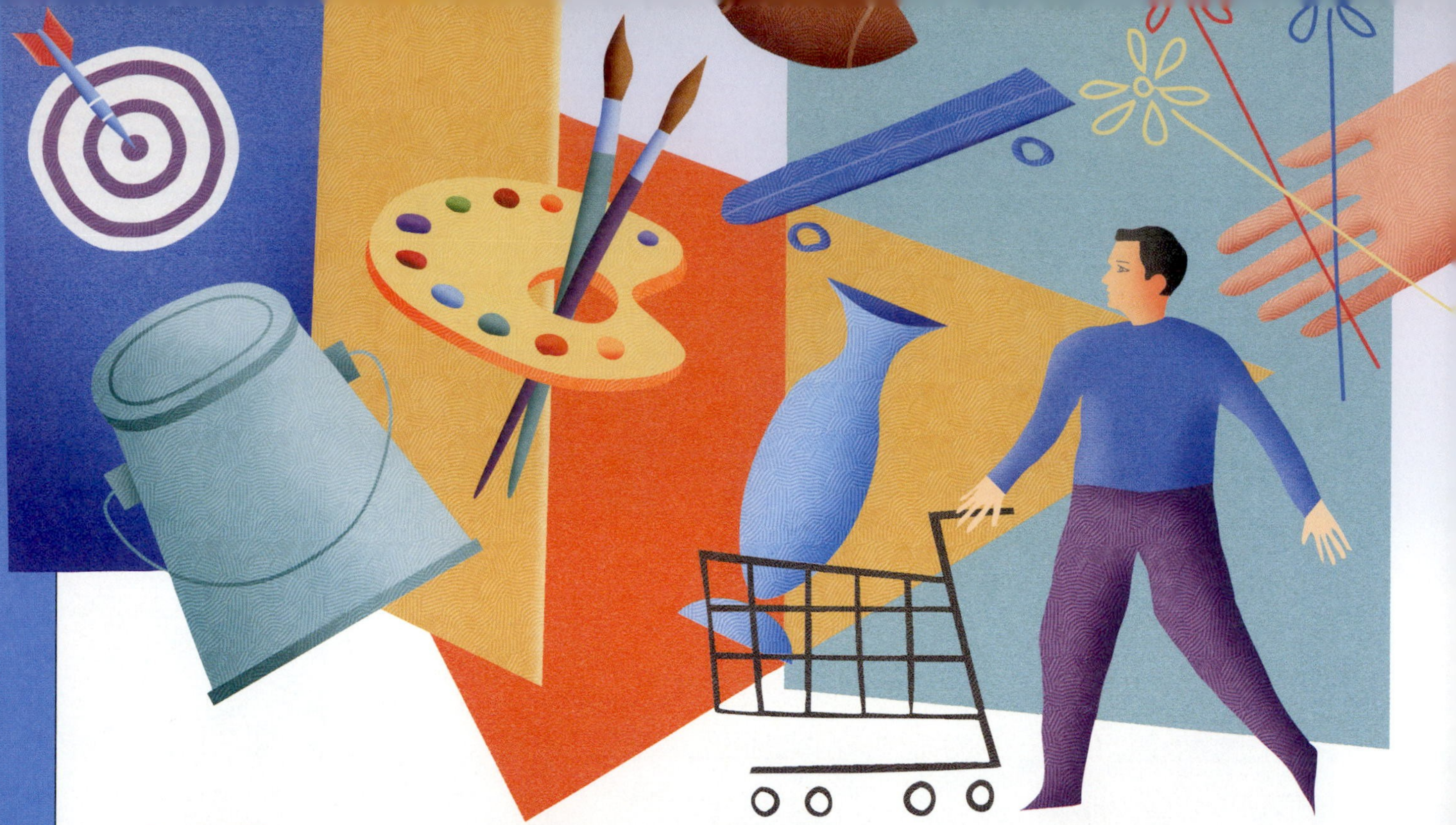

CHAPTER

10 Journalizing Sales and Cash Receipts Using Special Journals

OBJECTIVES & TERMS

After studying Chapter 10, you will be able to:

1. Define accounting terms related to sales and cash receipts for a merchandising business.
2. Identify accounting concepts and practices related to sales and cash receipts for a merchandising business.
3. Journalize sales on account using a sales journal.
4. Journalize cash receipts using a cash receipts journal.
5. Record sales returns and allowances using a general journal.

- customer
- sales tax
- sales journal
- cash sale
- credit card sale
- point-of-sale (POS) terminal
- terminal summary
- batch report
- batching out
- cash receipts journal
- sales discount
- sales return
- sales allowance
- credit memorandum

Point Your Browser
accountingxtra.swlearning.com

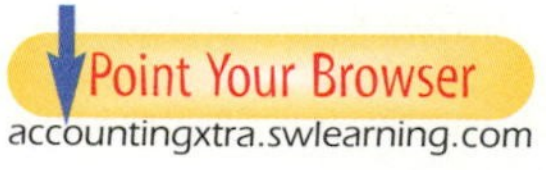

accounting in the real world

Best Buy

©DANIEL ACKER/BLOOMBERG NEWS/LANDOV

BEST BUY—INCREASING SALES RESULTS

A sluggish economy had caused consumer spending to drop, especially in the sales of desktop computers and CDs. Growth in comparable store sales—the sales at stores open for more than a year—were disappointing. This was not the ideal time to assume leadership of a leading specialty retailer of consumer electronics, personal computers, entertainment software, and appliances. But that is exactly what faced Bradbury H. Anderson as he became the new chief executive officer of Best Buy.

So how did Best Buy overcome this challenge? It went digital. Recognizing changes in consumer preferences, Best Buy increased its assortment of digital cameras and digital, LCD, and projection TVs. Mr. Anderson and his new management team undertook other strategic plans to reduce product costs and store expenses. These changes enabled Best Buy to achieve a 2.5% increase in comparable store sales, a 13% increase in total revenue, and an 8% increase in net income.

Critical Thinking

1. How can a company have a 13% increase in total revenue with just a 2.5% increase in comparable store sales?
2. For any local company, such as a fast-food restaurant, suggest changes in the products they offer that you believe could increase sales.

accountingxtra.swlearning.com

Source: Page 4 of Best Buy's 2003 Annual Report

internet activity

STATE SALES TAX RATES

Go to the homepage for the Federation of Tax Administrators (www.taxadmin.org) or search the Internet for state sales tax rates. Look for a chart or table that compares the sales tax rate for each state.

Instructions

1. Make a chart comparing the sales tax rate for your state with the sales tax rate for 10 other states.
2. Highlight the highest and lowest rates.

LESSON • LESSON • LESSON • LESSON • LESSON • LESSON

10-1 Journalizing Sales on Account Using a Sales Journal

SALES TAX

Purchases and sales of merchandise are the two major activities of a merchandising business. A person or business to whom merchandise or services are sold is called a **customer**. Hobby Shack sells merchandise to a variety of customers, including individuals, schools, and churches. Hobby Shack uses the special journals described in this chapter to record transactions related to sales.

Laws of most states and some cities require that a tax be collected from customers for each sale made. A tax on a sale of merchandise or services is called a **sales tax**. Sales tax rates are usually stated as a percentage of sales. Regardless of the tax rates used, accounting procedures are the same.

Businesses must file reports with the proper government unit and pay the amount of sales tax collected. Every business collecting a sales tax needs accurate records of the amount of (1) total sales and (2) total sales tax collected. The amount of sales tax collected is a business liability until paid to the government agency. Therefore, the sales tax amount is recorded in a separate liability account titled Sales Tax Payable, which has a normal credit balance.

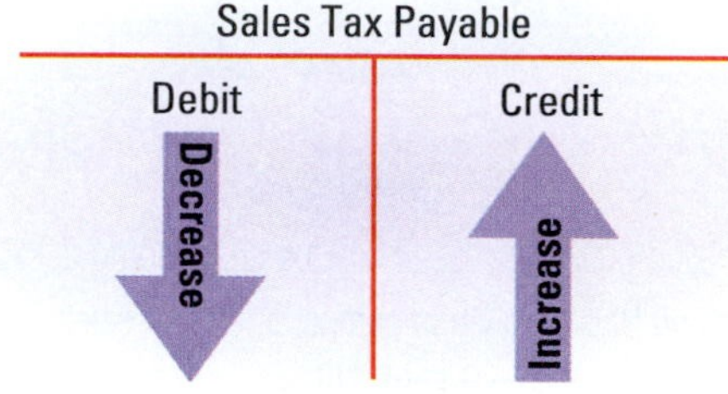

MAKING ETHICAL DECISIONS • MAKING ETHICAL DECISIONS • MAKING ETHICAL DECISIONS

making ethical decisions

Integrity—Doing What's Right

What does the word *integrity* mean to you? The word is derived from a Latin word meaning "wholeness," "completeness," and "purity." Many companies include an interpretation of integrity in their code of conduct.

"We always try to do the right thing." —Procter & Gamble

"To say what we mean, to deliver what we promise, to fulfill our commitments, and to stand for what is right." —Lockheed Martin

"We do the right thing without compromise. We avoid even the appearance of impropriety." —Intel

Companies with integrity have an absolute commitment to do what is right in all business activities. Integrity is ultimately the most critical component to long-term business success. A business that fails to act with integrity will soon find it difficult to hire employees, deal with suppliers, and enjoy repeat customers.

The American Institute of Certified Public Accountants recognizes that integrity is critical for maintaining public confidence in its members' professional services. "Integrity is an element of character fundamental to professional recognition. It is the quality from which the public trust derives and the benchmark against which a member must ultimately test all decisions."

Instructions

In private, write down five qualities that you believe people of high integrity possess. Using a typical grading schedule (A+, A, A−, etc.), identify how you believe your friends, teachers, and others would rate your integrity. Do you have integrity as defined by the three companies above?

SALES OF MERCHANDISE ON ACCOUNT

A sale of merchandise may be (1) on account or (2) for cash. A sale of merchandise increases the revenue of a business. Regardless of when payment is made, the revenue should be recorded at the time of a sale, not on the date cash is received. For example, on June 15 Hobby Shack sells merchandise on account to a customer. The customer pays Hobby Shack for the merchandise on July 12. Hobby Shack records the revenue on June 15, the date of the sale. The accounting concept *Realization of Revenue* is applied when revenue is recorded at the time goods or services are sold. [*CONCEPT: Realization of Revenue*]

A sale for which cash will be received at a later date is known as a sale on account. A sale on account is also referred to as a charge sale.

Hobby Shack summarizes the total due from all charge customers in a general ledger account titled Accounts Receivable. Accounts Receivable is an asset account with a normal debit balance. Therefore, the accounts receivable account is increased by a debit and decreased by a credit.

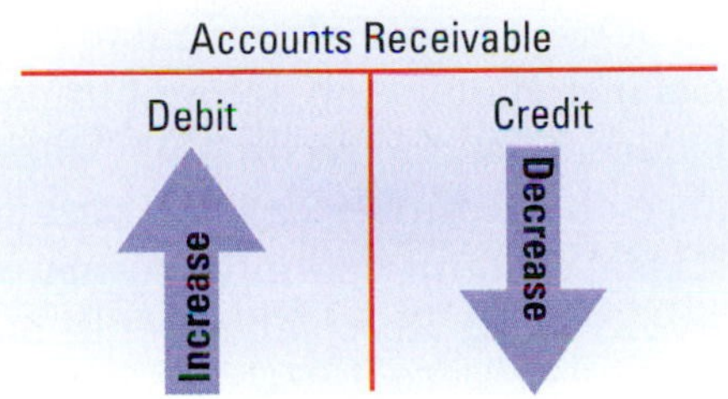

Advantages and Disadvantages of a Corporation

Organizing a corporation is as simple as filing an application with the appropriate state agency. The approved application establishes the corporation as a legal entity, giving the corporation many of the same legal rights and risks as individuals, including owning assets, borrowing money, paying taxes, and being sued.

The corporate form of business organization has several advantages over a sole proprietorship:

- *Limited liability.* The liability of stockholders is limited to their investment in the corporation.
- *Supply of capital.* Individuals are more willing to invest in a corporation because their personal assets are protected by limited liability.

However, there are also some disadvantages to a corporation:

- *Shared decision making.* Significant business decisions must be approved by a vote of the stockholders.
- *Shared profits.* The earnings of the corporation are divided among the stockholders.
- *Taxation.* The earnings of a corporation may be subject to federal and state income taxes. When the earnings of the corporation are distributed to the stockholders, individual stockholders may also have to pay income taxes on the dividends. Thus, the earnings of a corporation can be taxed twice, a concept known as double taxation.

Proper planning can offer stockholders the advantage of limited liability while avoiding the disadvantage of double taxation. Thus, although the organization application can be prepared without the help of an attorney or accountant, consulting with these professionals is recommended.

Critical Thinking

1. Think of two businesses you might be interested in starting. Describe whether the proprietorship or corporation form of organization would be better suited for this business.
2. Often a person who has started a proprietorship and run it successfully for many years sells the business to a corporation. Why would a corporation be interested in buying such a business?

SALES JOURNAL

SALES JOURNAL PAGE

	DATE		ACCOUNT DEBITED	SALE NO.	POST. REF.	1 ACCOUNTS RECEIVABLE DEBIT	2 SALES CREDIT	3 SALES TAX PAYABLE CREDIT	
1									1
2									2

Hobby Shack uses a special journal to record only sales of merchandise on account transactions. A special journal used to record only sales of merchandise on account is called a **sales journal**.

The special amount columns in this sales journal are Accounts Receivable Debit, Sales Credit, and Sales Tax Payable Credit. With these special amount columns, each sale on account transaction can be recorded on one line of the sales journal.

SALES INVOICE

HOBBY SHACK, INC.
1420 College Plaza
Atlanta, GA 30337-1726

Sold to: Village Crafts
120 Mountain Road
Marietta, GA 30060-1320
Cust. No. 150

No. 76
Date 11/3/--
Terms 30 days

Stock No.	Description	Quantity	Unit Price	Amount
4422	Deer and fawn bisque	25	12.00	300.00
7710	Lighthouse, 6" -- bisque	30	8.00	240.00
			Subtotal	540.00
Customer's Signature: *Max Schindler*		Salesclerk: *S.A.*	Sales Tax	32.40
			Total	572.40

When merchandise is sold on account, the seller prepares a form showing what has been sold. A form describing the goods or services sold, the quantity, and the price is known as an *invoice*. An invoice used as a source document for recording a sale on account is known as a *sales invoice*. [*CONCEPT: Objective Evidence*] A sales invoice is also referred to as a *sales ticket* or a *sales slip*.

The seller considers an invoice for a sale on account to be a sales invoice. The same invoice is considered by the customer to be a purchase invoice.

In the case of Hobby Shack, three copies of a sales invoice are prepared. The original copy is given to the customer. The second copy goes to Hobby Shack's shipping department. The third copy is used as the source document for the sale on account transaction. [*CONCEPT: Objective Evidence*] Sales invoices are numbered in sequence. Number 76 is the number of the sales invoice issued to Village Crafts.

Hobby Shack operates in a state with a 6% sales tax rate. The total amount of a sale of merchandise priced at \$300.00 is calculated as follows.

Price of Goods	×	Sales Tax Rate	=	Sales Tax
\$540.00	×	6%	=	\$32.40
Price of Goods	**+**	**Sales Tax**	**=**	**Total Amount**
\$540.00	+	\$32.40	=	\$572.40

SALE ON ACCOUNT

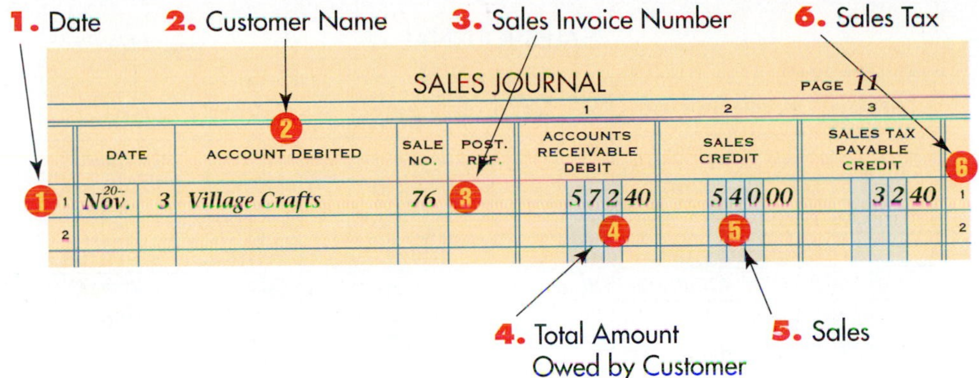

Hobby Shack sells on account only to businesses. Other customers must either pay cash or use a credit card.

November 3. Sold merchandise on account to Village Crafts, $540.00, plus sales tax, $32.40; total, $572.40. Sales Invoice No. 76.

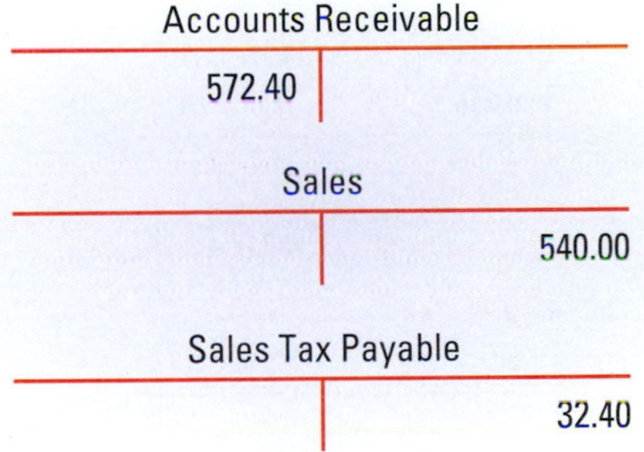

A sale on account transaction increases the amount to be collected later from a customer. Payment for this sale will be received at a later date. However, the sale is recorded at the time the sale is made because the sale has taken place and payment is due to Hobby Shack. [*CONCEPT: Realization of Revenue*]

Because Accounts Receivable has a normal debit balance, Accounts Receivable is debited for the total sales and sales tax, $572.40, to show the increase in this asset account. Sales has a normal credit balance. Therefore, Sales is credited for the price of the goods, $540.00, to show the increase in this revenue account. The sales tax payable account also has a normal credit balance. Therefore, Sales Tax Payable is credited for the amount of sales tax, $32.40, to show the increase in this liability account.

STEPS • STEPS • STEPS • STEPS • STEPS • STEPS • STEPS • STEPS • STEPS • STEPS

JOURNALIZING A SALE ON ACCOUNT

1. Write the date, *20--, Nov. 3,* in the Date column.
2. Write the customer name, *Village Crafts,* in the Account Debited column. The debit and credit amounts are recorded in special amount columns. Therefore, writing the titles of the general ledger accounts in the Account Debited column is not necessary. However, the name of the customer is written in the Account Debited column to show from whom the amount is due. Hobby Shack's procedures for keeping records of the amounts to be collected from each customer are described in Chapter 11.
3. Write the sales invoice number, *76,* in the Sale No. column.
4. Write the total amount owed by the customer, *$572.40,* in the Accounts Receivable Debit column.
5. Write the sales amount, *$540.00,* in the Sales Credit column.
6. Write the sales tax amount, *$32.40,* in the Sales Tax Payable Credit column.

   Some states exempt schools and other organizations from paying sales tax. A sale to a tax-exempt organization would be recorded using the same amount in the Sales Credit and Accounts Receivable Debit columns. No amount would be entered in the Sales Tax Payable Credit column.

TOTALING, PROVING, AND RULING A SALES JOURNAL

SALES JOURNAL — PAGE 11

	DATE		ACCOUNT DEBITED	SALE NO.	POST. REF.	1 ACCOUNTS RECEIVABLE DEBIT	2 SALES CREDIT	3 SALES TAX PAYABLE CREDIT	
1	20-- Nov.	3	Village Crafts	76		572 40	540 00	32 40	1
2		5	Fairview Church	77		1,908 00	1,908 00		2
3		9	Washington Schools	78		572 00	572 00		3
4		11	Country Crafters	79		768 50	725 00	43 50	4
5		16	Playtime Childcare	80		1,752 18	1,653 00	99 18	5
6		19	Village Crafts	81		2,549 30	2,405 00	144 30	6
7		24	Cumberland Center	82		158 00	158 00		7
8		24	Washington Schools	83		334 00	334 00		8
9		29	Country Crafters	84		453 68	428 00	25 68	9
10		30	Totals			9,068 06	8,723 00	345 06	10

At the end of each month, Hobby Shack totals, proves, and rules its sales journal. The procedures for proving and ruling a sales journal are the same as the procedures described for Hobby Shack's cash payments journal in Chapter 9.

The proof for Hobby Shack's sales journal is calculated as follows.

Col. No.	Column Title	Debit Totals	Credit Totals
1	Accounts Receivable Debit	$9,068.06	
2	Sales Credit		$8,723.00
3	Sales Tax Payable Credit		345.06
	Totals	$9,068.06	$9,068.06

The two totals, $9,068.06, are equal. Equality of debits and credits in Hobby Shack's sales journal for November is proved.

Posting from a sales journal is described in Chapter 11.

FYI FOR YOUR INFORMATION

Many states exempt food and drug sales for all customers. Some states even exempt clothing sales from sales tax.

©GETTY IMAGES/PHOTODISC

terms review

customer
sales tax
sales journal

audit your understanding

1. How does a merchandising business differ from a service business?
2. How are sales tax rates usually stated?
3. Why is sales tax collected considered a liability?
4. What is the title of the general ledger account used to summarize the total amount due from all charge customers?

work together 10-1

Journalizing sales on account; proving and ruling a sales journal

The sales journal for Distinctive Appliances is given in the *Working Papers.* Your instructor will guide you through the following examples.

1. Using the current year, journalize the following transactions on page 9 of the sales journal. The sales invoice source document is abbreviated as S.

Transactions:

Sept. 1. Sold merchandise on account to Adrian Makowski, $800.00, plus sales tax, $48.00; total, $848.00. S104.
11. Sold merchandise on account to Columbus City Schools, $875.00. Columbus City Schools is exempt from sales taxes. S105.
28. Sold merchandise on account to Swiss Delight, $1,460.00, plus sales tax, $87.60; total, $1,547.60. S106.

2. Total, prove, and rule the sales journal.

on your own 10-1

Journalizing sales on account; proving and ruling a sales journal

The sales journal for Parris Supplies is given in the *Working Papers.* Work these problems independently.

1. Using the current year, journalize the following transactions on page 6 of the sales journal. The sales invoice source document is abbreviated as S.

Transactions:

Jun. 5. Sold merchandise on account to Peter Gallaher, $650.00, plus sales tax, $39.00; total, $689.00. S410.
12. Sold merchandise on account to Spann Auto Supply, $590.00, plus sales tax, $35.40; total, $625.40. S411.
24. Sold merchandise on account to Fleming College, $545.00. Fleming College is exempt from sales taxes. S412.

2. Total, prove, and rule the sales journal.

LESSON

10-2 Journalizing Cash Receipts Using a Cash Receipts Journal

PROCESSING SALES TRANSACTIONS

Hobby Shack sells most of its merchandise for cash. A sale in which cash is received for the total amount of the sale at the time of the transaction is called a **cash sale**. Hobby Shack also sells merchandise to customers who have a bank-approved credit card. A sale in which a credit card is used for the total amount of the sale at the time of the transaction is called a **credit card sale**. Major bank-approved credit cards include VISA, MasterCard, and Discover Card. A customer who uses a credit card promises to pay the amount due for the credit card transaction to the bank issuing the credit card.

Some small businesses continue to use the traditional cash register to process sales transactions. After entering the price marked on each item sold, the sales clerk pushes a button instructing the cash register to total the sale, including any sales tax, and produce a cash register receipt for the customer. A typical cash register receipt is shown on the next page. At the end of every day, the cash register prints a summary of the sales recorded. The summary is adequate for journalizing the sales transaction, but it is unable to provide the business with information about what merchandise was sold, when it was sold, and to which customers.

Hobby Shack installed a modern version of a cash register. A computer used to collect, store, and report all the information of a sales transaction is called a **point-of-sale (POS) terminal**. Before any sale is entered, the number, description, price, and quantity on hand of each item of merchandise are stored in the POS terminal. When processing a sale, the sales clerk uses a scanning device to scan the universal product code (UPC) symbol on the item. A UPC code is shown on the next page.

The POS terminal matches the number represented by the UPC symbol with the merchandise number to obtain the description and price of the merchandise. When all the merchandise has been scanned, the sales clerk enters the customer's method of payment. For a cash sale, the sales clerk enters the cash tendered by the customer and the POS terminal computes the amount of change. For a credit card sale, the customer swipes the credit card in the card scanner. The POS system produces a receipt that contains detailed information about the sale. A customer receipt from a POS terminal is shown on the next page.

Periodically, Hobby Shack instructs the point-of-sale terminal to print a report of all cash and credit card sales. The report that summarizes the cash and credit card sales of a point-of-sale terminal is called a **terminal summary**. Hobby Shack uses the terminal summary as the source document for recording sales in its journals. [*CONCEPT: Objective Evidence*] A terminal summary is shown on the next page.

At any time, the POS system can produce a variety of informational reports to help management make decisions. For example:

1. A report of sales by sales clerk would assist management to analyze a sales clerk's efficiency.
2. A report of sales by time of day would assist management in scheduling sales clerks to match busy periods.
3. A report of merchandise having a quantity on hand below a predetermined reorder point alerts management to purchase additional merchandise.

Antique Shop
123 Eagle Street
Hanson, Iowa

	13.23
	2.45
	2.45
	10.34
Subtotal	28.47
Tax	1.71
Total	30.18

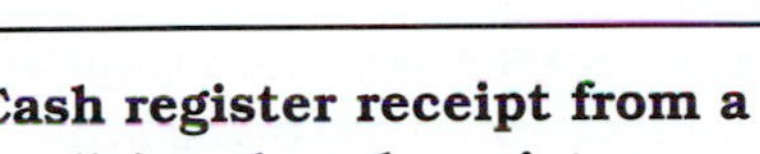

Cash register receipt from a traditional cash register

UPC (Universal Product Code) symbol on merchandise is scanned to enter data into a point-of-sale (POS) terminal

Hobby Shack, Inc.
1420 College Plaza
Atlanta, Georgia

latex paint, blue 1 oz.	
5 @ $1.45	7.25
paint brush, 3/4 glaze	
3 @ $3.25	9.75
Subtotal 1	17.00
Tax	1.02
TOTAL	18.02

VISA RECEIPT

Jan Windham	XXXXXXXXX1122
Exp 02/--	Ref3534423
04/01/--	
Register #: 002	Cashier #: 010

Thanks, Come Again

Point-of-sale (POS) terminal receipt

TERMINAL
SUMMARY
Hobby Shack, Inc.

Code:	34
Date:	11/27/--
Time:	18:24
Visa	*034*
Sales	295.38
Sales Tax	17.72
Total	313.10
MasterCard	*042*
Sales	107.21
Sales Tax	6.43
Total	113.64
Cash	*152*
Sales	5,057.41
Sales Tax	303.45
Total	5,360.86
Totals	
Sales	5,460.00
Sales Tax	327.60
Total	5,787.60

Terminal summary printed by POS terminal, used as source document for journalizing cash and credit card sales

BATCH REPORT

MERCHANT	02938493 234
TERMINAL	923874
DATE	04/03/--TIME 18:45
BATCH	45

VISA	
COUNT	= 007
SALES	= $ 325.23
RETURNS	= $ 12.13
NET	= $ 313.10
MASTERCARD	
COUNT	= 003
SALES	= $ 145.86
RETURNS	= $ 32.22
NET	= $ 113.64
TOTALS	
COUNT	= 010
SALES	= $ 471.09
RETURNS	= $ 44.35
NET	= $ 426.74

CONTROL NUMBER: 0938904235343

Batch Report for credit card sales printed by POS terminal (as discussed on page 278)

PROCESSING CREDIT CARDS

Sales information for credit card sales is stored in the POS terminal. When Hobby Shack produces the terminal summary, it also instructs the point-of-sale terminal to print a report of credit card sales. A report of credit card sales produced by a point-of-sale terminal is called a **batch report**. A batch report can be detailed, showing each credit card sale, or it can provide a summary of the number and total of sales by credit card type. The process of preparing a batch report of credit card sales from a point-of-sale terminal is called **batching out**. A batch report for credit card sales is shown on the previous page.

Hobby Shack has contracted with its bank, First American, to process its credit card sales. When Hobby Shack batches out, the POS terminal electronically transmits a summary batch report to First American. The bank combines the batch reports for all of its customers and submits the information to the nearest Federal Reserve Bank. The funds are transferred among the banks issuing the credit cards, similar to the way checks are transferred between banks.

For example, suppose a customer having a VISA card issued by Capital National Bank buys $500.00 worth of merchandise from Hobby Shack. When Hobby Shack batches out, an electronic message is sent to First American with the credit card number and amount of the sale. When the Federal Reserve Bank receives the information, $500.00 is transferred from Capital National's account to First American's account. First American then credits Hobby Shack's account for the sale. The cash is deposited in Hobby Shack's account 2–3 business days after the sale. However, Hobby Shack records the transaction on the date it occurs.

CASH RECEIPTS JOURNAL

CASH RECEIPTS JOURNAL PAGE

	DATE	ACCOUNT TITLE	DOC. NO.	POST. REF.	1 GENERAL DEBIT	2 GENERAL CREDIT	3 ACCOUNTS RECEIVABLE CREDIT	4 SALES CREDIT	5 SALES TAX PAYABLE CREDIT	6 SALES DISCOUNT DEBIT	7 CASH DEBIT	
1												1
2												2
3												3

Hobby Shack, Inc., has many transactions involving the receipt of cash. Because of the number of transactions, Hobby Shack uses a special journal for recording only cash receipts. A special journal used to record only cash receipt transactions is called a **cash receipts journal**.

Only those columns needed to record cash receipt transactions are included in Hobby Shack's cash receipts journal. Since all cash receipt transactions affect the cash account, a special column is provided for this general ledger account. In addition, Hobby Shack has many cash receipt transactions affecting the accounts receivable account, the sales account, and the sales tax payable account. Therefore, special columns are provided in Hobby Shack's cash receipts journal for these general ledger accounts.

To encourage early payment, Hobby Shack allows customers who purchase merchandise on account to take a deduction from the invoice amount. A cash discount on sales taken by a customer is called a **sales discount**. When a sales discount is taken, the customer pays less than the invoice amount previously recorded in the sales account. Sales discounts reduce the amount of cash Hobby Shack receives on sales on account. Because customers often take these discounts, Hobby Shack's cash receipts journal has a special column titled Sales Discount Debit. Because of these special columns, most of Hobby Shack's cash receipt transactions can be recorded on one line in the cash receipts journal. Cash receipts that do not occur often are recorded in the General columns.

CASH AND CREDIT CARD SALES

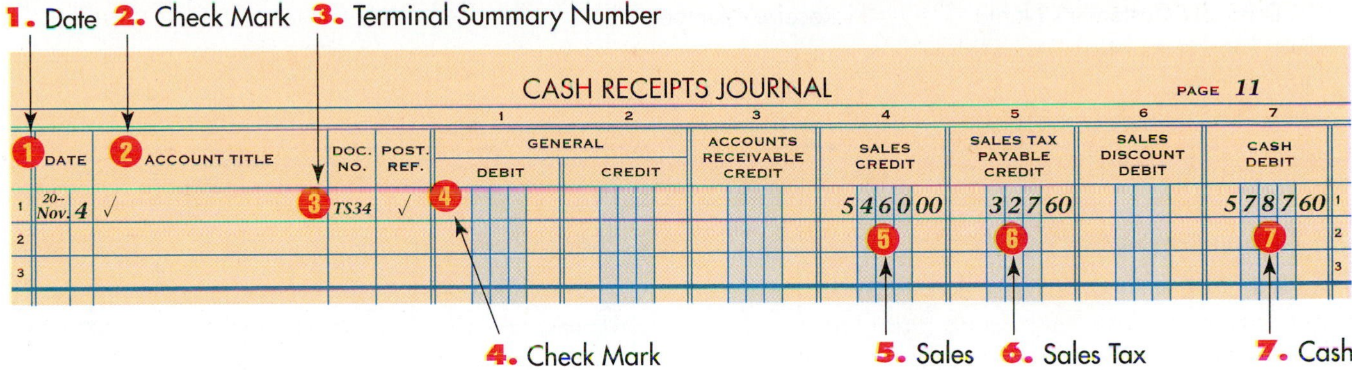

1. Date
2. Check Mark
3. Terminal Summary Number
CASH RECEIPTS JOURNAL
PAGE 11
DATE
ACCOUNT TITLE
DOC. NO.
POST. REF.
GENERAL
DEBIT
CREDIT
ACCOUNTS RECEIVABLE CREDIT
SALES CREDIT
SALES TAX PAYABLE CREDIT
SALES DISCOUNT DEBIT
CASH DEBIT
20--
Nov. 4
√
TS34
√
5 460 00
327 60
5 787 60
4. Check Mark
5. Sales
6. Sales Tax
7. Cash

Hobby Shack's POS terminal combines cash and credit card sales in the terminal summary. The total of the terminal summary is recorded as a single cash sales transaction.

November 4. Recorded cash and credit card sales, $5,460.00, plus sales tax, $327.60; total, $5,787.60. Terminal Summary 34.

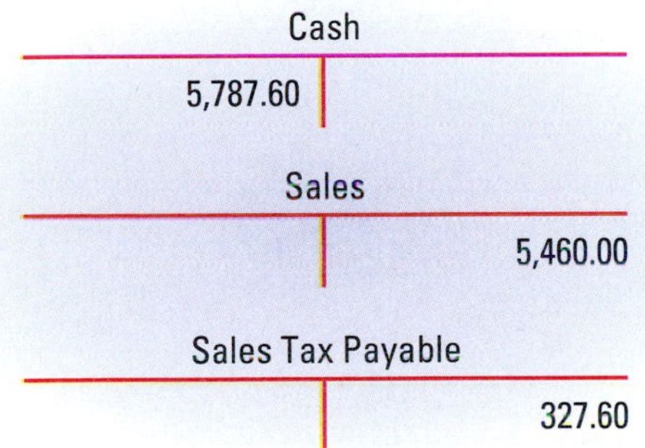

At the end of each week, Hobby Shack batches out and prints a terminal summary. The POS terminal assigns the summary a sequential number. The terminal summary is used by Hobby Shack as the source document for weekly cash and credit card sales transactions. [*CONCEPT: Objective Evidence*] Sales are also totaled at the end of each month so Hobby Shack can analyze monthly sales.

Management is responsible for determining how often the business should batch out, deposit cash, and record sales in the sales journal. Most businesses perform these tasks at the end of every business day. (The weekly processing demonstrated in this textbook was selected to simplify the textbook illustrations and problems.)

Because the asset account, Cash, has a normal debit balance, Cash is debited for the total sales and sales tax, $5,787.60, to show the increase in this asset account. The sales account has a normal credit balance. Therefore, Sales is credited for the total price of all goods sold, $5,460.00, to show the increase in this revenue account. The sales tax payable account also has a normal credit balance. Therefore, Sales Tax Payable is credited for the total sales tax, $327.60, to show the increase in this liability account.

STEPS • STEPS • STEPS • STEPS
JOURNALIZING CASH AND CREDIT CARD SALES

1. Write the date, *20--, Nov. 4*, in the Date column.
2. Place a check mark in the Account Title column to show that no account title needs to be written. The debit and credit amounts will be recorded in special amount columns.
3. Write the terminal summary document number, *TS34*, in the Doc. No. column.
4. Place a check mark in the Post. Ref. column to show that amounts on this line are not to be posted individually.
5. Write the sales amount, *$5,460.00*, in the Sales Credit column.
6. Write the sales tax amount, *$327.60*, in the Sales Tax Payable Credit column.
7. Write the cash amount, *$5,787.60*, in the Cash Debit column.

CASH RECEIPTS ON ACCOUNT

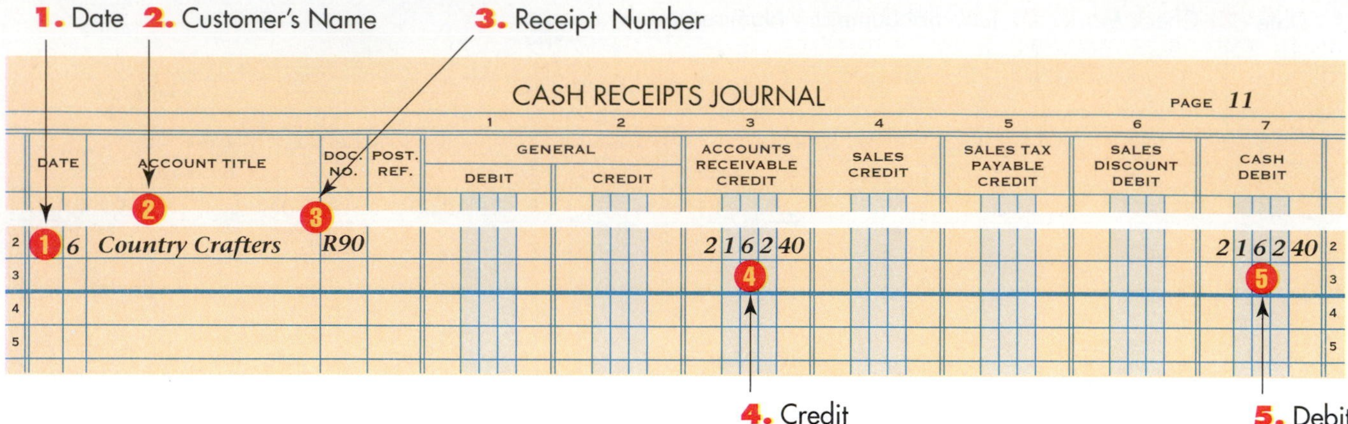

When cash is received on account from a customer, Hobby Shack prepares a receipt. The receipts are prenumbered so that all receipts can be accounted for. Receipts are prepared in duplicate. The original receipt is given to the customer. The copy of the receipt is used as the source document for the cash receipt on account transaction. [*CONCEPT: Objective Evidence*]

November 6. Received cash on account from Country Crafters, $2,162.40, covering S69. Receipt No. 90.

A cash receipt on account transaction decreases future amounts to be collected from a customer. This transaction increases the cash account balance and decreases the accounts receivable account balance. Because the cash account has a normal debit balance, Cash is debited for the amount of cash received, $2,162.40, to show the increase in this asset account. The accounts receivable account also has a normal debit balance. Therefore, Accounts Receivable is credited for $2,162.40 to show the decrease in this asset account.

Hobby Shack's procedures for keeping records of the amounts received from customers are described in Chapter 11. Posting procedures are also described in Chapter 11.

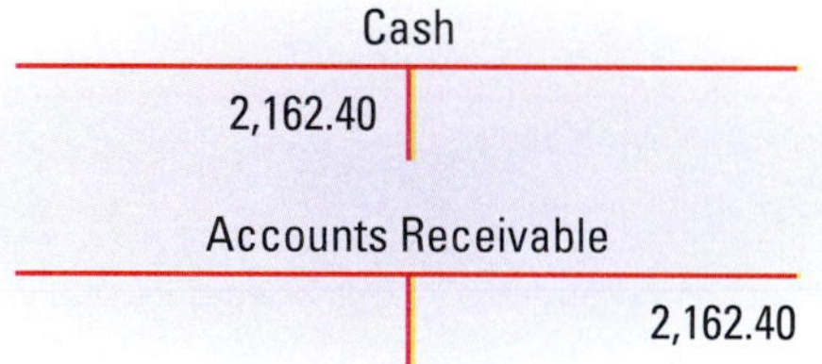

FYI FOR YOUR INFORMATION

All cash receipts are recorded in a cash receipts journal. Most cash receipts are for (1) cash received from customers on account and (2) cash and credit card sales.

STEPS • STEPS • STEPS • STEPS • STEPS • STEPS • STEPS • STEPS • STEPS • STEPS •

JOURNALIZING CASH RECEIPTS ON ACCOUNT

1. Write the date, *6*, in the Date column.
2. Write only the customer's name, *Country Crafters*, in the Account Title column. The debit and credit amounts are entered in special amount columns. Therefore, the titles of the two general ledger accounts do not need to be written in the Account Title column.
3. Write the receipt number, *R90*, in the Doc. No. column.
4. Write the credit amount, *$2,162.40*, in the Accounts Receivable Credit column.
5. Write the debit amount, *$2,162.40*, in the Cash Debit column.

CALCULATING CASH RECEIPTS ON ACCOUNT WITH SALES DISCOUNT

To encourage early payment for a sale on account, a deduction on the invoice amount may be allowed. A deduction that a vendor allows on the invoice amount to encourage prompt payment is known as a cash discount. A cash discount on sales is called a sales discount. When a sales discount is taken, a customer pays less cash than the invoice amount previously recorded in the sales account.

To encourage prompt payment, Hobby Shack gives credit terms of 2/10, n/30. When a customer pays the amount owed within 10 days, the sales invoice amount is reduced 2%. Otherwise, the net amount is due in 30 days.

On October 30, Hobby Shack sold merchandise on account to Cumberland Center for $1,200.00. On November 7, Hobby Shack received payment for this sale on account within the discount period. Because the payment is received within the discount period, the amount received is reduced by the amount of the sales discount.

Sales Invoice Amount	×	Sales Discount Rate	=	Sales Discount
$ 1,200.00	×	2%	=	$ 24.00

Computerized Accounting—Not Just for Corporations

For many years, only large corporations could afford to computerize their accounting functions. Today a variety of computer software programs are available to handle the record keeping and accounting needs of small and not-so-small businesses. Examples include Peachtree, Microsoft Small Business Manager, Oracle Small Business Suite, QuickBooks, and MYOB.

Depending on the needs of the business, there is a software program available to complete all or some accounting functions using a personal computer. These functions include the general ledger, accounts payable, accounts receivable, financial statements, and inventory. The software programs can print checks and maintain a check register, as well as reconcile bank statements. Some programs can process payroll, calculate taxes, and prepare tax forms.

Accounting software provides significant benefits. The software allows a business to improve the accuracy and completeness of financial records. Safeguards within the software alert the user to mistakes, problems, and inconsistencies. In addition, the software can create graphs and charts to complement financial reports and statements. The data is organized in a manner that enables management to create a variety of reports to analyze the effectiveness of its operations.

Instructions

1. Use Automated Accounting or some other accounting software to work one of the problems in this chapter. Report on any time that would be saved if this software were used to record the daily transactions of a real business.
2. Does the accounting software you used in question 1 have a graphing feature? If so, explore it to discover what kinds of graphs are available. Report on the usefulness of these graphs.

JOURNALIZING CASH RECEIPTS ON ACCOUNT WITH SALES DISCOUNTS

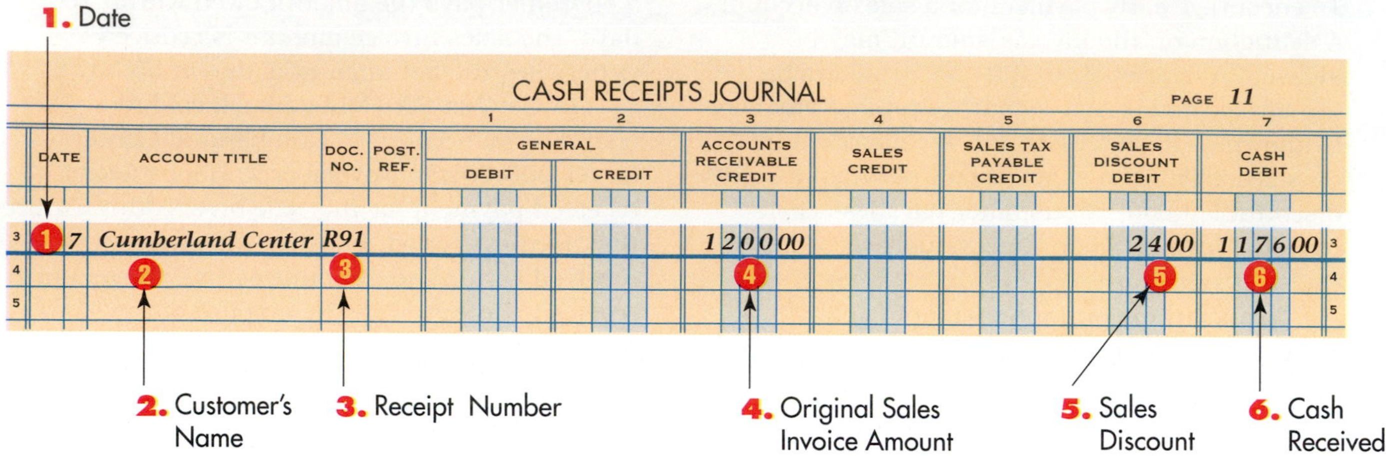

1. Date
CASH RECEIPTS JOURNAL
PAGE 11
DATE
ACCOUNT TITLE
DOC. NO.
POST. REF.
GENERAL DEBIT
GENERAL CREDIT
ACCOUNTS RECEIVABLE CREDIT
SALES CREDIT
SALES TAX PAYABLE CREDIT
SALES DISCOUNT DEBIT
CASH DEBIT
7 Cumberland Center R91 1 200 00 24 00 1 176 00
2. Customer's Name
3. Receipt Number
4. Original Sales Invoice Amount
5. Sales Discount
6. Cash Received

Sales discounts are recorded in a general ledger account titled Sales Discount. Since sales discounts decrease sales, the account Sales Discount is a contra account to Sales.

A business could debit Sales for the amount of the sales discount. However, better information is provided if these amounts are debited to Sales Discount. A separate account provides business managers with more information to evaluate whether a sales discount is a cost-effective method of encouraging early payments of sales on account.

November 7. Received cash on account from Cumberland Center, $1,176.00, covering Sales Invoice No. 74 for $1,200.00, less 2% discount, $24.00. Receipt No. 91.

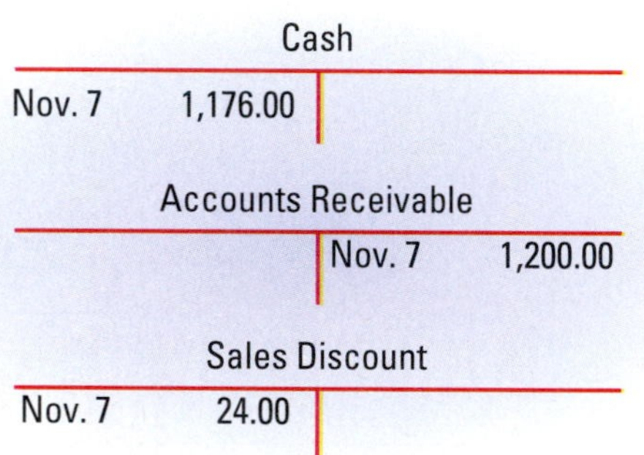

If a customer does not pay the amount owed within the sales discount period, the full invoice amount is due. If Cumberland Center had not taken the sales discount, the journal entry would be a debit to Cash, $1,200.00, and a credit to Accounts Receivable, $1,200.00.

STEPS: JOURNALIZING CASH RECEIPTS ON ACCOUNT WITH SALES DISCOUNTS

1. Write the date, *7*, in the Date column.
2. Write the customer's name, *Cumberland Center*, in the Account Title column.
3. Write the receipt number, *R91*, in the Doc. No. column.
4. Write the original invoice amount, *$1,200.00*, in the Accounts Receivable Credit column.
5. Write the amount of sales discount, *$24.00*, in the Sales Discount Debit column.
6. Write the debit to *Cash*, *$1,176.00*, in the Cash Debit column.

TOTALING, PROVING, AND RULING A CASH RECEIPTS JOURNAL

CASH RECEIPTS JOURNAL — PAGE 11

	DATE	ACCOUNT TITLE	DOC. NO.	POST. REF.	1 GENERAL DEBIT	2 GENERAL CREDIT	3 ACCOUNTS RECEIVABLE CREDIT	4 SALES CREDIT	5 SALES TAX PAYABLE CREDIT	6 SALES DISCOUNT DEBIT	7 CASH DEBIT	
22	30	√	T38	√				1,380.00	82.80		1,462.80	22
23	30	**Totals**					9,540.00	27,532.50	1,648.80	52.50	38,668.80	23
24												24

The procedures for totaling, proving, and ruling a cash receipts journal are the same as the procedures described for Hobby Shack's cash payments journal in Chapter 9. The use of the General Debit and General Credit columns is described in Part 3.

The proof for Hobby Shack's cash receipts journal for November is calculated as shown below. The two totals, $38,721.30, are equal. Equality of debits and credits is proved.

Col. No.	Column Title	Debit Totals	Credit Totals
1	General Debit	—	
2	General Credit		—
3	Accounts Receivable Credit		$ 9,540.00
4	Sales Credit		27,532.50
5	Sales Tax Payable Credit		1,648.80
6	Sales Discount Debit	$ 52.50	
7	Cash Debit	38,668.80	
	Totals	$38,721.30	$38,721.30

PROVING CASH AT THE END OF A MONTH

After the cash receipts journal is proved at the end of each month, cash is proved. Hobby Shack's cash proof at the end of November is calculated as shown.

The balance on the next unused check stub is $23,414.84. Since the balance on the next unused check stub is the same as the cash proof, cash is proved.

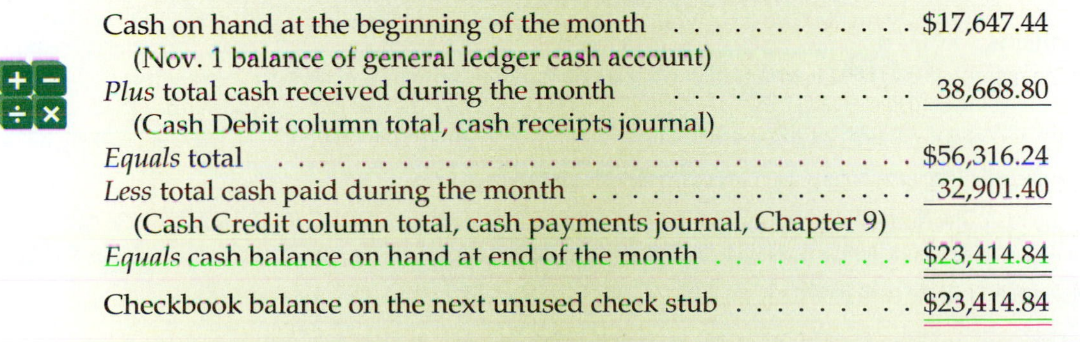

Cash on hand at the beginning of the month (Nov. 1 balance of general ledger cash account)	$17,647.44
Plus total cash received during the month (Cash Debit column total, cash receipts journal)	38,668.80
Equals total	$56,316.24
Less total cash paid during the month (Cash Credit column total, cash payments journal, Chapter 9)	32,901.40
Equals cash balance on hand at end of the month	$23,414.84
Checkbook balance on the next unused check stub	$23,414.84

terms review

cash sale
credit card sale
point-of-sale (POS) terminal
terminal summary
batch report
batching out
cash receipts journal
sales discount

audit your understanding

1. What is the difference in the receipt received by a customer from a cash register versus a point-of-sale terminal?
2. What are the two types of batch reports?
3. Who transfers funds between banks involved in the credit card sales?

work together 10-2

Journalizing cash receipts; proving and ruling a cash receipts journal

Cash receipts journal page 16 for Graphics Co. is given in the *Working Papers.* Your instructor will guide you through the following examples.

1. Using the current year, journalize the following transactions beginning on line 1. Source documents are abbreviated as follows: receipt, R; terminal summary, TS.

Transactions:

Oct. 4. Received cash on account from Oakely Company, $371.00, covering S96. R144.
13. Recorded cash and credit card sales, $8,361.60, plus sales tax, $501.70; total, $8,863.30. TS43.
30. Received cash on account from Sierra Supply, covering S97 for $5,989.00, less 2% discount. R145.

2. For the end of the month, total and prove cash receipts journal page 16.
3. Prove cash. The October 1 cash account balance in the general ledger was $11,764.96. The October 31 cash credit total in the cash payments journal is $8,779.53. On October 31, the balance on the next unused check stub was $18,088.95.
4. Rule page 16 of the cash receipts journal.

on your own 10-2

Journalizing cash receipts; proving and ruling a cash receipts journal

Cash receipts journal page 17 for Holloman Auto Parts is given in the *Working Papers.* Work these problems independently.

1. Using the current year, journalize the following transactions beginning on line 1. Source documents are abbreviated as follows: receipt, R; terminal summary, TS.

Transactions:

Nov. 2. Received cash on account from Wakeman Auto, $425.00, covering S298. R312.
13. Recorded cash and credit card sales, $3,254.30, plus sales tax, $189.55; total, $3,443.85. TS48.
27. Received cash on account from Cooley Used Cars, covering S295 for $1,459.00, less 2% discount. R313.

2. For the end of the month, total and prove cash receipts journal page 17.
3. Prove cash. The November 1 cash account balance in the general ledger was $2,848.10. The November 30 cash credit total in the cash payments journal is $4,284.25. On November 30, the balance on the next unused check stub was $3,862.52.
4. Rule page 17 of the cash receipts journal.

LESSON • LESSON • LESSON • LESSON • LESSON • LESSON

10-3 Recording Transactions Using a General Journal

CREDIT MEMORANDUM FOR SALES RETURNS AND ALLOWANCES

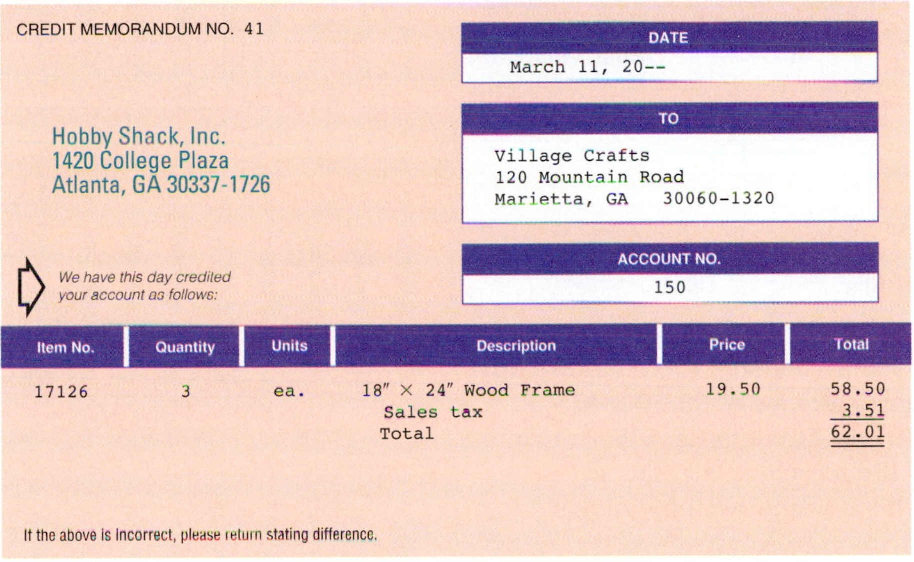

CREDIT MEMORANDUM NO. 41

DATE: March 11, 20--

Hobby Shack, Inc.
1420 College Plaza
Atlanta, GA 30337-1726

TO: Village Crafts
120 Mountain Road
Marietta, GA 30060-1320

We have this day credited your account as follows:

ACCOUNT NO. 150

Item No.	Quantity	Units	Description	Price	Total
17126	3	ea.	18″ × 24″ Wood Frame	19.50	58.50
			Sales tax		3.51
			Total		62.01

If the above is incorrect, please return stating difference.

In Chapter 9, purchases-related transactions other than purchases and cash payments were recorded in a general journal. Hobby Shack has a sales-related transaction that is recorded in a general journal rather than either the sales or the cash receipts journals.

Sales Returns and Allowances

Most merchandising businesses expect to have some merchandise returned. A customer may have received the wrong item or damaged goods. A customer may return merchandise for a credit on account or a cash refund. Credit allowed a customer for the sales price of returned merchandise, resulting in a decrease in the vendor's accounts receivable, is called a **sales return**.

Credit may be granted to a customer without requiring the return of merchandise. Credit also may be given because of a shortage in a shipment. Credit allowed a customer for part of the sales price of merchandise that is not returned, resulting in a decrease in the vendor's accounts receivable, is called a **sales allowance**.

A vendor usually informs a customer in writing when a sales return or a sales allowance is granted. A form prepared by the vendor showing the amount deducted for returns and allowances is called a **credit memorandum**. The original of a credit memorandum is given to the customer. The copy is used as the source document for recording the sales returns and allowances transaction. [*CONCEPT: Objective Evidence*]

Sales returns and sales allowances decrease the amount of sales. Therefore, the account Sales Returns and Allowances is a contra account to the revenue account Sales. Thus, the normal account balance of Sales Returns and Allowances is a debit, the opposite of the normal balance of Sales, a credit.

A business could debit the sales account for the amount of a return or allowance. However, better information is provided if these amounts are debited to Sales Returns and Allowances. This contra account enables management to quickly identify if the amount of sales returns and allowances compared to sales is greater than expected.

JOURNALIZING SALES RETURNS AND ALLOWANCES

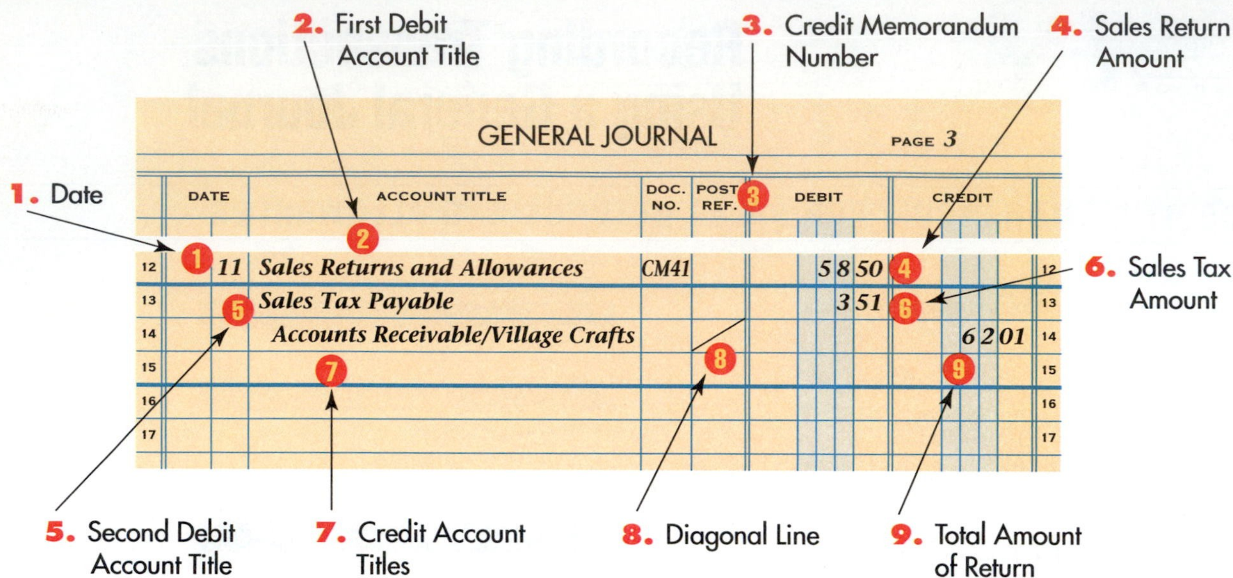

On March 8, Hobby Shack sold merchandise on account to Village Crafts for $503.50 ($475.00 sales plus $28.50 sales tax). Later, Village Crafts returned part of the merchandise. The sales return reduces the amount owed by Village Crafts by $62.01.

March 11. Granted credit to Village Crafts for merchandise returned, $58.50, plus sales tax, $3.51, from S160; total, $62.01. Credit Memorandum No. 41.

Sales Returns and Allowances

Mar. 11	58.50		

Sales Tax Payable

Mar. 11	3.51	Mar. 8	28.50

Accounts Receivable

Mar. 8	503.50	Mar. 11	62.01

STEPS • STEPS • STEPS • STEPS • STEPS • STEPS • STEPS • STEPS • STEPS • STEPS •

STEPS JOURNALIZING SALES RETURNS AND ALLOWANCES

1. Write the date, *11*, in the Date column.
2. Write *Sales Returns and Allowances* in the Account Title column.
3. Write *CM* and the credit memorandum number, *41*, in the Doc. No. column.
4. Write the amount of the sales return, *$58.50*, in the Debit column.
5. Write *Sales Tax Payable* on the next line in the Account Title column.
6. Write the sales tax amount, *$3.51*, in the Debit column.
7. On the next line, indented about 1 centimeter, write the accounts to be credited, *Accounts Receivable/Village Crafts*, in the Account Title column. Hobby Shack's procedures for keeping records of the amounts to be collected from each customer are described in Chapter 11.
8. Draw a diagonal line in the Post. Ref. column.
9. Write the total accounts receivable amount, *$62.01*, in the Credit column.

• terms review

sales return
sales allowance
credit memorandum

TERMS REVIEW • TERMS

• audit your understanding

1. What is the difference between a sales return and a sales allowance?
2. What is the source document for journalizing sales returns and allowances?
3. What general ledger accounts are affected, and how, by a sales returns and allowances transaction?
4. Why are sales returns and allowances not debited to the Sales account?

AUDIT YOUR UNDERSTANDING

work together 10-3

Journalizing sales returns and allowances using a general journal

The general journal for Cline Interiors is given in the *Working Papers.* Your instructor will guide you through the following examples.

1. Using the current year, journalize the following transactions on page 6 of a general journal. Source documents are abbreviated as: credit memorandum, CM; sales invoice, S.

Transactions:

June 3. Granted credit to Wilbanks and Associates for merchandise returned, $457.00, plus sales tax, $36.56, from S356; total, $493.56. CM41.

6. Granted credit to Westfall High School for damaged merchandise, $67.00 (no sales tax), from S345. CM42.

WORK TOGETHER • WORK TOGETHER

• on your own 10-3

Journalizing sales returns and allowances using a general journal

The general journal for City Lighting is given in the *Working Papers.* Work these problems independently.

1. Using the current year, journalize the following transactions on page 7 of a general journal. Source documents are abbreviated as: credit memorandum, CM; sales invoice, S.

Transactions:

July 3. Granted credit to Carver High School for damaged merchandise, $46.00 (no sales tax), from S642. CM87.

4. Granted credit to Karen's Fine Gifts for merchandise returned, $425.00, plus sales tax, $25.50, from S623; total, $450.50. CM86.

ON YOUR OWN • ON YOUR OWN

SUMMARY

After completing this chapter, you can

1. Define accounting terms related to sales and cash receipts for a merchandising business.
2. Identify accounting concepts and practices related to sales and cash receipts for a merchandising business.
3. Journalize sales on account using a sales journal.
4. Journalize cash receipts using a cash receipts journal.
5. Journalize sales returns and allowances using a general journal.

Explore Accounting

Journalizing Sales Discounts

Most sales of a merchandising business are to individuals for cash or credit card. Individual customers are expected to pay the full amount of the invoice at the time of the sale. In contrast, sales on account to business customers may involve a cash discount, such as 2/10, n/30. As discussed in Chapter 9, businesses often receive cash discounts to encourage early payment for a sale on account.

Sales on account that involve both sales taxes and a cash discount present an interesting accounting problem. Assume Country Crafters purchases $100.00 of merchandise, plus $6.00 sales tax, for a total sale of $106.00, with 2/10, n/30 payment terms. Nine days later, Country Crafters pays $103.88 in full payment of the invoice. How should the cash receipt be journalized?

Because the payment is received within the discount period, the sales amount is reduced by the amount of the sales discount, $2.12. The amount of sales tax should also be reduced because the amount of the sale is reduced. Thus, the following journal entry should be recorded:

Cash	103.88	
Sales Tax Payable	.12	
Sales Discount		2.00
Accounts Receivable		106.00

The net sales amount is $98.00—the original $100.00 sales less a 2% discount of $2.00. The net sales tax payable is $5.88—the original $6.00 sales tax less a 2% discount of $0.12. The end result is that a $98.00 sale was made on which $5.88 sales tax ($98.00 × 6%) was collected.

It is critically important for accounting employees to be familiar with sales tax laws in the states in which their companies do business. Each state regulates how sales taxes should be paid. In some states, state regulations require that sales taxes be paid only on actual sales realized—$5.88 for this transaction. Merchandising businesses in these states might modify the cash receipts journal to include a Sales Tax Payable Debit column.

In some states, sales taxes must be paid on the original invoice amount of sale—$6.00 for this transaction. In these states, a sales discount would not result in a reduction in the sales tax liability. The following journal entry would be recorded:

Cash	103.88	
Sales Discount	2.12	
Accounts Receivable		106.00

Instructions: With your instructor's permission, contact several local businesses to determine how they account for cash discounts on sales on account. Specifically, ask the manager (1) does the business offer cash discounts and (2) how do sales returns impact the amount of sales tax paid to the state.

10-1 APPLICATION PROBLEM

Journalizing sales on account; proving and ruling a sales journal

Audio Engineering is an electronics store specializing in sound systems.

Instructions:

1. Journalize the following transactions completed during September of the current year on page 10 of the sales journal given in the *Working Papers*. The sales invoice source document is abbreviated as S.

Transactions:

Sep. 2. Sold merchandise on account to Ketchum Clothing, $457.50, plus sales tax, $27.45; total, $484.95. S134.
5. Sold merchandise on account to Norton Industries, $345.00, plus sales tax, $20.70; total, $365.70. S135.
10. Sold merchandise on account to Jackson City Schools, $426.00. Jackson City Schools is exempt from paying sales tax. S136.
17. Sold merchandise on account to Riley & Slay, CPAs, $522.00, plus sales tax, $31.32; total, $553.32. S137.
23. Sold merchandise on account to Meadowbrook Church, $453.00. Meadowbrook Church is exempt from paying sales tax. S138.
30. Sold merchandise on account to Tang Construction, $512.00, plus sales tax, $30.72; total, $542.72. S139.

2. Total, prove, and rule page 10 of the sales journal.

10-2 APPLICATION PROBLEM

AUTOMATED ACCOUNTING

Journalizing cash receipts; proving and ruling a cash receipts journal

In Focus is a camera and film shop.

Instructions:

1. Journalize the following transactions completed during August of the current year on page 15 of the cash receipts journal given in the *Working Papers*. Source documents are abbreviated as follows: receipt, R; terminal summary, TS.

Transactions:

Aug. 1. Received cash on account from Reader Advertising, $345.60, covering S357. R288.
3. Recorded cash and credit card sales, $2,534.00, plus sales tax, $145.54; total, $2,679.54. TS28.
8. Received cash on account from WXGS Television, $312.60, covering S358. R289.
10. Recorded cash and credit card sales, $2,650.00, plus sales tax, $140.80; total, $2,790.80. TS29.
15. Received cash on account from Lambert News, covering S360 for $204.30, less 2% discount. R290.
17. Recorded cash and credit card sales, $2,372.00, plus sales tax, $132.43; total, $2,504.43. TS30.
24. Received cash on account from Kelly Modeling Agency, $236.96, covering S359. R291.
24. Recorded cash and credit card sales, $3,180.00, plus sales tax, $170.80; total, $3,350.80. TS31.
30. Received cash on account from JGN Industries, covering S361 for $201.40, less 2% discount. R292.
31. Recorded cash and credit card sales, $2,100.00, plus sales tax, $104.25; total, $2,204.25. TS32.

2. Total and prove the equality of debits and credits for cash receipts journal page 15.

3. Prove cash. The August 1 cash account balance in the general ledger was $2,548.25. The August 31 cash credit total in the cash payments journal was $15,485.25. On August 31, the balance on the next unused check stub was $1,885.56.
4. Rule page 15 of the cash receipts journal.

10-3 APPLICATION PROBLEM

Journalizing sales returns and allowances using a general journal

VanHorn Designs sells custom logo products.

Instructions:

1. Journalize the following transactions affecting sales completed during July of the current year. Use page 14 of the general journal given in the *Working Papers*. Source documents are abbreviated as follows: credit memorandum, CM; receipt, R; sales invoice, S.

Transactions:

July 2. Granted credit to Tahai Industries for merchandise returned, $253.00, plus sales tax, $15.18, from S456; total, $268.18. CM61.

4. Granted credit to Allergy Associates for damaged merchandise, $235.00, plus sales tax, $14.10, from S455; total, $249.10. CM62.

12. Granted credit to Jefferson School for damaged merchandise, $134.25, from S458. CM63.

10-4 MASTERY PROBLEM

QUICKBOOKS

Journalizing sales and cash receipts transactions; proving and ruling journals

Aqua Center installs and maintains swimming pools and spas.

Use page 19 of a sales journal, page 20 of a cash receipts journal, and page 14 of a general journal. Balances brought forward are provided on line 1 of each journal in the *Working Papers*.

Instructions:

1. Journalize the following transactions completed during the remainder of October in the appropriate journal. The sales tax rate is 4%. Source documents are abbreviated as follows: receipt, R; sales invoice, S; terminal summary, TS.

Transactions:

Oct. 26. Received cash on account from Slumber Inns, covering S435 for $1,356.00, less a 2% discount. R293.

27. Sold merchandise on account to County Hospital, $489.50, plus sales tax, $19.58; total, $509.08. S443.

28. Recorded cash and credit card sales, $4,315.00, plus sales tax, $126.60; total, $4,441.60. TS44.

29. Received cash on account from Summit Lodge, $467.24, covering S438. R294.

29. Granted credit to Slumber Inns for merchandise returned, $124.00, plus sales tax, $4.96, from S293; total, $128.96. CM54.

30. Sold merchandise on account to Southeastern University, $3,643.50. Southeastern University is exempt from sales tax. S444.

31. Recorded cash and credit card sales, $1,232.00, plus sales tax, $42.22; total, $1,274.22. TS45.

2. Total and prove the equality of debits and credits for the sales journal.
3. Rule the sales journal.
4. Total and prove the equality of debits and credits for the cash receipts journal.
5. Prove cash. The October 1 cash account balance in the general ledger was $4,483.25. The October 31 cash credit total in the cash payments journal was $39,315.22. On October 31, the balance on the next unused check stub was $8,918.50.
6. Rule the cash receipts journal.

10-5 CHALLENGE PROBLEM  

Journalizing transactions; proving and ruling special journals

Zone 6 is a lawn and garden store.

Instructions:

1. Journalize in the appropriate journal the following transactions completed during May of the current year. Use page 5 of a purchases and sales journal, page 8 of a cash payments journal, page 9 of a cash receipts journal, and page 7 of a general journal given in the *Working Papers*. The sales tax rate is 8%. Calculate and add the appropriate sales tax amount to each sale. Source documents are abbreviated as follows: check, C; memorandum, M; purchase invoice, P; receipt, R; sales invoice, S; terminal summary, TS.

Transactions:

May 1. Paid cash for rent, $1,400.00. C344.
3. Paid cash for electric bill, $186.00. C345.
3. Granted credit to Slippery Rock Inn for merchandise returned, $235.00, plus sales tax, $18.80, from S493; total, $253.80. CM67.
3. Purchased merchandise on account from Angelo Lawn Supplies, $1,340.00. P91.
4. Bought $120.00 worth of store supplies on account from Mosby Store Supplies, recorded on Memo 43, with 2/10, n/30 payment terms.
4. Paid cash on account to Northeast Nurseries, $7,632.00, covering P87. C346.
4. Sold merchandise on account to First National Bank, $546.00, plus sales tax. S567.
5. Bought office supplies for cash, $35.45. C347.
5. Paid cash for some merchandise, $89.40. C348.
6. Recorded cash and credit card sales, $3,235.00, plus sales tax of $239.40. TS23.
7. Received an invoice, stamped Purchase Invoice 92, for merchandise on account from Forde Collectibles for $3,250.00, less a 60% trade discount.
7. Houston Landscaping paid its $545.65 balance, less 2% discount. R490.
8. Bought office supplies on account from Office Mart, $81.60. M44.
10. Returned $260.00 of the merchandise purchased on Purchase Invoice 92 to Forde Collectibles, recorded on Debit Memorandum 23.
11. Paid the remaining balance of Purchase Invoice 92, less Debit Memorandum 23, to Forde Collectibles with Check No. 349, taking advantage of the 2/10, n/30 payment terms.
13. Cash and credit card sales for the week were $3,216.00, plus sales tax of $206.70. TS24.
14. Jackson Public Schools bought merchandise on account for $450.00. S568.
16. Purchased $2,900.00 of merchandise on account from Tom's Sod Farm on Purchase Invoice 93, with 2/10, n/30 payment terms.
17. Paid cash on account to Office Mart, $81.60, covering M44. C350.
20. Cash and credit card sales for the week were $2,554.00, plus sales tax, $184.23. TS25.
22. First National Bank paid $589.68 cash on its account, covering S567. R491.
23. SDR Investment Trust bought merchandise on account for $1,456.00, plus sales tax. S569.
23. Purchased merchandise on account from LawnScapes, Inc., $4,488.00. P94.
25. Paid $102.00 cash for advertising. C351.
27. Cash and credit card sales for the week were $2,742.00, plus sales tax, $184.25. TS26.
29. Slippery Rock Inn paid $2,345.64 on its account, covering S493. R492.
29. Granted credit to SDR Investment Trust for damaged merchandise, $45.00, plus sales tax, from S455. CM68. general general sales returns
31. Paid cash to replenish the petty cash fund, $361.60: office supplies, $74.40; store supplies, $85.00; advertising, $105.00; miscellaneous, $96.00. C352.
31. Recorded cash and credit card sales, $768.00, plus sales tax, $49.45. TS27.

2. Total the purchases, cash payments, sales, and cash receipts journals.
3. Prove the equality of debits and credits for the cash payments, sales, and cash receipts journals.
4. Prove cash. The May 1 cash account balance in the general ledger was $2,464.60. On May 31, the balance on the next unused check stub was $8,406.44.
5. Rule the purchases, cash payments, sales, and cash receipts journals.

applied communication

The tendency for prices to increase over time is referred to as *inflation*. Increasing prices reduce what an individual or company can purchase with the same amount of money.

Instructions: The following table represents the prices for selected consumer goods in 1990. Copy the table and add a column for the current year and a column for the percent of change. Use the newspaper and identify current prices for the products listed. Determine the percentage change in the price of each item. If an item decreased in price, can you explain the reason for the decrease?

Comparison of Prices for Selected Consumer Items

Item	1990 Price
19-inch color television	$149.00
Cassette tape	13.50
Milk (gallon)	1.99
Ground beef (pound)	1.69
Eggs, medium (dozen)	.99
Raisin bran	1.99
Film, 24 exposures	3.88
Theater ticket	6.50
Motor oil (quart)	.84
Refrigerator (19.1 cu. ft.)	790.00

case for critical thinking

Roshonda Compton, an accountant for an office supplies store, has noted a major increase in overdue amounts from charge customers. All invoice amounts from sales on account are due within 30 days. The amounts due have reduced the amount of cash available for the day-to-day operation of the business. Ms. Compton recommends that the business (1) stop all sales on account and (2) begin accepting bank credit cards. The owner is reluctant to accept the recommendations because the business might lose some reliable customers who do not have credit cards. Also, the business will have increased expenses because of the credit card fee. How would you respond to Ms. Compton's recommendations? What alternatives might the owner consider?

SCANS workplace competency

Basic Skill: Reading

Concept: Employers need employees at all levels who can read well. Reading includes locating, understanding, and interpreting written information. The written information may be in documents such as manuals, graphs, schedules, or even in software "Help" windows.

Application: Open a software application with which you are familiar, such as word processing, spreadsheet, or accounting software. Using either printed documentation or the Help function of the software, locate a software feature with which you are not familiar. Read the document and create a file in which you can practice applying this previously unknown feature. Write a statement about situations in which this new feature could save time.

using source documents

Journalizing sales and cash receipts transactions; proving and ruling journals

Golfer's Paradise sells golf and other recreational equipment. Source documents related to the sales and cash receipts are provided in the *Working Papers*.

Sales journal page 18, cash receipts journal page 24, and general journal page 15 for Golfer's Paradise are given in the *Working Papers*. Balances brought forward are provided on line 1 of each journal.

Instructions

1. Journalize the transactions shown in the source documents in the appropriate journal. The sales tax rate is 8%.
2. Total and prove the equality of debits and credits for the sales journal.
3. Rule the sales journal.
4. Total and prove the equality of debits and credits for the cash receipts journal.
5. Prove cash. The November 1 cash account balance in the general ledger was $2,551.18. The November 30 cash credit total in the cash payments journal was $49,158.84. On November 30, the balance on the next unused check stub was $5,106.41.
6. Rule the cash receipts journal.

analyzing Best Buy's financial statements

Comparable store sales—the sales at stores open for more than a year—is one of the best measures of financial success for a retail business. An increase in comparable store sales can be achieved by a combination of raising unit sales prices and selling more units. Regardless of the reason, an increase in comparable store sales demonstrates that the company's products are in demand.

Instructions

1. Use Best Buy's 11-Year Financial Highlights in Appendix B to identify the comparable store sales change for 2002–2004.
2. Use the 11-Year Financial Highlights to identify the types and number of stores open at the end of 2003 and 2004.
3. Refer to Note 1 in Appendix B to determine why Best Buy had no Musicland Stores at the end of 2004.

Automated Accounting

Automated Entries for Sales and Cash Receipts Using Special Journals

All transactions involving the receipt of cash are recorded in a special journal called the *cash receipts journal*. The sale of merchandise on account is recorded in the sales journal. All other sales-related transactions, such as sales returns and allowances, are recorded in the general journal.

A business or individual to whom merchandise or services are sold is called a *customer*. Businesses that have many customers maintain a separate customer file. The total owed by all customers maintained in a customer file is summarized in a single general ledger asset account called Accounts Receivable. Customer accounts may be added, changed, or deleted from the accounting system just as general ledger accounts are, as described in Chapter 9.

Sales

A sales transaction may be on account or for cash. The sales journal is used to enter sales on account transactions. Sales transactions may be entered directly into the computer from the invoice (source document). When the credit portion of a sales transaction is entered, the computer will automatically make the debit to Accounts Receivable.

To record transactions in the sales journal:

1. Click the Journal toolbar button.
2. Click the Sales tab.
3. Enter the transaction date and press Tab.
4. Enter the invoice number in the Refer. column and press Tab.
5. Enter the amount of the invoice in the Sales Credit column and press Tab. The Accounts Receivable debit amount is calculated and displayed automatically.
6. If the transaction involves sales tax, enter the amount in the Sales Tax Credit column and press Tab. If there is no sales tax, press Tab to bypass the Sales Tax Credit column.
7. Press Tab as necessary to position the cursor in the Customer column. Choose a customer name from the Customer drop-down list. You may also select the customer by striking the letter the customer name begins with until the correct name is displayed, and then striking Enter.
8. Click the Post button.

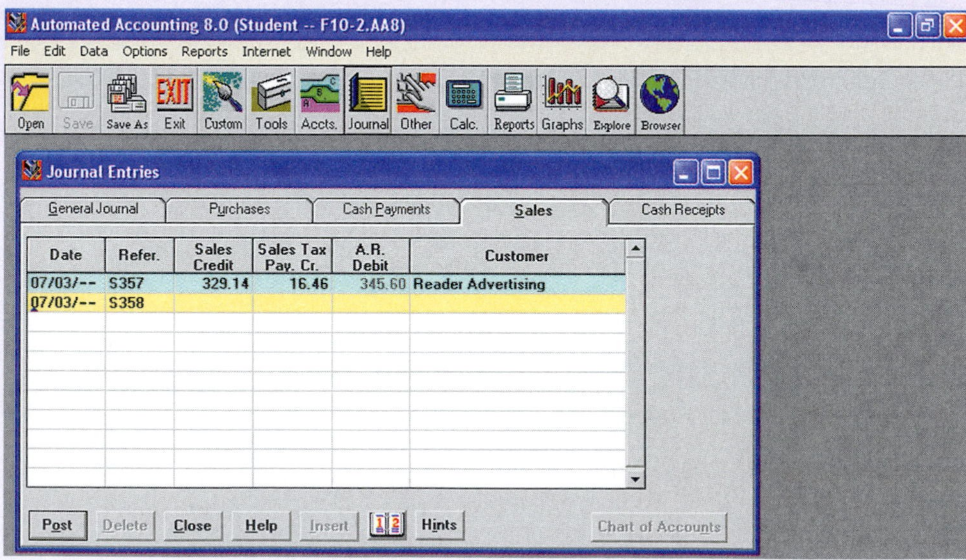

Cash Receipts

The cash receipts journal is used to enter all cash receipt transactions. The debit to cash is automatically calculated and displayed by the computer. There are two types of cash receipts:

1. Cash and credit card sales are cash receipts that do not affect Accounts Receivable.
2. Receipts on account are cash receipts that do affect Accounts Receivable.

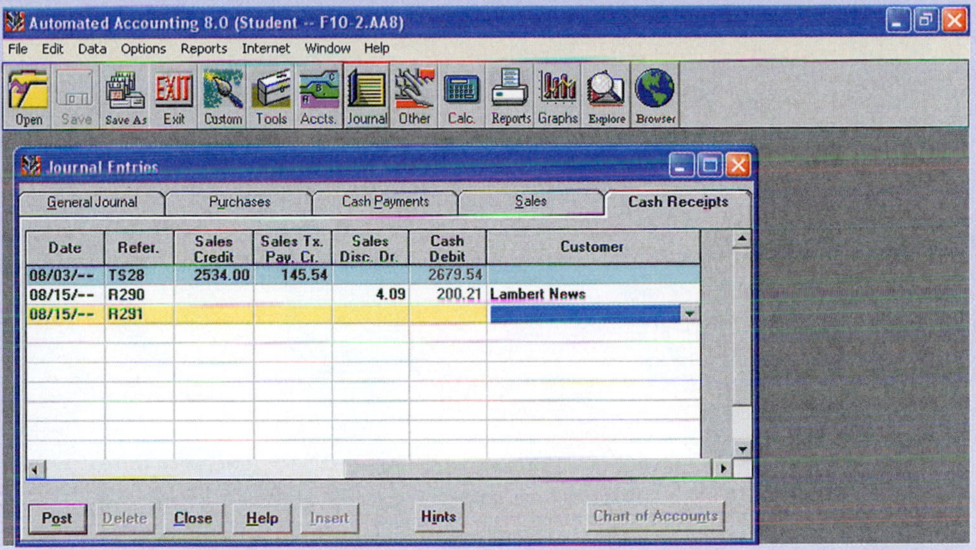

To record transactions in the cash receipts journal:

1. Click the Journal toolbar button.
2. Click the Cash Receipts tab.
3. Enter the transaction date and press Tab.
4. Enter the transaction reference and press Tab.
5. Enter the account number to debit or credit.
6. If recording a cash or credit card sale, press Tab until the cursor appears in the Sales Credit column. Enter the sales amount of the merchandise sold and press Tab. Enter the amount of sales tax in the Sales Tax Payable Credit column. The debit to Cash is automatically calculated and displayed.
7. If recording a receipt on account, press Tab until the cursor appears in the A.R. Credit column. Enter the amount. The debit to Cash is automatically calculated and displayed. Press Tab until the cursor appears in the Customer column. Choose the customer from the Customer drop-down list.
8. Click the Post button.

AUTOMATING APPLICATION PROBLEM 10-2: Journalizing cash receipts; proving and ruling a cash receipts journal

Instructions:

1. Load the *Automated Accounting 8.0* or higher software.
2. Select data file F10-2 from the appropriate directory/folder.
3. Select File from the menu bar and choose the Save As menu command. Key the path to the drive and directory that contains your data files. Save the data file with a filename of F10-2 XXX XXX (where the X's are your first and last name).
4. Access Problem Instructions through the Browser tool. Read the Problem Instructions screen.
5. Key the data listed in Application Problem 10-2.
6. Save your file and exit the Automated Accounting software.

AUTOMATING MASTERY PROBLEM 10-4: Journalizing sales and cash receipts transactions; proving and ruling journals

Instructions:

1. Load the *Automated Accounting 8.0* or higher software.
2. Select data file F10-4 from the appropriate directory/folder.
3. Select File from the menu bar and choose the Save As menu command. Key the path to the drive and directory that contains your data files. Save the data file with a filename of F10-4 XXX XXX (where the X's are your first and last name).
4. Access Problem Instructions through the Browser tool. Read the Problem Instructions screen.
5. Key the data listed in Mastery Problem10-4.
6. Save your file and exit the Automated Accounting software.

CHAPTER

11 Posting to General and Subsidiary Ledgers

OBJECTIVES & TERMS

After studying Chapter 11, you will be able to:

1. Define accounting terms related to posting to ledgers.
2. Identify accounting practices related to posting to ledgers.
3. Post separate items from a purchases, cash payments, and general journal to an accounts payable ledger.
4. Post separate items from a sales, cash receipts, and general journal to an accounts receivable ledger.
5. Post separate items from a cash payments and general journal to a general ledger.
6. Post special journal column totals to a general ledger.
7. Journalize and post correcting entries affecting customer accounts.

- subsidiary ledger
- accounts payable ledger
- accounts receivable ledger
- controlling account
- schedule of accounts payable
- schedule of accounts receivable

accounting in the real world

palmONE, INC.

©GETTY IMAGES

KEEPING UP WITH CHANGES AT palmOne, INC.

To keep up with the changes at palmOne, Inc., you need . . . well, you need a palmOne™ handheld!

Organizational changes are part of corporate life. Palm Computing, founded in 1992, was acquired by U.S. Robotics Corp. in 1995. The company later became part of 3Com Corp. in 1997, when U.S. Robotics was acquired by 3Com. In 2000, Palm again became an independent, publicly traded company. In its latest change, the company adopted the name palmOne, Inc., in October 2003, when it spun off PalmSource, Inc., maker of the Palm OS® platform software, and acquired Handspring, Inc.

Change is a constant at palmOne, Inc. Each change in corporate structure requires changes in the underlying accounting system. New accounts and different methods for combining those accounts are required to create financial statements.

Make a note in your handheld—accounting systems change.

Critical Thinking

1. What changes might occur in the chart of accounts when a business changes from being a sole proprietorship to a corporation?
2. Identify another business that has experienced changes in its corporate structure. What motivated the change(s)?

accountingxtra.swlearning.com

Source: www.palmone.com/us/company/pr/background.html

internet activity

AICPA—STUDENT RESOURCES

Go to the homepage for the American Institute of Certified Public Accountants (AICPA) (www.aicpa.org). Click on the "Students" link, and then click on "The Profession and You."

Instructions

1. Under the link "Fun CPA Facts," find and list three fun facts.
2. Under the "Frequently Asked Questions (FAQ)" link, read through the questions and answers. List one question and summarize the answer to the question.

LESSON

11-1 Posting to an Accounts Payable Ledger

LEDGERS AND CONTROLLING ACCOUNTS

A business's size, number of transactions, and type of transactions determine the number of ledgers used in an accounting system.

General Ledger

Hobby Shack's general ledger chart of accounts is on page 231. However, because of the business's size and the number and type of transactions, Hobby Shack also uses additional ledgers in its accounting system.

Subsidiary Ledgers

A business needs to know the amount owed each vendor as well as the amount to be collected from each charge customer. Therefore, a separate account is needed for each vendor and each customer. Hobby Shack keeps a separate ledger for vendors and a separate ledger for customers.

Each separate ledger is summarized in a single general ledger account. A ledger that is summarized in a single general ledger account is called a **subsidiary ledger**. A subsidiary ledger containing only accounts for vendors from whom merchandise is purchased on account or other items are bought on account is called an **accounts payable ledger**. A subsidiary ledger containing only accounts for charge customers is called an **accounts receivable ledger**. Total amounts are summarized in single general ledger accounts: Accounts Payable for vendors and Accounts Receivable for charge customers. An account in a general ledger that summarizes all accounts in a subsidiary ledger is called a **controlling account**. The balance of a controlling account equals the total of all account balances in its related subsidiary ledger.

MAKING ETHICAL DECISIONS • MAKING ETHICAL DECISIONS • MAKING ETHICAL DECISIONS

making ethical decisions

Whose Computer Is It Really?

John Melton is an accounting manager at Stegall Industries. John frequently walks through his department to make himself readily available for his employees to ask questions and provide feedback. With increasing frequency, John has observed that his employees have Internet auction sites open while they are working on their computers. Concerned that productivity in his department is suffering, he is considering installing some sort of monitoring system to gather evidence of the employees' computer usage.

In accordance with company policy, John began his planning by examining the company's code of conduct. Two statements appear relevant: "Employees should be treated with mutual respect, free from the threat of harassment and discrimination."

"Employees may occasionally use company computer systems, such as Internet and e-mail, for personal use. Such use should be on a limited basis and should not result in a measurable cost to the Company."

Instructions

Use the ethical model to evaluate John's proposed action to monitor his employees' Internet usage. Do you have any recommendations for John?

ACCOUNTS PAYABLE LEDGER AND GENERAL LEDGER CONTROLLING ACCOUNT

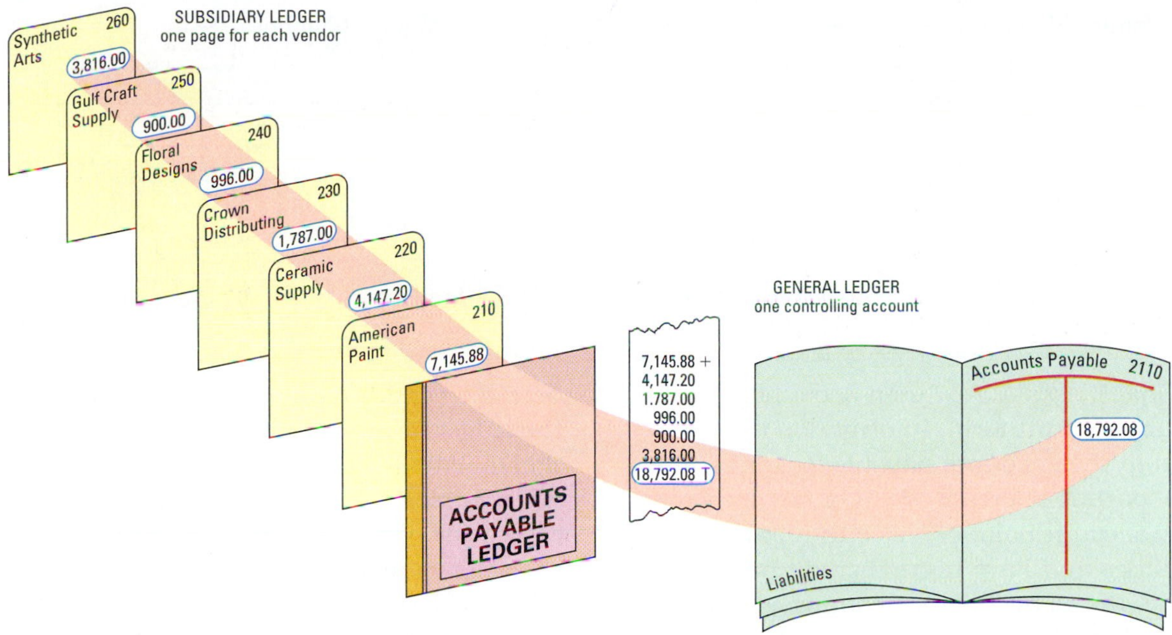

Hobby Shack assigns a vendor number to each account in the accounts payable ledger. A three-digit number is used. The first digit identifies the division in which the controlling account appears in the general ledger. The second two digits show each account's location within a subsidiary ledger. Accounts are assigned by 10s, beginning with the second digit. Accounts in the subsidiary ledgers can be located by either number or name.

The vendor number for American Paint is 210. The first digit, *2*, shows that the controlling account is a liability, Accounts Payable. The second and third digits, *10*, show the vendor number assigned to American Paint.

The procedure for adding new accounts to subsidiary ledgers is the same as described for TechKnow Consulting's general ledger in Chapter 4. Accounts are arranged in alphabetical order within the subsidiary ledgers. New accounts are assigned the unused middle number. If the proper alphabetical order places a new account as the last account, the next number in the sequence of 10s is assigned. Hobby Shack's chart of accounts for the subsidiary ledgers is on page 231.

When the balance of a vendor account in an accounts payable ledger is changed, the balance of the controlling account, Accounts Payable, is also changed. The total of all vendor account balances in the accounts payable ledger equals the balance of the controlling account, Accounts Payable.

REMEMBER The total amount owed to all vendors is summarized in a single general ledger account, *Accounts Payable.*

ACCOUNTS PAYABLE LEDGER FORMS

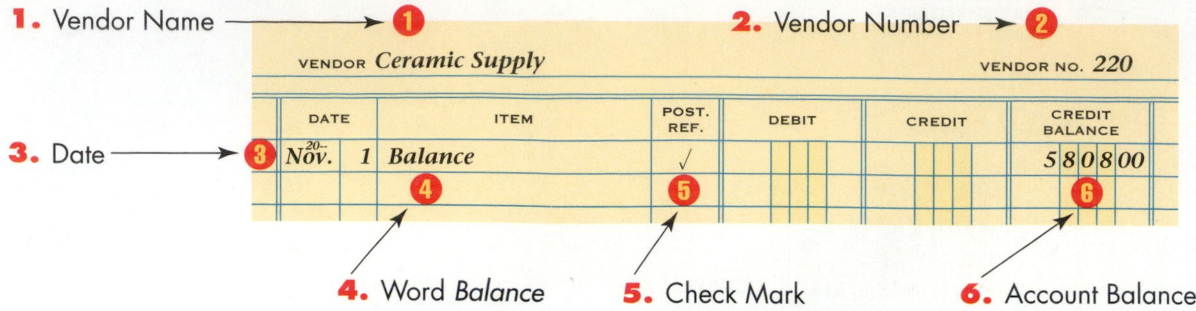

Hobby Shack uses a 3-column accounts payable subsidiary account form. Information to be recorded in the accounts payable ledger includes the date, posting reference, debit or credit amount, and new account balance. Accounts payable are liabilities and have normal credit balances. Therefore, the Debit Balance column is usually not needed for the accounts payable ledger accounts.

Each new account is opened by:

1. Writing the vendor name on the heading of the ledger account.
2. Writing the vendor number on the heading of the ledger account.

The vendor name is obtained from the first purchase invoice received. The vendor number is assigned using the three-digit numbering system previously described. Some businesses record both the vendor name and vendor address on the ledger form. However, the address information is usually kept in a separate name and address file. This practice eliminates having to record the vendor address on the ledger form each time a new ledger page is opened or the address changes.

The number of entries that may be recorded on each account form depends on the number of lines provided. When all lines have been used, a new page is prepared. The vendor name, vendor number, and account balance are recorded on the new page.

On November 1, Hobby Shack prepared a new page for Ceramic Supply in the accounts payable ledger because the existing page was full. On that day, the account balance was $5,808.00.

STEPS • STEPS • STEPS • STEPS • STEPS • STEPS • STEPS • STEPS • STEPS • STEPS •

STARTING A NEW PAGE IN THE ACCOUNTS PAYABLE LEDGER

1. Write the vendor name, *Ceramic Supply*, on the Vendor line.
2. Write the vendor number, *220*, on the Vendor No. line.
3. Write the date, *20--, Nov. 1*, in the date column.
4. Write the word *Balance* in the Item column.
5. Place a check mark in the Post. Ref. column to show that the amount has been carried forward from a previous page rather than posted from a journal.
6. Write the balance, *$5,808.00*, in the Credit Balance column.

REMEMBER A new vendor account is opened by writing the vendor name and vendor number on the heading of the ledger account and placing it in alphabetical order.

POSTING FROM A PURCHASES JOURNAL TO AN ACCOUNTS PAYABLE LEDGER

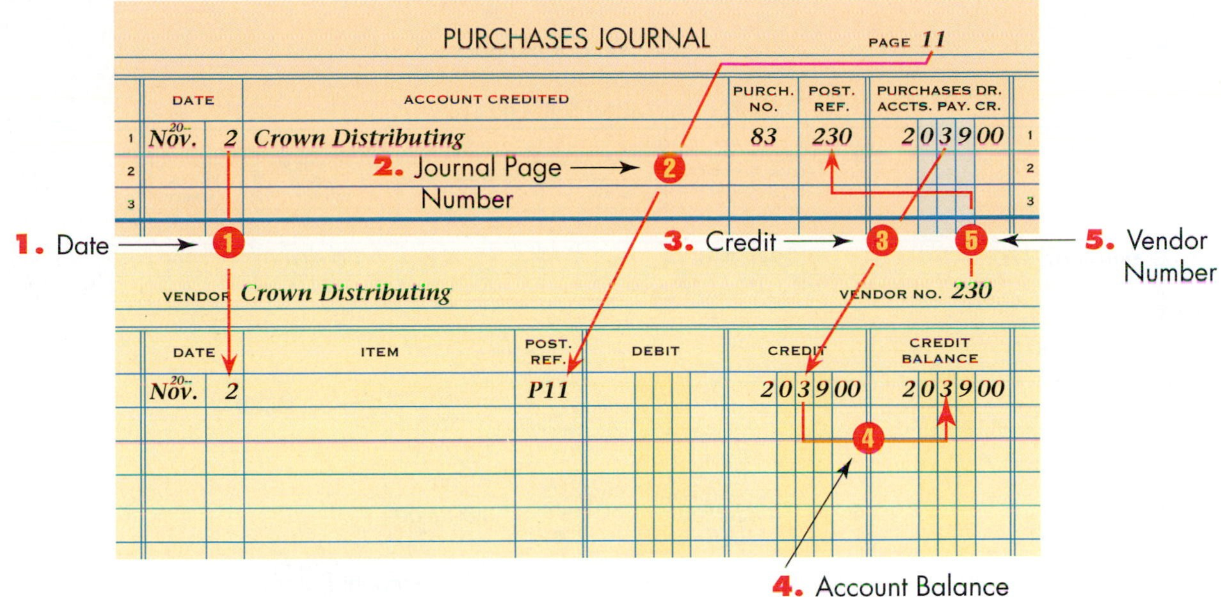

PURCHASES JOURNAL
PAGE 11
DATE
ACCOUNT CREDITED
PURCH. NO.
POST. REF.
PURCHASES DR. ACCTS. PAY. CR.
20-- Nov. 2 Crown Distributing 83 230 2 039 00
1. Date
2. Journal Page Number
3. Credit
4. Account Balance
5. Vendor Number
VENDOR Crown Distributing
VENDOR NO. 230
DATE
ITEM
POST. REF.
DEBIT
CREDIT
CREDIT BALANCE
20-- Nov. 2 P11 2 039 00 2 039 00

Each entry in the purchases journal affects the account of the vendor named in the Account Credited column. The amount on each line of a purchases journal is posted as a credit to a vendor account in the accounts payable ledger. Hobby Shack posts frequently to the accounts payable ledger. Posting frequently keeps each vendor account balance up to date.

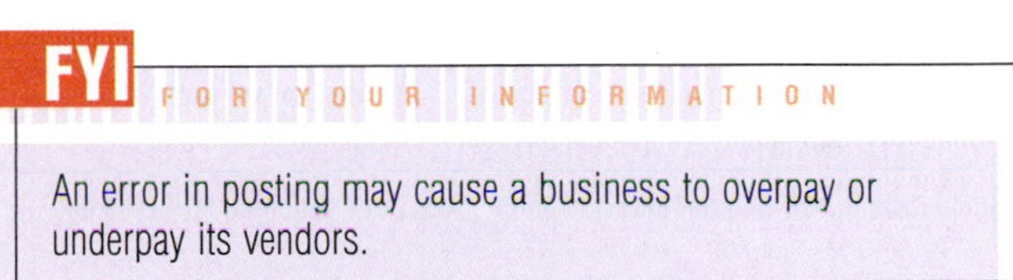

FYI FOR YOUR INFORMATION

An error in posting may cause a business to overpay or underpay its vendors.

STEPS

POSTING FROM A PURCHASES JOURNAL TO AN ACCOUNTS PAYABLE LEDGER

1. Write the date, *20--, Nov. 2*, in the Date column of the vendor account.
2. Write the journal page number, *P11*, in the Post. Ref. column of the account. When several journals are used, an abbreviation is used to show the journal from which the posting is made. *P* is the abbreviation used for the purchases journal. The abbreviation *P11* means page 11 of the purchases journal.
3. Write the credit amount, *$2,039.00*, in the Credit column of the account for *Crown Distributing*.
4. Add the amount in the Credit column to the previous balance in the Credit Balance column. (*Crown Distributing* has no previous balance; therefore, $0 + $2,039.00 = $2,039.00.) Write the new account balance, *$2,039.00*, in the Credit Balance column.
5. Write the vendor number, *230*, in the Post. Ref. column of the journal. The vendor number shows that the posting for this entry is complete.

POSTING FROM A CASH PAYMENTS JOURNAL TO AN ACCOUNTS PAYABLE LEDGER

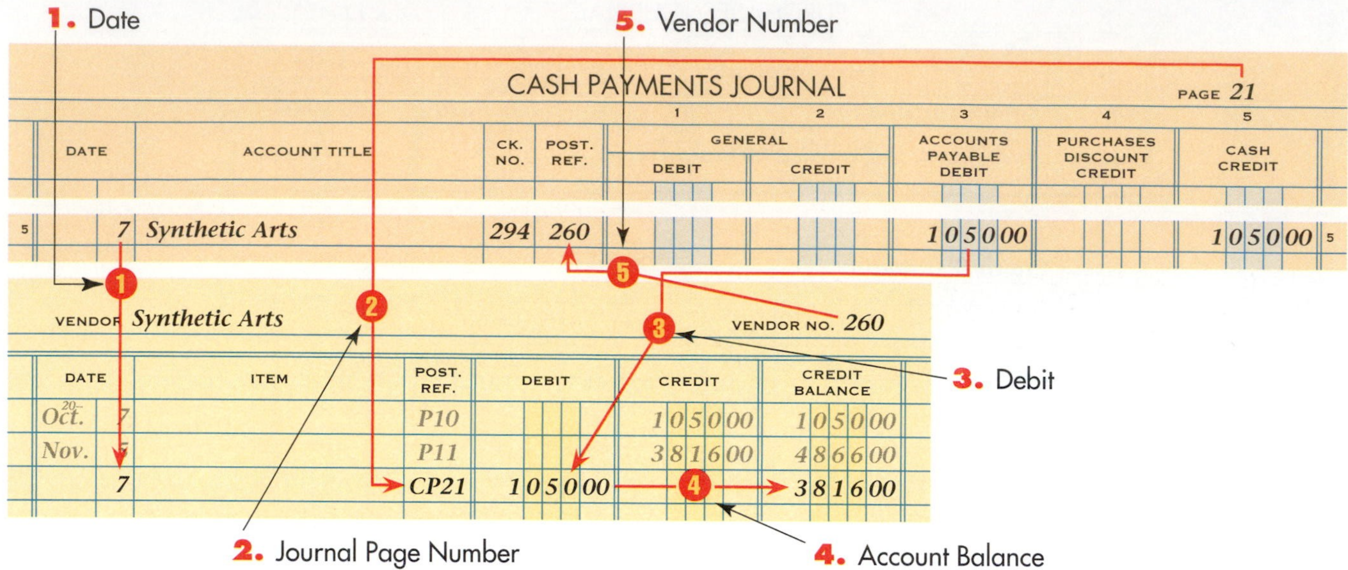

1. Date
5. Vendor Number
CASH PAYMENTS JOURNAL
PAGE 21
DATE
ACCOUNT TITLE
CK. NO.
POST. REF.
GENERAL DEBIT
GENERAL CREDIT
ACCOUNTS PAYABLE DEBIT
PURCHASES DISCOUNT CREDIT
CASH CREDIT
7 Synthetic Arts 294 260 1 050 00 1 050 00
VENDOR Synthetic Arts
VENDOR NO. 260
DATE
ITEM
POST. REF.
DEBIT
CREDIT
CREDIT BALANCE
20-- Oct. 7 P10 1 050 00 1 050 00
Nov. 5 P11 3 816 00 4 866 00
7 CP21 1 050 00 3 816 00
3. Debit
2. Journal Page Number
4. Account Balance

Each entry in the Accounts Payable Debit column of a cash payments journal affects a vendor account. Individual amounts in the Accounts Payable Debit column are posted frequently to the proper vendor account in the accounts payable ledger. Posting frequently keeps each vendor account balance up to date.

STEPS • STEPS • STEPS • STEPS

POSTING FROM A CASH PAYMENTS JOURNAL TO AN ACCOUNTS PAYABLE LEDGER

1. Write the date, *7*, in the Date column of the vendor account.
2. Write the journal page number, *CP21*, in the Post. Ref. column of the account. The abbreviation *CP21* means page 21 of the cash payments journal.
3. Write the debit amount, *$1,050.00*, in the Debit column of the vendor account.
4. Subtract the amount in the Debit column from the previous balance in the Credit Balance column ($4,866.00 − $1,050.00 = $3,816.00). Write the new balance, *$3,816.00*, in the Credit Balance column.
5. Write the vendor number, *260*, in the Post. Ref. column of the cash payments journal.

POSTING CREDIT AND DEBIT ENTRIES FROM A GENERAL JOURNAL TO AN ACCOUNTS PAYABLE LEDGER

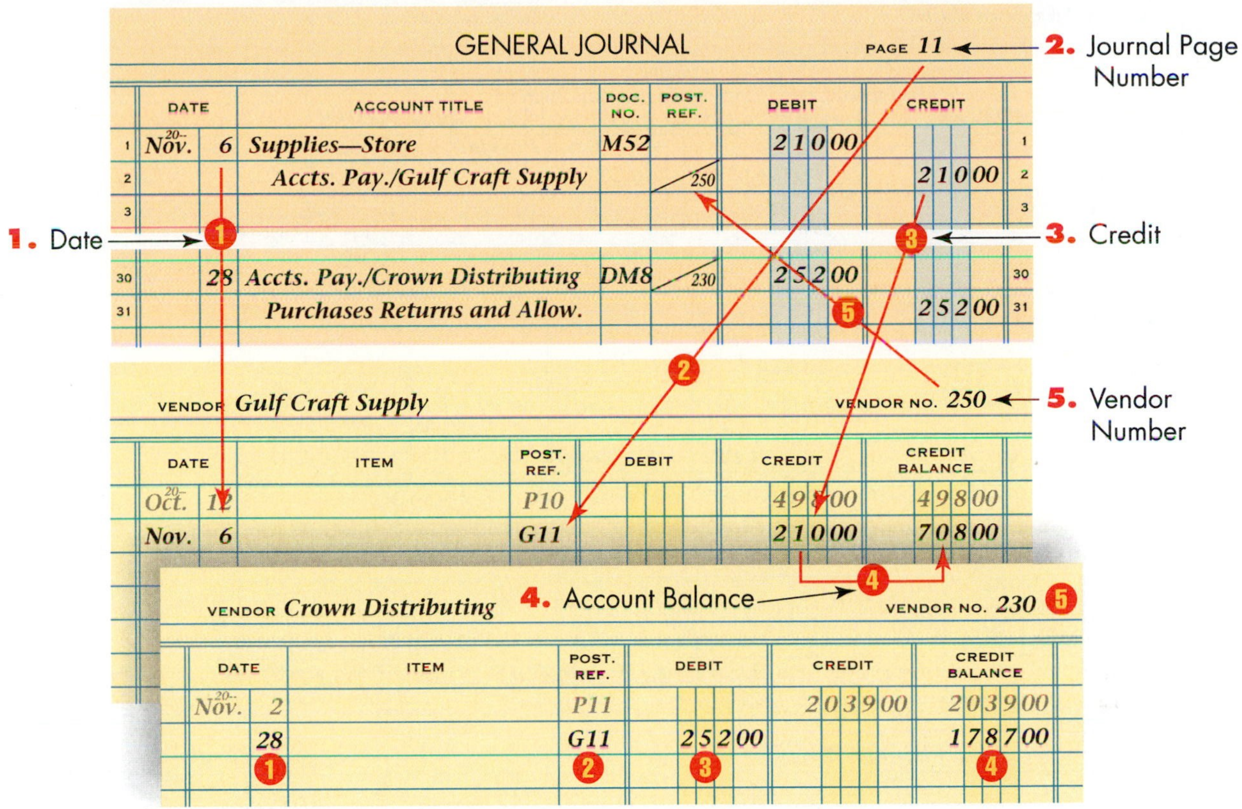

	DATE		ACCOUNT TITLE	DOC. NO.	POST. REF.	DEBIT	CREDIT	
1	20-- Nov.	6	Supplies—Store	M52		210 00		1
2			Accts. Pay./Gulf Craft Supply		250		210 00	2
3								3
30		28	Accts. Pay./Crown Distributing	DM8	230	252 00		30
31			Purchases Returns and Allow.				252 00	31

VENDOR Gulf Craft Supply — VENDOR NO. 250

DATE		ITEM	POST. REF.	DEBIT	CREDIT	CREDIT BALANCE
20-- Oct.	12		P10		498 00	498 00
Nov.	6		G11		210 00	708 00

VENDOR Crown Distributing — VENDOR NO. 230

DATE		ITEM	POST. REF.	DEBIT	CREDIT	CREDIT BALANCE
20-- Nov.	2		P11		2,039 00	2,039 00
	28		G11	252 00		1,787 00

Entries in a general journal may affect account balances in a general ledger and an accounts payable ledger. Posting from a general journal to a general ledger is described on pages 317–318.

STEPS

POSTING A CREDIT ENTRY FOR SUPPLIES BOUGHT ON ACCOUNT

1. Write the date, *Nov. 6*, in the Date column of the vendor account.
2. Write the general journal page number, *G11*, in the Post. Ref. column of the account. The abbreviation *G11* means page 11 of the general journal.
3. Write the amount, *$210.00*, in the Credit column of the vendor account.
4. Add the amount in the Credit column to the previous balance in the Credit Balance column ($498.00 + $210.00 = $708.00). Write the new balance, *$708.00*, in the Credit Balance column.
5. Write the vendor number, *250*, to the right of the diagonal line in the Post. Ref. column of the general journal.

POSTING A DEBIT ENTRY FOR A PURCHASES RETURN OR ALLOWANCE

1. Write the date, *28*, in the Date column of the vendor account.
2. Write the general journal page number, *G11*, in the Post. Ref. column of the account.
3. Write the amount, *$252.00*, in the Debit column of the vendor account.
4. Subtract the amount in the Debit column from the previous balance in the Credit Balance column ($2,039.00 − $252.00 = $1,787.00). Write the new balance, *$1,787.00*, in the Credit Balance column.
5. Write the vendor number, *230*, to the right of the diagonal line in the Post. Ref. column of the general journal.

COMPLETED ACCOUNTS PAYABLE LEDGER

VENDOR *American Paint* VENDOR NO. *210*

DATE		ITEM	POST. REF.	DEBIT	CREDIT	CREDIT BALANCE
20-- Nov.	1	Balance	√			2 650 00
	13		P11		3 768 00	6 418 00
	13		CP21	2 650 00		3 768 00
	20		P11		3 377 88	7 145 88

VENDOR *Ceramic Supply* VENDOR NO. *220*

DATE		ITEM	POST. REF.	DEBIT	CREDIT	CREDIT BALANCE
20-- Nov.	1	Balance	√			5 808 00
	5		P11		4 147 20	9 955 20
	20		CP21	5 808 00		4 147 20

VENDOR *Crown Distributing* VENDOR NO. *230*

DATE		ITEM	POST. REF.	DEBIT	CREDIT	CREDIT BALANCE
20-- Nov.	2		P11		2 039 00	2 039 00
	28		G11	252 00		1 787 00

VENDOR *Floral Designs* VENDOR NO. *240*

DATE		ITEM	POST. REF.	DEBIT	CREDIT	CREDIT BALANCE
20-- Nov.	1	Balance	√			744 00
	23		CP22	744 00		—
	24		G11		1 650 00	1 650 00
	26		G11		996 00	2 646 00
	30		CP22	1 650 00		996 00

VENDOR *Gulf Craft Supply* VENDOR NO. *250*

DATE		ITEM	POST. REF.	DEBIT	CREDIT	CREDIT BALANCE
20-- Nov.	1	Balance	√			498 00
	6		G11		210 00	708 00
	8		CP21	498 00		210 00
	23		G11		690 00	900 00

VENDOR *Synthetic Arts* VENDOR NO. *260*

DATE		ITEM	POST. REF.	DEBIT	CREDIT	CREDIT BALANCE
20-- Nov.	1	Balance	P11			1 050 00
	5		CP21		3 816 00	4 866 00
	7			1 050 00		3 816 00

Hobby Shack's accounts payable ledger has been posted for the month of November.

PROVING THE ACCOUNTS PAYABLE LEDGER

Hobby Shack, Inc.	
Schedule of Accounts Payable	
November 30, 20--	
American Paint	7 145 88
Ceramic Supply	4 147 20
Crown Distributing	1 787 00
Floral Designs	996 00
Gulf Craft Supply	900 00
Synthetic Arts	3 816 00
Total Accounts Payable	18 792 08

A controlling account balance in a general ledger must equal the sum of all account balances in a subsidiary ledger. Hobby Shack proves subsidiary ledgers at the end of each month.

A listing of vendor accounts, account balances, and total amount due all vendors is called a **schedule of accounts payable**. A schedule of accounts payable is prepared after all entries in a journal are posted. The balance of Accounts Payable in the general ledger is $18,792.08. The total of the schedule of accounts payable is $18,792.08. Because the two amounts are the same, the accounts payable ledger is proved.

The International Business Day

American business offices normally operate Monday through Friday, eight hours a day, with a 30- to 60-minute lunch break. This is not necessarily true in other countries, however. In the People's Republic of China, for example, employees usually work Monday through Saturday, eight hours a day, with lunch from 1:00 P.M. to 2:00 P.M.

When doing business internationally, both time zone differences and cultural factors affecting the business day must be taken into consideration. For example, in Spain, many businesses close at 2:00 P.M. so that employees may eat lunch with their families. The office reopens at 5:00 P.M. and stays open until about 8:00 P.M. Spain is in a time zone that is five hours ahead of Eastern Standard Time (EST), the time zone along the eastern coast of the United States. If doing business with a company in Spain, it would not be a good idea to try to call at 9:00 A.M. EST because the business might just be closing for lunch. A better time to call Spain from the EST time zone would be between noon and 3:00 P.M.

Critical Thinking

1. What are some ways you could reference time zones if you had to make frequent international phone calls?
2. If you work for a company with offices and customers all over the world, how could that affect the way you schedule projects?

Xtra! Study Tools
accountingxtra.swlearning.com

terms review

subsidiary ledger
accounts payable ledger
accounts receivable ledger
controlling account
schedule of accounts payable

TERMS REVIEW

audit your understanding

1. What is the relationship between a controlling account and a subsidiary ledger?
2. In which column of the cash payments journal are the amounts that are posted individually to the accounts payable ledger?

AUDIT YOUR

work together 11-1

Posting to an accounts payable ledger

Partial purchases, cash payments, and general journals for Graphics, Inc., are given in the *Working Papers.* Also given in the *Working Papers* are accounts payable ledger account forms for selected accounts and a blank form for a schedule of accounts payable. Your instructor will guide you through the following examples.

1. Start a new page for an accounts payable ledger account for Regal Designs. The account number is 240 and the balance on October 1 of the current year is $877.00.
2. Post the Accounts Payable Credit entry on line 7 of the purchases journal to the accounts payable account for Regal Designs.
3. Post the Accounts Payable Debit entry on line 15 of the cash payments journal to the accounts payable account for Electro-Graphics Supply.
4. Post the credit entry on line 5 of the general journal to the accounts payable account for Electro-Graphics Supply. Post the debit entry on line 6 of the general journal to the accounts payable account for Art and Things.
5. Prepare a schedule of accounts payable for Graphics, Inc., on October 31 of the current year for these selected accounts. Accounts Payable balance in the general ledger on October 31 is $6,558.20. Save your work to complete Work Together 11-2, 11-3, and 11-4.

WORK TOGETHER • WORK TOGETHER • WORK

on your own 11-1

Posting to an accounts payable ledger

Partial purchases, cash payments, and general journals for Amatera, Inc., are given in the *Working Papers.* Also given in the *Working Papers* are accounts payable ledger account forms for selected accounts and a blank form for a schedule of accounts payable. Work this problem independently.

1. Start a new page for an accounts payable ledger account for Swann Industries. The account number is 240 and the balance on September 1 of the current year is $1,248.00.
2. Post the Accounts Payable Credit entry on line 11 of the purchases journal to the accounts payable account for Swann Industries.
3. Post the Accounts Payable Debit entry on line 19 of the cash payments journal to the accounts payable account for Miller Supply.
4. Post the credit entry on line 5 of the general journal to the accounts payable account for Miller Supply. Post the debit entry on line 6 of the general journal to the accounts payable account for Franklin Mfg. Corp.
5. Prepare a schedule of accounts payable for Amatera, Inc., on September 30 of the current year for these selected accounts. Accounts Payable balance in the general ledger on September 30 is $9,142.25. Save your work to complete On Your Own 11-2, 11-3, and 11-4.

ON YOUR OWN • ON YOUR OWN • ON YOUR OWN

LESSON

11-2 Posting to an Accounts Receivable Ledger

ACCOUNTS RECEIVABLE LEDGER AND GENERAL LEDGER CONTROLLING ACCOUNT

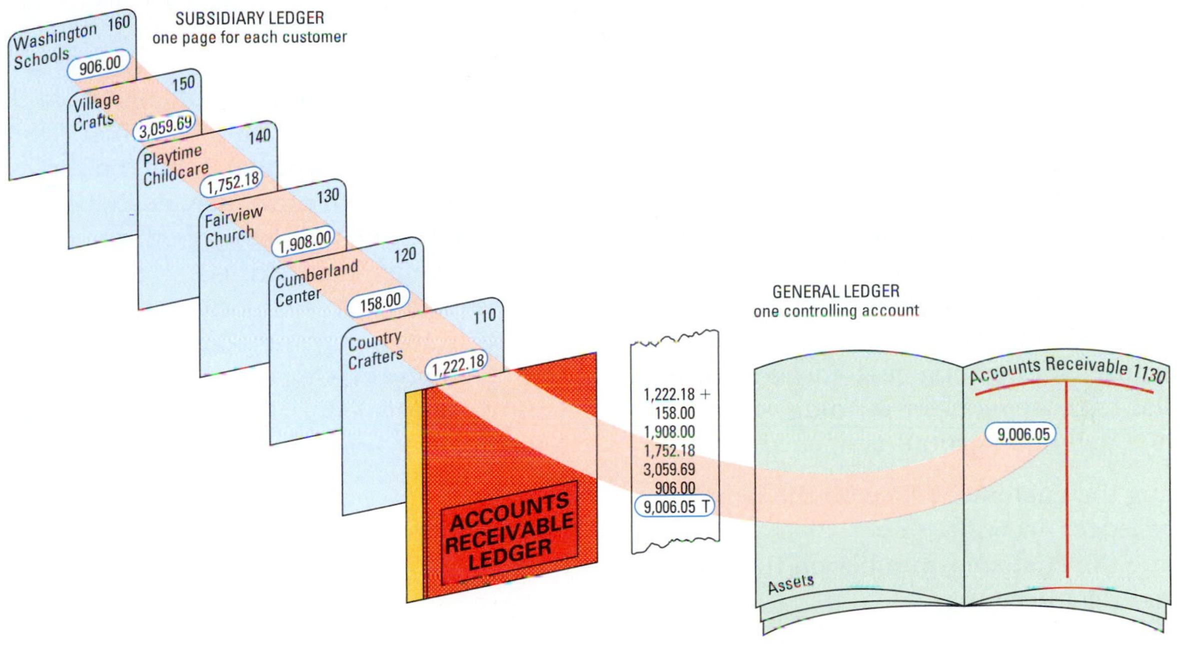

Hobby Shack assigns a customer number to each account in the accounts receivable ledger. A three-digit number is used.

The customer number for Country Crafters is 110. The first digit, *1*, shows that the controlling account is an asset, Accounts Receivable. The second and third digits, *10*, show the customer number assigned to Country Crafters.

When the balance of a customer account in an accounts receivable ledger is changed, the balance of the controlling account, Accounts Receivable, is also changed. The total of all customer account balances in the accounts receivable ledger equals the balance of the controlling account, Accounts Receivable.

REMEMBER The total amount to be collected from all charge customers is summarized in a single general ledger account, *Accounts Receivable.*

ACCOUNTS RECEIVABLE LEDGER FORMS

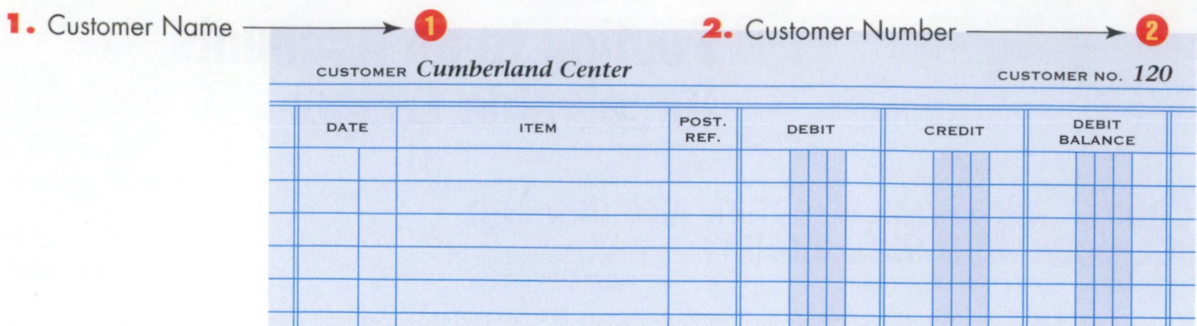

Hobby Shack uses a 3-column accounts receivable subsidiary account form. The accounts receivable account form is similar to the one used for the accounts payable ledger. Accounts receivable are assets, and assets have normal debit balances. Therefore, the form used in the accounts receivable ledger has a Debit Balance column instead of a Credit Balance column.

Procedures for opening customer accounts are similar to those used for opening vendor accounts. Each new account is opened by:

1. Writing the customer name on the heading of the ledger account.
2. Writing the customer number on the heading of the ledger account.

The customer name is obtained from the first sales invoice prepared for a customer. The customer number is assigned using the three-digit numbering system previously described.

Some businesses record both the customer name and customer address on the ledger form. However, the address information is usually kept in a separate name and address file. This practice eliminates having to record the customer address on the ledger form each time a new ledger page is started or the address changes.

FYI FOR YOUR INFORMATION

When an account that is no longer used is removed from the accounts receivable ledger, that customer number is available for assignment to a new customer.

POSTING FROM A SALES JOURNAL TO AN ACCOUNTS RECEIVABLE LEDGER

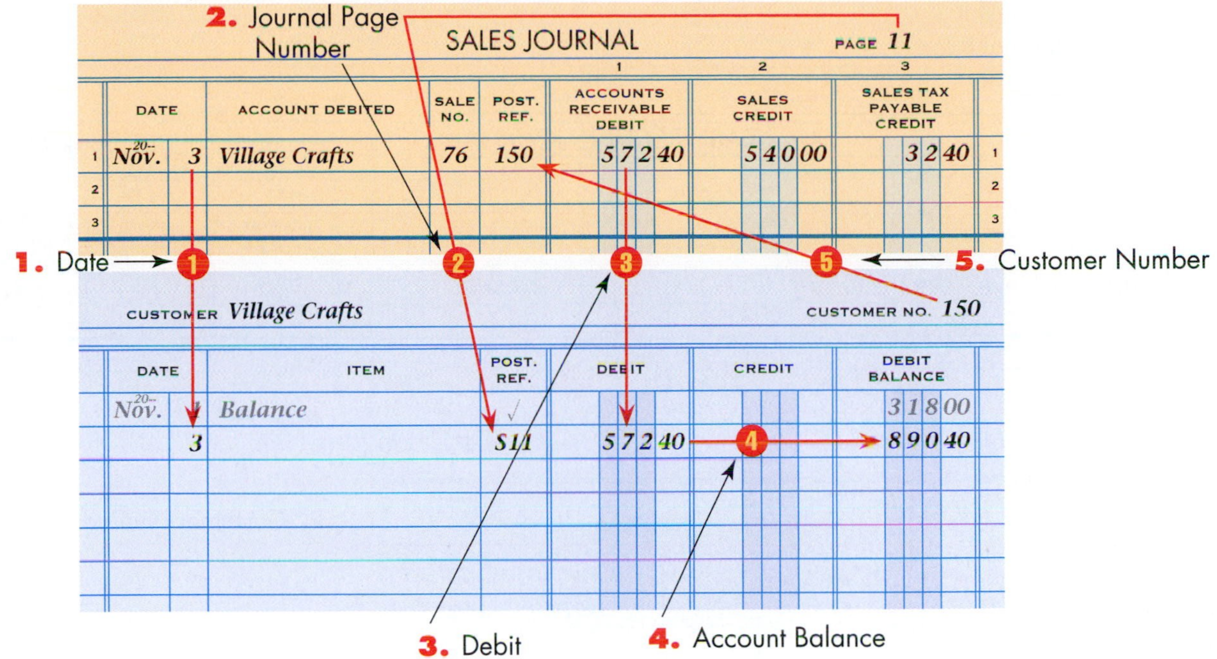

2. Journal Page Number
SALES JOURNAL
PAGE 11
DATE
ACCOUNT DEBITED
SALE NO.
POST. REF.
ACCOUNTS RECEIVABLE DEBIT
SALES CREDIT
SALES TAX PAYABLE CREDIT
20-- Nov. 3 Village Crafts 76 150 572 40 540 00 32 40
1. Date
5. Customer Number
CUSTOMER Village Crafts
CUSTOMER NO. 150
DATE
ITEM
POST. REF.
DEBIT
CREDIT
DEBIT BALANCE
20-- Nov. 1 Balance ✓ 318 00
3 S11 572 40 890 40
3. Debit
4. Account Balance

Each amount in a sales journal's Accounts Receivable Debit column is posted to the accounts receivable ledger. Each amount is posted as a debit to the customer account listed in the Account Debited column. Hobby Shack posts frequently to the accounts receivable ledger so that each customer account will show an up-to-date balance.

The controlling account in the general ledger, Accounts Receivable, is also increased by this entry.

At the end of the month, the journal's Accounts Receivable Debit column total is posted to the controlling account, Accounts Receivable.

Individual amounts in the Accounts Receivable Debit column are posted frequently to customer accounts in the accounts receivable ledger.

STEPS • STEPS • STEPS • STEPS • STEPS • STEPS • STEPS • STEPS • STEPS • STEPS

POSTING FROM A SALES JOURNAL TO AN ACCOUNTS RECEIVABLE LEDGER

1. Write the date, *3*, in the Date column of the account.
2. Write the sales journal page number, *S11*, in the Post. Ref. column of the account. *S* is the abbreviation used for the sales journal.
3. Write the debit amount, *$572.40*, in the Debit column of the customer account.
4. Add the amount in the Debit column to the previous balance in the Debit Balance column ($318.00 + $572.40 = $890.40). Write the new account balance, *$890.40*, in the Debit Balance column.
5. Write the customer number, *150*, in the Post. Ref. column of the sales journal. The customer number shows that the posting for this entry is complete.

POSTING FROM A CASH RECEIPTS JOURNAL TO AN ACCOUNTS RECEIVABLE LEDGER

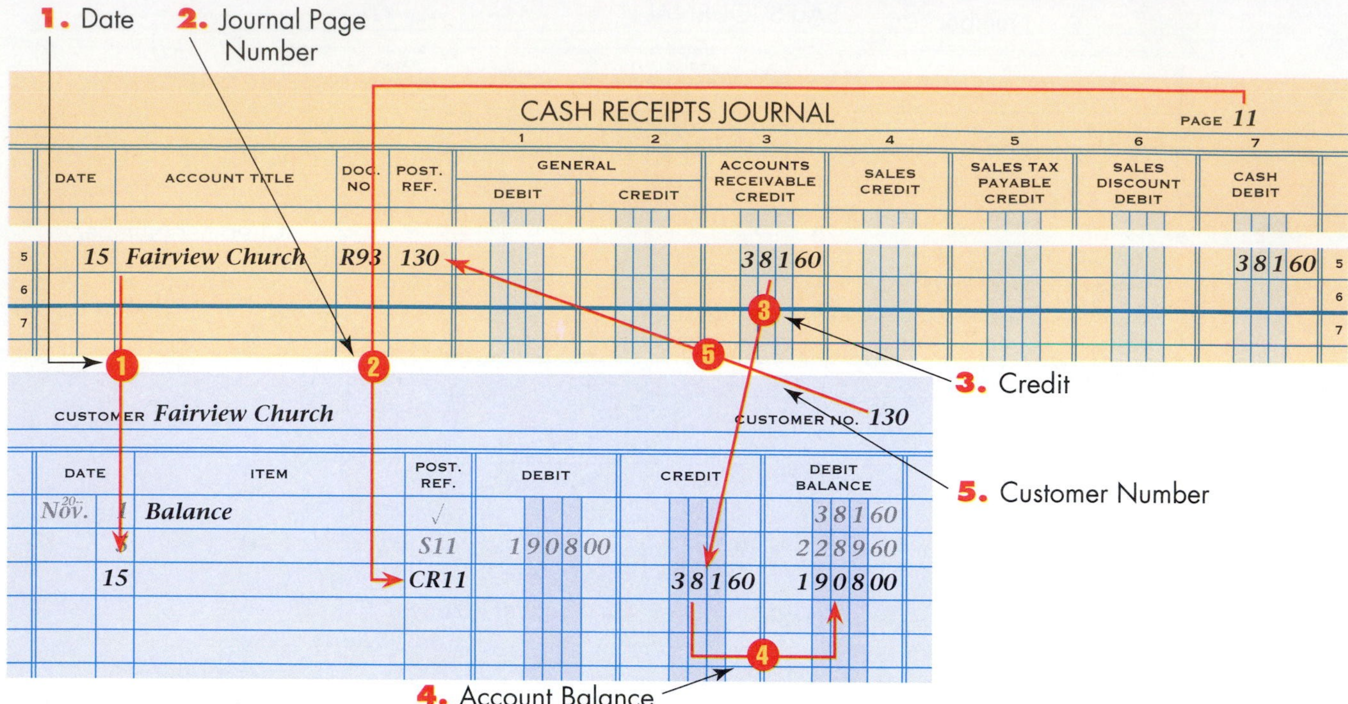

Each entry in the Accounts Receivable Credit column affects the customer named in the Account Title column. Each amount listed in the Accounts Receivable Credit column is posted to the proper customer account in the accounts receivable ledger. Hobby Shack posts frequently to the accounts receivable ledger so that each customer account will show an up-to-date balance.

STEPS: POSTING FROM A CASH RECEIPTS JOURNAL TO AN ACCOUNTS RECEIVABLE LEDGER

1. Write the date, *15*, in the Date column of the account.
2. Write the cash receipts journal page number, *CR11*, in the Post. Ref. column of the account. *CR* is the abbreviation for the cash receipts journal.
3. Write the credit amount, *$381.60*, in the Credit column of the customer account.
4. Subtract the amount in the Credit column from the previous balance in the Debit Balance column ($2,289.60 − $381.60 = $1,908.00). Write the new balance, *$1,908.00*, in the Debit Balance column.
5. Write the customer number, *130*, in the Post. Ref. column of the cash receipts journal.

©GETTY IMAGES/PHOTODISC

POSTING A CREDIT ENTRY FROM A GENERAL JOURNAL TO AN ACCOUNTS RECEIVABLE LEDGER

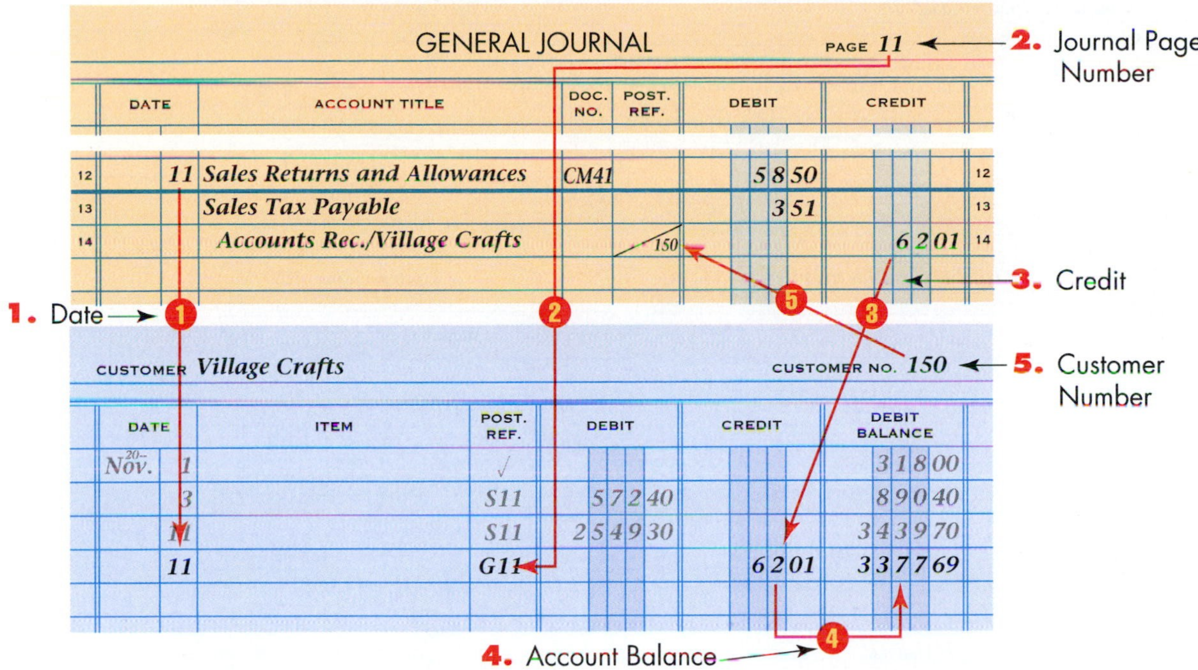

GENERAL JOURNAL
PAGE 11
DATE
ACCOUNT TITLE
DOC. NO.
POST. REF.
DEBIT
CREDIT
12 11 Sales Returns and Allowances CM41 58 50 12
13 Sales Tax Payable 3 51 13
14 Accounts Rec./Village Crafts 150 62 01 14
1. Date
2. Journal Page Number
3. Credit
4. Account Balance
5. Customer Number
CUSTOMER Village Crafts
CUSTOMER NO. 150
DATE
ITEM
POST. REF.
DEBIT
CREDIT
DEBIT BALANCE
20-- Nov. 1 ✓ 318 00
3 S11 572 40 890 40
10 S11 2,549 30 3,439 70
11 G11 62 01 3,377 69

Entries in a general journal may affect account balances in a general ledger and an accounts receivable ledger. Posting from a general journal to a general ledger is described on pages 317–318.

STEPS • STEPS • STEPS • STEPS • STEPS • STEPS • STEPS • STEPS • STEPS • STEPS

POSTING A CREDIT ENTRY FOR SALES RETURNS AND ALLOWANCES FROM A GENERAL JOURNAL TO AN ACCOUNTS RECEIVABLE LEDGER

1. Write the date, *Nov. 11*, in the Date column of the customer account.
2. Write the general journal page number, *G11*, in the Post. Ref. column of the account. The abbreviation *G11* means page 11 of the general journal.
3. Write the amount, *$62.01*, in the Credit column of the customer account.
4. Subtract the amount in the Credit column from the previous balance in the Debit Balance column ($3,439.70 – $62.01 = $3,377.69). Write the new balance, *$3,377.69*, in the Debit Balance column.
5. Write the customer number, *150*, to the right of the diagonal line in the Post. Ref. column of the general journal.

©GETTY IMAGES/PHOTODISC

COMPLETED ACCOUNTS RECEIVABLE LEDGER

CUSTOMER *Country Crafters* CUSTOMER NO. *110*

DATE		ITEM	POST. REF.	DEBIT	CREDIT	DEBIT BALANCE
20-- Nov.	1	Balance	✓			2,162.40
	6		CR11		2,162.40	—
	11		S11	768.50		768.50
	29		S11	453.68		1,222.18

CUSTOMER *Cumberland Center* CUSTOMER NO. *120*

DATE		ITEM	POST. REF.	DEBIT	CREDIT	DEBIT BALANCE
20-- Nov.	1	Balance	✓			4,189.20
	7		CR11		1,200.00	2,989.20
	24		S11	158.00		3,147.20
	25		CR11		2,989.20	158.00

CUSTOMER *Fairview Church* CUSTOMER NO. *130*

DATE		ITEM	POST. REF.	DEBIT	CREDIT	DEBIT BALANCE
20-- Nov.	1	Balance	✓			381.60
	5		S11	1,908.00		2,289.60
	15		CR11		381.60	1,908.00

CUSTOMER *Playtime Childcare* CUSTOMER NO. *140*

DATE		ITEM	POST. REF.	DEBIT	CREDIT	DEBIT BALANCE
20-- Nov.	1	Balance	✓			1,144.80
	16		S11	1,752.18		2,896.98
	18		CR11		1,144.80	1,752.18

CUSTOMER *Village Crafts* CUSTOMER NO. *150*

DATE		ITEM	POST. REF.	DEBIT	CREDIT	DEBIT BALANCE
20-- Nov.	1	Balance	✓			318.00
	3		S11	572.40		890.40
	11		S11	2,549.30		3,439.70
	11		G11		62.01	3,377.69
	19		CR11		318.00	3,059.69

CUSTOMER *Washington Schools* CUSTOMER NO. *160*

DATE		ITEM	POST. REF.	DEBIT	CREDIT	DEBIT BALANCE
20-- Nov.	1	Balance	✓			2,544.00
	9		S11	572.00		3,116.00
	12		CR11		2,544.00	572.00
	24		S11	334.00		906.00

Hobby Shack's accounts receivable ledger has been posted for the month of November.

PROVING THE ACCOUNTS RECEIVABLE LEDGER

Hobby Shack, Inc.		
Schedule of Accounts Receivable		
November 30, 20--		
Country Crafters	1222	18
Cumberland Center	158	00
Fairview Church	1908	00
Playtime Childcare	1752	18
Village Crafts	3059	69
Washington Schools	906	00
Total Accounts Receivable	9006	05

A listing of customer accounts, account balances, and total amount due from all customers is called a **schedule of accounts receivable**. A schedule of accounts receivable is prepared after all entries in a journal are posted. The balance of Accounts Receivable in the general ledger is $9,006.05. The total of the schedule of accounts receivable is $ 9,006.05. Because the two amounts are the same, the accounts receivable ledger is proved.

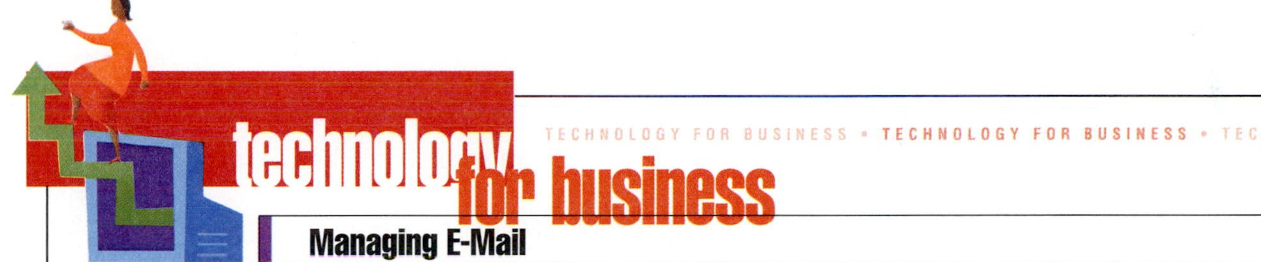

Managing E-Mail

Electronic mail (e-mail) has become an accepted method of business communication. E-mail is a convenient way to communicate with other colleagues, suppliers, and clients at any location, 24 hours a day, 365 days a year. E-mail is particularly useful in international communication, overcoming the inherent problems of phone communication with individuals in different time zones.

As with most innovations, however, e-mail is not without its unique problems. Business users often experience "e-mail overload," receiving unwanted e-mails that range from annoying to destructive:

1. *Personal e-mails*—Colleagues may use their business e-mail for personal communication, such as selling personal items, sharing jokes, and soliciting participation in civic activities.
2. *Spam*—Unsolicited commercial advertising via e-mail is known as spam. Many businesses advertise using spam because of its relatively inexpensive cost per contact.
3. *Viruses*—E-mails containing seemingly harmless subject lines from a colleague can actually contain a computer virus. Viruses are destructive computer programs that can display unwanted messages, delete data, or broadcast data to others via e-mail. Some viruses use e-mail address books to spread the virus when an attachment to a seemingly legitimate e-mail is opened.

These e-mails eat into productivity as workers spend time reading and managing messages. Computer system failures can cause a business to effectively shut down, thus losing sales. Businesses must take proactive steps to protect their computer system against spam and viruses by purchasing software and educating workers on proper e-mail procedures and etiquette.

Critical Thinking

1. E-mail sent and received through a company's server may be used as evidence in a lawsuit or criminal proceeding. What are some uses of e-mail that could be damaging to a company or employee?
2. Many people have been embarrassed when they sent e-mail with a very personal message to the wrong address. How could this be avoided at work?

term review

schedule of accounts receivable

TERM REVIEW • TERM

audit your understanding

1. To which accounts are the separate amounts in the sales journal posted individually?
2. In which column of the cash receipts journal are the amounts that are posted individually to the accounts receivable ledger?
3. What accounts are listed on a schedule of accounts receivable?

AUDIT YOUR UNDERSTANDING

work together 11-2

Posting to an accounts receivable ledger

Partial sales and cash receipts journals for Graphics, Inc. are given in the *Working Papers*. Also given in the *Working Papers* are one blank accounts receivable ledger account form and a blank form for preparation of a schedule of accounts receivable. You will also need the general journal from Work Together 11-1. Your instructor will guide you through the following examples.

1. Start a new page for an accounts receivable ledger account for Brandee Sparks. The account number is 140, and the balance for October 1 of the current year is $212.00.
2. Post the Accounts Receivable Debit entry on line 5 of the sales journal to the accounts receivable account for Brandee Sparks.
3. Post the Accounts Receivable Credit entry on line 9 of the cash receipts journal to the accounts receivable account for Alfredo Lopez.
4. Post the credit entry on line 3 of the general journal to the accounts receivable account for David Bishop.
5. Prepare a schedule of accounts receivable for Graphics, Inc., on October 31 of the current year. Accounts Receivable balance in the general ledger on October 31 is $2,530.22. Save your work to complete Work Together 11-4.

WORK TOGETHER • WORK TOGETHER

on your own 11-2

Posting to an accounts receivable ledger

Partial sales and cash receipts journals for Amatera, Inc. are given in the *Working Papers*. Also given in the *Working Papers* are one blank accounts receivable ledger account form and a blank form for preparation of a schedule of accounts receivable. You will also need the general journal from On Your Own 11-1. Work this problem independently.

1. Start a new page for an accounts receivable ledger account for Davis Sullivan. The account number is 140, and the balance for September 1 of the current year is $564.00.
2. Post the Accounts Receivable Debit entry on line 8 of the sales journal to the accounts receivable account for Davis Sullivan.
3. Post the Accounts Receivable Credit entry on line 21 of the cash receipts journal to the accounts receivable account for Harris Evans.
4. Post the credit entry on line 3 of the general journal to the accounts receivable account for Mary Burgin.
5. Prepare a schedule of accounts receivable for Amatera, Inc., on September 30 of the current year. Accounts Receivable balance in the general ledger on September 30 is $5,986.80. Save your work to complete On Your Own 11-4.

ON YOUR OWN • ON YOUR OWN • ON YOUR OWN

11-3 Posting from Journals to a General Ledger

STARTING A NEW PAGE FOR AN ACCOUNT IN A GENERAL LEDGER

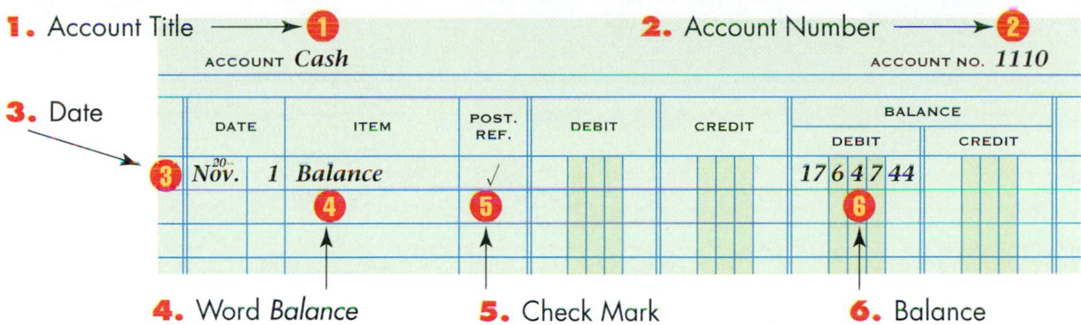

The number of entries that may be recorded on each general ledger account form depends on the number of lines provided. When all lines have been used, a new page is prepared. The account name, account number, and account balance are recorded on the new page.

On November 1, Hobby Shack prepared a new page for Cash in the general ledger because the existing page was full. On that day, the account balance was $17,647.44.

STEPS • STEPS • STEPS • STEPS • STEPS

STARTING A NEW PAGE FOR A GENERAL LEDGER ACCOUNT

1. Write the account title, *Cash*, at the top of the page.
2. Write the account number, *1110*, at the top of the page.
3. Write the date, *20--, Nov. 1*, in the Date column.
4. Write the word *Balance* in the Item column.
5. Place a check mark in the Post. Ref. column to show that the amount has been carried forward from a previous page rather than posted from a journal.
6. Write the balance, *$17,647.44*, in the Balance Debit column.

©GETTY IMAGES/PHOTODISC

POSTING FROM THE GENERAL AMOUNT COLUMNS OF A CASH PAYMENTS JOURNAL TO A GENERAL LEDGER

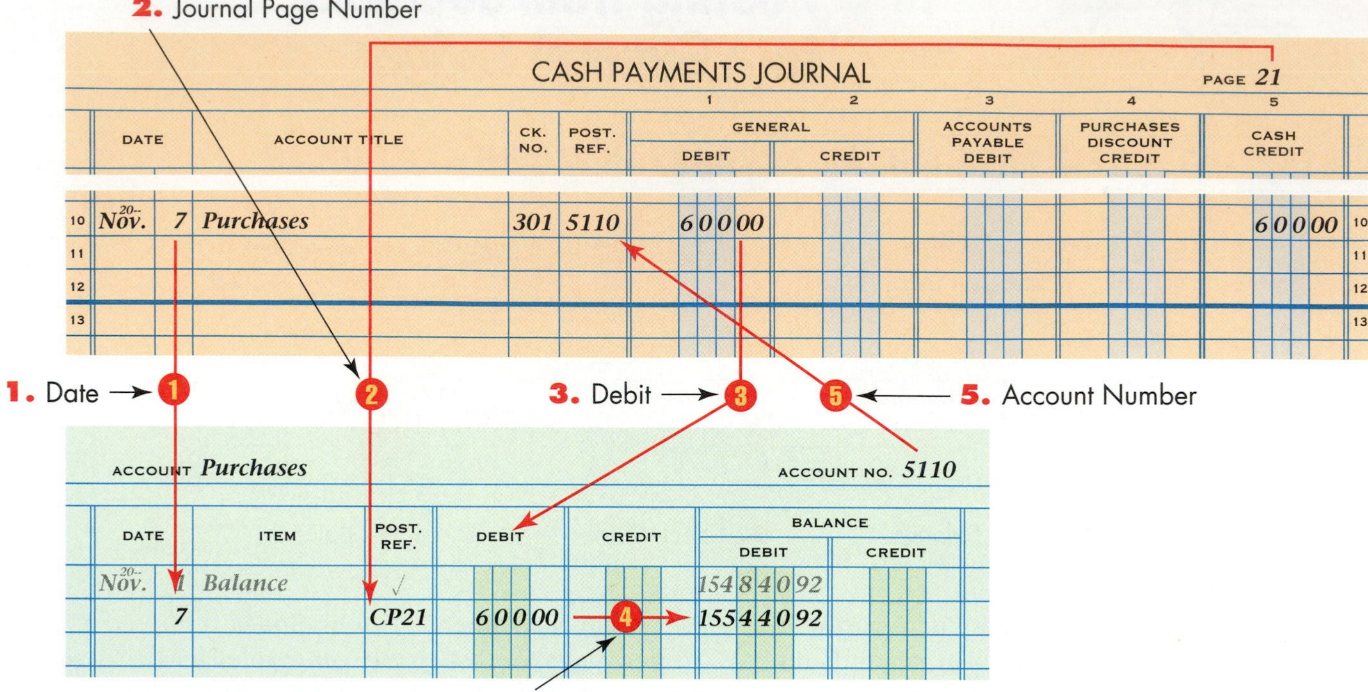

Amounts in cash payments journal entries are recorded in either general amount columns or special amount columns. Each amount in the General columns of a cash payments journal is posted individually to the general ledger account written in the Account Title column. However, only the monthly total of each special amount column is posted to a general ledger account.

STEPS: POSTING FROM THE GENERAL AMOUNT COLUMNS OF A CASH PAYMENTS JOURNAL TO A GENERAL LEDGER

1. Write the date, *7*, in the Date column of the account.
2. Write the journal page number, *CP21*, in the Post. Ref. column of the account. The abbreviation *CP21* means page 21 of the cash payments journal.
3. Write the debit amount, *$600.00*, in the account's Debit column. (A credit amount would be written in the Credit column.)
4. Add the amount in the Debit column to the previous balance in the Balance Debit column ($600.00 + $154,840.92 = $155,440.92). Write the new account balance, *$155,440.92*, in the Balance Debit column of the account.
5. Write the general ledger account number, *5110*, in the Post. Ref. column of the cash payments journal.

REMEMBER Separate amounts listed in special amount columns of a special journal are not posted individually to the general ledger—only the totals are posted.

POSTING A DEBIT ENTRY FROM A GENERAL JOURNAL TO A GENERAL LEDGER

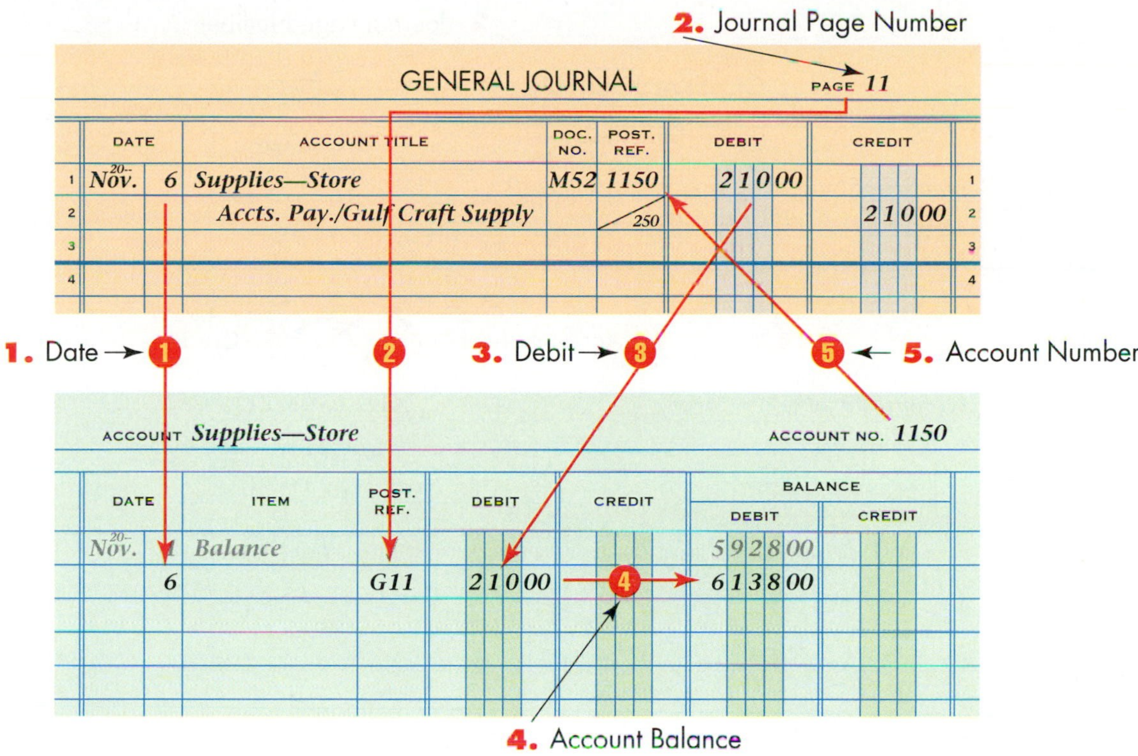

GENERAL JOURNAL — PAGE 11

	DATE		ACCOUNT TITLE	DOC. NO.	POST. REF.	DEBIT	CREDIT	
1	20-- Nov.	6	Supplies—Store	M52	1150	210 00		1
2			Accts. Pay./Gulf Craft Supply		250		210 00	2
3								3
4								4

ACCOUNT Supplies—Store — ACCOUNT NO. 1150

DATE		ITEM	POST. REF.	DEBIT	CREDIT	BALANCE DEBIT	BALANCE CREDIT
20-- Nov.	1	Balance	✓			5 928 00	
	6		G11	210 00		6 138 00	

STEPS

POSTING A DEBIT AMOUNT FROM A GENERAL JOURNAL TO A GENERAL LEDGER

1. Write the date, *6*, in the Date column of the account.
2. Write the general journal page number, *G11*, in the Post. Ref. column of the account. The abbreviation *G11* means page 11 of the general journal.
3. Write the amount, *$210.00*, in the Debit column of the account.
4. Calculate and write the new account balance, *$6,138.00*, in the Balance Debit column of the account.
5. Write the general ledger account number, *1150*, in the Post. Ref. column of the general journal.

©GETTY IMAGES/PHOTODISC

FYI FOR YOUR INFORMATION

Accuracy is very important in accounting. Following the proper sequence of steps for posting increases the accuracy of the task.

POSTING A CREDIT ENTRY FROM A GENERAL JOURNAL TO A GENERAL LEDGER

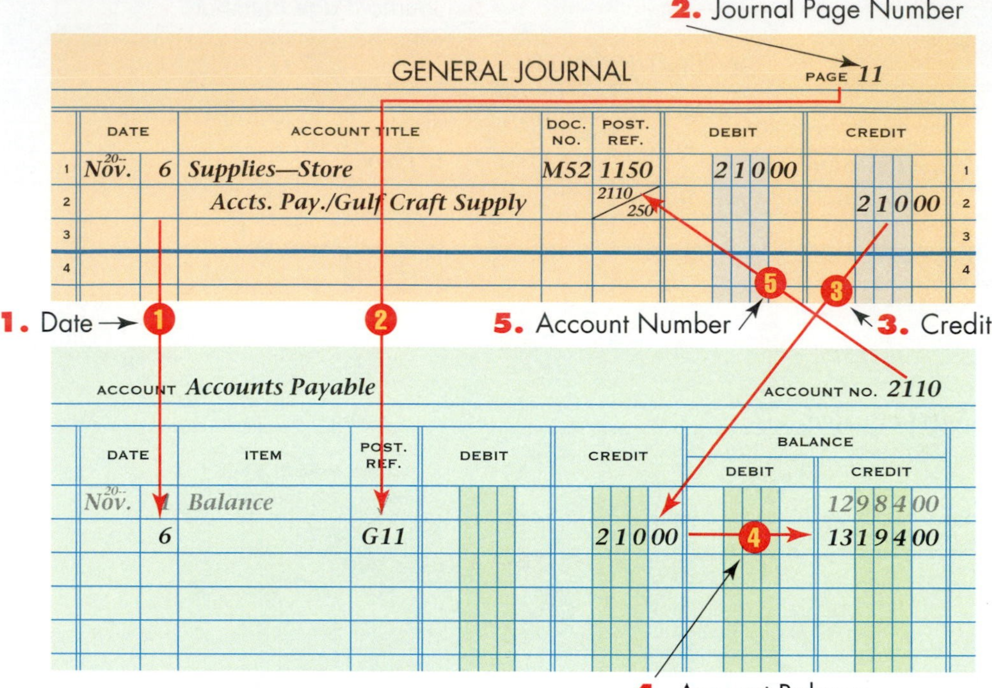

GENERAL JOURNAL PAGE 11

	DATE		ACCOUNT TITLE	DOC. NO.	POST. REF.	DEBIT	CREDIT	
1	20-- Nov.	6	Supplies—Store	M52	1150	210 00		1
2			Accts. Pay./Gulf Craft Supply		2110/250		210 00	2
3								3
4								4

ACCOUNT Accounts Payable ACCOUNT NO. 2110

DATE		ITEM	POST. REF.	DEBIT	CREDIT	BALANCE DEBIT	BALANCE CREDIT
20-- Nov.	1	Balance	✓				12984 00
	6		G11		210 00		13194 00

Transactions recorded in a general journal can affect both subsidiary ledger and general ledger accounts. Buying supplies on account, for example, results in a credit to Accounts Payable. The purchase should also be recorded as a credit in the subsidiary ledger account of the vendor, Gulf Craft Supply.

The diagonal line in the Post. Ref. column allows the posting reference of both the general ledger and subsidiary ledger account to be recorded.

STEPS • STEPS • STEPS • STEPS • STEPS

POSTING A CREDIT AMOUNT FROM A GENERAL JOURNAL TO A GENERAL LEDGER

1. Write the date, *6*, in the Date column of the account.
2. Write the general journal page number, *G11*, in the Post. Ref. column of the account.
3. Write the amount, *$210.00*, in the Credit column of the account.
4. Calculate and write the new account balance, *$13,194.00*, in the Balance Credit column of the account.
5. Write the general ledger account number, *2110*, to the left of the diagonal line in the Post. Ref. column of the general journal. The vendor account number, *250*, written to the right of the diagonal line, was described on page 303.

The major ways of starting a new small business are:

1. Buy an existing business.
2. Buy a franchise.
3. Start a business from scratch.

audit your understanding

1. Which amounts in a general journal are posted individually?
2. List the five steps for posting to a general ledger account.

AUDIT YOUR UNDERSTANDING

work together 11-3

Posting to a general ledger

Use the partial cash payments and general journals from Work Together 11-1. General ledger account forms are given in the *Working Papers.* Your instructor will guide you through the following examples.

1. Start a new page for a general ledger account for Supplies—Office. The account number is 1145, and the balance for October 1 of the current year is $3,824.00.
2. Post the October 19 General Debit entry of the cash payments journal to the appropriate general ledger account.
3. Post the October 12 general journal entry to the appropriate general ledger accounts.
4. Post the October 26 general journal entry to the appropriate general ledger accounts.
5. Post the October 28 general journal entry to the appropriate general ledger accounts. Save the general ledger accounts to complete Work Together 11-4.

WORK TOGETHER • WORK TOGETHER

on your own 11-3

Posting to a general ledger

Use the partial cash payments and general journals from On Your Own 11-1. General ledger account forms are given in the *Working Papers.* Work this problem independently.

1. Start a new page for a general ledger account for Supplies—Store. The account number is 1150, and the balance for September 1 of the current year is $3,158.00.
2. Post the September 21 General Debit entry of the cash payments journal to the appropriate general ledger account.
3. Post the September 15 general journal entry to the appropriate general ledger accounts.
4. Post the September 27 general journal entry to the appropriate general ledger accounts.
5. Post the September 29 general journal entry to the appropriate general ledger accounts. Save the general ledger accounts to complete On Your Own 11-4.

ON YOUR OWN • ON YOUR OWN

LESSON

11-4 Posting Special Journal Totals to a General Ledger

POSTING TOTALS OF A SALES JOURNAL TO A GENERAL LEDGER

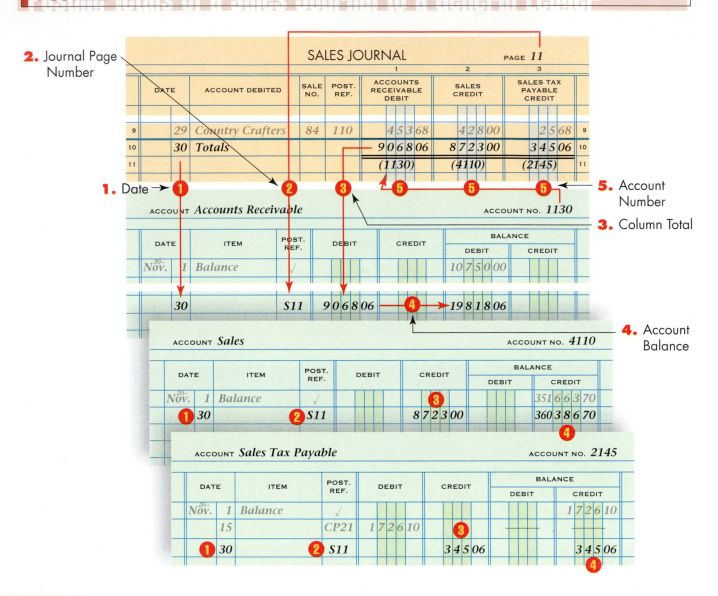

SALES JOURNAL — PAGE 11

	DATE	ACCOUNT DEBITED	SALE NO.	POST. REF.	1 ACCOUNTS RECEIVABLE DEBIT	2 SALES CREDIT	3 SALES TAX PAYABLE CREDIT	
9	29	Country Crafters	84	110	453 68	428 00	25 68	9
10	30	Totals			9,068 06	8,723 00	345 06	10
11					(1130)	(4110)	(2145)	11

ACCOUNT Accounts Receivable — ACCOUNT NO. 1130

DATE		ITEM	POST. REF.	DEBIT	CREDIT	BALANCE DEBIT	BALANCE CREDIT
20-- Nov.	1	Balance	✓			10,750 00	
	30		S11	9,068 06		19,818 06	

ACCOUNT Sales — ACCOUNT NO. 4110

DATE		ITEM	POST. REF.	DEBIT	CREDIT	BALANCE DEBIT	BALANCE CREDIT
20-- Nov.	1	Balance	✓				351,663 70
	30		S11		8,723 00		360,386 70

ACCOUNT Sales Tax Payable — ACCOUNT NO. 2145

DATE		ITEM	POST. REF.	DEBIT	CREDIT	BALANCE DEBIT	BALANCE CREDIT
20-- Nov.	1	Balance	✓				1,726 10
	15		CP21	1,726 10		—	—
	30		S11		345 06		345 06

1. Date
2. Journal Page Number
3. Column Total
4. Account Balance
5. Account Number

STEPS

POSTING EACH SPECIAL AMOUNT COLUMN TOTAL OF A SALES JOURNAL

1. Write the date, *30*, in the Date columns of the accounts.
2. Write the sales journal page number, *S11*, in the Post. Ref. columns of the accounts.
3. For each column and account, write the column total in the Debit or Credit column of the account.
4. For each account, calculate and write the new account balance in the Balance Debit or Credit column.
5. In the sales journal, write the general ledger account number in parentheses below each column total.

POSTING THE TOTAL OF A PURCHASES JOURNAL TO A GENERAL LEDGER

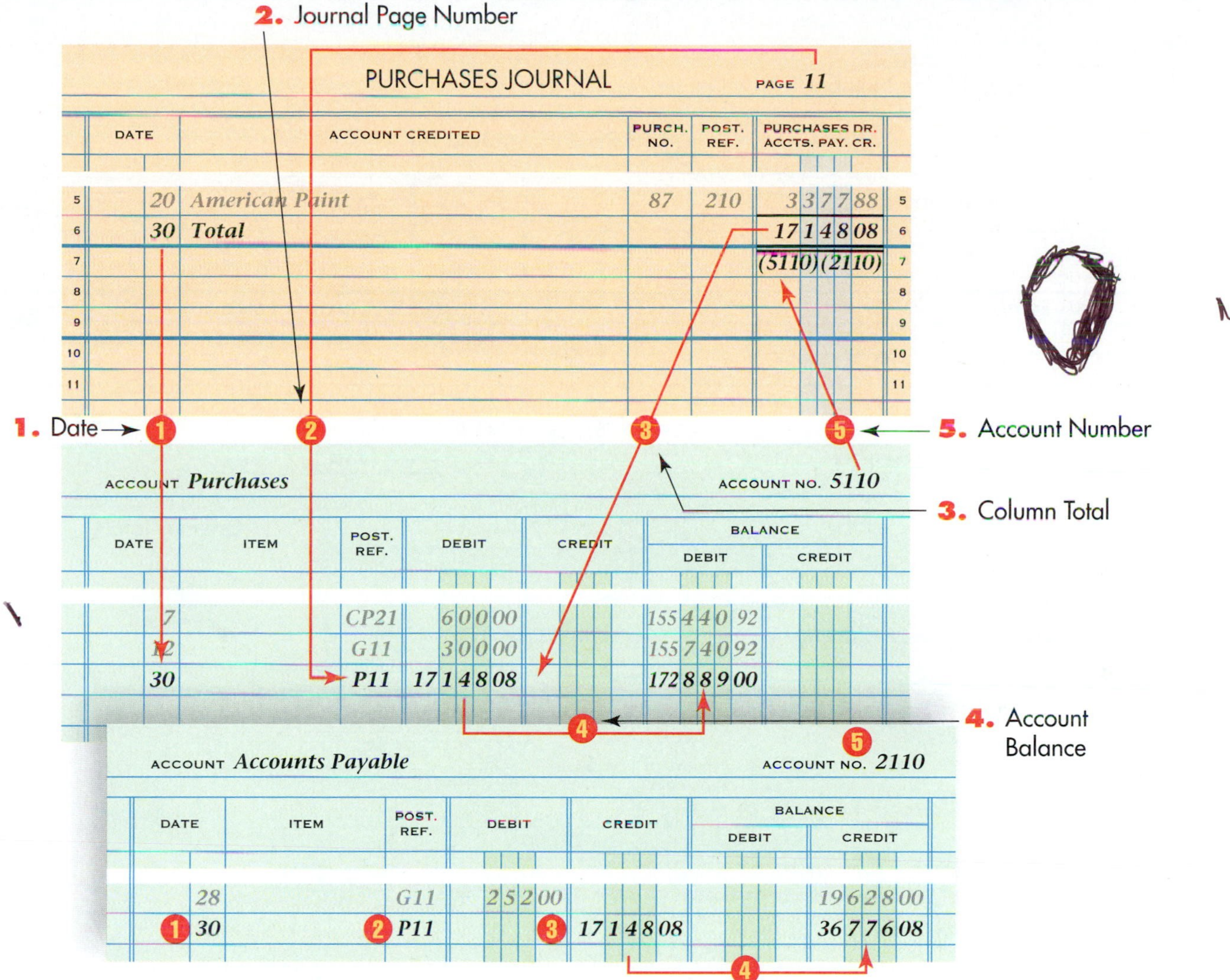

A purchases journal is totaled and ruled at the end of each month as described in Chapter 9. The total amount of the purchases journal is then posted to two general ledger accounts, Purchases and Accounts Payable.

STEPS • STEPS • STEPS • STEPS • STEPS • STEPS • STEPS • STEPS • STEPS • STEPS •

POSTING THE TOTAL OF A PURCHASES JOURNAL TO THE TWO GENERAL LEDGER ACCOUNTS

1. Write the date, *30*, in the Date columns of the accounts.
2. Write the purchases journal page number, *P11*, in the Post. Ref. columns of the accounts. The abbreviation *P11* means page 11 of the purchases journal.
3. For each account, write the purchases journal column total, *$17,148.08*, in the Debit or Credit column.
4. For each account, calculate and write the new account balance in the Balance Debit or Credit column.
5. Return to the purchases journal and write the purchases general ledger account number, *(5110)*, and the accounts payable general ledger account number, *(2110)*, in parentheses below the column total.

POSTING SPECIAL AMOUNT COLUMN TOTALS OF A CASH RECEIPTS JOURNAL TO A GENERAL LEDGER

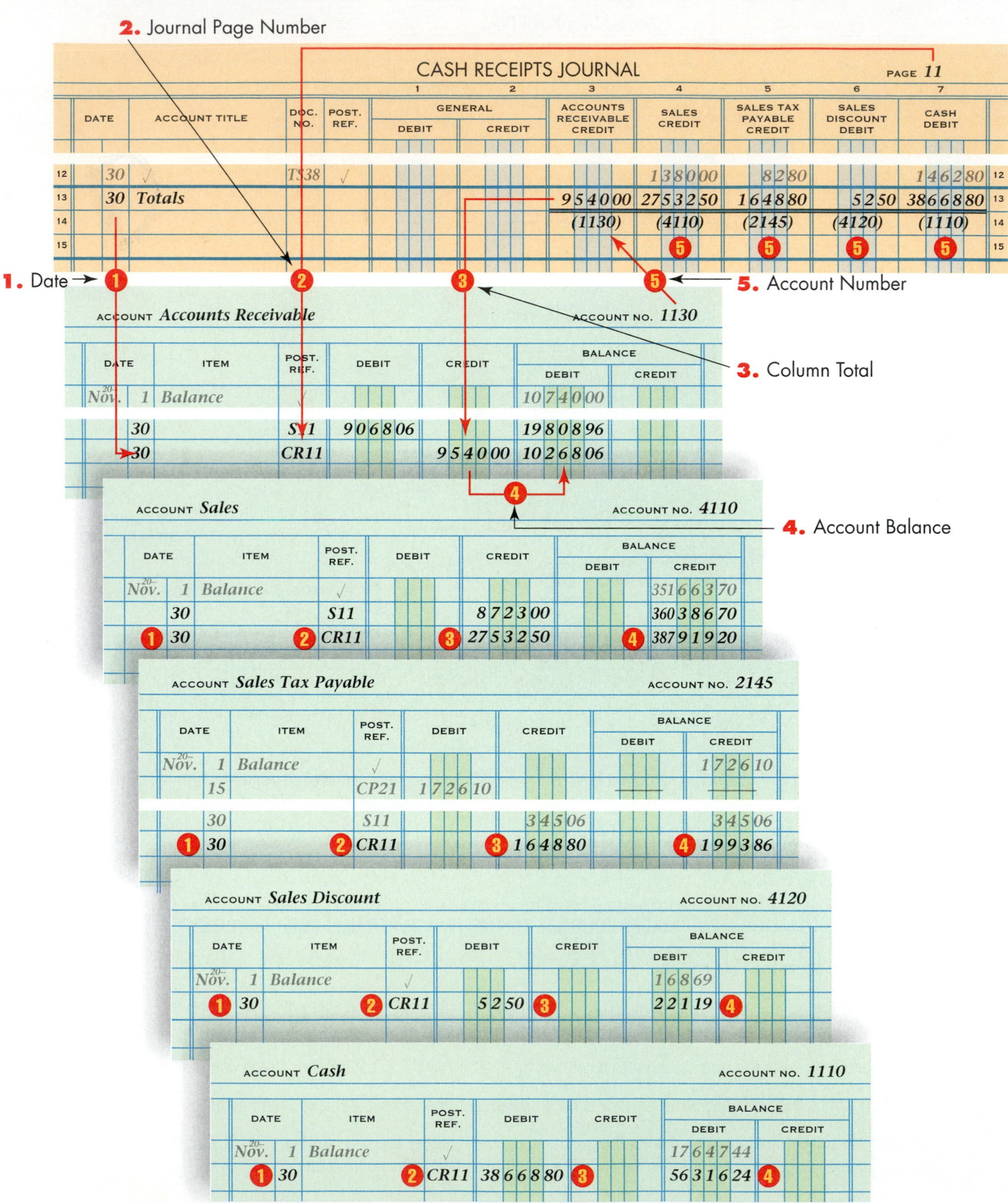

CASH RECEIPTS JOURNAL — PAGE 11

	DATE	ACCOUNT TITLE	DOC. NO.	POST. REF.	1 GENERAL DEBIT	2 GENERAL CREDIT	3 ACCOUNTS RECEIVABLE CREDIT	4 SALES CREDIT	5 SALES TAX PAYABLE CREDIT	6 SALES DISCOUNT DEBIT	7 CASH DEBIT	
12	30	✓	TS38	✓				1380 00	82 80		1462 80	12
13	30	Totals					9540 00	27532 50	1648 80	52 50	38668 80	13
14							(1130)	(4110)	(2145)	(4120)	(1110)	14
15												15

ACCOUNT Accounts Receivable — ACCOUNT NO. 1130

DATE		ITEM	POST. REF.	DEBIT	CREDIT	BALANCE DEBIT	BALANCE CREDIT
Nov. 20--	1	Balance	✓			10740 00	
	30		S11	9068 06		19808 96	
	30		CR11		9540 00	10268 06	

ACCOUNT Sales — ACCOUNT NO. 4110

DATE		ITEM	POST. REF.	DEBIT	CREDIT	BALANCE DEBIT	BALANCE CREDIT
Nov. 20--	1	Balance	✓				351663 70
	30		S11		8723 00		360386 70
	30		CR11		27532 50		387919 20

ACCOUNT Sales Tax Payable — ACCOUNT NO. 2145

DATE		ITEM	POST. REF.	DEBIT	CREDIT	BALANCE DEBIT	BALANCE CREDIT
Nov. 20--	1	Balance	✓				1726 10
	15		CP21	1726 10		—	—
	30		S11		345 06		345 06
	30		CR11		1648 80		1993 86

ACCOUNT Sales Discount — ACCOUNT NO. 4120

DATE		ITEM	POST. REF.	DEBIT	CREDIT	BALANCE DEBIT	BALANCE CREDIT
Nov. 20--	1	Balance	✓			168 69	
	30		CR11	52 50		221 19	

ACCOUNT Cash — ACCOUNT NO. 1110

DATE		ITEM	POST. REF.	DEBIT	CREDIT	BALANCE DEBIT	BALANCE CREDIT
Nov. 20--	1	Balance	✓			17647 44	
	30		CR11	38668 80		56316 24	

At the end of each month, equality of debits and credits is proved for a cash receipts journal. Cash is then proved as described in Chapter 10. After cash is proved, the cash receipts journal is ruled as described in Chapter 10. The total of each special amount column is then posted to the corresponding general ledger account.

STEPS • STEPS • STEPS • STEPS • STEPS • STEPS • STEPS • STEPS • STEPS • STEPS • STEPS •

POSTING EACH SPECIAL AMOUNT COLUMN TOTAL OF A CASH RECEIPTS JOURNAL

1. Write the date, *30*, in the Date columns of the accounts.
2. Write the cash receipts journal page number, *CR11*, in the Post. Ref. columns of the accounts. The abbreviation *CR11* means page 11 of the cash receipts journal.
3. For each special amount column and account, write the special amount column total in the Debit or Credit column of the account.
4. For each account, calculate and write the new account balance in the Balance Debit or Credit column.
5. Return to the cash receipts journal and write the general ledger account number in parentheses below the special amount column total.

CULTURAL DIVERSITY • CULTURAL DIVERSITY • CULTURAL DIVERSITY

Timeless Tools

Throughout history, people of different cultures and civilizations have devised tools for counting, calculating, and recordkeeping.

The Jibaro Indians living in the Amazon rain forest in South America use the most basic counting tools of all—their fingers. Jibaros use phrases to express the numbers five and ten that translate to "I have finished one hand" and "I have finished both hands."

A more complex device of ancient origin is the abacus. The abacus is a calculating device that developed in several different cultures. The Babylonians in Asia Minor had an early form of abacus, as did the Egyptians in northern Africa. The first abacus was known in China as early as the 6th century B.C. This abacus was a flat piece of wood divided into squares. Its use spread to the rest of the Asian world.

The abacus may be used to add, subtract, multiply, and divide. Twelfth-century Chinese mathematicians used the abacus to solve algebraic equations. Today some highly skilled people, particularly of Asian descent, still use the abacus for calculations.

Recordkeepers in the Incan civilization (in present-day Peru) memorized business transactions and recited them when necessary. Incan recordkeepers used small ropes of different colors and sizes and knotted and joined them in different ways to help remember financial data. These ropes, called *quipu*, were one of the earliest means of recording transactions.

Accounting tools have changed over the course of history. They will continue to evolve with future advances in technology.

Critical Thinking

1. What tools do most accounting workers today use for calculations?
2. Discuss whether the use of modern calculating tools results in the creation of more complex accounting transactions.

POSTING SPECIAL AMOUNT COLUMN TOTALS OF A CASH PAYMENTS JOURNAL TO A GENERAL LEDGER

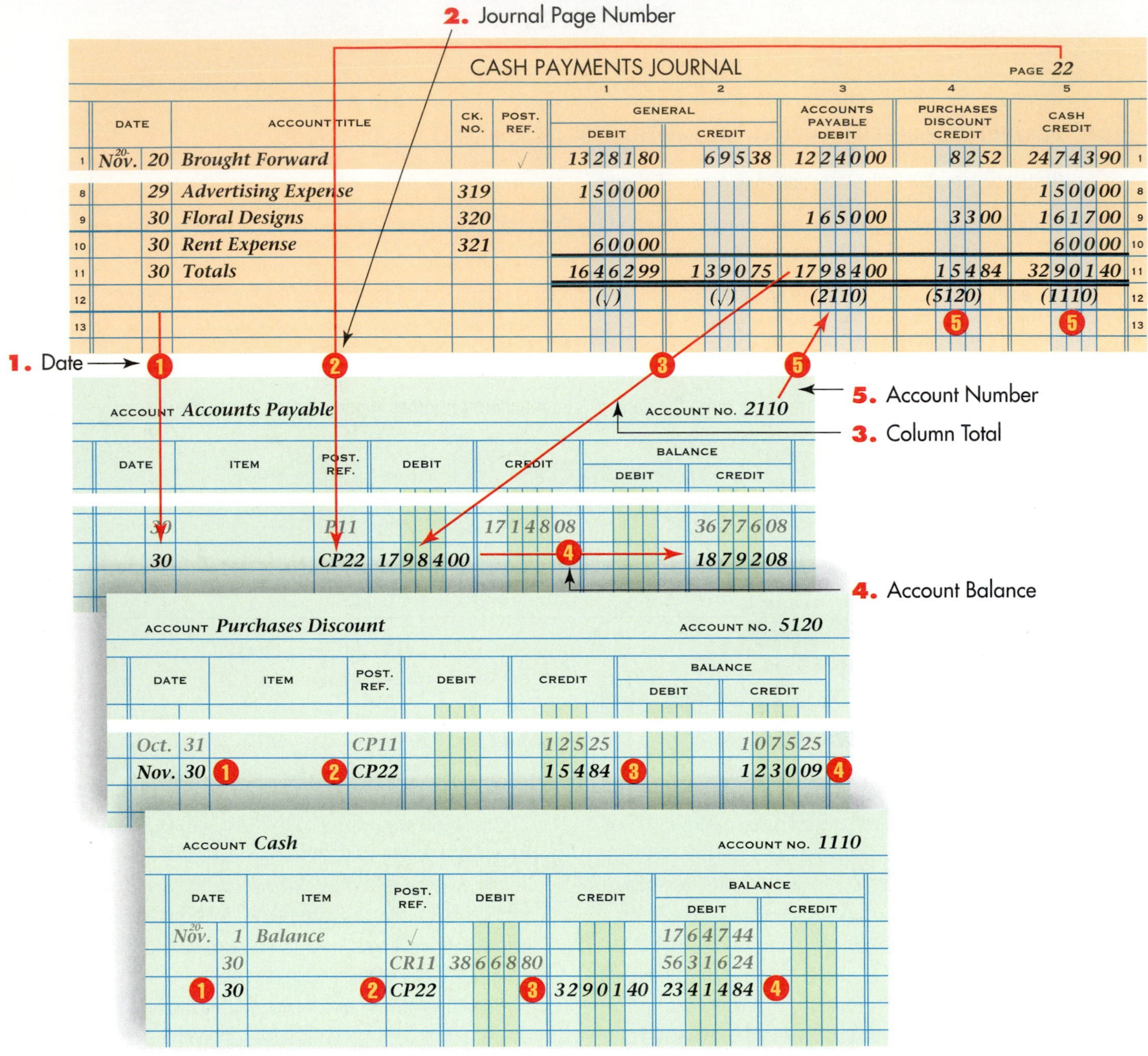

CASH PAYMENTS JOURNAL — PAGE 22

	DATE		ACCOUNT TITLE	CK. NO.	POST. REF.	1 GENERAL DEBIT	2 GENERAL CREDIT	3 ACCOUNTS PAYABLE DEBIT	4 PURCHASES DISCOUNT CREDIT	5 CASH CREDIT	
1	20-- Nov.	20	Brought Forward		✓	13281 80	695 38	12240 00	82 52	24743 90	1
8		29	Advertising Expense	319		1500 00				1500 00	8
9		30	Floral Designs	320				1650 00	33 00	1617 00	9
10		30	Rent Expense	321		600 00				600 00	10
11		30	Totals			16462 99	1390 75	17984 00	154 84	32901 40	11
12						(✓)	(✓)	(2110)	(5120)	(1110)	12
13											13

ACCOUNT Accounts Payable — ACCOUNT NO. 2110

DATE		ITEM	POST. REF.	DEBIT	CREDIT	BALANCE DEBIT	BALANCE CREDIT
	30		P11		17148 08		36776 08
	30		CP22	17984 00			18792 08

ACCOUNT Purchases Discount — ACCOUNT NO. 5120

DATE		ITEM	POST. REF.	DEBIT	CREDIT	BALANCE DEBIT	BALANCE CREDIT
Oct.	31		CP11		125 25		1075 25
Nov.	30		CP22		154 84		1230 09

ACCOUNT Cash — ACCOUNT NO. 1110

DATE		ITEM	POST. REF.	DEBIT	CREDIT	BALANCE DEBIT	BALANCE CREDIT
20-- Nov.	1	Balance	✓			17647 44	
	30		CR11	38668 80		56316 24	
	30		CP22		32901 40	23414 84	

The cash payments journal is totaled and ruled at the end of each month as described in Chapter 9. The total of each special column is then posted to a general ledger account. The total of each special amount column is posted to the account named in the journal's column headings.

The totals of the General amount columns are not posted. Each amount in these columns was posted individually to a general ledger account. To indicate that these totals are not to be posted, a check mark is placed in parentheses below each column total.

STEPS • STEPS • STEPS • STEPS • STEPS • STEPS • STEPS • STEPS • STEPS • STEPS • STEPS •

POSTING THE TOTALS OF EACH SPECIAL AMOUNT COLUMN TO THE GENERAL LEDGER ACCOUNT

1. Write the date, *30*, in the Date columns of the accounts.
2. Write the cash payments journal page number, *CP22*, in the Post. Ref. columns of the accounts.
3. For each special amount column and account, write the special amount column total in the Debit or Credit column of the account.
4. For each account, calculate and write the new account balance in the Balance Debit or Credit column.
5. Return to the cash payments journal and write the general ledger account number in parentheses below the special amount column total.

ORDER OF POSTING FROM SPECIAL JOURNALS

Items affecting customer or vendor accounts are posted periodically during the month. Hobby Shack posts frequently so that the balances of the subsidiary ledger accounts will be up to date. Since general ledger account balances are needed only when financial statements are prepared, the general ledger accounts are posted less often during the month. All items, including the totals of special columns, must be posted before a trial balance is prepared. Hobby Shack posts special amount column totals monthly.

The journals should be posted in the following order:

1. Sales journal.
2. Purchases journal.
3. General journal.
4. Cash receipts journal.
5. Cash payments journal.

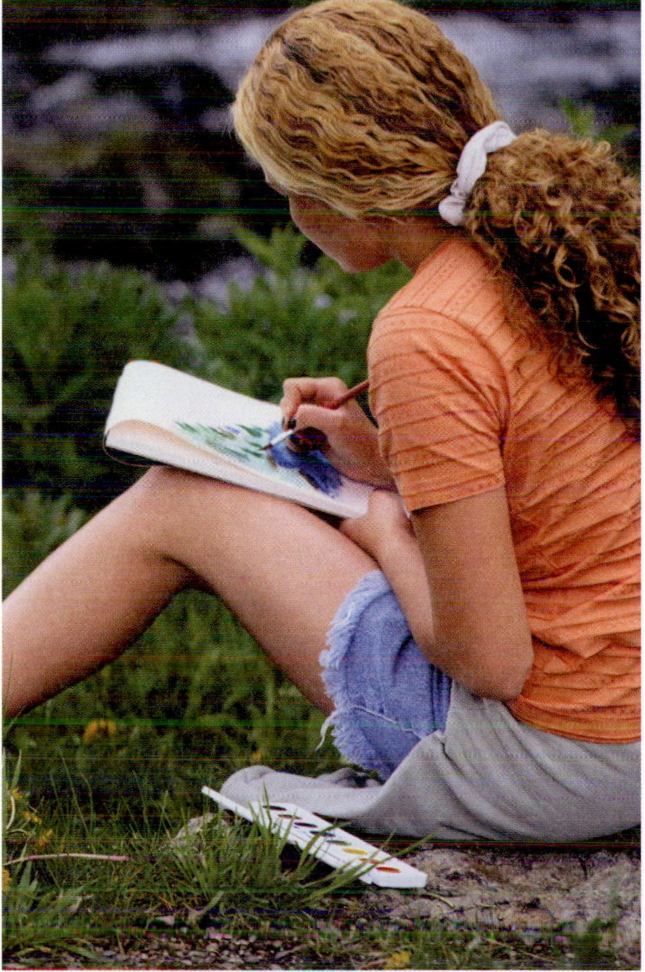

©GETTY IMAGES/PHOTODISC

FYI FOR YOUR INFORMATION

It is important to post the journals in the proper sequence. However, sometimes the entries will be out of chronological order. For example, if subsidiary accounts are posted for the week ended June 24, it is possible for a June 23 entry from the sales journal to appear before a June 20 entry from the cash receipts journal.

Xtra! Study Tools
accountingxtra.swlearning.com

audit your understanding

1. For which columns of a special journal are the column totals posted to the general ledger?
2. In what order should special journals be posted to the general ledger?

work together 11-4

Posting special journal totals to a general ledger

Use the journals that were used for Work Together 11-1 and 11-2. General ledger accounts are given in the *Working Papers*. Your instructor will guide you through the following examples.

1. Post the October 31 column totals of the sales journal.
2. Post the October 31 column total of the purchases journal.
3. Post the October 31 column totals of the cash receipts journal.
4. Post the October 31 column totals of the cash payments journal.

on your own 11-4

Posting special journal totals to a general ledger

Use the journals that were used for On Your Own 11-1 and 11-2. General ledger accounts are given in the *Working Papers*. Work this problem independently.

1. Post the September 30 column totals of the sales journal.
2. Post the September 30 column total of the purchases journal.
3. Post the September 30 column totals of the cash receipts journal.
4. Post the September 30 column totals of the cash payments journal.

LESSON

11-5 Correcting Errors in Subsidiary Ledger Accounts

JOURNALIZING CORRECTING ENTRIES AFFECTING CUSTOMER ACCOUNTS

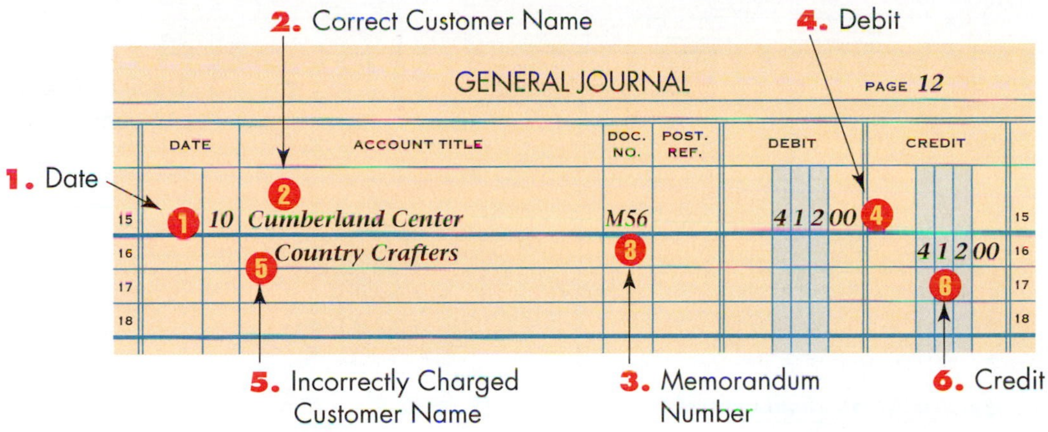

Errors may be made in recording amounts in subsidiary ledgers that do not affect the general ledger controlling account. For example, a sale on account may be recorded to the wrong customer in the sales journal. The column total posted from the sales journal to the general ledger is correct. The accounts receivable account shows the correct balance. However, two of the customer accounts in the accounts receivable ledger show incorrect balances.

December 10. Discovered that a sale on account to Cumberland Center on December 3 was incorrectly charged to the account of Country Crafters, $412.00. Memorandum No. 56.

The correcting entry recorded in the general journal involves only subsidiary ledger accounts. Cumberland Center's account is debited for $412.00 to record the charge sale in the correct account. Country Crafters' account is credited for $412.00 to cancel the incorrect entry.

ACCOUNTS RECEIVABLE LEDGER

Cumberland Center

Dec. 10	412.00		

Country Crafters

Dec. 3	412.00	Dec. 10	412.00

STEPS • STEPS • STEPS • STEPS • STEPS

JOURNALIZING CORRECTING ENTRIES AFFECTING CUSTOMER ACCOUNTS

1. Write the date, *10*, in the Date column of a general journal.
2. Write the name of the correct customer, *Cumberland Center*, in the Account Title column.
3. Write the memorandum number, *M56*, in the Doc. No. column.
4. Write the amount, *$412.00*, in the Debit column.
5. Indent and write the name of the incorrectly charged customer, *Country Crafters*, on the next line in the Account Title column.
6. Write the amount, *$412.00*, in the Credit column.

POSTING CORRECTING ENTRIES AFFECTING CUSTOMER ACCOUNTS

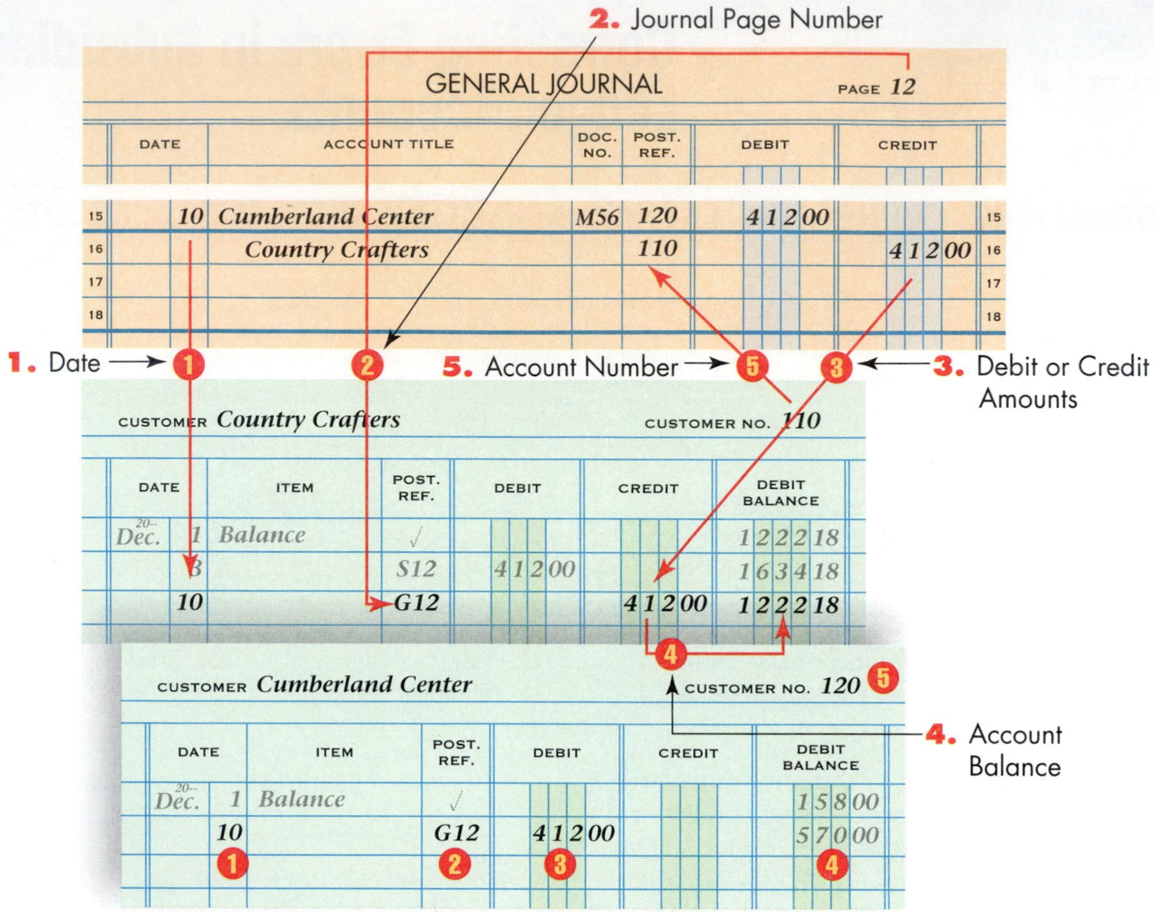

With one exception, the steps for posting a journal entry to correct customer accounts are the same as posting other transactions to subsidiary ledgers. However, a diagonal line is not needed in the Post. Ref. column to separate the references to the general ledger and subsidiary ledger account. Because the transaction does not affect a general ledger account, only a reference to the subsidiary ledger account is entered in the Post. Ref. column of the general journal.

STEPS • STEPS • STEPS • STEPS

POSTING CORRECTING ENTRIES AFFECTING CUSTOMER ACCOUNTS

1. Write the date, *10*, in the Date column of each customer account.
2. Write the general journal page number, *G12*, in the Post. Ref. column of the account.
3. Write the amount, *$412.00*, in the appropriate Debit or Credit column of each customer account.
4. For each account, calculate and write the new account balance in the Debit Balance column.
5. Write the appropriate vendor number in the Post. Ref. columns of the general journal.

FYI FOR YOUR INFORMATION

Recording a correcting entry establishes what accountants refer to as an *audit trail*. The original (incorrect) entry is retained in the accounting records. The reason for the correcting entry and the name of the employee who authorized the correction are recorded on the memo supporting the correcting entry. Thus, accountants can follow the history of the transactions to ensure that the net effect of the transactions is accurate.

audit your understanding

1. What is the source document for a correcting entry affecting customer accounts?
2. How does a correcting entry affecting customer accounts impact the general ledger accounts?
3. How does posting a correcting entry affecting customer accounts differ from recording other general journal entries that impact subsidiary ledger accounts?

work together 11-5

Journalizing and posting correcting entries affecting customer accounts

The general journal and accounts receivable ledger accounts for Cline Interiors are given in the *Working Papers*. Your instructor will guide you through the following examples.

1. Using the current year, journalize the following transaction on page 6 of a general journal. The memorandum source document is abbreviated as M.

Transaction:

June 3. Discovered that a sale on account to Howell Clinic on May 25, S346, was incorrectly charged to the account of Howsley Dance Studio, $414.99. M57.

2. Post the items to the accounts receivable ledger.

on your own 11-5

Journalizing and posting correcting entries affecting customer accounts

The general journal and accounts receivable ledger accounts for Gentry, Inc., are given in the *Working Papers*. Work this problem independently.

1. Using the current year, journalize the following transaction on page 7 of a general journal. The memorandum source document is abbreviated as M.

Transaction:

July 4. Discovered that a sale on account to Kellogg Co., on June 28, S143, was incorrectly charged to the account of Keller Corp., $715.98. M76.

2. Post the items to the accounts receivable ledger.

SUMMARY

After completing this chapter, you can

1. Define accounting terms related to posting to ledgers.
2. Identify accounting practices related to posting to ledgers.
3. Post separate items from a purchases, cash payments, and general journal to an accounts payable ledger.
4. Post separate items from a sales, cash receipts, and general journal to an accounts receivable ledger.
5. Post separate items from a cash payments and general journal to a general ledger.
6. Post special journal column totals to a general ledger.
7. Journalize and post correcting entries affecting customer accounts.

Explore Accounting

Categories of Internal Control

Posting transactions from a journal to both the general ledger and subsidiary ledgers presents opportunities for errors. Hobby Shack can fail to record a sales transaction to a customer's account. If the customer does not pay the amount owed, Hobby Shack may never collect the accounts receivable. To avoid errors and their resulting losses, businesses should institute effective internal controls.

Internal controls may be categorized in three phases: (1) preventive, (2) detective, and (3) corrective. A preventive control prevents the individual from making the error. Establishing and following consistent procedures for posting transactions is a preventive control. A detective control detects or finds the error. Preparing a trial balance is a detective control. A corrective control restores the business back to normal if an error occurs. Insurance, such as a fidelity bond on a cashier, is a corrective control.

Businesses with an adequate number of employees should split duties among several employees to reduce the chances of error. This segregation of duties enables one employee to check the work of another. For example, one employee should post transactions to the general ledger while another employee should post transactions to the subsidiary ledger.

Discussion

1. Describe internal control procedures that you have observed either as an employee or as a customer. Identify each procedure as (1) preventive, (2) detective, or (3) corrective.
2. Discuss whether a policeman monitoring a highway with radar is a preventive or detective control of the speed limit.

11-1 APPLICATION PROBLEM

Posting to an accounts payable ledger

Selected entries from the purchases, cash payments, and general journal for Healthy Nutrition, a health food store, are given in the *Working Papers*.

Instructions:

1. Start new pages for the following vendor accounts in the accounts payable ledger. Record the balances as of October 1 of the current year.

Vendor No.	Vendor Name	Account Balance
210	Cornucopia, Inc.	$3,090.00
220	Healthy Foods	5,064.00
230	Nutrition Center	—
240	Office Center	—
250	Sports Nutrition	4,512.00

2. Post the separate items recorded in the purchases, cash payments, and general journals to the appropriate accounts payable ledger accounts. Post in chronological order by date.
3. Prepare a schedule of accounts payable. Compare the total of the schedule with the balance of the controlling account, Accounts Payable, $13,352.00. If the totals are not the same, find and correct the errors.

11-2 APPLICATION PROBLEM

Posting to an accounts receivable ledger

Selected entries from the sales and cash receipts journals for Healthy Nutrition are given in the *Working Papers*.

Instructions:

1. Start new pages for the following customer accounts in the accounts receivable ledger. Record the balances as of October 1 of the current year.

Customer No.	Customer Name	Account Balance
110	Children's Center	$4,416.00
120	Eastman Sports Arena	2,220.00
130	Maple Tree Club	3,528.00
140	Southwest Community Club	—

2. Post the separate items recorded in the sales, cash receipts, and general journals to the appropriate accounts receivable ledger accounts. Post in chronological order by date.
3. Prepare a schedule of accounts receivable. Compare the total of the schedule with the balance of the controlling account, Accounts Receivable, $8,293.44. If the totals are not the same, find and correct the errors.

11-3 APPLICATION PROBLEM

Posting to a general ledger

Selected entries from the cash payments and general journals for Hartley Corporation are given in the *Working Papers.*

Instructions:

1. Start new pages for the following accounts in the general ledger. Record the balances as of November 1 of the current year.

General Ledger Account No.	Account Title	Balance
1110	Cash	$ 21,960.00
1130	Accounts Receivable	8,420.64
1150	Supplies—Office	4,416.00
1170	Prepaid Insurance	1,870.00
2110	Accounts Payable	15,396.00
2120	Sales Tax Payable	1,615.20
4110	Sales	206,904.00
4120	Sales Discount	2,051.23
5110	Purchases	115,800.00
5120	Purchases Discount	1,845.22
6160	Rent Expense	12,000.00

2. Post the separate general ledger items recorded in the cash payments and general journals. Save your work to complete Application Problem 11-4.

11-4 APPLICATION PROBLEM

Posting special journal column totals to a general ledger

The sales, purchases, and cash receipts journals for Hartley Corporation are given in the *Working Papers.* Use the general ledger accounts and cash payments journal from Application Problem 11-3.

Instructions:

Post the totals of the special columns of the sales, purchases, cash receipts, and cash payments journals.

11-5 APPLICATION PROBLEM AUTOMATED ACCOUNTING

Journalizing and posting correcting entries affecting customer accounts

The general journal and accounts receivable ledger accounts for Placid Marina are given in the *Working Papers.*

Instructions:

1. Using the current year, journalize the following transactions on page 6 of a general journal. Source documents are abbreviated as: sales invoices, S; memorandum, M.

Transactions:

July 14. Discovered that a sale on account to Mark Ford on July 5, S534, was incorrectly charged to the account of Andrew Forde, $253.32. M37.

15. Discovered that a sale on account to Sandy Patterson on July 8, S567, was incorrectly charged to the account of Daniel Patrick, $384.50. M38.

2. Post the items to the accounts receivable ledger.

11-6 MASTERY PROBLEM PEACHTREE QUICKBOOKS

Posting to general and subsidiary ledgers

The journals, subsidiary ledgers, and selected general ledger accounts for Auto Restoration, Inc., are given in the *Working Papers*.

Instructions:

1. Post the separate items in the following journals to the general and subsidiary ledgers. Use the current year. Note that some postings will be out of order by date because posting of individual amounts is not being done weekly.
   a. Sales journal to the accounts receivable ledger.
   b. Purchases journal to the accounts payable ledger.
   c. General journal to the accounts payable, accounts receivable, and general ledger.
   d. Cash receipts journal to the accounts receivable ledger.
   e. Cash payments journal to the accounts payable and general ledgers.
2. Post the totals of the special amount columns of the sales, purchases, cash receipts, and cash payments journals.
3. Prepare a schedule of accounts payable and a schedule of accounts receivable. Compare the totals of the schedules with the balances of the controlling accounts, Accounts Payable and Accounts Receivable, in the general ledger. If the totals are not the same, find and correct the errors.

11-7 CHALLENGE PROBLEM AUTOMATED ACCOUNTING PEACHTREE QUICKBOOKS

Journalizing and posting business transactions

The general, accounts payable, and accounts receivable ledgers for Custom Golf Land are given in the *Working Papers*.

Instructions:

1. Journalize the following transactions completed during October of the current year. Use page 11 of a sales journal, purchases journal, general journal, and cash receipts journal. Use page 21 of a cash payments journal. Add an 8% sales tax to all sales transactions. Source documents are abbreviated as follows: check, C; memorandum, M; purchase invoice, P; receipt, R; sales invoice, S; terminal summary, TS.

Transactions:

Oct. 2. Wrote a check for rent, $1,150.00. C265.
3. Received an invoice from Vista Golf Co. for merchandise purchased on account, $1,950.00. P71.
4. Paid for merchandise, $142.80. C266.
6. A check was received in payment on account from Viola Davis, $829.44, covering S45. R43.
7. Eagle Golf Equipment was paid on account, $2,358.00, covering P67. C267.
7. Cash and credit card sales, $5,676.00. TS31.
Posting. Post the items that are to be posted individually.
11. Merchandise was sold on account to Doris McCarley, $306.00. S49.
13. Store supplies were bought on account from Golf Source, $258.00. M34.
14. Cash and credit card sales, $5,808.00. TS32.
Posting. Post the items that are to be posted individually.
17. Wrote a check for electric bill, $220.20. C268.
20. Wrote a check to Vista Golf Co. on account, $3,216.00, less 2% discount, covering P68. C269.
21. Recorded cash and credit card sales, $5,376.00. TS33.
Posting. Post the items that are to be posted individually.
23. Design Golf was paid on account, $2,916.00, covering P69. C270.
24. Barry Fuller bought merchandise on account, $1,315.00. S50.
24. Received payment on account from Leona Silva, $285.12, covering S46. R44.

25. Merchandise was purchased on account from Pro Golf Supply, $1,542.00. P72.
27. A check was received in payment on account from David Bench, $972.00, covering S47. R45.
28. Received an invoice from Design Golf for merchandise purchased on account, $2,790.00. P73.
28. Merchandise was sold on account to Leona Silva, $1,314.00. S51.
28. Recorded cash and credit card sales, $5,556.00. TS34.
Posting. Post the items that are to be posted individually.
30. Discovered that a sale on account to David Bench on October 28, S51, was incorrectly charged to the account of Leona Silva, $1,419.12. M35.
30. Replenish the petty cash fund, $251.00: office supplies, $40.00; store supplies, $51.00; advertising, $62.00; miscellaneous, $98.00. C271.
31. Recorded cash and credit card sales, $1,680.00. TS35.
Posting. Post the items that are to be posted individually.

2. Prove and rule the sales journal. Post the totals of the special columns.
3. Total and rule the purchases journal. Post the total.
4. Prove the equality of debits and credits for the cash receipts and cash payments journals.
5. Prove cash. The balance on the next unused check stub is $38,140.56.
6. Rule the cash receipts journal. Post the totals of the special columns.
7. Rule the cash payments journal. Post the totals of the special columns.
8. Prepare a schedule of accounts payable and a schedule of accounts receivable. Prove the accuracy of the subsidiary ledgers by comparing the schedule totals with the balances of the controlling accounts in the general ledger. If the totals are not the same, find and correct the errors.

In states that have sales taxes, businesses are required to collect taxes on their sales and submit the taxes to the state. This additional activity requires considerable extra effort: keeping a separate record of the taxes collected at the time of sale, maintaining a separate account for the sales taxes collected, Sales Taxes Payable, and recording the collection and payment of the sales taxes in the account. These additional activities place an additional administrative burden on businesses, especially small businesses with few employees.

9. Can you think of a procedure that would not require the separate record for collecting and accounting for sales taxes, yet comply with a state's requirement to collect and submit sales taxes based on sale of merchandise sold? Write a brief response providing an alternative approach to collecting and paying sales taxes.

• applied communication

Instructions: Write a letter to the Cute and Cuddly Corporation explaining that you are returning an order of stuffed toys because of poor workmanship. You would like to receive a refund for the full amount of the order, $350.25. Explain that you are providing a copy of the invoice, and ask for written confirmation of the processing of the refund. Include information that will allow the Cute and Cuddly Corp. to comply with your request.

APPLIED

• cases for critical thinking

Case 1

Larry Hayes observes his accountant at work and says, "You post each individual accounts receivable entry in the journal. Then you post the totals of the Accounts Receivable columns. You are posting these entries twice, which will make the records wrong." The accountant does not agree that the posting procedure is incorrect. Is Mr. Hayes or his accountant correct? Why?

Case 2

Heritage House purchased merchandise on account six weeks ago for $600.00 from Lakmany Supply. A check for $600.00 was sent three weeks ago in payment of the account. Although no additional purchases have been made, Heritage House recently received a bill from Lakmany Supply that listed the balance due as $1,200.00. What probably caused this error? When would the error probably be discovered?

CASES FOR CRITICAL THINKING

• SCANS workplace competency

Interpersonal Competency: Participating as a member of a team

Concept: Many companies today use the team concept of a group of employees working together on a common function or project. Therefore, the ability to work as part of a team is a key skill employers look for. Brainstorming is a common group activity for generating ideas to find a solution to a problem or to start a project. In brainstorming, the goal is to generate a large number of ideas. The rules of brainstorming are simple: no idea is to be criticized or ridiculed. Even silly or impractical ideas might jog another group member's thoughts to an idea that will solve a problem.

Application: Form a group of about five students. Select one student to be the recorder who will write down all the ideas generated, ideally on a chalkboard where all group members can see them. The problem you will brainstorm is how to increase sales for Hobby Shack, Inc., the company used for illustrations in this part of the textbook. Do not stop brainstorming until you have at least 25 ideas.

SCANS WORKPLACE • SCANS

auditing for errors

Veronica Harper has just completed posting sales and cash receipts transactions to the general and subsidiary ledgers. According to the company's internal control procedures, you are assigned the task of checking her work.

Instructions: Three accounts receivable ledger accounts are shown below. Assume that the posting references and the amounts are correct. From your knowledge of the sales and cash receipts journals, determine whether any of the amounts are recorded in the incorrect column. List any incorrect amounts and calculate new ending balances for the accounts.

CUSTOMER *Gerald Adams* CUSTOMER NO. *110*

DATE		ITEM	POST. REF.	DEBIT	CREDIT	DEBIT BALANCE
20-- July	1	Balance	✓			624 25
	16		S7	554 53		1,178 78
	25		CR12	624 25		1,803 03

CUSTOMER *Betty Daigre* CUSTOMER NO. *120*

DATE		ITEM	POST. REF.	DEBIT	CREDIT	DEBIT BALANCE
20-- July	1	Balance	✓			2,315 48
	24		S7		230 24	2,085 24

CUSTOMER *Jackson Miller* CUSTOMER NO. *130*

DATE		ITEM	POST. REF.	DEBIT	CREDIT	DEBIT BALANCE
20-- July	1	Balance	✓			2,946 22
	5		CR7	1,758 95		4,705 17
	22		S7		2,946 22	1,758 95

analyzing Best Buy's financial statements

Best Buy's annual report (shown in Appendix B) contains a schedule that reports its financial highlights for the current and prior 10 years on pages B-2 and B-3. The schedule shows the dramatic increase in the size of the business over this period.

Instructions

1. Prepare a spreadsheet containing selected information from Best Buy's 11-Year Financial Highlights. If spreadsheet software is not available, use a sheet of paper with 12 columns. In the first column, beginning in the second row, enter the following headings:

   Cost of goods sold
   Selling, general, and administrative expenses
   Operating income
2. Across the first row, beginning in the second column, enter the years 2004 to 1994.
3. Calculate each year's cost of goods sold by subtracting gross profit from revenue.
4. Enter each year's amounts for selling, general, and administrative expenses and operating income.
5. Prepare a stacked column (bar) graph of the data.
6. What amount is represented by each year's bar?

Automated Accounting

Correction of Errors

In automated accounting, errors can be made even though care is taken in recording transactions. An incorrect entry can be journalized or posted. Account numbers or dollar amounts can be transposed, or the wrong customer, vendor, or general ledger account selected. If an error has been made, it is necessary to locate and correct the inaccurate journal entry.

It is important to detect incorrect entries early in order to eliminate reports that may be generated with incorrect amounts. Therefore, finding and correcting errors is very important in order to create accurate, reliable financial reports as well as to make decisions based on correct information.

The procedures for locating and correcting journal entries are identical for all journals.

Finding a Journal Entry

1. Click the desired journal tab: General, Purchases, Sales, Cash Payments, or Cash Receipts.
2. Choose Find from the Edit menu bar.
3. Enter the date, reference, name, or amount you want to find in the Find What text box. Click OK.
4. If a matching transaction is found, it will be highlighted in the journal.

Changing or Deleting Journal Transactions

1. Select (highlight) the specific transaction text box that you wish to change or delete.
2. To change the transaction, enter the correction and click the Post command button. To delete the entire transaction, choose the Delete command button.

AUTOMATING APPLICATION PROBLEM 11-5: Journalizing and posting correcting entries affecting customer accounts

Instructions:

1. Load the *Automated Accounting 8.0* or higher software.
2. Select data file F11-5 from the appropriate directory/folder.
3. Select File from the menu bar and choose the Save As menu command. Key the path to the drive and directory that contains your data files. Save the data file with a filename of F11-5 XXX XXX (where the X's are your first and last name).
4. Access Problem Instructions through the Browser tool. Read the Problem Instructions screen.
5. Refer to the data listed in Application Problem 11-5.
6. Save your file and exit the Automated Accounting software.

AUTOMATING CHALLENGE PROBLEM 11-7: Journalizing and posting business transactions

Instructions:

1. Load the *Automated Accounting 8.0* or higher software.
2. Select data file F11-7 from the appropriate directory/folder.
3. Select File from the menu bar and choose the Save As menu command. Key the path to the drive and directory that contains your data files. Save the data file with a filename of F11-7 XXX XXX (where the X's are your first and last name).
4. Access Problem Instructions through the Browser tool. Read the Problem Instructions screen.
5. Refer to the data listed in Challenge Problem 11-7.
6. Save your file and exit the Automated Accounting software.

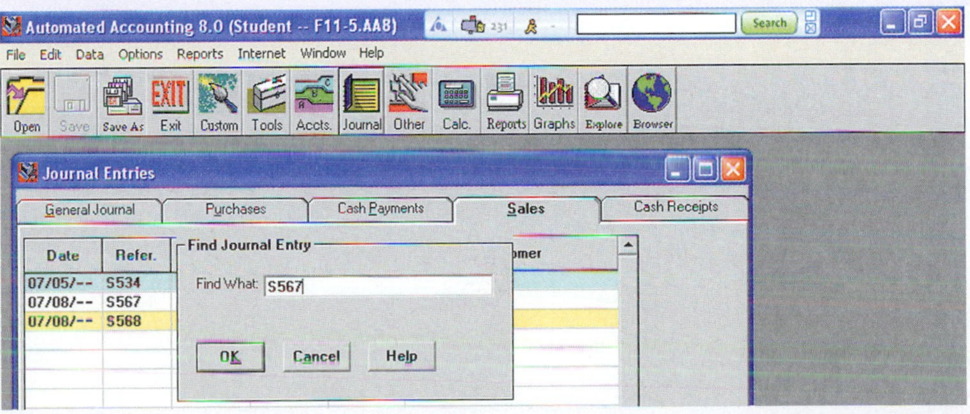

AUTOMATED ACCOUNTING • AUTOMATED ACCOUNTING • AUTOMATED ACCOUNTING • AUTOMATED ACCOUNTING • AUTOMATED ACCOUNTING

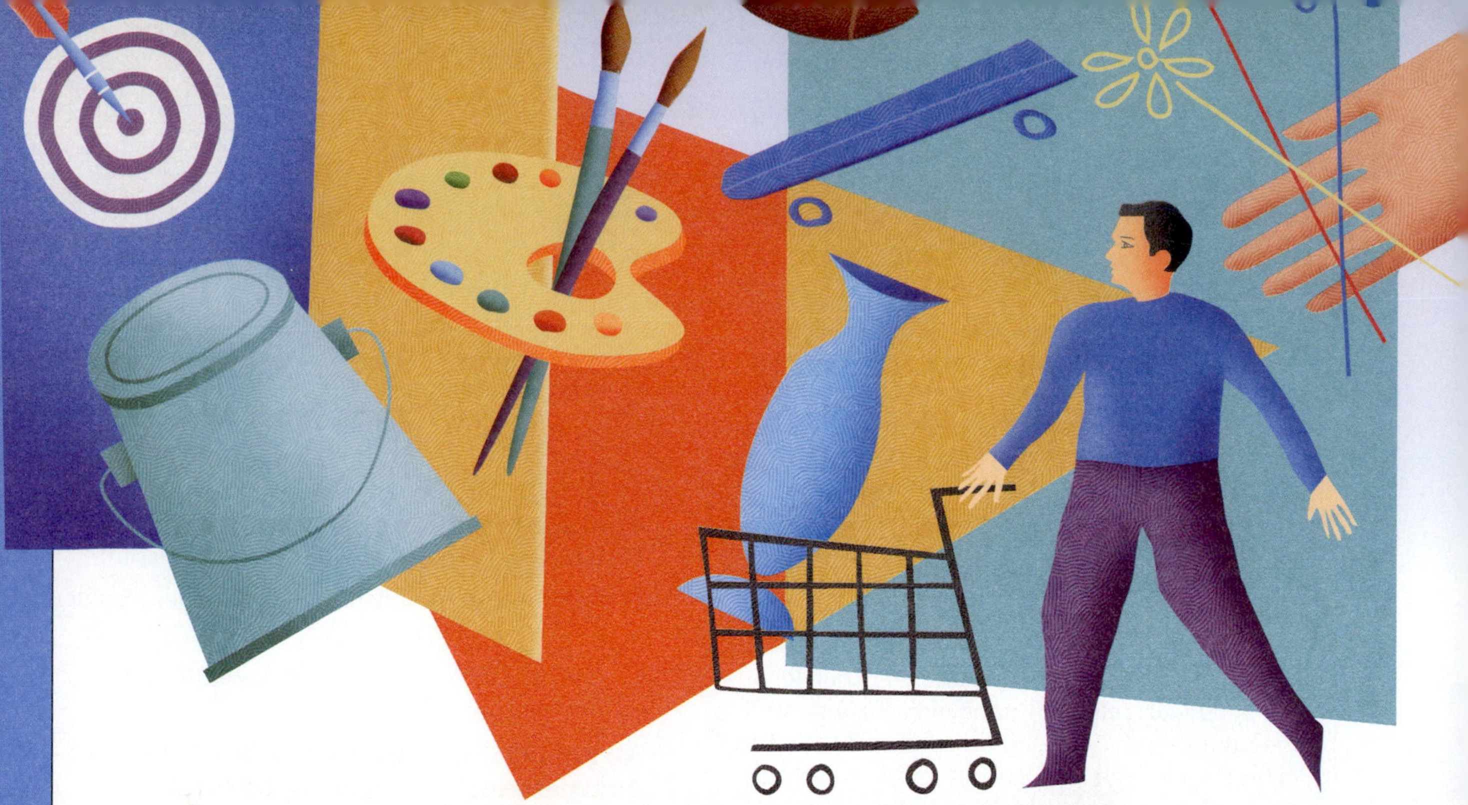

CHAPTER 12 Preparing Payroll Records

OBJECTIVES & TERMS

After studying Chapter 12, you will be able to:

1. Define accounting terms related to payroll records.
2. Identify accounting practices related to payroll records.
3. Complete a payroll time card.
4. Calculate payroll taxes.
5. Complete a payroll register and an employee earnings record.
6. Prepare payroll checks.

- salary
- pay period
- payroll
- total earnings
- payroll taxes
- withholding allowance
- social security tax
- Medicare tax
- tax base
- payroll register
- net pay
- employee earnings record

Point Your Browser
accountingxtra.swlearning.com

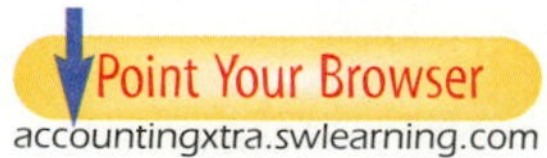

accounting in the real world

The Green Bay Packers

©STEVE APPS/EPA/LANDOV

THE PAYROLL PLAYBOOK OF THE GREEN BAY PACKERS

The Green Bay Packers have one of the richest and most enduring traditions of any professional franchise in any sport. Who hasn't watched the Packer faithful cheer their team to victory in snow-covered Lambeau Field? Twelve championships and three Super Bowls have been won under the leadership of legendary coaches like Vince Lombardi.

But did you know that the Green Bay Packers has been a publicly owned, nonprofit corporation since 1923? And, like every other corporation, the Green Bay Packers must pay its employees, withhold payroll taxes and benefits, and submit employee reports to the government.

The Packers employ a diverse group of talented individuals, including players, coaches, trainers, and scouts. However, many of its employees work off the field. From purchasing materials for the concession stands to planning advertising campaigns, individuals with a wide variety of talents are required for the Packers to continue as a viable corporation.

Critical Thinking

1. Identify at least 10 off-field jobs available with the Green Bay Packers.
2. How might payment of wages be different among the various types of employees?

accountingxtra.swlearning.com

Source: www.packers.com

ACCOUNTING IN THE REAL WORLD • ACCOUNTING IN THE REAL WORLD • ACCOUNTING IN THE REAL WORLD •

internet activity

CHILD LABOR LAWS

Go to the web site for the Department of Labor, Youth Rules (www.youthrules.dol.gov). Search the site for information about child labor laws.

Instructions

1. Make a chart showing which jobs youth can do at age 13 or younger, age 14, age 16, and age 18.
2. Make a chart showing what hours youth can work at age 14–15 and age 16.

INTERNET RESEARCH ACTIVITY • INTERNET RESEARCH ACTIVITY • INTERNET RESEARCH ACTIVITY •

LESSON

12-1 Preparing Payroll Time Cards

PAYING EMPLOYEES

Hobby Shack employs several people to work in the business. These employees record the time they work for Hobby Shack each day. Periodically, Hobby Shack pays its employees for the number of hours each employee has worked. The money paid for employee services is called a **salary**. The period covered by a salary payment is called a **pay period**. A business may decide to pay employee salaries every week, every two weeks, twice a month, or once a month. Hobby Shack uses a semimonthly pay period. Employees are paid twice a month, on the 15th and last day of each month.

The total amount earned by all employees for a pay period is called a **payroll**. The payroll is reduced by state and federal taxes and other deductions, such as health insurance, to determine the amount paid to all employees. Special payroll records support the recording of payroll transactions in a journal. The business also uses these records to inform employees of their annual earnings and to prepare payroll reports for the government.

FYI FOR YOUR INFORMATION

Salaries are usually stated as a fixed amount on a weekly, biweekly, semimonthly, or monthly basis. Salaried workers do not normally receive overtime pay. Money paid to employees on an hourly, daily, or even weekly basis is often referred to as *wages*. In practice, the terms *wages* and *salary* are often used interchangeably.

making ethical decisions

Is It Discrimination or Poor Judgment?

Your group at CyberMarket has an opening for a research analyst. You are on the search committee to pick candidates to be interviewed. Your company has a code of conduct that states the company will not discriminate on the basis of "race, color, religion, national origin, sex, sexual orientation or group affiliation, age, disability, or veteran status." In a recent meeting, committee members gave the following reasons for wanting to eliminate two candidates.

Candidate A: "She graduated from college before I was born. She can't possibly know anything about our business."

Candidate B: "The ad said two to five years of experience, but we really need someone with more than two years of experience."

Instructions

Use the ethical model to help evaluate hiring decisions based on each of the statements above. Use online sources, as appropriate, to determine whether any actions are illegal.

ANALYZING A PAYROLL TIME CARD

Hobby Shack

EMPLOYEE NO. 3

NAME Rick E. Selby

PAY PERIOD ENDED December 15, 20--

MORNING		AFTERNOON		OVERTIME		HOURS	
IN	OUT	IN	OUT	IN	OUT	REG	OT
1 7^{58}	12^{02}	12^{59}	5^{06}				

A payroll system must include an accurate record of the time each employee has worked. Several methods are used for keeping time records. One of the more frequently used methods is a time card. Time cards are used as the basic source of information to prepare a payroll.

Some time cards require employees to record only the total hours worked each day. Employees who record the total hours worked each day usually complete time cards by hand.

A business may use a time card that requires employees to record their arrival and departure times. Hobby Shack uses a time clock to record the daily arrival and departure times of its employees.

The time card shown here is for Rick E. Selby. Mr. Selby's employee number is at the top of the card. Below the employee number are the employee name and the ending date of the pay period.

Hobby Shack's time cards have three sections (Morning, Afternoon, and Overtime) with In and Out columns under each section. When Mr. Selby reported for work on December 1, he inserted the card in the time clock. The clock recorded his time of arrival, 7:58, on the first line of the time card. The other entries on this line indicate that he left for lunch at 12:02. He returned at 12:59 and left for the day at 5:06.

Hobby Shack calculates overtime pay for each employee who works more than 8 hours in one day. No employee works more than 5 days in any one week.

FYI FOR YOUR INFORMATION

Larger companies can afford more expensive systems to record employee arrival and departure times. A popular system requires employees to scan a personal identification card through a card scanner. At the end of the pay period, the system prints a report similar to the time card.

CALCULATING EMPLOYEE HOURS WORKED

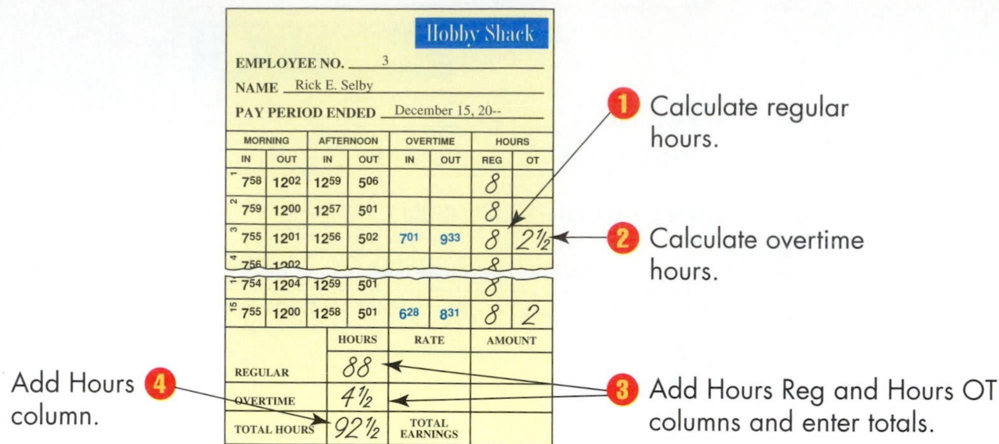

Hobby Shack

EMPLOYEE NO. 3

NAME Rick E. Selby

PAY PERIOD ENDED December 15, 20--

	MORNING		AFTERNOON		OVERTIME		HOURS	
	IN	OUT	IN	OUT	IN	OUT	REG	OT
1	7^{58}	12^{02}	12^{59}	5^{06}			8	
2	7^{59}	12^{00}	12^{57}	5^{01}			8	
3	7^{55}	12^{01}	12^{56}	5^{02}	7^{01}	9^{33}	8	$2\frac{1}{2}$
4	7^{56}	12^{02}					8	
14	7^{54}	12^{04}	12^{59}	5^{01}			8	
15	7^{55}	12^{00}	12^{58}	5^{01}	6^{28}	8^{31}	8	2

	HOURS	RATE	AMOUNT
REGULAR	88		
OVERTIME	$4\frac{1}{2}$		
TOTAL HOURS	$92\frac{1}{2}$	TOTAL EARNINGS	

1 Calculate regular hours.
2 Calculate overtime hours.
3 Add Hours Reg and Hours OT columns and enter totals.
Add Hours column. 4

The first task in preparing a payroll is to calculate the number of hours worked by each employee. When calculating hours worked, Hobby Shack rounds arrival and departure times to the nearest quarter hour.

STEPS CALCULATING EMPLOYEE HOURS WORKED

1. Calculate the number of regular hours for each day and enter the amounts in the Hours Reg column. Mr. Selby works 8 hours during a normal day. The hours worked on December 3, the third line of the time card, are calculated using the arrival and departure times imprinted on the time card.

   The hours worked in the morning and afternoon are calculated separately. The morning departure time of 12:01 is rounded to the nearest quarter hour, 12:00. The rounded arrival time, 8:00, subtracted from the departure time, 12:00, equals the morning hours worked. Hours worked of 4:00 means that Mr. Selby worked 4 hours and no (00) minutes. The total regular hours worked, 8, is recorded in the Hours Reg column.

	Departure Time	–	Arrival Time	=	Hours Worked
Morning:					
Time card	12:01		7:55		
Nearest quarter hour	12:00	–	8:00	=	4:00
Afternoon:					
Time card	5:02		12:56		
Nearest quarter hour	5:00	–	1:00	=	4:00
Total regular hours worked on December 3					8:00

2. Calculate the number of overtime hours for each day and enter the amounts in the Hours OT column. Overtime hours for December 3 are calculated using the same procedure as for regular hours.

   The hours worked of 2:30 means that Mr. Selby worked 2 hours and 30 minutes (½ hour) of overtime.

	Departure Time	–	Arrival Time	=	Hours Worked
Time card	9:33		7:01		
Nearest quarter hour	9:30	–	7:00	=	2:30

3. Add the hours worked in the Hours Reg and Hours OT columns and enter the totals in the spaces provided at the bottom of the time card. Mr. Selby worked 88 regular hours (8 hours × 11 days) and 4½ overtime hours during the semimonthly pay period.
4. Add the Hours column to calculate the total hours. Enter the total in the Hours column at the bottom of the time card. Mr. Selby worked 88 regular hours and 4½ overtime hours for a total of 92½ hours.

CALCULATING EMPLOYEE TOTAL EARNINGS

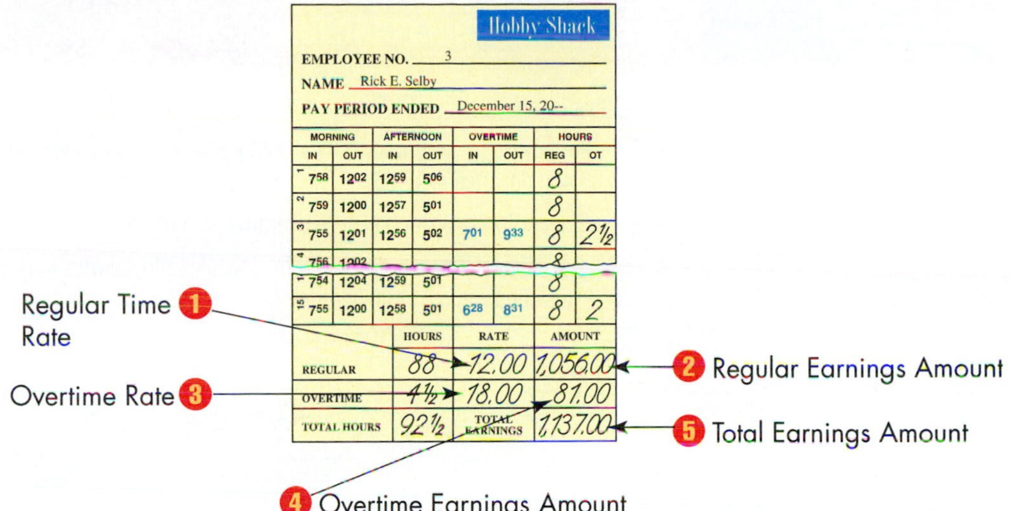

Hobby Shack

EMPLOYEE NO. 3

NAME Rick E. Selby

PAY PERIOD ENDED December 15, 20--

	MORNING IN	MORNING OUT	AFTERNOON IN	AFTERNOON OUT	OVERTIME IN	OVERTIME OUT	HOURS REG	HOURS OT
1	7 58	12 02	12 59	5 06			8	
2	7 59	12 00	12 57	5 01			8	
3	7 55	12 01	12 56	5 02	7 01	9 33	8	2½
4	7 56	12 02					8	
	7 54	12 04	12 59	5 01			8	
15	7 55	12 00	12 58	5 01	6 28	8 31	8	2

	HOURS	RATE	AMOUNT
REGULAR	88	12.00	1,056.00
OVERTIME	4½	18.00	81.00
TOTAL HOURS	92½	TOTAL EARNINGS	1,137.00

Once the total regular and overtime hours are determined, employee earnings can be calculated. The total pay due for a pay period before deductions is called **total earnings**. Total earnings are sometimes referred to as gross pay or gross earnings.

Hobby Shack owes Mr. Selby $1,137.00 for his work during the pay period ending December 15. However, taxes and other deductions must be subtracted from total earnings to determine the actual amount Hobby Shack will pay Mr. Selby.

STEPS • STEPS • STEPS • STEPS • STEPS • STEPS • STEPS • STEPS • STEPS • STEPS • STEPS •

CALCULATING AN EMPLOYEE'S TOTAL EARNINGS

1. Enter the rate for regular time in the Rate column. Mr. Selby's regular hourly rate is *$12.00*.
2. Calculate the regular earnings by multiplying regular hours times the regular rate. Enter the amount of regular earnings, *$1,056.00*, in the Regular Amount space.
3. Enter the rate for overtime, *$18.00*, in the Rate column. Mr. Selby is paid 1½ times his regular rate for overtime work.
4. Calculate the overtime earnings by multiplying overtime hours times the overtime rate. Enter the amount of overtime earnings, *$81.00*, in the Overtime Amount space.
5. Add the Amount column to calculate the total earnings. Enter the amount of total earnings, *$1,137.00*, in the Total Earnings space.

Regular Hours	×	Regular Rate	=	Regular Earnings
88	×	$12.00	=	$1,056.00

Regular Rate	×	1½	=	Overtime Rate
$12.00	×	1½	=	$18.00

Overtime Hours	×	Overtime Rate	=	Overtime Earnings
4½	×	$18.00	=	$81.00

• terms review

salary
pay period
payroll
total earnings

TERMS REVIEW • TERMS

• audit your understanding

1. What is a payroll?
2. How many hours were worked by a Hobby Shack employee who arrived at 8:29 and departed at 12:02?
3. How does Hobby Shack calculate overtime earnings?
4. What are the total earnings of a Hobby Shack employee who worked 44 hours in a week and earns $11.00 per hour?

AUDIT YOUR UNDERSTANDING

• work together 12-1

Calculating total earnings

Information taken from employee time cards is provided in the *Working Papers*. Your instructor will guide you through the following example.

1. For each employee, calculate the amount of regular, overtime, and total earnings. Overtime hours are paid at 1½ times the regular rate.

WORK TOGETHER

• on your own 12-1

Calculating total earnings

Information taken from employee time cards is provided in the *Working Papers*. Work this problem independently.

1. For each employee, calculate the amount of regular, overtime, and total earnings. Overtime hours are paid at 1½ times the regular rate.

ON YOUR OWN

LESSON • LESSON • LESSON • LESSON • LESSON • LESSON

12-2 Determining Payroll Tax Withholding

PAYROLL TAXES

Taxes based on the payroll of a business are called **payroll taxes**. A business is required by law to withhold certain payroll taxes from employee salaries. All payroll taxes are based on employee total earnings. Therefore, accurate and detailed payroll records must be maintained. Errors in payroll records could cause incorrect payroll tax payments. Federal and state governments may charge a business a penalty for failure to pay correct payroll taxes when they are due. Payroll taxes withheld represent a liability for the employer until payment is made to the government.

Employee Income Tax

A business must withhold federal income taxes from employee total earnings. Federal income taxes withheld must be forwarded periodically to the federal government. Federal income tax is withheld from employee earnings in all 50 states. Employers in many states also are required to withhold state, city, or county income taxes from employee earnings.

BUSINESS STRUCTURES • BUSINESS STRUCTURES • BUSINESS STRUCTURES

business structures

Selecting a Corporate Form

There exist several forms of corporations, each designed to meet the specific needs of its stockholders. The appropriate form is generally dependent on the size of the business and may be changed as the business grows.

1. *General Corporations.* Corporations that have more than 30 stockholders or offer to sell stock to the public must organize as a general or "C" corporation. These corporations must have a board of directors, conduct annual stockholders meetings, and publish financial reports with certain government agencies, such as the Securities and Exchange Commission. Large, well-known companies, such as Wal-Mart and General Motors, are C Corporations.
2. *Close Corporations.* In some states, corporations having fewer than 30 stockholders may elect to be a close corporation. This form of corporation reduces the governance requirements of a C Corporation. For example, a board of directors or annual stockholder meetings may not be required. Less than half of the states recognize this form of corporation.
3. *Subchapter S Corporation.* Named for the related section of the Internal Revenue Code, the Subchapter S or "S" Corporation is a special tax status available to C corporations. Unlike with C Corporations, distributions of earnings are not taxed to the stockholders, thus eliminating the "double taxation" of corporate earnings and distributions. Having 75 or fewer stockholders is the primary requirement for electing S corporation status.

Critical Thinking

1. You plan to expand your small proprietorship with an investment from several family members who will be stockholders. Which form of corporation would you probably use?
2. Considering your answer to question 1, what is the advantage to you? To your investors?

EMPLOYEE'S WITHHOLDING ALLOWANCE CERTIFICATE

3. Marital Status

2. Social Security Number

1. Name and Address

4. Withholding Allowances

Form **W-4** — Department of the Treasury, Internal Revenue Service

Employee's Withholding Allowance Certificate

For Privacy Act and Paperwork Reduction Act Notice, see page 2.

OMB No. 1545-0010 — 20--

1 Type or print your first name and middle initial: Rick E. — Last name: Selby

2 Your social security number: 450 70 6432

Home address (number and street or rural route): 1625 Northland Drive

3 ☐ Single ☒ Married ☐ Married, but withhold at higher Single rate.
Note: If married, but legally separated, or spouse is a nonresident alien, check the "Single" box.

City or town, state, and ZIP code: Clarkdale, GA 30020-6523

4 If your last name differs from that shown on your social security card, check here. You must call 1-800-772-1213 for a new card. ☐

5 Total number of allowances you are claiming (from line **H** above **or** from the applicable worksheet on page 2) . . . 5 — 4

6 Additional amount, if any, you want withheld from each paycheck . . . 6 — $-0-

7 I claim exemption from withholding for 20--, and I certify that I meet **both** of the following conditions for exemption:
Last year I had a right to a refund of **all** Federal income tax withheld because I had **no** tax liability **and**
This year I expect a refund of **all** Federal income tax withheld because I expect to have **no** tax liability.
If you meet both conditions, write "Exempt" here . . . ▶ 7

Under penalties of perjury, I certify that I am entitled to the number of withholding allowances claimed on this certificate, or I am entitled to claim exempt status.

Employee's signature (Form is not valid unless you sign it.) ▶ *Rick E. Selby* — Date ▶ *Feb. 15, 20 --*

8 Employer's name and address (Employer: Complete lines 8 and 10 only if sending to the IRS.) — 9 Office code (optional) — 10 Employer identification number

5. Signature and Date

The information used to determine the amount of income tax withheld is identified on Form W-4, Employee's Withholding Allowance Certificate. A deduction from total earnings for each person legally supported by a taxpayer, including the employee, is called a **withholding allowance**. Employers are required to have a current Form W-4 on file for all employees. The amount of income tax withheld is based on employee marital status and number of withholding allowances. A married employee will have less income tax withheld than a single employee with the same total earnings. The larger the number of withholding allowances claimed, the smaller the amount of income tax withheld.

Most employees are required to have federal income taxes withheld from their salaries. An exemption from withholding is available for certain low-income and part-time employees. The employee must meet the requirements listed in item 7 of the Form W-4. However, individuals cannot claim exemption from withholding if (1) their income exceeds $750 and includes more than $250 of unearned income such as interest and dividends and (2) another person can claim them as a dependent on their tax return.

STEPS • STEPS • STEPS • STEPS

PREPARING AN EMPLOYEE'S WITHHOLDING ALLOWANCE CERTIFICATE

1. Write the employee's name and address.
2. Write the employee's social security number.
3. Check the appropriate marital status block. Mr. Selby checked the married box for item 3.
4. Write the total number of withholding allowances claimed. Mr. Selby claimed four withholding allowances, one each for himself, his wife, and his two children.
5. The employee signs and dates the form.

FYI FOR YOUR INFORMATION

Each employee must have a social security number. Current law ensures that most infants who are at least one year old by the end of a tax year will have a social security number. Therefore, most employees will have received their social security number as a child. Employees without social security numbers can apply for a number at the nearest Social Security office.

FYI FOR YOUR INFORMATION

Employees are responsible for contacting their employer when the number of their dependents changes. A new W-4 form should be completed and a copy of the form sent to the Internal Revenue Service.

EMPLOYEE'S INCOME TAX WITHHOLDING—SINGLE PERSONS

SINGLE Persons—SEMIMONTHLY Payroll Period

If the wages are-		And the number of withholding allowances claimed is—										
At least	But less than	0	1	2	3	4	5	6	7	8	9	10
		The amount of income tax to be withheld is—										
$0	$115	$0	$0	$0	$0	$0	$0	$0	$0	$0	$0	$0
115	120	1	0	0	0	0	0	0	0	0	0	0
120	125	1	0	0	0	0	0	0	0	0	0	0
125	130	2	0	0	0	0	0	0	0	0	0	0
130	135	2	0	0	0	0	0	0	0	0	0	0
235	240	13	0	0	0	0	0	0	0	0	0	0
240	245	13	0	0	0	0	0	0	0	0	0	0
245	250	14	1	0	0	0	0	0	0	0	0	0
250	260	14	2	0	0	0	0	0	0	0	0	0
260	270	15	3	0	0	0	0	0	0	0	0	0
540	560	51	32	18	5	0	0	0	0	0	0	0
560	580	54	35	20	7	0	0	0	0	0	0	0
580	600	57	38	22	9	0	0	0	0	0	0	0
600	620	60	41	24	11	0	0	0	0	0	0	0
620	640	63	44	26	13	0	0	0	0	0	0	0
640	660	66	47	28	15	2	0	0	0	0	0	0
660	680	69	50	31	17	4	0	0	0	0	0	0
680	700	72	53	34	19	6	0	0	0	0	0	0
700	720	75	56	37	21	8	0	0	0	0	0	0
720	740	78	59	40	23	10	0	0	0	0	0	0
740	760	81	62	43	25	12	0	0	0	0	0	0
760	780	84	65	46	27	14	1	0	0	0	0	0
780	800	87	68	49	29	16	3	0	0	0	0	0
800	820	90	71	52	32	18	5	0	0	0	0	0
820	840	93	74	55	35	20	7	0	0	0	0	0
840	860	96	77	58	38	22	9	0	0	0	0	0
860	880	99	80	61	41	24	11	0	0	0	0	0
880	900	102	83	64	44	26	13	0	0	0	0	0
900	920	105	86	67	47	28	15	2	0	0	0	0
920	940	108	89	70	50	31	17	4	0	0	0	0
940	960	111	92	73	53	34	19	6	0	0	0	0
960	980	114	95	76	56	37	21	8	0	0	0	0
980	1,000	117	98	79	59	40	23	10	0	0	0	0
1,000	1,020	120	101	82	62	43	25	12	0	0	0	0
1,020	1,040	123	104	85	65	46	27	14	2	0	0	0
1,040	1,060	126	107	88	68	49	29	16	4	0	0	0
1,060	1,080	129	110	91	71	52	32	18	6	0	0	0
1,080	1,100	132	113	94	74	55	35	20	8	0	0	0
1,100	1,120	135	116	97	77	58	38	22	10	0	0	0
1,120	1,140	138	119	100	80	61	41	24	12	0	0	0
1,140	1,160	141	122	103	83	64	44	26	14	1	0	0
1,160	1,180	144	125	106	86	67	47	28	16	3	0	0
1,180	1,200	147	128	109	89	70	50	31	18	5	0	0
1,200	1,220	150	131	112	92	73	53	34	20	7	0	0
1,220	1,240	153	134	115	95	76	56	37	22	9	0	0
1,240	1,260	156	137	118	98	79	59	40	24	11	0	0
1,260	1,280	159	140	121	101	82	62	43	26	13	0	0
1,280	1,300	163	143	124	104	85	65	46	28	15	2	0
1,300	1,320	168	146	127	107	88	68	49	30	17	4	0
1,320	1,340	173	149	130	110	91	71	52	33	19	6	0

The amount of federal income tax withheld from each employee's total earnings is determined from withholding tables prepared by the Internal Revenue Service. These withholding tables are revised each year and are available from the Internal Revenue Service in Publication 15 (Circular E), Employer's Tax Guide. The withholding tables shown in this chapter are those available when this textbook was prepared.

Tables are prepared for various payroll periods—monthly, semimonthly, biweekly, weekly, and daily. Single persons are taxed at different levels of income than married persons. Therefore, one table is available for single persons and another table is available for married persons for each pay period.

Hobby Shack's pay period is semimonthly, so Hobby Shack uses the semimonthly withholding tables.

EMPLOYEE'S INCOME TAX WITHHOLDING—MARRIED PERSONS

MARRIED Persons—**SEMIMONTHLY** Payroll Period

1 Select the appropriate table.

If the wages are–		And the number of withholding allowances claimed is—										
At least	But less than	0	1	2	3	4	5	6	7	8	9	10
		The amount of income tax to be withheld is—										
720	**740**	40	27	14	1	0	0	0	0	0	0	0
740	**760**	42	29	16	3	0	0	0	0	0	0	0
760	**780**	44	31	18	5	0	0	0	0	0	0	0
780	**800**	46	33	20	7	0	0	0	0	0	0	0
800	**820**	48	35	22	9	0	0	0	0	0	0	0
820	**840**	50	37	24	11	0	0	0	0	0	0	0
840	**860**	52	39	26	13	0	0	0	0	0	0	0
860	**880**	54	41	28	15	2	0	0	0	0	0	0
880	**900**	56	43	30	17	4	0	0	0	0	0	0
900	**920**	58	45	32	19	6	0	0	0	0	0	0
920	**940**	60	47	34	21	8	0	0	0	0	0	0
940	**960**	63	49	36	23	10	0	0	0	0	0	0
960	**980**	66	51	38	25	12	0	0	0	0	0	0
980	**1,000**	69	53	40	27	14	1	0	0	0	0	0
1,000	**1,020**	72	55	42	29	16	3	0	0	0	0	0
1,020	**1,040**	75	57	44	31	18	5	0	0	0	0	0
1,040	**1,060**	78	59	46	33	20	7	0	0	0	0	0
1,060	**1,080**	81	61	48	35	22	9	0	0	0	0	0
1,080	**1,100**	84	64	50	37	24	11	0	0	0	0	0
1,100	**1,120**	87	67	52	39	26	13	0	0	0	0	0
1,120	**1,140**	90	70	54	41	28	15	2	0	0	0	0
1,140	**1,160**	93	73	56	43	30	17	4	0	0	0	0
1,160	**1,180**	96	76	58	45	32	19	6	0	0	0	0
1,180	**1,200**	99	79	60	47	34	21	8	0	0	0	0
1,200	**1,220**	102	82	63	49	36	23	10	0	0	0	0
1,220	**1,240**	105	85	66	51	38	25	12	0	0	0	0
1,240	**1,260**	108	88	69	53	40	27	14	1	0	0	0
1,260	**1,280**	111	91	72	55	42	29	16	3	0	0	0
1,280	**1,300**	114	94	75	57	44	31	18	5	0	0	0
1,300	**1,320**	117	97	78	59	46	33	20	7	0	0	0
1,320	**1,340**	120	100	81	62	48	35	22	9	0	0	0
1,340	**1,360**	123	103	84	65	50	37	24	11	0	0	0
1,360	**1,380**	126	106	87	68	52	39	26	13	0	0	0
1,380	**1,400**	129	109	90	71	54	41	28	15	2	0	0
1,400	**1,420**	132	112	93	74	56	43	30	17	4	0	0
1,420	**1,440**	135	115	96	77	58	45	32	19	6	0	0
1,440	**1,460**	138	118	99	80	60	47	34	21	8	0	0
1,460	**1,480**	141	121	102	83	63	49	36	23	10	0	0
1,480	**1,500**	144	124	105	86	66	51	38	25	12	0	0
1,500	**1,520**	147	127	108	89	69	53	40	27	14	1	0
1,820	**1,840**	195	175	156	137	117	98	78	59	46	33	21
1,840	**1,860**	198	178	159	140	120	101	81	62	48	35	23
1,860	**1,880**	201	181	162	143	123	104	84	65	50	37	25
1,880	**1,900**	204	184	165	146	126	107	87	68	52	39	27
1,900	**1,920**	207	187	168	149	129	110	90	71	54	41	29

2 Locate employee's total earnings.

3 Intersection of wages and number of withholding allowances column.

STEPS • STEPS • STEPS • STEPS • STEPS • STEPS • STEPS • STEPS • STEPS • STEPS •

DETERMINING AN EMPLOYEE'S INCOME TAX WITHHOLDING

1. Select the appropriate table. Married Persons—Semimonthly Payroll Period is selected to determine income tax withholding for employee Rick E. Selby.
2. Locate the employee's total earnings between the appropriate lines of the At Least and But Less Than columns. Mr. Selby's total earnings for the pay period ended December 15, 20--, are $1,137.00. Locate the line At Least $1,120.00 But Less Than $1,140.00.
3. Follow the selected wages line across to the column headed by the employee's number of withholding allowances. The amount listed at the intersection of the wages line and number of withholding allowances column is the employee's amount of income tax withholding. Mr. Selby's federal income tax withholding, with total earnings of $1,137.00 and withholding allowances of four, is $28.00 for the semimonthly pay period ended December 15, 20--.

EMPLOYEE SOCIAL SECURITY AND MEDICARE TAX

The Federal Insurance Contributions Act (FICA) provides for a federal system of old-age, survivors, disability, and hospital insurance. A federal tax paid for old-age, survivors, and disability insurance is called **social security tax**. A federal tax paid for hospital insurance is called **Medicare tax**. Each of these taxes is accounted for and reported separately.

Social security and Medicare taxes are paid by both employees and employer. Employers are required to withhold and deposit the employees' part of the taxes and pay a matching amount of these taxes.

Social security tax is calculated on employee earnings up to a maximum paid in a calendar year. The maximum amount of earnings on which a tax is calculated is called a **tax base**. Congress sets the tax base and the tax rates for social security tax. An act of Congress can change the tax base and tax rate at any time. The social security tax rate and base used in this text are 6.2% of earnings up to a maximum of $87,000.00 in each calendar year.

Between January 1 and December 15, Mr. Selby's earnings are less than the social security tax base. Therefore, Mr. Selby's social security tax deduction for the semimonthly pay period ended December 15, 20--, is calculated as shown.

Total Earnings	×	Social Security Tax Rate	=	Social Security Tax Deduction
$1,137.00	×	6.2%	=	$70.49

Medicare does not have a tax base. Therefore, Medicare tax is calculated on total employee earnings. The Medicare tax rate used in this text is 1.45% of total employee earnings.

Rick E. Selby's Medicare tax deduction for the semimonthly pay period ended December 15, 20--, is calculated as shown.

Total Earnings	×	Medicare Tax Rate	=	Medicare Tax Deduction
$1,137.00	×	1.45%	=	$16.49

FYI FOR YOUR INFORMATION

Accounting procedures are the same regardless of changes in the tax base and tax rate. The social security tax rate and the tax base shown above are assumed for all payroll calculations in this textbook.

REMEMBER When an employee's earnings exceed the tax base, no more social security tax is deducted.

terms review

payroll taxes
withholding allowance
social security tax
Medicare tax
tax base

TERMS REVIEW • TERMS

audit your understanding

1. Where does an employer get the information used to determine the amount of federal income tax to withhold from employees' earnings?
2. Employee federal income tax withholdings are based on what two factors?
3. Does the employer or employee pay social security tax and Medicare tax?

AUDIT YOUR UNDERSTANDING

work together 12-2

Determining payroll tax withholding

Information taken from a semimonthly payroll is given in the *Working Papers*. Your instructor will guide you through the following examples.

1. For each employee, determine the federal income tax that must be withheld. Use the tax withholding tables in this lesson.
2. Calculate the amount of social security tax and Medicare tax that must be withheld for each employee. Use a social security tax rate of 6.2% and a Medicare tax rate of 1.45%. None of the employees has accumulated earnings greater than the tax base.

WORK TOGETHER

on your own 12-2

Determining payroll tax withholding

Information taken from a semimonthly payroll is given in the *Working Papers*. Work this problem independently.

1. For each employee, determine the federal income tax that must be withheld. Use the tax withholding tables in this lesson.
2. Calculate the amount of social security tax and Medicare tax that must be withheld for each employee. Use a social security tax rate of 6.2% and a Medicare tax rate of 1.45%. None of the employees has accumulated earnings greater than the tax base.

ON YOUR OWN

12-3 Preparing Payroll Records

PAYROLL REGISTER

1. Pay Period Date
2. Payment Date
3. Employee Personal Data
4. Earnings
5. Federal Income Tax
6. Social Security Tax
7. Medicare Tax
8. Health Insurance
9. Other Deductions
10. Total Deductions
11. Net Pay
12. Total, Prove, and Rule
13. Check Number

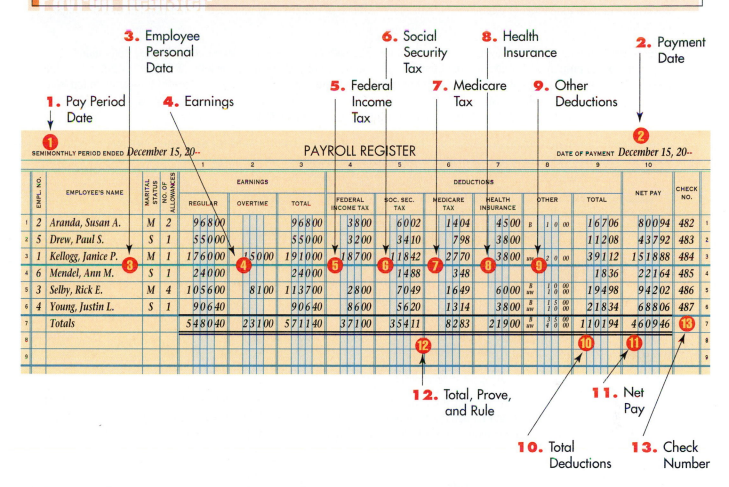

SEMIMONTHLY PERIOD ENDED *December 15, 20--* — PAYROLL REGISTER — DATE OF PAYMENT *December 15, 20--*

	EMPL. NO.	EMPLOYEE'S NAME	MARITAL STATUS	NO. OF ALLOWANCES	EARNINGS 1 REGULAR	EARNINGS 2 OVERTIME	EARNINGS 3 TOTAL	DEDUCTIONS 4 FEDERAL INCOME TAX	DEDUCTIONS 5 SOC. SEC. TAX	DEDUCTIONS 6 MEDICARE TAX	DEDUCTIONS 7 HEALTH INSURANCE	DEDUCTIONS 8 OTHER	DEDUCTIONS 9 TOTAL	10 NET PAY	CHECK NO.	
1	2	Aranda, Susan A.	M	2	968 00		968 00	38 00	60 02	14 04	45 00	B 10 00	167 06	800 94	482	1
2	5	Drew, Paul S.	S	1	550 00		550 00	32 00	34 10	7 98	38 00		112 08	437 92	483	2
3	1	Kellogg, Janice P.	M	1	1,760 00	150 00	1,910 00	187 00	118 42	27 70	38 00	uw 20 00	391 12	1,518 88	484	3
4	6	Mendel, Ann M.	S	1	240 00		240 00		14 88	3 48			18 36	221 64	485	4
5	3	Selby, Rick E.	M	4	1,056 00	81 00	1,137 00	28 00	70 49	16 49	60 00	B 10 00 uw 10 00	194 98	942 02	486	5
6	4	Young, Justin L.	S	1	906 40		906 40	86 00	56 20	13 14	38 00	B 15 00 uw 10 00	218 34	688 06	487	6
7		Totals			5,480 40	231 00	5,711 40	371 00	354 11	82 83	219 00	B 35 00 uw 40 00	1,101 94	4,609 46		7
8																8
9																9

A business form used to record payroll information is called a **payroll register**. A payroll register summarizes the payroll for one pay period and shows total earnings, payroll withholdings, and net pay of all employees. Hobby Shack prepares a separate payroll register for each semimonthly payroll.

STEPS PREPARING A PAYROLL REGISTER

1. Enter the last date of the semimonthly payroll period, *December 15, 20--*, at the top of the payroll register.
2. Enter the date of payment, *December 15, 20--*, also at the top of the payroll register.
3. For each employee, enter employee number, name, marital status, and number of allowances. This information is taken from personnel records. Entries for Rick E. Selby are on line 5 of the register.
4. Enter regular earnings, overtime earnings, and total earnings for each employee in columns 1, 2, and 3 of the payroll register. This information is taken from each employee's time card.

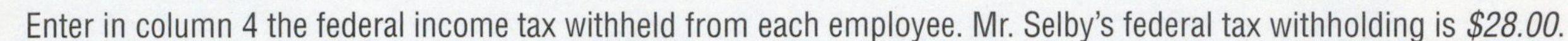

5 Enter in column 4 the federal income tax withheld from each employee. Mr. Selby's federal tax withholding is *$28.00*.

6 Enter in column 5 of the payroll register the social security tax withheld from each employee. Mr. Selby's social security tax deduction, *$70.49*, is recorded in column 5 of the payroll register. Mr. Selby's total earnings for the year have not exceeded the social security tax base, so his total earnings for the pay period are taxed.

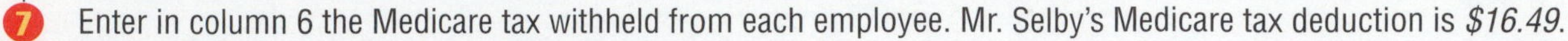

7 Enter in column 6 the Medicare tax withheld from each employee. Mr. Selby's Medicare tax deduction is *$16.49*.

8 Enter in column 7 the health insurance premium deductions. Full-time employees of Hobby Shack participate in a group health insurance plan to take advantage of lower group rates. Mr. Selby's semimonthly health insurance premium is *$60.00*. Premiums are set by the insurance company and are usually based on the employee marital status and whether coverage is for an individual or a family. Some health insurance premiums may be based on the number of individuals covered.

9 Enter in column 8 all other employee payroll deductions. The Other column is used to record voluntary deductions requested by an employee. Entries are identified by code letters. Hobby Shack uses the letter *B* to identify amounts withheld for buying U.S. Savings Bonds. *UW* is used to identify amounts withheld for employee contributions to United Way. Mr. Selby has authorized Hobby Shack to withhold *$10.00* each pay period to buy U.S. Savings Bonds for him. Mr. Selby has also authorized that *$10.00* be withheld as a contribution to the United Way.

10 After all deductions are entered in the payroll register, add all the deduction amounts for each employee and enter the totals in column 9. Mr. Selby's total deductions, *$194.98*, are calculated as shown.

Federal Income Tax	+	Social Security Tax	+	Medicare Tax	+	Health Insurance	+	Other	=	Total Deductions
$28.00	+	$70.49	+	$16.49	+	$60.00	+	$20.00	=	$194.98

11 Determine the net pay for each employee. The total earnings paid to an employee after payroll taxes and other deductions is called **net pay**. Subtract the total deductions, column 9, from total earnings, column 3, to determine net pay. Enter net pay in column 10. Mr. Selby's net pay, *$942.02*, is calculated as shown.

Total Earnings	−	Total Deductions	=	Net Pay
$1,137.00	−	$194.98	=	$942.02

12 Total, prove, and rule the payroll register. Total each amount column. Subtract the Total Deductions column from the Total Earnings column. The result should equal the total of the Net Pay column. If the totals do not agree, the errors must be found and corrected. Proving the accuracy of Hobby Shack's payroll register for the pay period ended December 15, 20--, is shown.

Total Earnings	−	Total Deductions	=	Net Pay
$5,711.40	−	$1,101.94	=	$4,609.46

The net pay, *$4,609.46*, is the same as the total of the Net Pay column. The payroll register is proved. After the payroll register is proved, rule double lines below all amount column totals to show the totals have been verified as correct.

13 Payroll checks are written after payroll calculations are verified and a manager approves the payroll. Write the payroll check numbers in the Check No. column.

EMPLOYEE EARNINGS RECORDS

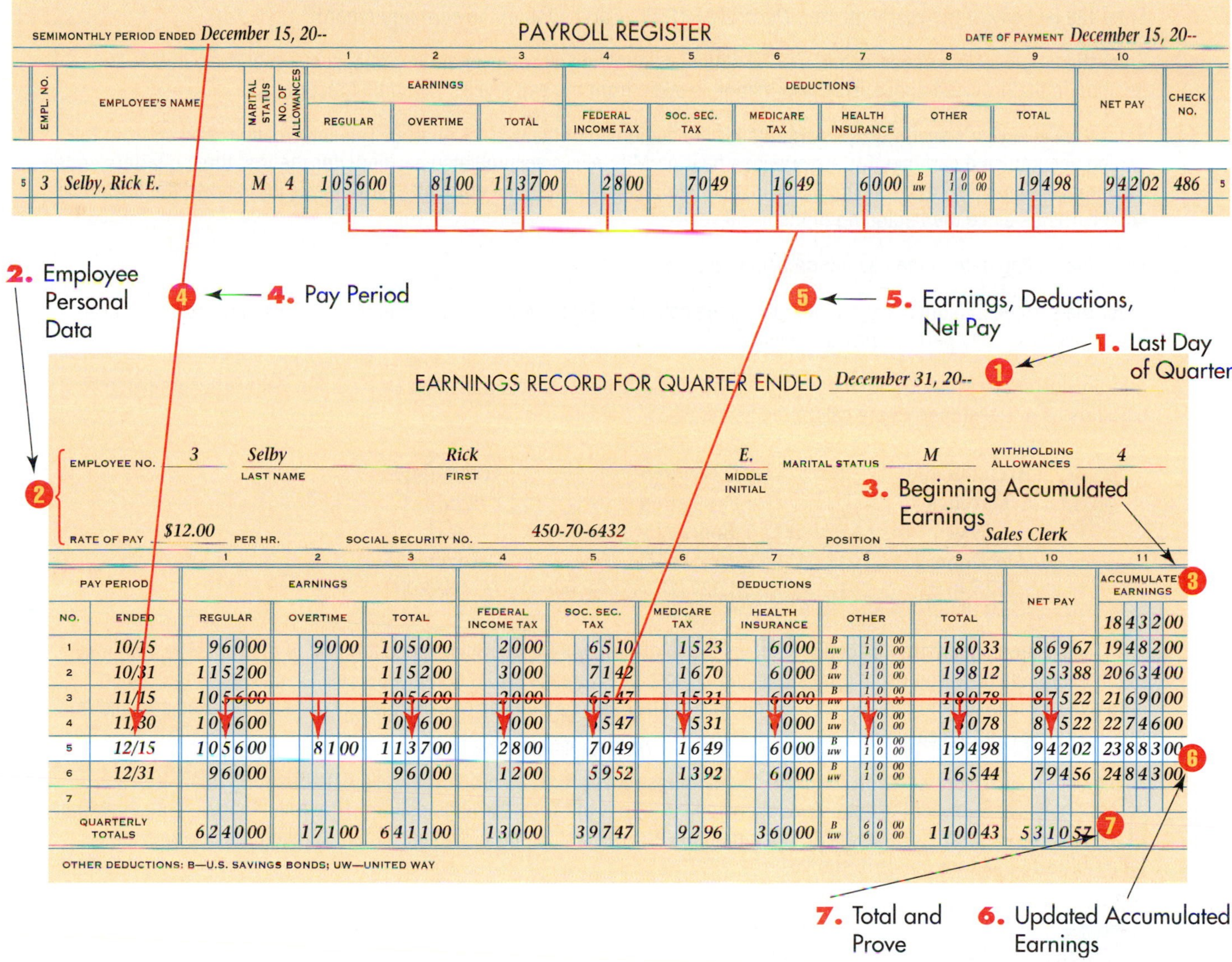

SEMIMONTHLY PERIOD ENDED *December 15, 20--* PAYROLL REGISTER DATE OF PAYMENT *December 15, 20--*

	EMPL. NO.	EMPLOYEE'S NAME	MARITAL STATUS	NO. OF ALLOWANCES	1 EARNINGS REGULAR	2 EARNINGS OVERTIME	3 EARNINGS TOTAL	4 DEDUCTIONS FEDERAL INCOME TAX	5 SOC. SEC. TAX	6 MEDICARE TAX	7 HEALTH INSURANCE	8 OTHER	9 TOTAL	10 NET PAY	CHECK NO.	
5	3	*Selby, Rick E.*	M	4	1056 00	81 00	1137 00	28 00	70 49	16 49	60 00	B 10 00 UW 10 00	194 98	942 02	486	5

EARNINGS RECORD FOR QUARTER ENDED *December 31, 20--*

EMPLOYEE NO. *3* LAST NAME *Selby* FIRST *Rick* MIDDLE INITIAL *E.* MARITAL STATUS *M* WITHHOLDING ALLOWANCES *4*

RATE OF PAY *$12.00* PER HR. SOCIAL SECURITY NO. *450-70-6432* POSITION *Sales Clerk*

PAY PERIOD NO.	PAY PERIOD ENDED	1 EARNINGS REGULAR	2 EARNINGS OVERTIME	3 EARNINGS TOTAL	4 DEDUCTIONS FEDERAL INCOME TAX	5 SOC. SEC. TAX	6 MEDICARE TAX	7 HEALTH INSURANCE	8 OTHER	9 TOTAL	10 NET PAY	11 ACCUMULATED EARNINGS
												18432 00
1	10/15	960 00	90 00	1050 00	20 00	65 10	15 23	60 00	B 10 00 UW 10 00	180 33	869 67	19482 00
2	10/31	1152 00		1152 00	30 00	71 42	16 70	60 00	B 10 00 UW 10 00	198 12	953 88	20634 00
3	11/15	1056 00		1056 00	20 00	65 47	15 31	60 00	B 10 00 UW 10 00	180 78	875 22	21690 00
4	11/30	10[illegible]6 00		10[illegible]6 00	[illegible]0 00	[illegible]5 47	[illegible]5 31	[illegible]0 00	B [illegible]0 00 UW [illegible]0 00	1[illegible]0 78	8[illegible]5 22	22746 00
5	12/15	1056 00	81 00	1137 00	28 00	70 49	16 49	60 00	B 10 00 UW 10 00	194 98	942 02	23883 00
6	12/31	960 00		960 00	12 00	59 52	13 92	60 00	B 10 00 UW 10 00	165 44	794 56	24843 00
7												
QUARTERLY TOTALS		6240 00	171 00	6411 00	130 00	397 47	92 96	360 00	B 60 00 UW 60 00	1100 43	5310 57	

OTHER DEDUCTIONS: B—U.S. SAVINGS BONDS; UW—UNITED WAY

A business must send a quarterly report to federal and state governments showing employee taxable earnings and taxes withheld from employee earnings. Detailed information about each employee's earnings is summarized in a single record for each employee. A business form used to record details affecting payments made to an employee is called an **employee earnings record**. An employee's earnings and deductions for each pay period are summarized on one line of the employee earnings record. A new earnings record is prepared for each employee each quarter. Rick E. Selby's earnings record for the fourth quarter is shown.

FYI FOR YOUR INFORMATION

The federal income tax withholding tables on pages 347–348 contain a column for 0 dependents. How can an employee have 0 dependents if the employee is a dependent? Some employees claim fewer dependents than they are allowed—even as low as zero—to increase the amount of tax withheld. An employee who has other taxable income, such as interest and dividends, can use payroll withholding to pay the additional income taxes owed on this income. As a result, the employee avoids having a large income tax payment when the tax return is filed.

STEPS • STEPS • STEPS • STEPS • STEPS • STEPS • STEPS • STEPS • STEPS • STEPS •

STEPS PREPARING AN EMPLOYEE EARNINGS RECORD

1. Enter the last day of the yearly quarter, *December 31, 20--*, at the top of the earnings record.
2. Enter the employee's number, name, marital status, withholding allowances, hourly rate, social security number, and position in the provided space. This information is taken from the employee's personnel records.
3. Enter the fiscal year's accumulated earnings for the beginning of the current quarter. This information is taken from the ending accumulated earnings for the previous quarter. Mr. Selby's accumulated earnings for the first three quarters ended September 30 are *$18,432.00*. The Accumulated Earnings column of the employee earnings record shows the accumulated earnings since the beginning of the fiscal year.
4. Enter the ending date of the pay period being recorded.
5. Enter the earnings, deductions, and net pay in the columns of the employee earnings record. This information is taken from the current pay period's payroll register.
6. Add the current pay period's total earnings to the previous period's accumulated earnings. Mr. Selby's accumulated earnings as of December 15 are calculated as shown.

Accumulated Earnings as of December 1	+	Total Earnings for Pay Period Ended December 15	=	Accumulated Earnings as of December 15
$22,746.00	+	$1,137.00	=	$23,883.00

The Accumulated Earnings column shows the total earnings for Mr. Selby since the first of the year. The amounts in the Accumulated Earnings column supply an up-to-date reference for an employee's year-to-date earnings. When employee earnings reach the tax base, certain payroll taxes do not apply. For example, social security taxes are paid only on the first $87,000 of earnings.

7. At the end of each quarter, total and prove the earnings record for each employee. Calculate quarterly totals for each amount column. Subtract the Total Deductions column from the Total Earnings column. The result should equal the total of the Net Pay column. If the totals do not agree, the errors must be found and corrected. Proving the accuracy of Mr. Selby's fourth quarterly totals is shown.

Total Earnings	–	Total Deductions	=	Net Pay
$6,411.00	–	$1,100.43	=	$5,310.57

The net pay, *$5,310.57*, is compared to the total of the Net Pay column. The earnings record is proved because these amounts are equal. These totals are needed to prepare required government reports.

REMEMBER Total earnings, not net pay, are added to the previous accumulated earnings amount on the earnings record. Total earnings is the amount compared to the tax base to determine whether social security taxes should be withheld.

Xtra! Study Tools
accountingxtra.swlearning.com

terms review

payroll register
net pay
employee earnings record

audit your understanding

1. What does the payroll register summarize?
2. How is net pay calculated?
3. Why do companies complete employee earnings records?

work together 12-3

Preparing payroll records

Selected payroll data for Antique Shop are provided in a payroll register in the *Working Papers.* Your instructor will guide you through the following examples.

1. Complete the payroll register entries for Judy Hensley and Mike McCune for the semimonthly pay period ended July 15, 20--. Use the tax withholding tables shown in Lesson 12-2. Use tax rates of 6.2% for social security tax and 1.45% for Medicare tax. Neither employee has reached the tax base. For each employee, withhold $60.00 for health insurance and $15.00 for U.S. Savings bonds, per pay period.
2. Total all the amount columns of the payroll register. Prove the payroll register.
3. Prepare a quarterly earnings record for Ms. Hensley for the quarter ended September 30, 20--, and enter the July 15 payroll information. Ms. Hensley's employee number is 5; rate of pay is $13.00; social security number is 543-69-0123; position is sales clerk. Accumulated earnings at the end of the second quarter are $13,520.00. Save your work to complete Work Together 12-4.

on your own 12-3

Preparing payroll records

Selected payroll data for Prosser Company are provided in a payroll register in the *Working Papers.* Work this problem independently.

1. Complete the payroll register entries for Allen P. Best and Tammy S. Edwards for the semimonthly pay period ended July 15, 20--. Use the tax withholding tables shown in Lesson 12-2. Use tax rates of 6.2% for social security tax and 1.45% for Medicare tax. For each employee, withhold $60.00 for health insurance and $10.00 for U.S. Savings Bonds per pay period. For Ms. Edwards, also withhold $20.00 for United Way per pay period.
2. Total all the amount columns of the payroll register. Prove the payroll register.
3. Prepare a quarterly earnings record for Mr. Best for the quarter ended September 30, 20--, and enter the July 15 payroll information. Mr. Best's employee number is 4; rate of pay is $12.25; social security number is 301-69-1427; position is sales clerk. Accumulated earnings at the end of the second quarter are $28,692.00. Save your work to complete On Your Own 12-4.

LESSON • LESSON • LESSON • LESSON • LESSON • LESSON

12-4 Preparing Payroll Checks

PAYROLL BANK ACCOUNT

1. Prepare the check stub.

2. Prepare the check.

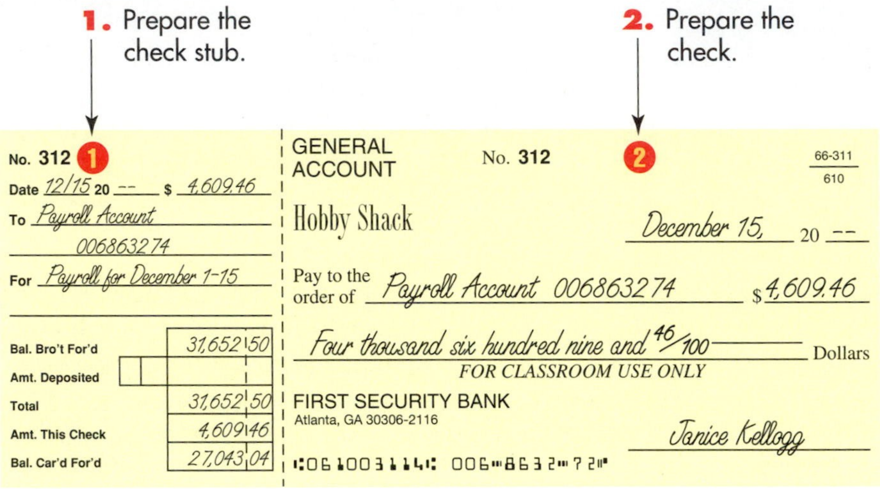

No. 312 (1)
Date 12/15 20 -- $ 4,609.46
To Payroll Account
006863274
For Payroll for December 1-15

Bal. Bro't For'd	31,652.50
Amt. Deposited	
Total	31,652.50
Amt. This Check	4,609.46
Bal. Car'd For'd	27,043.04

GENERAL ACCOUNT
No. 312 (2)
66-311/610
Hobby Shack
December 15, 20 --
Pay to the order of Payroll Account 006863274 $ 4,609.46
Four thousand six hundred nine and 46/100 Dollars
FOR CLASSROOM USE ONLY
FIRST SECURITY BANK
Atlanta, GA 30306-2116
Janice Kellogg
⑆061003114⑆ 006⑈8632⑈72⑈

Hobby Shack pays its employees with checks written on a special payroll checking account. A check for the total net pay is written on Hobby Shack's general checking account. The check is deposited in the payroll checking account.

A separate checking account for payroll checks helps to protect and control payroll payments. The exact amount needed to pay the payroll is deposited in the special payroll checking account. If amounts on checks are altered or unauthorized payroll checks are prepared, the amount in the special payroll account would be insufficient to cover all the checks. Thus, the bank and Hobby Shack would be alerted quickly to an unauthorized payroll check. Also, since payroll checks are drawn on the separate account, any balance in this account will correspond to the sum of outstanding payroll checks.

STEPS • STEPS • STEPS • STEPS • STEPS • STEPS • STEPS • STEPS • STEPS • STEPS

PREPARING A CHECK FOR TOTAL NET PAY

1. Prepare the check stub. The date of the check is *12/15*. The amount, *$4,609.46*, is the total of the Net Pay column of the payroll register. The check is payable to *Payroll Account 006863274*, Hobby Shack's special payroll checking account. The payment is for the payroll period from December 1 to 15. Calculate and record the new general checking account balance.

2. Prepare the check from the information on the check stub. Hobby Shack's check is drawn on the company's general account and is signed by Janice Kellogg.

REMEMBER Using a separate checking account for payroll checks provides internal control and helps to prevent fraud.

EMPLOYEE'S PAYROLL CHECK

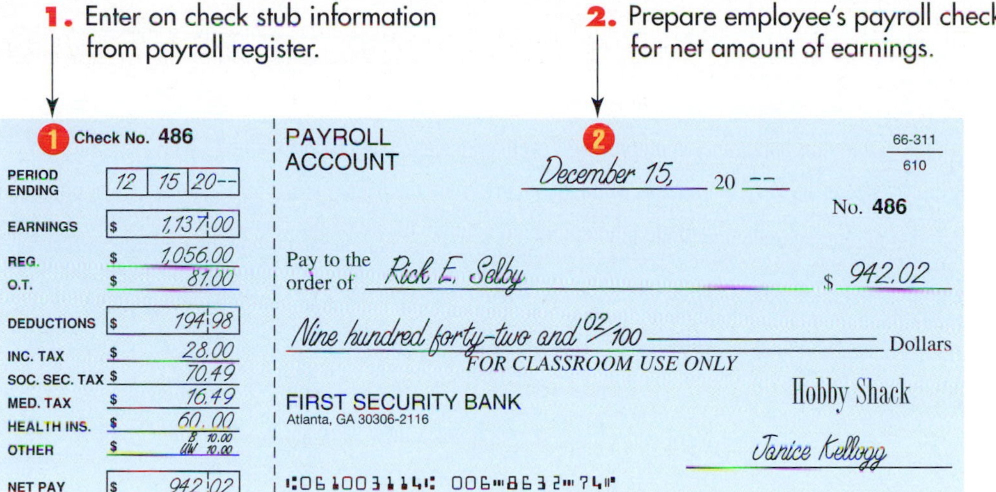

1. Enter on check stub information from payroll register.

2. Prepare employee's payroll check for net amount of earnings.

1 Check No. **486**

PERIOD ENDING	12 | 15 | 20--
EARNINGS	$ 1,137.00
REG.	$ 1,056.00
O.T.	$ 81.00
DEDUCTIONS	$ 194.98
INC. TAX	$ 28.00
SOC. SEC. TAX	$ 70.49
MED. TAX	$ 16.49
HEALTH INS.	$ 60.00
OTHER	$ B 10.00 / UW 10.00
NET PAY	$ 942.02

PAYROLL ACCOUNT

2 December 15, 20 --

66-311 / 610

No. **486**

Pay to the order of Rick E. Selby $ 942.02

Nine hundred forty-two and 02/100 ——— Dollars

FOR CLASSROOM USE ONLY

FIRST SECURITY BANK
Atlanta, GA 30306-2116

Hobby Shack

Janice Kellogg

⑆0610031114⑆ 006⑈8632⑈74⑈

The information used to prepare payroll checks is taken from a payroll register. A special payroll check form is used that has a detachable stub for recording earnings and amounts deducted. Employees keep the stubs for a record of deductions and cash received.

STEPS PREPARING AN EMPLOYEE'S PAYROLL CHECK

1. Prepare the check stub of each employee's payroll check. Enter information from the payroll register.
2. Prepare each employee's payroll check payable for the amount of net pay for the pay period. Rick E. Selby's net pay for the pay period ended December 15, 20--, is *$942.02*.

ELECTRONIC FUNDS TRANSFER

A computerized cash payments system that transfers funds without the use of checks, currency, or other paper documents is known as electronic funds transfer (EFT). Some businesses deposit employee net pay directly to each employee bank account by using EFT. When EFT is used, the bank's computer deducts the amount of net pay from the business's bank account and adds the amount to each employee bank account. The payroll must still be calculated, but individual checks are not written and do not have to be distributed. Under this system, each employee receives a statement of earnings and deductions similar to the detachable stub on a payroll check.

©GETTY IMAGES/PHOTODISC

audit your understanding

1. Why does Hobby Shack have a separate checking account for payroll checks?
2. What is the source of the information that is recorded on each employee's payroll check stub?
3. How do payroll procedures differ for employees who request that their pay be deposited through electronic funds transfer?

AUDIT YOUR UNDERSTANDING

work together 12-4

Preparing payroll checks

Use the payroll register from Work Together 12-3. In the *Working Papers* are three blank checks: one General Account check and two Payroll Account checks. Your instructor will guide you through the following examples.

1. Prepare Antique Shop's General Account check for the pay period ended July 15, 20--. The payment date is July 15. Balance brought forward from the previous check is $16,542.00. The Payroll Account number is 0639583. Sign your name as the manager of Antique Shop.
2. For the pay period ended July 15, 20--, prepare payroll checks for Judy Hensley and Mike McCune. The payment date is July 15. Sign your name as the manager of Antique Shop. Record the two payroll check numbers in the payroll register.

WORK TOGETHER • WORK

on your own 12-4

Preparing payroll checks

Use the payroll register from On Your Own 12-3. In the *Working Papers* are three blank checks: one General Account check and two Payroll Account checks. Work this problem independently.

1. Prepare Prosser Company's General Account check for the pay period ended July 15, 20--. The payment date is July 15. Balance carried forward from the previous check is $12,421.90. The Payroll Account number is 146-7219-6. Sign your name as the manager of Prosser Company.
2. For the pay period ended July 15, 20--, prepare payroll checks for Allen P. Best and Tammy S. Edwards. The payment date is July 15. Sign your name as the manager of Prosser Company. Record the two payroll checks in the payroll register.

ON YOUR OWN • ON YOUR OWN

After completing this chapter, you can

1. Define important accounting terms related to payroll records.
2. Identify accounting practices related to payroll records.
3. Complete a payroll time card.
4. Calculate payroll taxes.
5. Complete a payroll register and an employee earnings record.
6. Prepare payroll checks.

Explore Accounting

Employee vs. Independent Contractor

A business sometimes contracts with individuals to perform specified services for the business. Determining whether such an individual is an employee or a self-employed independent contractor is an important issue.

If the person is found to be an employee, the employer must withhold and submit employee income tax, social security tax, and Medicare tax to the Internal Revenue Service (IRS). The employer must pay an equal amount of social security and Medicare tax. Also, the employer will pay unemployment taxes (discussed in Chapter 13) and be subject to various employer reporting requirements.

A person who is found to be a self-employed independent contractor must pay an amount of social security and Medicare tax that is equivalent to both the employer and employee taxes.

If an employer incorrectly treats an employee as a self-employed independent contractor, the penalties can be severe. Therefore, it is important to a business to make an accurate determination of the status of all individuals performing work for the business. The IRS has provided guidelines to help businesses make the distinction. Every individual who performs services subject to the will and control of an employer both as to what shall be done and how it shall be done is considered an employee for withholding purposes. The major determining factor is whether the employer has the legal right to control both the method and result of the services. If the business has the right to control only the result of the service performed and not the means and methods of accomplishing the result, the individual is probably a self-employed independent contractor.

Research: Review federal tax publications or interview local businesses on the issues below. Then prepare a written or oral report to present to your class. (1) Why is it important to determine an individual's status? What is at stake for the individual, the employer, and the IRS? (2) What are the advantages and disadvantages of determining an individual to be an employee or independent contractor—to the individual? to the employer? to the IRS?

12-1 APPLICATION PROBLEM

Preparing payroll time cards

Employee time cards are given in the *Working Papers*.

Instructions:

1. Calculate the regular, overtime, and total hours worked by each employee. Any hours over the regular 8-hour day are considered overtime. Record the hours on the time cards.
2. Determine the regular, overtime, and total earnings for each employee. The overtime rate is 1½ times the regular rate. Complete the time cards.

12-2 APPLICATION PROBLEM

Determining payroll tax withholding

Information taken from the semimonthly payroll register is given in the *Working Papers*.

Instructions:

1. Determine the federal income tax that must be withheld for each of the eight employees. Use the tax withholding tables shown in Lesson 12-2.
2. Calculate the amount of social security tax and Medicare tax that must be withheld for each employee using 6.2% and 1.45% tax rates, respectively. None of the eight employees has accumulated earnings greater than the tax base.

12-3 APPLICATION PROBLEM 

Preparing a payroll register

The information for the semimonthly pay period October 1–15 of the current year is given in the *Working Papers*.

Instructions:

Complete a payroll register for Perez Company. The date of payment is October 15. Use the tax withholding tables shown in Lesson 12-2 for the income tax withholding for each employee. Calculate social security and Medicare taxes withholding using 6.2% and 1.45% tax rates, respectively. None of the employees has accumulated earnings greater than the social security tax base.

12-4 APPLICATION PROBLEM 

Preparing an employee earnings record

Grady R. Hurley's earnings for the six semimonthly pay periods in July, August, and September of the current year are given in the *Working Papers*. Deductions and net pay have been completed for July and August.

The following additional data about Grady R. Hurley are needed to complete the employee earnings record.

1. Employee number: 28
2. Marital status: married
3. Withholding allowances: 2
4. Rate of pay: regular, $15.00
5. Social security number: 462-81-5823
6. Position: service manager

7. Accumulated earnings for the end of second quarter: $15,750.00
8. Deductions from total earnings:
   a. Health insurance: $60.00 each semimonthly pay period
   b. U.S. Savings Bonds: $20.00 each semimonthly pay period
   c. Federal income tax: determined each pay period by using the withholding tables in Lesson 12-2.
   d. Social security taxes: 6.2% of total earnings each pay period
   e. Medicare taxes: 1.45% of total earnings each pay period

Instructions:

1. Calculate and record the accumulated earnings for the July and August pay periods.
2. Complete the earnings record for the pay periods ended September 15 and September 30.
3. Total all amount columns on the earnings record.
4. Verify the accuracy of the completed employee earnings record. The Quarter Total for Regular and Overtime Earnings should equal the Quarter Total for Net Pay plus Total Deductions. The Quarter Total for Total Earnings should equal the end-of-quarter Accumulated Earnings minus the beginning-of-quarter Accumulated Earnings.

12-5 APPLICATION PROBLEM  

Preparing payroll checks

Royal Appliances' net payroll for the semimonthly pay period ended May 15, 20--, is $7,498.80. Payroll checks are prepared May 15, 20--. Blank checks are provided in the *Working Papers*.

Instructions:

1. Prepare a General Account check for the total amount of the net pay. Make the check payable to Payroll Account 018-65-4237, and sign your name as manager of Royal Appliances. The beginning check stub balance is $10,138.95.
2. Prepare payroll checks for two employees of Royal Appliances. Payroll information for the two employees is as follows. Sign your name as a manager of Royal Appliances.
   a. Wanda M. Curtis

Check No. 823	
Regular Earnings	$740.00
Overtime Earnings	40.00
Deductions:	
Federal Income Tax	$33.00
Social Security Tax	48.36
Medicare Tax	11.31
Health Insurance	35.00

   b. Kevin R. Hayes

Check No. 827	
Regular Earnings	$920.00
Overtime Earnings	30.00
Deductions:	
Federal Income Tax	$23.00
Social Security	58.90
Medicare Tax	13.78
Health Insurance	60.00
Savings Bond	20.00

12-6 MASTERY PROBLEM

QUICKBOOKS

Preparing a semimonthly payroll

The following information for Arrow Company is for the semimonthly pay period August 16–31 of the current year. Forms are given in the *Working Papers*.

EMPL. NO.	EMPLOYEE'S NAME	MARITAL STATUS	NO. OF ALLOWANCES	EARNINGS		DEDUCTIONS	
				REGULAR	OVERTIME	HEALTH INSURANCE	SAVINGS BONDS
5	*Acron, Peter C.*	M	3	1,126.40	115.20	60.00	10.00
7	*Barenis, Mary P.*	S	1	1,155.00		25.00	
6	*Epps, John P.*	M	2	792.00		40.00	10.00
1	*Goforth, Alice A.*	S	2	1,135.20	77.40	40.00	
8	*Hiett, Franklin B.*	M	3	1,188.00		60.00	10.00
9	*Land, Keith*	S	1	954.60		25.00	10.00
2	*Malone, Lillie L.*	S	1	1,083.60		25.00	
4	*Rivers, Linda K.*	M	2	1,091.20	93.00	40.00	
10	*Sowell, Jacob S.*	M	2	1,161.60		40.00	10.00
3	*Vole, Ryan V.*	M	5	1,075.00		80.00	10.00

Instructions:

1. Prepare a payroll register. The date of payment is August 31. Use the income tax withholding tables shown in Lesson 12-2 to find the income tax withholding for each employee. Calculate social security and Medicare tax withholdings using 6.2% and 1.45% tax rates, respectively. None of the employees has accumulated earnings greater than the social security tax base.
2. Prepare a check for the total amount of the net pay. Make the check payable to Payroll Account 59-721-65, and sign your name as the manager of Arrow Company. The beginning check stub balance is $16,216.90.
3. Prepare payroll checks for Peter C. Acron, Check No. 1692, and Franklin B. Hiett, Check No. 1696. Sign your name as the manager of Arrow Company. Record the two payroll check numbers in the payroll register.

12-7 CHALLENGE PROBLEM

Calculating piecework wages

Production workers in factories are frequently paid on the basis of the number of units they produce. This payroll method is referred to as the *piecework incentive wage plan*. Most piecework incentive wage plans include a guaranteed hourly rate to employees regardless of the number of units they produce. This guaranteed hourly rate is referred to as the *base rate*.

Time and motion study engineers usually determine the standard time required for producing a single unit. Assume, for example, that time studies determine that one-third of an hour is the standard time required to produce a unit. Then the standard rate for an 8-hour day would be 24 units (8 hours divided by ⅓ hour = 24 units per day). If a worker's daily base pay is $96.00, the incentive rate per unit is $4.00 ($96.00 divided by 24 units × $4.00 per unit). Therefore, the worker who produces 24 or fewer units per day is paid the base pay, $96.00. However, each worker is paid an additional $4.00 for each unit over 24 produced each day.

Draker Furniture Company has eight employees in production departments that are paid on a piecework incentive wage plan. The following standard and incentive wage rates are listed by department.

Department	Standard Production per Employee	Incentive Rate per Unit
Cutting	32 units per day	$3.50
Assembly	20 units per day	$5.75
Finishing	45 units per day	$2.00

A payroll register is given in the *Working Papers*. Each employee worked eight hours a day during the semimonthly pay period, May 1–15. Payroll records for May 1–15 are summarized in the following table.

Employee No.	Employee Name	Marital Status	No. of Allow-ances	Guaranteed Daily Rate	Units Produced per Day, Pay Period May 1–15: 2	3	4	5	6	9	10	11	12	13
	Cutting Department													
C3	Bell, Julie M.	M	4	$112.00	33	30	28	32	32	32	32	33	35	33
C6	Hairston, Gary P.	M	2	$112.00	29	35	29	32	31	33	32	33	30	30
C9	Reeves, John M.	S	1	$112.00	31	30	35	34	34	31	35	28	31	32
	Assembly Department													
A2	Bullock, Amy C.	S	2	$115.00	22	20	20	20	22	22	22	22	23	20
A6	Green, Steven P.	S	1	$115.00	20	23	23	20	22	21	20	20	20	20
A9	Prine, Jacob R.	M	4	$115.00	23	22	21	22	22	21	22	22	20	23
	Finishing Department													
F5	Gerez, Dave A.	M	2	$90.00	39	47	38	47	43	41	40	41	39	46
F2	Kyle, Ryan G.	S	1	$90.00	41	43	47	38	42	39	43	39	43	39

Instructions:

Prepare a payroll register. The earnings column Incentive is used instead of Overtime. The date of payment is May 15. Use the income tax withholding tables shown in Lesson 12-2. Calculate the employee social security and Medicare tax withholdings using 6.2% and 1.45% tax rates, respectively. None of the employees has health insurance or other deductions. None of the employees has accumulated earnings greater than the social security tax base.

applied communication

The employees of Kaden Company currently use time cards and a time clock to record their arrival and departure times. Management plans to replace the time clock with a device that reads a magnetic strip on the back of each employee's name badge. The badge is scanned by a reader in the same manner that credit cards are scanned. Because the badge reader is connected to a computer, the information is recorded directly to a computer file. Thus, the new system will enable management to make daily analyses of employee hours and productivity. This information should allow managers to make more timely decisions and increase profits.

Instructions: Assume you work in the payroll department for Kaden Company. Write a memo to the employees informing them of the new system. Because some employees may not be happy with this new system, be sure to include reasons why the policy is being implemented.

case for critical thinking

Vadillo Lumber currently requires each employee to inform the accounting clerk of the total hours worked each day during the pay period. The total number of hours worked by all employees has been steadily increasing during the prior pay periods. The new store manager has suggested that a time clock be installed to record arrival and departure times. The accounting clerk believes the current system is satisfactory. Do you agree with the new manager or the accounting clerk? Explain your response.

SCANS workplace competency

Personal Qualities: Self-Esteem

Concept: A person with good self-esteem believes in his or her own self-worth and maintains a positive view of self. Employers may not specifically mention self-esteem as a desirable quality, but the positive attitude of a person who has self-esteem is an asset in the workplace.

Application: Self-esteem begins with knowledge of one's own skills and abilities. Make a list of the skills and abilities you would bring to the job market right now. Make a second list of skills and abilities you would like to develop because you think they are important to the job market.

SCANS WORKPLACE • SCANS

graphing workshop

Distribution of Gross Wages

The chart depicts data from the payroll register of Alectra Corporation. Analyze the graph to answer the following questions.

1. What was the largest payroll deduction?
2. What percent of employees' wages are withheld for taxes?
3. What amount is represented by the entire pie graph?

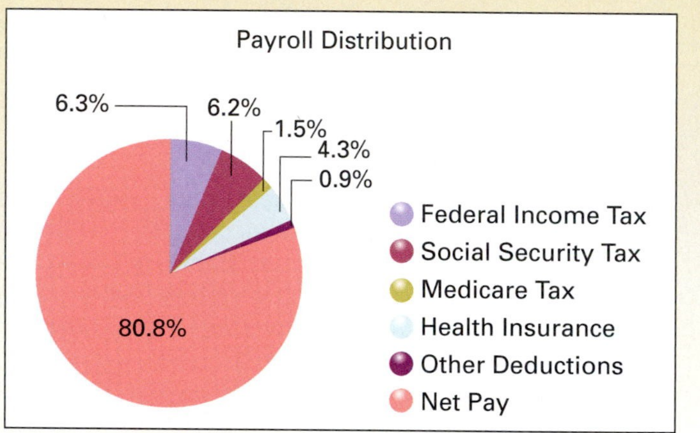

GRAPHING WORKSHOP

analyzing Best Buy's financial statements

Annual reports contain a report by management designed to inform potential investors and business partners about how the financial statements were prepared. The report describes, in detail, accounting and management policies that are followed to ensure that the amounts on the financial statements can be relied upon for making business decisions.

Instructions: Use the Report of Best Buy Management on Appendix B page B-17 to answer the following questions.

1. Who is responsible for the preparation of the Best Buy's financial statements?
2. What is the system of internal control designed to do?
3. What do internal auditors do?
4. What does the Audit Committee oversee?
5. What kind of assurance can the internal control system provide with respect to financial statement preparation?

ANALYZING BEST BUY'S FINANCIAL STATEMENTS

Automated Accounting

Automated Payroll Accounting

In an automated payroll system, the computer is used to maintain the employee database, record payroll transactions at the end of each pay period, calculate withholding taxes, and create all the related journal entries. The employee database identifies each employee by employee number. Other data required for each employee include the employee's name, social security number, marital status, number of withholding allowances, pay rate, and voluntary deductions. Employee accounts may be added, changed, or deleted from the accounting system.

Maintaining Employees

To perform employee maintenance in *Automated Accounting 8.0* or higher:

1. Click the Accounts toolbar button.
2. Click the Employees tab.
3. To add a new employee:
   - Enter the sequential employee number.
   - Enter information in all the data fields, including name, address, social security number, and marital status.
   - Press Enter or click Add Employee.
4. To change or delete data for a current employee:
   - Select the employee by clicking the grid cell containing the data you wish to change.
   - Enter the correct data.
   - Click the Change Employee button, or click the Delete button to remove the employee from the database. (Employees with cumulative earnings may be deleted only after the end of the calendar year.)

Entering Payroll Transactions

1. Click the Other toolbar button.
2. Click the Payroll tab.
3. Enter the date of the check.
4. Select the employee from the employee drop-down list.
5. Verify that the check number displayed is correct, or key the correct number.
6. For salaried employees, the salary amount will be automatically displayed. For hourly employees, enter the regular and overtime hours worked during the current payroll period.
7. Click the Calculate Taxes button to direct the software to calculate the employee taxes.
8. Enter the employee's voluntary deductions.
9. Click OK to generate and display the payroll check.
10. Click the Close button to dismiss the check and continue, or click Print to print the check.

AUTOMATING MASTERY PROBLEM 12-6: Preparing a semimonthly payroll

Instructions:

1. Load *Automated Accounting 8.0* or higher software.
2. Select database F12-6 from the appropriate directory/folder.
3. Select File from the menu bar and choose the Save As menu command. Key the path to the drive and directory that contains your data files. Save the data file with a filename of F12-6 XXX XXX (where the X's are your first and last name).
4. Access Problem Instructions through the Browser tool. Read the Problem Instructions screen.
5. Key the data listed in Mastery Problem 12-6. Note that there are some additional data in the problem instructions accessed through the Browser tool.
6. Save your file and exit the Automated Accounting software.

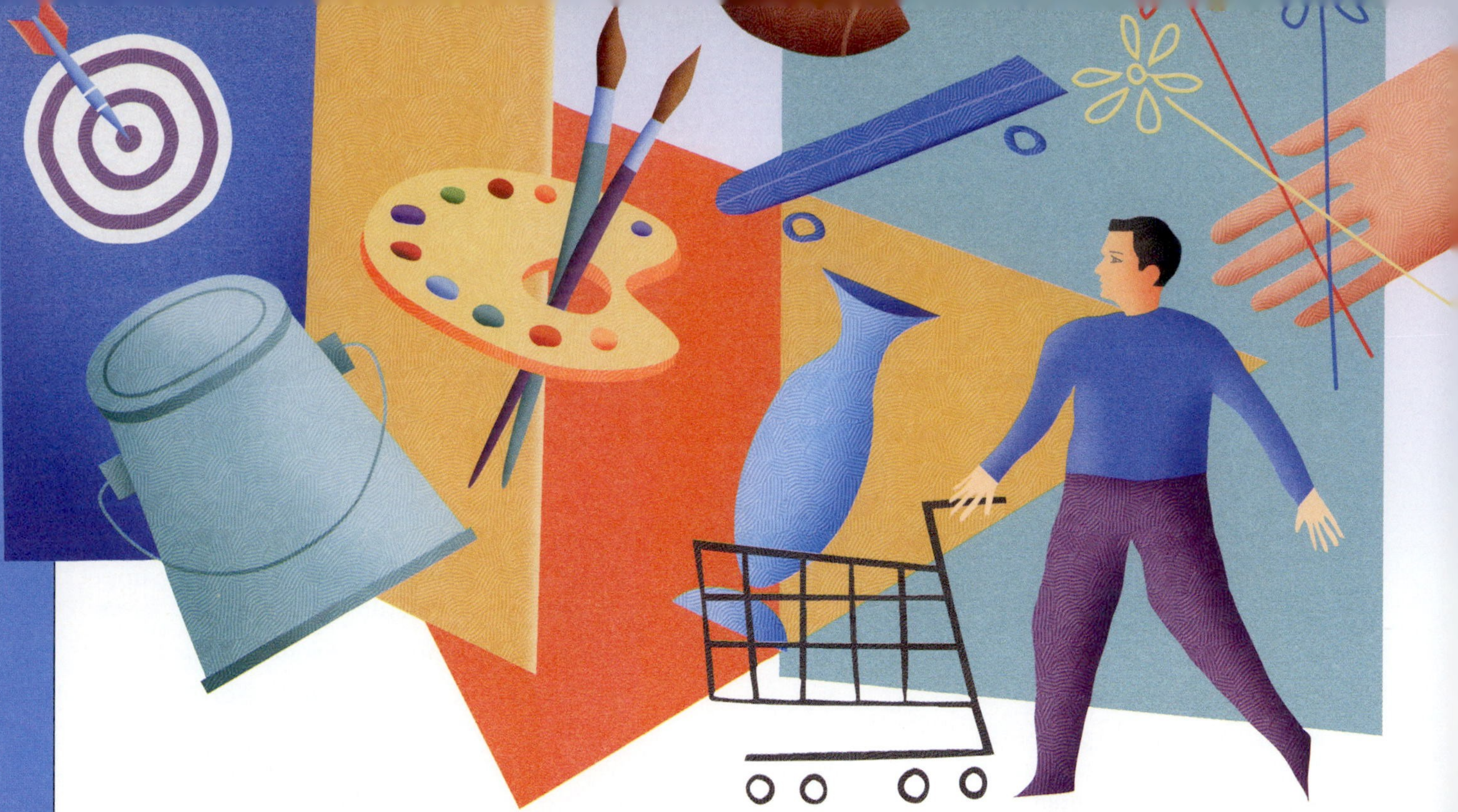

CHAPTER 13 Payroll Accounting, Taxes, and Reports

OBJECTIVES & TERMS

After studying Chapter 13, you will be able to:

1. Define accounting terms related to payroll accounting, taxes, and reports.
2. Identify accounting concepts and practices related to payroll accounting, taxes, and reports.
3. Analyze payroll transactions and record a payroll.
4. Record employer payroll taxes.
5. Prepare selected payroll tax reports.
6. Pay and record withholding and payroll taxes.

- federal unemployment tax
- state unemployment tax
- lookback period

Point Your Browser
accountingxtra.swlearning.com

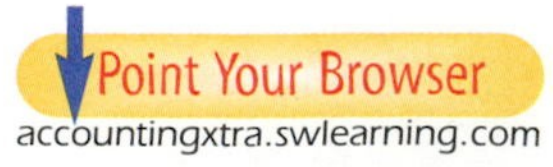

accounting in the real world

Intel

©DONN YOUNG/BLOOMBERG NEWS/LANDOV

EMPLOYEE BENEFITS AT INTEL

Innovative thinking comes from creative minds. Technology companies must continually develop new products and applications for those products in order to stay competitive in today's rapidly changing technology marketplace. To maintain a creative workforce, companies must create a comfortable work environment that encourages and rewards creativity.

An innovator in the design and production of computer processors, Intel is equally innovative in its employee benefits programs. In addition to the traditional medical and retirement plans, Intel employees receive the following benefits:

- They earn an 8-week paid vacation after 7 years of employment.
- They can design flexible work hours and locations.
- They have access to independent counselors to provide support if they or a family member is experiencing personal problems or crises, such as a chemical dependency.
- They have access to childcare programs.

Intel's LifeBalance Resource and Referral Program assists employees and their families with life issues, including childcare, tutoring, and eldercare.

Critical Thinking

1. Many Intel campuses offer other services to improve their employees' quality of life. Identify three services that you would suggest any company could offer its employees.
2. Why do you think Intel offers its employees the 8-week sabbatical?

accountingxtra.swlearning.com

Source: www.intel.com/jobs/usa/bencomp/benefits.htm

internet activity

IRS FORMS ONLINE

(NOTE: You will need to have Adobe Acrobat Reader on your computer to complete this activity.)

The Internal Revenue Service (IRS) makes some tax forms available online. Go to the homepage for the IRS (www.irs.gov). Click on "Forms and Publications." A W-4 Form is the form you fill out for your employer when you are hired. A 1040EZ Form is the form you use to file your income tax return each year.

Instructions

1. Search the site for a W-4 Form. Print out the form.
2. Search the site for a 1040EZ Form. Print out the form.
3. List one additional form that is available on the IRS site.

LESSON • LESSON • LESSON • LESSON • LESSON • LESSON

13-1 Recording a Payroll

DIFFERENT FORMS OF PAYROLL INFORMATION

Payroll information for each pay period is recorded in a payroll register. Each pay period the payroll information for each employee is also recorded on each employee earnings record. Separate payroll accounts for each employee are not kept in the general ledger. Instead, accounts are kept in the general ledger to summarize total earnings and deductions for all employees.

The payroll register and employee earnings records provide all the payroll information needed to prepare payroll and payroll tax reports. Journal entries are made to record the payment of the payroll and the employer payroll taxes. In addition, various quarterly and annual payroll tax reports are required to report the payment of payroll taxes.

making ethical decisions

MAKING ETHICAL DECISIONS • MAKING ETHICAL DECISIONS • MAKING ETHICAL DECISIONS

Your Call May Be Recorded

Janice Whitehead has just been fired for violating her employer's code of conduct. Over the last few months, Janice has been using her office phone to call former classmates to inform them of an upcoming class reunion. She believes her firing is unethical and is considering legal action against the company.

Cobb Manufacturing has the following statement in its code of conduct:

"Company telephones are to be used exclusively for company business. Employees needing to make personal phone calls should use their personal cellular phones."

During an ethics training program, employees were informed that the company uses a pen register. The device creates a list of all outgoing calls and the length of each call. Janice signed a statement that she understood the company has a "no tolerance" approach toward topics discussed in the training program.

Instructions

Was it ethical for Cobb Manufacturing to fire Janice for making personal phone calls?

PAYROLL REGISTER

SEMIMONTHLY PERIOD ENDED *December 15, 20--* — **PAYROLL REGISTER** — DATE OF PAYMENT *December 15, 20--*

	EMPL. NO.	EMPLOYEE'S NAME	MARITAL STATUS	NO. OF ALLOWANCES	EARNINGS 1 REGULAR	EARNINGS 2 OVERTIME	EARNINGS 3 TOTAL	DEDUCTIONS 4 FEDERAL INCOME TAX	DEDUCTIONS 5 SOC. SEC. TAX	DEDUCTIONS 6 MEDICARE TAX	DEDUCTIONS 7 HEALTH INSURANCE	DEDUCTIONS 8 OTHER	DEDUCTIONS 9 TOTAL	10 NET PAY	CHECK NO.	
1	2	Aranda, Susan A.	M	2	968 00		968 00	38 00	60 02	14 04	45 00	B 10 00	167 06	800 94	482	1
2	5	Drew, Paul S.	S	1	550 00		550 00	32 00	34 10	7 98	38 00		112 08	437 92	483	2
3	1	Kellogg, Janice P.	M	1	1,760 00	150 00	1,910 00	187 00	118 42	27 70	38 00	uw 20 00	391 12	1,518 88	484	3
4	6	Mendel, Ann M.	S	1	240 00		240 00		14 88	3 48			18 36	221 64	485	4
5	3	Selby, Rick E.	M	4	1,056 00	81 00	1,137 00	28 00	70 49	16 49	60 00	B 10 00 uw 10 00	194 98	942 02	486	5
6	4	Young, Justin L.	S	1	906 40		906 40	86 00	56 20	13 14	38 00	B 15 00 uw 10 00	218 34	688 06	487	6
7		Totals			5,480 40	231 00	5,711 40	371 00	354 11	82 83	219 00	B 35 00 uw 40 00	1,101 94	4,609 46		7
8																8
9																9

Similar to a special journal, the column totals of a payroll register provide the debit and credit amounts needed to journalize a payroll.

As you will learn in this chapter, the payroll journal entry is based on the totals of the Earnings Total column, each deduction column, and the Net Pay column. The totals of the Earnings Regular, Earnings Overtime, and Deductions Total columns are not used to journalize the payroll.

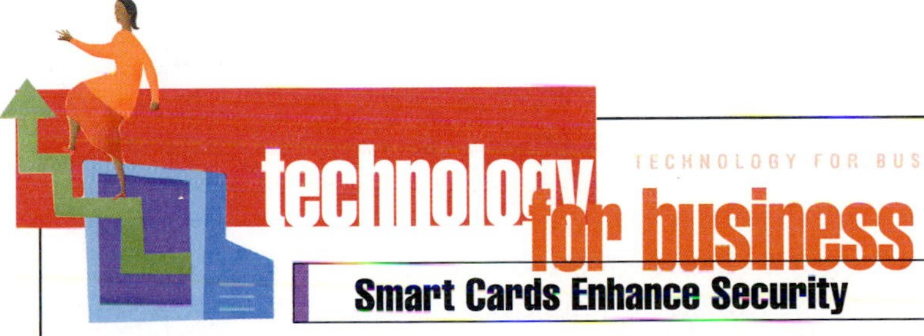

Smart Cards Enhance Security

Smart cards are quickly becoming a common method of conducting business and storing personal information. A smart card is a plastic card containing a computer chip. The first smart cards enabled customers to prepay for pay phone minutes. As minutes were used, the unused minutes were updated in the card's memory chip.

Businesses are finding innovative ways to use smart cards to manage their employees. An employee's arrival and departure time can be recorded by swiping the smart card in a card reader.

With the growing need for security, smart cards can limit an employee's physical access to secured areas of the business, such as warehouses, computer centers, and accounting offices.

The same card can also store a value of money that can be spent in the cafeteria. If the employee becomes seriously ill or is injured, the medical data stored on the smart card can be invaluable to medical personnel to provide prompt and effective treatment.

Critical Thinking

1. How could smart cards be used in your school?
2. Discuss whether employee smart cards compromise an employee's privacy rights.

ANALYZING PAYMENT OF A PAYROLL

Salary Expense			=	Account		
Dec. 15	5,711.40			Employee Income Tax Payable	Dec. 15	371.00
				Social Security Tax Payable	Dec. 15	354.11
				Medicare Tax Payable	Dec. 15	82.83
				Health Insurance Premiums Payable	Dec. 15	219.00
				U.S. Savings Bonds Payable	Dec. 15	35.00
				United Way Donations Payable	Dec. 15	40.00
				Cash	Dec. 15	4,609.46

Data about Hobby Shack's semimonthly pay period ended December 15, obtained from the payroll register, are summarized in the T accounts.

The Total Earnings column total, $5,711.40, is the salary expense for the period. Salary Expense is debited for this amount.

The Federal Income Tax column total, $371.00, is the amount withheld from employee salaries for federal income tax. The amount withheld is a liability of the business until the taxes are sent to the federal government. Employee Income Tax Payable is credited for $371.00 to record this liability.

The Social Security Tax column total, $354.11, is the amount withheld for social security tax. The amount is a liability of the business until the tax is paid to the government. Social Security Tax Payable is credited for $354.11.

The Medicare Tax column total, $82.83, is the amount withheld for Medicare tax. The amount is a liability of the business until the tax is paid to the government. Medicare Tax Payable is credited for $82.83.

The Health Insurance column total, $219.00, is the amount withheld for health insurance premiums. The amount is a liability of the business until the premiums are paid to the insurance company. Health Insurance Premiums Payable is credited for $219.00 to record this liability.

Two types of Other deductions are recorded in Hobby Shack's payroll register. The $35.00 Other column total identified with the letter *B* is withheld to buy savings bonds for employees. The $40.00 total identified with the letters *UW* is withheld for employee United Way pledges. Until these amounts have been paid by the employer, they are liabilities of the business. U.S. Savings Bonds Payable is credited for $35.00. United Way Donations Payable is credited for $40.00.

The Net Pay column total, $4,609.46, is the net amount paid to employees. Cash is credited for $4,609.46. A check for the total net pay amount, $4,609.46, is written on Hobby Shack's general checking account and is deposited in a special payroll checking account. Individual payroll checks are then written on the special payroll checking account.

JOURNALIZING PAYMENT OF A PAYROLL

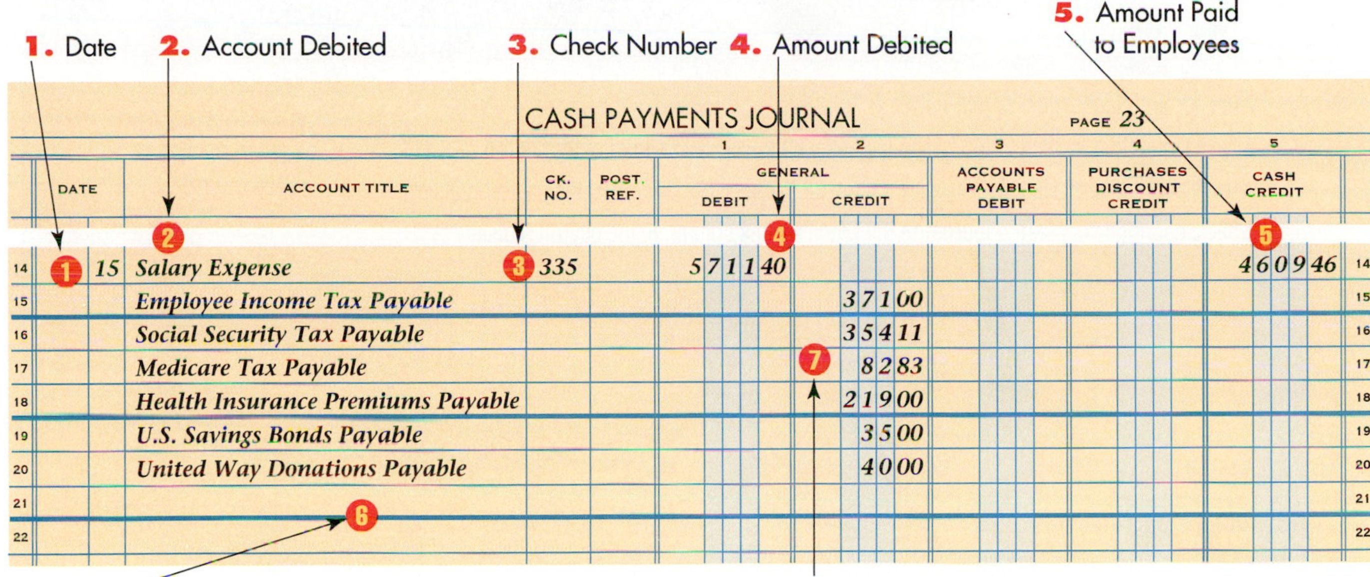

CASH PAYMENTS JOURNAL — PAGE 23

DATE		ACCOUNT TITLE	CK. NO.	POST. REF.	1 GENERAL DEBIT	2 GENERAL CREDIT	3 ACCOUNTS PAYABLE DEBIT	4 PURCHASES DISCOUNT CREDIT	5 CASH CREDIT
	15	Salary Expense	335		5,711 40				4,609 46
		Employee Income Tax Payable				371 00			
		Social Security Tax Payable				354 11			
		Medicare Tax Payable				82 83			
		Health Insurance Premiums Payable				219 00			
		U.S. Savings Bonds Payable				35 00			
		United Way Donations Payable				40 00			

Hobby Shack journalized the company's payroll for the semimonthly period ended December 15, 20--.

December 15. Paid cash for semimonthly payroll, $4,609.46 (total payroll, $5,711.40, less deductions: employee income tax, $371.00; social security tax, $354.11; Medicare tax, $82.83; health insurance premiums, $219.00; U.S. Savings Bonds, $35.00; United Way donations, $40.00). Check No. 335.

Amounts recorded in the General columns of a cash payments journal are posted individually to general ledger accounts. The credit to Cash, *$4,609.46*, is not posted separately to the cash account. The amount is included in the journal's Cash Credit column total that is posted at the end of the month. The same procedures are followed to post this journal entry to the appropriate accounts as were described in Chapter 11.

STEPS: JOURNALIZING PAYMENT OF A PAYROLL

1. Write the date, *15*, in the Date column.
2. Write the title of the account debited, *Salary Expense*, in the Account Title column.
3. Write the check number, *335*, in the Ck. No. column.
4. Write the amount debited to *Salary Expense, $5,711.40*, in the General Debit column.
5. On the same line, write the total amount paid to employees, *$4,609.46*, in the Cash Credit column.
6. On the next six lines, write the titles of the accounts credited, *Employee Income Tax Payable, Social Security Tax Payable, Medicare Tax Payable, Health Insurance Premiums Payable, U.S. Savings Bonds Payable,* and *United Way Donations Payable,* in the Account Title column.
7. On the same six lines, write the amounts credited to the corresponding liability accounts, *$371.00, $354.11, $82.83, $219.00, $35.00,* and *$40.00*, in the General Credit column.

REMEMBER Total Earnings is the debit amount for *Salary Expense*. Net Pay is the credit amount for cash.

• audit your understanding

1. What account title is used to journalize the Total Earnings column of the payroll register?
2. What account title is used to journalize the Federal Income Tax column of the payroll register?
3. What account title is used to journalize the Social Security Tax column of the payroll register?
4. What account title is used to journalize the Medicare Tax column of the payroll register?

AUDIT YOUR UNDERSTANDING

• work together 13-1

Recording a payroll

Metro Company's payroll register has the following totals for the semimonthly pay period, July 1–15 of the current year. T accounts and a cash payments journal page are provided in the *Working Papers*. Your instructor will guide you through the following examples.

Total Earnings	Federal Income Tax Withheld	Social Security Tax Withheld	Medicare Withheld
$12,600.00	$1,186.00	$781.20	$182.70

1. Use the T accounts provided to analyze Metro's July 1–15 payroll.
2. Journalize the payment of Metro's July 1–15 payroll on page 15 of the cash payments journal. The payroll was paid by Check No. 455 on July 15 of the current year.

WORK TOGETHER • WORK TOGETHER

• on your own 13-1

Recording a payroll

Butler Company's payroll register has the following totals for the semimonthly pay period, August 16–31 of the current year. T accounts and a cash payments journal page are provided in the *Working Papers*. Work this problem independently.

Total Earnings	Federal Income Tax Withheld	Social Security Tax Withheld	Medicare Withheld
$14,260.00	$1,562.00	$884.12	$206.77

1. Use the T accounts provided to analyze Butler's August 16–31 payroll.
2. Journalize the payment of Butler's August 16–31 payroll on page 16 of a cash payments journal. The payroll was paid by Check No. 628 on August 31 of the current year.

ON YOUR OWN • ON YOUR OWN

LESSON • LESSON • LESSON • LESSON • LESSON • LESSON

13-2 Recording Employer Payroll Taxes

CALCULATING EMPLOYER PAYROLL TAXES

Employers must pay to the government the taxes withheld from employee earnings. Hobby Shack has withheld federal income tax, social security tax, and Medicare tax from employee salaries. The amounts withheld are liabilities to the business until they are actually paid to the government. In addition, employers must pay several of their own payroll taxes. Employer payroll taxes are business expenses.

Most employers must pay four separate payroll taxes. These taxes are (1) employer social security tax, (2) Medicare tax, (3) federal unemployment tax, and (4) state unemployment tax. Employer payroll taxes expense is based on a percentage of employee earnings.

Employer Social Security and Medicare Taxes

The social security and Medicare taxes are the only payroll taxes paid by both the employees and the employer. Hobby Shack withheld $354.11 in social security tax and $82.83 in Medicare tax from employee wages for the pay period ended December 15. Hobby Shack owes the same amount of social security and Medicare taxes as the amount withheld from employees. Therefore, Hobby Shack's social security and Medicare taxes for the pay period ended December 15 are also $354.11 and $82.83 respectively.

Congress sets the social security and Medicare tax rates for employees and employers. Periodically, Congress may change the tax rates and tax base. The social security tax rate and base used in this text are 6.2% of earnings up to a maximum of $87,000.00 in each calendar year. Medicare does not have a tax base. Therefore, Medicare tax is calculated on total employee earnings. The Medicare tax rate used in this text is 1.45% of total employee earnings.

©GETTY IMAGES/PHOTODISC

REMEMBER Employers must pay four taxes on employee earnings—social security tax, Medicare tax, federal unemployment tax, and state unemployment tax.

UNEMPLOYMENT TAXABLE EARNINGS

HOBBY SHACK Taxable Earnings for December 15, 20--, Pay Period			
	Accumulated Earnings as of Nov. 30, 20--	Total Earnings for Dec. 15, 20-- Pay Period	Unemployment Taxable Earnings
Aranda, Susan A.	$21,115.00	$ 968.00	—
Drew, Paul S.	5,595.25	550.00	$550.00 ②
Kellogg, Janice P.	39,840.00	1,910.00	—
Mendel, Ann M.	① 2,030.00	① 240.00	240.00
Selby, Rick E.	22,746.00	1,137.00	—
Young, Justin L.	19,816.00	906.40	—
			③ $790.00

1. Enter accumulated earnings and total earnings for each employee.

2. Enter unemployment taxable earnings.

3. Total the unemployment taxable earnings column.

Federal unemployment insurance laws require that employers pay taxes for unemployment compensation. These tax funds are used to pay workers benefits for limited periods of unemployment and to administer the unemployment compensation program.

The total earnings subject to unemployment tax is referred to as *unemployment taxable earnings*. The unemployment tax is applied to the first $7,000.00 earned by each employee for each calendar year. The amount of unemployment taxable earnings for Hobby Shack's pay period ended December 15, 20--, is shown in the illustration.

STEPS: CALCULATING UNEMPLOYMENT TAXABLE EARNINGS

1. For each employee, enter accumulated earnings as of November 30 and total earnings for the December 15 pay period. These amounts are taken from each employee earnings record. Rick E. Selby's accumulated earnings as of November 30, *$22,746.00*, are recorded in the first column. His total earnings for the December 15 pay period, *$1,137.00*, are recorded in the second column.
2. Enter unemployment taxable earnings for the pay period in the Unemployment Taxable Earnings column for employees whose accumulated earnings are less than $7,000.00. The November 30 accumulated earnings for Paul S. Drew, *$5,595.25*, plus the December 15 earnings, *$550.00*, equal $6,145.25 and are less than $7,000.00. Therefore, his total earnings for the December 15 pay period, *$550.00*, are subject to unemployment tax and are recorded in the Unemployment Taxable Earnings column. Since the accumulated earnings for Mr. Selby are greater than $7,000.00, none of his current earnings are subject to unemployment tax. Thus, the amount of unemployment taxable earnings recorded in the third column is zero, which is represented by a dash.
3. Total the Unemployment Taxable Earnings column. This total amount, *$790.00*, is used to calculate the unemployment tax.

UNEMPLOYMENT TAXES

Hobby Shack pays two unemployment taxes, federal unemployment tax and state unemployment tax.

Federal Unemployment Tax

A federal tax used for state and federal administrative expenses of the unemployment program is called **federal unemployment tax**. The federal unemployment tax is 6.2% of the first $7,000.00 earned by each employee. An employer generally can deduct from federal unemployment payments the amounts paid to state unemployment funds. This deduction cannot be more than 5.4% of taxable earnings. The effective federal unemployment tax rate in most states is, therefore, 0.8% on the first $7,000.00 earned by each employee. (Federal, 6.2% − deductible for state, 5.4% = 0.8%.) All of the unemployment tax on the first $7,000.00 of salary is paid by the employer.

Hobby Shack's federal unemployment tax for the pay period ended December 15, 20--, is calculated as shown.

Unemployment Taxable Earnings	×	Federal Unemployment Tax Rate	=	Federal Unemployment Tax
$790.00	×	0.8%	=	$6.32

State Unemployment Tax

A state tax used to pay benefits to unemployed workers is called **state unemployment tax**. The Social Security Act specifies certain standards for unemployment compensation laws. Therefore, a high degree of uniformity exists in state unemployment laws. However, details of state unemployment laws do differ. Because of these differences, employers must know the requirements of the states in which they operate.

Many states require that employers pay unemployment tax of 5.4% on the first $7,000.00 earned by each employee. The unemployment taxable earnings used to calculate the federal unemployment tax are also used to calculate the state unemployment tax. Hobby Shack's state unemployment tax for the pay period ended December 15, 20--, is calculated as shown.

Unemployment Taxable Earnings	×	State Unemployment Tax Rate	=	State Unemployment Tax
$790.00	×	5.4%	=	$42.66

©GETTY IMAGES/PHOTODISC

JOURNALIZING EMPLOYER PAYROLL TAXES

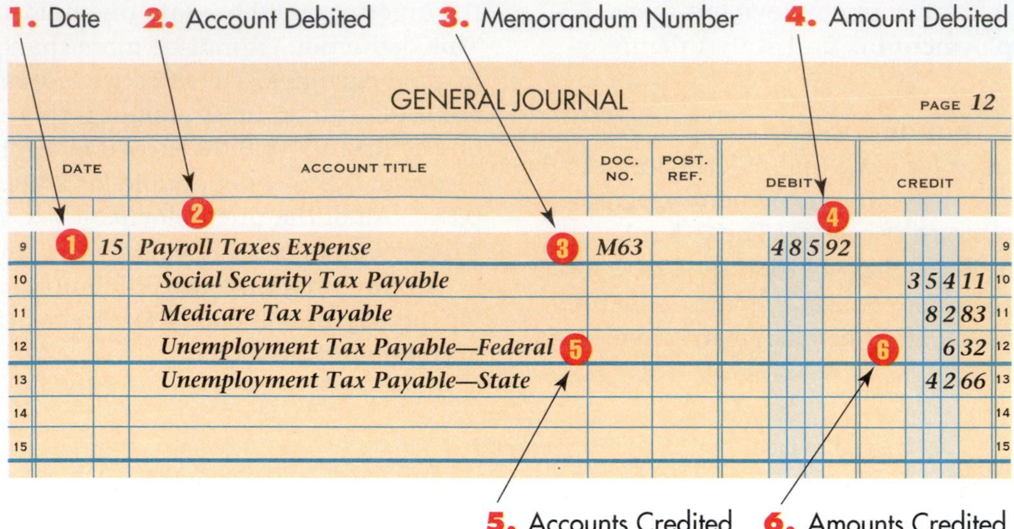

GENERAL JOURNAL — PAGE 12

	DATE		ACCOUNT TITLE	DOC. NO.	POST. REF.	DEBIT	CREDIT	
9		15	Payroll Taxes Expense	M63		485 92		9
10			Social Security Tax Payable				354 11	10
11			Medicare Tax Payable				82 83	11
12			Unemployment Tax Payable—Federal				6 32	12
13			Unemployment Tax Payable—State				42 66	13
14								14
15								15

Employer payroll taxes are paid to the government at a later date. However, the liability is incurred when salaries are paid. Therefore, the transaction to record employer payroll taxes expense is journalized on the same date the payroll is journalized. The salary expense and the employer payroll taxes expense are, therefore, both recorded in the same accounting period.

December 15. Recorded employer payroll taxes expense, $485.92, for the semimonthly pay period ended December 15. Taxes owed are: social security tax, $354.11; Medicare tax, $82.83; federal unemployment tax, $6.32; state unemployment tax, $42.66. Memorandum No. 63.

Payroll Taxes Expense is debited for $485.92 to show the increase in the balance of this expense account. Four liability accounts are credited to show the increase in payroll tax liabilities.

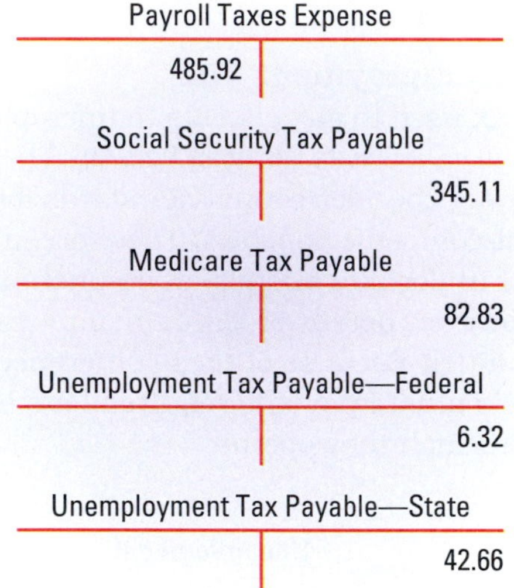

Amounts recorded in the general journal are posted individually to general ledger accounts. The same procedures are followed to post this journal entry to the appropriate accounts as were described in Chapter 11.

STEPS • STEPS • STEPS • STEPS • STEPS • STEPS • STEPS • STEPS • STEPS • STEPS •

STEPS: JOURNALIZING EMPLOYER PAYROLL TAXES

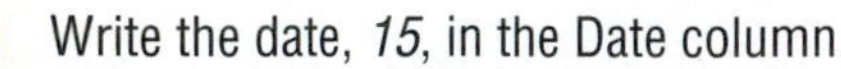

1. Write the date, *15*, in the Date column.
2. Write the title of the expense account debited, *Payroll Taxes Expense*, in the Account Title column.
3. Write the memorandum number, *M63*, in the Doc. No. column.
4. Write the debit amount, *$485.92*, in the Debit column.
5. Write the titles of the liability accounts credited, *Social Security Tax Payable, Medicare Tax Payable, Unemployment Tax Payable—Federal*, and *Unemployment Tax Payable—State*, on the next four lines of the Account Title column, indented about 1 centimeter.
6. Write the credit amounts, *$354.11, $82.83, $6.32,* and *$42.66*, respectively, in the Credit column.

terms review

federal unemployment tax
state unemployment tax

audit your understanding

1. What is the tax rate Hobby Shack must pay on employees for each of the following taxes: social security, Medicare, federal unemployment, and state unemployment?
2. What is the amount of each employee's earnings that is subject to federal and state unemployment taxes at Hobby Shack?

work together 13-2

Recording employer payroll taxes

Payroll information taken from employee earnings records is given below. A form and general journal page are provided in the *Working Papers*. Your instructor will guide you through the following examples.

Employee Name	Accumulated Earnings, April 30	Total Earnings for May 1–15 Pay Period
Beltran, Tamela C.	$5,100.00	$637.50
Cintron, Irma V.	7,350.00	920.00

1. Calculate the amount of earnings subject to unemployment taxes. Unemployment taxes are owed on the first $7,000.00 of earnings for each employee.
2. Calculate the amount of employer payroll taxes owed for the May 1–15 pay period. Use the employer payroll tax rates shown in this chapter.
3. Journalize the employer's payroll taxes for the May 1–15 pay period on May 15 of the current year. Use general journal page 10 and Memorandum No. 46.

on your own 13-2

Recording employer payroll taxes

Payroll information taken from employee earnings records is given below. A form and general journal page are provided in the *Working Papers*. Work this problem independently.

Employee Name	Accumulated Earnings, May 31	Total Earnings for June 1–15 Pay Period
Caldwell, Sarah H.	$6,020.00	$ 580.00
Easley, Benjamin P.	5,450.00	620.00
Franks, John J.	8,420.00	1,000.00

1. Calculate the amount of earnings subject to unemployment taxes. Unemployment taxes are owed on the first $7,000.00 of earnings for each employee.
2. Calculate the amount of employer payroll taxes owed for the June 1–15 pay period. Use the employer payroll tax rates shown in this chapter.
3. Journalize the employer's payroll taxes for the June 1–15 pay period on June 15 of the current year. Use general journal page 12 and Memorandum No. 83.

13-3 Reporting Withholding and Payroll Taxes

EMPLOYER ANNUAL REPORT TO EMPLOYEES OF TAXES WITHHELD

a Control number	22222	Void ☐	For Official Use Only ► OMB No. 1545-0008

b Employer identification number 31-0429632	1 Wages, tips, other compensation 24,843.00	2 Federal income tax withheld 648.00
c Employer's name, address, and ZIP code Hobby Shack, Inc. 1420 College Plaza Atlanta, GA 30337-1726	3 Social security wages 24,843.00	4 Social security tax withheld 1,540.24
	5 Medicare wages and tips 24,843.00	6 Medicare tax withheld 360.21
	7 Social security tips	8 Allocated tips
d Employee's social security number 450-70-6432	9 Advance EIC payment	10 Dependent care benefits
e Employee's first name and initial Rick E. — Last name Selby	11 Nonqualified plans	12a See instructions for box 12 (Code)
1625 Northland Drive Clarkdale, GA 30020-6523	13 Statutory employee ☐ Retirement plan ☐ Third-party sick pay ☐	12b (Code)
	14 Other	12c (Code)
f Employee's address and ZIP code		12d (Code)

15 State	Employer's state ID number	16 State wages, tips, etc.	17 State income tax	18 Local wages, tips, etc.	19 Local income tax	20 Locality name

Form **W-2** **Wage and Tax Statement** 20--

Department of the Treasury—Internal Revenue Service

For Privacy Act and Paperwork Reduction Act Notice, see back of Copy D.

Copy A For Social Security Administration — Send this entire page with Form W-3 to the Social Security Administration; photocopies are **not** acceptable.

Cat. No. 10134D

Each employer who withholds income tax, social security tax, and Medicare tax from employee earnings must furnish each employee with an annual report of these withholdings. The report shows total year's earnings and the amounts withheld for taxes for an employee. These amounts are obtained from the employee earnings records. The report is prepared on the Internal Revenue Service Form W-2, Wage and Tax Statement. The Form W-2 prepared by Hobby Shack for Rick E. Selby is shown.

Employers are required to furnish Form W-2 to each employee by January 31 of the next year. If an employee ends employment before December 31, Form W-2 must be furnished within 30 days of the last date of employment.

Four copies (A to D) of Form W-2 are prepared for each employee. Copies B and C are given to the employee. The employee attaches Copy B to a personal federal income tax return and keeps Copy C for a personal record. The employer sends Copy A to the Social Security Administration and keeps Copy D for the business's records.

Businesses in states with state income tax must prepare additional copies of Form W-2. The employee attaches the additional copy to the personal state income tax return.

EMPLOYER'S QUARTERLY FEDERAL TAX RETURN

1. Heading

Form **941** (Rev. January 2004) Department of the Treasury Internal Revenue Service (99)

Employer's Quarterly Federal Tax Return

▶ See separate instructions revised January 2004 for information on completing this return.

Please type or print.

Enter state code for state in which deposits were made **only** if different from state in address to the right ▶ (see page 2 of separate instructions).

Name (as distinguished from trade name): Hobby Shack, Inc.
Trade name, if any
Address (number and street): 1420 College Plaza

Date quarter ended: December 31, 20--
Employer identification number: 31-0429532
City, state, and ZIP code: Atlanta GA 30337-1726

OMB No. 1545-0029

T
FF
FD
FP
I
T

If address is different from prior return, check here ▶ ☐ IRS Use

A If you **do not have to file** returns in the future, check here ▶ ☐ and enter date final wages paid ▶

B If you are a seasonal employer, see **Seasonal employers** on page 1 of the instructions and check here ▶ ☐

Line	Description		Amount
1	Number of employees in the pay period that includes March 12th . ▶	1 6	
2	Total wages and tips, plus other compensation (see separate instructions)	2	32,980.00
3	Total income tax withheld from wages, tips, and sick pay	3	2,168.00
4	Adjustment of withheld income tax for preceding quarters of **this calendar year**	4	-0-
5	Adjusted total of income tax withheld (line 3 as adjusted by line 4)	5	2,168.00
6	Taxable social security wages . . . 6a 32,980.00 × 12.4% (.124) =	6b	4,089.52
	Taxable social security tips . . . 6c -0- × 12.4% (.124) =	6d	-0-
7	Taxable Medicare wages and tips . . . 7a 32,980.00 × 2.9% (.029) =	7b	956.42
8	Total social security and Medicare taxes (add lines 6b, 6d, and 7b). **Check here if wages are not subject to social security and/or Medicare tax** ▶ ☐	8	5,045.94
9	Adjustment of social security and Medicare taxes (see instructions for required explanation) Sick Pay $ ______ ± Fractions of Cents $ ______ ± Other $ ______ =	9	-0-
10	Adjusted total of social security and Medicare taxes (line 8 as adjusted by line 9)	10	5,045.94
11	**Total taxes** (add lines 5 and 10)	11	7,213.94
12	Advance earned income credit (EIC) payments made to employees (see instructions)	12	-0-
13	Net taxes (subtract line 12 from line 11). **If $2,500 or more, this must equal line 17, column (d) below (or line D of Schedule B (Form 941))**	13	7,213.94
14	Total deposits for quarter, including overpayment applied from a prior quarter	14	7,213.94
15	**Balance due** (subtract line 14 from line 13). See instructions	15	-0-
16	**Overpayment.** If line 14 is more than line 13, enter excess here ▶ $ ______ and check if to be: ☐ Applied to next return **or** ☐ Refunded.		

- **All filers:** If line 13 is less than $2,500, **do not** complete line 17 **or** Schedule B (Form 941).
- **Semiweekly schedule depositors:** Complete Schedule B (Form 941) and check here . . . ▶ ☐
- **Monthly schedule depositors:** Complete line 17, columns (a) through (d), and check here. . . ▶ ☒

17 Monthly Summary of Federal Tax Liability. (Complete **Schedule B (Form 941)** instead, if you were a semiweekly schedule depositor.)

(a) First month liability	(b) Second month liability	(c) Third month liability	(d) Total liability for quarter
2,271.44	2,394.70	2,547.80	7,213.94

Third Party Designee Do you want to allow another person to discuss this return with the IRS (see separate instructions)? ☐ **Yes.** Complete the following. ☐ **No**

Designee's name ▶ Phone no. ▶ ( ) Personal identification number (PIN) ▶

Sign Here Under penalties of perjury, I declare that I have examined this return, including accompanying schedules and statements, and to the best of my knowledge and belief, it is true, correct, and complete.

Signature ▶ Janice Kellogg Print Your Name and Title ▶ Janice Kellogg, Manager Date ▶ 1/24/--

For Privacy Act and Paperwork Reduction Act Notice, see back of Payment Voucher. Cat. No. 17001Z Form **941** (Rev. 1-2004)

2. Number of Employees

3. Total Quarterly Earnings

4. Income Tax Withheld

5. Employee and Employer Social Security and Medicare Taxes

6. Social Security plus Medicare Taxes

7. Total Taxes

9. Total Taxes

8. Total Taxes for Each Month

PREPARING EMPLOYER'S QUARTERLY FEDERAL TAX RETURN

Each employer is required by law to periodically report the payroll taxes withheld from employee salaries and the employer payroll taxes due the government. Some reports are submitted quarterly and others, annually.

Each employer must file a quarterly federal tax return showing the federal income tax, social security tax, and Medicare tax due the government. This information is submitted every three months on Form 941, Employer's Quarterly Federal Tax Return. Form 941 is filed before the last day of the month following the end of a calendar quarter. Hobby Shack's Form 941 for the quarter ended December 31 is shown on the previous page. The information needed to prepare Form 941 is obtained from employee earnings records.

STEPS • STEPS • STEPS • STEPS • STEPS • STEPS • STEPS • STEPS • STEPS • STEPS •

STEPS PREPARING AN EMPLOYER'S QUARTERLY FEDERAL TAX RETURN

1. Enter the company name, address, employer identification number, and the date the quarter ended in the heading section of Form 941.
2. Enter the number of employees, *6*, on line 1 of Form 941.
3. Enter total quarterly earnings, *$32,980.00*, on line 2. This amount is the sum of the fourth quarter total earnings of all employees. Total earnings, *$32,980.00*, is also recorded on lines 6a and 7a.
4. Enter the income tax withheld, *$2,168.00*, on line 3. The amount is the total of the fourth quarter federal income tax withheld from all employees. The same amount is entered on line 5.
5. Enter the quarterly employee and employer social security taxes, *$4,089.52*, and Medicare taxes, *$956.42*, on lines 6b and 7b, respectively. The taxes due are calculated as shown.

	Total Earnings	×	Tax Rate	=	Tax
Social Security	$32,980.00	×	12.4%	=	$4,089.52
Medicare	$32,980.00	×	2.9%	=	$ 956.42

The 12.4% tax rate is the sum of the employee 6.2% and the employer 6.2% social security tax rates. The 2.9% tax rate is the sum of the employee 1.45% and the employer 1.45% Medicare tax rates.

6. Enter the total social security tax plus Medicare tax, *$5,045.94* ($4,089.52 + $956.42 = $5,045.94), on line 8. Since Hobby Shack has no adjustment to its taxes, the total is also entered on line 10.
7. Enter the total taxes, *$7,213.94*, on lines 11 and 13. Hobby Shack is required to pay the federal government the sum of the federal income tax withheld and the employee and employer's shares of the social security tax and Medicare tax.
8. Enter on lines 17a, 17b, and 17c the total amounts of employee income tax withheld and employee and employer social security and Medicare taxes for each month of the quarter. For the month of December, the amount of taxes owed is calculated as shown and recorded on line 17.

	Federal Income Tax Withheld	+	Employee Social Security and Medicare Tax	+	Employer Social Security and Medicare Tax	=	Federal Tax Liability
Dec. 1–15	$371.00	+	$436.94	+	$436.94	=	$1,244.88
Dec. 16–31	$386.00	+	$458.46	+	$458.46	=	$1,302.92
Totals	$757.00	+	$895.40	+	$895.40	=	$2,547.80

9. Enter the total quarterly withholding and payroll taxes, *$7,213.94*, on line 17d. This total is the sum of the three monthly totals reported on line 17 ($2,271.44 + $2,394.70 + $2,547.80 = $7,213.94).

EMPLOYER ANNUAL REPORTING OF PAYROLL TAXES

DO NOT STAPLE OR FOLD

a Control number	33333	For Official Use Only ▶ OMB No. 1545-0008	
b Kind of Payer: 941 [X], Military [ ], 943 [ ], CT-1 [ ], Hshld. emp. [ ], Medicare govt. emp. [ ], Third-party sick pay [ ]		1 Wages, tips, other compensation 104,525.00	2 Federal income tax withheld 6,790.00
		3 Social security wages 104,525.00	4 Social security tax withheld 6,480.55
c Total number of Forms W-2	d Establishment number	5 Medicare wages and tips 104,525.00	6 Medicare tax withheld 1,515.61
e Employer identification number 31-0429632		7 Social security tips	8 Allocated tips
f Employer's name Hobby Shack, Inc. 1420 College Plaza Atlanta, GA 30337-1726		9 Advance EIC payments	10 Dependent care benefits
		11 Nonqualified plans	12 Deferred compensation
		13 For third-party sick pay use only	
g Employer's address and ZIP code		14 Income tax withheld by payer of third-party sick pay	
h Other EIN used this year			
15 State	Employer's state ID number	16 State wages, tips, etc.	17 State income tax
		18 Local wages, tips, etc.	19 Local income tax
Contact person Janice Kellogg		Telephone number (404) 555-9368	For Official Use Only
Email address jkellogg@hobbyshack.com		Fax number ( )	

Under penalties of perjury, I declare that I have examined this return and accompanying documents, and, to the best of my knowledge and belief, they are true, correct, and complete.

Signature ▶ *Janice Kellogg* Title ▶ *Manager* Date ▶ *2/27/--*

Form **W-3 Transmittal of Wage and Tax Statements** 20-- Department of the Treasury Internal Revenue Service

Send this entire page with the entire Copy A page of Form(s) W-2 to the Social Security Administration. Photocopies are not acceptable.

Form W-3, Transmittal of Wage and Tax Statements, is sent to the Social Security Administration by February 28 each year. Form W-3 reports the previous year's earnings and payroll taxes withheld for all employees. Attached to Form W-3 is Copy A of each employee Form W-2. Employers with more than 250 employees must send the information to the Internal Revenue Service in computer files rather than the actual Forms W-2 and W-3.

At the end of a calendar year, employers must also report to the federal and state governments a summary of all earnings paid to employees during the twelve months.

©GETTY IMAGES/PHOTODISC

audit your understanding

1. When must employers furnish a W-2 statement to their employees?
2. What taxes are included in the quarterly federal tax return filed by the employer?

work together 13-3

Reporting withholding and payroll taxes

A Form 941, Employer's Quarterly Federal Tax Return, is given in the *Working Papers.* Your instructor will guide you through the following example. The following data is for Audio Solutions.

Date Paid	Total Earnings	Federal Income Tax Withheld	Employee Social Security Tax Withheld	Employee Medicare Tax Withheld
Jan. 31	$10,440.00	$731.00	$647.28	$151.38
Feb. 28	10,960.00	767.00	679.52	158.92
Mar. 31	12,400.00	868.00	768.80	179.80

a. Company address: 625 Sandpiper Street, Ormond Beach, Florida 32074-4060

b. Employer identification number: 70-7818356

c. Number of employees: 6

1. Prepare a Form 941 for Audio Solutions for the first quarter of the current year. Use the preparation date of April 24. Sign your name as the manager of the company.

on your own 13-3

Reporting withholding and payroll taxes

A Form 941, Employer's Quarterly Federal Tax Return, is given in the *Working Papers.* Work this problem independently. The following data is for Audio Solutions. The company address, employer identification number, and number of employees are the same as in Work Together 13-3.

Date Paid	Total Earnings	Federal Income Tax Withheld	Employee Social Security Tax Withheld	Employee Medicare Tax Withheld
Apr. 30	$11,760.00	$823.00	$729.12	$170.52
May 31	11,820.00	827.00	732.84	171.39
June 30	10,900.00	763.00	675.80	158.05

1. Prepare a Form 941 for Audio Solutions for the second quarter of the current year. Use the preparation date of July 22. Sign your name as the manager of the company.

LESSON • LESSON • LESSON • LESSON • LESSON • LESSON

13-4 Paying Withholding and Payroll Taxes

PAYING THE LIABILITY FOR EMPLOYEE INCOME TAX, SOCIAL SECURITY TAX, AND MEDICARE TAX

Employers must pay to the federal, state, and local governments all payroll taxes withheld from employee earnings as well as the employer payroll taxes. The payment of payroll taxes with the government is referred to as a *deposit*. Two amounts determine how often deposits are made to the federal government: (1) the amount of payroll taxes collected during the current deposit period and (2) the amount of payroll taxes owed during a prior 12-month period. The 12-month period that ends on June 30th of the prior year is called the **lookback period**. The Internal Revenue Service provides businesses with the following flowchart to assist them in determining when to make tax deposits.

When to Deposit Form 941 Employment Taxes

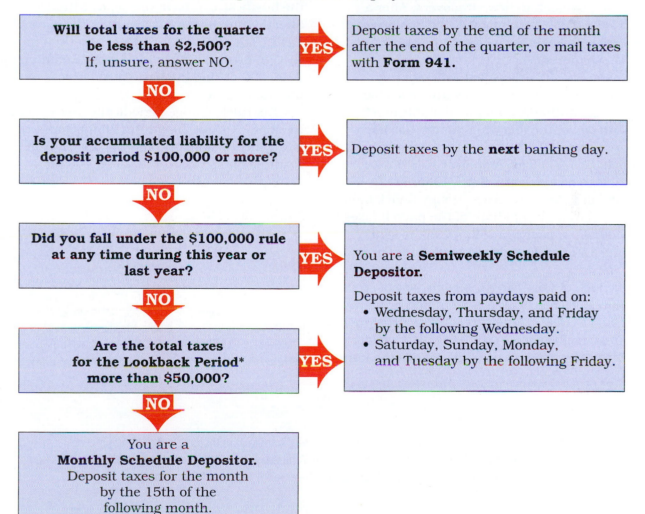

Will total taxes for the quarter be less than $2,500? If, unsure, answer NO.

YES → Deposit taxes by the end of the month after the end of the quarter, or mail taxes with **Form 941.**

NO ↓

Is your accumulated liability for the deposit period $100,000 or more?

YES → Deposit taxes by the **next** banking day.

NO ↓

Did you fall under the $100,000 rule at any time during this year or last year?

YES → (see Semiweekly Schedule Depositor below)

NO ↓

Are the total taxes for the Lookback Period* more than $50,000?

YES → You are a **Semiweekly Schedule Depositor.**

Deposit taxes from paydays paid on:
- Wednesday, Thursday, and Friday by the following Wednesday.
- Saturday, Sunday, Monday, and Tuesday by the following Friday.

NO ↓

You are a **Monthly Schedule Depositor.** Deposit taxes for the month by the 15th of the following month.

FORM 8109, FEDERAL DEPOSIT COUPON

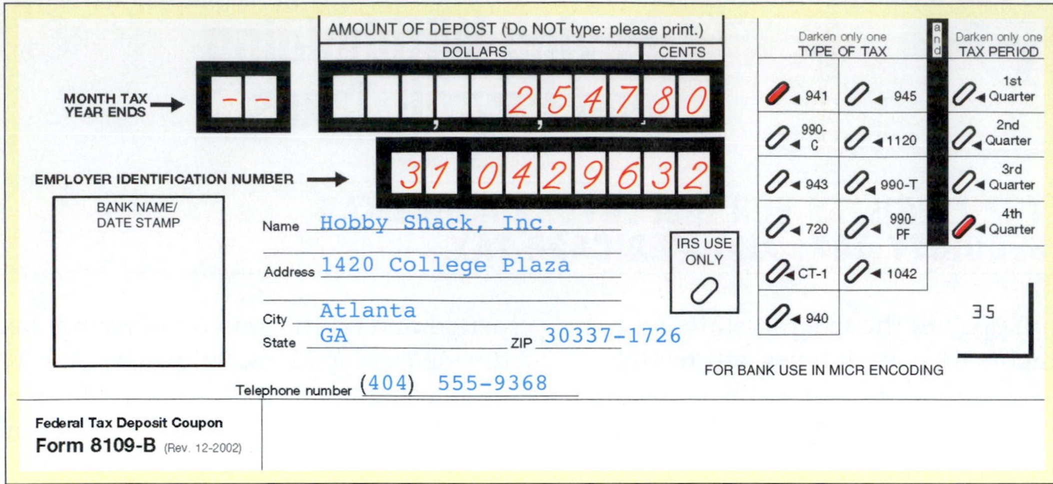
AMOUNT OF DEPOST (Do NOT type: please print.)

DOLLARS | CENTS

MONTH TAX YEAR ENDS - -

2547 80

EMPLOYER IDENTIFICATION NUMBER 31 0429632

BANK NAME/ DATE STAMP

Name Hobby Shack, Inc.

Address 1420 College Plaza

City Atlanta

State GA ZIP 30337-1726

Telephone number (404) 555-9368

IRS USE ONLY

Darken only one TYPE OF TAX: 941, 945, 990-C, 1120, 943, 990-T, 720, 990-PF, CT-1, 1042, 940

and

Darken only one TAX PERIOD: 1st Quarter, 2nd Quarter, 3rd Quarter, 4th Quarter

35

FOR BANK USE IN MICR ENCODING

Federal Tax Deposit Coupon
Form 8109-B (Rev. 12-2002)

New employers are monthly schedule depositors for the first calendar year of business. The Internal Revenue Service issues a monthly Form 8109 coupon book to new employers. After a lookback period is established, the business must evaluate whether a change in its deposit period is required.

Hobby Shack is classified as a monthly depositor. So, the payroll taxes are deposited with a local authorized financial institution by the 15th day of the following month, accompanied by Form 8109. In December, Hobby Shack withheld $757.00 from employee salaries for federal income taxes and $895.40 for social security and Medicare taxes. Hobby Shack must also pay the employer share of the payroll taxes. The federal tax payment, $2,547.80, is sent January 15 to an authorized bank with Form 8109 as shown.

The type of tax—federal income, social security, and Medicare taxes—is identified by marking the 941 circle. These taxes are reported to the government using Form 941. The calendar quarter is identified on the right side of the form.

Deposits can also be made using the Electronic Federal Tax Payment System (EFTPS). Using either a personal computer or telephone, the business can have the deposit transferred directly from its bank account to the government. Although any business can enroll in the EFTPS, businesses having deposits of more than $200,000 during the past calendar year must use the EFTPS.

Tax rules change periodically. Always check the most current tax information before calculating any tax amount and the tax deposit requirements.

FYI FOR YOUR INFORMATION

Some federal tax forms can be printed from copies available on the Internet. Other tax forms, such as the W-2, W-3, and 8109, are designed to be machine readable and must be obtained directly from the Internal Revenue Service.

REMEMBER Social security tax and Medicare tax are the only payroll taxes paid by both the employer and employee. A business pays the same amount of social security tax and Medicare tax as the amount withheld from employees.

JOURNALIZING PAYMENT OF LIABILITY FOR EMPLOYEE INCOME TAX, SOCIAL SECURITY TAX, AND MEDICARE TAX

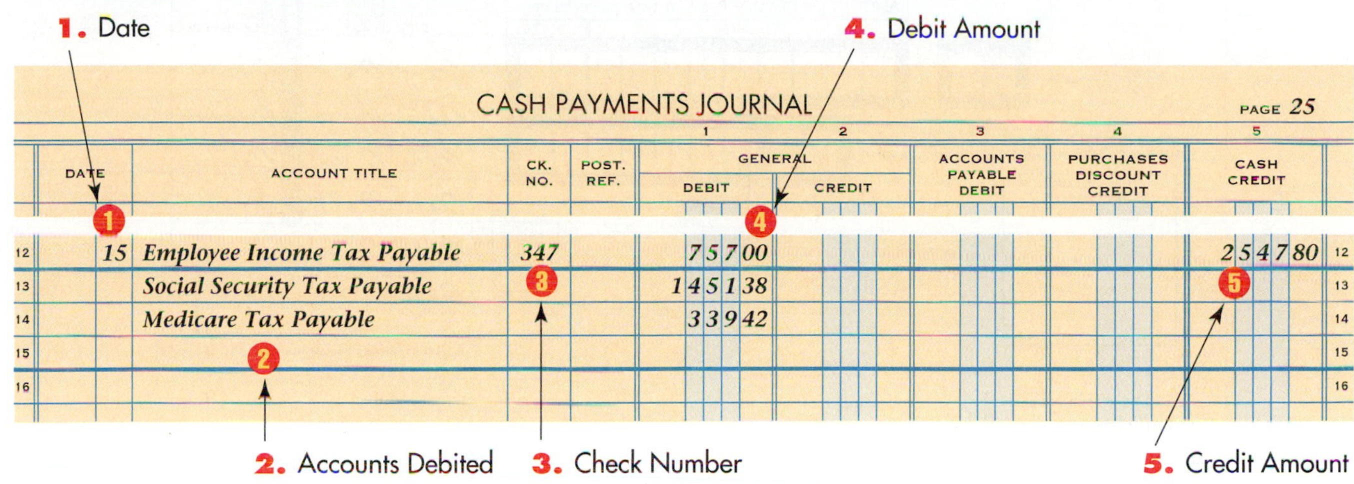

CASH PAYMENTS JOURNAL — PAGE 25

	DATE		ACCOUNT TITLE	CK. NO.	POST. REF.	1 GENERAL DEBIT	2 GENERAL CREDIT	3 ACCOUNTS PAYABLE DEBIT	4 PURCHASES DISCOUNT CREDIT	5 CASH CREDIT	
12		15	Employee Income Tax Payable	347		757 00				2 547 80	12
13			Social Security Tax Payable			1 451 38					13
14			Medicare Tax Payable			339 42					14
15											15
16											16

January 15. Paid cash for liability for employee income tax, $757.00; social security tax, $1,451.38; and Medicare tax, $339.42; total, $2,547.80. Check No. 347.

Employee Income Tax Payable	
757.00	Jan. 15 Bal. 757.00

Social Security Tax Payable	
1,451.38	Jan. 15 Bal. 1,451.38

Medicare Tax Payable	
339.42	Jan. 15 Bal. 339.42

Cash	
	2,547.80

The balances of the liability accounts are reduced by this transaction. Therefore, Employee Income Tax Payable is debited for $757.00. Social Security Tax Payable is debited for $1,451.37. Medicare Tax Payable is debited for $339.42. The balance of Cash is decreased by a credit for the total payment, $2,547.80.

STEPS • STEPS • STEPS • STEPS • STEPS

JOURNALIZING A PAYMENT OF LIABILITY FOR EMPLOYEE INCOME TAX, SOCIAL SECURITY TAX, AND MEDICARE TAX

1. Write the date, *15*, in the Date column.
2. Write the titles of the three accounts debited, *Employee Income Tax Payable, Social Security Tax Payable*, and *Medicare Tax Payable*, in the Account Title column.
3. Write the check number, *347*, in the Ck. No. column.
4. Write the three debit amounts, *$757.00, $1,451.38,* and *$339.42*, in the General Debit column.
5. Write the amount of the credit to *Cash*, *$2,547.80*, in the Cash Credit column.

FOR YOUR INFORMATION

Semimonthly pay periods are paid twice a month. Biweekly pay periods are paid every two weeks.

PAYING THE LIABILITY FOR FEDERAL UNEMPLOYMENT TAX

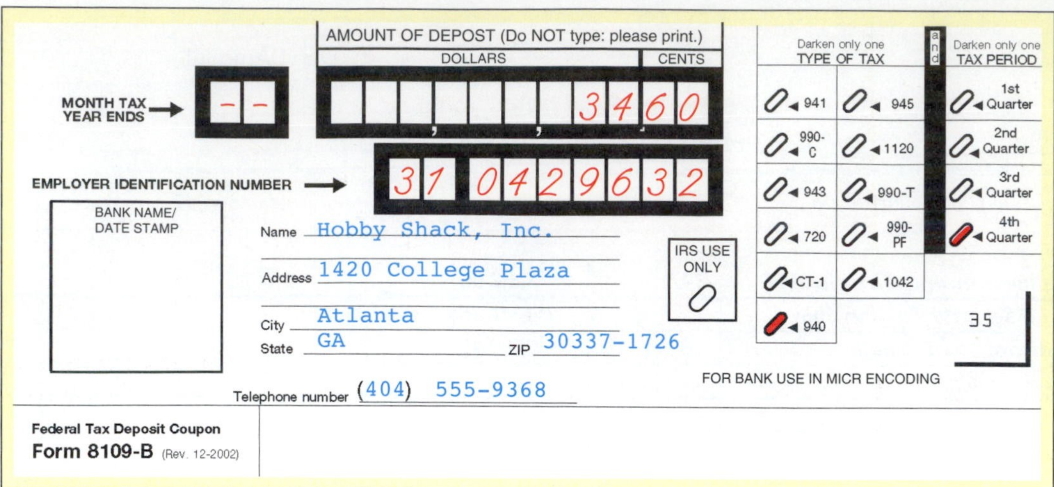
AMOUNT OF DEPOST (Do NOT type: please print.)

DOLLARS | CENTS

MONTH TAX YEAR ENDS: – –

3460

EMPLOYER IDENTIFICATION NUMBER: 31 0429632

BANK NAME/ DATE STAMP

Name Hobby Shack, Inc.

Address 1420 College Plaza

City Atlanta

State GA ZIP 30337-1726

Telephone number (404) 555-9368

IRS USE ONLY

Darken only one TYPE OF TAX: 941, 945, 990-C, 1120, 943, 990-T, 720, 990-PF, CT-1, 1042, 940

Darken only one TAX PERIOD: 1st Quarter, 2nd Quarter, 3rd Quarter, 4th Quarter

35

FOR BANK USE IN MICR ENCODING

Federal Tax Deposit Coupon
Form 8109-B (Rev. 12-2002)

Federal unemployment insurance is paid by the end of the month following each quarter if the liability amount is more than $100. However, all unemployment tax liabilities outstanding at the end of a calendar year should be paid. Federal unemployment tax is paid to the federal government by making a tax deposit with an authorized bank. The deposit for federal unemployment tax is similar to the deposit required for income tax, social security tax, and Medicare tax. Form 8109, Federal Tax Deposit Coupon accompanies the unemployment tax deposit.

The total of federal unemployment taxes paid during a calendar year is reported on Form 940. Hobby Shack's federal unemployment tax liability at the end of December 31 is $34.60. Hobby Shack's Form 8109 for the fourth quarter is shown. The type of tax, federal unemployment tax, is identified by marking the 940 circle since this tax is reported to the government using Form 940. The calendar quarter is identified on the right side of the form.

©GETTY IMAGES/PHOTODISC

JOURNALIZING PAYMENT OF LIABILITY FOR FEDERAL UNEMPLOYMENT TAX

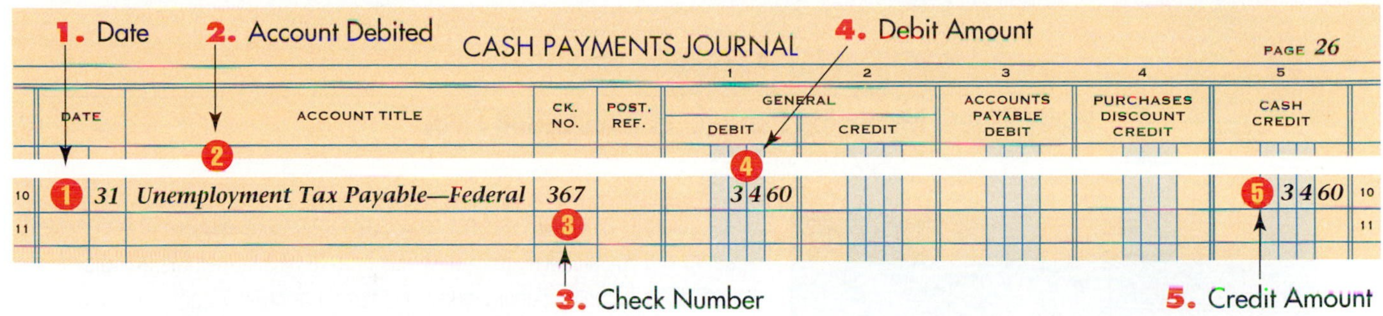

1. Date
2. Account Debited
CASH PAYMENTS JOURNAL
4. Debit Amount
PAGE 26
DATE
ACCOUNT TITLE
CK. NO.
POST. REF.
GENERAL
DEBIT
CREDIT
ACCOUNTS PAYABLE DEBIT
PURCHASES DISCOUNT CREDIT
CASH CREDIT
31
Unemployment Tax Payable—Federal
367
34 60
34 60
3. Check Number
5. Credit Amount

January 31. Paid cash for federal unemployment tax liability for quarter ended December 31, $34.60. Check No. 367.

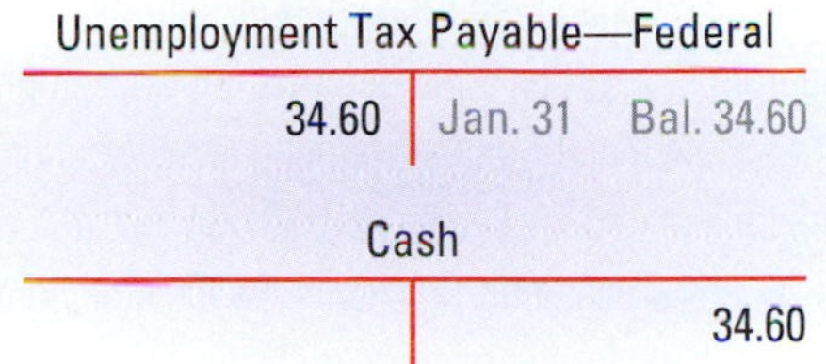

The balance of the liability account is reduced by this transaction. Therefore, Unemployment Tax Payable—Federal is debited for $34.60. The balance of the asset account, Cash, is decreased by a credit for the payment, $34.60.

STEPS JOURNALIZING A PAYMENT OF LIABILITY FOR FEDERAL UNEMPLOYMENT TAX

1. Write the date, *31*, in the Date column.
2. Write the title of the account debited, *Unemployment Tax Payable—Federal*, in the Account Title column.
3. Write the check number, *367*, in the Ck. No. column.
4. Write the debit amount, *$34.60*, in the General Debit column.
5. Write the amount of the credit to *Cash*, *$34.60*, in the Cash Credit column.

JOURNALIZING PAYMENT OF LIABILITY FOR STATE UNEMPLOYMENT TAX

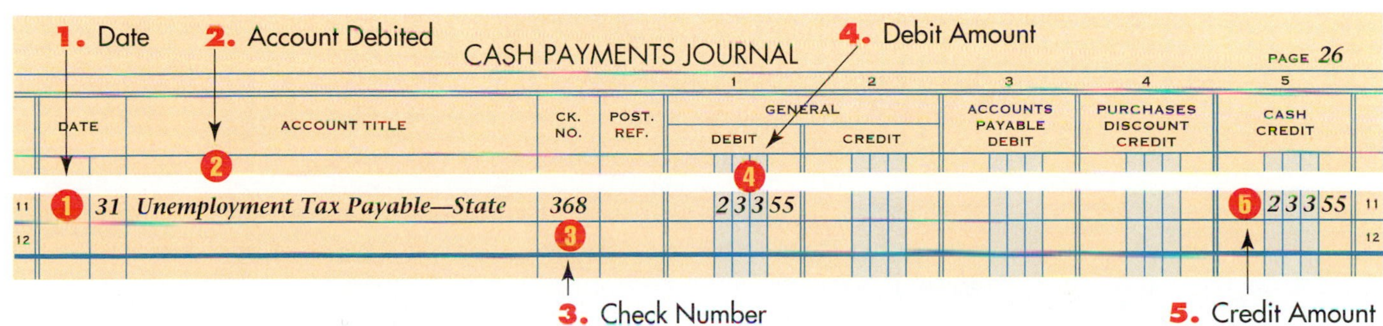

1. Date
2. Account Debited
CASH PAYMENTS JOURNAL
4. Debit Amount
PAGE 26
DATE
ACCOUNT TITLE
CK. NO.
POST. REF.
GENERAL
DEBIT
CREDIT
ACCOUNTS PAYABLE DEBIT
PURCHASES DISCOUNT CREDIT
CASH CREDIT
31
Unemployment Tax Payable—State
368
233 55
233 55
3. Check Number
5. Credit Amount

The same steps are followed as for federal unemployment tax. State requirements for reporting and paying state unemployment taxes vary. In general, employers are required to pay the state unemployment tax during the month following each calendar quarter.

January 31. Paid cash for state unemployment tax liability for quarter ended December 31, $233.55. Check No. 368.

careers in accounting

CAREERS IN ACCOUNTING • CAREERS IN ACCOUNTING • CAREERS IN ACCOUNTIN

Wally Wood, Managing Partner of Accounting Firm

COURTESY OF WALLY WOOD

Stop a farmer as he harvests his crop. Ask him how he decided to become a farmer and you are likely to hear, "I was born to be a farmer. My grandfather started this farm. My father worked this farm. I've never thought of doing anything else."

Likewise, Wally Wood was born into the accounting profession. Wally began working part-time for his father, K. Dale Wood, CPA, in 1973 at the age of 16. He started his accounting career doing write-up work for clients, recording their accounting transactions in accounting records, and preparing their financial statements. He also began preparing short tax returns.

After graduating from high school, he became a full-time employee of his father's accounting firm while majoring in accounting at the local university. "After about two years, due to circumstances beyond our control, I became the in-charge on several tax and small write-up clients. By the time I graduated from college, I was responsible for the majority of the tax and write-up clients."

Soon after graduating from college and passing the CPA examination, Wally became a partner in the firm, now called Wood and Wood, Ltd. Within three years, before the age of 30, Wally became managing partner of the firm. As the managing partner, Wally is ultimately responsible for the quality of all services provided by the firm. A managing partner also markets the firm's services to obtain new clients. Like the owner of any small business, the managing partner manages the firm's employees, technology, equipment, and accounting records.

The firm recently expanded by buying another CPA firm, becoming Wood, Wood and Taylor, Ltd. Wally notes, "As a small firm, we are uniquely positioned to provide personalized tax, audit, and consulting services to our clients, including individuals, small businesses, and government agencies. We also perform peer reviews for other accounting firms, evaluating their work to ensure that proper accounting and auditing standards are being applied."

As managing partner of an accounting firm, Wally recognizes his obligation to be involved in the growth and governance of his profession. As a member of several committees of his state society of certified public accountants, he is working to ensure that accountants provide quality services to their clients.

Salary Range: According to the 2005 salary survey conducted by financial recruiting company Robert Half International, directors (partners) of small public accounting firms earned between $69,000 and $87,750 a year. Graduate degrees and professional certifications can increase these salaries by up to 10 percent.

Qualifications: Starting your own accounting firm requires a combination of expertise and experience. After earning a Certified Public Accountant license, you should obtain several years' experience in another accounting firm.

Occupational Outlook: The Sarbanes-Oxley Act of 2002 has dramatically increased the demand for accountants who can establish, document, and evaluate the internal accounting controls required to prepare accurate financial statements. Clients continue to need tax planning and other consulting services.

term review

TERM REVIEW

lookback period

audit your understanding

AUDIT YOUR

1. For a monthly schedule depositor, when are payroll taxes paid to the federal government?
2. What are two different uses for Form 8109?

work together 13-4

WORK TOGETHER • WORK TOGETHER • WORK

Paying withholding and payroll taxes

A cash payments journal page is given in the *Working Papers*. Your instructor will guide you through the following examples. The following payroll data is for Digital Supplies for the monthly pay period ended March 31 of the current year.

Date Paid	Federal Income Tax Withheld	Employee Social Security Tax Withheld	Employee Medicare Tax Withheld
Mar. 31	$1,386.00	$1,322.05	$309.25

Credit balances on March 31 for the unemployment tax accounts for the first quarter are as follows: Unemployment Tax Payable—Federal, $511.75; Unemployment Tax Payable—State, $3,454.34. Digital Supplies pays both unemployment taxes each quarter.

1. Prepare a journal entry for payment of the withheld taxes. Digital Supplies is a monthly schedule depositor. Journalize Check No. 383 on cash payments journal page 14 using the date the taxes are due to the federal government.
2. Prepare journal entries for payment of the federal and state unemployment taxes liability. Assume both checks were prepared on the due date for the federal tax deposit. Check Nos. 401 and 402.

on your own 13-4

ON YOUR OWN • ON YOUR OWN • ON YOUR OWN

Paying withholding and payroll taxes

A cash payments journal page is given in the *Working Papers*. Work this problem independently. The following payroll data is for River Hardware for the monthly pay period ended June 30 of the current year.

Date Paid	Federal Income Tax Withheld	Employee Social Security Tax Withheld	Employee Medicare Tax Withheld
June 30	$1,052.00	$1,004.40	$234.95

Credit balances on June 30 for the unemployment tax accounts for the second quarter are as follows: Unemployment Tax Payable—Federal, $274.80; Unemployment Tax Payable—State, $1,922.40. River Hardware pays both unemployment taxes each quarter, regardless of the amount owed.

1. Prepare a journal entry for payment of the withheld taxes. River Hardware is a monthly schedule depositor. Journalize Check No. 678 on cash payments journal page 19 using the date the taxes are due to the federal government.
2. Prepare journal entries for payment of the federal and state unemployment taxes liability. Assume both checks were prepared on the due date for the federal tax deposit. Check Nos. 711 and 712.

SUMMARY

After completing this chapter, you can

1. Define important accounting terms related to payroll accounting, taxes, and reports.
2. Identify accounting concepts and practices related to payroll accounting, taxes, and reports.
3. Analyze payroll transactions and record a payroll.
4. Record employer payroll taxes.
5. Prepare selected payroll tax reports.
6. Pay and record withholding and payroll taxes.

Explore Accounting

Net Income vs. Taxable Income

Financial statements should provide important information that is accurate, reliable, comparable, and consistent. Over the years, a set of principles and concepts for maintaining accounting records and preparing financial statements has been developed. These guidelines are known as Generally Accepted Accounting Principles (GAAP). Most businesses use GAAP in preparing their financial statements and determining their net income.

The Internal Revenue Service (IRS) is responsible for collecting money to operate the federal government. Federal income taxes are calculated as a percentage of business or individual income. To accomplish its task, the IRS prepares Internal Revenue Service Regulations.

The objectives of the accounting profession and business community, however, are not necessarily the same as those of the federal government and the IRS. For example, a GAAP concept, Matching Expenses with Revenue, requires that the cost of business equipment be allocated over the usable life of the equipment. However, to encourage businesses to replace equipment more rapidly, IRS Regulations may permit the cost of equipment to be allocated more rapidly. Thus, in a certain year the expense for allocating cost would be greater for tax purposes than for financial reporting purposes. These types of differences create different amounts reported as net income for financial reporting purposes and for tax reporting purposes.

Thus, most businesses follow GAAP in preparing their financial statements but must follow IRS Regulations in preparing their tax returns. As a result, net income on financial statements generally differs from taxable income reported on tax returns.

Research: Examine several company annual reports. Study the financial statements and the notes connected with those statements. Is there any information indicating a difference between net income reported on the financial statements and taxable income for tax purposes? What are they, if any?

13-1 APPLICATION PROBLEM

Recording a payroll

Dana's payroll register has the following totals for two semimonthly pay periods, July 1–15 and July 16–31 of the current year.

Period	Total Earnings	Deductions					Net Pay
		Federal Income Tax	Social Security Tax	Medicare Tax	Other	Total	
July 1–15	$6,970.00	$685.00	$432.14	$101.07	B $180.00	$1,398.21	$5,571.79
July 16–31	6,040.00	572.00	374.48	87.58	B 150.00	1,184.06	4,855.94
Other Deductions: B—U.S. Savings Bonds							

Instructions:

Journalize payment of the two payrolls on page 15 of the cash payments journal given in the *Working Papers*. The first payroll was paid by Check No. 547 on July 15 of the current year. The second payroll was paid by Check No. 568 on July 31 of the current year.

13-2 APPLICATION PROBLEM

Recording employer payroll taxes

Use Malone's selected payroll information for the two semimonthly pay periods, April 1–15 and April 16–30 of the current year. Forms and a general journal are given in the *Working Papers*.

Employee Name	Accumulated Earnings, March 31	Total Earnings for April 1–15 Pay Period	Total Earnings for April 16–30 Pay Period
Bolser, Frank T.	$4,860.00	$ 810.00	$ 795.00
Denham, Beth R.	5,670.00	945.00	980.00
Harjo, Teresa S.	7,500.00	1,250.00	1,250.00
Knutzen, John L.	3,720.00	620.00	635.00
Prescott, Laura F.	4,560.00	760.00	740.00
Schmidt, Ian T.	6,900.00	1,150.00	1,125.00

Employer payroll tax rates are as follows: social security, 6.2%; Medicare, 1.45%; federal unemployment, 0.8%; state unemployment, 5.4%. Unemployment taxes are owed on the first $7,000.00 of earnings for each employee.

Instructions:

1. Calculate the amount of earnings subject to unemployment taxes for the April 1–15 pay period. Note that Ian T. Schmidt has accumulated earnings on March 31 of $6,900.00. Therefore, only $100.00 ($7,000.00 – $6,900.00) of his April 1–15 earnings is subject to unemployment tax.
2. Calculate the employer payroll tax amounts for the April 1–15 pay period.
3. Journalize the employer payroll taxes on page 16 of a general journal. Use the date of April 15 of the current year. The source document is Memorandum No. 69.
4. Calculate the employer payroll taxes for the April 16–30 pay period. Calculate April 15 accumulated earnings by adding total earnings for the April 1–15 pay period to the March 31 accumulated earnings. Note that only part of Beth R. Denham's earnings for April 16–20 are subject to unemployment tax.
5. Journalize the employer payroll taxes on page 16 of a general journal. Use the date of April 30 of the current year. The source document is Memorandum No. 76.

13-3 APPLICATION PROBLEM

Reporting withholding and payroll taxes

The following payroll data is for Eagle Toys for the second quarter of the current year.

Date Paid	Total Earnings	Federal Income Tax Withheld	Employee Social Security Tax Withheld	Employee Medicare Tax Withheld
Apr. 30	$ 9,166.00	$654.00	$568.29	$132.91
May 31	10,382.00	687.00	643.68	150.54
June 30	9,872.00	718.00	612.06	143.14

Additional data:

1. Company address: 784 McDonald Street, Mesa, AZ 85201
2. Employer identification number: 80-7818356
3. Number of employees: 5
4. Federal tax payments have been made on May 15, June 15, and July 15.

Instructions:

Prepare the Form 941, Employer's Quarterly Federal Tax Return, given in the *Working Papers*. Use the date July 21. Sign your name as the manager of the company. Amounts on lines 13 and 17d may not equal, due to rounding.

13-4 APPLICATION PROBLEM

Paying withholding and payroll taxes

The following payroll data is for Zimmerman Company for the first quarter of the current year.

Period	Total Earnings	Federal Income Tax Withheld
March	$17,560.00	$1,548.00
First Quarter	$52,210.00	—

In addition, total earnings are subject to 6.2% employee and 6.2% employer social security tax, plus 1.45% employee and 1.45% employer Medicare tax. The federal unemployment tax rate is 0.8% and the state unemployment tax rate is 5.4% of total earnings. No total earnings have exceeded the tax base for calculating unemployment taxes.

Instructions:

1. Calculate the appropriate liability amount of social security and Medicare taxes for March. Journalize the payment of the withheld taxes on page 8 of the cash payments journal given in the *Working Papers*. The taxes were paid by Check No. 813 on April 15 of the current year.
2. Calculate the appropriate federal unemployment tax liability for the first quarter. Journalize payment of this liability in the cash payments journal. The tax was paid by Check No. 830 on April 30 of the current year.
3. Calculate the appropriate state unemployment tax liability for the first quarter. Journalize payment of this liability in the cash payments journal. The tax was paid by Check No. 831 on April 30 of the current year.

13-5 MASTERY PROBLEM

AUTOMATED ACCOUNTING PEACHTREE QUICKBOOKS

Journalizing payroll transactions

Keller Systems, Inc., completed payroll transactions during the period May 1 to June 15 of the current year. Payroll tax rates are as follows: social security, 6.2%; Medicare, 1.45%; federal unemployment, 0.8%; state unemployment, 5.4%. The company buys savings bonds for employees as accumulated withholdings reach the necessary amount to purchase a bond. No total earnings have exceeded the tax base for calculating unemployment taxes. Keller Systems is a monthly schedule depositor for payroll taxes.

Instructions:

1. Journalize the following transactions on page 14 of the cash payments journal and page 10 of the general journal given in the *Working Papers*. Source documents are abbreviated as follows: check, C, and memorandum, M.

Transactions:

May 15. Paid cash for April's payroll tax liability. Withheld taxes from April payrolls: employee income tax, $532.00; social security tax, $634.88; and Medicare tax, $148.48. C421.

15. Paid cash for semimonthly payroll. Total earnings, $5,250.00; withholdings: employee income tax, $273.00; U.S. Savings Bonds, $60.00 (calculate the social security and Medicare deductions). C422.

15. Recorded employer payroll taxes expense for the May 15 payroll. M42.

15. Paid cash for U.S. Savings Bonds for employees, $300.00. C423.

31. Paid cash for semimonthly payroll. Gross wages, $5,310.00; withholdings: employee income tax, $276.00; U.S. Savings Bonds, $60.00. C461.

31. Recorded employer payroll taxes expense for the May 31 payroll. M46.

31. Paid cash for federal unemployment tax liability for quarter ended March 31, $245.76. C462.

31. Paid cash for state unemployment tax liability for quarter ended March 31, $1,658.88. C463.

June 15. Paid cash for the May liability for employee income tax, social security tax, and Medicare tax, C487. (Calculate the social security and Medicare tax liabilities by multiplying total earnings for the period by 12.4% for social security tax and 2.9% for Medicare tax.)

15. Paid cash for semimonthly payroll. Gross wages, $5,280.00; withholdings: employee income tax, $274.00; U.S. Savings Bonds, $75.00. C488.

15. Recorded employer payroll taxes expense. M53.

2. Prove and rule the cash payments journal.

13-6 CHALLENGE PROBLEM

PEACHTREE QUICKBOOKS

Journalizing and posting payroll transactions

Golf Design, Inc., completed payroll transactions during the period January 1 to April 30 of the current year. Payroll tax rates are as follows: social security, 6.2%; Medicare, 1.45%; federal unemployment, 0.8%; and state unemployment, 5.4%. The company buys savings bonds for employees as the accumulated withholdings reach the necessary amount to purchase a bond. No total earnings have exceeded the tax base for calculating unemployment taxes.

The balances in the general ledger as of January 1 of the current year are recorded in the *Working Papers*.

Chart of Accounts

Account Number	Account Title
2120	Employee Income Tax Payable
2130	Social Security Tax Payable
2140	Medicare Tax Payable
2150	Unemployment Tax Payable—Federal
2160	Unemployment Tax Payable—State
2180	U.S. Savings Bonds Payable
6150	Payroll Taxes Expense
6170	Salary Expense

Instructions:

1. Journalize the following transactions on page 1 of the cash payments journal and the general journal given in the *Working Papers*. Payroll withholdings for employee income tax and U.S. Savings Bonds are provided. Calculate other payroll withholdings using the tax rates provided. Source documents are abbreviated as follows: check, C, and memorandum, M.

Transactions:

Jan. 2. Wrote a check for 15 U.S. Savings Bonds at $25.00 each for employees. C195.
15. Paid the December liability for employee income tax, social security tax, and Medicare tax. C204.
31. Wrote a check for federal unemployment tax liability for quarter ended December 31. C210.
31. Wrote a check for state unemployment tax liability for quarter ended December 31. C211.
31. Paid January payroll (total payroll, $12,200.00, less deductions: employee income tax, $805.00; U.S. Savings Bonds, $125.00). C216.
31. Recorded employer payroll taxes expense. M98.
Posting. Post the items that are to be posted individually.

Feb. 15. Wrote a check for January liability for employee income tax and for social security tax and Medicare tax. C222.
28. Paid February payroll (total payroll, $12,360.00, less deductions: employee income tax, $816.00; U.S. Savings Bonds, $125.00). C232.
28. Recorded employer payroll taxes expense. M107.
Posting. Post the items that are to be posted individually.

2. Prove and rule cash payments journal page 1. Carry the column totals forward to page 2 of the cash payments journal.
3. Journalize the following transactions on page 2 of the cash payments journal and continuing on page 1 of the general journal.

Transactions:

Mar. 15. Wrote a check for February liability for employee income tax, social security tax, and Medicare tax. C237.
31. Paid March payroll (total payroll, $11,860.00, less deductions: employee income tax, $783.00; U.S. Savings Bonds, $125.00). C258.
31. Recorded employer payroll taxes expense. M116.
Posting. Post the items that are to be posted individually.

Apr. 1. Paid cash for 15 U.S. Savings Bonds at $25.00 each for employees. C259.
15. Wrote a check for March liability for employee income tax, social security tax, and Medicare tax. C270.
30. Wrote a check for federal unemployment tax liability for quarter ended March 31. C276.
30. Wrote a check for state unemployment tax liability for quarter ended March 31. C277.
Posting. Post the items that are to be posted individually.

4. Prove and rule cash payments journal page 2.

applied communication

One of the unwritten rules of business is that payroll information is private and confidential. People usually do not want their co-workers to know how much they are paid. This common business practice presents a challenge for employees responsible for payroll accounting. Payroll workers handle many different types of data. The payroll department records personal information about employees, such as addresses and social security numbers, and verifies and totals time cards. In addition, each pay period, payroll accountants calculate each employee's earnings, deductions, and net pay. It is important for payroll employees to be trustworthy and able to maintain confidentiality.

Instructions: In the form of a memorandum, write a statement of a company's policy regarding the confidentiality of payroll information. The memorandum should be addressed to the employees of the payroll department.

APPLIED COMMUNICATION

cases for critical thinking

Case 1

Wyatt Company has decided to hire a sales representative. The business can afford to pay the representative a salary of only $30,000.00. The accounting assistant informs the manager that hiring the representative will cost the business more than the $30,000.00 salary. Do you agree with the accounting assistant? Explain your response.

Case 2

One of the unwritten rules of business is that payroll information is private and confidential. People usually do not want their co-workers to know how much they are paid. This common business practice presents a challenge for employees responsible for payroll accounting. Payroll workers handle many different types of data. The payroll department records personal information about employees, such as addresses and social security numbers, and verifies and totals time cards. In addition, each pay period, payroll accountants calculate each employee's earnings, deductions, and net pay. Why is it important for payroll employees to be trustworthy and able to maintain confidentiality?

CASES FOR CRITICAL THINKING • CASES

SCANS workplace competency

Basic Skill: Reading

Concept: Information can be critical to the success of a company. In addition to its own internal information, a company needs information its workers acquire about technology, the industry, and competitors, as well as information about the business climate. Much of this information can be found by locating, understanding, and interpreting written information in prose and in documents such as manuals, graphs, and schedules.

Application: Whether you have a part-time or full-time job, you will have social security tax and Medicare tax withheld from your paycheck. These taxes provide benefits to citizens who meet qualifications established by the government. Look up the Social Security Act in an encyclopedia or other reference work in your library or on the Internet. Write a brief analysis of social security. Describe its history, current issues and concerns, and its impact on society and business.

SCANS WORKPLACE COMPETENCY

• auditing for errors

In June, the liability for federal and state unemployment tax for Excelsior Corporation is recorded at about the same amount as for previous months. Jackie Blette suggests that it usually begins to decrease in June, except when many new graduates are hired that month. You have been asked to investigate the payroll data to discover whether there is a problem.

Instructions

1. Why would the liability for unemployment tax begin to decline in June?
2. If there is an error in the unemployment liability amounts, what is the likely cause?
3. Examine the information below and on a separate sheet of paper write the correct amounts for the unemployment tax liabilities.

Accumulated Earnings Jan.–May	June Total Earnings	Federal Unemployment Tax	State Unemployment Tax
4,260.00	810.00	6.48	43.74
5,200.00	1,100.00	8.80	59.40
6,450.00	1,250.00	10.00	67.50
6,800.00	1,350.00	10.80	72.90
3,600.00	1,200.00	9.60	64.80

• analyzing Best Buy's financial statements

Every publicly traded company is required to have an annual audit of its financial statements. Independent auditors examine how the company records transactions and prepares financial statements. The auditors issue an opinion that states whether the financial statements present fairly the financial position of the company.

Instructions: Use Best Buy's Report of Independent Auditors on Appendix B page B-18 to answer the following questions.

1. What is the auditor's responsibility with respect to the financial statements?
2. What standards are used to conduct the audit?
3. Is the auditor required to obtain absolute assurance that the financial statements are exactly correct?
4. Must auditors examine every transaction?
5. What public accounting firm audits Best Buy?

Payroll Taxes and Journal Entries

In an automated payroll system, the computer is used to maintain the employee database, to record payroll transactions at the end of each pay period, and to display and print various payroll reports.

Generating Payroll Journal Entries

Automated Accounting 8.0 can generate the current payroll journal entry.

1. Choose the Current Payroll Journal Entry menu item from the Options menu. Note that you must first have a payroll entered into the system before payroll journal entries can be generated.
2. When the confirmation dialog box appears, click Yes.
3. Click the Post button.

Generating the Employer's Payroll Taxes Journal Entries

Automated Accounting 8.0 can also generate the current payroll taxes journal entry.

1. Choose the Employer's Payroll Taxes menu item from the Options menu.
2. When the confirmation dialog box appears, click Yes.
3. Click the Post button.

Generating Payroll Reports

1. Click the Reports toolbar button.
2. Choose the Payroll Reports option from the Select a Report Group list.

There are four types of payroll reports available:

1. *Employee List Report:* The report provides a complete listing of the employee payroll information.
2. *Payroll Report:* The report shows employee earnings and withholding information for the month, quarter, and year. Information is listed by employee and is summarized.
3. *Quarterly Report:* The report summarizes wages subject to social security and Medicare taxes. The information is listed by employee.
4. *W-2 Statements:* The report summarizes an employee's taxable wages and various withholdings for both the employee and the Internal Revenue Service.

After each payroll period, the appropriate reports may be generated as needed. The W-2 statement is generated only at the end of the calendar year.

AUTOMATING MASTERY PROBLEM 13-5: Journalizing payroll transactions

Instructions:

1. Load the *Automated Accounting 8.0* or higher software.
2. Select data file F13-5 from the appropriate directory/folder.
3. Select File from the menu bar and choose the Save As menu command. Key the path to the drive and directory that contains your data files. Save the data file with a filename of F13-5 XXX XXX (where X's are your first and last names).
4. Access Problem Instructions through the Browser tool. Read the Problem Instructions screen.
5. Journalize the transactions listed in Mastery Problem 13-5.
6. Save your file and exit the Automated Accounting software.

Automating Payroll Journal Entries (optional)

This problem requires that you first complete a payroll. Therefore, you must have already completed Automated Accounting Problem 12-6.

Instructions:

1. Load the *Automated Accounting 8.0* or higher software.
2. Select the file that is your solution to Problem 12-6 in Chapter 12. It should be saved as F12-6 XXX XXX (where the X's are your first and last name).
3. Select File from the menu bar and choose the Save As menu command. Key the path to the drive and directory that contains your data files. Save the data file with a filename of F13-Opt XXX XXX (where the X's are your first and last name).
4. Access Problem Instructions through the Browser tool. Read the Problem Instructions screen.
5. Complete the problem.
6. Save your file and exit the Automated Accounting software.

An Accounting Cycle for a Corporation: Journalizing and Posting Transactions

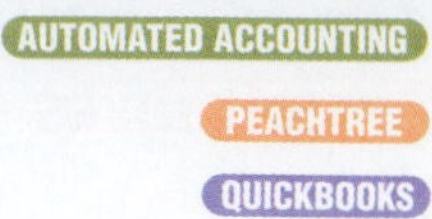

Reinforcement Activity 2 reinforces learning from Part 2, Chapters 9 through 16. Activities cover a complete accounting cycle for a merchandising business organized as a corporation. Reinforcement Activity 2 is a single problem divided into two parts. Part A includes learning from Chapters 9 through 13. Part B includes learning from Chapters 14 through 16.

The accounting work of a single merchandising business for the last month of a yearly fiscal period is used in this reinforcement activity. The records kept and reports prepared, however, illustrate the application of accounting concepts for all merchandising businesses.

MEDICAL SERVICES COMPANY (MSC)

Medical Services Company (MSC), a merchandising business, is organized as a corporation. The business sells a complete line of medical accessories, from crutches to lift chairs. MSC is located in a medical office plaza adjacent to the hospital and is open for business Monday through Saturday. A monthly rent is paid for the building. MSC accepts credit cards from customers.

CHART OF ACCOUNTS

MSC uses the chart of accounts shown on the next page.

JOURNALS AND LEDGERS

The journals and ledgers used by MSC are listed below. Models of the journals and ledgers are shown in the textbook chapters indicated.

Journals and Ledgers	Chapter
Purchases journal	9
Cash payments journal	9
General journal	9
Sales journal	10
Cash receipts journal	10
Accounts payable ledger	11
Accounts receivable ledger	11
General ledger	11

CHART OF ACCOUNTS

GENERAL LEDGER

Balance Sheet Accounts

(1000) ASSETS
1100 Current Assets
1110 Cash
1120 Petty Cash
1130 Accounts Receivable
1135 Allowance for Uncollectible Accounts
1140 Merchandise Inventory
1145 Supplies—Office
1150 Supplies—Store
1160 Prepaid Insurance
1200 Plant Assets
1210 Office Equipment
1220 Accumulated Depreciation—Office Equipment
1230 Store Equipment
1240 Accumulated Depreciation—Store Equipment

(2000) LIABILITIES
2110 Accounts Payable
2115 Federal Income Tax Payable
2120 Employee Income Tax Payable
2130 Social Security Tax Payable
2135 Medicare Tax Payable
2140 Sales Tax Payable
2150 Unemployment Tax Payable—Federal
2160 Unemployment Tax Payable—State
2170 Health Insurance Premiums Payable
2180 U.S. Savings Bonds Payable
2190 United Way Donations Payable
2195 Dividends Payable

(3000) OWNER'S EQUITY
3110 Capital Stock
3120 Retained Earnings
3130 Dividends
3140 Income Summary

Income Statement Accounts

(4000) OPERATING REVENUE
4110 Sales
4120 Sales Discount
4130 Sales Returns and Allowances

(5000) COST OF MERCHANDISE
5110 Purchases
5120 Purchases Discount
5130 Purchases Returns and Allowances

(6000) OPERATING EXPENSES
6110 Advertising Expense
6115 Cash Short and Over
6120 Credit Card Fee Expense
6125 Depreciation Expense—Office Equipment
6130 Depreciation Expense—Store Equipment
6135 Insurance Expense
6140 Miscellaneous Expense
6150 Payroll Taxes Expense
6160 Rent Expense
6165 Repairs Expenses
6170 Salary Expense
6175 Supplies Expense—Office
6180 Supplies Expense—Store
6185 Uncollectible Accounts Expense
6190 Utilities Expense

(7000) INCOME TAX EXPENSE
7105 Federal Income Tax Expense

SUBSIDIARY LEDGERS

Accounts Receivable Ledger

110 Bratton Clinic
120 Clegg Medical Center
130 Glenmore School
140 Jamacus Clinic
150 Odom Daycare
160 Treet Retirement Home

Accounts Payable Ledger

210 Armstrong Medical
220 Cross Office Supply
230 Evans Supply
240 Ogden Instruments
250 Spencer Industries
260 Ziegler, Inc.

RECORDING TRANSACTIONS

The December 1 account balances for the general and subsidiary ledgers are given in the *Working Papers.*

Instructions:

1. Journalize the following transactions completed during December of the current year. Use page 12 of a sales journal, page 12 of a purchases journal, page 12 of a general journal, page 12 of a cash receipts journal, and page 23 of a cash payments journal. MSC offers sales terms of 2/10, n/30. The sales tax rate is 6%. Source documents are abbreviated as follows: check, C; memorandum, M; purchase invoice, P; receipt, R; sales invoice, S; terminal summary, TS; debit memorandum, DM; credit memorandum, CM.

Dec. 1. Paid cash for rent, $1,200.00. C372.
2. Paid cash for electric bill, $346.20. C373.
2. Received cash on account from Clegg Medical Center, covering S64 for $413.40, less 2% sales discount. R92.
3. Paid cash for miscellaneous expense, $72.00. C374.
3. Paid cash on account to Spencer Industries, covering P73 for $580.00, less 2% discount. C375.
4. Sold merchandise on account to Bratton Clinic, $450.00, plus sales tax, $27.00; total, $477.00. S67.
5. Recorded cash and credit card sales, $5,796.00, plus sales tax, $347.76; total, $6,143.76. TS45.

Posting. Post the items that are to be posted individually. Post the journals in this order: sales journal, purchases journal, general journal, cash receipts journal, and cash payments journal.

7. Sold merchandise on account to Glenmore School, $462.00. Glenmore School is exempt from sales tax. S68.
7. Received cash on account from Treet Retirement Home, $432.48, covering S65. R93.
8. Bought office supplies on account from Cross Office Supply, $351.60. M43.
9. Purchased merchandise on account from Ogden Instruments, $2,250, less a 40% trade discount. P77.
9. Bought store supplies on account from Ziegler, Inc., $330.00. M44.
10. Paid cash for office supplies, $174.00. C376.
11. Paid cash on account to Evans Supply, $1,170.00, covering P74. C377.
11. Purchased merchandise on account from Spencer Industries, $1,032.00. P78.
12. Paid cash for store supplies, $264.00. C378.
12. Recorded cash and credit card sales, $7,125.00, plus sales tax, $427.50; total, $7,552.50. TS46.

Posting. Post the items that are to be posted individually.

14. Purchased merchandise on account from Evans Supply, $3,276.00. P79.
14. Sold merchandise on account to Odom Daycare, $170.00, plus sales tax, $10.20; total, $180.20. S69.
14. Paid cash for advertising, $415.00. C379.
15. Returned $226.00 of merchandise to Evans Supply from P79, $226.00. DM4.
15. Paid cash on account to Armstrong Medical, $1,272.00, covering P75. C380.
15. Received cash on account from Jamacus Clinic, $821.50, covering S66. R94.
15. Sold merchandise on account to Clegg Medical Center, $490.00, plus sales tax, $29.40; total, $519.40. S70.
15. Paid cash for liability for employee income tax, $342.00, social security tax, $767.00, and Medicare tax, $179.38; total, $1,288.38. C381.
15. Paid cash for semimonthly payroll, $2,313.85 (total payroll, $2,930.00, less deductions: employee income tax, $162.00; social security tax, $181.66; Medicare tax, $42.49; health insurance, $170.00; U.S. Savings Bonds, $30.00; United Way donations, $30.00). C382.

15. Recorded employer payroll taxes, $248.95, for the semimonthly pay period ended December 15. Taxes owed are: social security tax, $181.66; Medicare tax, $42.49; federal unemployment tax, $3.20; and state unemployment tax, $21.60. M45.
19. Recorded cash and credit card sales, $6,925.00, plus sales tax, $415.50; total, $7,340.50. TS47.
Posting. Post the items that are to be posted individually.
23. Paid cash on account to Ogden Instruments, $2,200.00, covering P76. C383.
24. Received cash on account from Odom Daycare, covering S69 for $180.20, less 2% discount. R95.
24. Granted credit to Clegg Medical Center for merchandise returned, $120.00, plus sales tax, $7.20, from S70; total, $127.20. CM5.
26. Recorded cash and credit card sales, $6,980.00, plus sales tax, $418.80; total, $7,398.80. TS48.
Posting. Post the items that are to be posted individually.

MSC's bank charges a fee for handling the collection of credit card sales deposited during the month. The credit card fee is deducted from Audio Solutions' bank account. The amount is then shown on the bank statement. The credit card fee is recorded in the cash payments journal as a reduction in cash.

Dec. 28. Recorded credit card fee expense, $342.00. M46. (Debit Credit Card Fee Expense; credit Cash.)

2. Prove and rule page 23 of the cash payments journal.
3. Carry the column totals forward to page 24 of the cash payments journal.
4. Journalize the following transactions.

Dec. 30. Purchased merchandise on account from Armstrong Medical, $1,940.00. P80.
31. Paid cash to replenish the petty cash fund, $145.20: office supplies, $35.00; store supplies, $19.00; advertising, $64.00; miscellaneous, $26.00; cash short, $1.20. C384.
31. Paid cash for semimonthly payroll, $2,462.32 (total payroll, $3,120.00, less deductions: employee income tax, $189.00; social security tax, $193.44; Medicare tax, $45.24; health insurance, $170.00; U.S. Savings Bonds, $30.00; United Way donations, $30.00). C385.
31. Recorded employer payroll taxes, $263.48, for the semimonthly pay period ended December 31. Taxes owed are: social security tax, $193.44: Medicare tax, $45.24; federal unemployment tax, $3.20; and state unemployment tax, $21.60. M47.
31. Recorded cash and credit card sales, $3,890.00, plus sales tax, $233.40; total, $4,123.40. TS49.
Posting. Post the items that are to be posted individually.

5. Prove and rule the sales journal. Post the totals of the special columns.
6. Total and rule the purchases journal. Post the total.
7. Prove the equality of debits and credits for the cash receipts and cash payments journals.
8. Prove cash. The balance on the next unused check stub is $40,126.14.
9. Rule the cash receipts journal. Post the totals of the special columns.
10. Rule the cash payments journal. Post the totals of the special columns.
11. Prepare a schedule of accounts receivable and a schedule of accounts payable. Prove the accuracy of the subsidiary ledgers by comparing the schedule totals with the balances of the controlling accounts in the general ledger. If the totals are not the same, find and correct the errors.

The ledgers used in Reinforcement Activity 2—Part A are needed to complete Reinforcement Activity 2—Part B.

CHAPTER 14 Distributing Dividends and Preparing a Work Sheet for a Merchandising Business

OBJECTIVES & TERMS

After studying Chapter 14, you will be able to:

1. Define accounting terms related to distributing dividends and preparing a work sheet for a merchandising business.
2. Identify accounting concepts and practices related to distributing dividends and preparing a work sheet for a merchandising business.
3. Journalize the declaration and payment of a dividend.
4. Begin a work sheet for a merchandising business.
5. Plan work sheet adjustments for merchandise inventory, supplies, prepaid expenses, uncollectible accounts, and depreciation.
6. Calculate federal income tax and plan the work sheet adjustment for federal income tax.
7. Complete a work sheet for a merchandising business.

- retained earnings
- dividends
- board of directors
- declaring a dividend
- merchandise inventory
- uncollectible accounts
- allowance method of recording losses from uncollectible accounts
- book value
- book value of accounts receivable
- current assets
- plant assets
- depreciation expense
- estimated salvage value
- straight-line method of depreciation
- accumulated depreciation
- book value of a plant asset

accounting in the real world

Lowe's

©EMILE WAMSTEKER/BLOOMBERG NEWS/LANDOV

LOWE'S—THE GOOD NEIGHBOR

Welcome to the neighborhood! That's the reaction Lowe's wants when it opens a store in your neighborhood. Lowe's is working to make home improvement more convenient for its customers. By providing the right products at the right price, whether in local stores or at Lowes.com, the company seeks to make it easy for its customers to improve the quality and value of their homes.

Lowe's is also investing in its community. The company provides relief supplies to victims of natural disasters, financial support for Habitat for Humanity, and educational grants to K-12 public education systems.

Community involvement is important to the employees at Lowe's. The company encourages volunteerism through Lowe's Heroes, a program focused on home safety. Looking out for your neighbor—that's what being a good neighbor is all about.

Critical Thinking

1. Beyond having quality products at a fair price, how do Lowe's and other home improvement companies assist customers to improve their homes?
2. How should Lowe's account for a donation of lumber to a Habitat for Humanity house?

accountingxtra.swlearning.com

Source: http://images.lowes.com/general/a/anreport03/Annual_Report.pdf

internet activity

FINDING STOCK PRICES

Many company web sites give a history of the stock prices for the company's stock. Go to the homepage for a company of your choice. Look under a heading such as "About Us" or "Investor Relations" to find information about the price of the company's stock.

Instructions

1. Find the closing stock price from the previous day's trading.
2. Find the highest price for which the stock sold on the previous day.
3. Find the lowest price for which the stock sold on the previous day.

LESSON • LESSON • LESSON • LESSON • LESSON • LESSON

14-1 Distributing Corporate Earnings to Stockholders

FINANCIAL INFORMATION

Management decisions about future business operations are often based on financial information. This information shows whether a profit is being made or a loss is being incurred. Profit or loss information helps an owner or manager determine future changes. Financial information is also needed to prepare required tax reports.

Hobby Shack uses a fiscal year that begins on January 1 and ends on December 31. Therefore, Hobby Shack summarizes its financial information on December 31 of each year.

©GETTY IMAGES/PHOTODISC

MAKING ETHICAL DECISIONS • MAKING ETHICAL DECISIONS • MAKING ETHICAL DECISIONS

making ethical decisions

He's Guilty!

A company that believes one of its employees is stealing may obtain the services of a Certified Fraud Examiner (CFE). The CFE is trained to examine accounting records and obtain other evidence related to the alleged theft. CFEs often serve as expert witnesses in court. The Code of Professional Ethics of the Association of Certified Fraud Examiners provides its members with guidance on how to serve as an expert witness. The Code states that the CFE should obtain evidence that provides a reasonable basis for his or her opinion. However, the CFE should never express an opinion on the guilt or innocence of any person.

Instructions

Access the ACFE Code of Professional Ethics of the Association of Certified Fraud Examiners at www.cfenet.com. Citing the section, what other advice does the Code provide a CFE when serving as an expert witness?

STOCKHOLDERS' EQUITY ACCOUNTS USED BY A CORPORATION

(3000) STOCKHOLDERS' EQUITY

3110 Capital Stock
3120 Retained Earnings
3130 Dividends
3140 Income Summary

A corporation's ownership is divided into units. Each unit of ownership in a corporation is known as a *share of stock*. An owner of one or more shares of a corporation is known as a *stockholder*. Each stockholder is an owner of a corporation.

Owners' equity accounts for a corporation normally are listed under a major chart of accounts division titled Stockholders' Equity.

Most corporations have many stockholders. It is not practical to have a separate owner's equity account for each stockholder. Instead, a single owners' equity account, titled Capital Stock, is used for the investment of all owners.

A second stockholders' equity account is used to record a corporation's earnings. Net income increases a corporation's total stockholders' equity. Some income may be retained by a corporation for business expansion. An amount earned by a corporation and not yet distributed to stockholders is called **retained earnings**. Retained Earnings is the title of the account used to record a corporation's earnings.

Some income may be given to stockholders as a return on their investments. A third stockholders' equity account is used to record the distribution of a corporation's earnings to stockholders. Earnings distributed to stockholders are called **dividends**. A corporation's dividend account is a temporary account similar to a proprietorship's drawing account. Each time a dividend is declared, an account titled Dividends is debited. At the end of each fiscal period, the balance in the dividends account is closed to Retained Earnings.

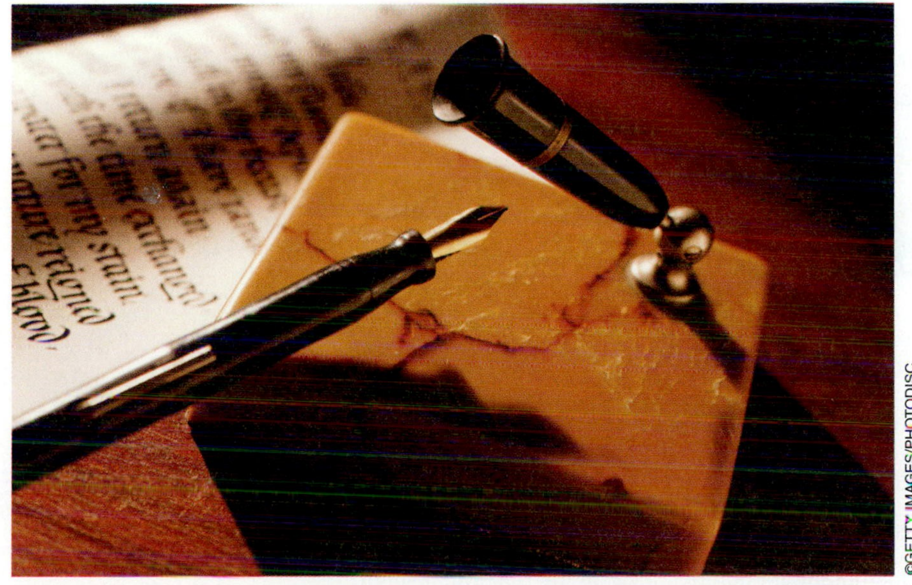

©GETTY IMAGES/PHOTODISC

REMEMBER *Dividends* is a temporary account that is closed to *Retained Earnings* at the end of the fiscal period.

DECLARING A DIVIDEND

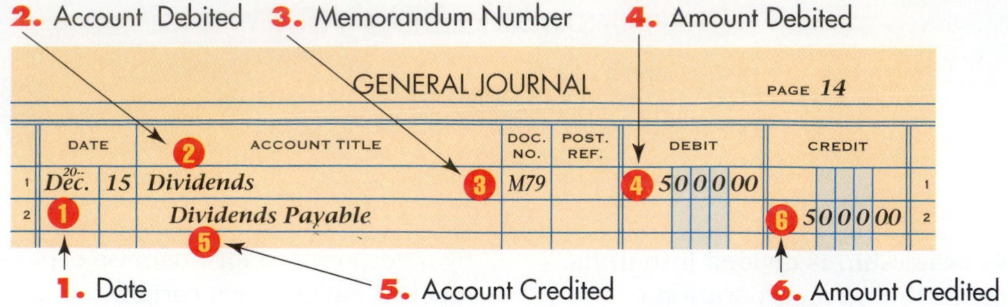

A group of persons elected by the stockholders to manage a corporation is called a **board of directors**. Dividends can be distributed to stockholders only by formal action of a corporation's board of directors. [*CONCEPT: Business Entity*]

Action by a board of directors to distribute corporate earnings to stockholders is called **declaring a dividend**. Dividends normally are declared on one date and paid on a later date. If a board of directors declares a dividend, the corporation is then obligated to pay the dividend. The dividend is a liability that must be recorded in the corporation's accounts.

Hobby Shack declares dividends each March 15, June 15, September 15, and December 15. The dividends are then paid on the 15th of the following month.

The stockholders' equity account, Dividends, has a normal debit balance and is increased by a $5,000.00 debit. Dividends Payable is credited for $5,000.00 to show the increase in this liability account.

December 15. Hobby Shack's board of directors declared a quarterly dividend of $2.00 per share; capital stock issued is 2,500 shares; total dividend, $5,000.00. Date of payment is January 15. Memorandum No. 79.

Dividends

3/15 Decl.	5,000.00		
6/15 Decl.	5,000.00		
9/15 Decl.	5,000.00		
12/15 Decl.	5,000.00		

Dividends Payable

4/15 Paid	5,000.00	3/15 Decl.	5,000.00
7/15 Paid	5,000.00	6/15 Decl.	5,000.00
10/15 Paid	5,000.00	9/15 Decl.	5,000.00
		12/15 Decl.	5,000.00

Number of Shares Outstanding	×	Quarterly Dividend per Share	=	Total Quarterly Dividend
2,500	×	$2.00	=	$5,000.00

STEPS • STEPS • STEPS • STEPS • STEPS • STEPS • STEPS • STEPS • STEPS • STEPS

JOURNALIZING DECLARING A DIVIDEND

1. Write the date, *20--, Dec. 15*, in the Date column.
2. Write the title of the account debited, *Dividends*, in the Account Title column.
3. Write the memorandum number, *M79*, in the Doc. No. column.
4. Write the debit amount, *$5,000.00*, in the Debit column.
5. Write the title of the account credited, *Dividends Payable*, on the next line of the Account Title column, indented about 1 centimeter.
6. Write the credit amount, *$5,000.00*, in the Credit column.

PAYING A DIVIDEND

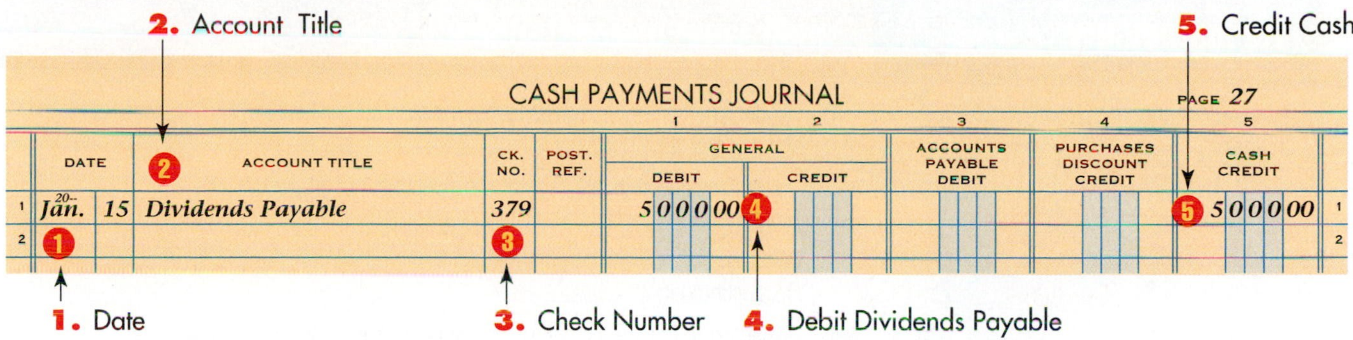

Hobby Shack issues one check for the amount of the total dividend to be paid. This check is deposited in a special dividend checking account. A separate check for each stockholder is drawn on this special account. The special account avoids a large number of cash payments journal entries and also reserves cash specifically for paying dividends.

A check is often made payable to an agent, such as a bank. The agent then handles the details of sending dividend checks to individual stockholders.

January 15. Paid cash for quarterly dividend declared December 15, $5,000.00. Check No. 379.

Dividends Payable

4/15 Paid	5,000.00	3/15 Decl.	5,000.00
7/15 Paid	5,000.00	6/15 Decl.	5,000.00
10/15 Paid	5,000.00	9/15 Decl.	5,000.00
1/15 Paid	5,000.00	12/15 Decl.	5,000.00

Cash

		1/15 Paid	5,000.00

When this entry is posted, the dividends payable account has a zero balance.

STEPS: JOURNALIZING THE PAYMENT OF DIVIDENDS

1. Write the date, *20--, Jan. 15*, in the Date column.
2. Write the account title, *Dividends Payable*, in the Account Title column.
3. Write the check number, *379*, in the Ck. No. column.
4. Write the debit amount, *$5,000.00*, in the General Debit column.
5. Write the credit amount, *$5,000.00*, in the Cash Credit column.

FYI — FOR YOUR INFORMATION

Dividends are declared on one date and paid on a later date. Only stockholders owning the stock on the date of record specified by the board of directors receive the dividend. Stockholders owning the stock on the date of record receive the entire dividend, regardless of how long they have owned the stock.

terms review

retained earnings
dividends
board of directors
declaring a dividend

audit your understanding

1. Under what major chart of accounts division are the owners' equity accounts for a corporation normally listed?
2. How many accounts are kept for the investment of all owners of a corporation?
3. What account does a corporation use to record earnings not yet distributed to stockholders?
4. What action is required before a corporation can distribute income to its stockholders?

work together 14-1

Journalizing dividends

Journals are given in the *Working Papers*. Your instructor will guide you through the following examples.

Coastal Aquatics completed the following transactions during December of the current year and January of the next year.

Transactions:

Dec. 15. The board of directors declared a dividend of $3.00 per share; capital stock issued is 1,750 shares. M162.
Jan. 15. Paid cash for dividend declared December 15. C687.

1. Use page 14 of a general journal. Journalize the dividend declared on December 15.
2. Use page 21 of a cash payments journal. Journalize payment of the dividend on January 15.

on your own 14-1

Journalizing dividends

Journals are given in the *Working Papers*. Work this problem independently.

Sonoma Treasures completed the following transactions during December of the current year and January of the next year.

Transactions:

Dec. 15. The board of directors declared a dividend of $1.00 per share; capital stock issued is 21,000 shares. M321.
Jan. 15. Paid cash for dividend declared December 15. C721.

1. Use page 22 of a general journal. Journalize the dividend declared on December 15.
2. Use page 24 of a cash payments journal. Journalize payment of the dividend.

LESSON

14-2 Beginning an 8-Column Work Sheet for a Merchandising Business

A columnar accounting form on which the financial information needed to prepare financial statements is summarized is known as a *work sheet*. A work sheet is used to plan adjustments and summarize the information necessary to prepare financial statements. The steps used to prepare a work sheet are similar for proprietorships and corporations.

ENTERING A TRIAL BALANCE ON A WORK SHEET

To prepare a work sheet, a trial balance is first entered in the Trial Balance columns. All general ledger accounts and balances are listed in the same order as they appear in the general ledger. Trial Balance columns are totaled to prove equality of debits and credits.

The worksheet for Hobby Shack is different from the work sheet completed for TechKnow in Chapter 6. Unlike a service business, a merchandising business will have an account for merchandise inventory. A corporation's accounts are similar to those of a proprietorship except for the capital stock, retained earnings, dividends, and federal income tax accounts.

PLANNING ADJUSTMENTS ON A WORK SHEET

Some general ledger accounts need to be brought up to date before financial statements are prepared. Accounts are brought up to date by planning and entering adjustments on a work sheet. Adjustments are planned in the Adjustments columns of a work sheet. Adjustments recorded on a work sheet are for planning purposes only. The general ledger account balances are not changed until entries are journalized and posted. Journal entries made to bring general ledger accounts up to date are known as *adjusting entries*.

Hobby Shack's adjustments for supplies and prepaid insurance are the same as those for TechKnow described in Chapter 6. Hobby Shack also makes adjustments to these accounts: (1) Merchandise Inventory, (2) Uncollectible Accounts Expense, (3) Depreciation Expense, and (4) Federal Income Tax Expense.

The adjustment for merchandise inventory is unique to a merchandising business. Adjustments for uncollectible accounts expense and depreciation expense could also be made by a service business. The adjustment for federal income tax is unique to corporations. This adjustment is not made for a proprietorship because taxes are paid by the owner, not the business.

Small businesses represent approximately 99 percent of employers, employ nearly 50 percent of non-government employees, and are responsible for about two-thirds to three-quarters of net new jobs, according to the Office of Advocacy of the U.S. Small Business Administration.

RECORDING A TRIAL BALANCE ON A WORK SHEET

ACCOUNT *Cash* **1.** Account Titles ACCOUNT NO. *1110*

DATE		ITEM	POST. REF.	DEBIT	CREDIT	BALANCE DEBIT	BALANCE CREDIT
20-- Dec.	1	Balance	✓			28 260 00	
	31		CR12	37 180 80		65 440 80	
	31		CP24		36 360 52	29 080 28	

2. Account Balances

Hobby Shack, Inc.
Work Sheet
For Year Ended December 31, 20--

	❶ ACCOUNT TITLE	1 TRIAL BALANCE DEBIT	2 TRIAL BALANCE CREDIT
1	Cash	29 080 28 ❷	
2	Petty Cash	300 00	
3	Accounts Receivable	14 698 40	
4	Allow. for Uncoll. Accts.		127 52
5	Merchandise Inventory	140 480 00	
6	Supplies—Office	3 480 00	
7	Supplies—Store	3 944 00	
8	Prepaid Insurance	5 800 00	
9	Office Equipment	35 864 50	
10	Acc. Depr.—Office Equipment		6 497 00
11	Store Equipment	40 849 50	
12	Acc. Depr.—Store Equipment		5 069 00
13	Accounts Payable		11 583 03
14	Federal Income Tax Payable		
40	Insurance Expense		
41	Miscellaneous Expense	2 564 90	
42	Payroll Taxes Expense	9 105 00	
43	Rent Expense	18 000 00	
44	Salary Expense	104 525 00	
45	Supplies Expense—Office		
46	Supplies Expense—Store		
47	Uncollectible Accounts Expense		
48	Utilities Expense	3 820 00	
49	Federal Income Tax Expense	18 000 00	
50		670 861 59	670 861 59 ❸

3. Total, prove and rule the debit and credit columns.

STEPS • STEPS • STEPS • STEPS • STEPS • STEPS • STEPS • STEPS • STEPS • STEPS •

STEPS RECORDING A TRIAL BALANCE ON A WORK SHEET

1. Write the title of each general ledger account in the work sheet's Account Title column in the same order they appear in the general ledger. All accounts are listed regardless of whether there is a balance or not. Listing all accounts reduces the possibility of overlooking an account that needs to be brought up to date.
2. Write the balance of each account in the appropriate work sheet's Trial Balance Debit or Credit column. The amounts are taken from the general ledger accounts.
3. Total, prove, and rule the Trial Balance Debit and Credit columns of the work sheet.

ANALYZING AND RECORDING SUPPLIES ADJUSTMENTS

The balance of Supplies—Office in the trial balance, $3,480.00, is the cost of office supplies on hand at the beginning of the year plus the office supplies purchased during the year. The supplies on hand on December 31 are counted and determined to be $750.00. The difference is the value of office supplies used during the year, which is an expense.

Likewise, the balance of Supplies—Store in the trial balance, $3,944.00, is the cost of store supplies on hand at the beginning of the year plus the store supplies purchased during the year. The value of store supplies on hand on December 31 is determined to be $1,034.00.

Analyzing Supplies Adjustments

Four questions are asked to analyze the adjustments for the supplies accounts.

1. **What is the balance of the Supplies accounts?**
   Supplies—Office, *$3,480.00*
   Supplies—Store, *$3,944.00*
2. **What should the balance be for these accounts?**
   Supplies—Office, *$750.00*
   Supplies—Store, *$1,034.00*
3. **What must be done to correct the account balances?**
   Decrease Supplies—Office, *$2,730.00 ($3,480.00 − 750.00)*
   Decrease Supplies—Store, *$2,910.00 ($3,944.00 − 1,034.00)*
4. **What adjustment is made?**
   Debit:
   Supplies Expense—Office, *$2,730.00*
   Supplies Expense—Store, *$2,910.00*
   Credit:
   Supplies—Office, *$2,730.00*
   Supplies—Store, *$2,910.00*

The supplies adjustments are shown in the T accounts. The December 31 balance shown in faded type is the balance before the adjustments.

Supplies Expense—Office

	Debit		Credit
Adj. (a)	2,730.00		

Supplies—Office

	Debit		Credit
Dec. 31 Bal.	3,480.00	Adj. (a)	2,730.00
(Adj. Bal.	*750.00)*		

Supplies Expense—Store

	Debit		Credit
Adj. (b)	2,910.00		

Supplies—Store

	Debit		Credit
Dec. 31 Bal.	3,944.00	Adj. (b)	2,910.00
(Adj Bal.	*1,034.00)*		

©GETTY IMAGES/PHOTODISC

RECORDING SUPPLIES ADJUSTMENTS ON A WORK SHEET

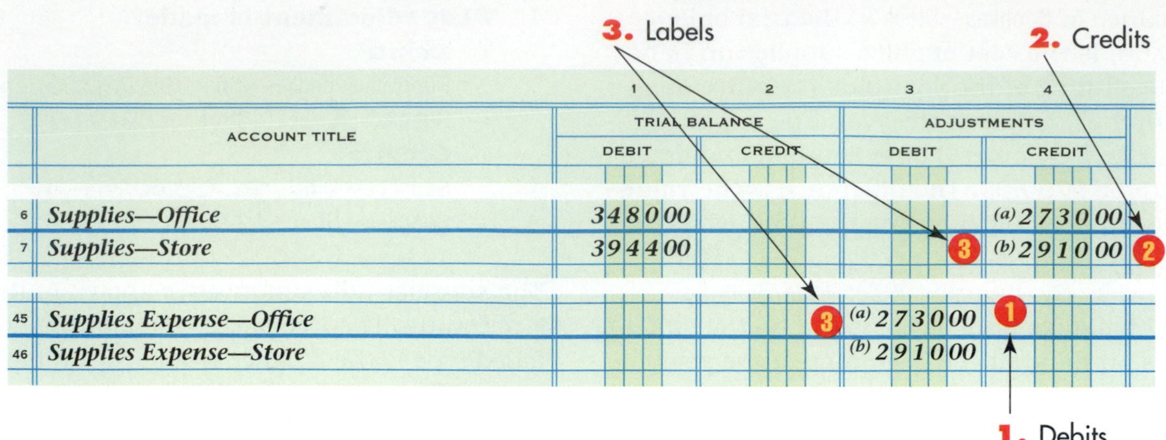

STEPS: RECORDING WORK SHEET ADJUSTMENTS FOR SUPPLIES

1. Write the debit amounts in the Adjustments Debit column on the lines with the appropriate account titles: *$2,730.00* with *Supplies Expense—Office* and *$2,910.00* with *Supplies Expense—Store*.
2. Write the credit amounts in the Adjustments Credit column on the lines with the appropriate account titles: *$2,730.00* with *Supplies—Office* and *$2,910.00* with *Supplies—Store*.
3. Label the two parts of the *Supplies—Office* adjustment with a small letter *a* in parentheses, *(a)*. Label the two parts of the *Supplies—Store* adjustment with a small letter *b* in parentheses, *(b)*.

ANALYZING AND RECORDING A PREPAID INSURANCE ADJUSTMENT

Insurance premiums are debited to a prepaid insurance account when paid. During the year, Hobby Shack paid $5,800.00 of insurance premiums.

Analyzing a Prepaid Insurance Adjustment

Hobby Shack determined that the value of prepaid insurance on December 31 is $2,630.00. Therefore, the value of insurance used during the year is $3,170.00 ($5,800.00 – $2,630.00). This difference is the amount of insurance expense for the year. Prepaid Insurance is credited and Insurance Expense is debited at the end of the fiscal period for the value of insurance used.

The prepaid insurance adjustment is shown in the T accounts. The December 31 balance shown in faded type is the balance before the adjustment.

1. **What is the balance of Prepaid Insurance?**
   $5,800.00
2. **What should the balance be for this account?**
   $2,630.00
3. **What must be done to correct the account balance?**
   Decrease $3,170.00 ($5,800.00 – $2,630.00)
4. **What adjustment is made?**
   Debit Insurance Expense, *$3,170.00*
   Credit Prepaid Insurance, *$3,170.00*

Insurance Expense

Adj. (c)	3,170.00		

Prepaid Insurance

Dec. 31 Bal.	5,800.00	Adj. (c)	3,170.00
(New Bal.	*2,630.00)*		

Recording a Prepaid Insurance Adjustment

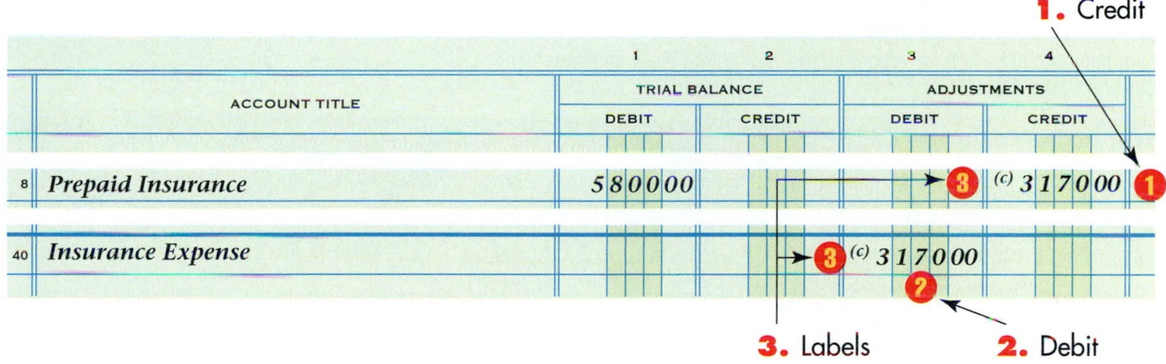

	ACCOUNT TITLE	TRIAL BALANCE DEBIT (1)	TRIAL BALANCE CREDIT (2)	ADJUSTMENTS DEBIT (3)	ADJUSTMENTS CREDIT (4)
8	*Prepaid Insurance*	5 800 00			(c) 3 170 00
40	*Insurance Expense*			(c) 3 170 00	

STEPS

RECORDING WORK SHEET ADJUSTMENTS FOR PREPAID INSURANCE

1. Enter the amount of insurance used, *$3,170.00*, in the Adjustments Credit column on the Prepaid Insurance line of the work sheet.
2. Enter the same amount, *$3,170.00*, in the Adjustments Debit column on the Insurance Expense line of the work sheet.
3. Label the two parts of the adjustment with a small letter *c* in parentheses, *(c)*.

Xtra! Study Tools
accountingxtra.swlearning.com

audit your understanding

1. What accounts are used for the adjustment to office supplies?
2. What accounts are used for the adjustment to prepaid insurance?

work together 14-2

Beginning an 8-column work sheet for a merchandising business

A partially completed work sheet for Coastal Aquatics is given in the *Working Papers*. Four general ledger accounts are shown below. Your instructor will guide you through the following examples.

1. Enter the accounts and account balances on the following lines.

Line	Account	Account Balance
3	Accounts Receivable	$ 15,485.25
13	Accounts Payable	18,482.28
29	Sales	845,828.09
32	Purchases	389,184.01

2. Total, prove, and rule the trial balance.
3. From a physical count of the following, December 31 balances are determined to be:

Supplies—Office	$657.15
Supplies—Store	633.11
Prepaid Insurance	800.00

Analyze adjustments that need to be made for the accounts above and enter the adjustments on the work sheet. Label the adjustments *(a) – (c)*. Save your work to complete Work Together 14-3.

on your own 14-2

Beginning an 8-column work sheet for a merchandising business

A partially completed work sheet for Sonoma Treasures is given in the *Working Papers*. Four general ledger accounts are shown below. Work this problem independently.

1. Enter the accounts and account balances on the following lines.

Line	Account	Account Balance
8	Prepaid Insurance	$ 12,000.00
25	Capital Stock	210,000.00
30	Sales Discount	715.25
43	Rent Expense	30,000.00

2. Total, prove, and rule the trial balance.
3. From a physical count of the following, December 31 balances are determined to be:

Supplies—Office	$ 633.61
Supplies—Store	983.36
Prepaid Insurance	3,000.00

Analyze adjustments that need to be made for the accounts above and enter the adjustments on the work sheet. Label the adjustments *(a)–(c)*. Save your work to complete On Your Own 14-3.

376-377

LESSON

14-3 Planning and Recording a Merchandise Inventory Adjustment

MERCHANDISE INVENTORY

In addition to supplies and prepaid insurance, Hobby Shack needs to adjust the merchandise inventory account. Planning the adjustment is similar to the adjustment for supplies. However, the adjusting entry includes a new account.

The amount of goods on hand for sale to customers is called **merchandise inventory**. The general ledger account in which merchandise inventory is recorded is titled Merchandise Inventory. Merchandise Inventory is an asset account with a normal debit balance.

Merchandise Inventory	
Debit	Credit
Increase ↑	Decrease ↓

Hobby Shack's merchandise inventory account on January 1, the beginning of the fiscal year, has a debit balance of $140,480.00.

Merchandise Inventory		
Jan. 1 Bal.	140,480.00	

The balance of the merchandise inventory account on December 31, the end of the fiscal year, is the same amount, $140,480.00. The January 1 and December 31 balances are the same because no entries have been made in the account during the fiscal year. The changes in inventory resulting from purchases and sales transactions have not been recorded in the merchandise inventory account.

During a fiscal period, the amount of merchandise on hand increases each time merchandise is purchased. However, all purchases are recorded in the purchases account. The amount of merchandise on hand decreases each time merchandise is sold. However, all sales are recorded in the sales account. This procedure makes it easier to determine the total purchases and sales during a fiscal period. The merchandise inventory account balance, therefore, must be adjusted to reflect the changes resulting from purchases and sales during a fiscal period.

©GETTY IMAGES/PHOTODISC

ANALYZING AND RECORDING A MERCHANDISE INVENTORY ADJUSTMENT

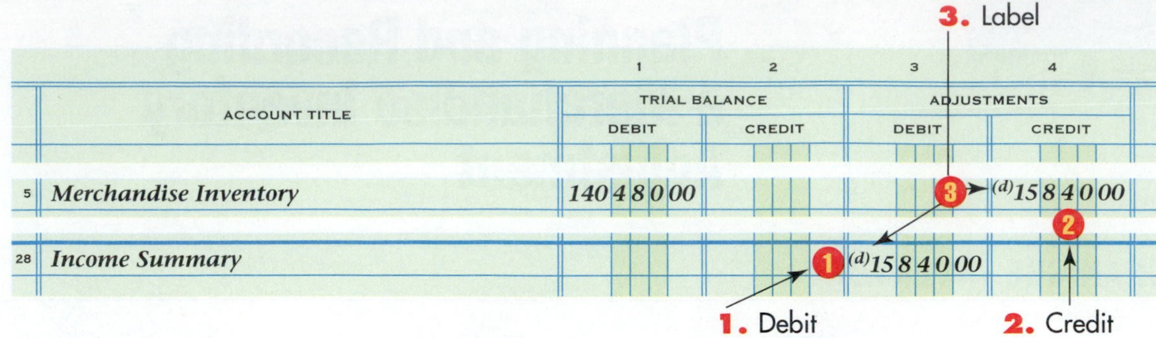

3. Label
ACCOUNT TITLE
TRIAL BALANCE
ADJUSTMENTS
DEBIT
CREDIT
Merchandise Inventory
140 480 00
(d)15 840 00
Income Summary
(d)15 840 00
1. Debit
2. Credit

The two accounts used to adjust the merchandise inventory are Merchandise Inventory and Income Summary.

Before the adjustment, the merchandise inventory account has a January 1 debit balance of $140,480.00. The merchandise inventory account balance, however, is not up-to-date. The actual count of merchandise on December 31 shows that the inventory is valued at $124,640.00. Therefore, the merchandise inventory account balance must be adjusted to show the current value of merchandise on hand.

Most accounts needing adjustment at the end of a fiscal period have a related temporary account. For example, when the account Prepaid Insurance is adjusted, Insurance Expense is the related expense account, a temporary account. Merchandise Inventory, however, does not have a related expense account. Therefore, Income Summary, a temporary account, is used to adjust the merchandise inventory account at the end of a fiscal period.

Four questions are asked in analyzing the adjustment for merchandise inventory.

1. **What is the balance of Merchandise Inventory?** *$140,480.00*
2. **What should the balance be for this account?** *$124,640.00*
3. **What must be done to correct the account balance?** *Decrease $15,840.00*
4. **What adjustment is made?**
   Debit Income Summary, *$15,840.00*
   Credit Merchandise Inventory, *$15,840.00*

Merchandise Inventory			
Jan. 1 Bal.	140,480.00	Adj. (d)	15,840.00
(New Bal.	*124,640.00)*		

Income Summary			
Adj. (d)	15,840.00		

Income Summary is debited and Merchandise Inventory is credited for $15,840.00. The beginning debit balance of Merchandise Inventory, *$140,480.00*, minus the adjustment credit amount, *$15,840.00*, equals the ending debit balance of Merchandise Inventory, *$124,640.00*.

STEPS • STEPS • STEPS • STEPS • STEPS • STEPS • STEPS • STEPS • STEPS • STEPS

RECORDING A WORK SHEET ADJUSTMENT FOR MERCHANDISE INVENTORY

1. Write the debit amount, *$15,840.00*, in the Adjustments Debit column on the line with the account title *Income Summary*.
2. Write the credit amount, *$15,840.00*, in the Adjustments Credit column on the line with the account title *Merchandise Inventory*.
3. Label the two parts of this adjustment with the small letter *d* in parentheses, *(d)*.

ANALYZING AN ADJUSTMENT WHEN ENDING MERCHANDISE INVENTORY IS GREATER THAN BEGINNING MERCHANDISE INVENTORY

If the amount of merchandise inventory on hand is greater than the January 1 balance of Merchandise Inventory, opposite entries would be made—debit Merchandise Inventory and credit Income Summary. For example, Venable Company's merchandise inventory account on January 1 has a debit balance of $294,700.00. The count of merchandise on December 31 shows that the inventory is valued at $298,900.00. The merchandise on hand is $4,200.00 greater than the January 1 balance of Merchandise Inventory.

Four questions are asked in analyzing the adjustment for merchandise inventory.

1. **What is the balance of Merchandise Inventory?** *$294,700.00*
2. **What should the balance be for this account?** *$298,900.00*
3. **What must be done to correct the account balance?** *Increase $4,200.00*
4. **What adjustment is made?**
   Debit Merchandise Inventory, *$4,200.00*
   Credit Income Summary, *$4,200.00*

The merchandise inventory adjustment is shown in the T accounts.

Merchandise Inventory

Jan. 1 Bal.	294,700.00		
Adj. (d)	4,200.00		
(New Bal.	*298,900.00)*		

Income Summary

		Adj. (d)	4,200.00

Merchandise Inventory is debited and Income Summary is credited for $4,200.00. The beginning debit balance of Merchandise Inventory, *$294,700.00*, plus the adjustment debit amount, *$4,200.00*, equals the ending debit balance of Merchandise Inventory, *$298,900.00*.

©GETTY IMAGES/PHOTODISC

REMEMBER When an account that requires adjusting does not have a related expense account, the temporary account *Income Summary* is used.

term review

merchandise inventory

audit your understanding

1. In what order should general ledger accounts be listed on a work sheet?
2. What accounts are used for the adjustment for merchandise inventory?
3. What adjusting entry is entered on a work sheet when the ending merchandise inventory is less than the beginning value?
4. When is the temporary account Income Summary used?

work together 14-3

Analyzing and recording an adjustment for merchandise inventory

Use the work sheet from Work Together 14-2. Your instructor will guide you through the following example.

1. From a physical count of merchandise inventory, the December 31 balance is determined to be $234,904.20. Analyze the merchandise inventory adjustment and enter the adjustment on the work sheet. Label the adjustment *(d)*. Save your work to complete Work Together 14-4.

on your own 14-3

Analyzing and recording an adjustment for merchandise inventory

Use the work sheet from On Your Own 14-2. Work this problem independently.

1. From a physical count of merchandise inventory, the December 31 balance is determined to be $261,089.97. Analyze the merchandise inventory adjustment and enter the adjustment on the work sheet. Label the adjustment *(d)*. Save your work to complete On Your Own 14-4.

14-4 Planning and Recording an Allowance for Uncollectible Accounts Adjustment

ALLOWANCE METHOD OF RECORDING LOSSES FROM UNCOLLECTIBLE ACCOUNTS

Uncollectible Accounts Expense	
Debit	Credit
Increase	Decrease

Accounts Receivable	
Debit	Credit
Increase	Decrease

Allowance for Uncollectible Accounts	
Debit	Credit
Decrease	Increase

With each sale on account, a business takes a risk that customers will not pay their accounts. Accounts receivable that cannot be collected are called **uncollectible accounts**. This risk is a cost of doing business that should be recorded as an expense in the same accounting period that the revenue is earned. Accurate financial reporting requires that expenses be recorded in the fiscal period in which the expenses contribute to earning revenue. [*CONCEPT: Matching Expenses with Revenue*]

At the end of a fiscal year, a business does not know which customer accounts will become uncollectible. If a business knew exactly which accounts would become uncollectible, it could credit Accounts Receivable and each customer account for the uncollectible amounts and debit Uncollectible Accounts Expense for the same amounts.

To solve this accounting problem, a business can calculate and record an estimated amount of uncollectible accounts expense. Estimating uncollectible accounts expense at the end of a fiscal period accomplishes two objectives:

1. It reports a balance sheet amount for Accounts Receivable that reflects the amount the business expects to collect in the future.
2. It recognizes the expense of uncollectible accounts in the same period in which the related revenue is recorded.

To record estimated uncollectible accounts, an adjusting entry is made affecting two accounts. The estimated amount of uncollectible accounts is debited to Uncollectible Accounts Expense and credited to an account titled Allowance for Uncollectible Accounts.

An account that reduces a related account is known as a *contra account.* Allowance for Uncollectible Accounts is a contra account to its related asset account, Accounts Receivable.

Crediting the estimated value of uncollectible accounts to a contra account is called the **allowance method of recording losses from uncollectible accounts**. The difference between an asset's account balance and its related contra account balance is called **book value**. The difference between the balance of Accounts Receivable and its contra account, Allowance for Uncollectible Accounts, is called the **book value of accounts receivable**. The book value of accounts receivable, which is reported on the balance sheet, represents the total amount of accounts receivable the business expects to collect in the future.

A contra account is usually assigned the next number of the account number sequence after its related account in the chart of accounts. Hobby Shack's Accounts Receivable account is numbered 1130 and the Allowance for Uncollectible Accounts contra account is numbered 1135.

ESTIMATING UNCOLLECTIBLE ACCOUNTS EXPENSE

Total Sales on Account	×	Percentage	=	Estimated Uncollectible Accounts Expense
$124,500.00	×	1%	=	$1,245.00

Many businesses use a percentage of total sales on account to estimate uncollectible accounts expense. Each sale on account represents a risk of loss from an uncollectible account. Therefore, if the estimated percentage of loss is accurate, the amount of uncollectible accounts expense will be accurate regardless of when the actual losses occur.

Since a sale on account creates a risk of loss, estimating the percentage of uncollectible accounts expense for the same period matches sales revenue with the related uncollectible accounts expense. [*CONCEPT: Matching Expenses with Revenue*]

Hobby Shack estimates uncollectible accounts expense by calculating a percentage of total sales on account. A review of Hobby Shack's previous experience in collecting sales on account shows that actual uncollectible accounts expense has been about 1% of total sales on account. The company's total sales on account for the year is $124,500.00. Thus, Hobby Shack estimates that $1,245.00 of the current fiscal year's sales on account will eventually be uncollectible.

FYI FOR YOUR INFORMATION

Allowance for Bad Debts and *Allowance for Doubtful Accounts* are account titles sometimes used instead of *Allowance for Uncollectible Accounts*.

technology for business

TECHNOLOGY FOR BUSINESS • TECHNOLOGY FOR BUSINESS • TECHNOLOGY FOR BUSINE

Spending More than Time on the Web

The World Wide Web is changing and growing every day. While some companies target customers for on-line sales, others use the Internet as a key part of their marketing strategy.

Every day thousands of companies invite consumers to visit company and product web sites with the phrase "Visit our web site" followed by the address. Web sites offer contests, discount offers, coupons, recipes, and product information. These sites feature more data than you get from a print ad or television commercial.

Business-to-business selling via the web is growing, and it has a name—electronic commerce or E-commerce. Wal-Mart, General Motors, and Eastman Kodak are among the companies that pioneered E-commerce with their customers and suppliers. Additional information about accounting for Internet sales is provided in Chapter 24.

Critical Thinking

1. Customers who buy merchandise on the Internet usually have to pay shipping charges to receive the merchandise. Why would customers prefer to shop this way than to visit a store and avoid shipping charges?
2. Consider methods companies must use to receive payment for merchandise purchased on their web sites. What kinds of additional procedures would companies need to consider?

ANALYZING AND RECORDING AN ADJUSTMENT FOR UNCOLLECTIBLE ACCOUNTS EXPENSE

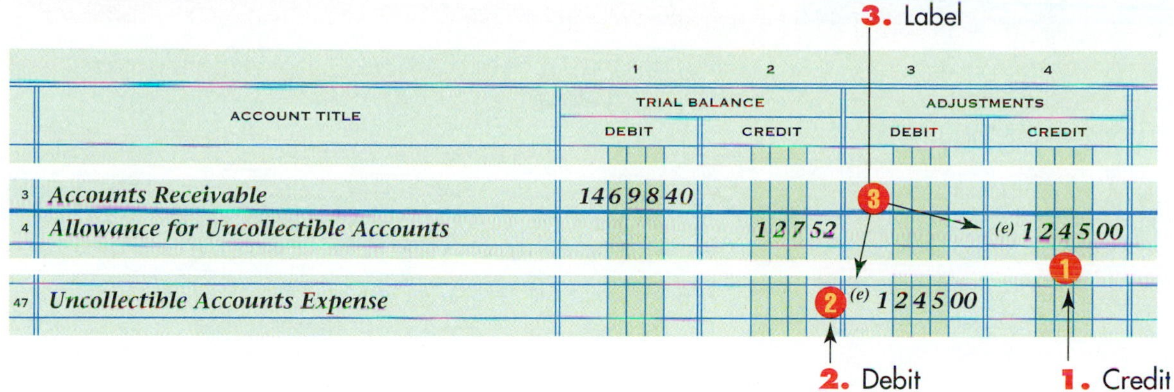

The percentage of total sales on account method of estimating uncollectible accounts expense assumes that a portion of every sale on account dollar will become uncollectible. Hobby Shack has estimated that 1% of its $124,500.00 sales on account, or $1,245.00, will eventually become uncollectible.

At the end of a fiscal period, an adjustment for uncollectible accounts expense is planned on a work sheet.

The Allowance for Uncollectible Accounts balance in the Trial Balance Credit column, $127.52, is the allowance estimate from the previous fiscal period that has not yet been identified as uncollectible.

When the allowance account has a previous credit balance, the amount of the adjustment is added to the previous balance.

Accounts Receivable

Dec. 31 Bal.	14,698.40	

Uncollectible Accounts Expense

Adj. (e)	1,245.00	

Allowance for Uncollectible Accounts

		Bal.	127.52
		Adj. (e)	1,245.00
		(New Bal.	*1,372.52)*

This new balance of the allowance account, $1,372.52, is the estimated amount of accounts receivable that will eventually become uncollectible. This amount, subtracted from the accounts receivable account balance, $14,698.40, is the book value of accounts receivable. Notice in the T accounts that Accounts Receivable is not affected by this adjustment. Also notice that Uncollectible Accounts Expense did not have a balance before the adjustment.

Accounts Receivable	–	Balance of Allowance for Uncollectible Accounts	=	Book Value of Accounts Receivable
$14,698.40	–	$1,372.52	=	$13,325.88

Hobby Shack estimates that it will collect $13,325.88 from its outstanding accounts receivable.

STEPS • STEPS • STEPS • STEPS

RECORDING A WORK SHEET ADJUSTMENT FOR UNCOLLECTIBLE ACCOUNTS

1. Enter the estimated uncollectible amount, *$1,245.00*, in the Adjustments Credit column on the *Allowance for Uncollectible Accounts* line of the work sheet.
2. Enter the same amount, *$1,245.00*, in the Adjustments Debit column on the *Uncollectible Accounts Expense* line of the work sheet.
3. Label the two parts of this adjustment with the small letter *e* in parentheses, *(e)*.

Xtra! Study Tools
accountingxtra.swlearning.com

terms review

uncollectible accounts
allowance method of recording losses from uncollectible accounts
book value
book value of accounts receivable

audit your understanding

1. Why is an uncollectible account recorded as an expense rather than a reduction in revenue?
2. When do businesses normally estimate the amount of their uncollectible accounts expense?
3. What two objectives will be accomplished by recording an estimated amount of uncollectible accounts expense?
4. Why is *Allowance for Uncollectible Accounts* called a *contra account*?
5. How is the book value of accounts receivable calculated?

work together 14-4

Analyzing and recording an adjustment for uncollectible accounts expense

Use the work sheet from Work Together 14-3. Your instructor will guide you through the following example.

1. Coastal Aquatics estimates uncollectible accounts expense as 0.5% of its total sales on account. During the current year, Coastal Aquatics had sales on account of $424,000.00. Record the uncollectible accounts expense adjustment on the work sheet. Label the adjustment *(e)*. Save your work to complete Work Together 14-5.

on your own 14-4

Analyzing and recording an adjustment for uncollectible accounts expense

Use the work sheet from On Your Own 14-3. Work independently to complete this problem.

1. Sonoma Treasures estimates uncollectible accounts expense as 0.4% of its total sales on account. During the current year, Sonoma Treasures had sales on account of $462,500.00. Record the uncollectible accounts expense adjustment on the work sheet. Label the adjustment *(e)*. Save your work to complete On Your Own 14-5.

LESSON • LESSON • LESSON • LESSON • LESSON • LESSON

14-5 Planning and Recording Depreciation Adjustments

CATEGORIES OF ASSETS

Most businesses use two broad categories of assets in their operations. Cash and other assets expected to be exchanged for cash or consumed within a year are called **current assets**. Assets that will be used for a number of years in the operation of a business are called **plant assets**. Some of Hobby Shack's plant assets are computers, cash registers, sales display cases, and furniture.

Businesses may have three major types of plant assets—equipment, buildings, and land. Hobby Shack records its equipment in two different equipment accounts—Office Equipment and Store Equipment. Because it rents the building and the land where the business is located, Hobby Shack does not need plant asset accounts for buildings and land. [*CONCEPT: Adequate Disclosure*]

Depreciating Plant Assets

A business buys plant assets to use in earning revenue. Hobby Shack bought a new lighted display case. Hobby Shack knows that the display case will be useful only for a limited period of time. After several years, most display cases become worn from use and no longer attractively display the products. Hobby Shack will replace worn display cases with newer models. Thus, each display case has a limited useful life to the business.

In order to match revenue with the expenses used to earn the revenue, the cost of a plant asset should be expensed over the plant asset's useful life. A portion of a plant asset's cost is transferred to an expense account in each fiscal period that a plant asset is used to earn revenue. [*CONCEPT: Matching Expenses with Revenue*] The portion of a plant asset's cost that is transferred to an expense account in each fiscal period during a plant asset's useful life is called **depreciation expense**.

Three factors are considered in calculating the annual amount of depreciation expense for a plant asset.

1. *Original Cost.* The original cost of a plant asset includes all costs paid to make the asset usable to a business. These costs include the price of the asset, delivery costs, and any necessary installation costs.
2. *Estimated Salvage Value.* Generally, a business removes a plant asset from use and disposes of it when the asset is no longer usable. The amount that will be received for an asset at the time of its disposal is not known when the asset is bought. Thus, the amount that may be received at disposal must be estimated. The amount an owner expects to receive when a plant asset is removed from use is called **estimated salvage value**. Estimated salvage value may also be referred to as *residual value* or *scrap value*.
3. *Estimated Useful Life.* The total amount of depreciation expense is distributed over the estimated useful life of a plant asset. When a plant asset is bought, the exact length of useful life is not known. Therefore, the number of years of useful life must be estimated. Two factors affect the useful life of a plant asset: (1) physical depreciation and (2) functional depreciation. Physical depreciation is caused by wear from use and deterioration from aging and weathering. Functional depreciation occurs when a plant asset becomes inadequate or obsolete. An asset is inadequate when it can no longer satisfactorily perform the needed service. An asset is obsolete when a newer asset can operate more efficiently or produce better service.

CALCULATING DEPRECIATION EXPENSE AND BOOK VALUE

Straight-Line Depreciation

Charging an equal amount of depreciation expense for a plant asset in each year of useful life is called the **straight-line method of depreciation**.

Hobby Shack summarizes the depreciation expense for each plant asset to calculate the total depreciation expense recorded on the work sheet.

On January 2, 20X1, Hobby Shack bought a lighted display case for $1,250.00, with an estimated salvage value of $250.00 and an estimated useful life of 5 years. Using the straight-line method of depreciation, the annual depreciation expense, $200.00, is the same for each year in which the asset is used.

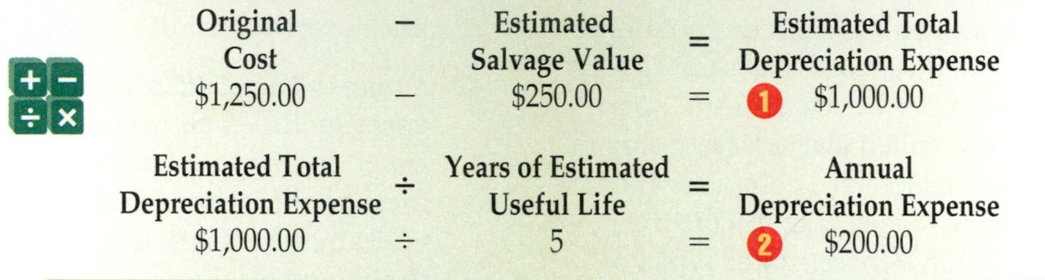

STEPS — CALCULATING ANNUAL DEPRECIATION EXPENSE

1. Subtract the asset's estimated salvage value from the asset's original cost. This difference is the estimated total depreciation expense for the asset's entire useful life.
2. Divide the estimated total depreciation expense by the years of estimated useful life. The result is the annual depreciation expense.

Calculating Accumulated Depreciation

The total amount of depreciation expense that has been recorded since the purchase of a plant asset is called **accumulated depreciation**. The amount accumulates each year of the plant asset's useful life.

First, the depreciation expense that has accumulated over all prior years is determined. Second, the depreciation expense for the current year is calculated. Third, the prior accumulated depreciation and the current depreciation expense are added.

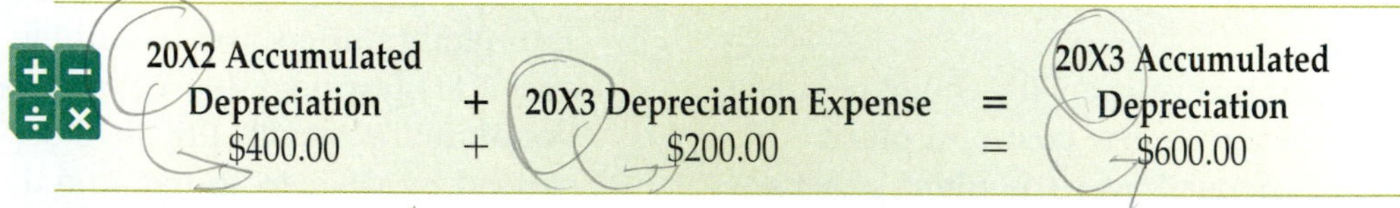

20X2 Accumulated Depreciation + 20X3 Depreciation Expense = 20X3 Accumulated Depreciation
$400.00 + $200.00 = $600.00

Calculating Book Value

The original cost of a plant asset minus accumulated depreciation is called the **book value of a plant asset**. The book value is calculated by subtracting the accumulated depreciation from the original cost of the asset.

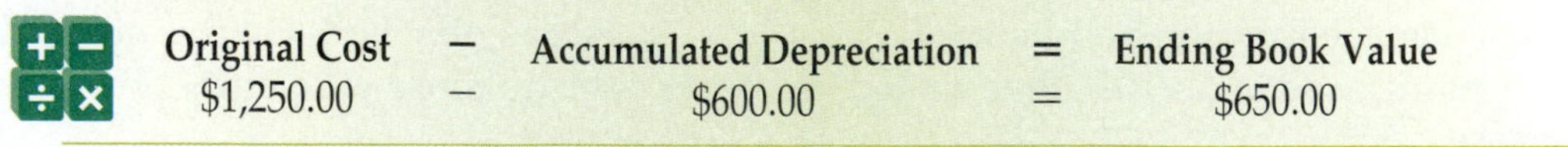

Procedures for recording the accumulated depreciation and book value of individual assets are presented in Chapter 18.

ANALYZING AND RECORDING ADJUSTMENTS FOR DEPRECIATION EXPENSE

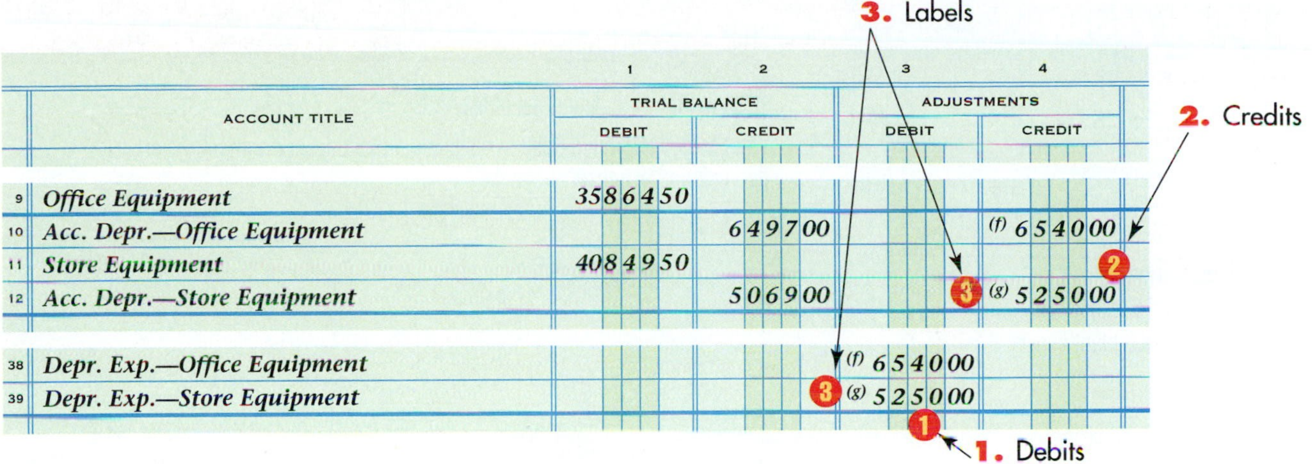

	ACCOUNT TITLE	TRIAL BALANCE DEBIT (1)	TRIAL BALANCE CREDIT (2)	ADJUSTMENTS DEBIT (3)	ADJUSTMENTS CREDIT (4)
9	*Office Equipment*	35,864.50			
10	*Acc. Depr.—Office Equipment*		6,497.00		(f) 6,540.00
11	*Store Equipment*	40,849.50			
12	*Acc. Depr.—Store Equipment*		5,069.00		(g) 5,250.00
38	*Depr. Exp.—Office Equipment*			(f) 6,540.00	
39	*Depr. Exp.—Store Equipment*			(g) 5,250.00	

At the end of the fiscal year, Hobby Shack calculates the depreciation expense for each plant asset. Hobby Shack determined that total depreciation expense is $6,540.00 for store equipment and $5,250.00 for office equipment. Adjustments are planned in the Adjustments columns of the work sheet.

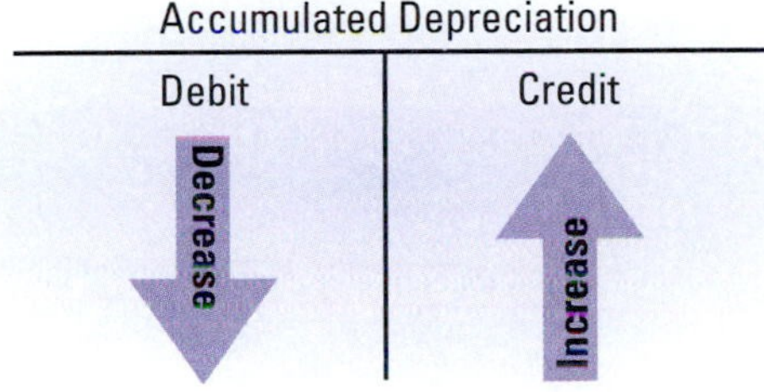

It is important to retain original cost information for plant assets. Therefore, rather than credit the plant asset account, depreciation is recorded in the contra asset account Accumulated Depreciation.

Office Equipment

Debit		Credit	
Dec. 31 Bal.	*35,864.50*		

Accumulated Depreciation—Office Equipment

Debit		Credit	
		Jan. 1 Bal.	6,497.00
		Dec. 31 Adj.	6,540.00
		Dec. 31 Bal.	*13,037.00*

Depreciation Expense—Office Equipment

Debit		Credit	
Dec. 31 Adj.	6,540.00		

Store Equipment

Debit		Credit	
Dec. 31 Bal.	*40,849.50*		

Accumulated Depreciation—Store Equipment

Debit		Credit	
		Jan. 1 Bal.	5,069.00
		Dec. 31 Adj.	5,250.00
		Dec. 31 Bal.	*10,319.00*

Depreciation Expense—Store Equipment

Debit		Credit	
Dec. 31 Adj.	5,250.00		

At any time, the book value of plant assets can be calculated by subtracting Accumulated Depreciation from its related plant asset account.

STEPS • STEPS • STEPS • STEPS

RECORDING WORK SHEET ADJUSTMENTS FOR DEPRECIATION

1. Write the debit amounts in the Adjustments Debit column on the lines with the appropriate account titles: *$6,540.00* with *Depreciation Expense—Office Equipment* and *$5,250.00* with *Depreciation Expense—Store Equipment.*
2. Write the credit amounts in the Adjustments Credit column on the lines with the appropriate account titles: *$6,540.00* with *Accumulated Depreciation—Office Equipment* and *$5,250.00* with *Accumulated Depreciation—Store Equipment.*
3. Label the two parts of the Office Equipment adjustment with the small letter *f* in parentheses, *(f)*. Label the two parts of the Store Equipment adjustment with the small letter *g* in parentheses, *(g)*.

Xtra! Study Tools
accountingxtra.swlearning.com

terms review

current assets
plant assets
depreciation expense
estimated salvage value
straight-line method of depreciation
accumulated depreciation
book value of a plant asset

TERMS REVIEW • TERMS

audit your understanding

1. What are the two categories of assets?
2. What three factors are used to calculate a plant asset's annual depreciation expense?

AUDIT YOUR UNDERSTANDING

work together 14-5

Planning and recording adjustments for depreciation

Use the work sheet from Work Together 14-4. Your instructor will guide you through the following example.

1. Calculate depreciation expense for a computer printer costing $1,600; estimated salvage value, $100.00, useful life, 5 years.
2. Calculate the book value of the computer printer at the end of its second year of service.
3. On December 31, Coastal Aquatics determined the total depreciation expense: office equipment, $6,120.00; store equipment, $5,060.00. Plan the work sheet adjustments and label the adjustments *(f)* and *(g)*. Save your work to complete Work Together 14-6.

WORK TOGETHER • WORK

on your own 14-5

Planning and recording adjustments for depreciation

Use the work sheet from On Your Own 14-4. Your instructor will guide you through the following example. Work independently to complete this problem.

1. Calculate depreciation expense for a display rack costing $2,350.00; estimated salvage value, $600.00, useful life, 7 years.
2. Calculate the book value of the display rack at the end of its third year of service.
3. On December 31, Sonoma Treasures determined the total depreciation expense: office equipment, $5,184.00; store equipment, $6,480.00. Plan the work sheet adjustments and label the adjustments *(f)* and *(g)*. Save your work to complete On Your Own 14-6.

ON YOUR OWN • ON YOUR OWN

14-6 Calculating Federal Income Tax and Completing a Work Sheet

FEDERAL INCOME TAX EXPENSE ADJUSTMENT

Corporations anticipating annual federal income taxes of $500.00 or more are required to pay their estimated taxes each quarter. Estimated income tax is paid in quarterly installments in April, June, September, and December. However, the actual federal income tax owed is calculated at the end of a fiscal year. Based on the actual income tax owed for a year, a corporation must file an annual return. Any additional tax owed that was not paid in quarterly installments must be paid when the final return is filed.

Early in the current year, Hobby Shack estimated $18,000.00 federal income tax for the year. Hobby Shack paid $4,500.00 in each quarterly installment for a total of $18,000.00. Each tax payment is recorded as a debit to Federal Income Tax Expense and a credit to Cash.

Federal income tax is an expense of a corporation. However, the amount of tax depends on net income before the tax is recorded.

Federal Income Tax Expense is an expense account. The account appears under a major division titled *Income Tax Expense* in Hobby Shack's chart of accounts. Federal Income Tax Payable, a liability account, appears under the heading *Current Liabilities*.

In order to make adjustments to federal income tax, you must first determine the net income before federal income tax expense. To calculate, follow these steps:

1. Complete all other adjustments on a work sheet.
2. Extend all amounts except Federal Income Tax Expense to the Income Statement or Balance Sheet columns.
3. On a separate sheet of paper, total the work sheet's Income Statement columns.
4. Calculate the difference between the Income Statement Debit column total and the Income Statement Credit column total. This difference between the totals of these two income statement columns is the net income before federal income tax expense.

Total of Income Statement Credit column	$ 500,253.10
Less total of Income Statement Debit column before federal income tax	−396,049.91
Equals Net Income before Federal Income Tax	$ 104,203.19

©GETTY IMAGES/PHOTODISC

CALCULATING FEDERAL INCOME TAX

15% of net income before taxes, zero to $50,000.00 (15% tax on the *first* $50,000.00 of net income)
Plus 25% of net income before taxes, $50,000.00 to $75,000.00 (25% tax on the *next* $25,000.00 of net income)
Plus 34% of net income before taxes, $75,000.00 to $100,000.00 (34% tax on the *next* $25,000.00 of net income)
Plus 39% of net income before taxes, $100,000.00 to $335,000.00 (39% tax on the *next* $225,000.00 of net income)
Plus 34% of net income before taxes over $335,000.00 (34% tax on net income *above* $335,000.00)

Step 1:

First Net Income Amount	×	**First Tax Rate**	=	**Federal Income Tax on First $50,000.00 of Net Income**
$50,000.00	×	15%	=	$7,500.00

Step 2:

Second Net Income Amount	×	**Second Tax Rate**	=	**Federal Income Tax on Next $25,000.00 of Net Income**
$25,000.00	×	25%	=	$6,250.00

Step 3:

Third Net Income Amount	×	**Third Tax Rate**	=	**Federal Income Tax on Next $25,000.00 of Net Income**
$25,000.00	×	34%	=	$8,500.00

Step 4:

Total Net Income	–	**Lowest Dollar Amount of Fourth Tax Range**	=	**Amount of Net Income to Which Fourth Tax Rate Is Applied**
$104,203.19	–	$100,000.00	=	$4,203.19

Step 5:

Fourth Net Income Amount	×	**Fourth Tax Rate**	=	**Federal Income Tax on Next $140,914.00 of Net Income**
$4,203.19	×	39%	=	$1,639.24

Step 6:

First Federal Tax Amount	+	**Second Federal Tax Amount**	+	**Third Federal Tax Amount**	+	**Fourth Federal Tax Amount**	=	**Total Federal Tax Amount**
$7,500.00	+	$6,250.00	+	$8,500.00	+	$1,639.24	=	$23,889.24

The amount of federal income tax expense a corporation must pay is calculated using a tax rate table furnished by the Internal Revenue Service. Different tax percentages are applied to different portions of the net income to determine the total federal income tax owed. Hobby Shack's net income before federal income tax is $104,203.19. Corporation tax rates in effect when this text was written are used to calculate Hobby Shack's federal income tax expense.

STEPS • STEPS • STEPS • STEPS • STEPS • STEPS • STEPS • STEPS • STEPS • STEPS •

CALCULATING FEDERAL INCOME TAX

1. Multiply $50,000.00 by a tax rate of 15% to calculate the first federal income tax amount. This is the tax Hobby Shack must pay on its first $50,000.00 of net income.
2. Multiply $25,000.00 by a tax rate of 25% to calculate the second federal income tax amount. This is the tax Hobby Shack must pay on the next $25,000.00 of net income.
3. Multiply $25,000.00 by a tax rate of 34% to calculate the third federal income tax amount. This is the tax Hobby Shack must pay on the next $25,000.00 of net income.
4. The tax rate of 39% applies to all net income that falls in the range of $100,000.00 to $335,000.00. Hobby Shack's net income is $104,203.19. When the net income does not equal or exceed the highest dollar amount given in a range, the amount of net income to which the tax rate is applied is determined by subtracting the lowest dollar amount in the range from the total net income. ($104,203.19 – $100,000.00 = $4,203.19)
5. Multiply $4,203.19 by a tax rate of 39% to calculate the fourth federal income tax amount, $1,639.24. This is the tax Hobby Shack must pay on the remainder of its net income.
6. Add the four tax amounts together to determine Hobby Shack's federal income tax expense for the fiscal year.

RECORDING THE FEDERAL INCOME TAX ADJUSTMENT

	ACCOUNT TITLE	1 TRIAL BALANCE DEBIT	2 TRIAL BALANCE CREDIT	3 ADJUSTMENTS DEBIT	4 ADJUSTMENTS CREDIT	5 INCOME STATEMENT DEBIT	6 INCOME STATEMENT CREDIT	7 BALANCE SHEET DEBIT	8 BALANCE SHEET CREDIT	
9	*Office Equipment*	35864 50						35864 50		9
10	*Acc. Depr.—Office Equipment*		6497 00		(f) 6540 00				13037 00	10
11	*Store Equipment*	40849 50						40849 50		11
12	*Acc. Depr.—Store Equipment*		5069 00		(g) 5250 00				10319 00	12
13	*Accounts Payable*		11583 03						11583 03	13
14	*Federal Income Tax Payable*				(h) 5889 24				5889 24	14
46	*Supplies Expense—Store*			(b) 2910 00		2910 00				46
47	*Uncollectible Accounts Expense*			(e) 1245 00		1245 00				47
48	*Utilities Expense*	3820 00				3820 00				48
49	*Federal Income Tax Expense*	18000 00		(h) 5889 24		23889 24				49
50		670861 59	670861 59	43574 24	43574 24					50
51										51

1. Calculate and enter the federal income tax adjustment.

2. Total and rule the adjustment columns.

3. Extend the account balances.

STEPS • STEPS • STEPS • STEPS • STEPS • STEPS • STEPS • STEPS • STEPS • STEPS

RECORDING A WORK SHEET ADJUSTMENT FOR FEDERAL INCOME TAX EXPENSE

1. Calculate the amount of the federal income tax expense adjustment. The adjustment is the difference between the federal income tax for the year and the taxes paid during the year.

Federal Income Tax.	$23,889.24
Less Total of Quarterly Installments.	−18,000.00
Equals Federal Income Tax Adjustment.	$ 5,889.24

Enter the federal income tax expense adjustment, *$5,889.24*, in the Adjustments Credit column on the *Federal Income Tax Payable* line of the work sheet. Enter the same amount in the Adjustments Debit column of the *Federal Income Tax Expense* line of the work sheet. Label both parts of the adjustment *(h)*.

2. Total and rule the Adjustments columns.

3. Extend the *Federal Income Tax Expense* account balance, *$23,889.24*, to the Income Statement Debit column. Extend the amount for *Federal Income Tax Payable*, *$5,889.24*, to the Balance Sheet Credit column.

Federal Income Tax Expense

Debit		Credit
4/15	4,500.00	
6/15	4,500.00	
9/15	4,500.00	
12/15	4,500.00	
(12/15 Bal.	*18,000.00)*	
12/31 Adj. (h)	5,889.24	
(New Bal.	*23,889.24)*	

Federal Income Tax Payable

Debit	Credit	
	12/31 Adj. (h)	5,889.24

©GETTY IMAGES/PHOTODISC

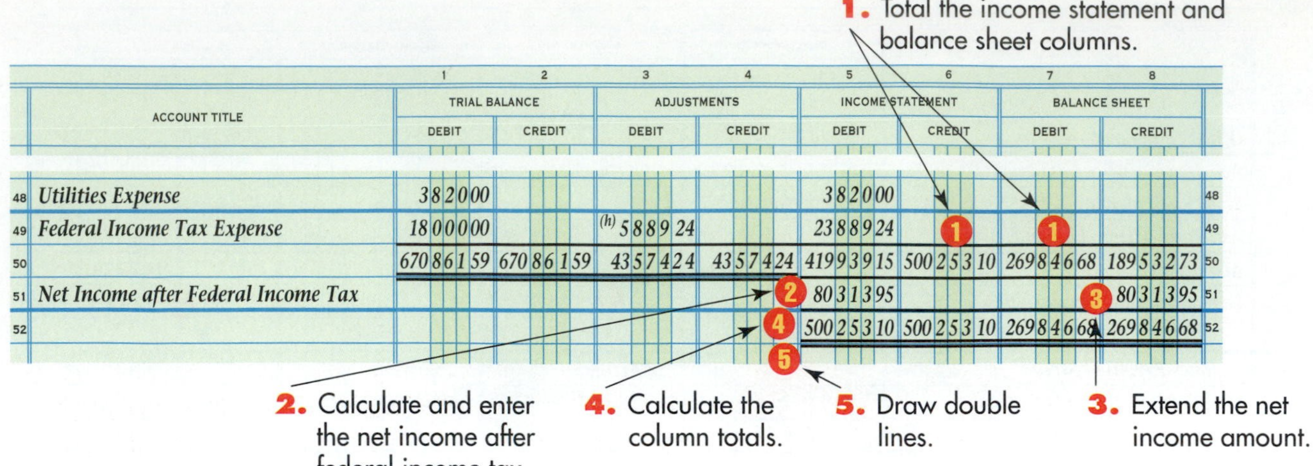

	ACCOUNT TITLE	1 TRIAL BALANCE DEBIT	2 TRIAL BALANCE CREDIT	3 ADJUSTMENTS DEBIT	4 ADJUSTMENTS CREDIT	5 INCOME STATEMENT DEBIT	6 INCOME STATEMENT CREDIT	7 BALANCE SHEET DEBIT	8 BALANCE SHEET CREDIT	
48	*Utilities Expense*	3820 00				3820 00				48
49	*Federal Income Tax Expense*	18000 00		(h) 5889 24		23889 24				49
50		670861 59	670861 59	43574 24	43574 24	419939 15	500253 10	269846 68	189532 73	50
51	*Net Income after Federal Income Tax*					80313 95			80313 95	51
52						500253 10	500253 10	269846 68	269846 68	52

1. Total the income statement and balance sheet columns.
2. Calculate and enter the net income after federal income tax.
4. Calculate the column totals.
5. Draw double lines.
3. Extend the net income amount.

After the adjustment for federal income tax expense has been recorded, the work sheet is ready to be completed. Income Statement column totals are used to calculate net income after federal income tax.

Hobby Shack follows the same procedures for completing a work sheet as described for TechKnow in Chapter 6, with the exception of the Income Summary account. TechKnow sells a service, not merchandise. Therefore, TechKnow has no amount recorded in the Income Summary account, a related account used to adjust Merchandise Inventory. Hobby Shack sells merchandise. Therefore, the Income Summary account is used as the related account to adjust Merchandise Inventory. The merchandise inventory adjustment reflects the increases and decreases in the amount of goods on hand resulting from purchases and sales. Therefore, the amount recorded in Income Summary is extended to the work sheet's Income Statement Debit or Credit column. An Income Summary debit amount is extended to the Income Statement Debit column. An Income Summary credit amount is extended to the Income Statement Credit column.

Hobby Shack's completed work sheet for the year ended December 31, 20--, is shown on pages 432–433.

STEPS: COMPLETING A WORK SHEET

1. Total the Income Statement and Balance Sheet columns.
2. Write the words *Net Income after Federal Income Tax* on line 51 of the work sheet. Calculate and enter the net income after federal income tax, *$80,313.95*, in the Income Statement Debit column on this new line of the work sheet.

Total of Income Statement Credit column	$500,253.10
Less Total of Income Statement Debit column	−419,939.15
Equals Net Income after Federal Income Tax	$ 80,313.95

3. Extend the net income after federal income tax amount, *$80,313.95*, to the Balance Sheet Credit column.
4. Total the four Income Statement and Balance Sheet columns. Determine that the totals of each pair of columns are in balance.
5. Rule double lines across the Income Statement and Balance Sheet columns to show that the totals have been verified as correct.

CAREERS IN ACCOUNTING • CAREERS IN ACCOUNTING • CAREERS IN ACCOUNTING

careers in accounting

Everlyn Johnson, Small Business Owner

COURTESY OF EVERLYN JOHNSON

By the age of 18, you will have gained experiences that will change your life in ways you might never imagine. These experiences may come from an extracurricular activity, a part-time job, or a hobby, and they may influence the direction of your career or retirement.

For Everlyn Johnson, the youthful experience that would affect her life was learning to sew. Her mother taught her the basics when Everlyn was 11. Advancing from quilts to doll clothes to her prom dress, Everlyn learned that human sciences (formerly home economics) would lead her to a fulfilling career. Earning bachelor's, master's, and doctoral degrees in the area, Dr. Johnson worked with her state's cooperative extension service for over 27 years. In her role as a county agent, she was responsible for educating the public on home living skills—including sewing. Later she advanced to a position where she was responsible for gathering and communicating current knowledge and research with other county agents.

Most people plan to relax in their retirement. But not Dr. Johnson. She says, "I constantly heard people say that they wish they knew how to sew. I saw a niche that needed filling and decided I was the person to fulfill it." So after just three years of retirement, Everlyn decided to open a fabric store.

One of her first tasks to prepare for the store opening was to enroll in an income tax course at the local university. She recalls, "I felt the tax course would help me do a better job of keeping the records of the business and would ensure that I planned the business to take advantage of tax laws." Then she started doing her homework, meeting with a variety of small business owners to learn the rewards and pitfalls of small business ownership.

Everlyn visited fabric stores outside her market area. "The owners of many stores painted less than a rosy picture of the prospect of opening a store," she remarks. "I felt they were missing something—that main ingredient that would make the store successful. Then I visited two stores that were constantly conducting sewing classes. It was clear to see that these classes were the key to the success of the stores. Perfect!" Having spent most of her career teaching classes, Everlyn now plans sewing classes, teaching some herself, to serve her customers and to promote the sale of fabric and accessories in her store.

Salary: Approximately $70,000, depending on experience.

Qualifications: A master's degree requires one year of university courses beyond the bachelor's degree. Most doctoral programs require another four years of university study and research.

Occupational Outlook: The budgetary constraints of county, state, and federal governments have reduced the financial resources devoted to cooperative education. Thus, the opportunities for individuals in this career have been declining. However, in Dr. Johnson's situation, she was able to use her background to move into a successful business venture.

A COMPLETED 8-COLUMN WORK SHEET

Hobby Shack, Inc.

Work Sheet

For Year Ended December 31, 20--

	ACCOUNT TITLE	1 TRIAL BALANCE DEBIT	2 TRIAL BALANCE CREDIT	3 ADJUSTMENTS DEBIT	4 ADJUSTMENTS CREDIT	5 INCOME STATEMENT DEBIT	6 INCOME STATEMENT CREDIT	7 BALANCE SHEET DEBIT	8 BALANCE SHEET CREDIT	
1	Cash	2908028						2908028		1
2	Petty Cash	30000						30000		2
3	Accounts Receivable	1469840						1469840		3
4	Allow. for Uncoll. Accts.		12752		(e) 124500				137252	4
5	Merchandise Inventory	14048000			(d) 1584000			12464000		5
6	Supplies—Office	348000			(a) 273000			75000		6
7	Supplies—Store	394400			(b) 291000			103400		7
8	Prepaid Insurance	580000			(c) 317000			263000		8
9	Office Equipment	3586450						3586450		9
10	Acc. Depr.—Office Equipment		649700		(f) 654000				1303700	10
11	Store Equipment	4084950						4084950		11
12	Acc. Depr.—Store Equipment		506900		(g) 525000				1031900	12
13	Accounts Payable		1158303						1158303	13
14	Federal Income Tax Payable				(h) 588924				588924	14
15	Employee Income Tax Payable		75700						75700	15
16	Social Security Tax Payable		145138						145138	16
17	Medicare Tax Payable		39942						39942	17
18	Sales Tax Payable		255670						255670	18
19	Unemployment Tax Payable—Federal		3460						3460	19
20	Unemployment Tax Payable—State		23355						23355	20
21	Health Insurance Premiums Payable		100800						100800	21
22	U.S. Savings Bonds Payable		6000						6000	22
23	United Way Donations Payable		7000						7000	23
24	Dividends Payable		500000						500000	24
25	Capital Stock		12500000						12500000	25
26	Retained Earnings		1076129						1076129	26
27	Dividends	2000000						2000000		27
28	Income Summary			(d) 1584000		1584000				28

29	Sales		49512000				49512000			29
30	Sales Discount	25848				25848				30
31	Sales Returns and Allowances	312728				312728				31
32	Purchases	20996000				20996000				32
33	Purchases Discount		164815				164815			33
34	Purch. Returns and Allowances		348495				348495			34
35	Advertising Expense	360000				360000				35
36	Cash Short and Over	1925				1925				36
37	Credit Card Fee Expense	338500				338500				37
38	Depr. Exp.—Office Equipment			(f) 654000		654000				38
39	Depr. Exp.—Store Equipment			(g) 525000		525000				39
40	Insurance Expense			(c) 317000		317000				40
41	Miscellaneous Expense	256490				256490				41
42	Payroll Taxes Expense	910500				910500				42
43	Rent Expense	1800000				1800000				43
44	Salary Expense	10452500				10452500				44
45	Supplies Expense—Office			(a) 273000		273000				45
46	Supplies Expense—Store			(b) 291000		291000				46
47	Uncollectible Accounts Expense			(e) 124500		124500				47
48	Utilities Expense	382000				382000				48
49	Federal Income Tax Expense	1800000		(h) 588924		2388924				49
50		67086159	67086159	4357424	4357424	41993915	50025310	26984668	18953273	50
51	Net Income after Federal Income Tax					8031395			8031395	51
52						50025310	50025310	26984668	26984668	52

A 10-COLUMN WORK SHEET (LEFT PAGE)

1. Trial balance 2. Adjustments 3.

Hobby Shack, Inc.
Work Sheet
For Year Ended December 31, 20--

		1	2	3	4	5	6
	ACCOUNT TITLE	TRIAL BALANCE		ADJUSTMENTS		ADJUSTED TRIAL BALANCE	
		DEBIT	CREDIT	DEBIT	CREDIT	DEBIT	CREDIT
1	*Cash*	29080 28				29080 28	
2	*Petty Cash*	300 00				300 00	
3	*Accounts Receivable*	14698 40				14698 40	
4	*Allow. for Uncoll. Accts.*		127 52		(e) 1245 00		1372 52
5	*Merchandise Inventory*	140480 00			(d) 15840 00	124640 00	
6	*Supplies—Office*	3480 00			(a) 2730 00	750 00	
7	*Supplies—Store*	3944 00			(b) 2910 00	1034 00	
8	*Prepaid Insurance*	5800 00			(c) 3170 00	2630 00	
9	*Office Equipment*	35864 50				35864 50	
10	*Acc. Depr.—Office Equipment*		6497 00		(f) 6540 00		13037 00
11	*Store Equipment*	40849 50				40849 50	
12	*Acc. Depr.—Store Equipment*		5069 00		(g) 5250 00		10319 00
13	*Accounts Payable*		11583 03				11583 03
14	*Federal Income Tax Payable*				(h) 5889 24		5889 24
24	*Dividends Payable*		5000 00				5000 00
25	*Capital Stock*		125000 00				125000 00
26	*Retained Earnings*		10761 29				10761 29
27	*Dividends*	20000 00				20000 00	
28	*Income Summary*			(d) 15840 00		15840 00	
29	*Sales*		495120 00				495120 00
30	*Sales Discount*	258 48				258 48	
31	*Sales Returns and Allowances*	3127 28				3127 28	
32	*Purchases*	209960 00				209960 00	
33	*Purchases Discount*		1648 15				1648 15
34	*Purch. Returns and Allowances*		3484 95				3484 95
35	*Advertising Expense*	3600 00				3600 00	
36	*Cash Short and Over*	19 25				19 25	
37	*Credit Card Fee Expense*	3385 00				3385 00	
38	*Depr. Exp.—Office Equipment*			(f) 6540 00		6540 00	
39	*Depr. Exp.—Store Equipment*			(g) 5250 00		5250 00	
40	*Insurance Expense*			(c) 3170 00		3170 00	
41	*Miscellaneous Expense*	2564 90				2564 90	
42	*Payroll Taxes Expense*	9105 00				9105 00	
43	*Rent Expense*	18000 00				18000 00	
44	*Salary Expense*	104525 00				104525 00	
45	*Supplies Expense—Office*			(a) 2730 00		2730 00	
46	*Supplies Expense—Store*			(b) 2910 00		2910 00	
47	*Uncollectible Accounts Expense*			(e) 1245 00		1245 00	
48	*Utilities Expense*	3820 00				3820 00	
49	*Federal Income Tax Expense*	18000 00		(h) 5889 24		23889 24	
50		670861 59	670861 59	43574 24	43574 24	689785 83	689785 83
51	*Net Income after Federal Income Tax*						
52							

4. Total, prove, and rule

A 10-COLUMN WORK SHEET (RIGHT PAGE)

Extend Adjusted Balances

5. Extend Balances

	7	8	9	10	
	INCOME STATEMENT		BALANCE SHEET		
	DEBIT	CREDIT	DEBIT	CREDIT	
			29080 28		1
			300 00		2
			14698 40		3
				1372 52	4
			124640 00		5
			750 00		6
			1034 00		7
			2630 00		8
			35864 50		9
				13037 00	10
			40849 50		11
				10319 00	12
				11583 03	13
				5889 24	14
				5000 00	24
				125000 00	25
				10761 29	26
			20000 00		27
	15840 00				28
		495120 00			29
	258 48				30
	3127 28				31
	209960 00				32
		1648 15			33
		3484 95			34
	3600 00				35
	19 25				36
	3385 00				37
	6540 00				38
	5250 00				39
	3170 00				40
	2564 90				41
	9105 00				42
	18000 00				43
	104525 00				44
	2730 00				45
	2910 00				46
	1245 00				47
	3820 00				48
	23889 24				49
	419939 15	500253 10	269846 68	189532 73	50
	80313 95			80313 95	51
	500253 10	500253 10	269846 68	269846 68	52

6. Calculate net income; total, prove, and rule

Some large businesses with many accounts to be adjusted at the end of a fiscal period may use a 10-column work sheet. A 10-column work sheet includes an additional pair of amount columns titled Adjusted Trial Balance.

Any business with adjustments to make at the end of a fiscal period could use either an 8-column or a 10-column work sheet. However, completing two extra amount columns when most of the account balances are not adjusted requires extra time and work. Account balances not adjusted must be extended from the Trial Balance columns to the Adjusted Trial Balance columns; whereas, with an 8-column work sheet, account balances not adjusted are extended directly to the Balance Sheet or Income Statement columns.

STEPS • STEPS • STEPS • STEPS

COMPLETING A 10-COLUMN WORK SHEET

1. Record the trial balance on the work sheet.
2. Plan the adjustments on the work sheet.
3. Extend the balances in the Trial Balance Debit and Credit columns to the Adjusted Trial Balance Debit and Credit columns. Calculate up-to-date adjusted balances for all accounts affected by adjustments.
4. Total, prove, and rule the Adjusted Trial Balance Debit and Credit columns.
5. Extend the amounts in the Adjusted Trial Balance Debit and Credit columns to the appropriate Income Statement and Balance Sheet columns.
6. Calculate net income and total, prove, and rule the Income Statement and Balance Sheet columns in the same way as on an 8-column work sheet.

REMEMBER A 10-column work sheet is often used by large merchandising companies with many accounts to be adjusted.

Xtra! Study Tools
accountingxtra.swlearning.com

audit your understanding

1. In what column is the Income Summary amount extended?
2. To which Balance Sheet column is a net loss amount extended?
3. What extra step is required when a 10-column work sheet is prepared instead of an 8-column work sheet?

AUDIT YOUR UNDERSTANDING

work together 14-6

Completing an 8-column work sheet for a merchandising business organized as a corporation

Use the work sheet from Work Together 14-5. Your instructor will guide you through the following examples.

1. Extend all amounts except Federal Income Tax Expense to the appropriate Income Statement or Balance Sheet columns. Do not total the columns.
2. On the form provided in the *Working Papers*, total the work sheet's Income Statement columns. Calculate the difference between the debit and credit totals. This difference becomes the net income before federal income tax expense.
3. Using the tax table shown in this chapter, calculate federal income tax expense and record the income tax adjustment on the work sheet. Label the adjustment *(h)*.
4. Complete the work sheet.

WORK TOGETHER • WORK TOGETHER

on your own 14-6

Completing an 8-column work sheet for a merchandising business organized as a corporation

Use the work sheet from On Your Own 14-5. Work this problem independently.

1. Extend all amounts except Federal Income Tax Expense to the appropriate Income Statement or Balance Sheet columns. Do not total the columns.
2. On the form provided in the *Working Papers*, total the work sheet's Income Statement columns. Calculate the difference between the debit and credit totals.
3. Using the tax table shown in this chapter, calculate federal income tax expense and record the income tax adjustment on the work sheet. Label the adjustment *(h)*.
4. Complete the work sheet.

ON YOUR OWN • ON YOUR OWN

SUMMARY

After completing this chapter, you can

1. Define accounting terms related to distributing dividends and preparing a work sheet for a merchandising business.
2. Identify accounting concepts and practices related to distributing dividends and preparing a work sheet for a merchandising business.
3. Journalize the declaration and payment of a dividend.
4. Begin a work sheet for a merchandising business.
5. Plan work sheet adjustments for merchandise inventory, supplies, prepaid expenses, uncollectible accounts, and depreciation.
6. Calculate federal income tax and plan the work sheet adjustment for federal income tax.
7. Complete a work sheet for a merchandising business.

Explore Accounting

Accounting Systems Design

An important role of accountants is to prepare financial statements for businesses. In addition, many accountants design accounting systems used to prepare the various financial reports important to successful business operations.

An accounting system should be designed to meet the needs of the business it serves. Factors to consider are size of the company, number of facility locations, geographic area of operations (local, statewide, national, international), number of employees, and type of organization (service, merchandising, manufacturing). Also to be considered are the intended uses of the information: traditional financial statements (income statement, balance sheet, cash flow statement), income tax information, management decision information, management control information, and product pricing information.

An accounting system is built around a chart of accounts, which provides the organizational system around which information will be collected, filed, and made available for various types of financial reports.

A small business owned and operated by one person may not need detailed information. However, as a business grows in size and complexity, more detailed information is required. Large international businesses need very complex accounting systems with thousands of accounts to furnish management with the information needed to make decisions and the data for various reports required by governments and other agencies. As businesses grow, accountants constantly look for ways to provide better information. Thus, accountants play a key role in the successful growth of a business.

Activity: Assume Hobby Shack has made the decision to change from a merchandising business to a manufacturing business. It will create its own ceramic molds that will enable it to produce its own line of ceramic images. As the accountant, how would you recommend the chart of accounts be modified to meet the changing needs of the company?

14-1 APPLICATION PROBLEM

Journalizing dividends

Drake Corporation completed the following transactions during December of the current year and January of the next year.

Instructions:

1. Use page 17 of a general journal. Journalize the dividend declared on December 15.
2. Use page 28 of a cash payments journal. Journalize payment of the dividend on January 15.

Transactions:

Dec.	15.	The board of directors declared a dividend of $1.50 per share; capital stock issued is 2,100 shares. M258.
Jan.	15.	Paid cash for dividend declared December 15. C721.

14-2 APPLICATION PROBLEM

Beginning an 8-column work sheet for a merchandising business

A partially completed work sheet for Branson Amusement Company is given in the *Working Papers*. Four general ledger accounts are shown below.

Instructions:

1. Enter the accounts and account balances on the following lines.

Line	Account	Account Balance
6	Supplies—Office	$ 5,210.98
13	Accounts Payable	17,558.16
33	Purchases Discount	5,155.28
44	Salary Expense	193,971.80

2. Total, prove, and rule the trial balance.
3. From a physical count of the following, December 31 balances are determined to be:

Supplies—Office	$489.73
Supplies—Store	701.19
Prepaid Insurance	500.00

Analyze the supplies and prepaid insurance adjustments and enter the adjustments on the work sheet. Label the adjustments *(a)–(c)*. Save your work to complete Application Problem 14-3.

14-3 APPLICATION PROBLEM

EXCEL

Analyzing and recording a merchandise inventory adjustment on a work sheet

Use the work sheet prepared in Application Problem 14-2.

Instructions:

1. From a physical count of merchandise inventory, the December 31 balance is determined to be $226,766.38. Analyze the merchandise inventory adjustment and enter the adjustment on the work sheet. Label the adjustment *(d)*. Save your work to complete Application Problem 14-4.

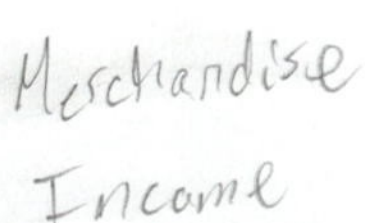

14-4 APPLICATION PROBLEM

Analyzing and recording an allowance for uncollectible accounts adjustment on a work sheet

Use the work sheet prepared in Application Problem 14-3.

Instructions:

1. Branson Amusement Company estimates uncollectible accounts expense as 0.8% of its total sales on account. During the current year, Branson had credit sales of $248,500.00. As of December 31, record the uncollectible accounts expense adjustment on the work sheet and label the adjustment *(e)*. Save your work to complete Application Problem 14-5.

14-5 APPLICATION PROBLEM

Planning and recording adjustments for depreciation

Use the work sheet prepared in Application Problem 14-4.

Instructions:

1. Wave Dive Company tests scuba equipment. Calculate depreciation expense for scuba testing equipment costing $10,540.00; estimated salvage value, $2,500.00; useful life, 3 years.
2. Calculate the book value of the scuba testing equipment at the end of its second year of service.
3. On December 31, Branson Amusement Company determined total depreciation expense: office equipment, $5,850.00; store equipment, $5,250.00. Plan the work sheet adjustments and label the adjustments *(f)* and *(g)*. Save your work to complete Application Problem 14-6.

14-6 APPLICATION PROBLEM

Calculating federal income tax and completing an 8-column work sheet for a merchandising business

Use the work sheet prepared in Application Problem 14-5.

Instructions:

1. Extend all amounts except Federal Income Tax Expense to the appropriate Income Statement or Balance Sheet columns. Do not total the columns.
2. On the form provided in the *Working Papers*, calculate the net income before federal income tax expense.
3. Using the tax table shown in this chapter, calculate federal income tax expense and record the income tax adjustment on the work sheet. Label the adjustment *(h)*.
4. Finish the work sheet.

14-7 MASTERY PROBLEM  

Preparing an 8-column work sheet for a merchandising business

The trial balance for Carol's Closet as of December 31 of the current year is recorded on a work sheet in the *Working Papers*.

Instructions:

1. Analyze the following adjustment information collected on December 31 and record the adjustments on the work sheet. Label each adjustment using labels *(a)* through *(g)*.

a. Office supplies inventory	$ 1,407.00
b. Store supplies inventory	570.11
c. Merchandise inventory	238,830.61
d. Uncollectible accounts are 1.2% of credit sales of:	458,200.00
e. Value of prepaid insurance	2,000.00
f. Estimate of office equipment depreciation	5,216.00
g. Estimate of store equipment depreciation	4,820.00

2. Using the tax table shown in this chapter, calculate federal income tax expense and record the income tax adjustment on the work sheet. Label the adjustment *(h)*.
3. Complete the work sheet.

14-8 CHALLENGE PROBLEM

Preparing a 10-column work sheet for a merchandising business

Hillside Ski Shop's trial balance as of December 31 of the current year is recorded on a work sheet in the *Working Papers*.

Instructions:

1. Analyze the following adjustment information collected on December 31 and record the adjustments on the work sheet. Label each adjustment using labels *(a)* through *(g)*.

a. Office supplies inventory	$ 343.42
b. Store supplies inventory	309.41
c. Merchandise inventory	167,000.46
d. Uncollectible accounts are 1.0% of credit sales of:	158,900.00
e. Value of prepaid insurance	3,000.00
f. Estimate of office equipment depreciation	3,890.00
g. Estimate of store equipment depreciation	3,460.00

2. Using the tax table shown in this chapter, calculate federal income tax expense and record the income tax adjustment on the work sheet. Label the adjustment *(h)*.
3. Complete the work sheet.

applied communication

Sometimes a credit customer does not pay off the amount due on an account receivable by the deadline specified in the terms of the sale on account. In this situation, a business wants to (1) receive the amount owed and (2) preserve a long-term relationship so there can be repeated sales to that customer.

Instructions: Write a first-notice letter to a customer who has not yet paid an amount due. Balance your business's need to receive payment with the desire to keep the customer's goodwill now and in the future. Use a supportive opening and closing.

cases for critical thinking

Case 1

After completing a work sheet, Park's Boutique finds that garment bags still in boxes were overlooked in calculating the supplies inventory. The value of the garment bags overlooked is $600.00. Jerry Park suggests that the accountant not worry because the oversight does not have any effect on balancing the Income Statement and Balance Sheet columns of the work sheet. Mr. Park says that the oversight will be corrected when the store supplies are counted at the end of the next fiscal period. The accountant recommends that the work sheet be redone to reflect the recalculated supplies inventory. Do you agree with Mr. Park or the accountant? Explain your answer.

Case 2

High Five Sports Equipment paid $1,800.00 for a one-year fire insurance policy. The company prepares an income statement and balance sheet every three months. However, the accountant prepares a prepaid insurance adjustment only at the end of the year. Yang Chu, one of the business's managers, thinks the prepaid insurance should be adjusted every three months. Who is correct? Why?

SCANS workplace competency

Technology Competency: Maintaining and Troubleshooting Equipment

Concept: Company offices are filled with equipment that is used in daily operations, such as copying machines, telephone systems, and computers and computer networks. An important function is to keep all the equipment well maintained so that there are no interruptions in the business's daily operations. Usually a facilities manager or technology manager has a plan for preventing, identifying, and solving problems with equipment.

Application: Identify five problems that can occur with the use of computers or computer networks. Suggest how each problem can be solved.

• auditing for errors

Martin Grotte has just completed the year-end work sheet for Lancing Corporation. Part of the work sheet is shown below.

Account Title	Trial Balance Debit	Trial Balance Credit	Adjustments Debit	Adjustments Credit
Accounts Receivable	42,518.25			
Allow. for Uncoll. Accts.		251.66		(e) 496.41
Merchandise Inventory	251,486.36		(d) 9,548.25	
Supplies—Office	5,141.84			(a) 4,154.22
Supplies—Store	3,148.28			(b) 2,974.22
Prepaid Insurance	6,000.00			(c) 5,000.00
Office Equipment	28,550.00			
Acc. Depr.—Office Equipment		12,480.00		(f) 5,210.00
Store Equipment	58,940.00			
Acc. Depr.—Store Equipment		16,420.00		(g) 8,420.00
Federal Income Tax Payable				(h) 45,813.38
Sales		992,818.10		
Utilities Expense	5,485.22			
Federal Income Tax Expense	60,000.00		(h) 45,813.38	

Martin used the following information to prepare the work sheet adjustments:

a. Uncollectible accounts are estimated to be 0.5% of gross sales (the amount of sales before discounts and returns and allowances are subtracted).
b. Office supplies inventory on hand, $987.62.
c. Store supplies inventory on hand, $174.06.
d. Merchandise inventory on hand, $241,938.11.
e. The six-month insurance premium was paid on July 1.
f. Office equipment has a 5-year useful life and a $2,500 salvage value.
g. Store equipment has a 7-year useful life and a $3,500 salvage value.

Instructions

Audit the work sheet to determine if the work sheet adjustments were recorded properly. Prepare a list that describes any errors you discover and how they should be corrected.

• analyzing Best Buy's financial statements

Best Buy issued a dividend for the first time in the 2004 fiscal year. Investors use a ratio known as the *dividend yield* when making investment decisions. The dividend yield is calculated as follows:

$$\text{Dividend Yield} = \frac{\text{Dividend per Share}}{\text{Market Price per Share}}$$

Companies with large dividend yields (greater than 3%) are typically considered to be *income stocks*, meaning that investors own the stock primarily to earn the dividend. In contrast, companies with small dividend yields (less than 2%) are often referred to as *growth stocks*, meaning that investors are counting on the market value of the stock to increase over time.

Instructions: Use Best Buy's financial statements in Appendix B to answer the following questions.

1. Calculate the dividend yield for Best Buy, assuming the current market price is $60.00 per share.
2. Would you classify Best Buy as an income or growth stock?

Automated Accounting

Understanding Graphs

Charts and graphs provide a picture of numeric data and help explain it. They are commonly used to track sales goals, monitor expenses, identify trends, and make forecasts. Computer presentations and printed reports frequently include charts and graphs.

Graphs and charts effectively communicate summary data such as component percentages. Different styles of graphs are used to display different types of financial information. A pie graph is used to illustrate parts of a whole. For example, a pie graph could be used to show cost of goods sold, operating expenses, and net income as percentages of net sales. Bar graphs are used to show the relative size of related items, such as expenses. Line graphs are used to illustrate trends, such as net sales or net income over a period of years. To be effective, charts and graphs should be clearly labeled.

Many accounting software packages are capable of producing charts and graphs from data contained within their files. *Automated Accounting 8.0* can generate the following graphs:

1. Income statement
2. Expense distribution
3. Top customers
4. Balance sheet
5. Sales

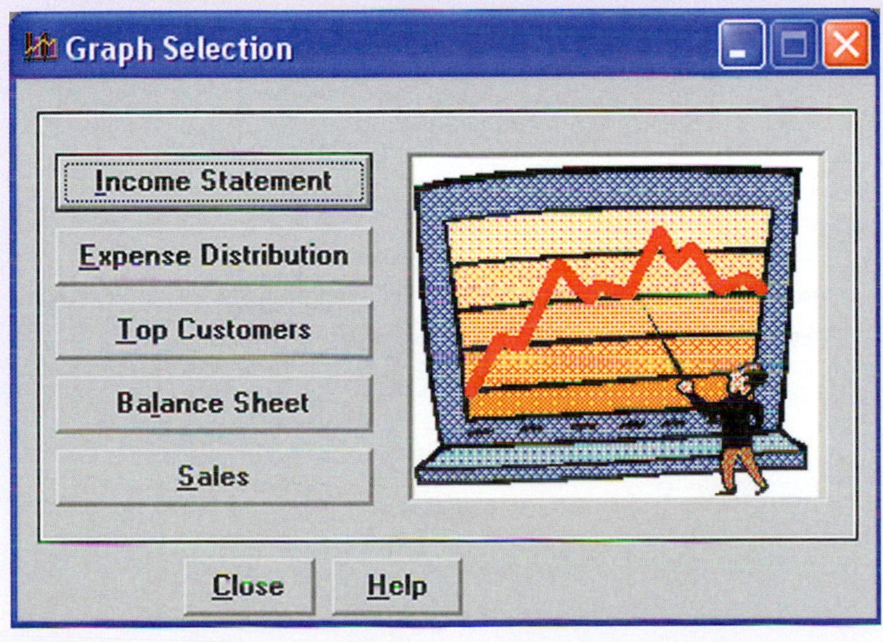

To prepare a graph based on financial data when a data file is open:

1. Choose the Graph Selection menu item from the Reports menu or click the Graphs toolbar button.
2. Click the type of graph you would like to display.
3. You may choose to print the graph by clicking the Print button.
4. Click the Close button to close the Graph Selection window.

Automated Accounting Graphing Problem (optional)

Instructions:

1. Open the data file that is your solution to Automated Accounting Problem F11-5. If it is available, the filename should be F11-5 XXX XXX (where the X's are your first and last name). There is no Help file available for this graphing problem.
2. Click the Graphs toolbar button.
3. Click the Income Statement button to display a graph of the income statement.
4. View the other graphs available. Note that some are not very meaningful because this particular problem does not have a wide range of data available for graphing.
5. Exit Automated Accounting without saving your file.

OBJECTIVES & TERMS

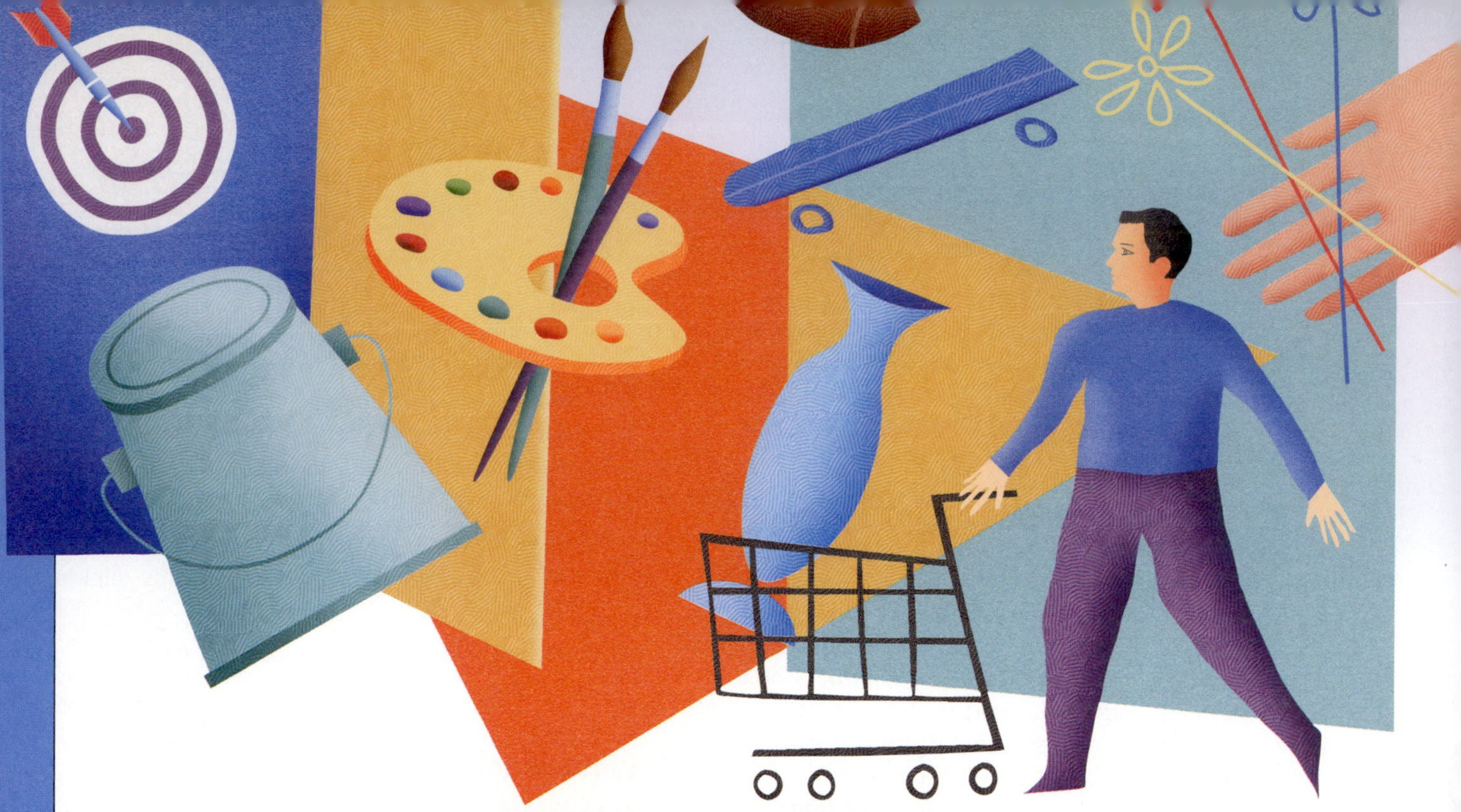

CHAPTER 15 Financial Statements for a Corporation

After studying Chapter 15, you will be able to:

1. Define accounting terms related to financial statements for a merchandising business organized as a corporation.
2. Identify accounting concepts and practices related to financial statements for a merchandising business organized as a corporation.
3. Prepare an income statement for a merchandising business organized as a corporation.
4. Analyze an income statement using component percentages and financial ratios.
5. Prepare a statement of stockholders' equity for a merchandising business organized as a corporation.
6. Prepare a balance sheet for a merchandising business organized as a corporation.

- net sales
- cost of merchandise sold
- gross profit on sales
- financial ratio
- earnings per share
- price-earnings ratio
- statement of stockholder's equity
- par value
- current liabilities
- long-term liabilities
- supporting schedule

Point Your Browser
accountingxtra.swlearning.com

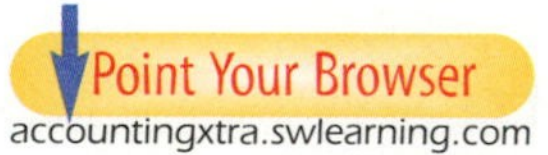

accounting in the real world

Gap, Inc.

©GETTY IMAGES

THE EVOLUTION OF GAP, INC.

Many of today's most notable companies had very humble beginnings. Gap, Inc., began in 1969 when Don and Doris Fisher opened a clothing store in San Francisco. The company grew quickly, becoming a publicly traded company in just seven years.

The company expanded beyond its Gap store concept in 1983 by purchasing Banana Republic, a small safari and travel clothing company. Gap further extended its penetration into the clothing market by introducing the Old Navy brand in 1994. The rest, as they say, is history. With over 3,000 stores, Gap, Inc., is now a major force in the apparel industry.

Each of its clothing brands targets different customers. The original Gap brand targets style-conscious customers in the casual specialty market. Banana Republic targets men and women who want more sophisticated seasonal fashions, shoes, personal care products, intimate apparel, and gifts for the home. Old Navy is more value focused, providing families with great fashions at affordable prices.

Critical Thinking

1. Should a single set of financial statements be prepared for Gap Inc., or should financial statements be prepared for each brand?
2. How would the chart of accounts differ among the three brands?

accountingxtra.swlearning.com

Source: www.oldnavy.com/html/ourcompany/aboutourstores.asp

ACCOUNTING IN THE REAL WORLD • ACCOUNTING IN THE REAL WORLD • ACCOUNTING IN THE REAL WORLD •

internet activity

EDGAR—PART 1

Go to the homepage for the Securities and Exchange Commission (SEC) (www.sec.gov). The SEC provides almost instant access to forms filed with the SEC. Investors can access these forms through a system called EDGAR. Click on "Filings and Forms (EDGAR)." Search the site to find out more about EDGAR.

Instructions

1. Each letter in "EDGAR" is an abbreviation for a word. List the word connected with each letter in EDGAR.
2. Briefly state how EDGAR helps investors.

INTERNET RESEARCH ACTIVITY • INTERNET RESEARCH ACTIVITY • INTERNET RESEARCH ACTIVITY •

LESSON • LESSON • LESSON • LESSON • LESSON • LESSON

15-1 Preparing an Income Statement

USES OF FINANCIAL STATEMENTS

Financial statements provide the primary source of information needed by owners and managers to make decisions on the future activity of a business. All financial information must be reported in order to make sound business decisions. The financial statements should provide information about a business's financial condition, changes in this financial condition, and the progress of operations. [*CONCEPT: Adequate Disclosure*]

Comparing financial condition and progress for more than one fiscal period also helps owners and managers make sound business decisions. Therefore, financial information must be reported the same way from one fiscal period to the next. [*CONCEPT: Consistent Reporting*]

Hobby Shack prepares three financial statements to report financial progress and condition. A corporation prepares an income statement and a balance sheet similar to those used by a proprietorship. A corporation also prepares a statement of stockholders' equity.

©GETTY IMAGES/PHOTODISC

making ethical decisions

MAKING ETHICAL DECISIONS • MAKING ETHICAL DECISIONS • MAKING ETHICAL DECISIONS

Can You Share Client Names?

After working six years with a national public accounting firm, Elena Espinoza decided to venture out on her own. Elena's new firm, Espinoza Consulting, specializes in helping companies that are facing severe financial difficulties. When delivering proposals to potential clients, Elena proudly lists the names of her current clients.

The Code of Professional Conduct for the American Institute of Certified Public Accountants "prohibits a member in public practice from disclosing confidential information without the client's consent." Elena is aware of the rule but believes she is not violating this rule.

Instructions

Access the AICPA Code of Professional Conduct. Determine if Elena's actions violate the confidentiality rule. (Hint: Remember that the Code includes rules, interpretations, and ethics rulings.)

careers in accounting

CAREERS IN ACCOUNTING • CAREERS IN ACCOUNTING • CAREERS IN ACCOUNTI

Ken Harrison, Computer and Information Systems Manager

COURTESY OF KEN HARRISON

As a high school student, Ken Harrison knew he didn't want to do the same thing for his entire career. Ken recalls, "I was the only one in my college freshman orientation group who firmly knew their intended major. 'Accounting!' I proudly responded to our group leader." Ken had been advised that an accounting degree was a good background for law school. However, when presented with attractive accounting job offers in the first semester of his senior year, he thought that "perhaps law school could wait!"

Ken began his career with PricewaterhouseCoopers. During five years in public accounting, he was exposed to numerous accounting issues and became acquainted with the upper-level managers and officers of his clients.

Networking in his profession and community has brought Ken numerous opportunities. At age 28, he was offered the chief financial officer (CFO) position for a start-up general aviation company. Later, as its general manager, he was involved in sales, marketing, human resources, finance, and information technology. "As a successful entrepreneurial business, our little company soon became the target of larger companies in the industry. I hadn't studied much about mergers and acquisitions in college, but 'deal making' soon became a requirement." The sale of the company to a much larger out-of-state corporation, which brought in their own leadership, resulted in Ken's position being eliminated.

Another opportunity soon appeared—to go to work for a publicly held client who needed a CPA familiar with mergers and acquisitions. Seven years later, when Ken's personal desires turned to a more humanitarian calling, he accepted the CFO position of an international not-for-profit organization working to provide impoverished people with the skills and means to improve their lives. In that role, he experienced different and interesting challenges, including travel to many developing countries. "Who would have imagined an accounting degree would take me to remote Africa!" he remarks.

Ken is now working in state government for another former colleague. He explains, "Our mission is to help improve business processes of the state government by installing and supporting an enterprise resource planning (ERP) system." Ken helps direct 80 individuals who assist the users of the ERP throughout the government.

Salary Range: The median annual salary for a computer and information systems manager was $85,240 in 2002 (Bureau of Labor Statistics, *Occupational Outlook Handbook, 2004–05*, at www.bls.gov). The middle 50 percent of these managers earned between $64,150 and $109,950.

Qualifications: Ken believes networking is the key to opportunity. Developing relationships with colleagues and individuals in professional and civic organizations will open doors to opportunities in the most unexpected places. A Certified Public Accountant (CPA) license and public accounting experience provide a solid foundation. Communication skills and a willingness to work in every aspect of the organization, from sales to technology, are important to take advantage of job opportunities.

Occupational Outlook: The U.S. Department of Labor expects jobs for computer and information systems managers to increase much faster than the national average for all occupations. The continued application of technology to business operations will increase the number of jobs that use computer technology, thus requiring more individuals to manage the technology

INCOME STATEMENT INFORMATION ON A WORK SHEET

Hobby Shack, Inc.
Work Sheet
For Year Ended December 31, 20--

	Account Title	1 Trial Balance Debit	2 Trial Balance Credit	3 Adjustments Debit	4 Adjustments Credit	5 Income Statement Debit	6 Income Statement Credit	7 Balance Sheet Debit	8 Balance Sheet Credit	
5	Merchandise Inventory	140480 00			(d) 15840 00			124640 00		5
29	Sales		495120 00				495120 00			29
30	Sales Discount	258 48				258 48				30
31	Sales Returns and Allowances	3127 28				3127 28				31
32	Purchases	209960 00				209960 00				32
33	Purchases Discount		1648 15				1648 15			33
34	Purch. Returns and Allowances		3484 95				3484 95			34
35	Advertising Expense	3600 00				3600 00				35
36	Cash Short and Over	19 25				19 25				36
37	Credit Card Fee Expense	3385 00				3385 00				37
38	Depr. Exp.—Office Equipment			(f) 6540 00		6540 00				38
39	Depr. Exp.—Store Equipment			(g) 5250 00		5250 00				39
40	Insurance Expense			(c) 3170 00		3170 00				40
41	Miscellaneous Expense	2564 90				2564 90				41
42	Payroll Taxes Expense	9105 00				9105 00				42
43	Rent Expense	18000 00				18000 00				43
44	Salary Expense	104525 00				104525 00				44
45	Supplies Expense—Office			(a) 2730 00		2730 00				45
46	Supplies Expense—Store			(b) 2910 00		2910 00				46
47	Uncollectible Accounts Expense			(e) 1245 00		1245 00				47
48	Utilities Expense	3820 00				3820 00				48
49	Federal Income Tax Expense	18000 00		(h) 5889 24		23889 24				49
50		670861 59	670861 59	43574 24	43574 24	419939 15	500253 10	269846 68	189532 73	50
51	Net Income after Federal Income Tax					80313 95			80313 95	51
52						500253 10	500253 10	269846 68	269846 68	52

An income statement is used to report a business's financial progress. Merchandising businesses report revenue, cost of merchandise sold, gross profit on sales, expenses, and net income or loss. Current and previous income statements can be compared to determine the reasons for increases or decreases in net income. This comparison is helpful in making management decisions about future operations.

Information from a completed work sheet is used to prepare an income statement. Amounts in all revenue and expense accounts and Merchandise Inventory are reported on an income statement.

The income statement of a merchandising business has three main sections: (1) revenue section, (2) cost of merchandise sold section, and (3) expenses section.

REVENUE SECTION OF AN INCOME STATEMENT FOR A MERCHANDISING BUSINESS

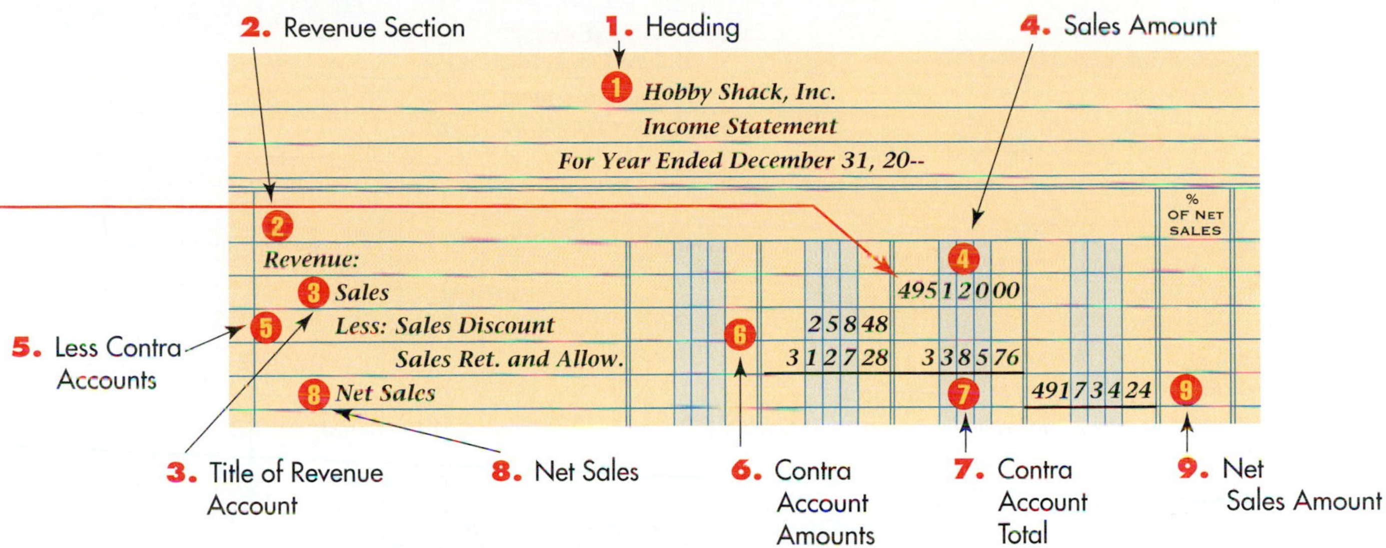

Hobby Shack's income statement differs from TechKnow's income statement shown in Part 1. Hobby Shack has more accounts to report on the income statement. The account Sales and its contra accounts, Sales Discounts and Sales Returns and Allowances, are reported in the Revenue section. Total sales less sales discount and sales returns and allowances is called **net sales**.

STEPS • STEPS • STEPS • STEPS • STEPS • STEPS • STEPS • STEPS • STEPS • STEPS

PREPARING THE REVENUE SECTION OF AN INCOME STATEMENT

1. Write the income statement heading on three lines.
2. Write the name of this section, *Revenue:*, at the extreme left of the wide column on the first line.
3. Write the title of the revenue account, *Sales*, on the next line, indented about one centimeter.
4. Write the balance of the sales account, *$495,120.00*, in the third amount column.
5. Write *Less:* on the next line, indented about one centimeter, followed by *Sales Discount* and *Sales Returns and Allowances* on the next line.
6. Write the balances of the sales discount account, *$258.48*, and sales returns and allowances account, *$3,127.28*, in the second amount column.
7. Add sales discounts, *$258.48*, and sales returns and allowances, *$3,127.28*, and write the amount, *$3,385.76*, in the third amount column.
8. Write *Net Sales* on the next line, indented about one centimeter.
9. Subtract the total of the contra accounts, *$3,385.76*, from sales, *$495,120.00*, to calculate net sales, *$491,734.24*. Write this amount in the fourth amount column.

COST OF MERCHANDISE SOLD SECTION OF AN INCOME STATEMENT FOR A MERCHANDISING BUSINESS

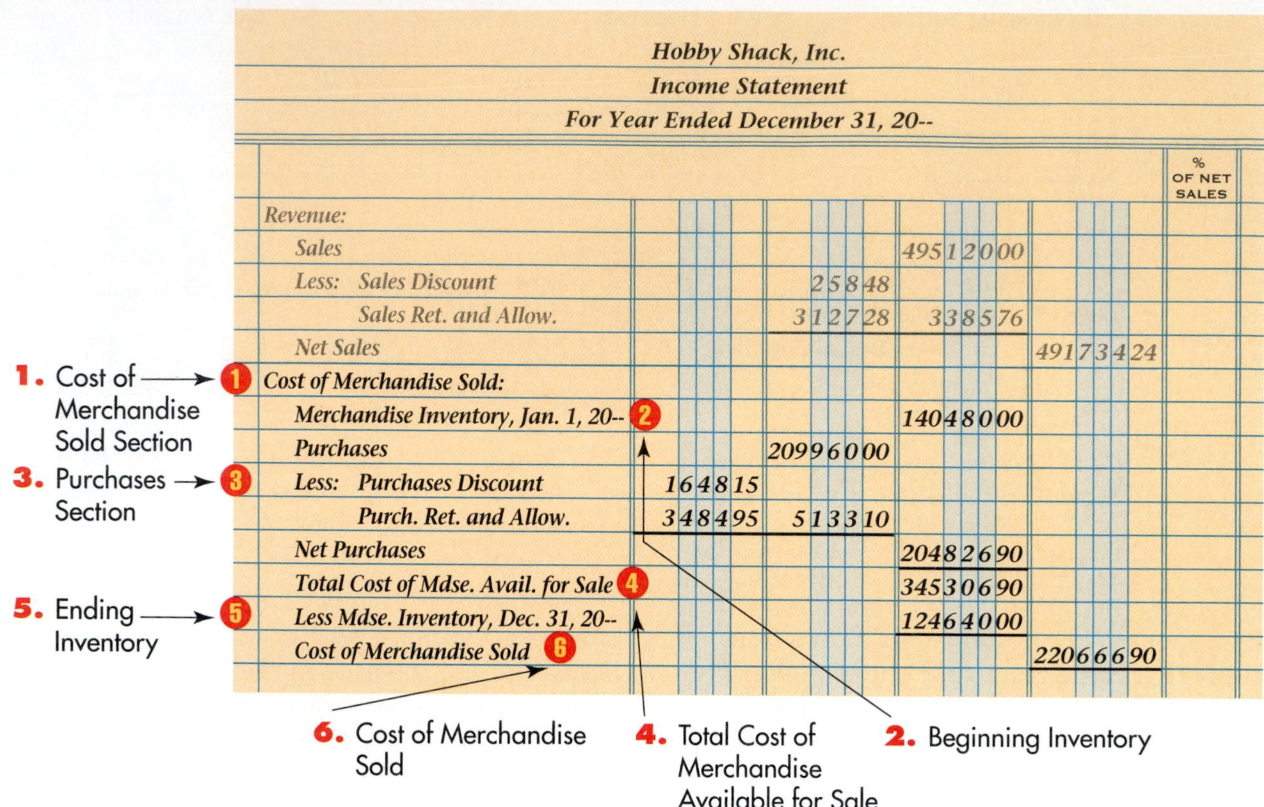

The original price of all merchandise sold during a fiscal period is called the **cost of merchandise sold.** [*CONCEPT: Historical Cost*] Cost of merchandise sold is also known as *cost of goods sold* or *cost of sales.*

STEPS • STEPS • STEPS • STEPS • STEPS • STEPS • STEPS • STEPS • STEPS • STEPS •

PREPARING THE COST OF MERCHANDISE SOLD SECTION OF AN INCOME STATEMENT

1. Write the name of this section, *Cost of Merchandise Sold:*, at the extreme left of the wide column.
2. Write the beginning inventory found in the Trial Balance Debit column of the work sheet.
   a. Indent about one centimeter on the next line and write *Merchandise Inventory, Jan. 1, 20--.*
   b. Write the beginning merchandise inventory balance, *$140,480.00*, in the third amount column.
3. Prepare the Purchases section.
   a. Indent about one centimeter on the next line and write *Purchases.* Enter the purchases amount, *$209,960.00*, in the second amount column.
   b. Write *Less:* on the next line, indented about one centimeter, followed by *Purchases Discount* and *Purchases Returns and Allowances* on the next line. It is permissible to abbreviate long titles when necessary.
   c. Write the balances of the purchases discount account, *$1,648.15*, and purchases returns and allowances account, *$3,484.95*, in the first amount column.
   d. Add purchases discounts, *$1,648.15*, and purchases returns and allowances, *$3,484.95*, and write the amount, *$5,133.10*, in the second amount column.
   e. Write *Net Purchases* on the next line, indented about one centimeter.
   f. Subtract the total of the contra accounts, *$5,133.10*, from purchases, *$209,960.00*, to calculate net purchases, *$204,826.90.* Write this amount in the third amount column.

4. Calculate the total cost of merchandise available for sale.
   a. Indent about one centimeter on the next line, and write *Total Cost of Merchandise Available for Sale.*
   b. Add the beginning merchandise inventory balance, *$140,480.00*, and net purchases, *$204,826.90*, to calculate the total cost of merchandise available for sale, *$345,306.90*. Write this amount in the third amount column.

5. Write the ending inventory found in the Balance Sheet Debit column of the work sheet.
   a. Indent about one centimeter on the next line, and write *Less Merchandise Inventory, Dec. 31, 20--.*
   b. Write the ending merchandise inventory balance, *$124,640.00*, found in the Balance Sheet Debit column of the work sheet, in the third amount column.

6. Calculate the cost of merchandise sold.
   a. Indent about one centimeter on the next line, and write *Cost of Merchandise Sold.*
   b. Subtract the ending merchandise inventory balance, *$124,640.00*, from the total cost of merchandise available for sale, *$345,306.90*, to calculate the cost of merchandise sold, *$220,666.90*. Write the amount in the fourth amount column.

Most calculated amounts reported on a financial statement have a related description. Net sales and net purchases are two examples. However, the totals of the sales contra accounts, *$3,385.76*, and the purchases contra accounts, *$5,133.10*, are not described. Instead, the reader of the financial statement is expected to understand the amount by its physical position on the statement. Each amount is immediately to the right of an amount column ruled with a single line.

The single ruled line indicates that the column is being totaled. The amount adjacent to the column is the sum of that column.

Hobby Shack, Inc.
Income Statement
For Year Ended December 31, 20--

					% OF NET SALES
Revenue:					
Sales			495120 00		
Less: Sales Discount		258 48			
Sales Ret. and Allow.		3127 28	3385 76		
Net Sales				491734 24	

Total of adjacent column

©GETTY IMAGES/PHOTODISC

COMPLETING AN INCOME STATEMENT FOR A MERCHANDISING BUSINESS

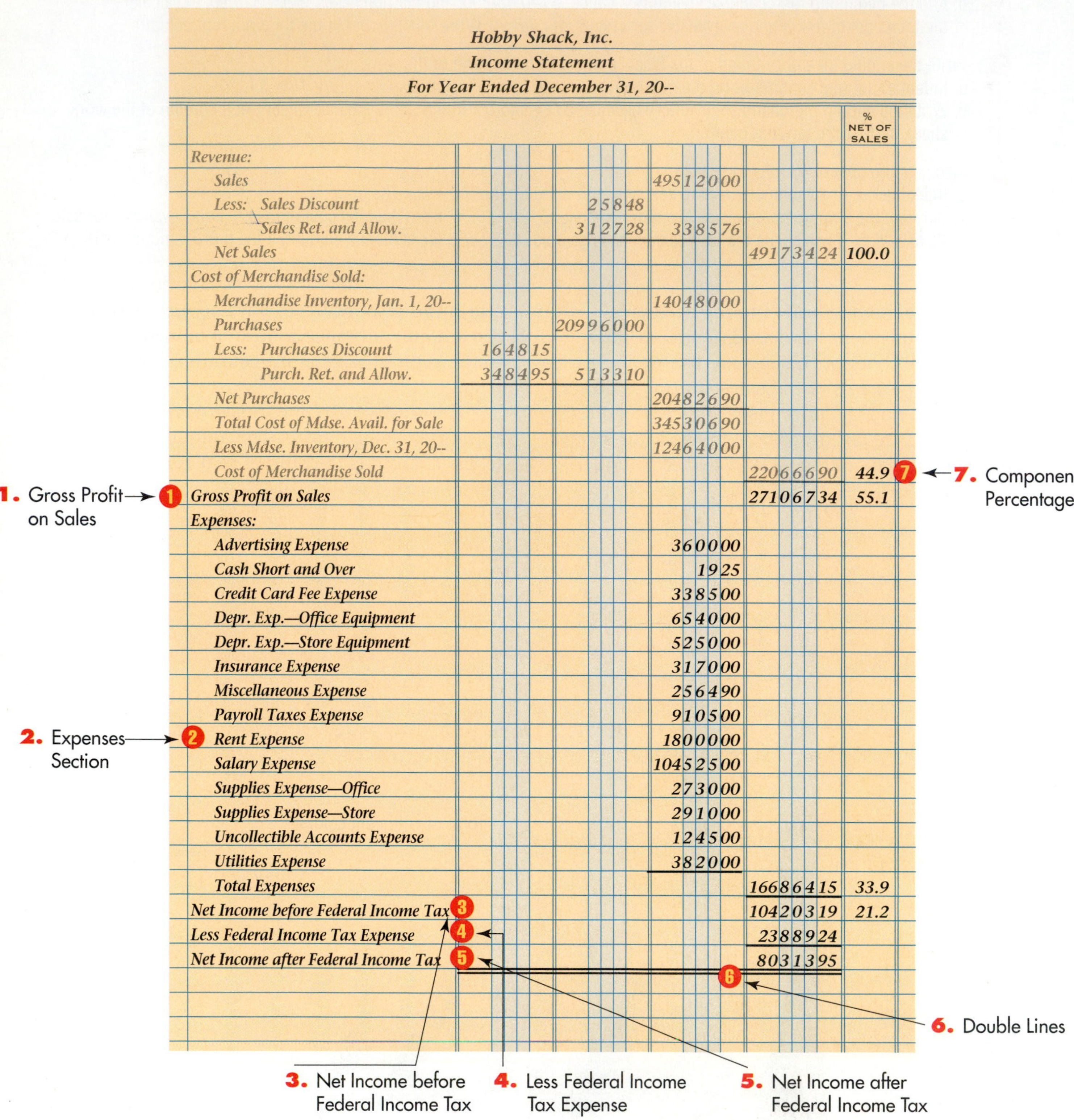

Hobby Shack, Inc.
Income Statement
For Year Ended December 31, 20--

					% NET OF SALES
Revenue:					
Sales			495120 00		
Less: Sales Discount		258 48			
Sales Ret. and Allow.		3127 28	3385 76		
Net Sales				491734 24	100.0
Cost of Merchandise Sold:					
Merchandise Inventory, Jan. 1, 20--			140480 00		
Purchases		209960 00			
Less: Purchases Discount	1648 15				
Purch. Ret. and Allow.	3484 95	5133 10			
Net Purchases			204826 90		
Total Cost of Mdse. Avail. for Sale			345306 90		
Less Mdse. Inventory, Dec. 31, 20--			124640 00		
Cost of Merchandise Sold				220666 90	44.9
Gross Profit on Sales				271067 34	55.1
Expenses:					
Advertising Expense			3600 00		
Cash Short and Over			19 25		
Credit Card Fee Expense			3385 00		
Depr. Exp.—Office Equipment			6540 00		
Depr. Exp.—Store Equipment			5250 00		
Insurance Expense			3170 00		
Miscellaneous Expense			2564 90		
Payroll Taxes Expense			9105 00		
Rent Expense			18000 00		
Salary Expense			104525 00		
Supplies Expense—Office			2730 00		
Supplies Expense—Store			2910 00		
Uncollectible Accounts Expense			1245 00		
Utilities Expense			3820 00		
Total Expenses				166864 15	33.9
Net Income before Federal Income Tax				104203 19	21.2
Less Federal Income Tax Expense				23889 24	
Net Income after Federal Income Tax				80313 95	

The revenue remaining after cost of merchandise sold has been deducted is called **gross profit on sales**. Management uses gross profit on sales as a measure for how effectively the business is performing in its primary functions of buying and selling merchandise. Calculating a ratio between gross profit on sales and net sales enables management to compare its performance to prior fiscal periods. The percentage relationship between one financial statement item and the total that includes that item is known as a *component percentage*. Hobby Shack calculates a component percentage for most calculated amounts reported in the fourth column of the income statement.

STEPS • STEPS • STEPS • STEPS • STEPS • STEPS • STEPS • STEPS • STEPS • STEPS •

STEPS COMPLETING AN INCOME STATEMENT

1. Calculate the gross profit on sales.
   a. Write *Gross Profit on Sales* on the next line at the extreme left of the wide column.
   b. Write the gross profit on sales amount, *$271,067.34*, in the second amount column. (Total revenue, *$491,734.24*, less cost of merchandise sold, *$220,666.90*, equals gross profit on sales, *$271,067.34*.)

2. Prepare the expenses section. Use the information from the Income Statement Debit column of the work sheet.
   a. Write the name of this section, *Expenses:*, at the extreme left of the wide column.
   b. On the next line, indented about one centimeter, list the expense account titles, one per line, in the order in which they appear on the work sheet.
   c. Write the amount of each expense account balance in the third amount column.
   d. Indent about one centimeter, and write *Total Expenses* on the next line in the wide column below the last expense account title.
   e. Total the individual expense amounts and write the total, *$166,864.15*, in the fourth amount column on the total line.

3. Calculate the net income before federal income tax.
   a. Write *Net Income before Federal Income Tax* on the next line at the extreme left of the wide column.
   b. Write the amount, *$104,203.19*, in the fourth amount column. (Gross profit on sales, *$271,067.34*, less total expenses, *$166,864.15*, equals net income before federal income tax, *$104,203.19*.)

4. Write *Less Federal Income Tax Expense* on the next line at the extreme left of the wide column. Write the amount, *$23,889.24*, on the same line in the fourth amount column.

5. Calculate net income after federal income tax.
   a. Write *Net Income after Federal Income Tax* on the next line at the extreme left of the wide column.
   b. Write the amount, *$80,313.95*, in the fourth amount column. (Net income before federal income tax, *$104,203.19*, less federal income tax expense, *$23,889.24*, equals net income after federal income tax, *$80,313.95*.)
   c. Verify accuracy by comparing the amount of net income after federal income tax calculated on the income statement, *$80,313.95*, with the amount on the work sheet, *$80,313.95*. The two amounts must be the same.

6. Rule double lines across the four amount columns to show that the income statement has been verified as correct.

7. Calculate a component percentage for each amount in the fourth amount column through the Net Income before Federal Income Tax. Divide the amount of each component by the amount of net sales. Round each component percentage to the nearest 0.1%. Write the component percentage in the % of Net Sales column.

Income Statement Component	Amount	÷	Net Sales	=	Component Percentage
Cost of Merchandise Sold	$220,666.90	÷	$491,734.24	=	44.9%
Gross Profit on Sales	$271,067.34	÷	$491,734.24	=	55.1%
Total Expenses	$166,864.15	÷	$491,734.24	=	33.9%
Net Income before Federal Income Tax	$104,203.19	÷	$491,734.24	=	21.2%

Xtra! Study Tools
accountingxtra.swlearning.com

terms review

net sales
cost of merchandise sold
gross profit on sales

TERMS REVIEW • TERMS

audit your understanding

1. What is the major difference between the income statement for a merchandising business and a service business?
2. How is the cost of merchandise sold calculated?
3. How can the amount of net income calculated on the income statement be verified?

AUDIT YOUR UNDERSTANDING

work together 15-1

Preparing an income statement for a merchandising business

The work sheet for Interstate Tires, Inc., for the year ended December 31 of the current year is given in the *Working Papers*. Your instructor will guide you through the following examples.

1. Prepare an income statement.
2. Calculate and record on the income statement the following component percentages: (a) cost of merchandise sold, (b) gross profit on sales, (c) total expenses, and (d) net income before federal income tax. Round percentage calculations to the nearest 0.1%. Save your work to complete Work Together 15-2.

WORK TOGETHER • WORK

on your own 15-1

Preparing an income statement for a merchandising business

Osborn Corporation's work sheet for the year ended December 31 of the current year is given in the *Working Papers*. Work independently to complete this problem.

1. Prepare an income statement.
2. Calculate and record on the income statement the following component percentages: (a) cost of merchandise sold, (b) gross profit on sales, (c) total expenses, and (d) net income before federal income tax. Round percentage calculations to the nearest 0.1%. Save your work to complete On Your Own 15-2.

ON YOUR OWN • ON YOUR

LESSON • LESSON • LESSON • LESSON • LESSON • LESSON

15-2 Analyzing an Income Statement

USING COMPONENT PERCENTAGES

A percentage relationship between one financial statement item and the total that includes that item is known as a *component percentage*. For Hobby Shack, a merchandising business, every sales dollar reported on the income statement includes four components: (1) cost of merchandise sold, (2) gross profit on sales, (3) total expenses, and (4) net income before income tax. To help make decisions about future operations, Hobby Shack analyzes relationships between these four income statement components and sales. Hobby Shack calculates a component percentage for each of the four components. The relationship between each component and sales is shown in a separate column on the income statement.

Acceptable Component Percentages

	Acceptable Industry Standards	Hobby Shack Component Percentages
Sales	100%	100%
Cost of merchandise sold	not more than 46.0%	44.9%
Gross profit on sales	not less than 54.0%	55.1%
Total expenses	not more than 35.0%	33.9%
Net income before federal income tax	not less than 19.0%	21.2%

For a component percentage to be useful, a business must know acceptable percentages. This information is determined by making comparisons with prior fiscal periods as well as with industry standards published by industry organizations. Based on these sources, Hobby Shack determines acceptable component percentages for the current fiscal period. Each percentage represents the amount of each sales dollar that is considered acceptable. For example, Hobby Shack determines that the cost of merchandise sold should be no more than 46.0%, or 46 cents, of each sales dollar.

FYI FOR YOUR INFORMATION

Unacceptable component percentages serve as a warning that management action is necessary. Calculating and reporting component percentages is an example of how accounting information can help management planning and decision making. Effective managers rely on the information provided from accounting records.

ANALYSIS OF COMPONENT PERCENTAGES

Hobby Shack compares four of its component percentages to its acceptable component percentages. The four component percentages are for cost of merchandise sold, gross profit on sales, total expenses, and net income before federal income tax.

Cost of Merchandise Sold Component Percentage

The cost of merchandise sold is a major cost and must be kept as low as possible. Analysis of Hobby Shack's component percentages shows that the cost of merchandise sold is 44.9% of sales.

The component percentage for cost of merchandise sold, *44.9%*, is less than the maximum acceptable percentage, *46.0%*. Therefore, Hobby Shack's component percentage for cost of merchandise sold is considered acceptable.

Gross Profit on Sales Component Percentage

Gross profit must be large enough to cover total expenses and the desired amount of net income. Acceptable industry standards show that at least 54 cents, or 54.0%, of each sales dollar should result in gross profit. Hobby Shack's component percentage for gross profit on sales is 55.1%.

The component percentage for gross profit on sales, *55.1%*, is not less than the minimum acceptable percentage, *54.0%*. Therefore, Hobby Shack's component percentage for gross profit on sales is considered acceptable.

Total Expenses Component Percentage

Total expenses must be less than gross profit on sales to provide a desirable net income. Acceptable industry standards show that no more than 35 cents, or 35.0%, of each sales dollar should be devoted to total expenses. Hobby Shack's component percentage for total expenses is 33.9%.

The component percentage for total expenses, *33.9%*, is not more than the maximum acceptable percentage, *35.0%*. Therefore, Hobby Shack's component percentage for total expenses is considered acceptable.

Net Income before Federal Income Tax Component Percentage

The component percentage for net income before federal income tax shows the progress being made by a business. Acceptable industry standards show that at least 19 cents, or 19.0%, of each sales dollar should result in net income. Hobby Shack's component percentage for net income is 21.25%.

The component percentage for net income, *21.2%*, is not less than the minimum acceptable percentage, *19.0%*. Therefore, Hobby Shack's component percentage for net income is considered acceptable.

REMEMBER The cost of merchandise sold and total expenses reduce owner's equity. For this reason, a business wants actual component percentages of these financial statement totals to be less than the acceptable component percentage. A business wants the gross profit on sales and net income before federal income tax to be as high as possible. Thus, a business wants the actual component percentage for these financial statement totals to be higher than the acceptable component percentages.

ANALYZING AN INCOME STATEMENT SHOWING A NET LOSS

Cloth Circuit					
Income Statement					
For Year Ended December 31, 20--					
					% OF NET SALES
Revenue:					
Sales			848 184 10		
Cost of Merchandise Sold				485 763 95	58.0
Gross Profit on Sales				351 956 98	42.0
Expenses:					
Advertising Expense			32 550 00		
Credit Card Fee Expense			5 118 20		
Utilities Expense			5 184 00		
Total Expenses				393 726 94	47.0
Net Loss before Federal Income Tax				(41 769 96)	(5.0)
Less Federal Income Tax Expense				(6 265 49)	
Net Loss after Federal Income Tax				(35 504 47)	

When a business's total expenses are greater than the gross profit on sales, the difference is known as a *net loss.* Cloth Circuit's total expenses, *$393,726.94*, less gross profit on sales, *$351,956.98*, equals net loss before federal income taxes, *$41,769.96*. The net loss before federal income taxes, *$41,769.96*, is written in parentheses in the fourth amount column on the line with the words *Net Loss before Federal Income Taxes*. An amount written in parentheses on a financial statement indicates a negative amount.

Cloth Circuit's managers can compare its component percentages to acceptable component percentages. The component percentage for cost of merchandise sold, *58.0%*, is less than Cloth Circuit's maximum acceptable component percentage, *60.0%*. The component percentage for gross profit on sales, *42.0%*, is greater than the minimum acceptable component percentage, *40.0%*. These component percentages indicate that management is doing a good job controlling the cost of merchandise inventory.

The component percentage for total expenses, *47.0%*, is more than the maximum acceptable component percentage, *37.0%*. Because a net loss occurred, the component percentage for net income before federal income tax, *(5.0%)*, means that Cloth Circuit lost 5.0 cents on each sales dollar. These component percentages indicate that management is not effective in controlling its expenses.

To return to profitability, management must take action to reduce its expenses. Advertising and salary expense are the two largest expenses that management could quickly control. Rent expense, although one of the three largest expenses, is more difficult to control in the short term since most lease agreements are signed for a year or more.

FYI FOR YOUR INFORMATION

A corporation having a net loss before federal income taxes can file for a tax refund from the federal government. To qualify for a refund, the corporation must have paid at least an equal amount of federal income taxes in the previous three years. Cloth Circuit calculates its tax refund using the same tax schedule Hobby Shack used to calculate its federal income tax expense. Cloth Circuit's tax refund, *$6,265.49*, is shown as a negative amount, thus reducing the amount of the net loss to $35,504.47.

ACTIONS TO CORRECT UNACCEPTABLE COMPONENT PERCENTAGES

The goal of any business is to earn an acceptable net income. When component percentages are not acceptable, regardless of whether a net income or net loss occurred, management action is necessary.

Unacceptable Component Percentage for Gross Profit on Sales

The component percentage for gross profit on sales is directly related to sales revenue and cost of merchandise sold. An unacceptable component percentage for gross profit on sales requires one of three actions: (1) increase sales revenue, (2) decrease cost of merchandise sold, or (3) increase sales revenue and also decrease cost of merchandise sold.

Increasing sales revenue while keeping the cost of merchandise sold the same will increase gross profit on sales. To increase sales revenue, management may consider increasing the markup on merchandise purchased for sale. However, a business must be cautious on the amount of the markup increase. If the increase in markup is too large, a decrease in sales revenue could occur for two reasons: (1) the sales price is beyond what customers are willing to pay or (2) the sales price is higher than what competing businesses charge for the same merchandise.

Decreasing the cost of merchandise sold while keeping the sales revenue the same will also increase gross profit on sales. To decrease cost of merchandise sold, management should review purchasing practices. For example, would purchasing merchandise in larger quantities or from other vendors result in a lower cost?

Combining a small increase in sales revenue and a small decrease in the cost of merchandise sold may also result in an acceptable component percentage for gross profit on sales.

Unacceptable Component Percentage for Total Expenses

Each expense account balance must be reviewed to determine if major increases have occurred. This review should include comparisons with prior fiscal periods as well as with industry standards. Actions must then be taken to reduce any expenses for which major increases have occurred or that are beyond industry standards.

Unacceptable Component Percentage for Net Income before Federal Income Tax

If the component percentages for cost of merchandise sold, gross profit on sales, and total expenses are brought within acceptable ranges, net income before federal income tax will also be acceptable.

FYI FOR YOUR INFORMATION

Net income after federal income tax is typically referred to as *net income.*

FINANCIAL RATIOS

Individual amounts reported on an income statement have little meaning without being compared to another amount. Suppose a company has net income before federal income taxes of $1,000,000.00. Is the company successful? Only by calculating the net income before federal income taxes component percentage could this question begin to be answered.

Comparisons between other financial items can also provide valuable information about the financial performance of a business. A comparison between two items of financial information is called a **financial ratio**. Most financial ratios include at least one amount reported on the financial statements.

Earnings per Share

Net Income after Federal Income Tax	÷	Number of Shares Outstanding	=	Earnings per Share
$80,313.95	÷	2,500	=	$32.13

The amount of net income after federal income tax belonging to a single share of stock is called **earnings per share**. The ratio is calculated by dividing net income after federal income taxes by the number of shares outstanding.

Earnings per share is one of the most widely recognized measures of a corporation's financial performance. The financial ratio is often referred to as *EPS*. Unlike component percentages, earnings per share cannot be compared to industry standards. Instead, earnings per share is compared to (1) prior year's earnings per share or (2) the market price of the stock.

©GETTY IMAGES/PHOTODISC

Price-Earnings Ratio

Market Price per Share	÷	Earnings per Share	=	Price-Earnings Ratio
$345.00	÷	$32.13	=	10.7

The relationship between the market value per share and earnings per share of a stock is called the **price-earnings ratio**. The ratio is calculated as the market price per share divided by the earnings per share as determined by the stock markets. The ratio is often referred to as the *P-E ratio*.

The price-earnings ratio provides investors with information concerning the price of the stock relative to the earnings. Low price-earnings ratios are typically associated with slow growth companies, such as public utilities. Companies expected to have dynamic growth in future earnings typically have a high price-earnings ratio.

Online sources of financial information highlight the earnings per share and price-earnings ratio over several years. Investors can analyze the trends in the earnings per share to project future earnings of the company. Then, using historical price-earnings ratios, investors can predict future market prices of the company's stock.

FYI FOR YOUR INFORMATION

Some financial ratios are unique to companies in a particular industry. For example, a critical financial ratio for the airline industry is revenue per passenger mile, calculated as sales divided by total passenger miles. Managers of airline companies rely on this ratio to measure how effectively the airline is pricing its tickets.

terms review

financial ratio
earnings per share
price-earnings ratio

audit your understanding

1. For a merchandising business, every sales dollar includes what four components?
2. How does a company determine acceptable component percentages?
3. What is the result if total expenses are greater than gross profit on sales?

work together 15-2

Analyzing an income statement

Use the income statement for Interstate Tires, Inc., from Work Together 15-1. A form for completing this problem is given in the *Working Papers*. Your instructor will guide you through the following examples.

1. Interstate Tires determines that no more than 53 cents, or 53.0%, of each sales dollar should be devoted to cost of merchandise sold. Compare the actual component percentage for cost of merchandise sold to the acceptable percentage. Indicate if the actual component percentage is acceptable or unacceptable. If it is unacceptable, suggest an action that corrects it.
2. Acceptable auto parts industry standards show that at least 47 cents, or 47.0%, of each sales dollar should result in gross profit. For Interstate Tires, compare the actual component percentage for gross profit on sales to the acceptable percentage. Indicate if the actual component percentage is acceptable or unacceptable. If it is unacceptable, suggest an action that corrects it.
3. Interstate Tires currently has 110,000 of shares outstanding with a market price of $13.75 per share. Calculate the earnings per share and price-earnings ratio.

on your own 15-2

Analyzing an income statement

Use the income statement for Osborn Corporation from On Your Own 15-1. A form for completing this problem is given in the *Working Papers*. Work independently to complete this problem.

1. Acceptable game industry standards show that no more than 30 cents, or 30.0%, of each sales dollar should be devoted to total expenses. For Osborn Corporation, compare the actual component percentage for total expenses to the acceptable percentage. Indicate if the actual component percentage is acceptable or unacceptable. If it is unacceptable, suggest an action that corrects it.
2. Acceptable game industry standards show that at least 15 cents, or 15.0%, of each sales dollar should result in net income. For Osborn Corporation, compare the actual component percentage for net income to the acceptable percentage. Indicate if the actual component percentage is acceptable or unacceptable. If it is unacceptable, suggest an action that corrects it.
3. Osborn Corporation currently has 8,000 shares outstanding with a market price of $104.50 per share. Calculate the earnings per share and price-earnings ratio.

LESSON

15-3 Preparing a Statement of Stockholders' Equity

CAPITAL STOCK SECTION OF THE STATEMENT OF STOCKHOLDERS' EQUITY

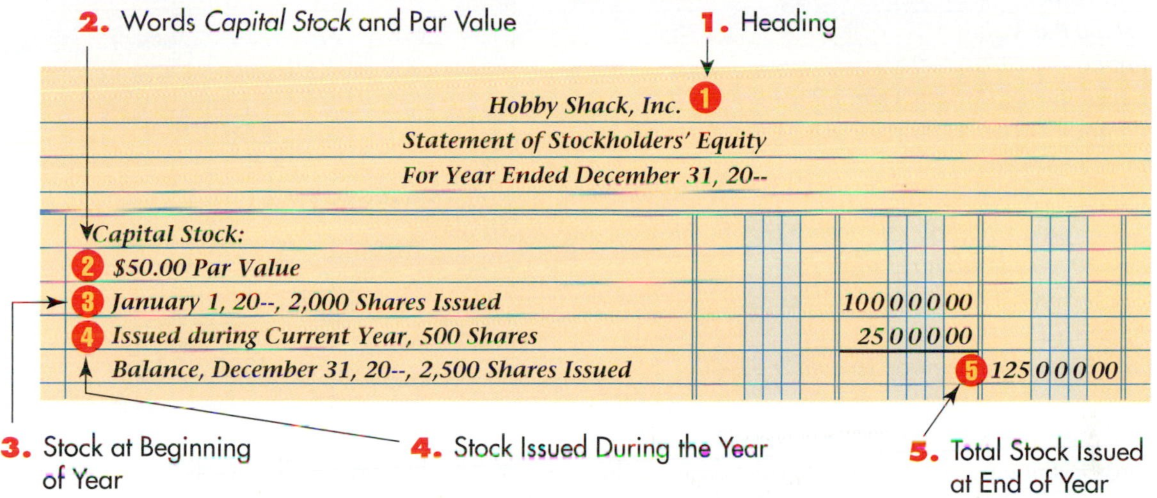

Hobby Shack, Inc.
Statement of Stockholders' Equity
For Year Ended December 31, 20--

Capital Stock:			
$50.00 Par Value			
January 1, 20--, 2,000 Shares Issued		100 000 00	
Issued during Current Year, 500 Shares		25 000 00	
Balance, December 31, 20--, 2,500 Shares Issued			125 000 00

A financial statement that shows changes in a corporation's ownership for a fiscal period is called a **statement of stockholders' equity**. A statement of stockholders' equity contains two major sections: (1) capital stock and (2) retained earnings.

The amount of capital stock issued as of the beginning of the year is the beginning balance of the capital stock account. Any additional stock transactions recorded in the general ledger during the fiscal year would be added up to calculate the amount of stock issued during the fiscal year. Thus, the amounts in the capital stock section of the statement of stockholders' equity are obtained from the general ledger account, Capital Stock.

Each share of stock issued by a corporation has a monetary value. A value assigned to a share of stock and printed on the stock certificate is called **par value**.

STEPS: PREPARING THE CAPITAL STOCK SECTION OF A STATEMENT OF STOCKHOLDERS' EQUITY

1. Write the heading: company name, *Hobby Shack, Inc.*; statement name, *Statement of Stockholders' Equity*; and fiscal period, *For Year Ended December 31, 20--*, in the statement heading.
2. Write the heading *Capital Stock:* and on the next line write the par value of the stock, *$50.00 Par Value*, indented about 1 centimeter.
3. Write the number of shares, *2,000*, and dollar amount, *$100,000.00*, of stock issued as of the beginning of the year.
4. Write the number of shares, *500*, and dollar amount, *$25,000.00*, of stock issued during the year.
5. Calculate the total dollar amount of stock issued as of the end of the year, *$125,000.00*, by adding the dollar amount of beginning stock, *$100,000.00*, and the dollar amount of shares issued during the year, *$25,000.00*.

RETAINED EARNINGS SECTION OF THE STATEMENT OF STOCKHOLDERS' EQUITY

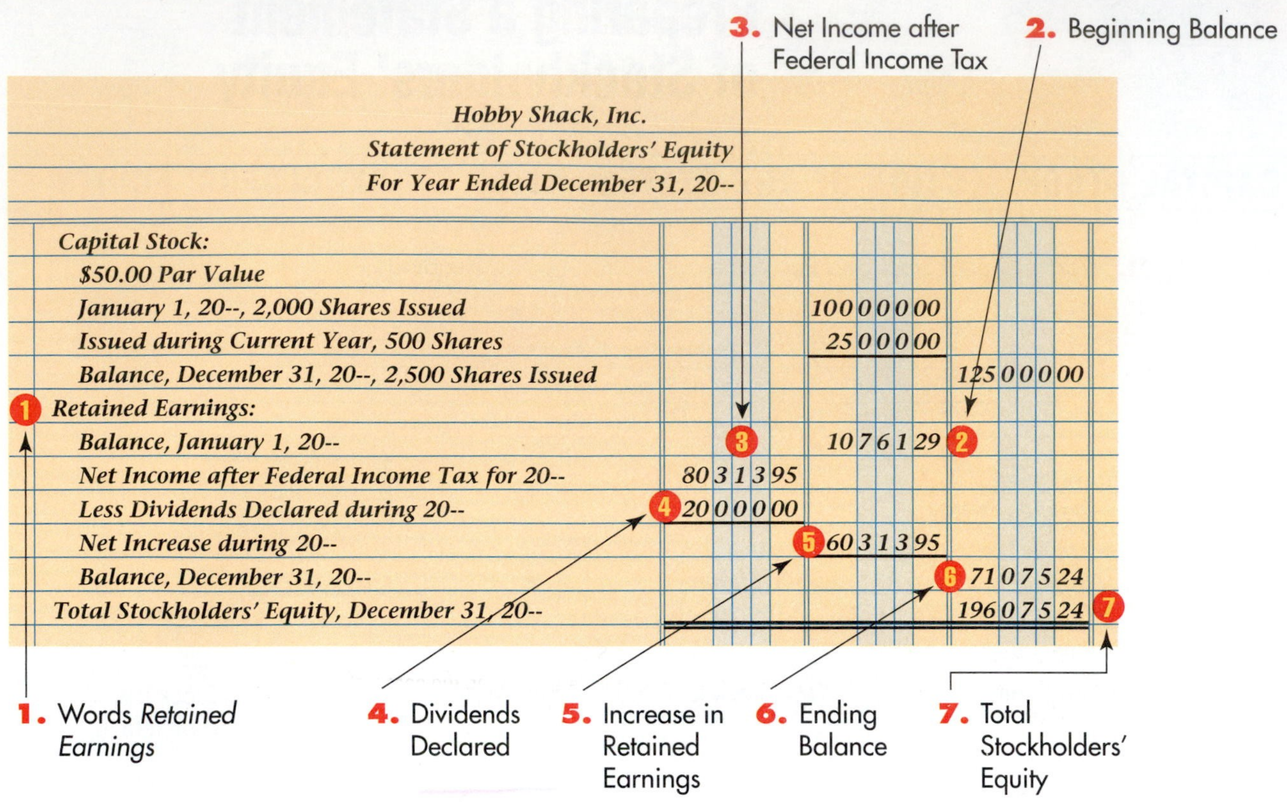

Hobby Shack, Inc.			
Statement of Stockholders' Equity			
For Year Ended December 31, 20--			
Capital Stock:			
$50.00 Par Value			
January 1, 20--, 2,000 Shares Issued		100 000 00	
Issued during Current Year, 500 Shares		25 000 00	
Balance, December 31, 20--, 2,500 Shares Issued			125 000 00
Retained Earnings:			
Balance, January 1, 20--		10 761 29	
Net Income after Federal Income Tax for 20--	80 313 95		
Less Dividends Declared during 20--	20 000 00		
Net Increase during 20--		60 313 95	
Balance, December 31, 20--			71 075 24
Total Stockholders' Equity, December 31, 20--			196 075 24

Net income increases a corporation's total capital. Some income may be retained by a corporation for business expansion. Some income may be distributed as dividends to provide stockholders with a return on their investments. During the year, Hobby Shack's board of directors declared $20,000.00 in dividends.

Amounts used to prepare the statement of stockholders' equity are obtained from the income statement and balance sheet columns of the work sheet shown in Chapter 14.

STEPS: PREPARING THE RETAINED EARNINGS SECTION OF A STATEMENT OF STOCKHOLDERS' EQUITY

1. Write the heading *Retained Earnings.*
2. Write the beginning balance of *Retained Earnings, $10,761.29,* from the Balance Sheet Credit column, indented about 1 centimeter.
3. Write the net income after federal income tax, *$80,313.95,* from the Income Statement Debit column.
4. Write the amount of dividends, *$20,000.00,* from the Balance Sheet Debit column.
5. Subtract dividends, *$20,000.00,* from net income after federal income tax, *$80,313.95,* to calculate the increase in retained earnings, *$60,313.95.*
6. Add the beginning balance of retained earnings, *$10,761.29,* and the increase in retained earnings, *$60,313.95,* to calculate the ending balance of retained earnings, *$71,075.24.*
7. Add the ending amounts of capital stock, *$125,000.00,* and retained earnings, *$71,075.24,* to calculate the total amount of stockholders' equity, *$196,075.24.*

terms review

statement of stockholders' equity
par value

audit your understanding

1. What financial information does a statement of stockholders' equity report?
2. What are the two major sections of a statement of stockholders' equity?
3. Where is the information found to prepare the capital stock section of a statement of stockholders' equity?
4. Where is the beginning balance of retained earnings found?
5. How does a corporation distribute a portion of income to stockholders?
6. Where is the amount of dividends found?

work together 15-3

Preparing a statement of stockholders' equity

Use the work sheet and income statement for Interstate Tires, Inc., from Work Together 15-2. A form for the statement of stockholders' equity is given in the *Working Papers*. Your instructor will guide you through the following example.

1. Prepare a statement of stockholders' equity for the current year. As of January 1, Interstate Tires, Inc., had issued 100,000 shares of capital stock with a par value of $1.00 per share. During the fiscal year, the corporation issued 10,000 additional shares of capital stock. Save your work to complete Work Together 15-4.

on your own 15-3

Preparing a statement of stockholders' equity

Use the work sheet and income statement for Osborn Corporation from On Your Own 15-2. A form for the statement of stockholders' equity is given in the *Working Papers*. Work this problem independently.

1. Prepare a statement of stockholders' equity for the current year. As of January 1, Osborn Corporation had issued 7,500 shares of capital stock with a par value of $25.00 per share. During the fiscal year, the corporation issued 500 additional shares of stock. Save your work to complete On Your Own 15-4.

15-4 Preparing a Balance Sheet

BALANCE SHEET INFORMATION ON A WORK SHEET

Hobby Shack, Inc.
Work Sheet
For Year Ended December 31, 20--

		1	2	3	4	5	6	7	8	
	ACCOUNT TITLE	TRIAL BALANCE		ADJUSTMENTS		INCOME STATEMENT		BALANCE SHEET		
		DEBIT	CREDIT	DEBIT	CREDIT	DEBIT	CREDIT	DEBIT	CREDIT	
1	Cash	29 080 28						29 080 28		1
2	Petty Cash	300 00						300 00		2
3	Accounts Receivable	14 698 40						14 698 40		3
4	Allow. for Uncoll. Accts.		127 52		(e) 1 245 00				1 372 52	4
5	Merchandise Inventory	140 480 00			(d) 15 840 00			124 640 00		5
6	Supplies—Office	3 480 00			(a) 2 730 00			750 00		6
7	Supplies—Store	3 944 00			(b) 2 910 00			1 034 00		7
8	Prepaid Insurance	5 800 00			(c) 3 170 00			2 630 00		8
9	Office Equipment	35 864 50						35 864 50		9
10	Acc. Depr.—Office Equipment		6 497 00		(f) 6 540 00				13 037 00	10
11	Store Equipment	40 849 50						40 849 50		11
12	Acc. Depr.—Store Equipment		5 069 00		(g) 5 250 00				10 319 00	12
13	Accounts Payable		11 583 03						11 583 03	13
14	Federal Income Tax Payable				(h) 5 889 24				5 889 24	14
15	Employee Income Tax Payable		757 00						757 00	15
16	Social Security Tax Payable		1 451 38						1 451 38	16
17	Medicare Tax Payable		399 42						399 42	17
18	Sales Tax Payable		2 556 70						2 556 70	18
19	Unemployment Tax Payable—Federal		34 60						34 60	19
20	Unemployment Tax Payable—State		233 55						233 55	20
21	Health Insurance Premiums Payable		1 008 00						1 008 00	21
22	U.S. Savings Bonds Payable		60 00						60 00	22
23	United Way Donations Payable		70 00						70 00	23
24	Dividends Payable		5 000 00						5 000 00	24

A corporation's balance sheet reports assets, liabilities, and stockholders' equity on a specific date. [*CONCEPT: Accounting Period Cycle*] Some management decisions can best be made after owners have analyzed the balance sheet. For example, balance sheet information would enable management to determine whether the corporation should incur additional liabilities to acquire additional plant assets.

The information used to prepare a balance sheet is obtained from two sources: (1) the Balance Sheet columns of a work sheet and (2) the owners' equity statement.

Procedures for preparing Hobby Shack's balance sheet are similar to those used by TechKnow in Part 1. A balance sheet may be prepared in account form or report form. As described in Chapter 7, TechKnow uses the account form. Hobby Shack uses the report form.

CURRENT ASSETS SECTION OF A BALANCE SHEET

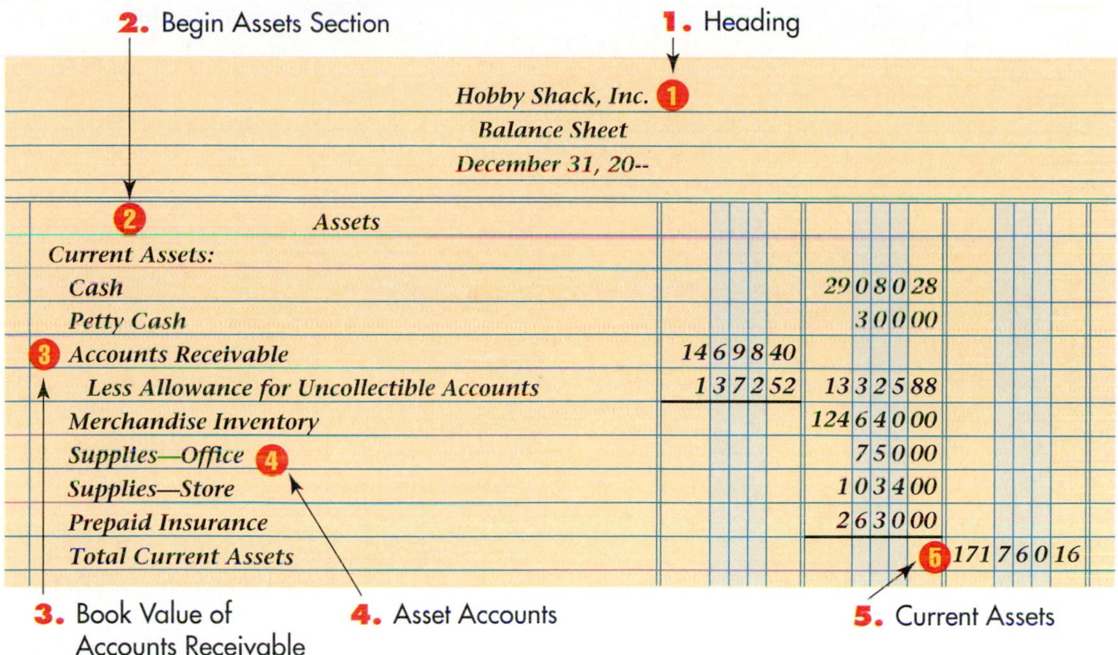

2. Begin Assets Section
1. Heading
Hobby Shack, Inc.
Balance Sheet
December 31, 20--
Assets
Current Assets:
Cash
Petty Cash
Accounts Receivable
Less Allowance for Uncollectible Accounts
Merchandise Inventory
Supplies—Office
Supplies—Store
Prepaid Insurance
Total Current Assets
29 080 28
300 00
14 698 40
1 372 52
13 325 88
124 640 00
750 00
1 034 00
2 630 00
171 760 16
3. Book Value of Accounts Receivable
4. Asset Accounts
5. Current Assets

Hobby Shack classifies its assets as current assets and plant assets. A business owning both current and plant assets usually lists them under separate headings on a balance sheet. Some of Hobby Shack's asset accounts have related contra accounts that reduce the related account on the balance sheet. The difference between an asset's account balance and its related contra account balance is known as *book value*. An asset's book value is reported on a balance sheet by listing three amounts: (1) the balance of the asset account, (2) the balance of the asset's contra account, and (3) the book value.

STEPS • STEPS • STEPS • STEPS • STEPS • STEPS • STEPS • STEPS • STEPS • STEPS •

PREPARING THE CURRENT ASSETS SECTION OF A BALANCE SHEET

1. Write the balance sheet heading on three lines.
2. Begin preparing the assets section of the balance sheet. Use information from the work sheet.
   a. Write the section title, *Assets*, on the first line in the middle of the wide column.
   b. Write the section title, *Current Assets:*, on the next line at the extreme left of the wide column.
   c. Beginning on the next line, indented about one centimeter, write the *Cash* and *Petty Cash* account titles in the order in which they appear on the work sheet.
   d. Write the balance of each asset account in the second column.
3. Calculate the book value of accounts receivable.
   a. Write *Accounts Receivable* on the next line, indented about one centimeter.
   b. Write the total amount of accounts receivable, *$14,698.40*, in the first amount column.
   c. Write *Less Allowance for Uncollectible Accounts* on the next line, indented about two centimeters.
   d. Write the amount of the allowance for uncollectible accounts, *$1,372.52*, in the first amount column.
   e. Subtract the allowance for uncollectible accounts, *$1,372.52*, from the total amount of accounts receivable, *$14,698.40*, to calculate the book value of accounts receivable, *$13,325.88*. Write the amount in the second amount column on the same line.
4. Write the remaining asset account titles and amounts.
5. Calculate total current assets.
   a. Write *Total Current Assets* on the next line, indented about one centimeter.
   b. Add the amounts in the second amount column and write the total, *$171,760.16*, in the third amount column.

PLANT ASSETS SECTION OF A BALANCE SHEET

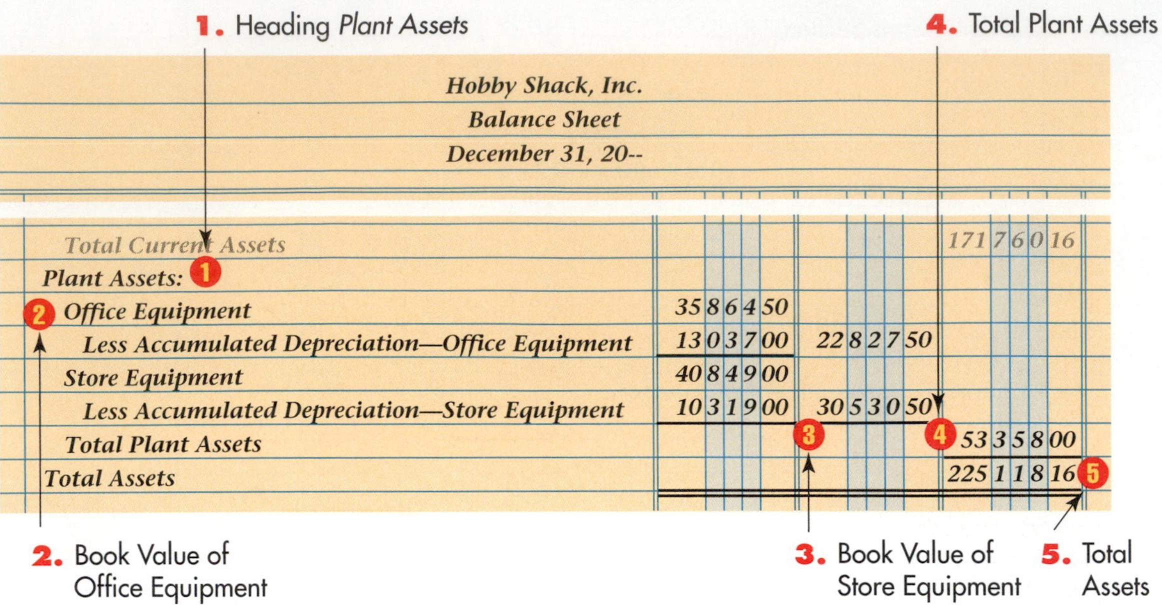

Hobby Shack, Inc.
Balance Sheet
December 31, 20--

Total Current Assets			171 760 16
Plant Assets: ①			
② *Office Equipment*	35 864 50		
Less Accumulated Depreciation—Office Equipment	13 037 00	22 827 50	
Store Equipment	40 849 00		
Less Accumulated Depreciation—Store Equipment	10 319 00	30 530 50	
Total Plant Assets		③	④ 53 358 00
Total Assets			225 118 16 ⑤

STEPS • STEPS • STEPS • STEPS • STEPS • STEPS • STEPS • STEPS • STEPS • STEPS •

PREPARING THE PLANT ASSETS SECTION OF A BALANCE SHEET

1. Write the heading *Plant Assets* on the next line at the extreme left of the wide column.

2. Calculate the book value of office equipment using information from the work sheet.
   a. Write *Office Equipment* on the next line, indented about one centimeter.
   b. Write the total amount of office equipment, *$35,864.50*, in the first amount column.
   c. Write *Less Accumulated Depreciation—Office Equipment* on the next line, indented about two centimeters.
   d. Write the amount of the accumulated depreciation—office equipment, *$13,037.00*, in the first amount column.
   e. Subtract the accumulated depreciation—office equipment, *$13,037.00*, from the total amount of office equipment, *$35,864.50*, to calculate the book value of office equipment, *$22,827.50*. Write the amount in the second amount column on the same line.

3. Use the same procedure to calculate the book value of store equipment.

4. Calculate total plant assets.
   a. Write *Total Plant Assets* on the next line, indented about one centimeter.
   b. Add the amounts in the second amount column and write the total, *$53,358.00*, in the third amount column.

5. Calculate total assets.
   a. Write *Total Assets* on the next line at the extreme left of the wide column.
   b. Add the current and plant asset totals and write the amount, *$225,118.16*, on the same line in the third amount column.

©GETTY IMAGES/PHOTODISC

LIABILITIES SECTION OF A BALANCE SHEET

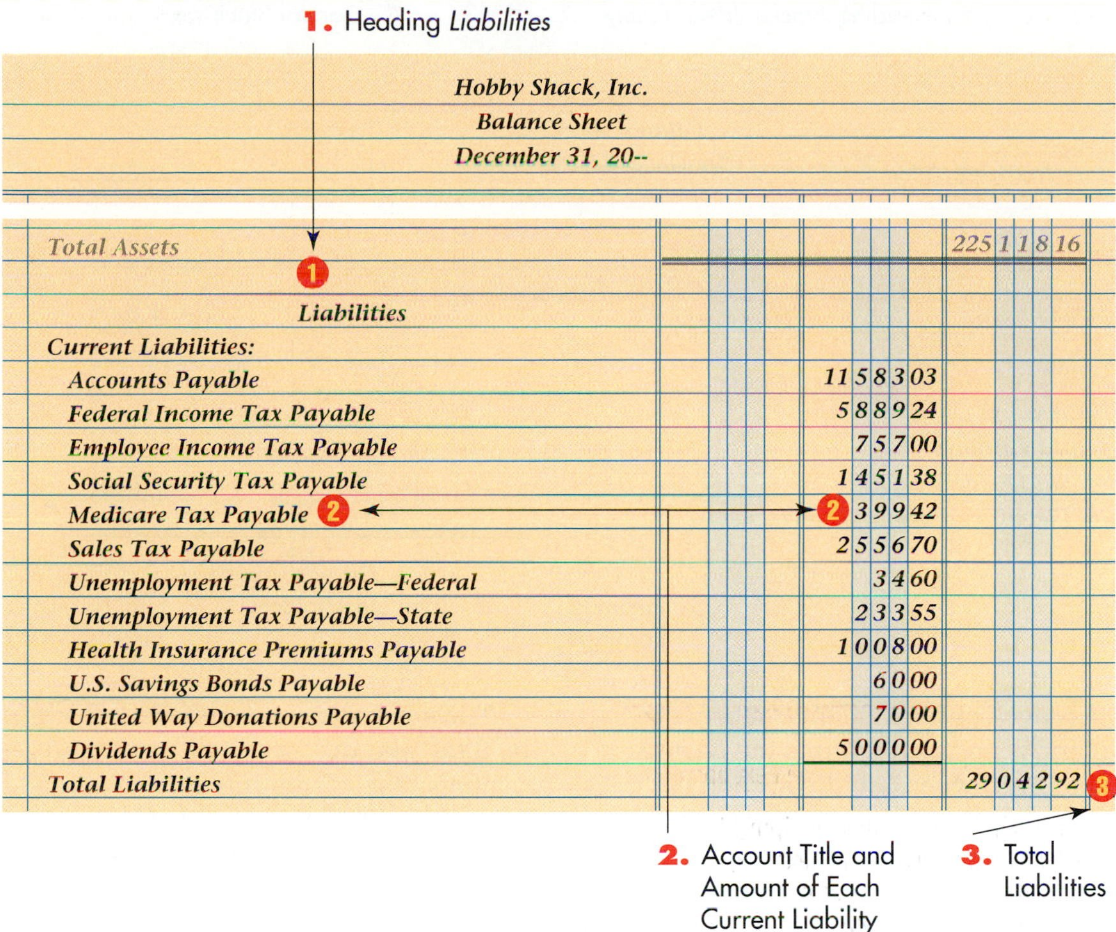

Hobby Shack, Inc.			
Balance Sheet			
December 31, 20--			
Total Assets			225118 16
Liabilities			
Current Liabilities:			
Accounts Payable		11583 03	
Federal Income Tax Payable		5889 24	
Employee Income Tax Payable		757 00	
Social Security Tax Payable		1451 38	
Medicare Tax Payable		399 42	
Sales Tax Payable		2556 70	
Unemployment Tax Payable—Federal		34 60	
Unemployment Tax Payable—State		233 55	
Health Insurance Premiums Payable		1008 00	
U.S. Savings Bonds Payable		60 00	
United Way Donations Payable		70 00	
Dividends Payable		5000 00	
Total Liabilities			29042 92

Liabilities are classified according to the length of time until they are due. Liabilities due within a short time, usually within a year, are called **current liabilities.**

Liabilities owed for more than a year are called **long-term liabilities**. An example of a long-term liability is Mortgage Payable. On December 31 of the current year, Hobby Shack does not have any long-term liabilities.

To prepare the liabilities section of the balance sheet, use information from the work sheet.

STEPS • PREPARING THE LIABILITIES SECTION OF A BALANCE SHEET

1. Write the section title, *Liabilities*, on the next line in the middle of the wide column.
2. Write the title *Current Liabilities:* on the next line at the extreme left of the wide column.
   a. Beginning on the next line, indented about one centimeter, write the liability account titles in the order in which they appear on the work sheet.
   b. Write the balance of each liability account in the second amount column.
3. Calculate total liabilities.
   a. Write *Total Liabilities* on the next line below the last liability account title at the extreme left of the wide column.
   b. Write the total liabilities, *$29,042.92*, on the same line in the third amount column.

FYI FOR YOUR INFORMATION

A company having both current liabilities and long-term liabilities would include headings and totals for each category. The process is similar to preparing the assets section of a balance sheet.

STOCKHOLDERS' EQUITY SECTION OF A BALANCE SHEET

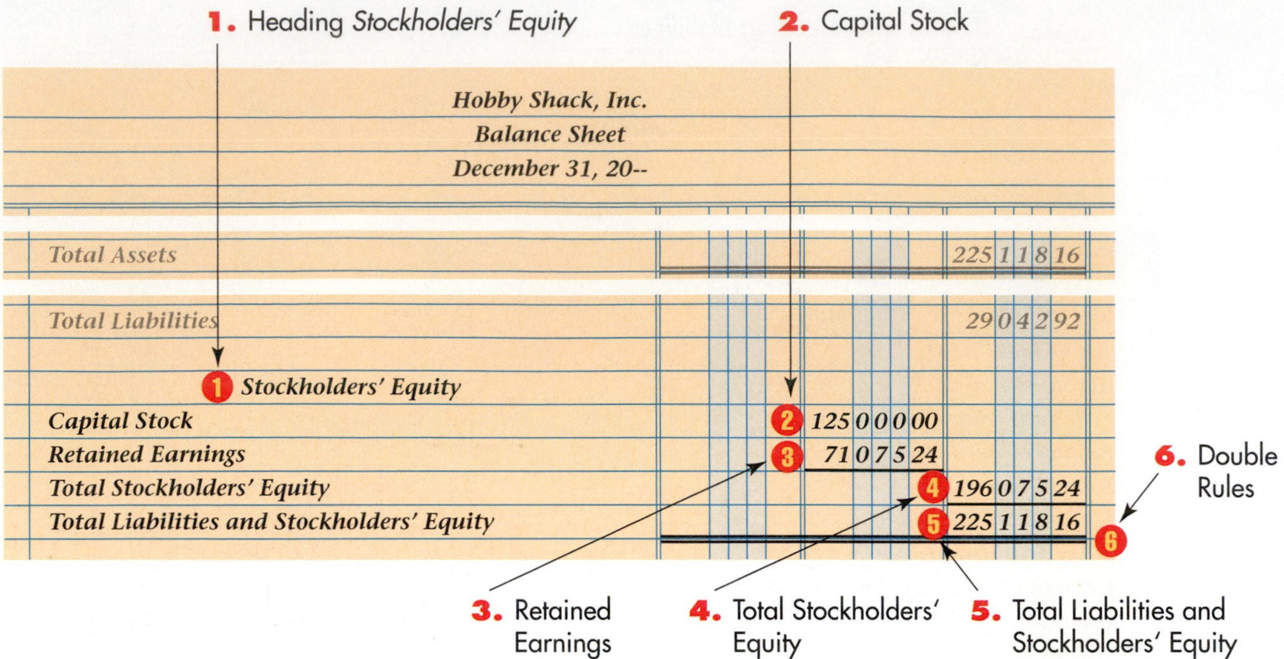

A major difference between balance sheets of a corporation and a proprietorship is the owners' equity section. The owners' equity section of Hobby Shack's balance sheet is labeled *Stockholders' Equity*. Some corporations use the same label, *Owners' Equity*, as proprietorships. Either label is acceptable.

The stockholders' equity section contains the total amounts of capital stock and retained earnings. These amounts are calculated and reported on the statement of stockholders' equity.

Hobby Shack's completed balance sheet is shown on the following page.

STEPS • STEPS • STEPS • STEPS • STEPS • STEPS • STEPS • STEPS • STEPS • STEPS •

PREPARING THE STOCKHOLDERS' EQUITY SECTION OF A BALANCE SHEET

1. Write the heading *Stockholders' Equity* on the next line centered in the wide column.
2. Write the title and amount of *Capital Stock, $125,000.00*, calculated on the statement of stockholders' equity.
3. Write the title and amount of *Retained Earnings, $71,075.24*, calculated on the statement of stockholders' equity.
4. Add the amount of capital stock, *$125,000.00*, and retained earnings, *$71,075.24*, to calculate the total of stockholders' equity, *$196,075.24*.
5. Add the amount of total liabilities, *$29,042.92*, and total stockholders' equity, *$196,075.24*, to calculate the total of liabilities and stockholders' equity, *$225,118.16*. Verify accuracy by comparing the total amount of assets and the total amount of liabilities and stockholders' equity. These two amounts must be the same.
6. Draw double rules across the three columns at the end of the Assets section and the Stockholders' Equity section to show that assets equal liabilities plus owners' equity.

REMEMBER Total assets must equal the total of liabilities and stockholders' equity. If these totals are not equal, identify the errors before preparing adjusting and closing entries.

COMPLETED BALANCE SHEET

Hobby Shack, Inc.			
Balance Sheet			
December 31, 20--			
Assets			
Current Assets:			
Cash		29,080.28	
Petty Cash		300.00	
Accounts Receivable	14,698.40		
Less Allowance for Uncollectible Accounts	1,372.52	13,325.88	
Merchandise Inventory		124,640.00	
Supplies—Office		750.00	
Supplies—Store		1,034.00	
Prepaid Insurance		2,630.00	
Total Current Assets			171,760.16
Plant Assets:			
Office Equipment	35,864.50		
Less Accumulated Depreciation—Office Equipment	13,037.00	22,827.50	
Store Equipment	40,849.00		
Less Accumulated Depreciation—Store Equipment	10,319.00	30,530.50	
Total Plant Assets			53,358.00
Total Assets			225,118.16
Liabilities			
Current Liabilities:			
Accounts Payable		11,583.03	
Federal Income Tax Payable		5,889.24	
Employee Income Tax Payable		757.00	
Social Security Tax Payable		1,451.38	
Medicare Tax Payable		399.42	
Sales Tax Payable		2,556.70	
Unemployment Tax Payable—Federal		34.60	
Unemployment Tax Payable—State		233.55	
Health Insurance Premiums Payable		1,008.00	
U.S. Savings Bonds Payable		60.00	
United Way Donations Payable		70.00	
Dividends Payable		5,000.00	
Total Liabilities			29,042.92
Stockholders' Equity			
Capital Stock		125,000.00	
Retained Earnings		71,075.24	
Total Stockholders' Equity			196,075.24
Total Liabilities and Stockholders' Equity			225,118.16

SUPPORTING SCHEDULES FOR A BALANCE SHEET

A report prepared to give details about an item on a principal financial statement is called a **supporting schedule**. A supporting schedule is sometimes referred to as a *supplementary report* or an *exhibit*.

Hobby Shack prepares two supporting schedules to accompany the balance sheet. The supporting schedules are a schedule of accounts payable and a schedule of accounts receivable. A balance sheet shows only the accounts payable total amount. The account balance for each vendor is not shown. When detailed information is needed, a supporting schedule of accounts payable is prepared, showing the balance for each vendor. A balance sheet also shows only the accounts receivable total amount. When information about the account balance for each customer is needed, a supporting schedule of accounts receivable is prepared. Hobby Shack's supporting schedules on December 31 are similar to the supporting schedules for November 30 shown in Chapter 11.

BUSINESS STRUCTURES • BUSINESS STRUCTURES • BUSINESS STRUCTURES

Who Owns the Corporation?

A share of stock is a unit of ownership in a corporation. Stock may be purchased by individuals, investment companies, pension funds, institutions, banks, and other companies. Publicly traded stocks are bought and sold on stock exchanges throughout the world. Ownership of a corporation's stock entitles the owner to distributions of earnings if there are dividends declared. Many stock owners, however, buy stock with the expectation that the stock will increase in value and they can then sell the stock at a profit.

Stock ownership also entitles the owner to vote at stockholders' meetings, where important issues regarding the corporation may be decided. The membership of the board of directors of the corporation is also determined at stockholders' meetings. Sometimes individuals or other stock owners will attempt to gain a majority holding of a company's stock in order to take control of the company.

Sometimes investors determine which corporation's stock they will purchase based on political or social issues. For example, one investor might buy stocks only of companies that have good reputations on environmental issues. Others might buy stocks only of companies that have good policies regarding racial or gender discrimination.

Critical Thinking

1. If you were buying stock as an investment for your retirement years, would you be more concerned with the future resale value of the stock or its dividends? Would the answer be different for 18-year-olds and 60-year-olds?
2. What are some other kinds of social issues that might be important considerations for some people in purchasing corporate stock?

terms review

current liabilities
long-term liabilities
supporting schedule

TERMS REVIEW • TERMS

audit your understanding

1. How does Hobby Shack classify its assets?
2. What three items are listed on the balance sheet for an account having a related contra asset account?
3. What is an example of a long-term liability?
4. Where are the amounts obtained for the stockholders' equity section of the balance sheet?
5. What are two supporting schedules that might accompany a balance sheet?

AUDIT YOUR UNDERSTANDING

work together 15-4

Preparing a balance sheet for a corporation

Use Interstate Tires' work sheet and statement of stockholders' equity from Work Together 15-3. A form for the balance sheet is given in the *Working Papers*. Your instructor will guide you through the following examples.

1. Prepare a balance sheet for the current year.

WORK TOGETHER

on your own 15-4

Preparing a balance sheet for a corporation

Use Osborn Corporation's work sheet and statement of stockholders' equity from On Your Own 15-3. A form for the balance sheet is given in the *Working Papers*. Work this problem independently.

1. Prepare a balance sheet for the current year.

ON YOUR OWN

SUMMARY

After completing this chapter, you can

1. Define accounting terms related to financial statements for a merchandising business organized as a corporation.
2. Identify accounting concepts and practices related to financial statements for a merchandising business organized as a corporation.
3. Prepare an income statement for a merchandising business organized as a corporation.
4. Analyze an income statement using component percentages and financial ratios.
5. Prepare a statement of stockholders' equity for a merchandising business organized as a corporation.
6. Prepare a balance sheet for a merchandising business organized as a corporation.

Explore Accounting

Alternative Fiscal Years

Most small companies use a fiscal year that is the same as the calendar year, January 1 to December 31. However, there may be several reasons why a different fiscal period would be beneficial. If the calendar year end comes in the middle of a high sales period, a fiscal year ending at this time can be more difficult. All employees are extremely busy with sales and shipping. Because of this activity, accurately identifying sales, inventory, and accounts receivable is more difficult. If the calendar year end comes just before the high sales period begins, an analysis of the company's financial condition will not be as favorable. The company may have borrowed money to buy a high level of inventory, so the company has higher debt and high inventory levels. Therefore, some companies choose to use a natural business year as the fiscal year, as discussed in Chapter 6.

FanciFoods is a corporation that makes and sells decorative cakes, cookies, and candies. Approximately 90% of its sales are made between November 1 and February 15 because of the three holidays of Thanksgiving, Christmas, and Valentine's Day. The company spends six months—May to November—preparing for its heavy sales period. The company has selected April 1 to March 31 as its fiscal year. By March 31, inventory is low, most accounts receivable have been collected, and the company has not yet replaced inventory to begin preparing for the next season. Thus, this is an ideal time to end the fiscal period. Inventory is easier to count, the level of accounts receivable is lower, and more employees are available to help with the closing activities.

Research: What other types of companies may find it beneficial to use a fiscal year different from the calendar year? What would be the ideal fiscal period for these companies? You may wish to find a local business that has a fiscal period different from the calendar year. If so, determine the reasons for selecting the fiscal period it now uses.

15-1 APPLICATION PROBLEM 

Preparing an income statement for a merchandising business

A work sheet for Historic Doors, Inc., for the year ended December 31 of the current year is given in the *Working Papers*.

Instructions:

1. Prepare an income statement.
2. Calculate and record on the income statement the following component percentages: (a) cost of merchandise sold, (b) gross profit on sales, (c) total expenses, and (d) net income before federal income tax. Round percentage calculations to the nearest 0.1%.

15-2 APPLICATION PROBLEM

Analyzing component percentages and financial ratios

The income statement for Custom Jewelry, Inc., and a form for completing this problem are given in the *Working Papers*. The managers of Custom Jewelry have established the following target component percentages:

Cost of Merchandise Sold	35.0%
Gross Profit on Sales	65.0%
Expenses	40.0%
Net Income before Federal Income Tax	25.0%

Instructions:

1. Compare the actual component percentages to the target percentage. Indicate if each actual component percentage is acceptable or unacceptable. If a percentage is unacceptable, suggest a possible action to correct the unacceptable component percentage.
2. Custom Jewelry has 110,000 shares of stock outstanding on December 31. The company's market price is $13.75 per share. Calculate the earnings per share and price-earnings ratio.

15-3 APPLICATION PROBLEM 

Preparing a statement of stockholders' equity

A form for completing this problem is given in the *Working Papers*.

Instructions:

1. Prepare a statement of stockholders' equity for Classic Interiors, Inc., for the fiscal year ended on December 31 of the current year. Use the following additional information.

Capital stock outstanding on January 1	50,000 shares
Capital stock issued during the year	10,000 shares
Capital stock par value	$5.00
Retained earnings, January 1	$59,485.50
Dividends declared during year	$66,000.00
Net income after federal income tax	$110,635.34

15-4 APPLICATION PROBLEM

Preparing a balance sheet for a corporation

Henderson Corporation's partial work sheet for the year ended December 31 of the current year is given in the *Working Papers*. A form for completing this problem is also given in the *Working Papers*. The December 31 balance in retained earnings reported on the statement of stockholders' equity is $97,294.85.

Instructions:

1. Prepare a balance sheet in report form.

15-5 MASTERY PROBLEM

PEACHTREE QUICKBOOKS

Preparing financial statements

The work sheet for Lighting Center, Inc., for the year ended December 31 of the current year and forms for completing this problem are given in the *Working Papers*.

Instructions:

1. Prepare an income statement. Calculate and record the following component percentages: (a) cost of merchandise sold, (b) gross profit on sales, (c) total expenses, and (d) net income or loss before federal income tax. Round percentage calculations to the nearest 0.1%.
2. Prepare a statement of stockholders' equity. The company had 90,000 shares of $1.00 par value stock outstanding on January 1. The company issued an additional 10,000 shares during the year.
3. Prepare a balance sheet in report form.
4. Calculate the earnings per share and price-earnings ratio. The current market price of the stock is $28.50.

15-6 CHALLENGE PROBLEM

Analyzing component percentages and financial ratios

Instructions:

1. Obtain the financial statements of two corporations in similar industries. Calculate the income statement component percentages, earnings per share, and price-earnings ratio of each corporation. The current market price of each stock can be obtained from a newspaper or online. *Note: Annual reports may be available in your classroom, school library, or public library. They can also be found online.*
2. Contrast the component percentages of the companies. Identify which company you believe is performing better.

• applied communication

A long written report should contain numerous headings. A heading enables the reader to focus on the primary idea of the next section. An outline is a special document that lists only the headings of a report. By reviewing an outline before and after reading a report, the reader can gain a better understanding of the relationship among the topics being presented.

Each chapter of this textbook is similar to a long report. Headings are used to separate and emphasize major concepts.

Instructions: Prepare an outline of this chapter.

APPLIED COMMUNICATION

• cases for critical thinking

Case 1

Rayshawn Washington manages a paint and decorating store. At the end of each fiscal year, an accountant is hired to prepare financial statements. At the end of each month during the year, Mr. Washington prepares a work sheet. The work sheet is prepared to determine if the business made or lost money that month. The accountant suggests that monthly financial statements also be prepared. Mr. Washington believes, however, that the monthly work sheet is sufficient to determine how the business is doing. Do you agree with Mr. Washington or the accountant? Why?

Case 2

Christy Burch and Myung Lim, business managers, compared their current income statement with the income statement of a year ago. They noted that sales were 12.0% higher than a year ago. They also noted that the total expenses were 20.0% higher than a year ago. What type of analysis should be done to determine whether the increase in expenses is justified?

CASES FOR CRITICAL • CASES FOR

• SCANS workplace competency

Thinking Skills: Reasoning

Concept: Employers want to hire workers who can think on the job. Employees should be able to build on past experience and discover a rule or principle that underlies the relationship between two or more objects and then apply the principle to solving a problem.

Application: Use the financial statements illustrated in this chapter to describe the major differences between the financial statements of a service business and a merchandising business. Describe how these differences affect the investment needed to start each kind of business and the ability of the business to grow.

SCANS WORKPLACE • SCANS

graphing workshop

Evaluating Department Sales

Collinsville Home Center made a strategic decision in 1999 to carry a line of home appliances. The following graph depicts sales for the company's three departments for the recent eight-year period. Analyze the graph to answer the following questions.

1. Describe the sales growth in the Appliances department.
2. State the approximate total company sales for 2004.
3. Describe the performance of the Lumber Department.

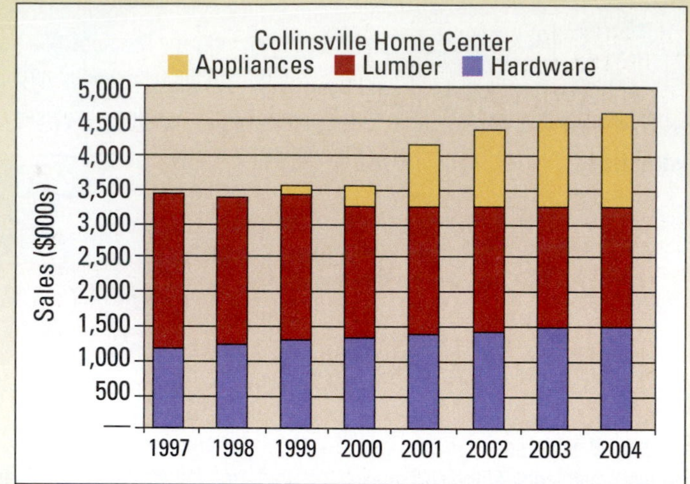

GRAPHING WORKSHOP • GRAPHING WORKSHOP

analyzing Best Buy's financial statements

Gross profit on sales indicates the amount of revenue remaining after the cost of merchandise has been deducted. Best Buy's gross profit on sales, labeled simply as "gross profit" on its income statement, has increased dramatically over the past three fiscal periods, a very favorable trend. But sales have also increased, making it difficult to determine how effectively Best Buy has been controlling its cost of merchandise sold.

The component percentage for gross profit on sales is also referred to as the *gross margin* or *gross profit rate.*

Instructions

1. Use Best Buy's 11-Year Financial Highlights in Appendix B to identify the gross profit rate for 2002–2004.
2. Is the trend in the gross profit rate favorable or unfavorable?
3. Demonstrate how amounts on Best Buy's Consolidated Statement of Earnings were used to calculate the gross profit rate for 2004.

ANALYZING BEST BUY'S FINANCIAL STATEMENTS

Automated Accounting

Generating Automated Financial Statements

As you have already learned, a work sheet on which adjustments are planned in order to update and prove the general ledger is not prepared in Automated Accounting. The *Automated Accounting 8.0* software keeps up-to-date general ledger account balances. Adjusting entries are planned from a trial balance and then journalized and posted. Financial statements are then prepared from the updated general ledger.

Financial statements selected in the Automated Accounting Reports Selection window are automatically displayed. They can then be printed for a permanent record.

To display financial statements:

1. Click the Reports toolbar button, or choose the Report Selection menu item from the Reports menu.
2. When the Report Selection dialog appears, choose the Financial Statements option from the Select a Report Group list.
3. Choose the financial statement report you would like to display from the Choose a Report to Display list.
4. Click the OK button.

Ways of Using Financial Statement Information

Sometimes it is not enough to simply display or print a financial statement. It might be desirable to paste a copy of the income statement or balance sheet in a memo or report. There could be an advantage in copying and pasting a financial statement in a spreadsheet where different assumptions could be tried to see how the business could be improved. For example, you might change the cost of purchases and see what effect the change has on net income.

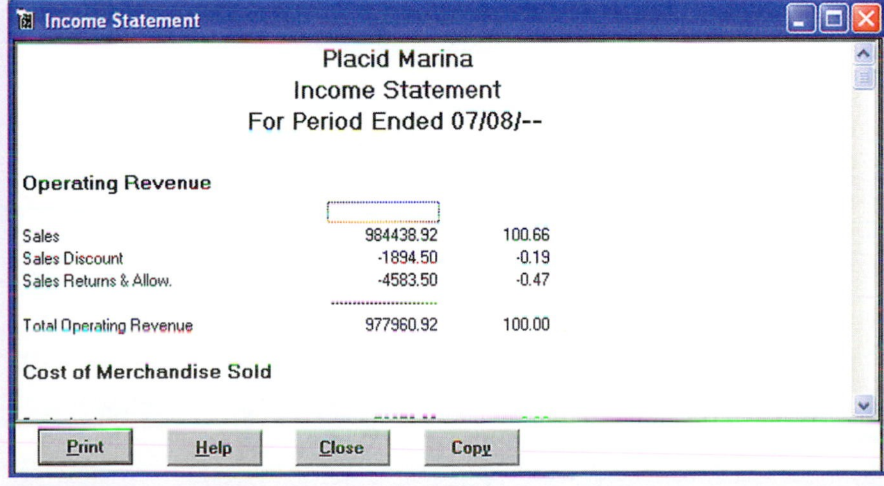

Copying a Financial Statement

Automated Accounting has a Copy function in the report window that allows you to copy the displayed financial statement in either a word processing or a spreadsheet format. When the report is displayed, click the Copy button. You then must choose either a word processing or a spreadsheet format. The report is saved on the operating system's Clipboard. You can then open an existing word processing document or start a new one, and click the Paste tool on the toolbar or select Edit, Paste. The report is copied into a word processing document. To make columns align, it is necessary to reformat the entire report in a monotype font, such as Courier New, so that each character occupies the same amount of space. A similar process is used to copy a report to a spreadsheet.

Automated Accounting Problem: Copying and Pasting Data from the Automated Accounting System (optional)

Instructions:

1. Load the *Automated Accounting 8.0* or higher software.
2. Select data file F15-CP from the appropriate folder/directory.
3. Select File from the menu bar and choose the Save As menu command. Key the path to the drive and directory that contains your data files. Save the data file with a filename of F15-CP XXX XXX (where the X's are your first and last names).
4. Access Problem Instructions through the Browser Tool. Read the Problem Instructions screen.
5. Save your file and exit the Automated Accounting software.

CHAPTER 16 Recording Adjusting and Closing Entries for a Corporation

OBJECTIVES & TERMS

After studying Chapter 16, you will be able to:

1. Identify accounting concepts and practices related to adjusting and closing entries for a merchandising business organized as a corporation.
2. Record adjusting entries.
3. Record closing entries for income statement accounts.
4. Record closing entry for dividends.
5. Prepare a post-closing trial balance.

accounting in the real world

• Apple

©KYODO/LANDOV

APPLE SPREADS ITS WINGS

Recent world history would be incomplete without a reference to three computers—Apple II, Macintosh, and iMac—that pushed computer technology beyond the standard of their day.

The Apple II was the first personal computer to gain wide distribution and put the Apple Computer company on the technology map. The Macintosh introduced the graphical interface and mouse technologies we now take for granted. The iMac merged digital audio and video into traditional computer technology to enable stunning editing of video and audio files.

Although Apple's foundation is in computers, the company has spread its wings into related technology markets. The widely successful iPod is the driving force in the popular digital music player market. iTunes was the first Internet site to offer legal, digital copies of music files. Together, iPod and iTunes have revolutionized how people access and play music.

Apple has clearly demonstrated that it can be a player in any market that requires the innovative application of computer technology.

Critical Thinking

1. Identify other companies that have extended their product lines beyond their original market.
2. Identify at least five expenses Apple incurs to support its iTunes business.

Source: www.apple.com, www.apple-history.com

ACCOUNTING IN THE REAL WORLD • ACCOUNTING IN THE REAL WORLD • ACCOUNTING IN THE REAL WORLD •

internet activity

EDGAR—PART 2

Go to the homepage for EDGAR (www.sec.gov/edgar.shtml). Click on "Search for Company Filings," and then click on "Latest Filings."

Instructions

1. Look at the most recent filing (top of the list) and record the company name and the date and time the filing was accepted.
2. Click the "Back" button to return to "Search the EDGAR Database" page. Again, click on "Latest Filings." Scroll down the list to find the company filing you recorded in instruction 1. Count and record the number of additional filings that are listed.

INTERNET RESEARCH ACTIVITY • INTERNET RESEARCH ACTIVITY •

LESSON • LESSON • LESSON • LESSON • LESSON • LESSON

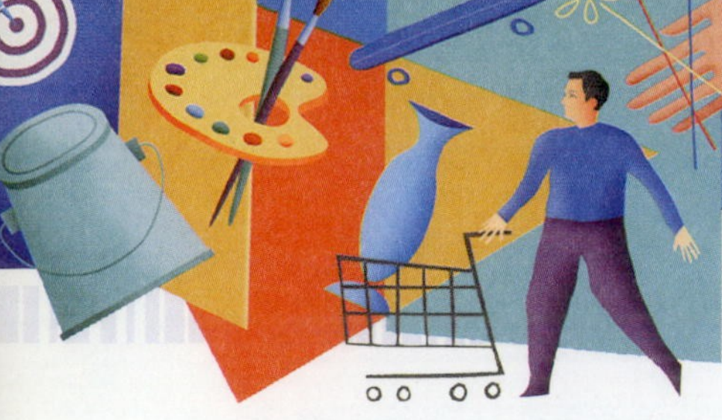

16-1 Recording Adjusting Entries

ADJUSTING ENTRIES RECORDED FROM A WORK SHEET

	ACCOUNT TITLE	1 TRIAL BALANCE DEBIT	2 TRIAL BALANCE CREDIT	3 ADJUSTMENTS DEBIT	4 ADJUSTMENTS CREDIT	
1	*Cash*	29,080.28				1
2	*Petty Cash*	300.00				2
3	*Accounts Receivable*	14,698.40				3
4	*Allow. for Uncoll. Accts.*		127.52		(e) 1,245.00	4
5	*Merchandise Inventory*	140,480.00			(d) 15,840.00	5
6	*Supplies—Office*	3,480.00			(a) 2,730.00	6
7	*Supplies—Store*	3,944.00			(b) 2,910.00	7
8	*Prepaid Insurance*	5,800.00			(c) 3,170.00	8
28	*Income Summary*			(d) 15,840.00		28
45	*Supplies Expense—Office*			(a) 2,730.00		45
46	*Supplies Expense—Store*			(b) 2,910.00		46
47	*Uncollectible Accounts Expense*			(e) 1,245.00		47
48	*Utilities Expense*	3,820.00				48
49	*Federal Income Tax Expense*	18,000.00		(h) 5,889.24		49

3. Identify the first adjustment.

2. Date **1.** Heading **4.** Account Debited **5.** Debit **7.** Credit

GENERAL JOURNAL PAGE *15*

	DATE		ACCOUNT TITLE	DOC. NO.	POST. REF.	DEBIT	CREDIT	
1			① *Adjusting Entries*					1
② 2	*20--* *Dec.*	*31*	*Uncollectible Accounts Expense* ④			⑤ 1,245.00		2
3			*Allowance for Uncoll. Accounts* ⑥				1,245.00 ⑦	3
4		*31*	*Income Summary*			15,840.00		4
5			*Merchandise Inventory*				15,840.00	5
6		*31*	*Supplies Expense—Office*			2,730.00		6
7			*Supplies—Office*				2,730.00	7
16		*31*	*Federal Income Tax Expense*			5,889.24		16
17			*Federal Income Tax Payable*				5,889.24	17
18								18

6. Account Credited

General ledger account balances are changed only by posting journal entries. Two types of journal entries change general ledger account balances at the end of a fiscal period: (1) Adjusting entries bring general ledger account balances up to date. (2) Closing entries prepare temporary accounts for the next fiscal period. [*CONCEPT: Matching Expenses with Revenue*] Adjusting entries recorded in a work sheet are journalized in a general journal. Hobby Shack begins the adjusting entries on a new general journal page. The adjusting entries are entered in the Debit and Credit columns of the general journal.

STEPS • STEPS • STEPS • STEPS • STEPS • STEPS • STEPS • STEPS • STEPS • STEPS

STEPS RECORDING ADJUSTING ENTRIES IN A GENERAL JOURNAL

1. Write the heading, *Adjusting Entries*, in the middle of the general journal's Account Title column. This heading explains all of the adjusting entries that follow. Therefore, indicating a source document is unnecessary. The first adjusting entry is recorded on the first two lines below the heading.
2. For the first adjusting entry in the work sheet Adjustments columns, write the date, *Dec. 31, 20--*, in the Date column.
3. Scan down the Adjustments column of the work sheet to identify the first adjustment, *(e)*, to *Allowance for Uncollectible Accounts*. Identify the debit and credit parts of this entry.
4. Write the title of the account debited in the Account Title column.
5. Write the debit adjustment amount in the Debit column.
6. Write the title of the account credited in the Account Title column, indented about 1 centimeter.
7. Write the credit adjustment amount in the Credit column.
8. Continue down the Adjustments columns, repeating Steps 4 through 7 for each of the additional adjustments.

REMEMBER Remember to start a new general journal page for adjusting entries.

MAKING ETHICAL DECISIONS • MAKING ETHICAL DECISIONS • MAKING ETHICAL DECISIONS

making ethical decisions

Insider Trading

Midori Watanabe works in the research unit of a large chemical company. Her group has recently discovered a new chemical process that will revolutionize how household cleaning products are manufactured. The discovery should have a significant positive impact on her company's profitability and its stock price.

Midori purchases shares of her company every month through a payroll deduction program. She is considering using a large portion of her savings to buy additional shares of the company. Since you are the ethics officer of the company, she has asked your opinion on her proposed stock purchase.

Instructions

Access the *Code of Business Conduct* of Dow at www.dow.com. Using this code of conduct as a guide, provide Midori with guidance on her proposed stock purchase. Can Midori continue her monthly purchases?

ADJUSTING ENTRY FOR ALLOWANCE FOR UNCOLLECTIBLE ACCOUNTS

GENERAL JOURNAL PAGE 15

	DATE		ACCOUNT TITLE	DOC. NO.	POST. REF.	DEBIT	CREDIT	
1			*Adjusting Entries*					1
2	20-- Dec.	31	*Uncollectible Accounts Expense*			1 245 00		2
3			*Allowance for Uncoll. Accounts*				1 245 00	3

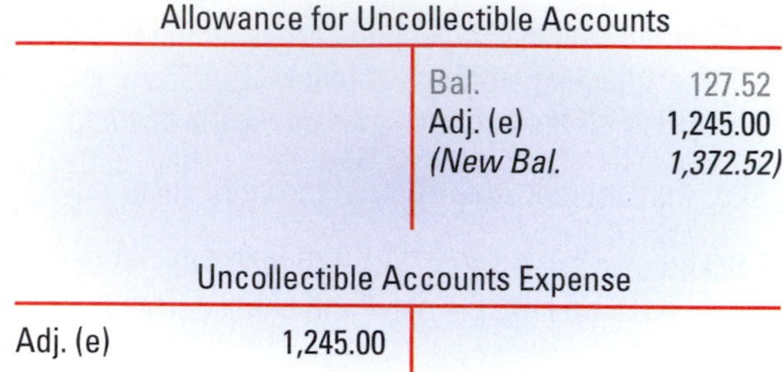

Allowance for Uncollectible Accounts
Bal. 127.52
Adj. (e) 1,245.00
(New Bal. 1,372.52)
Uncollectible Accounts Expense
Adj. (e) 1,245.00

Hobby Shack estimated that $1,245.00 of the current fiscal year's sales on account will eventually be uncollectible. The amount is added to the existing balance in Allowance for Uncollectible Accounts, $127.52. The adjusted balance of Allowance for Uncollectible Accounts, $1,372.52, is the amount of the current accounts receivable that Hobby Shack expects to become uncollectible.

The effect of posting the adjusting entry (e) for Uncollectible Accounts is shown in the T accounts. The debit to Uncollectible Accounts Expense recognizes this as an expense for the fiscal period.

ADJUSTING ENTRY FOR MERCHANDISE INVENTORY

GENERAL JOURNAL PAGE 15

	DATE		ACCOUNT TITLE	DOC. NO.	POST. REF.	DEBIT	CREDIT	
4		31	*Income Summary*			15 840 00		4
5			*Merchandise Inventory*				15 840 00	5

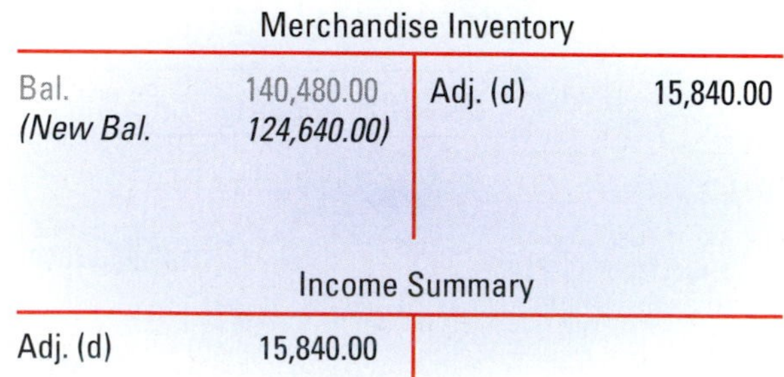

Merchandise Inventory
Bal. 140,480.00
(New Bal. 124,640.00)
Adj. (d) 15,840.00
Income Summary
Adj. (d) 15,840.00

The merchandise inventory account has a January 1 debit balance of $140,480.00. The inventory was counted at the end of the fiscal period and determined to cost $124,640.00. Adjustment *(d)* for $15,840.00 reduces the cost of inventory, $140,480.00, to $124,640.00. The effect of posting the adjusting entry for merchandise inventory is shown in the T accounts.

ADJUSTING ENTRY FOR SUPPLIES—OFFICE

GENERAL JOURNAL — PAGE 15

	DATE		ACCOUNT TITLE	DOC. NO.	POST. REF.	DEBIT	CREDIT	
6		31	Supplies Expense—Office			2 730 00		6
7			Supplies—Office				2 730 00	7

Hobby Shack counted $750.00 of office supplies on hand at the end of the fiscal period. The balance of Supplies—Office in the trial balance, $3,480.00, is the cost of office supplies on hand at the beginning of the year plus the office supplies purchased during the year. Adjustment *(a)* for $2,730.00 reduces the balance in Supplies—Office from $3,480.00 to $750.00.

The effect of posting the adjusting entry for office supplies is shown in the T accounts. The debit to Supplies Expense—Office recognizes the amount of supplies used during the period as an expense.

Supplies—Office

	Debit		Credit
Bal.	3,480.00	Adj. (a)	2,730.00
(New Bal.	*750.00)*		

Supplies Expense—Office

	Debit		Credit
Adj. (a)	2,730.00		

ADJUSTING ENTRY FOR SUPPLIES—STORE

GENERAL JOURNAL — PAGE 15

	DATE		ACCOUNT TITLE	DOC. NO.	POST. REF.	DEBIT	CREDIT	
8		31	Supplies Expense—Store			2 910 00		8
9			Supplies—Store				2 910 00	9

Hobby Shack also counted $1,034.00 of store supplies on hand at the end of the fiscal period. Adjustment *(b)* for $2,910.00 reduces the balance in Supplies—Store, $3,944.00, to the current cost of store supplies on hand, $1,034.00. The effect of posting the adjusting entry for store supplies inventory is shown in the T accounts. The debit to Supplies Expense—Store recognizes the amount of supplies used during the period as an expense.

Supplies—Store

	Debit		Credit
Bal.	3,944.00	Adj. (b)	2,910.00
(New Bal.	*1,034.00)*		

Supplies Expense—Store

	Debit		Credit
Adj. (b)	2,910.00		

ADJUSTING ENTRY FOR PREPAID INSURANCE

GENERAL JOURNAL PAGE 15

	DATE	ACCOUNT TITLE	DOC. NO.	POST. REF.	DEBIT	CREDIT	
10	31	*Insurance Expense*			3 170 00		10
11		*Prepaid Insurance*				3 170 00	11

During the fiscal period, Hobby Shack paid $5,800.00 for future insurance coverage. At the end of the fiscal year, Hobby Shack determined that the value of prepaid insurance on December 31 is $2,630.00. Adjustment *(c)* reduces Prepaid Insurance by $3,170.00, the value of insurance used during the year.

The effect of posting the adjusting entry for Prepaid Insurance is shown in the T accounts. The debit to Insurance Expense recognizes the amount of insurance used during the fiscal period as an expense.

Prepaid Insurance

Bal.	5,800.00	Adj. (c)	3,170.00
(New Bal.	*2,630.00)*		

Insurance Expense

Adj. (c)	3,170.00		

ADJUSTING ENTRY FOR DEPRECIATION—OFFICE EQUIPMENT

GENERAL JOURNAL PAGE 15

	DATE	ACCOUNT TITLE	DOC. NO.	POST. REF.	DEBIT	CREDIT	
12	31	*Depreciation Exp.—Office Equip.*			6 540 00		12
13		*Accum. Depr.—Office Equip.*				6 540 00	13

Hobby Shack estimated its depreciation of office equipment during the fiscal year to be $6,540.00. Adjustment *(f)* increases Accum. Depr.—Office Equip. by $6,540.00, resulting in a new balance of $13,037.00.

The effect of posting the adjusting entry for office equipment depreciation is shown in the T accounts. The debit to Depreciation Exp.—Office Equip. recognizes the depreciation as an expense for the fiscal period.

Accum. Depr.—Office Equip.

		Bal.	6,497.00
		Adj. (f)	6,540.00
		(New Bal.	*13,037.00)*

Depreciation Exp.—Office Equip.

Adj. (f)	6,540.00		

ADJUSTING ENTRY FOR DEPRECIATION—STORE EQUIPMENT

GENERAL JOURNAL — PAGE 15

	DATE	ACCOUNT TITLE	DOC. NO.	POST. REF.	DEBIT	CREDIT	
14	31	*Depreciation Exp.—Store Equip.*			5 250 00		14
15		*Accum. Depr.—Store Equip.*				5 250 00	15

Hobby Shack estimated its depreciation of store equipment during the fiscal year to be $5,250.00. Adjustment *(g)* increases Accum. Depr.—Store Equip. by $5,250.00, resulting in a new balance of $10,319.00.

The effect of posting the adjusting entry for store equipment depreciation is shown in the T accounts. The debit to Depreciation Exp.—Store Equip. recognizes the depreciation as an expense for the fiscal period.

Accum. Depr.—Store Equip.

Debit		Credit	
		Bal.	5,069.00
		Adj. (g)	5,250.00
		(New Bal.	*10,319.00)*

Depreciation Exp.—Store Equip.

Debit		Credit
Adj. (g)	5,250.00	

ADJUSTING ENTRY FOR FEDERAL INCOME TAXES

GENERAL JOURNAL — PAGE 15

	DATE	ACCOUNT TITLE	DOC. NO.	POST. REF.	DEBIT	CREDIT	
16	31	*Federal Income Tax Expense*			5 889 24		16
17		*Federal Income Tax Payable*				5 889 24	17

Hobby Shack made four quarterly estimated payments of $4,500.00. The actual federal income tax expense, $23,889.24, was calculated based on the company's net income before federal income tax. Hobby Shack must make an extra payment of $5,889.24 to pay its tax liability. Adjustment *(h)* increases Federal Income Tax Expense by $5,889.24, resulting in a new balance of $23,889.24. The adjustment also creates the $5,889.24 tax liability.

The effect of posting the adjusting entry for federal income tax is shown in the T accounts.

Federal Income Tax Payable

Debit		Credit	
		Adj. (h)	5,889.24
		(New Bal.	*5,889.24)*

Federal Income Tax Expense

Debit		Credit
Bal.	18,000.00	
Adj. (h)	5,889.24	
(New Bal.	*23,889.24)*	

• audit your understanding

1. When adjusting entries are journalized, why is no source document recorded?
2. What adjusting entry is recorded for a merchandising business that is not recorded for a service business?
3. What balance sheet account is increased from a zero balance after adjusting entries are journalized and posted?

AUDIT YOUR UNDERSTANDING

• work together 16-1

Journalizing adjusting entries

The work sheet for Discount Books, Inc., is given in the *Working Papers.* Your instructor will guide you through the following example.

1. Record the appropriate adjusting entries on page 18 of a general journal provided in the *Working Papers.* Use December 31 of the current year as the date. Save your work to complete Work Together 16-2.

WORK TOGETHER

• on your own 16-1

Journalizing adjusting entries

The work sheet for Sturgis Supply, Inc., is given in the *Working Papers.* Work this problem independently.

1. Record the appropriate adjusting entries on page 24 of a general journal provided in the *Working Papers.* Use December 31 of the current year as the date. Save your work to complete On Your Own 16-2.

ON YOUR OWN

16-2 Recording Closing Entries for Income Statement Accounts

Closing entries for a corporation are made from information in a work sheet. Closing entries for revenue and expense accounts are similar to those for proprietorships. A corporation's closing entries to close net income and temporary equity accounts are also similar to those for a proprietorship. However, these closing entries affect different accounts. A corporation records four closing entries:

1. A closing entry for income statement accounts with credit balances (revenue and contra cost accounts)
2. A closing entry for income statement accounts with debit balances (cost, contra revenue, and expense accounts)
3. A closing entry to record net income or net loss in the retained earnings account and close the income summary account
4. A closing entry for the dividends account

THE INCOME SUMMARY ACCOUNT

At the end of a fiscal period, the temporary accounts are closed to prepare the general ledger for the next fiscal period. [*CONCEPT: Matching Expenses with Revenue*] To close a temporary account, an amount equal to its balance is recorded on the side opposite the balance.

Amounts needed for the closing entries are obtained from the Income Statement and Balance Sheet columns of the work sheet and from the statement of stockholders' equity. Closing entries are recorded in the general journal.

Chapter 8 discusses the difference between permanent accounts and temporary accounts. Permanent accounts, also referred to as *real accounts*, include the asset and liability accounts as well as the owners' capital accounts. The ending account balances of permanent accounts for one fiscal period are the beginning account balances for the next fiscal period. Temporary accounts, also referred to as *nominal accounts*, include the revenue, cost, expense, and dividend accounts.

Another temporary account is used to summarize the closing entries for revenue, cost, and expenses. The account is titled Income Summary because it is used to summarize information about net income. Income Summary is used only at the end of a fiscal period to help prepare other accounts for a new fiscal period.

The income summary account is unique because it does not have a normal balance side. The balance of this account is determined by the amounts posted to the account at the end of a fiscal period. When revenue is greater than total expenses, resulting in a net income, the income summary account has a credit balance, as shown in the T account.

Income Summary	
Debit Total expenses	Credit Revenue (greater than expenses) (Credit balance is the net income.)

REMEMBER The income summary account is used only at the end of the fiscal period to help prepare other accounts for a new fiscal period.

CLOSING ENTRY FOR ACCOUNTS WITH CREDIT BALANCES

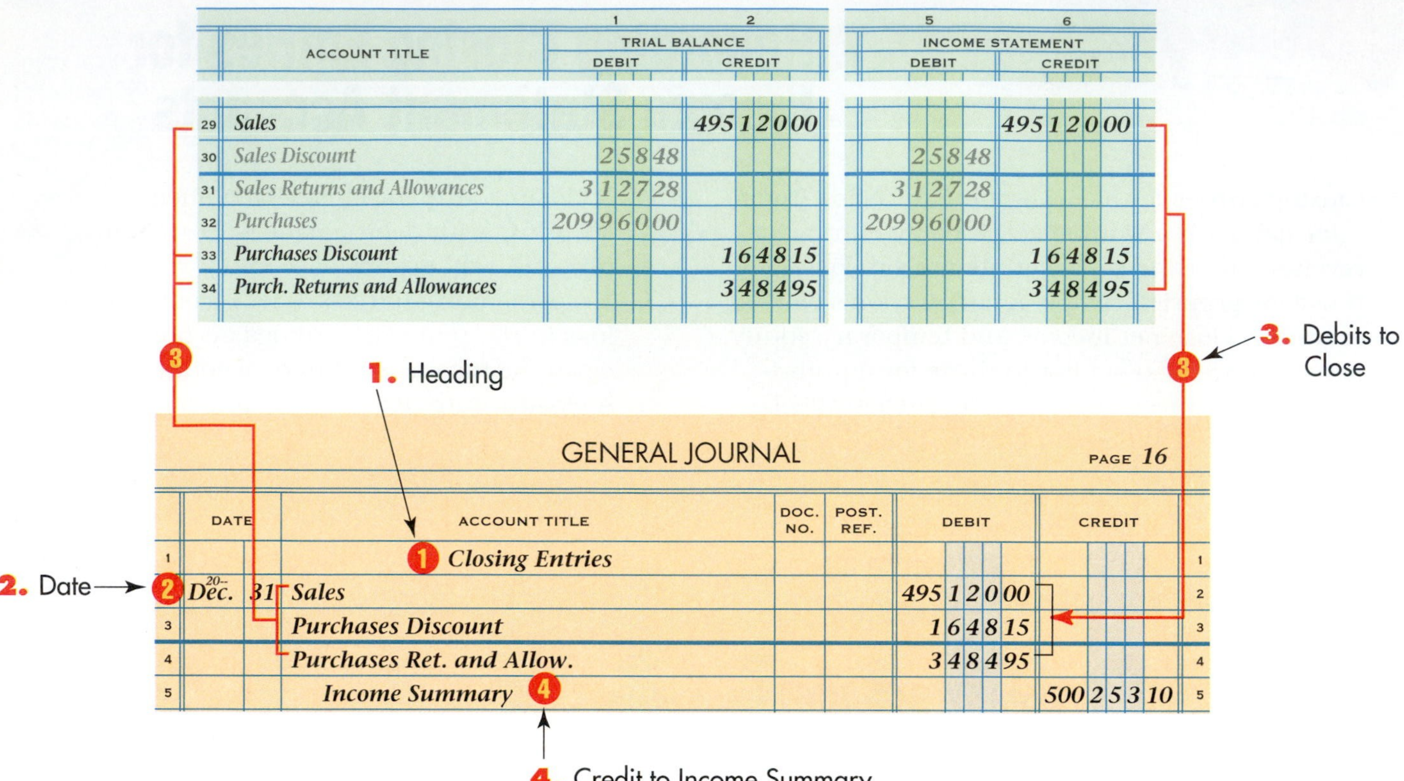

Hobby Shack's work sheet has three income statement accounts with credit balances. One account, Sales, is a revenue account. The other two accounts, Purchases Discount and Purchases Returns and Allowances, are contra cost accounts. Each account has a normal credit balance that must be reduced to zero to prepare the account for the next fiscal period. [*CONCEPT: Matching Expenses with Revenue*]

To reduce each balance to zero, each account is debited for the amount of the balance. The impact of the closing entry on the sales account is shown in the T account.

Sales			
Closing	495,120.00	Bal.	495,120.00
		(New Bal. zero)	

Income Summary is credited for $500,253.10, the total of the three debits in this closing entry.

Income Summary			
Adj. (mdse. inv.)	15,840.00	Closing (credit accounts)	500,253.10

The balance in Income Summary will be adjusted by other closing entries.

STEPS • STEPS • STEPS • STEPS • STEPS

CLOSING INCOME STATEMENT ACCOUNTS WITH CREDIT BALANCES

1. Write the heading, *Closing Entries,* in the middle of the general journal's Account Title column on a new page. This heading explains all of the closing entries that follow. Therefore, indicating a source document is unnecessary. The first closing entry is recorded on the first four lines below the heading.
2. Write the date, *Dec. 31, 20--*, in the Date column.
3. Write the account title of each revenue and contra cost account in the Account Title column. Write the balance of each revenue and contra cost account in the Debit column.
4. Write the title of the account credited, *Income Summary*, in the Account Title column, indented about 1 centimeter. Write the amount, *$500,253.10*, in the Credit column.

CLOSING ENTRY FOR INCOME STATEMENT ACCOUNTS WITH DEBIT BALANCES

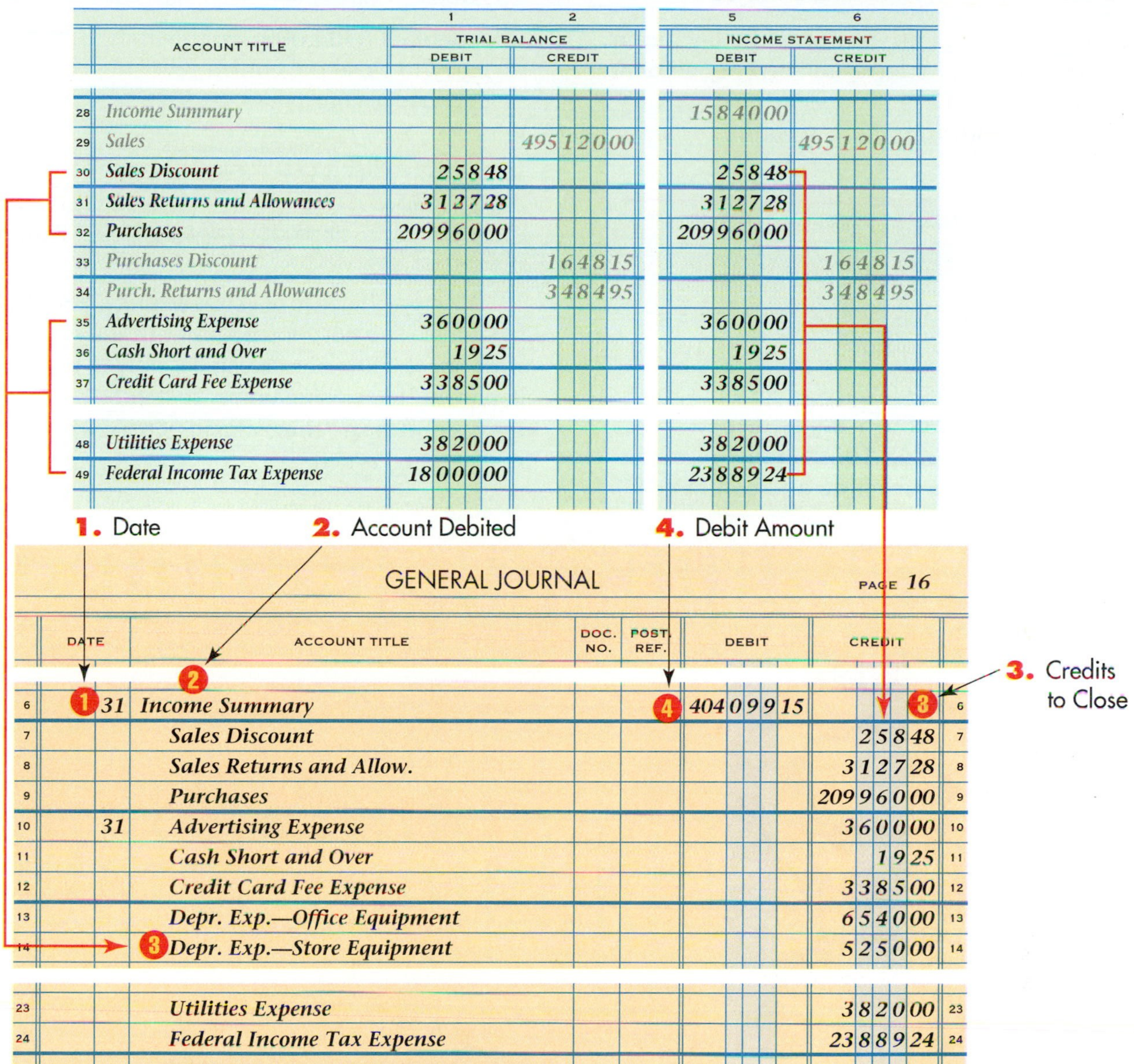

	ACCOUNT TITLE	TRIAL BALANCE DEBIT (1)	TRIAL BALANCE CREDIT (2)	INCOME STATEMENT DEBIT (5)	INCOME STATEMENT CREDIT (6)
28	Income Summary			15,840.00	
29	Sales		495,120.00		495,120.00
30	Sales Discount	258.48		258.48	
31	Sales Returns and Allowances	3,127.28		3,127.28	
32	Purchases	209,960.00		209,960.00	
33	Purchases Discount		1,648.15		1,648.15
34	Purch. Returns and Allowances		3,484.95		3,484.95
35	Advertising Expense	3,600.00		3,600.00	
36	Cash Short and Over	19.25		19.25	
37	Credit Card Fee Expense	3,385.00		3,385.00	
48	Utilities Expense	3,820.00		3,820.00	
49	Federal Income Tax Expense	18,000.00		23,889.24	

GENERAL JOURNAL — PAGE 16

	DATE		ACCOUNT TITLE	DOC. NO.	POST. REF.	DEBIT	CREDIT	
6		31	Income Summary			404,099.15		6
7			Sales Discount				258.48	7
8			Sales Returns and Allow.				3,127.28	8
9			Purchases				209,960.00	9
10		31	Advertising Expense				3,600.00	10
11			Cash Short and Over				19.25	11
12			Credit Card Fee Expense				3,385.00	12
13			Depr. Exp.—Office Equipment				6,540.00	13
14			Depr. Exp.—Store Equipment				5,250.00	14
23			Utilities Expense				3,820.00	23
24			Federal Income Tax Expense				23,889.24	24

Hobby Shack's work sheet has many income statement accounts with debit balances—contra revenue accounts, Purchases, and the expense accounts. These debit balances must be reduced to zero to prepare the accounts for the next fiscal period. [*CONCEPT: Matching Expenses with Revenue*] To reduce the balances to zero, the accounts are credited for the amount of their balances. Income Summary is debited for the total amount.

STEPS: CLOSING INCOME STATEMENT ACCOUNTS WITH DEBIT BALANCES

1. Write the date, *31*, in the Date column.
2. Write the title of the account debited, *Income Summary*, in the Account Title column. The debit to *Income Summary* is not entered in the amount column until all cost and expense balances have been journalized and the total amount calculated.
3. Write the account title of each contra revenue, cost, and expense account in the Account Title column, each indented about 1 centimeter. Write the balance of each cost and expense account in the Credit column.
4. Add the credit amounts for this entry. Write the total of the cost and expense accounts, *$404,099.15*, in the Debit column on the same line as the account title *Income Summary*.

SUMMARY OF CLOSING ENTRY FOR INCOME STATEMENT ACCOUNTS WITH DEBIT BALANCES

The second closing entry reduces the balance of the contra revenue, Purchases, and expense accounts to a zero balance. The effect of the closing entry on Purchases is shown in the T account.

Purchases			
Bal.	209,960.00	Closing	209,960.00
(New Bal. zero)			

After recording this closing entry, Income Summary has three amounts:

1. A debit of $15,840.00, the amount of the merchandise inventory adjustment
2. A credit of $500,253.10, the amount of the entry to close the revenue and contra cost accounts
3. A debit of $404,099.15, the amount of the entry to close the contra revenue, cost, and expense accounts

Income Summary			
Adj. (mdse. inv.)	15,840.00	Closing (credit amounts)	500,253.10
Closing (debit accounts)	404,099.15	*(New Bal.*	*80,313.95)*

The credit balance of Income Summary, *$80,313.95*, is equal to the net income amount shown on the work sheet. However, Income Summary is not closed as part of this closing entry. Instead, the account is closed with the third closing entry when net income is recorded.

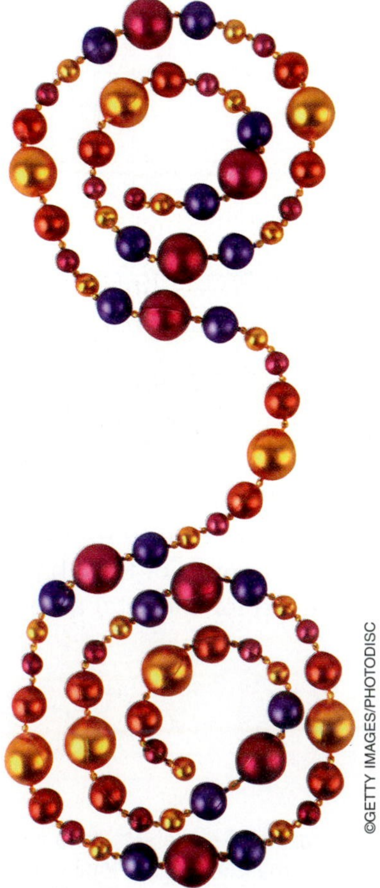

©GETTY IMAGES/PHOTODISC

A document that outlines the mission and goals of a corporation is known as a *strategic plan*. The management of a corporation uses the strategic plan as a guiding light to ensure that all business decisions work toward achieving its goals.

Buying a franchise is a popular way to start a small business. Franchises are particularly appealing to people with less experience because the failure rate is much lower than that of other new businesses. Advantages of purchasing a franchise include the franchise's proven reputation, established customers, and time-tested business procedures. Disadvantages include the franchisee's sometimes-limited control over the new business and the relatively high initial fees attached to the purchase of a franchise.

CLOSING ENTRY TO RECORD NET INCOME

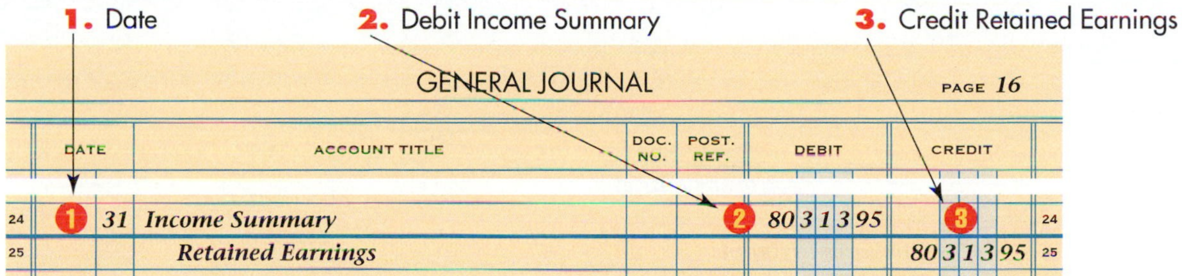

After closing entries for the income statement accounts are posted, Income Summary has a credit balance of $80,313.95. This credit balance equals the net income calculated on the work sheet.

A corporation's net income should be recorded in the retained earnings account at the end of the fiscal year. After the closing entry is posted, Income Summary has a zero balance.

Retained Earnings

Debit		Credit	
		Bal.	10,761.29
		Closing (Income Summary)	80,313.95
		(New Bal.	*91,075.24)*

Income Summary

Debit		Credit	
Adj. (mdse. inv.)	15,840.00	Closing (credit accounts)	500,253.10
Closing (debit accounts)	404,099.15		
Closing (retained earnings)	80,313.95	*(New Bal. zero)*	

The new balance in retained earnings, *$91,075.24*, does not yet equal the amount reported on the statement of stockholder's equity. The fourth closing entry is required to adjust Retained Earnings to the correct amount.

CLOSING ENTRY FOR DIVIDENDS

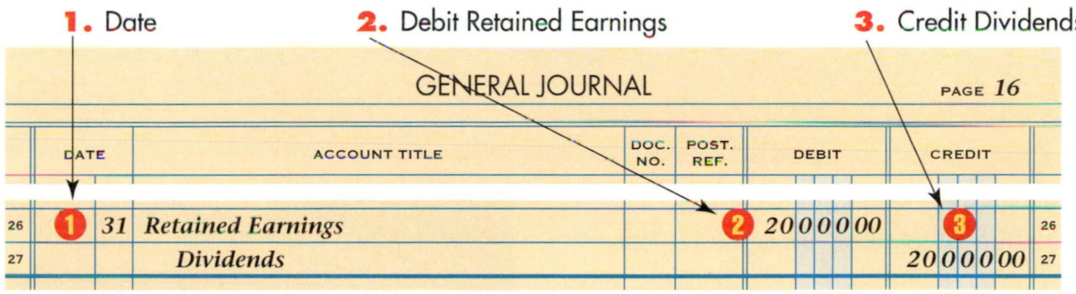

Because dividends decrease the earnings retained by a corporation, the dividends account is closed to Retained Earnings. After the closing entry for the dividends account is posted, Dividends has a zero balance. The amount of the dividends, *$20,000.00*, has reduced the balance of Retained Earnings.

Retained Earnings

Debit		Credit	
		Bal.	10,761.29
Closing (dividends)	20,000.00	Closing (Income Summary)	80,313.95
		(New Bal.	*71,075.24)*

Dividends

Debit		Credit	
Bal.	20,000.00	Closing (dividends)	20,000.00
(New Bal. zero)			

COMPLETED CLOSING ENTRIES FOR A CORPORATION RECORDED IN A JOURNAL

GENERAL JOURNAL — PAGE 16

DATE		ACCOUNT TITLE	DOC. NO.	POST. REF.	DEBIT	CREDIT
		Closing Entries				
20-- Dec.	31	Sales			495 120 00	
		Purchases Discount			1 648 15	
		Purchases Ret. and Allow.			3 484 95	
		Income Summary				500 253 10
	31	Income Summary			404 099 15	
		Sales Discount				258 48
		Sales Returns and Allow.				3 127 28
		Purchases				209 960 00
		Advertising Expense				3 600 00
		Cash Short and Over				19 25
		Credit Card Fee Expense				3 385 00
		Depr. Exp.—Office Equipment				6 540 00
		Depr. Exp.—Store Equipment				5 250 00
		Insurance Expense				3 170 00
		Miscellaneous Expense				2 564 90
		Payroll Taxes Expense				9 105 00
		Rent Expense				18 000 00
		Salary Expense				104 525 00
		Supplies Expense—Office				2 730 00
		Supplies Expense—Store				2 910 00
		Uncollectible Accounts Expense				1 245 00
		Utilities Expense				3 820 00
		Federal Income Tax Expense				23 889 24
	31	Income Summary			80 313 95	
		Retained Earnings				80 313 95
	31	Retained Earnings			20 000 00	
		Dividends				20 000 00

Hobby Shack's general journal appears as shown above, after all closing entries have been recorded.

The next step would be to post the adjusting and closing entries to the general ledger.

FYI FOR YOUR INFORMATION

If a corporation has a net loss, *Income Summary* has a debit balance. *Retained Earnings* would then be debited and *Income Summary* credited for the net loss amount.

©GETTY IMAGES/PHOTODISC

• audit your understanding

1. Where is the information obtained for journalizing closing entries for revenue, cost, and expenses?
2. What is the name of the temporary account that is used to summarize the closing entries for revenue, cost, and expenses?

AUDIT YOUR UNDERSTANDING

• work together 16-2

Journalizing closing entries

Use the work sheet of Discount Books, Inc., from Work Together 16-1. A general journal is given in the *Working Papers*. Your instructor will guide you through the following example.

1. Record the following closing entries on page 19 of the general journal.
   a. Close the income statement accounts with credit balances.
   b. Close the income statement accounts with debit balances.
   c. Close Income Summary.
   d. Close the dividend account.

WORK TOGETHER • WORK

• on your own 16-2

Journalizing closing entries

Use the work sheet of Sturgis Supply, Inc., from On Your Own 16-1. A general journal is given in the *Working Papers*. Work this problem independently.

1. Record the following closing entries on page 25 of the general journal.
   a. Close the income statement accounts with credit balances.
   b. Close the income statement accounts with debit balances.
   c. Close Income Summary.
   d. Close the dividend account.

ON YOUR OWN • ON YOUR OWN

LESSON

16-3 Preparing a Post-Closing Trial Balance

COMPLETED GENERAL LEDGER AFTER ADJUSTING AND CLOSING ENTRIES ARE POSTED

ACCOUNT *Cash* ACCOUNT NO. *1110*

DATE		ITEM	POST. REF.	DEBIT	CREDIT	BALANCE DEBIT	BALANCE CREDIT
20-- Dec.	31	Balance	✓			29,080.28	

ACCOUNT *Petty Cash* ACCOUNT NO. *1120*

DATE		ITEM	POST. REF.	DEBIT	CREDIT	BALANCE DEBIT	BALANCE CREDIT
20-- Dec.	31	Balance	✓			300.00	

ACCOUNT *Accounts Receivable* ACCOUNT NO. *1130*

DATE		ITEM	POST. REF.	DEBIT	CREDIT	BALANCE DEBIT	BALANCE CREDIT
20-- Dec.	31	Balance	✓			14,698.40	

ACCOUNT *Allow. for Uncoll. Acc.* ACCOUNT NO. *1135*

DATE		ITEM	POST. REF.	DEBIT	CREDIT	BALANCE DEBIT	BALANCE CREDIT
20-- Dec.	31	Balance	✓				127.52
	31		G15		1,245.00		1,372.52

ACCOUNT *Merchandise Inventory* ACCOUNT NO. *1140*

DATE		ITEM	POST. REF.	DEBIT	CREDIT	BALANCE DEBIT	BALANCE CREDIT
20-- Dec.	31	Balance	✓			140,480.00	
	31		G15		15,840.00	124,640.00	

ACCOUNT *Supplies—Office* ACCOUNT NO. *1145*

DATE		ITEM	POST. REF.	DEBIT	CREDIT	BALANCE DEBIT	BALANCE CREDIT
20-- Dec.	31	Balance	✓			3,480.00	
	31		G15		2,730.00	750.00	

ACCOUNT *Supplies—Store* ACCOUNT NO. *1150*

DATE		ITEM	POST. REF.	DEBIT	CREDIT	BALANCE DEBIT	BALANCE CREDIT
20-- Dec.	31	Balance	✓			3,944.00	
	31		G15		2,910.00	1,034.00	

ACCOUNT *Prepaid Insurance* ACCOUNT NO. *1160*

DATE		ITEM	POST. REF.	DEBIT	CREDIT	BALANCE DEBIT	BALANCE CREDIT
20-- Dec.	31	Balance	✓			5,800.00	
	31		G15		3,170.00	2,630.00	

ACCOUNT *Office Equipment* ACCOUNT NO. *1205*

DATE		ITEM	POST. REF.	DEBIT	CREDIT	BALANCE DEBIT	BALANCE CREDIT
20-- Dec.	31	Balance	✓			35,864.50	

ACCOUNT *Acc. Depr.— Office Equipment* ACCOUNT NO. *1210*

DATE		ITEM	POST. REF.	DEBIT	CREDIT	BALANCE DEBIT	BALANCE CREDIT
20-- Dec.	31	Balance	✓				6,497.00
	31		G15		6,540.00		13,037.00

ACCOUNT *Store Equipment* ACCOUNT NO. *1215*

DATE		ITEM	POST. REF.	DEBIT	CREDIT	BALANCE DEBIT	BALANCE CREDIT
20-- Dec.	31	Balance	✓			40,849.50	

ACCOUNT *Acc. Depr.— Store Equipment* ACCOUNT NO. *1220*

DATE		ITEM	POST. REF.	DEBIT	CREDIT	BALANCE DEBIT	BALANCE CREDIT
20-- Dec.	31	Balance	✓				5,069.00
	31		G15		5,250.00		10,319.00

ACCOUNT *Accounts Payable* ACCOUNT NO. *2110*

DATE		ITEM	POST. REF.	DEBIT	CREDIT	BALANCE DEBIT	BALANCE CREDIT
20-- Dec.	31	Balance	✓				11,583.03

ACCOUNT *Federal Income Tax Payable* ACCOUNT NO. *2120*

DATE		ITEM	POST. REF.	DEBIT	CREDIT	BALANCE DEBIT	BALANCE CREDIT
20-- Dec.	31	Balance	G15		5,889.24		5,889.24

ACCOUNT *Employee Income Tax Payable* ACCOUNT NO. *2130*

DATE		ITEM	POST. REF.	DEBIT	CREDIT	BALANCE DEBIT	BALANCE CREDIT
20-- Dec.	31	Balance	✓				757.00

ACCOUNT *Social Security Tax Payable* ACCOUNT NO. *2135*

DATE		ITEM	POST. REF.	DEBIT	CREDIT	BALANCE DEBIT	BALANCE CREDIT
20-- Dec.	31	Balance	✓				1,451.38

ACCOUNT *Medicare Tax Payable* ACCOUNT NO. *2140*

DATE		ITEM	POST. REF.	DEBIT	CREDIT	BALANCE DEBIT	BALANCE CREDIT
20-- Dec.	31	Balance	✓				399.42

ACCOUNT *Sales Tax Payable* ACCOUNT NO. *2145*

DATE		ITEM	POST. REF.	DEBIT	CREDIT	BALANCE DEBIT	BALANCE CREDIT
20-- Dec.	31	Balance	✓				2,556.70

ACCOUNT *Unemployment Tax Payable—Federal* ACCOUNT NO. *2150*

DATE		ITEM	POST. REF.	DEBIT	CREDIT	BALANCE DEBIT	BALANCE CREDIT
20-- Dec.	31	Balance	✓				34.60

ACCOUNT *Unemployment Tax Payable—State* ACCOUNT NO. *2155*

DATE		ITEM	POST. REF.	DEBIT	CREDIT	BALANCE DEBIT	BALANCE CREDIT
20-- Dec.	31	Balance	✓				233.55

ACCOUNT *Health Insurance Premiums Payable* ACCOUNT NO. *2160*

DATE		ITEM	POST. REF.	DEBIT	CREDIT	BALANCE DEBIT	BALANCE CREDIT
20-- Dec.	31	Balance	✓				1,008.00

ACCOUNT *U.S. Savings Bonds Payable* ACCOUNT NO. *2165*

DATE		ITEM	POST. REF.	DEBIT	CREDIT	BALANCE DEBIT	BALANCE CREDIT
20-- Dec.	31	Balance	✓				60.00

ACCOUNT *United Way Donations Payable* ACCOUNT NO. *2170*

DATE		ITEM	POST. REF.	DEBIT	CREDIT	BALANCE DEBIT	BALANCE CREDIT
20-- Dec.	31	Balance	✓				70.00

ACCOUNT *Dividends Payable* ACCOUNT NO. *2180*

DATE		ITEM	POST. REF.	DEBIT	CREDIT	BALANCE DEBIT	BALANCE CREDIT
20-- Dec.	31	Balance	✓				5,000.00

Hobby Shack's completed general ledger after adjusting and closing entries are posted is shown above and on the following page.

Balance sheet accounts (asset, liability, and capital accounts) have up-to-date balances to begin the new fiscal period.

Income statement accounts (revenue, cost, and expense accounts) have zero balances to begin the new fiscal period. [*CONCEPT: Matching Expenses with Revenue*]

COMPLETED GENERAL LEDGER AFTER ADJUSTING AND CLOSING ENTRIES ARE POSTED (CONCLUDED)

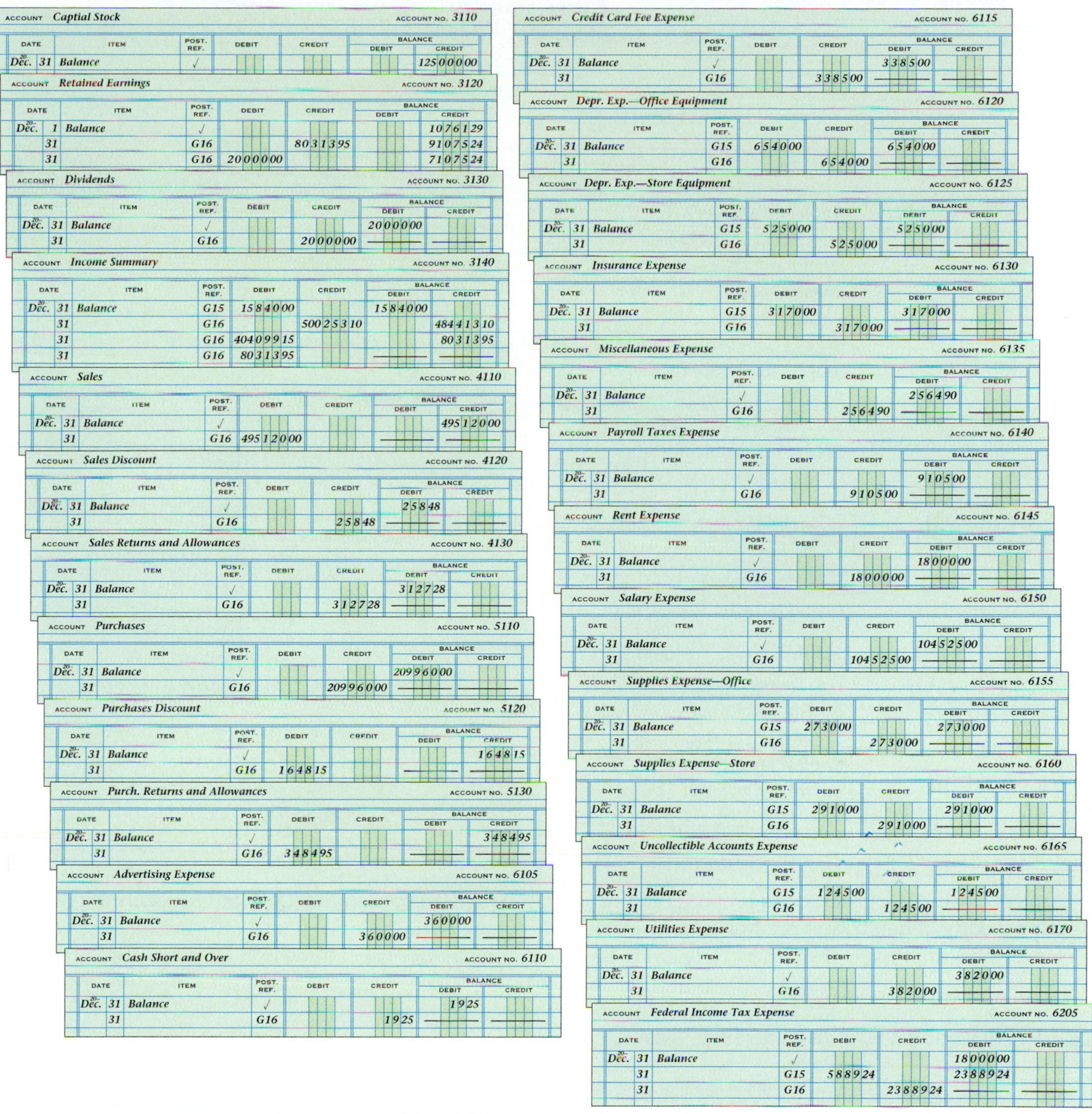

ACCOUNT Captial Stock — ACCOUNT NO. 3110

DATE		ITEM	POST. REF.	DEBIT	CREDIT	BALANCE DEBIT	BALANCE CREDIT
20-- Dec.	31	Balance	✓				125 000 00

ACCOUNT Retained Earnings — ACCOUNT NO. 3120

DATE		ITEM	POST. REF.	DEBIT	CREDIT	BALANCE DEBIT	BALANCE CREDIT
20-- Dec.	1	Balance	✓				10 761 29
	31		G16		80 313 95		91 075 24
	31		G16	20 000 00			71 075 24

ACCOUNT Dividends — ACCOUNT NO. 3130

DATE		ITEM	POST. REF.	DEBIT	CREDIT	BALANCE DEBIT	BALANCE CREDIT
20-- Dec.	31	Balance	✓			20 000 00	
	31		G16		20 000 00	—	—

ACCOUNT Income Summary — ACCOUNT NO. 3140

DATE		ITEM	POST. REF.	DEBIT	CREDIT	BALANCE DEBIT	BALANCE CREDIT
20-- Dec.	31	Balance	G15	15 840 00		15 840 00	
	31		G16		500 253 10		484 413 10
	31		G16	404 099 15			80 313 95
	31		G16	80 313 95		—	—

ACCOUNT Sales — ACCOUNT NO. 4110

DATE		ITEM	POST. REF.	DEBIT	CREDIT	BALANCE DEBIT	BALANCE CREDIT
20-- Dec.	31	Balance	✓				495 120 00
	31		G16	495 120 00		—	—

ACCOUNT Sales Discount — ACCOUNT NO. 4120

DATE		ITEM	POST. REF.	DEBIT	CREDIT	BALANCE DEBIT	BALANCE CREDIT
20-- Dec.	31	Balance	✓			258 48	
	31		G16		258 48	—	—

ACCOUNT Sales Returns and Allowances — ACCOUNT NO. 4130

DATE		ITEM	POST. REF.	DEBIT	CREDIT	BALANCE DEBIT	BALANCE CREDIT
20-- Dec.	31	Balance	✓			3 127 28	
	31		G16		3 127 28	—	—

ACCOUNT Purchases — ACCOUNT NO. 5110

DATE		ITEM	POST. REF.	DEBIT	CREDIT	BALANCE DEBIT	BALANCE CREDIT
20-- Dec.	31	Balance	✓			209 960 00	
	31		G16		209 960 00	—	—

ACCOUNT Purchases Discount — ACCOUNT NO. 5120

DATE		ITEM	POST. REF.	DEBIT	CREDIT	BALANCE DEBIT	BALANCE CREDIT
20-- Dec.	31	Balance	✓				1 648 15
	31		G16	1 648 15		—	—

ACCOUNT Purch. Returns and Allowances — ACCOUNT NO. 5130

DATE		ITEM	POST. REF.	DEBIT	CREDIT	BALANCE DEBIT	BALANCE CREDIT
20-- Dec.	31	Balance	✓				3 484 95
	31		G16	3 484 95		—	—

ACCOUNT Advertising Expense — ACCOUNT NO. 6105

DATE		ITEM	POST. REF.	DEBIT	CREDIT	BALANCE DEBIT	BALANCE CREDIT
20-- Dec.	31	Balance	✓			3 600 00	
	31		G16		3 600 00	—	—

ACCOUNT Cash Short and Over — ACCOUNT NO. 6110

DATE		ITEM	POST. REF.	DEBIT	CREDIT	BALANCE DEBIT	BALANCE CREDIT
20-- Dec.	31	Balance	✓			19 25	
	31		G16		19 25	—	—

ACCOUNT Credit Card Fee Expense — ACCOUNT NO. 6115

DATE		ITEM	POST. REF.	DEBIT	CREDIT	BALANCE DEBIT	BALANCE CREDIT
20-- Dec.	31	Balance	✓			3 385 00	
	31		G16		3 385 00	—	—

ACCOUNT Depr. Exp.—Office Equipment — ACCOUNT NO. 6120

DATE		ITEM	POST. REF.	DEBIT	CREDIT	BALANCE DEBIT	BALANCE CREDIT
20-- Dec.	31	Balance	G15	6 540 00		6 540 00	
	31		G16		6 540 00	—	—

ACCOUNT Depr. Exp.—Store Equipment — ACCOUNT NO. 6125

DATE		ITEM	POST. REF.	DEBIT	CREDIT	BALANCE DEBIT	BALANCE CREDIT
20-- Dec.	31	Balance	G15	5 250 00		5 250 00	
	31		G16		5 250 00	—	—

ACCOUNT Insurance Expense — ACCOUNT NO. 6130

DATE		ITEM	POST. REF.	DEBIT	CREDIT	BALANCE DEBIT	BALANCE CREDIT
20-- Dec.	31	Balance	G15	3 170 00		3 170 00	
	31		G16		3 170 00	—	—

ACCOUNT Miscellaneous Expense — ACCOUNT NO. 6135

DATE		ITEM	POST. REF.	DEBIT	CREDIT	BALANCE DEBIT	BALANCE CREDIT
20-- Dec.	31	Balance	✓			2 564 90	
	31		G16		2 564 90	—	—

ACCOUNT Payroll Taxes Expense — ACCOUNT NO. 6140

DATE		ITEM	POST. REF.	DEBIT	CREDIT	BALANCE DEBIT	BALANCE CREDIT
20-- Dec.	31	Balance	✓			9 105 00	
	31		G16		9 105 00	—	—

ACCOUNT Rent Expense — ACCOUNT NO. 6145

DATE		ITEM	POST. REF.	DEBIT	CREDIT	BALANCE DEBIT	BALANCE CREDIT
20-- Dec.	31	Balance	✓			18 000 00	
	31		G16		18 000 00	—	—

ACCOUNT Salary Expense — ACCOUNT NO. 6150

DATE		ITEM	POST. REF.	DEBIT	CREDIT	BALANCE DEBIT	BALANCE CREDIT
20-- Dec.	31	Balance	✓			104 525 00	
	31		G16		104 525 00	—	—

ACCOUNT Supplies Expense—Office — ACCOUNT NO. 6155

DATE		ITEM	POST. REF.	DEBIT	CREDIT	BALANCE DEBIT	BALANCE CREDIT
20-- Dec.	31	Balance	G15	2 730 00		2 730 00	
	31		G16		2 730 00	—	—

ACCOUNT Supplies Expense—Store — ACCOUNT NO. 6160

DATE		ITEM	POST. REF.	DEBIT	CREDIT	BALANCE DEBIT	BALANCE CREDIT
20-- Dec.	31	Balance	G15	2 910 00		2 910 00	
	31		G16		2 910 00	—	—

ACCOUNT Uncollectible Accounts Expense — ACCOUNT NO. 6165

DATE		ITEM	POST. REF.	DEBIT	CREDIT	BALANCE DEBIT	BALANCE CREDIT
20-- Dec.	31	Balance	G15	1 245 00		1 245 00	
	31		G16		1 245 00	—	—

ACCOUNT Utilities Expense — ACCOUNT NO. 6170

DATE		ITEM	POST. REF.	DEBIT	CREDIT	BALANCE DEBIT	BALANCE CREDIT
20-- Dec.	31	Balance	✓			3 820 00	
	31		G16		3 820 00	—	—

ACCOUNT Federal Income Tax Expense — ACCOUNT NO. 6205

DATE		ITEM	POST. REF.	DEBIT	CREDIT	BALANCE DEBIT	BALANCE CREDIT
20-- Dec.	31	Balance	✓			18 000 00	
	31		G15	5 889 24		23 889 24	
	31		G16		23 889 24	—	—

POST-CLOSING TRIAL BALANCE

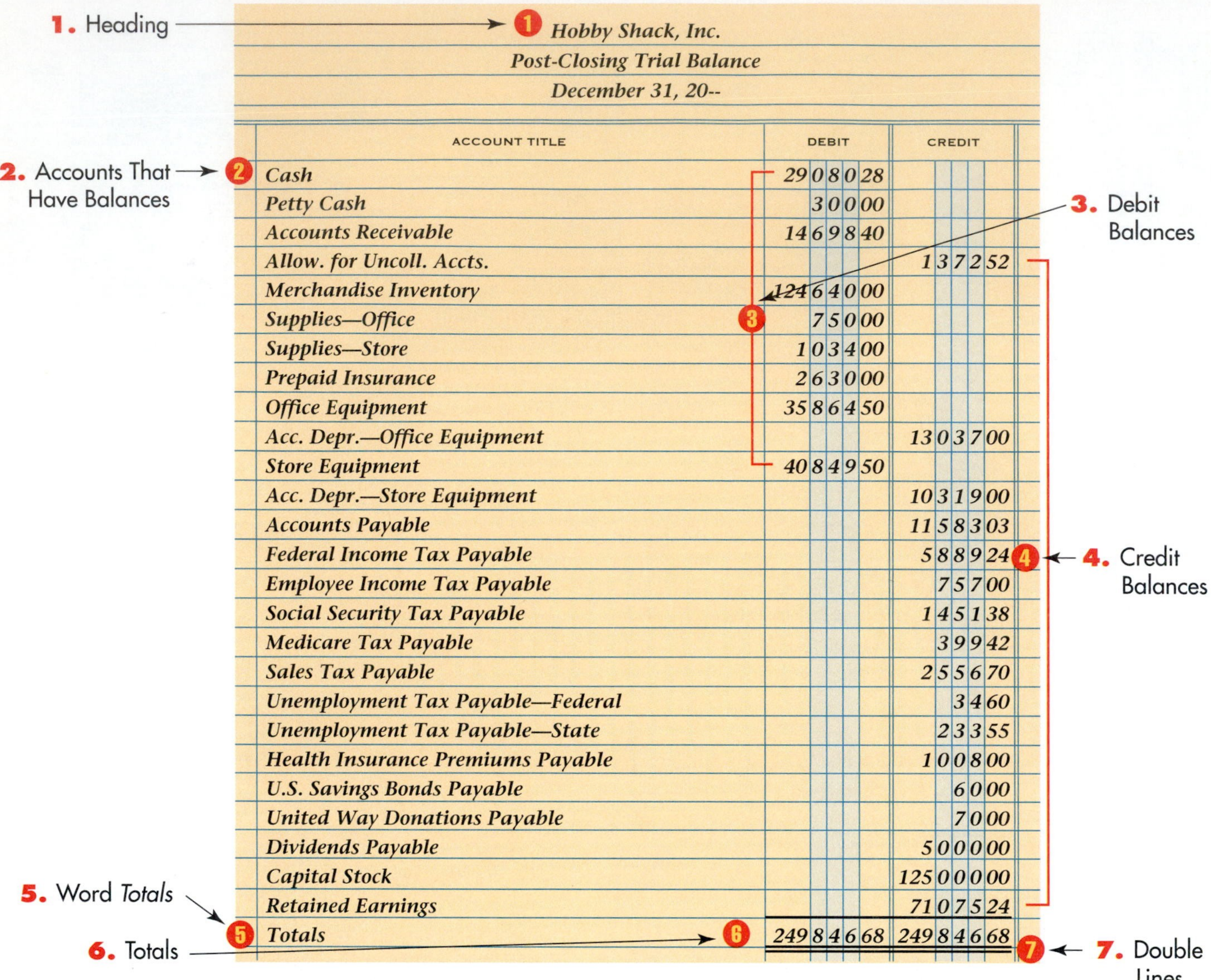

Hobby Shack, Inc.
Post-Closing Trial Balance
December 31, 20--

ACCOUNT TITLE	DEBIT	CREDIT
Cash	29 080 28	
Petty Cash	300 00	
Accounts Receivable	14 698 40	
Allow. for Uncoll. Accts.		1 372 52
Merchandise Inventory	124 640 00	
Supplies—Office	750 00	
Supplies—Store	1 034 00	
Prepaid Insurance	2 630 00	
Office Equipment	35 864 50	
Acc. Depr.—Office Equipment		13 037 00
Store Equipment	40 849 50	
Acc. Depr.—Store Equipment		10 319 00
Accounts Payable		11 583 03
Federal Income Tax Payable		5 889 24
Employee Income Tax Payable		757 00
Social Security Tax Payable		1 451 38
Medicare Tax Payable		399 42
Sales Tax Payable		2 556 70
Unemployment Tax Payable—Federal		34 60
Unemployment Tax Payable—State		233 55
Health Insurance Premiums Payable		1 008 00
U.S. Savings Bonds Payable		60 00
United Way Donations Payable		70 00
Dividends Payable		5 000 00
Capital Stock		125 000 00
Retained Earnings		71 075 24
Totals	249 846 68	249 846 68

A post-closing trial balance is prepared to prove the equality of debits and credits in the general ledger and to prepare the general ledger for the next fiscal period. Account balances on the post-closing trial balance agree with the balances on the balance sheet shown in Chapter 15.

STEPS: PREPARING A POST-CLOSING TRIAL BALANCE

1. Write the post-closing trial balance heading on three lines.
2. List all general ledger accounts that have balances in the Account Title column.
3. Write the balance of each asset account in the Debit column. Write the balance of each contra account in the Credit column.
4. Write the balance of each liability and capital account in the Credit column.
5. Write the word *Totals* on the next line below the last account title.
6. Total the columns and write the totals, *$249,846.68*, on the Totals line.
7. Verify equality. Rule double lines below both column totals.

ACCOUNTING CYCLE FOR A MERCHANDISING BUSINESS ORGANIZED AS A CORPORATION

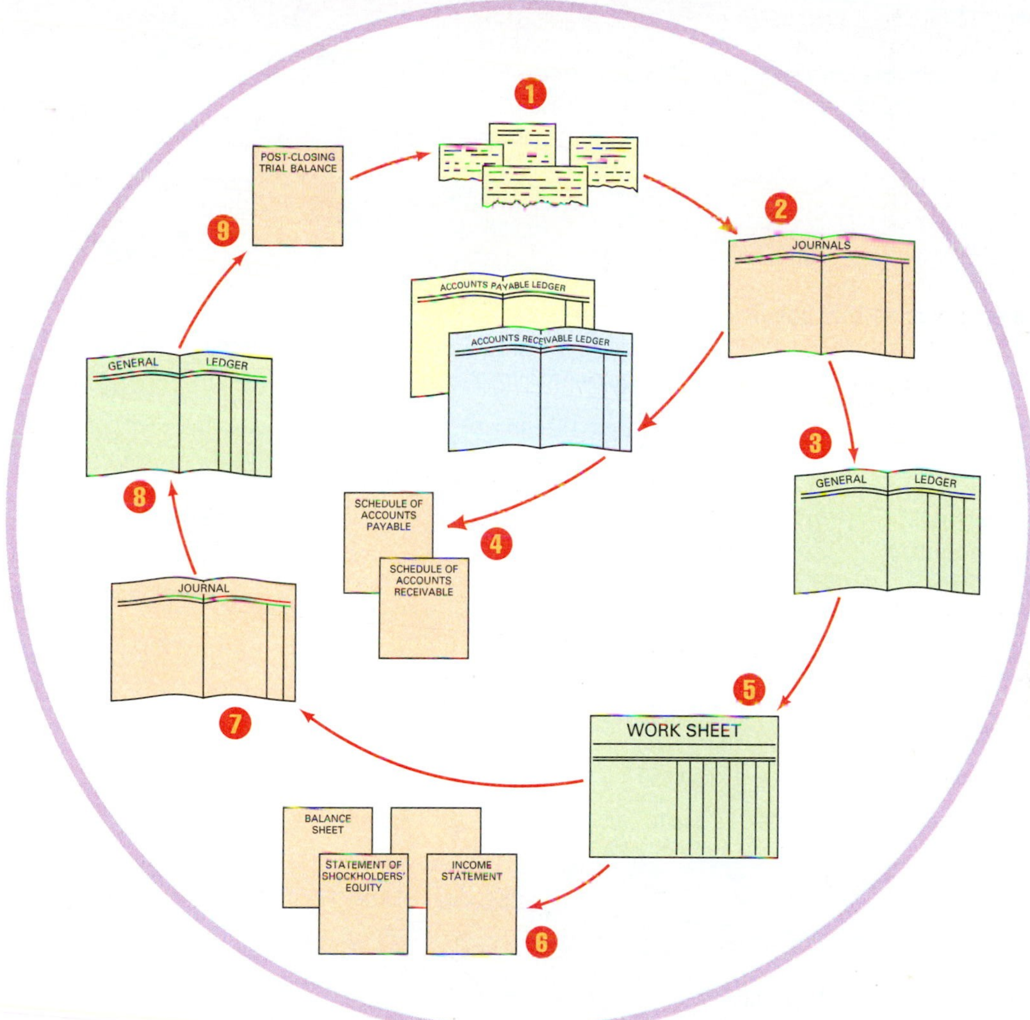

Service and merchandising businesses use a similar accounting cycle. The accounting cycles are also similar for a proprietorship and a corporation. Variations occur when subsidiary ledgers are used. Variations also occur in preparing financial statements.

STEPS

ACCOUNTING CYCLE FOR A MERCHANDISING BUSINESS

1. Source documents are checked for accuracy, and transactions are analyzed into debit and credit parts.
2. Transactions, from information on source documents, are recorded in journals.
3. Journal entries are posted to the accounts payable ledger, the accounts receivable ledger, and the general ledger.
4. Schedules of accounts payable and accounts receivable are prepared from the subsidiary ledgers.
5. A work sheet, including a trial balance, is prepared from the general ledger.
6. Financial statements are prepared from the work sheet.
7. Adjusting and closing entries are journalized from the work sheet.
8. Adjusting and closing entries are posted to the general ledger.
9. A post-closing trial balance of the general ledger is prepared.

audit your understanding

1. Which accounts are listed on a post-closing trial balance?
2. What is the purpose of preparing a post-closing trial balance?
3. In what order should accounts be listed on a post-closing trial balance?

work together 16-3

Preparing a post-closing trial balance

For the current year, the December 31 balances for Visual Art Center's balance sheet accounts after adjusting and closing entries have been posted are given below. Your instructor will guide you through the following example.

Account	Balance
Cash	$ 21,810.20
Petty Cash	350.00
Accounts Receivable	8,398.80
Merchandise Inventory	190,980.00
Supplies—Office	1,314.00
Supplies—Store	2,268.00
Prepaid Insurance	1,980.00
Accounts Payable	11,676.50
Sales Tax Payable	1,584.00
Capital Stock	100,000.00
Retained Earnings	113,840.50

1. Prepare a post-closing trial balance on the form provided in the *Working Papers*.

on your own 16-3

Preparing a post-closing trial balance

For the current year, the December 31 balances for Welding Supply's balance sheet accounts after adjusting and closing entries have been posted are given below. Work this problem independently.

Account	Balance
Cash	$ 26,485.00
Petty Cash	500.00
Accounts Receivable	15,487.00
Allow. for Uncoll. Accts.	1,457.00
Merchandise Inventory	134,152.00
Supplies	741.00
Prepaid Insurance	1,000.00
Equipment	25,487.00
Acc. Dep.—Equipment	12,450.00
Accounts Payable	13,154.00
Federal Income Tax Payable	2,489.00
Sales Tax Payable	1,548.00
Dividends Payable	5,000.00
Capital Stock	50,000.00
Retained Earnings	117,754.00

1. Prepare a post-closing trial balance on the form provided in the *Working Papers*.

SUMMARY

After completing this chapter, you can

1. Identify accounting concepts and practices related to adjusting and closing entries for a merchandising business organized as a corporation.
2. Record adjusting entries.
3. Record closing entries for income statement accounts.
4. Record closing entry for dividends.
5. Prepare a post-closing trial balance.

Explore Accounting

Freight Charges

When a business purchases merchandise from a vendor, ordinarily a third-party freight company is used to deliver the merchandise from the seller (vendor) to the buyer (purchasing business). As part of the terms of sale, the buyer and seller must agree on who is responsible for the freight charges. Those terms will be listed on the seller's sales invoice as either FOB shipping point or FOB destination. *FOB* is an abbreviation for the phrase "Free on Board." *FOB shipping point* means that the buyer is responsible for the freight charges. *FOB destination* means that the seller is responsible for the freight charges. *Shipping point* is the location where the freight company receives the merchandise from the seller. *Destination* refers to the receiving point of the buyer.

The accounting entries for freight charges can be complicated when one business is responsible for the freight charges according to the terms of sale, but the other business pays the freight company. For example, terms of sale may be FOB shipping point, meaning that the buyer is responsible for the freight charges. However, the freight company may require payment in advance. Therefore, the seller pays the freight company for the freight charges.

Four different situations may occur:

1. FOB shipping point, seller pays freight company
2. FOB shipping point, buyer pays freight company
3. FOB destination, seller pays freight company
4. FOB destination, buyer pays freight company

Research: Investigate this issue by reviewing collegiate Principles of Accounting or Intermediate Accounting textbooks. Also, you might interview a merchandising business manager to determine how the business accounts for freight charges. After completing your research, write a report on the issue of freight charges that would clearly explain the correct accounting procedures to a new accounting department employee.

16-1 APPLICATION PROBLEM

Journalizing adjusting entries

A partial work sheet for Cellar Books, Inc., for the year ended December 31 is given in the *Working Papers*.

Instructions:

1. Record the appropriate adjusting entries on page 22 of the general journal provided in the *Working Papers*. Use December 31 of the current year as the date.

16-2 APPLICATION PROBLEM

Journalizing closing entries

Use the partial work sheet for Cellar Books, Inc., given in Problem 16-1.

Instructions:

Prepare the following closing entries on page 23 of the general journal provided in the *Working Papers*.

1. Close the income statement accounts with credit balances.
2. Close the income statement accounts with debit balances.
3. Close Income Summary.
4. Close the dividend account.

16-3 APPLICATION PROBLEM 

Preparing a post-closing trial balance

For the current year, the December 31 balances for the balance sheet accounts of Cellar Books, Inc., after adjusting and closing entries have been posted are given below.

Account	Balance	Account	Balance
Cash	$ 16,485.00	Federal Income Tax Payable	$ 3,660.23
Petty Cash	400.00	Employee Income Tax Payable	1,248.20
Accounts Receivable	41,483.15	Social Security Tax Payable	903.96
Allow. for Uncoll. Accts.	2,406.15	Medicare Tax Payable	211.41
Merchandise Inventory	246,598.05	Sales Tax Payable	2,458.25
Supplies—Office	329.62	Unemployment Tax Payable—Federal	28.00
Supplies—Store	326.81	Unemployment Tax Payable—State	189.00
Prepaid Insurance	2,000.00	Health Insurance Premiums Payable	400.00
Office Equipment	38,458.25	U.S. Savings Bonds Payable	25.00
Acc. Dep.—Office Equipment	23,960.00	United Way Donations Payable	40.00
Store Equipment	41,478.50	Dividends Payable	3,000.00
Acc. Dep.—Store Equipment	31,100.00	Capital Stock	60,000.00
Accounts Payable	19,948.80	Retained Earnings	237,980.38

Instructions:

1. Prepare a post-closing trial balance on the form provided in the *Working Papers*.

16-4 APPLICATION PROBLEM   

Journalizing and posting adjusting and closing entries; preparing a post-closing trial balance

Use the following partial work sheet of Wilson Paint, Inc., for the year ended December 31 of the current year. The general ledger accounts and their balances as well as forms for completing this problem are in the *Working Papers*.

Instructions:

1. Journalize the adjusting entries using page 22 of a general journal.
2. Post the adjusting entries.
3. Journalize the closing entries using page 23 of a general journal.
4. Post the closing entries.
5. Prepare a post-closing trial balance.

	ACCOUNT TITLE	1 TRIAL BALANCE DEBIT	2 TRIAL BALANCE CREDIT	3 ADJUSTMENTS DEBIT	4 ADJUSTMENTS CREDIT	5 INCOME STATEMENT DEBIT	6 INCOME STATEMENT CREDIT
1	Cash	15,482.00					
2	Petty Cash	500.00					
3	Accounts Receivable	42,158.80					
4	Allow. for Uncoll. Accts.		684.20		(e) 3,560.00		
5	Merchandise Inventory	274,535.33		(d) 1,483.60			
6	Supplies—Office	6,158.84			(a) 5,847.10		
7	Supplies—Store	5,548.55			(b) 4,918.50		
8	Prepaid Insurance	8,000.00			(c) 7,200.00		
9	Office Equipment	22,158.66					
10	Acc. Depr.—Office Equipment		4,848.00		(f) 3,580.00		
11	Store Equipment	34,158.11					
12	Acc. Depr.—Store Equipment		12,480.00		(g) 6,140.00		
13	Accounts Payable		15,487.99				
14	Federal Income Tax Payable				(h) 1,356.14		
15	Employee Income Tax Payable		1,125.58				
16	Social Security Tax Payable		903.96				
17	Medicare Tax Payable		211.41				
18	Sales Tax Payable		2,345.99				
19	Unemployment Tax Pay.—Federal		25.60				
20	Unemployment Tax Pay.—State		172.80				
21	Health Insurance Premiums Payable		350.00				
22	U.S. Savings Bonds Payable		50.00				
23	United Way Donations Payable		60.00				
24	Dividends Payable		5,000.00				
25	Capital Stock		125,000.00				
26	Retained Earnings		136,843.68				
27	Dividends	20,000.00					
28	Income Summary				(d) 1,483.60		1,483.60
29	Sales		724,183.99				724,183.99
30	Sales Discount	1,694.48				1,694.48	
31	Sales Returns and Allowances	4,189.64				4,189.64	
32	Purchases	331,805.18				331,805.18	
33	Purchases Discount		3,418.47				3,418.47
34	Purch. Returns and Allowances		4,684.69				4,684.69
35	Advertising Expense	14,518.00				14,518.00	
36	Cash Short and Over	4.60				4.60	
37	Credit Card Fee Expense	12,180.00				12,180.00	
38	Depr. Exp.—Office Equipment			(f) 3,580.00		3,580.00	
39	Depr. Exp.—Store Equipment			(g) 6,140.00		6,140.00	
40	Insurance Expense			(c) 7,200.00		7,200.00	
41	Miscellaneous Expense	6,481.00				6,481.00	
42	Payroll Taxes Expense	14,184.60				14,184.60	
43	Rent Expense	20,150.00				20,150.00	
44	Salary Expense	168,483.60				168,483.60	
45	Supplies Expense—Office			(a) 5,847.10		5,847.10	
46	Supplies Expense—Store			(b) 4,918.50		4,918.50	
47	Uncollectible Accounts Expense			(e) 3,560.00		3,560.00	
48	Utilities Expense	5,484.97				5,484.97	
49	Federal Income Tax Expense	30,000.00		(h) 1,356.14		31,356.14	
50		1,037,876.36	1,037,876.36	34,085.34	34,085.34	641,777.81	733,770.75
51	Net Income after Federal Income Tax					91,992.94	
52						733,770.75	733,770.75

16-5 MASTERY PROBLEM

AUTOMATED ACCOUNTING PEACHTREE QUICKBOOKS

Journalizing and posting adjusting and closing entries; preparing a post-closing trial balance

Use the partial work sheet of Northern Lights for the year ended December 31 of the current year, on page 503. The general ledger accounts and their balances as well as forms for completing this problem are in the *Working Papers*.

Instructions:

1. Journalize the adjusting entries using page 18 of a general journal.
2. Post the adjusting entries.
3. Journalize the closing entries using page 19 of a general journal.
4. Post the closing entries.
5. Prepare a post-closing trial balance.

16-6 CHALLENGE PROBLEM

Inventory auditing challenges

For most businesses, merchandise inventory is a major portion of the business's assets. Therefore, reporting an accurate amount on the financial statements is important to accurate financial reporting. Whether a member of the business's accounting staff or an outside auditor audits the merchandise inventory of the business, determining an accurate count of the merchandise inventory is very important. Different types of merchandise present different kinds of challenges for the auditor.

a. *Actual count, common costs:* A sports store has 50 tennis rackets, all the same model. The rackets should be counted and multiplied times the cost per racket to determine the inventory value.
b. *Actual count, unique costs:* An automobile dealer has 60 new automobiles. Since each automobile probably has a unique and significant cost, the cost of each automobile should be totaled to determine the inventory value.
c. *Sampling:* A hardware store has many machine bolts. Since the value of each is low and there are many items, a small quantity may be counted or weighed. Then estimate the total cost based on the sample size or weight.
d. *Measuring/calculating:* An oil company stores crude oil in large tanks. The depth of the oil in the tank can be measured with a measuring rod; then the circumference of the tank can be measured. The total volume of crude oil can be calculated, then divided by the volume of one barrel of crude oil to determine the total barrels. This number can then be multiplied by the cost per barrel of crude oil.

Instructions:

How would you determine the value of the following inventory items? Record your answers in the *Working Papers*.

1. Grain in a grain elevator
2. Lumber in a lumber yard
3. Diamond rings in a jewelry store
4. Nails in a home improvement store

	ACCOUNT TITLE	1 TRIAL BALANCE DEBIT	2 TRIAL BALANCE CREDIT	3 ADJUSTMENTS DEBIT	4 ADJUSTMENTS CREDIT	5 INCOME STATEMENT DEBIT	6 INCOME STATEMENT CREDIT
1	Cash	5124 12					
2	Petty Cash	250 00					
3	Accounts Receivable	14843 30					
4	Allow. for Uncoll. Accts.		124 55		(e) 2120 00		
5	Merchandise Inventory	154318 22			(d) 3488 14		
6	Supplies—Office	3415 58			(a) 3148 66		
7	Supplies—Store	6184 56			(b) 5348 84		
8	Prepaid Insurance	7000 00			(c) 6000 00		
9	Office Equipment	21482 66					
10	Acc. Depr.—Office Equipment		6480 00		(f) 3580 00		
11	Store Equipment	40481 66					
12	Acc. Depr.—Store Equipment		18480 00		(g) 6140 00		
13	Accounts Payable		8418 36				
14	Federal Income Tax Payable				(h) 965 64		
15	Employee Income Tax Payable		458 00				
16	Social Security Tax Payable		528 24				
17	Medicare Tax Payable		123 54				
18	Sales Tax Payable		1415 30				
19	Unemployment Tax Pay.—Federal		4 00				
20	Unemployment Tax Pay.—State		27 00				
21	Health Insurance Premiums Payable		250 00				
22	U.S. Savings Bonds Payable		40 00				
23	United Way Donations Payable		60 00				
24	Dividends Payable		4000 00				
25	Capital Stock		80000 00				
26	Retained Earnings		89761 21				
27	Dividends	16000 00					
28	Income Summary			(d) 3488 14		3488 14	
29	Sales		514815 35				514815 35
30	Sales Discount	2154 94				2154 94	
31	Sales Returns and Allowances	6184 74				6184 74	
32	Purchases	301548 60				301548 60	
33	Purchases Discount		2154 65				
34	Purch. Returns and Allowances		2889 41				2154 65
35	Advertising Expense	2491 95				2491 95	2889 41
36	Cash Short and Over	5 25				5 25	
37	Credit Card Fee Expense	8154 62				8154 62	
38	Depr. Exp.—Office Equipment			(f) 3580 00		3580 00	
39	Depr. Exp.—Store Equipment			(g) 6140 00		6140 00	
40	Insurance Expense			(c) 6000 00		6000 00	
41	Miscellaneous Expense	410 00				410 00	
42	Payroll Taxes Expense	14184 60				14184 60	
43	Rent Expense	15400 00				15400 00	
44	Salary Expense	102240 30				102240 30	
45	Supplies Expense—Office			(a) 3148 66		3148 66	
46	Supplies Expense—Store			(b) 5348 84		5348 84	
47	Uncollectible Accounts Expense			(e) 2120 00		2120 00	
48	Utilities Expense	4154 51				4154 51	
49	Federal Income Tax Expense	4000 00		(h) 965 64		4965 64	
50		730029 61	730029 61	30791 28	30791 28	491720 79	519859 41
51	Net Income after Federal Income Tax					28138 62	
52						519859 41	519859 41

applied communication

Public speakers are judged by the ability of the audience to remember important points of their presentation. Effective public speakers use a variety of techniques to encourage the audience to listen to their message.

Instructions: Contact an instructor in your school or a local businessperson you have heard speak at school or community functions. Ask the person to describe the techniques used to help the audience listen and remember the message. Write a short report summarizing these techniques. Be prepared to present your report orally in class.

case for critical thinking

Antwan Jones, a new accounting clerk, has just experienced his first closing of a fiscal period. He questions why the adjustments on the work sheet have to be recorded in a general journal. Antwan maintains that the adjustments can simply be posted from the work sheet. As the senior accounting clerk, how would you respond to his statement?

SCANS workplace competency

Thinking Skills: Knowing how to learn

Concept: One way to learn new concepts is to build on knowledge already acquired. For example, you might learn how to create your own filing system after using a filing system created by someone else.

Application: Describe how the financial statements and adjusting and closing entries for a corporation differ from those of a proprietorship. Could a proprietorship prepare a statement of stockholders' equity?

auditing for errors

Editing an Accounting Policies Manual

The Sarbanes-Oxley Act requires publicly traded corporations to document and test their accounting systems. The documentation for Mateen Supply Corporation contains the following section on the preparation of closing entries. Identify the errors in this section of Mateen's accounting systems documentation.

Closing Entries

After the worksheet has been completed and verified, journal entries are recorded to close temporary accounts. Three entries are recorded:

1. Sales and contra purchases accounts are debited for their year-end balances. The total of the accounts is credited to Income Summary.
2. Purchasing and expense accounts are credited for their year-balances. The total of the accounts is debited to Income Summary.
3. If the company had a net income, record a debit to Income Summary for the difference of the closing entries recorded in steps 1 and 2. If the company had a net loss, record a credit to Income Summary for this difference. In either case, record the same amount to Retained Earnings to balance the entry.

analyzing Best Buy's financial statements

Generally accepted accounting principles require several forms of earnings per share to be reported. Earnings per share from the normal operations of the business is presented first. The effect on earnings per share from unusual, nonrecurring events is added or deducted. The net of these items is the earnings per share that is typically reported in the financial news.

Instructions

1. Use Best Buy's Consolidated Statement of Earnings in Appendix B to identify the components of basic earnings per share.
2. Determine the nature of each of the adjustments to earnings per share.
3. What is the label given to the net earnings per share amount?

Automated Accounting

End-of-Fiscal-Period Work for a Corporation

Adjusting Entries

At the end of a fiscal period, many accounts need to be adjusted to recognize changes and expenses of the fiscal period. Supplies accounts need to be adjusted to reflect the portion of supplies that are an expense of the period and the portion that remains on hand as an asset. The period's depreciation on plant assets needs to be recorded as an expense. Federal income tax needs to be calculated and recorded. Merchandise inventory must be adjusted to show the amount of inventory on hand as an asset and the amount sold as part of the cost of goods sold. Adjusting entries are recorded in the general journal. The reference used for adjusting entries is *Adj.Ent.*

After all adjusting entries have been entered and posted, the file should be saved with the letters *BC* in the filename. *BC* stands for "Before Closing." Once closing entries are posted, it is very difficult to correct any errors that may have been made during the fiscal period. Therefore, having a file saved before the closing entries ensures that a before-closing file exists if corrections are necessary.

Closing Entries

In an automated accounting system, closing entries are generated and posted by the software. *Automated Accounting 8.0* automatically prepares all closing entries.

1. Choose Generate Closing Journal Entries from the Options menu.
2. Click Yes to generate the closing entries.

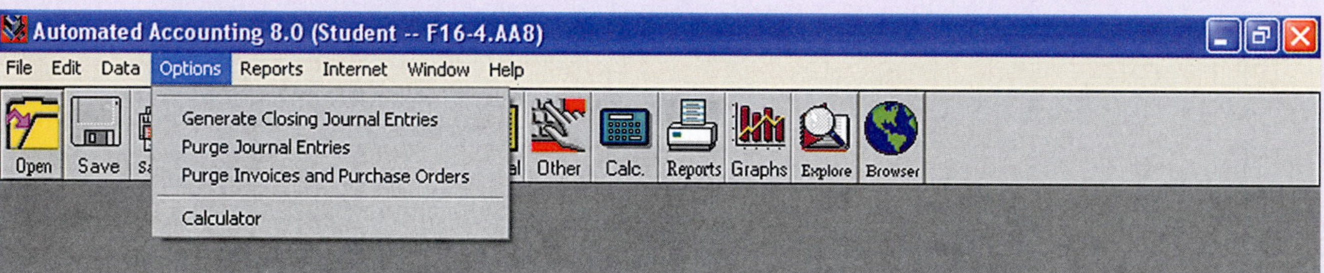

3. The general journal will appear, containing the journal entries. The journal entries should be examined for accuracy.
4. Click the Post button.
5. Display a post-closing trial balance report.
   a. Click on the Reports toolbar button, or choose the Report Selection menu item from the Reports menu.
   b. Select the Ledger Reports option button from the Select a Report Group list.
   c. Choose Trial Balance from the Choose a Report to Display list.
6. After closing entries are generated and posted, the file should be saved again with the letters *AC* in the filename. *AC* stands for "After Closing."

AUTOMATING APPLICATION PROBLEM 16-4: Journalizing and posting adjusting and closing entries; preparing a post-closing trial balance

Instructions:

1. Load *Automated Accounting 8.0* or higher software.
2. Select data file F16-4 from the appropriate directory/folder.
3. Select File from the menu bar and choose the Save As menu command. Key the path to the drive and directory that contains your data files. Save the data file with a filename of F16-4BC XXX XXX (where the X's are your first and last name and *BC* stands for "Before Closing").

4. Access Problem Instructions through the Browser Tool. Read the Problem Instructions screen.
5. Key the adjusting entries from the work sheet in Application Problem 16-4.
6. Save your file and exit the Automated Accounting software.

AUTOMATING MASTERY PROBLEM 16-5: Journalizing and posting adjusting and closing entries; preparing a post-closing trial balance

Instructions:

1. Load *Automated Accounting 8.0* or higher software.
2. Select data file F16-5 from the appropriate directory/folder.
3. Select File from the menu bar and choose the Save As menu command. Key the path to the drive and directory that contains your data files. Save the data file with a filename of F16-5BC XXX XXX (where the X's are your first and last name and *BC* stands for "Before Closing").
4. Access Problem Instructions through the Browser Tool. Read the Problem Instructions screen.
5. Key the adjusting entries from the work sheet in Mastery Problem 16-5.
6. Save your file and exit the Automated Accounting software.

An Accounting Cycle for a Corporation: End-of-Fiscal-Period Work

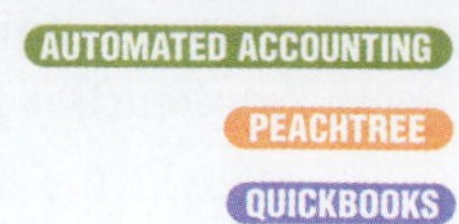

The ledgers used in Reinforcement Activity 2—Part A are needed to complete Reinforcement Activity 2—Part B.

Reinforcement Activity 2—Part B includes those accounting activities needed to complete the accounting cycle of Medical Services Company (MSC).

END-OF-FISCAL-PERIOD WORK

Instructions:

12. Prepare a trial balance on a work sheet. Use December 31 of the current year as the date.
13. Complete the work sheet using the following adjustment information:

a.	Office supplies inventory	$ 476.60
b.	Store supplies inventory	817.00
c.	Merchandise inventory	33,278.01
d.	Uncollectible accounts are 2.0% of credit sales of $65,000.00	
e.	Value of prepaid insurance	$ 500.00
f.	Estimate of office equipment depreciation	3,520.00
g.	Estimate of store equipment depreciation	2,240.00

14. Using the tax table shown in Chapter 14, calculate federal income tax expense and record the income tax adjustment on the work sheet.
15. Prepare an income statement. Figure and record the following component percentages: (a) cost of merchandise sold, (b) gross profit on sales, (c) total expenses, and (d) net income or loss before federal income tax. Round percentage calculations to the nearest 0.1%.
16. Prepare a statement of stockholders' equity. The company had 9,500 shares of $1.00 par value stock outstanding on January 1. The company issued an additional 500 shares during the year.
17. Prepare a balance sheet in report form.
18. Calculate the earnings per share and price-earnings ratio. The current market price of the stock is $87.50.
19. Use page 13 of a general journal. Journalize and post the adjusting entries.
20. Use page 14 of a general journal. Journalize and post the closing entries.
21. Prepare a post-closing trial balance.

The following activities are included in the Zenith Global Imports simulation:

1. Recording transactions in special journals from source documents.
2. Posting items to be posted individually to a general ledger and subsidiary ledgers.
3. Recording a payroll in a payroll register. Updating the employee earnings records. Recording payroll journal entries.
4. Posting column totals to a general ledger.
5. Preparing schedules of accounts receivable and accounts payable from subsidiary ledgers.
6. Preparing a trial balance on a work sheet.
7. Planning adjustments and completing a work sheet.
8. Preparing financial statements.
9. Journalizing and posting adjusting entries.
10. Journalizing and posting closing entries.
11. Preparing a post-closing trial balance.

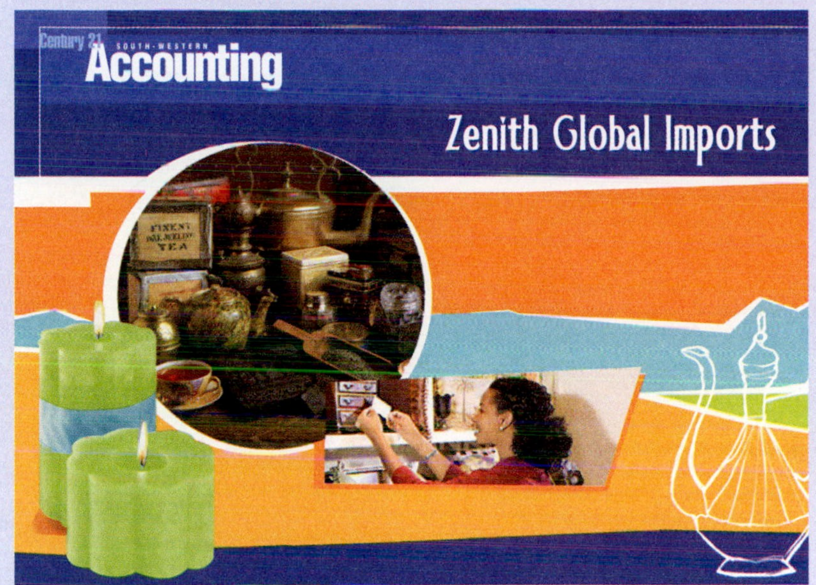

Zenith Global Imports

This simulation covers the realistic transactions completed by Zenith Global Imports. The business sells imported goods, including fabrics, clothing, furniture, and decorative accessories.

Transactions are recorded in special journals similar to the ones used by Hobby Shack, Inc., in this accounting cycle. The activities included in the accounting cycle for Zenith Global Imports are listed at the left.

This real-life business simulation comes with source documents. It is available in manual and automated versions. The automated version is used with *Automated Accounting* software.

APPENDIX A

Statement of Cash Flows

CASH FLOW ANALYSIS

Financial statements provide managers, investors, and other individuals with financial information about the operating efficiency and financial condition of a business. The income statement, balance sheet, and statement of stockholders' equity are prepared using accounting records of a business. On the income statement, revenues are recorded when the revenue is earned, regardless of when the cash is received. Expenses are recorded when incurred, regardless of when the cash is paid. The accounting method that records revenues when they are earned and expenses when they are incurred is called the *accrual basis of accounting*.

Accrual-based financial statements report useful information. Some individuals, however, may need more information about why cash is received and how cash is spent in a business. The cash receipts and cash payments of a company are called *cash flows*. A financial statement that reports the cash flows of a business for a fiscal period is called a *statement of cash flows*. The statement reports the source of all cash receipts and the reason for all cash payments during a fiscal period.

The statement of cash flows is divided into three sections: cash flows from operating activities, cash flows from investing activities, and cash flows from financing activities.

CASH FLOWS FROM OPERATING ACTIVITIES

The cash receipts and payments necessary to operate a business on a day-to-day basis are called *operating activities*. Cash inflows and outflows from operating activities are listed below.

Operating Activities	
Cash Inflows	**Cash Outflows**
Cash sales of merchandise	Cash paid for salaries
Cash sales of services	Cash paid for merchandise
Cash received on account	Cash paid on account
Interest income	Cash paid for supplies
	Cash paid for utilities
	Cash paid for interest

CASH FLOWS FROM INVESTING ACTIVITIES

Cash receipts and cash payments involving the sale or purchase of assets used to earn revenue over a period of time are called *investing activities*. Cash inflows and outflows from investing activities are listed below.

Investing Activities	
Cash Inflows	**Cash Outflows**
Sale of property/building Sale of investments Sale of machinery/equipment	Purchase of property/building Cash paid for investment Purchase of machinery/equipment

CASH FLOWS FROM FINANCING ACTIVITIES

Cash receipts and payments involving debt or equity transactions are called *financing activities*. Cash inflows and outflows from financing activities are listed below.

Financing Activities	
Cash Inflows	**Cash Outflows**
Issuing stock Long-term loans Issuing bonds	Payment of cash dividends Repayment of loan principal Retirement of bond principal

PREPARING THE OPERATING ACTIVITIES SECTION OF A STATEMENT OF CASH FLOWS

The first item listed in the operating activities section is the net income for the period. Since this amount is calculated using the accrual basis of accounting, several adjustments must be made to adjust the net income to actual cash flow from operating activities.

Adjusting Net Income for Depreciation

Depreciation expense is recorded on the income statement and reduces net income. However, depreciation expense is a non-cash expense, because cash is not paid out for depreciation. Therefore, even though it is an expense, it is not an outflow of cash. Since it has already been subtracted to determine net income, it has to be added back in when adjusting net income to cash flow. Sanibel Sports recorded $1,500.00 of depreciation expense for 20X2. The adjustment to add back in the amount of depreciation expense is the first adjustment listed on the statement of cash flows for Sanibel Sports on page A-5.

Adjusting Net Income for Changes in Current Assets

Increases and decreases in current assets affect cash flows and require adjustments. The balance in accounts receivable for Sanibel Sports on December 31, 20X1, was $78,550.00. On December 31, 20X2, the balance was $64,270.00. The accounts receivable account balance decreased by $14,280.00 during the year. A decrease in accounts receivable means that the sales amount reported on the income statement was less than the cash received on account. The $14,280.00 decrease in accounts receivable represents additional cash that has been received and is added to net income to determine cash flow on Sanibel Sports' statement of cash flows.

The balance in the supplies account for Sanibel Sports on December 31, 20X1, was $6,702.00. On December 31, 20X2, the balance was $7,377.00. The supplies account balance increased by $675.00 during the year. An

land sold by Sanibel during this period. Further investigation reveals that Sanibel sold the land for $10,300.00 during 20X2. The sale of land is an inflow of cash of $10,300.00. This amount is shown as an inflow of cash on Sanibel Sports' statement of cash flows.

When the changes in all long-term asset accounts have been analyzed and cash flows listed, the net cash flows from investing activities ($39,700.00), is calculated and recorded.

PREPARING THE FINANCING ACTIVITIES SECTION OF A STATEMENT OF CASH FLOWS

The third section of the statement of cash flows reports the cash effect of financing activities. Cash flows resulting from a company's financial activities are identified by analyzing the changes in long-term debt and stockholders' equity accounts. The balance in the loans payable account for Sanibel Sports on December 31, 20X1, was zero. On December 31, 20X2, the balance was $12,500.00. The $12,500.00 increase represents the proceeds from a loan Sanibel Sports received. This amount is shown as an inflow of cash on Sanibel Sports' statement of cash flows.

The balance in the retained earnings account for Sanibel Sports on December 31, 20X1, was $73,670.00. On December 31, 20X2, the balance was $128,020.00. The change in this account is caused by two items. The retained earnings account increases by the amount of net income for a period and decreases by the amount of dividends paid during a period. The beginning balance of $73,670.00, plus the net income of $62,350.00, would give a balance of $136,020.00. Any difference between that amount and the actual ending balance in retained earnings is caused by dividends. Therefore, the amount of dividends declared by Sanibel Sports this period equals $8,000.00. Since this was a cash dividend, this amount is shown as an outflow of cash on Sanibel Sports' statement of cash flows.

Retained Earnings, beginning balance	$ 73,670.00
Plus net income	62,350.00
Equals	$136,020.00
Minus current balance of Retained Earnings	128,020.00
Equals dividend paid	$ 8,000.00

When all the changes in long-term debt and stockholder equity accounts have been analyzed and cash flows listed, the net cash flows from financing activities, $4,500.00, is calculated and recorded.

increase in supplies means that Sanibel Sports bought more supplies than it used during the period. The amount of supplies used is listed on the income statement as an expense and reduces net income. The $675.00 increase in supplies represents additional cash that was used and is deducted from net income to determine cash flow on Sanibel Sports' statement of cash flows.

In a similar manner, all decreases in current assets will be added to net income as an adjustment. All increases in current assets will be deducted from net income as an adjustment.

Effect of Changes in Current Assets on Cash Flows	
Increases in current assets →	Deducted from net income
Decreases in current assets →	Added to net income

Adjusting Net Income for Changes in Current Liabilities

Increases and decreases in current liabilities also affect cash flows and require adjustments. The balance in accounts payable for Sanibel Sports on December 31, 20X1, was $79,290.00. On December 31, 20X2, the balance was $63,400.00. The accounts payable account balance decreased by $15,890.00 during the year. A decrease in accounts payable means that the cash flow for purchases on account was more than the amount of purchases reported on the income statement. The $15,890.00 decrease in accounts payable represents additional cash that has been paid out and is deducted from net income to determine cash flow on Sanibel Sports' statement of cash flows.

The balance in the salaries payable account for Sanibel Sports on December 31, 20X1, was $12,500.00. On December 31, 20X2, the balance was $20,900.00. The salaries payable account balance increased by $8,400.00 during the year. An increase in salaries payable means that not all of the salaries earned during the year were paid. The amount of salaries earned is listed on the income statement and reduces net income. The $8,400.00 increase in salaries payable represents a cash savings and is added to net income to determine cash flow on Sanibel Sports' statement of cash flows.

In a similar manner, all decreases in current liabilities will be deducted from net income as an adjustment. All increases in current liabilities will be added to net income as an adjustment.

Effect of Changes in Current Liabilities on Cash Flows	
Increases in current liabilities →	Added to net income
Decreases in current liabilities →	Deducted from net income

When all adjustments are recorded, the total adjustment to net income, $7,615.00, is calculated and entered on the statement of cash flows. Finally, net cash flows from operating activities, $69,965.00, are calculated and recorded.

PREPARING THE INVESTING ACTIVITIES SECTION OF A STATEMENT OF CASH FLOWS

The second section of the statement of cash flows reports the cash effect of investing activities. Cash flows resulting from a company's investing activities are identified by analyzing the changes in long-term asset accounts.

The balance in the equipment account for Sanibel Sports on December 31, 20X1, was $45,000.00. On December 31, 20X2, the balance was $95,000.00. The $50,000.00 increase represents the cost of new equipment purchased for cash. This amount is shown as an outflow of cash on Sanibel Sports' statement of cash flows.

The balance in the land account for Sanibel Sports on December 31, 20X1, was $35,500.00. On December 31, 20X2, the balance was $25,200.00. The $10,300.00 decrease represents

Sanibel Sports			
Statement of Cash Flows			
For Year Ended December 31, 20X2			
Cash Flows from Operating Activities:			
Net Income		62,350.00	
Adjustments to Net Income:			
Depreciation Expense	1,500.00		
Changes in current assets and liabilities:			
Decrease in accounts receivable	14,280.00		
Increase in supplies	(675.00)		
Decrease in accounts payable	(15,890.00)		
Increase in salaries payable	8,400.00		
Total adjustments to net income		7,615.00	
Net cash flows from operating activities			69,965.00
Cash Flows from Investing Activities:			
Purchased equipment		(50,000.00)	
Sold land		10,300.00	
Net cash flows from investing activities			(39,700.00)
Cash Flows from Financing Activities:			
Proceeds from loan payable		12,500.00	
Dividend payment		(8,000.00)	
Net cash flows from financing activities			4,500.00
Net Change in Cash			34,765.00
Cash Balance, Beginning of Period			62,750.00
Cash Balance, End of Period			97,515.00

COMPLETING THE STATEMENT OF CASH FLOWS

The sum of the operating, investing, and financing activities sections of the statement of cash flows are added in order to calculate the net increase or decrease in cash. If all cash transactions have been accounted for, the change in cash plus the beginning cash balance should equal the ending cash balance reported on the balance sheet.

Sanibel Sports' increase in cash, $34,765.00, is added to the beginning cash balance, $62,750.00, to calculate the ending cash balance, $97,515.00. The ending cash balance equals the cash balance reported on Sanibel Sports' balance sheet. Thus, the statement of cash flows has been prepared accurately.

PRACTICE PROBLEM A-1: PREPARING A STATEMENT OF CASH FLOWS

The following information was taken from the financial records of Bonita Body Shop for the year ending December 31, 20X2:

Net Income	$15,495.00
Depreciation Expense	2,300.00

Account Title	Balance Dec. 31, 20X1	Balance Dec. 31, 20X2
Cash	$70,700.00	$51,795.00
Accounts Receivable	10,500.00	12,300.00
Prepaid Insurance	7,000.00	6,000.00
Accounts Payable	13,000.00	15,500.00
Interest Payable	1,400.00	0.00
Equipment	18,000.00	22,000.00
Loans Payable	40,000.00	10,000.00
Retained Earnings	42,000.00	54,495.00

Additional information: Equipment was purchased for $4,000.00 cash.
All dividends were paid in cash.

Statement paper is provided in the *Working Papers.*

Instructions:

1. Complete a statement of cash flows for the year ending December 31, 20X2, for Bonita Body Shop.

PRACTICE PROBLEM A-2: PREPARING A STATEMENT OF CASH FLOWS

The following information was taken from the financial records of Terrace Yard Care for the year ending December 31, 20X2:

Net Income	$3,500.00
Depreciation Expense	2,000.00

Account Title	Balance Dec. 31, 20X1	Balance Dec. 31, 20X2
Cash	$13,300.00	$15,000.00
Accounts Receivable	20,500.00	25,900.00
Supplies	700.00	400.00
Accounts Payable	18,600.00	16,600.00
Salaries Payable	0.00	800.00
Equipment	4,000.00	5,500.00
Land	8,000.00	6,000.00
Loans Payable	0.00	3,000.00
Retained Earnings	11,200.00	13,700.00

Additional information: Equipment was purchased for $1,500.00 cash.
Land was sold for $2,000.00 cash.
All dividends were paid in cash.

Statement paper is provided in the *Working Papers.*

Instructions:

1. Complete a statement of cash flows for the year ending December 31, 20X2, for Terrace Yard Care.

Best Buy's Fiscal 2004 Annual Report and Form 10-K

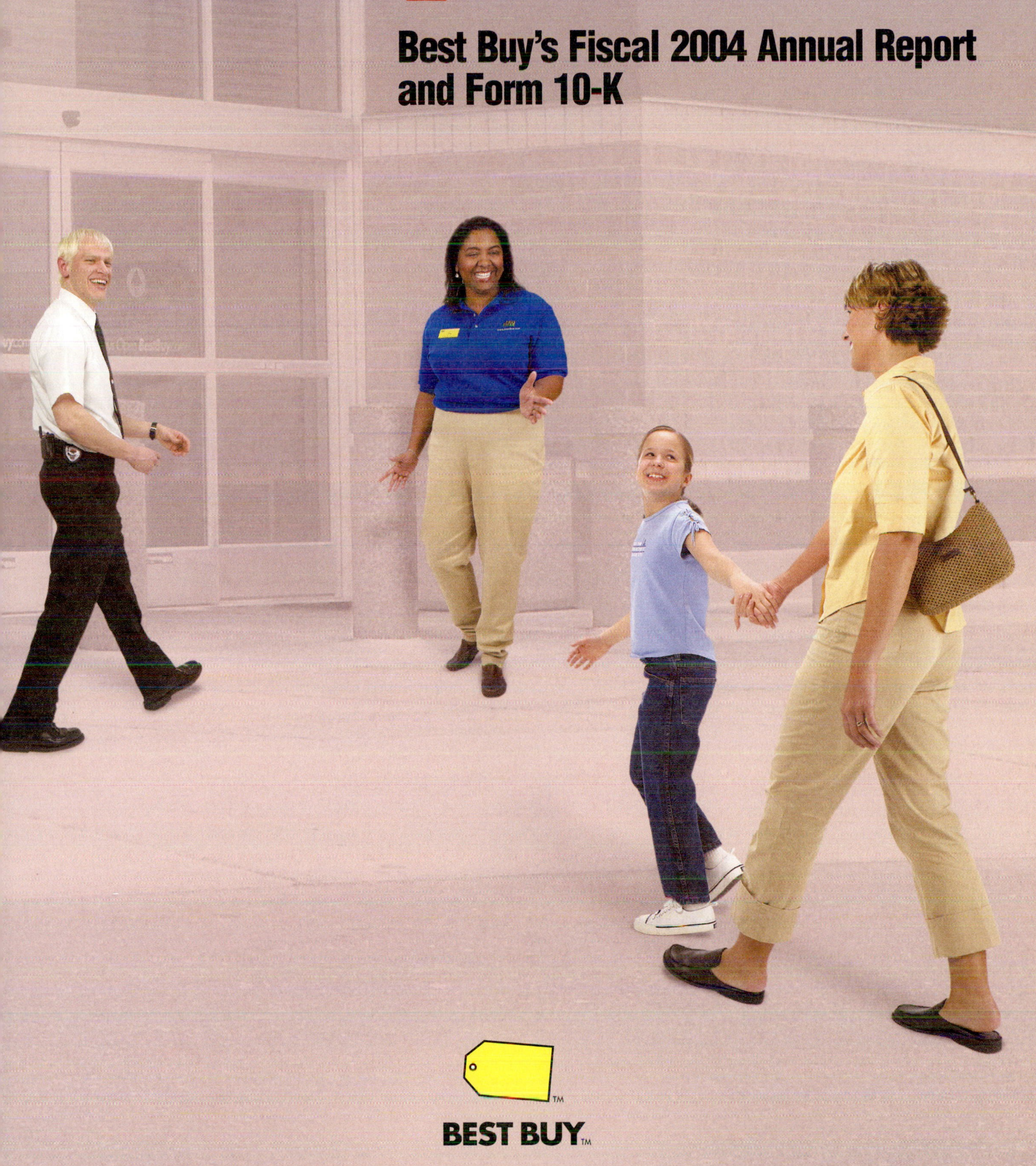

BEST BUY™

Fiscal 2004 Annual Report

11-Year Financial Highlights

$ in millions, except per share amounts

Fiscal Year[1]	2004	2003[2]	2002[3]	2001[3]
Statement of Earnings Data				
Revenue	$ 24,547	$ 20,946	$ 17,711	$ 15,189
Gross profit	6,197	5,236	3,770	3,012
Selling, general and administrative expenses	4,893	4,226	2,862	2,401
Operating income	1,304	1,010	908	611
Earnings (loss) from continuing operations	800	622	570	401
Loss from discontinued operations, net of tax	(29)	(441)	—	(5)
Loss on disposal of discontinued operations, net of tax	(66)	—	—	—
Cumulative effect of change in accounting principles, net of tax[2]	—	(82)	—	—
Net earnings (loss)	705	99	570	396
Per Share Data[4]				
Continuing operations	$ 2.44	$ 1.91	$ 1.77	$ 1.26
Discontinued operations	(0.09)	(1.36)	—	(0.02)
Loss on disposal of discontinued operations	(0.20)	—	—	—
Cumulative effect of accounting changes	—	(0.25)	—	—
Net earnings (loss)	2.15	0.30	1.77	1.24
Cash dividends declared and paid	0.40	—	—	—
Common stock price: High	62.70	53.75	51.47	59.25
Low	25.55	16.99	22.42	14.00
Operating Statistics				
Comparable store sales change[5]	7.1%	2.4%	1.9%	4.9%
Gross profit rate	25.2%	25.0%	21.3%	19.8%
Selling, general and administrative expense rate	19.9%	20.2%	16.2%	15.8%
Operating income rate	5.3%	4.8%	5.1%	4.0%
Year-End Data				
Working capital[6]	$ 1,223	$ 1,074	$ 895	$ 214
Total assets[6]	8,652	7,694	7,367	4,840
Long-term debt, including current portion[6]	850	834	820	296
Convertible preferred securities	—	—	—	—
Shareholders' equity	3,422	2,730	2,521	1,822
Number of stores				
U.S. Best Buy stores	608	548	481	419
Magnolia Audio Video stores	22	19	13	13
International stores	127	112	95	—
Musicland stores	—	1,195	1,321	1,309
Total retail square footage (000s)				
U.S. Best Buy stores	26,421	24,243	21,599	19,010
Magnolia Audio Video stores	218	189	133	133
International stores	2,800	2,375	1,923	—
Musicland stores	—	8,305	8,806	8,772

Please read this table in conjunction with Management's Discussion and Analysis of Financial Condition and Results of Operations, as well as the Consolidated Financial Statements and Notes, included in Item 7 and Item 8, respectively, of our Annual Report on Form 10-K. Certain prior-year amounts have been reclassified to conform to the current-year presentation. Results for fiscal 2004, 2003, 2002 and 2001 reflect the classification of Musicland's financial results as discontinued operations.

(1) Both fiscal 2001 and 1996 included 53 weeks. All other periods presented included 52 weeks.

(2) Effective on March 3, 2002, we adopted Statement of Financial Accounting Standards (SFAS) No. 142, *Goodwill and Other Intangible Assets.* During fiscal 2003, we completed the required goodwill impairment testing and recognized an after-tax, non-cash impairment charge of $40 that is reflected in our fiscal 2003 financial results as a cumulative effect of a change in accounting principle. Also effective on March 3, 2002, we changed our method of accounting for vendor allowances in accordance with Emerging Issues Task Force (EITF) Issue No. 02-16, *Accounting by a Reseller for Cash Consideration Received from a Vendor.* The change resulted in an after-tax, non-cash charge of $42 that also is reflected in our fiscal 2003 financial results as a cumulative effect of a change in accounting principle. Refer to Note 1 of the Notes to Consolidated Financial Statements included in Item 8 of our Annual Report on Form 10-K. Prior fiscal years have not been restated to reflect the pro forma effects of these changes. During fiscal 1994, we adopted SFAS No. 109, *Accounting for Income Taxes*, resulting in a cumulative effect adjustment of $1.

(3) During the third quarter of fiscal 2002, we acquired the common stock of Future Shop Ltd. During the fourth quarter of fiscal 2001, we acquired the common stock of Musicland Stores Corporation (Musicland) and Magnolia Hi-Fi, Inc. (Magnolia Hi-Fi). During fiscal 2004, Magnolia Hi-Fi began doing business as Magnolia Audio Video. The results of operations of these businesses are included from their respective dates of acquisition. As noted previously, Musicland's financial results are included in discontinued operations.

2000	1999	1998	1997	1996	1995	1994[2]
$ 12,494	$ 10,065	$ 8,338	$ 7,758	$ 7,215	$ 5,080	$ 3,007
2,393	1,815	1,312	1,046	934	690	457
1,854	1,464	1,146	1,006	814	568	380
539	351	166	40	120	122	77
347	216	82	(6)	46	58	42
—	—	—	—	—	—	—
—	—	—	—	—	—	—
—	—	—	—	—	—	(1)
347	216	82	(6)	46	58	41
$ 1.09	$ 0.69	$ 0.30	$ (0.02)	$ 0.18	$ 0.21	$ 0.17
—	—	—	—	—	—	—
—	—	—	—	—	—	—
—	—	—	—	—	—	—
1.09	0.69	0.30	(0.02)	0.18	0.21	0.17
—	—	—	—	—	—	—
53.67	32.67	10.20	4.37	4.94	7.54	5.24
27.00	9.83	1.44	1.31	2.13	3.69	1.81
11.1%	13.5%	2.0%	(4.7%)	5.5%	19.9%	26.9%
19.2%	18.0%	15.7%	13.5%	12.9%	13.6%	15.2%
14.8%	14.5%	13.7%	13.0%	11.3%	11.2%	12.6%
4.3%	3.5%	2.0%	0.5%	1.7%	2.4%	2.6%
$ 453	$ 662	$ 666	$ 563	$ 585	$ 609	$ 363
2,995	2,532	2,070	1,740	1,892	1,507	952
31	61	225	238	230	241	220
—	—	230	230	230	230	—
1,096	1,034	536	429	430	376	311
357	311	284	272	251	204	151
—	—	—	—	—	—	—
—	—	—	—	—	—	—
—	—	—	—	—	—	—
16,205	14,017	12,694	12,026	10,771	8,041	5,072
—	—	—	—	—	—	—
—	—	—	—	—	—	—
—	—	—	—	—	—	—

(4) Earnings per share is presented on a diluted basis and reflects a three-for-two stock split in May 2002; two-for-one stock splits in March 1999, May 1998 and April 1994; and a three-for-two stock split in September 1993.

(5) Comprised of revenue at stores and Internet sites operating for at least 14 full months, as well as remodeled and expanded locations. Relocated stores are excluded from the comparable store sales calculation until at least 14 full months after reopening. Acquired stores are included in the comparable store sales calculation beginning with the first full quarter following the first anniversary of the date of acquisition. The calculation of the comparable store sales percentage change excludes the impact of fluctuations in foreign currency exchange rates.

In the third quarter of fiscal 2004, we refined our methodology for calculating our comparable store sales percentage change. It now reflects the impact of non-point-of-sale (non-POS) revenue transactions. We refined our comparable store sales calculation in light of changes in our business. Previously, our comparable store sales calculation was based on store POS revenue. The comparable store sales change for fiscal 2004 has been computed based on the refined methodology. The comparable store sales changes for prior fiscal years have not been computed using the refined methodology. Refining the methodology for calculating our comparable store sales percentage change did not impact previously reported revenue, earnings or cash flows.

(6) Includes both continuing and discontinued operations.

Item 8. Financial Statements and Supplementary Data.

Consolidated Balance Sheets

$ in millions, except per share amounts

Assets	February 28, 2004	March 1, 2003
Current Assets		
Cash and cash equivalents	$ 2,600	$ 1,914
Receivables	343	312
Merchandise inventories	2,607	2,077
Other current assets	174	198
Current assets of discontinued operations	—	397
Total current assets	5,724	4,898
Property and Equipment		
Land and buildings	484	208
Leasehold improvements	861	719
Fixtures and equipment	2,151	2,108
Property under master and capital lease	78	54
	3,574	3,089
Less accumulated depreciation and amortization	1,330	1,027
Net property and equipment	2,244	2,062
Goodwill, Net	477	429
Intangible Assets	37	33
Other Assets	170	115
Noncurrent Assets of Discontinued Operations	—	157
Total Assets	$ 8,652	$ 7,694

See Notes to Consolidated Financial Statements.

Consolidated Balance Sheets

$ in millions, except per share amounts

Liabilities and Shareholders' Equity	February 28, 2004	March 1, 2003
Current Liabilities		
Accounts payable	$ 2,535	$ 2,195
Unredeemed gift card liabilities	300	222
Accrued compensation and related expenses	269	174
Accrued liabilities	649	538
Accrued income taxes	380	374
Current portion of long-term debt	368	1
Current liabilities of discontinued operations	—	320
Total current liabilities	4,501	3,824
Long-Term Liabilities	247	287
Long-Term Debt	482	828
Noncurrent Liabilities of Discontinued Operations	—	25
Shareholders' Equity		
Preferred stock, $1.00 par value: Authorized — 400,000 shares; Issued and outstanding — none	—	—
Common stock, $.10 par value: Authorized — 1 billion shares; Issued and outstanding — 324,648,000 and 321,966,000 shares, respectively	32	32
Additional paid-in capital	836	778
Retained earnings	2,468	1,893
Accumulated other comprehensive income	86	27
Total shareholders' equity	3,422	2,730
Total Liabilities and Shareholders' Equity	$ 8,652	$ 7,694

See Notes to Consolidated Financial Statements.

Consolidated Statements of Earnings

$ in millions, except per share amounts

For the Fiscal Years Ended	February 28, 2004	March 1, 2003	March 2, 2002
Revenue	$ 24,547	$ 20,946	$ 17,711
Cost of goods sold	18,350	15,710	13,941
Gross profit	6,197	5,236	3,770
Selling, general and administrative expenses	4,893	4,226	2,862
Operating income	1,304	1,010	908
Net interest (expense) income	(8)	4	18
Earnings from continuing operations before income tax expense	1,296	1,014	926
Income tax expense	496	392	356
Earnings from continuing operations	800	622	570
Loss from discontinued operations (Note 2), net of $17 and $119 tax	(29)	(441)	—
Loss on disposal of discontinued operations (Note 2), net of $0 tax	(66)	—	—
Cumulative effect of change in accounting principle for goodwill (Note 1), net of $24 tax	—	(40)	—
Cumulative effect of change in accounting principle for vendor allowances (Note 1), net of $26 tax	—	(42)	—
Net earnings	$ 705	$ 99	$ 570
Basic earnings (loss) per share:			
Continuing operations	$ 2.47	$ 1.93	$ 1.80
Discontinued operations	(0.09)	(1.37)	—
Loss on disposal of discontinued operations	(0.20)	—	—
Cumulative effect of accounting changes	—	(0.25)	—
Basic earnings per share	$ 2.18	$ 0.31	$ 1.80
Diluted earnings (loss) per share:			
Continuing operations	$ 2.44	$ 1.91	$ 1.77
Discontinued operations	(0.09)	(1.36)	—
Loss on disposal of discontinued operations	(0.20)	—	—
Cumulative effect of accounting changes	—	(0.25)	—
Diluted earnings per share	$ 2.15	$ 0.30	$ 1.77
Basic weighted average common shares outstanding (in millions)	323.3	321.1	316.0
Diluted weighted average common shares outstanding (in millions)	328.0	324.8	322.5
Pro forma effect of change in accounting principle for vendor allowances (Note 1):			
Earnings from continuing operations			$ 564
Basic earnings per share			1.78
Diluted earnings per share			1.75
Net earnings			$ 564
Basic earnings per share			1.78
Diluted earnings per share			1.75

See Notes to Consolidated Financial Statements.

Consolidated Statements of Cash Flows

$ in millions

For the Fiscal Years Ended	February 28, 2004	March 1, 2003	March 2, 2002
Operating Activities			
Net earnings	$ 705	$ 99	$ 570
Loss from and disposal of discontinued operations, net of tax	95	441	—
Cumulative effect of change in accounting principles, net of tax	—	82	—
Earnings from continuing operations	800	622	570
Adjustments to reconcile earnings from continuing operations to total cash provided by operating activities from continuing operations:			
Depreciation	385	310	242
Asset impairment charges	22	11	20
Deferred income taxes	(14)	(37)	15
Amortization of goodwill	—	—	3
Other	12	13	16
Changes in operating assets and liabilities, net of acquired assets and liabilities:			
Receivables	(27)	(89)	1
Merchandise inventories	(507)	(256)	(324)
Other assets	(22)	(36)	(24)
Accounts payable	318	(20)	575
Other liabilities	250	117	196
Accrued income taxes	197	111	253
Total cash provided by operating activities from continuing operations	1,414	746	1,543
Investing Activities			
Additions to property and equipment	(545)	(725)	(581)
Decrease in recoverable costs from developed properties	4	69	25
Acquisitions of businesses, net of cash acquired	(3)	(3)	(368)
Other, net	1	—	—
Total cash used in investing activities from continuing operations	(543)	(659)	(924)
Financing Activities			
Dividends paid	(130)	—	—
Issuance of common stock	114	40	48
Repurchase of common stock	(100)	—	—
Long-term debt payments	(17)	(13)	(5)
Net proceeds from issuance of long-term debt	—	18	726
Total cash (used in) provided by financing activities from continuing operations	(133)	45	769
Effect of Exchange Rate Changes on Cash	1	—	—
Net Cash Used in Discontinued Operations	(53)	(79)	(270)
Increase in Cash and Cash Equivalents	686	53	1,118
Cash and Cash Equivalents at Beginning of Year	1,914	1,861	743
Cash and Cash Equivalents at End of Year	$ 2,600	$ 1,914	$ 1,861
Supplemental Disclosure of Cash Flow Information			
Income tax paid	$ 306	$ 283	$ 139
Interest paid	22	24	25
Capital lease obligation incurred	26	—	—

See Notes to Consolidated Financial Statements.

Consolidated Statements of Changes in Shareholders' Equity

$ and shares in millions

	Common Shares	Common Stock	Additional Paid-In Capital	Retained Earnings	Accumulated Other Comprehensive Income (Loss)	Total
Balances at March 3, 2001	**312**	**$ 31**	**$ 567**	**$ 1,224**	**$ —**	**$1,822**
Net earnings	—	—	—	570	—	570
Other comprehensive loss, net of tax:						
Foreign currency translation adjustments	—	—	—	—	(5)	(5)
Other	—	—	—	—	(1)	(1)
Total comprehensive income						564
Stock options exercised	7	—	49	—	—	49
Tax benefit from stock options exercised	—	—	86	—	—	86
Balances at March 2, 2002	**319**	**31**	**702**	**1,794**	**(6)**	**2,521**
Net earnings	—	—	—	99	—	99
Other comprehensive income (loss), net of tax:						
Foreign currency translation adjustments	—	—	—	—	34	34
Other	—	—	—	—	(1)	(1)
Total comprehensive income						132
Stock options exercised	3	1	43	—	—	44
Tax benefit from stock options exercised	—	—	33	—	—	33
Balances at March 1, 2003	**322**	**32**	**778**	**1,893**	**27**	**2,730**
Net earnings	—	—	—	705	—	705
Foreign currency translation adjustments	—	—	—	—	59	59
Total comprehensive income						764
Stock options exercised	5	—	114	—	—	114
Tax benefit from stock options exercised	—	—	41	—	—	41
Vesting of restricted stock awards	—	—	3	—	—	3
Common stock dividends, $0.40 per share	—	—	—	(130)	—	(130)
Repurchase of common stock	(2)	—	(100)	—	—	(100)
Balances at February 28, 2004	**325**	**$ 32**	**$ 836**	**$ 2,468**	**$ 86**	**$3,422**

See Notes to Consolidated Financial Statements.

Notes to Consolidated Financial Statements

$ in millions, except per share amounts

1. Summary of Significant Accounting Policies

Description of Business

Best Buy Co., Inc. is a specialty retailer of consumer electronics, home-office products, entertainment software, appliances and related services with fiscal 2004 revenue from continuing operations of $24.5 billion. We operate two reportable segments: Domestic and International. The Domestic segment is comprised of U.S. Best Buy and Magnolia Audio Video (formerly operating as Magnolia Hi-Fi) operations. U.S. Best Buy stores offer a wide variety of consumer electronics, home-office products, entertainment software, appliances and related services, and operated 608 stores in 48 states and the District of Columbia at the end of fiscal 2004. Magnolia Audio Video stores offer high-end audio and video products with 22 stores in Washington, Oregon and California. Magnolia Audio Video was acquired in the fourth quarter of fiscal 2001. The International segment is comprised of Future Shop and Best Buy operations in Canada. At the end of fiscal 2004 we operated 108 Future Shop and 19 Canadian Best Buy stores. Future Shop and Canadian Best Buy stores offer products similar to those offered by U.S. Best Buy stores. Future Shop stores operate in all Canadian provinces, while the Canadian Best Buy stores operate in Ontario, Alberta and Manitoba. Future Shop was acquired in the third quarter of fiscal 2002.

On June 16, 2003, we sold our interest in Musicland to an affiliate of Sun Capital Partners Inc. As described in Note 2, Discontinued Operations, below, we have classified Musicland's financial results as discontinued operations for all periods presented. Prior to fiscal 2003, the Musicland business was included in our Domestic segment. These Notes to Consolidated Financial Statements, except where otherwise indicated, relate to continuing operations only.

Basis of Presentation

The consolidated financial statements include the accounts of Best Buy Co., Inc. and its subsidiaries. We have eliminated significant intercompany accounts and transactions. All subsidiaries are wholly owned.

Reclassifications

Certain previous-year amounts have been reclassified to conform to the current-year presentation. These reclassifications had no impact on net earnings, financial position or cash flows.

Use of Estimates in the Preparation of Financial Statements

The preparation of financial statements in conformity with accounting principles generally accepted in the United States (GAAP) requires us to make estimates and assumptions. These estimates and assumptions affect the reported amounts in the consolidated balance sheets and statements of earnings, as well as the disclosure of contingent liabilities. Actual results could differ from these estimates and assumptions.

Fiscal Year

Our fiscal year ends on the Saturday nearest the end of February. Fiscal 2004, 2003 and 2002 each included 52 weeks.

Cash and Cash Equivalents

We consider highly liquid investments with a maturity of three months or less when purchased to be cash equivalents. We carry these investments at cost, which approximates market value.

Merchandise Inventories

Merchandise inventories are recorded at the lower of average cost or market.

Property and Equipment

Property and equipment are recorded at cost. Property under master and capital lease is comprised of retail locations under our master lease program and point-of-sale equipment used in our retail stores. The related depreciation for master and capital lease assets is included in depreciation expense. Accumulated depreciation for property under master and capital lease was $12 and $3 as of February 28, 2004, and March 1, 2003, respectively. We compute depreciation using the straight-line method over the estimated useful lives of the assets or, in the case of leasehold improvements, over the shorter of the estimated useful lives or lease terms. Repairs and maintenance costs are charged directly to expense as incurred. Major renewals or replacements that substantially extend the useful life of an asset are capitalized and depreciated.

Estimated useful lives by major asset category are as follows:

Asset	Life (in years)
Buildings	30-40
Leasehold improvements	10-25
Fixtures and equipment	3-15
Property under master and capital lease	3-35

Impairment of Long-Lived Assets and Costs Associated with Exit Activities

We account for the impairment or disposal of long-lived assets in accordance with Statement of Financial Accounting Standards (SFAS) No. 144, *Accounting for the Impairment or Disposal of Long-Lived Assets,* which requires long-lived assets, such as property and equipment, to be evaluated for impairment whenever events or changes in circumstances indicate the carrying value of an asset may not be recoverable. An impairment loss is recognized when estimated undiscounted cash flows expected to result from the use of the asset plus net proceeds expected from disposition of the asset (if any) are less than the carrying value of the asset. When an impairment loss is recognized, the carrying amount of the asset is reduced to its estimated fair value.

We recorded pre-tax asset impairment charges of $22, $11 and $20, in fiscal 2004, 2003 and 2002, respectively. The impairment charges in fiscal 2004 related to corporate technology assets that were taken out of service based on changes in our business. The asset impairment charges in fiscal 2003 related to charges associated with vacating existing corporate facilities in connection with the relocation to our new corporate campus in fiscal 2004. The impairment charges in fiscal 2002 related to corporate technology assets, certain fixed assets and an e-commerce investment. Asset impairment charges are included in selling, general and administrative expenses (SG&A).

We adopted SFAS No. 146, *Accounting for Costs Associated with Exit or Disposal Activities,* on January 1, 2003. Since adoption, the present value of costs associated with location closings, primarily future lease costs, are charged to earnings when a location is vacated. Prior to adoption of SFAS No. 146, we recognized a liability when we made the decision to relocate or close the location.

Goodwill and Intangible Assets

Goodwill is the excess of the purchase price over the fair value of identifiable net assets acquired in business combinations accounted for under the purchase method. Effective March 3, 2002, we adopted SFAS No. 142, *Goodwill and Other Intangible Assets,* which eliminated the systematic amortization of goodwill. The Statement also requires that we review goodwill for impairment at adoption and at least annually thereafter.

$ in millions, except per share amounts

A reconciliation of reported earnings adjusted to reflect the adoption of SFAS No. 142, as if it were effective for all fiscal years presented, is provided below.

	2004	2003	2002
Reported earnings from continuing operations	$ 800	$ 622	$ 570
Add back goodwill amortization, net of tax	—	—	2
Adjusted earnings from continuing operations	800	622	572
Reported loss from discontinued operations, net of tax	(29)	(441)	—
Add back goodwill amortization, net of tax	—	—	16
Adjusted (loss) earnings from discontinued operations	(29)	(441)	16
Loss on disposal of discontinued operations, net of tax	(66)	—	—
Cumulative effect of change in accounting principles, net of tax	—	(82)	—
Adjusted net earnings	$ 705	$ 99	$ 588
Reported basic earnings per share from continuing operations	$2.47	$1.93	$1.80
Add back goodwill amortization	—	—	0.01
Adjusted basic earnings per share from continuing operations	2.47	1.93	1.81
Reported basic loss per share from discontinued operations	(0.09)	(1.37)	—
Add back goodwill amortization	—	—	0.05
Adjusted basic (loss) earnings per share from discontinued operations	(0.09)	(1.37)	0.05
Loss on disposal of discontinued operations	(0.20)	—	—
Cumulative effect of change in accounting principles	—	(0.25)	—
Adjusted basic earnings per share	$2.18	$0.31	$1.86
Reported diluted earnings per share from continuing operations	$2.44	$1.91	$1.77
Add back goodwill amortization	—	—	0.01
Adjusted diluted earnings per share from continuing operations	2.44	1.91	1.78
Reported diluted loss per share from discontinued operations	(0.09)	(1.36)	—
Add back goodwill amortization	—	—	0.05
Adjusted diluted (loss) earnings per share from discontinued operations	(0.09)	(1.36)	0.05
Loss on disposal of discontinued operations	(0.20)	—	—
Cumulative effect of change in accounting principles	—	(0.25)	—
Adjusted diluted earnings per share	$2.15	$0.30	$1.83

During the second quarter of fiscal 2003, we completed the transitional requirements for goodwill impairment testing. As a result of the transitional goodwill impairment testing, we determined that the carrying value of the assets of our Musicland and Magnolia Audio Video businesses, which were acquired in the fourth quarter of fiscal 2001, exceeded their current fair values. We determine fair values utilizing widely accepted valuation techniques, including discounted cash flows and market multiple analyses. We based Musicland's fair value on the then-current expectations for the business in light of the then-existing retail environment and the uncertainty associated with future trends in prerecorded music products. We based Magnolia Audio Video's fair value on the then-current expectations for the business in light of recent sales trends and the then-existing business environment, including an economic slowdown in the Pacific Northwest. The resulting after-tax, non-cash impairment charge was $348, of which $308 was associated with Musicland and $40 was associated with Magnolia Audio Video. The charge represented a complete write-off of the goodwill associated with these businesses. As described in Note 2, Discontinued Operations, below, we have classified Musicland's financial results as discontinued operations, including the related goodwill impairment charge.

During the fourth quarter of fiscal 2004, we completed our annual impairment testing of goodwill and tradename recorded in our International segment, using the same techniques as described above, and determined there was no impairment.

Goodwill totaled $477 and $429 at February 28, 2004, and March 1, 2003, respectively. The change in the International segment's goodwill balance from March 1, 2003, was the result of fluctuations in foreign currency exchange rates.

Intangible assets totaled $37 and $33 at February 28, 2004, and March 1, 2003, respectively. The only identifiable intangible asset included in our balance sheet is an indefinite-lived intangible tradename related to Future Shop, which is included in the International segment. The change in the intangible asset balance from March 1, 2003, was the result of fluctuations in foreign currency exchange rates.

The changes in the carrying amount of goodwill by segment for continuing operations were as follows:

	Domestic	International	Total
Balances at March 3, 2001	$ 67	$ —	$ 67
Goodwill resulting from acquisition	—	406	406
Systematic amortization of goodwill	(3)	—	(3)
Changes in foreign currency exchange rates	—	(5)	(5)
Balances at March 2, 2002	64	401	465
Goodwill resulting from acquisition	3	—	3
Final purchase price allocation adjustment	—	(5)	(5)
Impairment charge	(64)	—	(64)
Changes in foreign currency exchange rates	—	30	30
Balances at March 1, 2003	3	426	429
Changes in foreign currency exchange rates	—	48	48
Balances at February 28, 2004	$ 3	$ 474	$ 477

Insurance

We are self-insured for certain costs related to health, workers' compensation and general liability insurance, although we obtain third-party insurance coverage to limit our exposure to these claims. We estimate our self-insured liabilities using historical experience and valuations provided by independent third-party actuaries.

Income Taxes

We account for income taxes under the liability method. Under this method, deferred tax assets and liabilities are recognized for the estimated future tax consequences attributable to differences between the financial statement carrying amounts of existing assets and liabilities and their respective tax bases, and operating loss and tax credit carryforwards. Deferred tax assets and liabilities are measured using enacted tax rates in effect for the year in which those temporary differences are expected to be recovered or settled. The effect on deferred tax assets and liabilities of a change in tax rates is recognized in our statement of earnings in the period that includes the enactment date. A valuation allowance is recorded to reduce the carrying amounts of deferred tax assets if it is more likely than not that such assets will not be realized.

Long-Term Liabilities

The major components of long-term liabilities at February 28, 2004, and March 1, 2003, included deferred compensation plan liabilities, long-term rent-related liabilities, deferred income taxes and advances received under vendor alliance programs.

Foreign Currency

Foreign currency denominated assets and liabilities are translated into U.S. dollars using the exchange rates in effect at the balance sheet date. Results of operations and cash flows are translated using the average exchange rates throughout the period. The effect of exchange rate fluctuations on translation of assets and liabilities is included as a component of shareholders' equity in accumulated other comprehensive income. Gains and losses from foreign currency transactions have not been significant.

Revenue Recognition

We recognize revenue from the sale of merchandise at the time the customer takes possession of the merchandise. We recognize service revenue at the time the service is provided, the sales price is fixed or determinable, and collectibility is reasonably assured. Proceeds from the sales of gift cards are deferred until redeemed by the customer. Amounts billed to customers for shipping and handling are included in revenue.

We sell extended service contracts on behalf of an unrelated third party. In jurisdictions where we are not deemed to be the obligor on the contract, commissions are recognized in revenue at the time of sale. In jurisdictions where we are deemed to be the obligor on the contract, commissions are recognized in revenue ratably over the term of the service contract.

Sales Incentives

We frequently offer sales incentives that entitle our customers to receive a reduction in the price of a product or service. Sales incentives include discounts, coupons and any other offers that entitle a customer to receive a reduction in the price of a product or service by submitting a claim for a refund or rebate. For sales incentives in which we are the obligor, the reduction in revenue is recognized at the time the product is sold.

During fiscal 2004, we initiated a customer loyalty program which allows members to earn points for each purchase completed at U.S. Best Buy stores. Points earned enable members to receive a certificate that may be redeemed on future purchases at U.S. Best Buy stores. We account for our customer loyalty program in accordance with Emerging Issues Task Force (EITF) Issue No. 00-22, *Accounting for "Points" and Certain Other Time-Based or Volume-Based Sales Incentive Offers, and Offers for Free Products or Services to Be Delivered in the Future.* The value of points earned by our loyalty program members is included as a liability and a reduction of revenue at the time the points are earned based on the percentage of points that are projected to be redeemed.

Cost of Goods Sold

Cost of goods sold includes the total cost of products sold, costs of services provided, certain vendor allowances, customer shipping and handling charges, in-bound freight expenses, physical inventory losses, and handling and delivery costs associated with our online and direct-to-consumer businesses.

Vendor Allowances

We receive allowances from vendors as a result of purchasing and promoting their products. Vendor allowances provided as a reimbursement of specific, incremental and identifiable costs incurred to promote a vendor's products are included as an expense reduction when the cost is incurred. Subsequent to fiscal 2002, all other vendor allowances, including vendor allowances received in excess of our cost to promote a vendor's product, are initially deferred and recorded as a reduction of merchandise inventories. The deferred amounts are then included as a reduction of cost of goods sold when the related product is sold. Vendor allowances included in SG&A were approximately $92 and $118, in fiscal 2004 and 2003, respectively.

Prior to fiscal 2003, the majority of vendor allowances were included as a reduction of advertising expenses in SG&A (see Change in Accounting Principles — Goodwill and Vendor Allowances, below).

Selling, General & Administrative Expenses

SG&A includes payroll and benefit costs; occupancy costs; depreciation; advertising; vendor allowances that are a reimbursement of specific, incremental and identifiable costs to promote a vendor's products; outside service fees; costs associated with operating our distribution network that primarily relate to moving merchandise from distribution centers to stores; and long-lived asset impairment charges.

Advertising Costs

Advertising costs, which are included in SG&A, are expensed the first time the advertisement runs. Gross advertising expenses, before expense reimbursement from vendor allowances, for fiscal 2004, 2003 and 2002 were $675, $567 and $493, respectively.

Pre-Opening Costs

Non-capital expenditures associated with opening new stores are expensed as incurred.

Stock-Based Compensation

In December 2002, the Financial Accounting Standards Board (FASB) issued SFAS No. 148, *Accounting for Stock-Based Compensation — Transition and Disclosure*. SFAS No. 148 amends SFAS No. 123, *Accounting for Stock-Based Compensation*, to provide alternative methods of transition for a voluntary change to the fair value-based method of accounting for stock-based employee compensation. In addition, SFAS No. 148 requires expanded and more prominent disclosure in both annual and interim financial statements about the method of accounting for stock-based employee compensation and the effect of the method on reported results.

We have stock-based compensation plans including fixed stock option plans, restricted stock and an employee stock purchase plan. We have not adopted a method under SFAS No. 148 to expense stock options, but continue to apply Accounting Principles Board (APB) Opinion No. 25, *Accounting for Stock Issued to Employees*, and related Interpretations in accounting for these plans. Accordingly, no compensation expense has been recognized for stock option grants, as the exercise price equals the stock price on the date of grant. In addition, compensation expense has not been recognized for our employee stock purchase plan as it is intended to be a plan that qualifies under Section 423 of the Internal Revenue Code of 1986, as amended. Restricted stock awards result in compensation expense as discussed in Note 5, Shareholders' Equity, below.

$ in millions, except per share amounts

The table below illustrates the effect on net earnings and earnings per share as if we had applied the fair value recognition provisions of SFAS No. 123 to stock-based compensation for each of the last three fiscal years.

	2004	2003	2002
Net earnings, as reported	$ 705	$ 99	$ 570
Add: Stock-based compensation expense included in reported net earnings, net of tax[1]	5	1	1
Deduct: Stock-based compensation expense determined under fair value method for all awards, net of tax	(101)	(85)	(59)
Net earnings, pro forma	$ 609	$ 15	$ 512
Earnings per share:			
Basic — as reported	$2.18	$0.31	$1.80
Basic — pro forma	$1.88	$0.05	$1.62
Diluted — as reported	$2.15	$0.30	$1.77
Diluted — pro forma	$1.88	$0.05	$1.61

(1) Amounts represent the after-tax compensation costs for restricted stock awards.

The fair value of each stock option was estimated on the date of the grant using the Black-Scholes option-pricing model with the following assumptions:

	2004	2003	2002
Risk-free interest rate	3.3%	4.2%	4.9%
Expected dividend yield	0.8%	—	—
Expected stock price volatility	60%	60%	55%
Expected life of stock options	5.5 years	5.0 years	4.5 years

The weighted average fair value of stock options granted during fiscal 2004, 2003 and 2002 used in computing pro forma compensation expense was $30.93, $23.91 and $18.60 per share, respectively.

Derivative Financial Instruments

SFAS No. 133, *Accounting for Derivative Instruments and Hedging Activities,* requires that all derivatives be included on the balance sheet at fair value. Our only derivative financial instrument was an interest rate swap with a fair value of $4 and $5 as of February 28, 2004, and March 1, 2003, respectively. Our interest rate swap is included in long-term debt.

Change in Accounting Principles — Goodwill and Vendor Allowances

The adoption of SFAS No. 142 related to goodwill described above has been accounted for as a cumulative effect of a change in accounting principle and applied cumulatively as if the change had occurred at March 3, 2002, the beginning of fiscal 2003.

In September 2002, the EITF released Issue No. 02-16, *Accounting by a Reseller for Cash Consideration Received from a Vendor,* with final consensus reached in March 2003. EITF No. 02-16 establishes the accounting standards for recording vendor allowances in a retailer's income statement.

During fiscal 2003, we changed our method of accounting for vendor allowances in accordance with EITF No. 02-16. Based on the new standard, vendor allowances are considered a reduction in the price of a vendor's products or services and included as a component of cost of goods sold when the related product or service is sold, unless the allowance represents a reimbursement of a specific, incremental and identifiable cost incurred to sell a vendor's products or services. We continue to record vendor allowances that represent a reimbursement of a specific, incremental and identifiable cost incurred to sell a vendor's products or services as a reduction of the related cost in SG&A. Previously, and in accordance with GAAP, we had recognized and classified a majority of vendor allowances as a reduction of advertising costs in SG&A. The cumulative effect of the change in our method of accounting for vendor allowances resulted in an after-tax, non-cash charge to net earnings of $50, of which $8 was associated with Musicland. The effect of the change on the fiscal year ended March 1, 2003, was a decrease in net earnings from continuing operations of $1. As described in Note 2, Discontinued Operations, below, we have classified Musicland's financial results as discontinued operations, including the related cumulative effect of the change in accounting principle.

New Accounting Standards

In January 2003, the FASB issued Interpretation (FIN) No. 46, *Consolidation of Variable Interest Entities*, which requires the consolidation of, and disclosures about, variable interest entities (VIEs). VIEs are entities for which control is achieved through means other than voting rights. In December 2003, the FASB revised FIN No. 46 to incorporate all decisions, including those in previously issued FASB Staff Positions, into one Interpretation. The revised Interpretation supersedes the original Interpretation. In most circumstances, the requirements were effective immediately for all VIEs in which an interest was acquired after January 31, 2003. For variable interests in special purpose entities in which an interest was acquired before February 1, 2003, the requirements were effective for us at the end of fiscal 2004. Requirements for non-special purpose entities acquired before February 1, 2003, are effective for us at the end of the first quarter of fiscal 2005. FIN No. 46 has not had, and is not expected to have, a significant impact on our consolidated financial statements.

During fiscal year 2004, we adopted EITF Issue No. 03-10, *Application of Issue No. 02-16 by Resellers to Sales Incentives Offered to Consumers by Manufacturers*, which amends EITF No. 02-16. According to the amended guidance, if certain criteria are met, consideration received by a reseller in the form of reimbursement from a vendor for honoring the vendor's sales incentives offered directly to consumers (e.g., manufacturers' coupons) should not be recorded as a reduction of the cost of the reseller's purchases from the vendor. The adoption of EITF No. 03-10 did not impact reported net earnings, financial position or cash flows.

2. Discontinued Operations

During the fourth quarter of fiscal 2003, we committed to a plan to sell our interest in Musicland. On June 16, 2003, we sold our interest in Musicland to an affiliate of Sun Capital Partners Inc. The affiliate of Sun Capital Partners Inc. assumed all of Musicland's liabilities, including approximately $500 in lease obligations, in exchange for all of the capital stock of Musicland and paid no cash consideration. The transaction also resulted in the transfer of all of Musicland's assets, other than a distribution center in Franklin, Indiana, and selected nonoperating assets. The loss from discontinued operations for fiscal 2004 includes a loss on the disposal of discontinued operations (which was primarily non-cash) of $66, net of tax, related to the sale of Musicland. In connection with the sale, Musicland is purchasing transition support services from us for up to one year from the date of the sale, until Musicland is able to develop long-term service providers for these services. In accordance with SFAS No. 144, Musicland's financial results are reported separately as discontinued operations for all periods presented.

During fiscal 2003, we recorded an after-tax, non-cash impairment charge of $308 for the full write-off of goodwill related to our acquisition of Musicland. In addition, we recorded an after-tax, non-cash charge of $8 for the change in our method of accounting for Musicland vendor allowances. The charges are classified as cumulative effects of changes in accounting principles in discontinued operations (see Note 1, Summary of Significant Accounting Policies, above).

Report of Best Buy Management

To Our Shareholders:

Our management is responsible for the preparation, integrity and objectivity of the accompanying consolidated financial statements and the related financial information. The financial statements have been prepared in conformity with accounting principles generally accepted in the United States and necessarily include certain amounts that are based on estimates and informed judgments. Our management also prepared the related financial information included in this Annual Report on Form 10-K and is responsible for its accuracy and consistency with the financial statements.

The consolidated financial statements have been audited by Ernst & Young LLP, independent auditor, who were given unrestricted access to all financial records and related data, including minutes of all meetings of shareholders, the Board of Directors and committees of the Board of Directors. We believe that all representations made to the independent auditors during its audit were valid and appropriate. The independent auditor's role is to form an opinion as to the fairness with which such financial statements present our financial position and results of operations in accordance with accounting principles generally accepted in the United States. The report of Ernst & Young LLP is presented on the following page.

We maintain a system of internal control over financial reporting that is designed to provide reasonable assurance to management, the Audit Committee and the Board of Directors as to the reliability of our financial records and the protection of our shareholders' interests. The system includes a documented organizational structure and division of responsibility; established policies and procedures, including a code of conduct to foster a strong ethical climate, which are communicated throughout Best Buy; and the careful selection, training and development of employees. Internal auditors monitor the operation of the internal control system and report findings and recommendations to management and the Audit Committee, and corrective actions are taken to address control deficiencies and other opportunities for improving the system as they are identified. The Audit Committee, which is comprised completely of independent directors, further augments our system of internal control. The Audit Committee oversees our system of internal control, accounting practices, financial reporting and audits, and assesses whether their quality, integrity and objectivity are sufficient to protect shareholders' investments.

There are inherent limitations in the effectiveness of any system of internal control, including the possibility of circumvention or overriding of controls. Furthermore, the effectiveness of an internal control system can change with circumstances. Accordingly, even an effective internal control system can provide only reasonable assurance with respect to financial statement preparation. The concept of reasonable assurance is based on the recognition that the cost of a system of internal control should not exceed the related benefits. We believe our system provides the appropriate balance.

As of February 28, 2004, we believe our system of internal control over financial reporting was effective for providing reliable financial statements. We further believe the information contained in the accompanying consolidated financial statements and related financial information included in this Annual Report on Form 10-K fairly presents, in all material respects, the financial condition and results of operations of our Company.

Bradbury H. Anderson
Vice Chairman
and Chief Executive Officer

Darren R. Jackson
Executive Vice President — Finance
and Chief Financial Officer

Report of Independent Auditors

Shareholders and Board of Directors
Best Buy Co., Inc.

We have audited the accompanying consolidated balance sheets of Best Buy Co., Inc. and subsidiaries (the Company) as of February 28, 2004, and March 1, 2003, and the related consolidated statements of earnings, changes in shareholders' equity, and cash flows for each of the three years in the period ended February 28, 2004. Our audits also included the financial statement schedule listed in Item 15(a). These financial statements and schedule are the responsibility of the Company's management. Our responsibility is to express an opinion on these financial statements and schedule based on our audits.

We conducted our audits in accordance with auditing standards generally accepted in the United States. Those standards require that we plan and perform the audit to obtain reasonable assurance about whether the financial statements are free of material misstatement. An audit includes examining, on a test basis, evidence supporting the amounts and disclosures in the financial statements. An audit also includes assessing the accounting principles used and significant estimates made by management, as well as evaluating the overall financial statement presentation. We believe that our audits provide a reasonable basis for our opinion.

In our opinion, the financial statements referred to above present fairly, in all material respects, the consolidated financial position of Best Buy Co., Inc. and subsidiaries at February 28, 2004, and March 1, 2003, and the consolidated results of their operations and their cash flows for each of the three years in the period ended February 28, 2004, in conformity with accounting principles generally accepted in the United States. Also, in our opinion, the related financial statement schedule, when considered in relation to the basic financial statements taken as a whole, presents fairly, in all material respects, the information set forth therein.

As discussed in Notes 1 and 2 to the consolidated financial statements, the Company changed its method of accounting for goodwill to conform to Statement of Financial Accounting Standards No. 142 and its method of accounting for cash consideration received from a vendor to conform to Emerging Issues Task Force No. 02-16 effective March 3, 2002.

Ernst & Young LLP

Minneapolis, Minnesota
March 29, 2004

APPENDIX C

Accounting Concepts

The following accounting concepts and their definitions are provided in this appendix for ready reference.

ACCOUNTING CONCEPTS

Accounting personnel are guided in their work by generally accepted accounting concepts. Ten commonly accepted accounting concepts are described in this appendix. Each concept is fully explained in the text the first time an application of the concept is described. Throughout the textbook, each time a concept application occurs, a concept reference is given, such as [*CONCEPT: Business Entity*].

1. ACCOUNTING PERIOD CYCLE [Chapter 6]
   Changes in financial information are reported for a specific period of time in the form of financial statements.
2. ADEQUATE DISCLOSURE [Chapter 7]
   Financial statements contain all information necessary to understand a business's financial condition.
3. BUSINESS ENTITY [Chapter 1]
   Financial information is recorded and reported separately from the owner's personal financial information.
4. CONSISTENT REPORTING [Chapter 6]
   The same accounting procedures are followed in the same way in each accounting period.
5. GOING CONCERN [Chapter 7]
   Financial statements are prepared with the expectation that a business will remain in operation indefinitely.
6. HISTORICAL COST [Chapter 9]
   The actual amount paid for merchandise or other items bought is recorded.
7. MATCHING EXPENSES WITH REVENUE [Chapter 6]
   Revenue from business activities and expenses associated with earning that revenue are recorded in the same accounting period.
8. OBJECTIVE EVIDENCE [Chapter 3]
   A source document is prepared for each transaction.
9. REALIZATION OF REVENUE [Chapter 1]
   Revenue is recorded at the time goods or services are sold.
10. UNIT OF MEASUREMENT [Chapter 1]
   Business transactions are stated in numbers that have common values—that is, using a common unit of measurement.

Using a Calculator and Computer Keypad

KINDS OF CALCULATORS

Many different models of calculators, both desktop and handheld, are available. All calculators have their own features and particular placement of operating keys. Therefore, it is necessary to refer to the operator's manual for specific instructions and locations of the operating keys for the calculator being used. A typical keyboard of a desktop calculator is shown in the illustration.

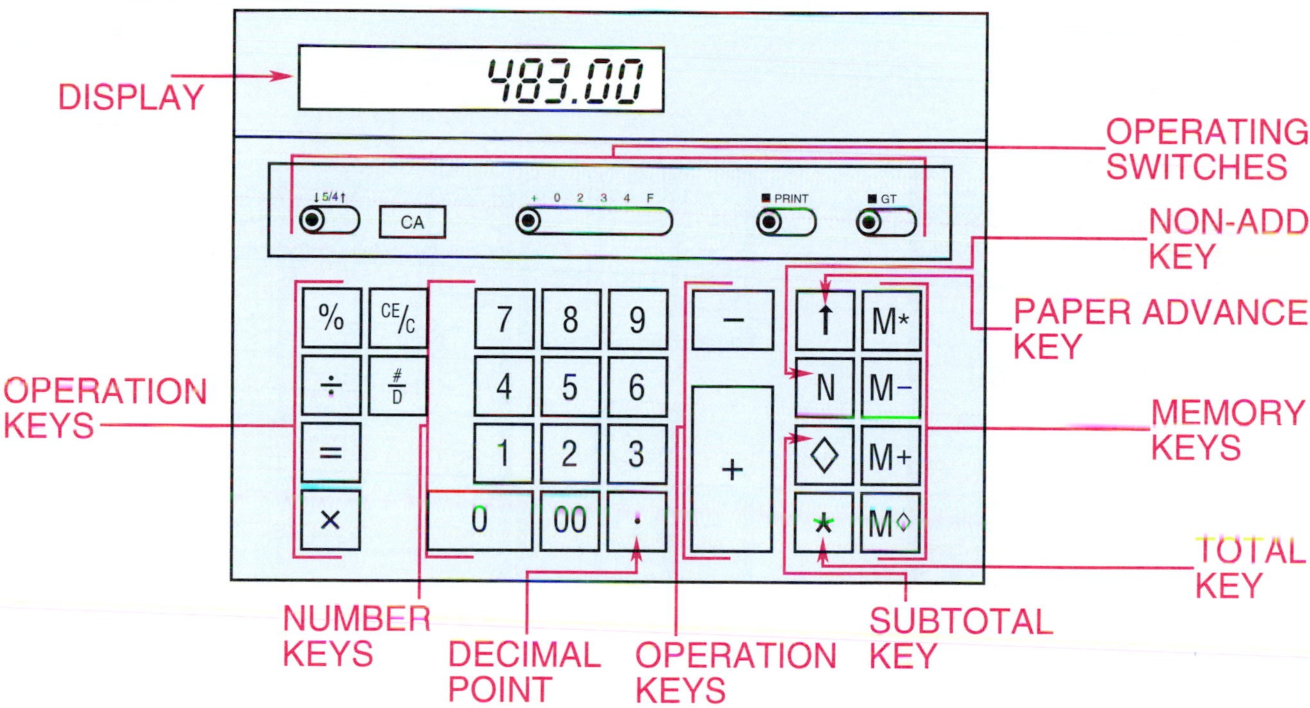

DESKTOP CALCULATOR SETTINGS

Several operating switches on a desktop calculator must be engaged before the calculator will produce the desired results.

The *decimal selector* sets the appropriate decimal places necessary for the numbers that will be entered. For example, if the decimal selector is set at 2, both the numbers entered and the answer will have two decimal places. If the decimal selector is set at F, the calculator automatically sets the decimal places. The F setting allows the answer to be unrounded and carried out to the maximum number of decimal places possible.

The *decimal rounding selector* rounds the answers. The down arrow position will drop any digits beyond the last digit desired. The up arrow position will drop any digits beyond the last digit desired and round the last digit up. In the 5/4 position, the calculator rounds the last desired digit up only when the following digit is 5 or greater. If the following digit is less than 5, the last desired digit remains unchanged.

The *GT* or *grand total switch* in the on position accumulates totals.

KINDS OF COMPUTER KEYBOARDS

The computer has a keypad on the right side of the keyboard, called the *numeric keypad*. Even though several styles of keyboards are found, there are two basic layouts for the numeric keypad. The standard layout and enhanced layout are shown in the illustration. On the standard keyboard, the directional arrow keys are found on the number keys. To use the numbers, press the key called *Num Lock*. (This key is found above the "7" key.) When the Num Lock is turned on, numbers are entered when the keys on the keypad are pressed. When the Num Lock is off, the arrow, Home, Page Up, Page Down, End, Insert, and Delete keys can be used.

The enhanced keyboards have the arrow keys and the other directional keys mentioned above to the left of the numeric keypad. When using the keypad on an enhanced keyboard, Num Lock can remain on.

The asterisk (*) performs a different function on the computer than the calculator. The asterisk on the calculator is used for the total while the computer uses it for multiplication.

Another difference is the division key. The computer key is the forward slash key (/). The calculator key uses the division key (÷).

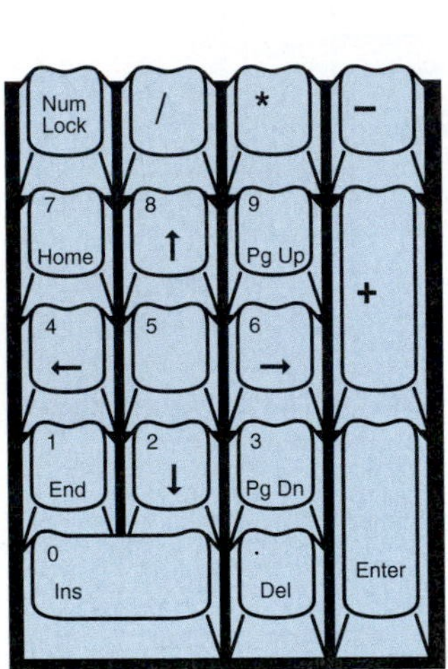

Standard Keyboard Layout

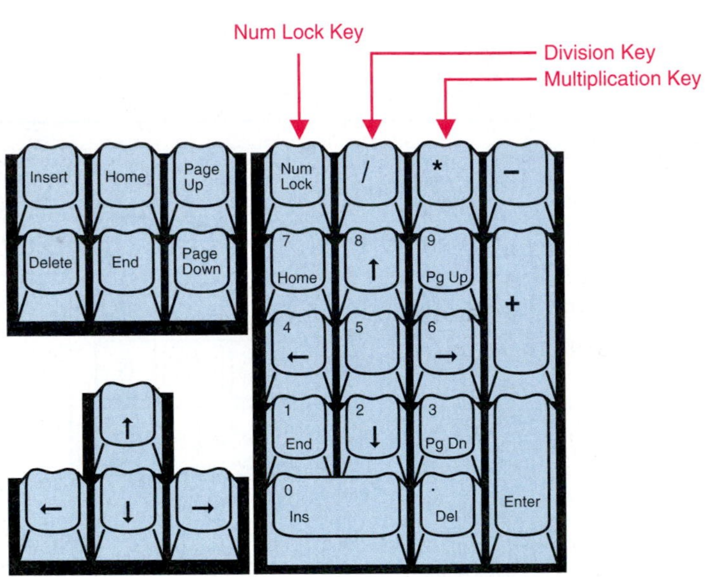

Enhanced Keyboard Layout

TEN-KEY TOUCH SYSTEM

Striking the numbers 0 to 9 on a calculator or numeric keypad without looking at the keyboard is called the *touch system*. Using the touch system develops both speed and accuracy.

The 4, 5, and 6 keys are called the *home row*. If the right hand is used for the keyboard, the index finger is placed on the 4 key, the middle finger on the 5 key, and the ring finger on the 6 key. If the left hand is used, the ring finger is placed on the 4 key, the middle finger on the 5 key, and the index finger on the 6 key.

Place the fingers on the home row keys. Curve the fingers and keep the wrist straight. These keys may feel slightly concaved or the 5 key may have a raised dot. The differences in the home row allow the operator to recognize the home row by touch rather than by sight.

Maintain the position of the fingers on the home row. The finger used to strike the 4 key will also strike the 7 key and the 1 key. Stretch the finger up to reach the 7; then stretch the finger down to reach the 1 key. Visualize the position of these keys.

Again, place the fingers on the home row. Stretch the finger that strikes the 5 key up to reach the 8 key, then down to reach the 2 key. Likewise, stretch the finger that strikes the 6 key up to strike the 9 and down to strike the 3 key. This same finger will stretch down again to hit the decimal point.

If the right hand is used, the thumb will be used to strike the 0 and 00 keys and the little finger to strike the addition key. If the left hand is used, the little finger will be used to strike the 0 and 00 keys and the thumb to strike the addition key.

HANDHELD CALCULATORS

Handheld calculators are slightly different from desktop calculators, not only in their size and features but also in their operation. Refer to the operator's manual for specific instructions for the calculator being used.

On a handheld calculator, the numeric keys are usually very close together. In addition, the keys do not respond to touch as easily as on a desktop calculator. Therefore, the touch system is usually not used on a handheld calculator.

PERFORMING MATHEMATICAL OPERATIONS ON DESKTOP CALCULATORS

Mathematical operations can be performed on a calculator both quickly and efficiently. The basic operations of addition, subtraction, multiplication, and division are used frequently on a calculator.

Addition

Each number to be added is called an *addend*. The answer to an addition problem is called the *sum*.

Addition is performed by entering an addend and striking the addition key (+). All numbers are entered on a calculator in the exact order they are given. To enter the number 4,455.65, strike the 4, 4, 5, 5, decimal, 6, and 5 keys in that order, and then strike the addition key. Commas are not entered. Continue in this manner until all addends have been entered. To obtain the sum, strike the total key on the calculator.

Subtraction

The top number or first number of a subtraction problem is called the *minuend*. The number to be subtracted from the minuend is called the *subtrahend*. The answer to a subtraction problem is called the *difference*.

Subtraction is performed by first entering the minuend and striking the addition key (+). The subtrahend is then entered, followed by the minus key (−), followed by the total key.

Multiplication

The number to be multiplied is called the *multiplicand*. The number of times the multiplicand will be multiplied is called the *multiplier*. The answer to a multiplication problem is called the *product*.

Multiplication is performed by entering the multiplicand and striking the multiplication key (×). The multiplier is then entered, followed by the equals key (=). The calculator will automatically multiply and give the product.

Division

The number to be divided is called the *dividend*. The number the dividend will be divided by is called the *divisor*. The answer to a division problem is called the *quotient*.

Division is performed by entering the dividend and striking the division key (÷). The divisor is then entered, followed by the equals key (=). The calculator will automatically divide and give the quotient.

Correcting Errors

If an error is made while using a calculator, several methods of correction may be used. If an incorrect number has been entered and the addition key or equals key has not yet been struck, strike the clear entry (CE) key one time.

This key will clear only the last number that was entered. However, if the clear entry key is depressed more than one time, the entire problem will be cleared on some calculators. If an incorrect number has been entered and the addition key has been struck, strike the minus key one time only. This will automatically subtract the last number added, thus removing it from the total.

PERFORMING MATHEMATICAL OPERATIONS ON COMPUTERS AND HANDHELD CALCULATORS

On a computer keypad or a handheld calculator, addition is performed in much the same way as on a desktop calculator. However, after the + key is depressed, the display usually shows the accumulated total. Therefore, the total key is not found. Some computer programs will not calculate the total until Enter is pressed.

Subtraction is performed differently on many computer keypads and handheld calculators. The minuend is usually entered, followed by the minus (−) key. Then the subtrahend is entered. Pressing either the + key or the = key will display the difference. Some computer programs will not calculate the difference until Enter is pressed.

Multiplication and division are performed the same way on a computer keypad and handheld calculator as on a desktop calculator. Keep in mind that computers use the * for multiplication and / for division.

SAFETY CONCERNS

Whenever electrical equipment such as a calculator or computer is being operated in a classroom or office, several safety rules apply. These rules protect the operator of the equipment, other persons in the environment, and the equipment itself.

1. Do not unplug equipment by pulling on the electrical cord. Instead, grasp the plug at the outlet and remove it.
2. Do not stretch electrical cords across an aisle where someone might trip over them.
3. Avoid food and beverages near the equipment where a spill might result in an electrical short.
4. Do not attempt to remove the cover of a calculator, computer, or keyboard for any reason while the power is turned on.
5. Do not attempt to repair equipment while it is plugged in.
6. Always turn the power off or unplug equipment when finished using it.

CALCULATION DRILLS

Instructions for Desktop Calculators

Complete each drill using the touch method. Set the decimal selector at the setting indicated in each drill. Compare the answer on the calculator to the answer in the book. If the two are the same, progress to the next problem. It is not necessary to enter 00 in the cents column if the decimal selector is set at 0-F. However, digits other than zeros in the cents column must be entered preceded by a decimal point.

Instructions for Computer Keypads

Complete each drill using the touch method. There is no decimal selector on computer keypads. Set the number of decimal places as directed in the instructions for the computer program. In spreadsheets, for example, use the formatting options to set the number of decimal places. When the drill indicates "F" for floating, leave the computer application in its default format. Compare the answer on the computer monitor to the answer in the book. If the two are the same, progress to the next problem. It is not necessary to enter 00 in the cents column. However, digits other than zeros in the cents column must be entered preceded by a decimal point.

DRILL D-1 Performing addition using the home row keys
Decimal Selector—2

4.00	44.00	444.00	4,444.00	44,444.00
5.00	55.00	555.00	5,555.00	55,555.00
6.00	66.00	666.00	6,666.00	66,666.00
5.00	45.00	455.00	4,455.00	44,556.00
4.00	46.00	466.00	4,466.00	44,565.00
5.00	54.00	544.00	5,544.00	55,446.00
6.00	56.00	566.00	5,566.00	55,664.00
5.00	65.00	655.00	6,655.00	66,554.00
4.00	64.00	644.00	6,644.00	66,555.00
5.00	66.00	654.00	6,545.00	65,465.00
49.00	561.00	5,649.00	56,540.00	565,470.00

DRILL D-2 Performing addition using the 0, 1, 4, and 7 keys
Decimal Selector—2

4.00	11.00	444.00	4,440.00	44,000.00
7.00	44.00	777.00	7,770.00	77,000.00
4.00	74.00	111.00	1,110.00	11,000.00
1.00	71.00	741.00	4,400.00	41,000.00
4.00	70.00	740.00	1,100.00	71,000.00
7.00	10.00	101.00	4,007.00	10,000.00
4.00	14.00	140.00	7,001.00	10,100.00
1.00	17.00	701.00	1,007.00	40,100.00
4.00	40.00	700.00	1,004.00	70,100.00
7.00	77.00	407.00	7,700.00	74,100.00
43.00	428.00	4,862.00	39,539.00	448,400.00

DRILL D-3 Performing addition using the 2, 5, and 8 keys
Decimal Selector—2

5.00	58.00	588.00	8,888.00	88,855.00
8.00	52.00	522.00	5,555.00	88,822.00
5.00	85.00	888.00	2,222.00	88,852.00
2.00	52.00	222.00	8,525.00	88,222.00
5.00	25.00	258.00	2,585.00	85,258.00
8.00	58.00	852.00	8,258.00	22,255.00
5.00	82.00	225.00	8,585.00	22,288.00
2.00	28.00	885.00	5,258.00	22,258.00
5.00	88.00	882.00	2,852.00	22,888.00
8.00	22.00	228.00	2,288.00	25,852.00
53.00	550.00	5,550.00	55,016.00	555,550.00

DRILL D-4 Performing addition using the 3, 6, 9, and decimal point keys
Decimal Selector—2

6.00	66.66	666.66	6,666.99	66,699.33
9.00	99.99	999.99	9,999.66	99,966.66
6.00	33.33	333.33	3,333.99	33,366.33
3.00	33.66	666.99	3,366.99	36,963.36
6.36	33.99	999.66	6,699.33	69,636.36
3.36	99.66	333.66	9,966.33	33,333.66
9.36	99.33	696.36	9,636.69	66,666.99
9.63	33.36	369.63	3,696.36	99,999.33
6.33	33.69	336.69	6,963.99	96,369.63
9.93	69.63	963.36	6,699.33	36,963.36
68.97	603.30	6,366.33	67,029.66	639,965.01

DRILL D-5 Performing subtraction using all number keys
Decimal Selector—F

456.73	789.01	741.00	852.55	987.98
−123.21	−456.00	−258.10	−369.88	−102.55
333.52	333.01	482.90	482.67	885.43

DRILL D-6 Performing multiplication using all number keys
Decimal Selector—F

654.05	975.01	487.10	123.56	803.75
× 12.66	× 27.19	× 30.21	× 50.09	× 1.45
8,280.273	26,510.5219	14,715.291	6,189.1204	1,165.4375

DRILL D-7 Performing division using all number keys
Decimal Selector—F

900.56	÷	450.28	=	2.
500.25	÷	100.05	=	5.
135.66	÷	6.65	=	20.4
269.155	÷	105.55	=	2.550023685*
985.66	÷	22.66	=	43.49779346*

**Number of decimal places may vary, due to machine capacity.*

Recycling Problems

RECYCLING PROBLEM 1-1

Determining how transactions change an accounting equation

Brian Frizza is a personal trainer and operates a business called FitnessPro. FitnessPro uses the accounts shown in the following accounting equation. Use the form given in the *Recycling Problem Working Papers* to complete this problem.

	Assets							=	Liabilities	+	Owner's Equity
Trans. No.	Cash	+	Accts. Rec.— Dean Mills	+	Supplies	+	Prepaid Insurance	=	Accts. Pay.— Topline	+	Brian Frizza, Capital
Beg. Bal. 1.	2,200 *−120*		—0—		1,100		200		200		3,300 *−120 (expense)*
New Bal. 2.	*2,080*		*—0—*		*1,100*		*200*		*200*		*3,180*

Transactions:

1. Paid cash for telephone bill, $120.00.
2. Received cash from owner as an investment, $400.00.
3. Paid cash for rent, $600.00.
4. Received cash from sales, $425.00.
5. Bought supplies on account from Topline, $310.00.
6. Sold services on account to Dean Mills, $500.00.
7. Paid cash for supplies, $250.00.
8. Paid cash for advertising, $700.00.
9. Received cash on account from Dean Mills, $400.00.
10. Paid cash on account to Topline, $200.00.
11. Paid cash for insurance, $225.00.
12. Received cash from sales, $675.00.
13. Paid cash to owner for personal use, $1,000.00.

Instructions:

For each transaction, complete the following. Transaction 1 is given as an example.

1. Analyze the transaction to determine which accounts in the accounting equation are affected.
2. Write the amount in the appropriate columns, using a plus (+) if the account increases or a minus (−) if the account decreases.
3. For transactions that change owner's equity, write in parentheses a description of the transaction to the right of the amount.
4. Calculate the new balance for each account in the accounting equation.
5. Before going on to the next transaction, determine that the accounting equation is still in balance.

RECYCLING PROBLEM 2-1

Analyzing transactions into debit and credit parts

Luke Harris owns a business called Colato Copies. Colato Copies uses the following accounts.

Cash
Accounts Receivable—Flowerama
Accounts Receivable—Seaside Inn
Supplies
Prepaid Insurance
Accounts Payable—Pacific Paper
Accounts Payable—Raffi Supplies
Luke Harris, Capital
Luke Harris, Drawing
Sales
Advertising Expense
Miscellaneous Expense
Rent Expense
Repair Expense
Utilities Expense

Instructions:

Use the forms given in the *Recycling Problem Working Papers*.

1. Prepare a T account for each account.
2. Analyze each transaction into its debit and credit parts. Write the debit and credit amounts in the proper T accounts to show how each transaction changes account balances. Write the date of the transaction in parentheses before each amount.

Transactions:

July 1. Received cash from owner as an investment, $4,500.00.
2. Paid cash for rent, $520.00.
4. Paid cash for supplies, $300.00.
4. Received cash from sales, $400.00.
5. Paid cash for insurance, $200.00.
8. Sold services on account to Flowerama, $450.00.
9. Bought supplies on account from Raffi Supplies, $700.00.
10. Paid cash for rent, $120.00.
11. Received cash from owner as an investment, $2,300.00.
11. Received cash from sales, $800.00.
12. Bought supplies on account from Pacific Paper, $300.00.
13. Received cash on account from Flowerama, $250.00.
15. Paid cash for miscellaneous expense, $40.00.
16. Paid cash on account to Raffi Supplies, $350.00.
22. Paid cash for electric bill (utilities expense), $70.00.
23. Paid cash for advertising, $160.00.
25. Sold services on account to Seaside Inn, $640.00.
26. Paid cash to owner for personal use, $1,200.00.
30. Received cash on account from Seaside Inn, $300.00.

RECYCLING PROBLEM 3-1

Journalizing transactions and proving and ruling a journal

Adeline Stein owns a service business called Stein Express, which uses the following accounts:

Cash	Accts. Pay.—Rim Supply	Sales	Repair Expense
Supplies	Accts. Pay.— Parks Co.	Advertising Expense	Utilities Expense
Prepaid Insurance	Adeline Stein, Capital	Miscellaneous Expense	
Accts. Rec.—M. Bien	Adeline Stein, Drawing	Rent Expense	

Transactions:

Aug. 1. Received cash from owner as an investment, $8,750.00. R1.
2. Paid cash for supplies, $500.00. C1.
3. Paid cash for rent, $300.00. C2.
4. Bought supplies on account from Rim Supply, $1,200.00. M1.
5. Paid cash for electric bill, $250.00. C3.
8. Paid cash on account to Rim Supply, $700.00. C4.
8. Received cash from sales, $425.00. T8.
8. Sold services on account to M. Bien, $125.00. S1.
9. Paid cash for insurance, $1,900.00. C5.
10. Paid cash for miscellaneous expense, $27.00. C6.
10. Received cash from sales, $297.00. T10.
11. Paid cash for supplies, $770.00. C7.
11. Received cash from sales, $493.00. T11.
12. Received cash from sales, $294.00. T12.
15. Paid cash to owner for personal use, $125.00. C8.
15. Received cash from sales, $275.00. T15.
16. Paid cash for repairs, $88.00. C9.
17. Received cash on account from M. Bien, $125.00. R2.
17. Bought supplies on account from Parks Co., $345.00. M2.
17. Received cash from sales, $200.00. T17.
18. Received cash from sales, $600.00. T18.
19. Received cash from sales, $175.00. T19.
22. Bought supplies on account from Parks Co., $80.00. M3.
22. Received cash from sales, $450.00. T22.
23. Paid cash for telephone bill, $50.00. C10.
23. Sold services on account to M. Bien, $425.00. S2.
24. Paid cash for advertising, $80.00. C11.
24. Received cash from sales, $250.00. T24.
25. Received cash from sales, $325.00. T25.
26. Paid cash for supplies, $45.00. C12.
26. Received cash from sales, $310.00. T26.
29. Received cash on account from M. Bien, $425.00. R3.
30. Paid cash to owner for personal use, $150.00. C13.
31. Received cash from sales, $450.00. T31.

Instructions:

1. Use page 1 of the journal given in the *Recycling Problem Working Papers*. Journalize the transactions for August 1 through August 19 of the current year. Source documents are abbreviated as follows: check, C; memorandum, M; receipt, R; sales invoice, S; calculator tape, T.
2. Prove and rule page 1 of the journal. Carry the column totals forward to page 2 of the journal.
3. Use page 2 of the journal to journalize the transactions for the remainder of August.
4. Prove page 2 of the journal.
5. Prove cash. The beginning cash balance on August 1 is zero. The balance on the next unused check stub is $8,859.00.
6. Rule page 2 of the journal.

RECYCLING PROBLEM 4-1

Journalizing transactions and posting to a general ledger

Janet Porter owns a service business called Porter's Parties. Porter's Parties' general ledger accounts are given in the *Recycling Problem Working Papers.*

Transactions:

Aug. 1. Received cash from owner as an investment, $4,500.00. R1.
3. Paid cash for supplies, $300.00. C1.
5. Sold services on account to Nicholas Calendo, $650.00. S1.
6. Received cash from sales, $630.00. T6.
9. Paid cash for electric bill, $130.00. C2.
11. Paid cash for rent, $530.00. C3.
13. Bought supplies on account from Jordan Supplies, $800.00. M1.
13. Received cash from sales, $650.00. T13.
16. Paid cash for miscellaneous expense, $55.00. C4.
18. Paid cash on account to Jordan Supplies, $500.00. C5.
20. Paid cash for supplies, $105.00. C6.
20. Received cash on account from Nicholas Calendo, $350.00. R2.
25. Paid cash for advertising, $250.00. C7.
27. Paid cash for supplies, $75.00. C8.
27. Received cash from sales, $1,200.00. T27.
30. Paid cash to owner for personal use, $800.00. C9.
31. Received cash from sales, $780.00. T31.

Instructions:

1. Open an account for Utilities Expense. Use the 3-digit numbering system described in the chapter.
2. Journalize the transactions completed during August of the current year. Use page 1 of a journal. Source documents are abbreviated as follows: check, C; memorandum, M; receipt, R; sales invoice, S; calculator tape, T.
3. Prove the journal.
4. Prove cash. The beginning cash balance on August 1 is zero. The balance on the next unused check stub is $5,365.00.
5. Rule the journal.
6. Post from the journal to the general ledger.

RECYCLING PROBLEM 5-1

Reconciling a bank statement; journalizing a bank service charge, a dishonored check, and petty cash transactions

Tao Vang owns a business called Fast Print. Selected general ledger accounts are given below. Forms are given in the *Recycling Problem Working Papers.*

110 Cash	140 Prepaid Insurance	535 Repair Expense
115 Petty Cash	320 Tao Vang, Drawing	540 Supplies Expense
120 Accts. Rec.—Corner Cafe	520 Miscellaneous Expense	550 Utilities Expense
130 Supplies	530 Rent Expense	

Instructions:

1. Journalize the following transactions completed during May of the current year. Use page 12 of a journal. Source documents are abbreviated as follows: check, C; memorandum, M.

Transactions:

May 21. Paid cash to establish a petty cash fund, $150.00. C51.
24. Paid cash for supplies, $72.00. C52.
26. Paid cash for repairs, $85.00. C53.

27. Received notice from the bank of a dishonored check from Corner Cafe, $70.00, plus $25.00 fee; total, $95.00. M22.
28. Paid cash for miscellaneous expense, $42.00. C54.
31. Paid cash to owner for personal use, $200.00. C55.
31. Paid cash to replenish the petty cash fund, $105.00: supplies, $85.00; miscellaneous expense, $20.00. C56.

2. On May 31 of the current year, Fast Print received a bank statement dated May 30. Prepare a bank statement reconciliation. Use May 31 of the current year as the date. The following information is obtained from the May 30 bank statement and from the records of the business.

Bank statement balance	$1,586.00
Bank service charge	25.00
Outstanding deposit, May 31	285.00
Outstanding checks, Nos. 55 and 56	
Checkbook balance on Check Stub No. 57	$1,591.00

3. Continue using the journal and journalize the following transaction.

Transaction:

May 31. Received bank statement showing May bank service charge, $25.00. M23.

RECYCLING PROBLEM 6-1

Completing a work sheet

On February 28 of the current year, Hibbing Hair Care has the following general ledger accounts and balances. The business uses a monthly fiscal period.

	Account Balances	
Account Titles	**Debit**	**Credit**
Cash	$2,609.00	
Petty Cash	300.00	
Accounts Receivable—Robert Perpich	581.00	
Supplies	895.00	
Prepaid Insurance	1,200.00	
Accounts Payable—Ely Supplies		$ 450.00
Jens Miller-Smith, Capital		4,550.00
Jens Miller-Smith, Drawing	300.00	
Income Summary		
Sales		3,100.00
Advertising Expense	425.00	
Insurance Expense		
Miscellaneous Expense	250.00	
Rent Expense	1,100.00	
Supplies Expense		
Utilities Expense	440.00	

Instructions:

1. Prepare the heading and trial balance on the work sheet given in the *Recycling Problem Working Papers*. Total and rule the Trial Balance columns.
2. Analyze the following adjustment information into debit and credit parts. Record the adjustments on the work sheet.

Adjustment Information, February 28

Supplies inventory	$ 450.00
Value of prepaid insurance	1,000.00

3. Total and rule the Adjustments columns.
4. Extend the up-to-date balances to the Balance Sheet or Income Statement columns.
5. Rule a single line across the Income Statement and Balance Sheet columns. Total each column. Calculate and record the net income or net loss. Label the amount in the Account Title column.
6. Total and rule the Income Statement and Balance Sheet columns.

RECYCLING PROBLEM 7-1

Preparing financial statements

The following information is obtained from the work sheet of SuperClean for the month ended August 31 of the current year. Forms are given in the *Recycling Problem Working Papers*.

		5	6	7	8	
	ACCOUNT TITLE	INCOME STATEMENT		BALANCE SHEET		
		DEBIT	CREDIT	DEBIT	CREDIT	
1	*Cash*			5,632 00		1
2	*Accounts Receivable—D. Dawson*			175 00		2
3	*Accounts Receivable—K. Keene*			315 00		3
4	*Supplies*			467 00		4
5	*Prepaid Insurance*			900 00		5
6	*Accounts Payable—DV Supply*				593 00	6
7	*Accounts Payable—Supply Warehouse*				700 00	7
8	*Michelle Delist, Capital*				5,031 00	8
9	*Michelle Delist, Drawing*			1,500 00		9
10	*Income Summary*					10
11	*Sales*		5,881 00			11
12	*Advertising Expense*	625 00				12
13	*Insurance Expense*	150 00				13
14	*Miscellaneous Expense*	145 00				14
15	*Supplies Expense*	925 00				15
16	*Utilities Expense*	1,371 00				16
17		3,216 00	5,881 00	8,989 00	6,324 00	17
18	*Net Income*	2,665 00			2,665 00	18
19		5,881 00	5,881 00	8,989 00	8,989 00	19
20						20

Instructions:

1. Prepare an income statement for the month ended August 31 of the current year.
2. Calculate and record the component percentages for total expenses and net income. Round percentage calculations to the nearest 0.1%.
3. Prepare a balance sheet for August 31 of the current year.

RECYCLING PROBLEM 8-1

Journalizing adjusting and closing entries

The following information is obtained from the partial work sheet of SuperClean for the month ended August 31 of the current year.

		3	4	5	6	7	8	
	ACCOUNT TITLE	ADJUSTMENTS		INCOME STATEMENT		BALANCE SHEET		
		DEBIT	CREDIT	DEBIT	CREDIT	DEBIT	CREDIT	
1	*Cash*					5632 00		1
2	*Accounts Receivable—D. Dawson*					175 00		2
3	*Accounts Receivable—K. Keene*					315 00		3
4	*Supplies*		(a) 925 00			467 00		4
5	*Prepaid Insurance*		(b) 150 00			900 00		5
6	*Accounts Payable—DV Supply*						593 00	6
7	*Accounts Payable—Supply Warehouse*						700 00	7
8	*Michelle Delist, Capital*						5031 00	8
9	*Michelle Delist, Drawing*					1500 00		9
10	*Income Summary*							10
11	*Sales*				5881 00			11
12	*Advertising Expense*			625 00				12
13	*Insurance Expense*	(b) 150 00		150 00				13
14	*Miscellaneous Expense*			145 00				14
15	*Supplies Expense*	(a) 925 00		925 00				15
16	*Utilities Expense*			1371 00				16
17		1075 00	1075 00	3216 00	5881 00	8989 00	6324 00	17
18	*Net Income*			2665 00			2665 00	18
19				5881 00	5881 00	8989 00	8989 00	19
20								20

Instructions:

1. Use page 16 of the journal given in the *Recycling Problem Working Papers*. Journalize the adjusting entries.
2. Continue to use page 16 of the journal. Journalize the closing entries.

RECYCLING PROBLEM 9-1

Journalizing purchases, cash payments, and other transactions

Backwoods, Inc., is a sporting goods store organized as a corporation.

Instructions:

1. Using the journals given in the *Recycling Problem Working Papers*, journalize the following transactions completed during August of the current year. Use page 9 of a purchases journal, page 15 of a cash payments journal, and page 12 of a general journal. Source documents are abbreviated as follows: check, C; memorandum, M; purchase invoice, P; debit memorandum, DM.

Transactions:

Aug. 1. Paid cash to Keller Realty for rent, $1,000.00. C772.
2. Paid cash to LWAP Radio for advertising, $720.00. C773.
3. Bought office supplies on account from Johnson Office Supply, $420.00. M62.
4. Paid cash on account to Arrowhead Supply, $4,210.00, covering P436. No cash discount was offered. C774.
6. Paid cash to City Utilities for electric bill, $420.00. C775.
7. Paid cash on account to Johnson Office Supply covering M62, less 2% discount. C776.
9. Paid cash to Mark's Discount Stores for store supplies, $224.00. C777.

9. Purchased merchandise on account from Peterson Sports, $3,560.00. P445.
11. Purchased merchandise for cash from Atlas Sports Co., $3,480.00, less a 60% trade discount. C778.
13. Returned merchandise to Peterson Sports from P445, $233.00. DM19.
13. Purchased merchandise for cash from Duck Crafts, $495.00. C779.
15. Returned merchandise to Evans Sports Corporation from P438, $112.00. DM20.
15. Paid cash on account to Peterson Sports covering P445 after a purchase return, DM19, less 2% discount. C780.
20. Purchased merchandise for cash from Atlas Sports Co., $156.00. C781.
21. Paid cash on account to Evans Sports Corporation, $1,950.00. No cash discount was offered. C782.
22. Purchased merchandise on account from Camo Clothing, $8,100, less a 50% trade discount. P446.
23. Bought store supplies on account from Mancil Marketing, $120.00. M63.
24. Paid cash to Velmar Company for store supplies, $245.00. C783.
29. Purchased merchandise for cash from Paintball Central, $1,154.00. C784.

2. Total the amount columns of cash payments journal page 15. Prove the equality of debits and credits and rule the cash payments journal to carry the totals forward.
3. Record the totals brought forward from cash payments journal page 15 to line 1 of page 16 of the cash payments journal.
4. Journalize the following transactions.

Transactions:

Aug. 31. Paid cash on account to Camo Clothing covering P446, less 2% cash discount. C785.
31. Paid cash to replenish the petty cash fund, $127.80: supplies—office, $25.66; supplies—store, $48.25; miscellaneous, $54.33; and cash over, $0.44. C786.

5. Total and rule page 9 of the purchases journal.
6. Total the amount columns of cash payments journal page 16. Prove the equality of debits and credits of cash payments journal page 16.
7. Rule page 16 of the cash payments journal.

RECYCLING PROBLEM 10-1

Journalizing sales and cash receipts transactions; proving and ruling journals

Burge Supply sells lumber, brick, and other construction materials.

Sales journal page 22, cash receipts journal page 23, and general journal page 17 for Aqua Central are given in the *Recycling Problem Working Papers*. Balances brought forward are provided on line 1 of the sales and cash receipts journals.

Instructions:

1. Journalize the following transactions completed during the remainder of November in the appropriate journal. Sales tax rate is 6%. Source documents are abbreviated as follows: receipt, R; sales invoice, S; terminal summary, TS.

Transactions:

Nov. 25. Received cash on account from Davis Construction, $1,379.84, covering S845 for $1,408.00, less 2% cash discount, $28.16. R334.
26. Recorded cash and credit card sales, $4,844.00, plus sales tax, $290.64; total, $5,134.64. TS38.
28. Sold merchandise on account to Margaret Sienna, $664.00, plus sales tax, $39.84; total, $703.84. S889.
28. Received cash on account from Ventura Fencing, $2,849.00, covering S861. R335.
29. Granted credit to Davis Construction for merchandise returned, $1,820.00, plus sales tax, $109.20; total, $1,929.20. CM43.

30. Sold merchandise on account to State University, $2,118.00. State University is exempt from sales tax. S890.

30. Recorded cash and credit card sales, $839.00, plus sales tax, $50.34; total, $889.34. TS39.

2. Total and prove the equality of debits and credits for the sales journal.
3. Rule the sales journal.
4. Total and prove the equality of debits and credits for the cash receipts journal.
5. Prove cash. The November 1 cash account balance in the general ledger was $8,483.31. The November 31 cash credit total in the cash payments journal was $42,194.33. On November 31 the balance on the next unused check stub was $16,626.70.
6. Rule the cash receipts journal.

RECYCLING PROBLEM 11-1

Posting to general and subsidiary ledgers

The journals and ledgers for Custom Boots are given in the *Recycling Problem Working Papers.*

Instructions:

1. Post the separate items in the following journals to the general and subsidiary ledgers. Use the current year.
   a. Sales journal.
   b. Purchases journal.
   c. General journal.
   d. Cash receipts journal.
   e. Cash payments journal.
2. Prove and rule the sales journal. Post the totals of the special amount columns.
3. Total and rule the purchases journal. Post the total.
4. Prove and rule the cash receipts journal. Post the totals of the special amount columns.
5. Prove and rule the cash payments journal. Post the totals of the special amount columns.
6. Prepare a schedule of accounts payable and a schedule of accounts receivable. Compare the totals of the schedules with the balances of the controlling accounts, Accounts Payable and Accounts Receivable, in the general ledger. If the totals are not the same, find and correct the errors.

RECYCLING PROBLEM 12-1

Preparing a semimonthly payroll

The following information is for the semimonthly pay period July 16–31 of the current year. Forms are given in the *Recycling Problem Working Papers.*

SEMIMONTHLY PERIOD ENDED *July 31, 20--*

	EMPL. NO.	EMPLOYEE'S NAME	MARITAL STATUS	NO. OF ALLOWANCES	EARNINGS: REGULAR	EARNINGS: OVERTIME	DEDUCTIONS: HEALTH INSURANCE
1	5	Abrams, Thomas	S	1	892 00		35 00
2	6	Carroll, John	M	2	880 00	90 00	60 00
3	1	Harris, Jonathan	S	1	924 00		35 00
4	4	Kennard, Mary	S	1	1056 00	72 00	35 00
5	2	Locke, Anna	M	2	994 00		60 00
6	7	Rayford, Stan	M	2	812 00		60 00
7	3	Suell, Nicole	M	3	860 00		80 00
8							
9							
10							
11							
12							

Instructions:

1. Prepare a payroll register. The date of payment is July 31. Use the income tax withholding tables shown in Chapter 12 to find the income tax withholding for each employee. Calculate social security and Medicare tax withholdings using 6.2% and 1.45% tax rates, respectively. None of the employee-accumulated earnings has exceeded the social security tax base.
2. Prepare a check for the total amount of the net pay. Make the check payable to Payroll Account 982-561-4732 and sign your name as the manager of Sanford Company. The beginning check stub balance is $11,530.50.
3. Prepare payroll checks for Thomas Abrams, Check No. 558, and Anna Locke, Check No. 562. Sign your name as the manager of Sanford Company. Record the two payroll check numbers in the payroll register.

RECYCLING PROBLEM 13-1

Journalizing payroll transactions

Wooden Cycles completed payroll transactions during the period January 1 to March 31 of the current year. Payroll tax rates are as follows: social security, 6.2%; Medicare, 1.45%; federal unemployment, 0.8%; state unemployment, 5.4%. No total earnings have exceeded the tax base for calculating unemployment taxes. Wooden Cycles is a monthly schedule depositor for payroll taxes.

Instructions:

1. Journalize the following transactions on page 14 of the cash payments journal and page 10 of the general journal given in the *Recycling Problem Working Papers*. Source documents are abbreviated as follows: check, C, and memorandum, M.

Transactions:

Jan.	31.	Paid cash for monthly payroll. Gross wages, $5,920.00; withholdings: employee income tax, $360.00; calculate social security and Medicare taxes. C555.
	31.	Recorded employer payroll taxes expense for the January payroll. M24.
Feb.	15.	Paid cash for the January liability for employee income tax, social security tax, and Medicare tax. C575.
	28.	Paid cash for monthly payroll. Gross wages, $6,058.00; withholdings: employee income tax, $372.00; calculate social security and Medicare taxes. C601.
	28.	Recorded employer payroll taxes expense for the February payroll. M28.
Mar.	15.	Paid cash for the February liability for employee income tax, social security tax, and Medicare tax. C624.
	31.	Paid cash for monthly payroll. Gross wages, $6,120.00; withholdings: employee income tax, $394.00; calculate social security and Medicare taxes. C658.
	31.	Recorded employer payroll taxes expense for the March payroll. M35.
Apr.	15.	Paid cash for the March liability for employee income tax, social security tax, and Medicare tax. C699.
	15.	Paid cash for federal unemployment tax liability for quarter ended March 31. C700.
	15.	Paid cash for state unemployment tax liability for quarter ended March 31. C701.

2. Prove and rule the cash payments journal.

RECYCLING PROBLEM 14-1

Preparing an 8-column work sheet for a merchandising business

The trial balance for Audio Source, Inc., as of December 31 of the current year is recorded on a work sheet in the *Recycling Problem Working Papers*. Audio Source completed the following transactions during December of the current year and January of the next year.

Transactions:

Dec. 15. The board of directors declared a dividend of $0.375 per share; capital stock issued is 20,000 shares. M114.

Jan. 15. Paid cash for dividend declared December 15. C924.

Instructions:

1. Use page 12 of a general journal. Journalize the dividend declared on December 15.
2. Use page 18 of a cash payments journal. Journalize payment of the dividend on January 15.
3. Analyze the following adjustment information collected on December 31 and record the adjustments on the work sheet. Label each adjustment using labels *(a)* through *(g)*.
   a. Uncollectible accounts are 0.4% of credit sales of $620,000.00.
   b. Merchandise inventory $270,461.36
   c. Office supplies inventory 1,081.34
   d. Store supplies inventory 1,585.90
   e. Value of prepaid insurance 160.00
   f. Estimate of office equipment depreciation 6,140.00
   g. Estimate of store equipment depreciation 5,520.00
4. Using the federal income tax table shown in Chapter 14, calculate federal income tax expense and record the income tax adjustment on the work sheet. Label the adjustment *(h)*.
5. Complete the work sheet.

RECYCLING PROBLEM 15-1

Preparing financial statements

The completed work sheet for Hawkins Parts, Inc., for the year ended December 31 of the current year and forms for completing this problem are given in the *Recycling Problem Working Papers*.

Instructions:

1. Prepare an income statement. Calculate and record the following component percentages: (a) cost of merchandise sold, (b) gross profit on sales, (c) total expenses, and (d) net income or loss before federal income tax. Round percentage calculations to the nearest 0.1%.
2. Prepare a statement of stockholders' equity. The company had 30,000 shares of $1.00 par value stock outstanding on January 1. The company issued an additional 2,000 shares during the year.
3. Prepare a balance sheet in report form.
4. Calculate the earnings per share and price-earnings ratio. The current market price of the stock is $89.00.

RECYCLING PROBLEM 16-1

Journalizing and posting adjusting and closing entries; preparing a post-closing trial balance

Use the following partial work sheet of Southern Fixtures, Inc., for the year ended December 31 of the current year. The general ledger accounts and their balances as well as forms for completing this problem are in the *Recycling Problem Working Papers*.

Southern Fixtures, Inc.

Work Sheet

For Year Ended December 31, 20--

		3	4	5	6
		ADJUSTMENTS		INCOME STATEMENT	
	ACCOUNT TITLE	DEBIT	CREDIT	DEBIT	CREDIT
4	Allow. for Uncoll. Accts.		(a) 2,215.00		
5	Merchandise Inventory	(b) 4,819.00			
6	Supplies—Office		(c) 6,106.00		
7	Supplies—Store		(d) 3,154.00		
8	Prepaid Insurance		(e) 9,600.00		
9	Office Equipment				
10	Acc. Depr.—Office Equipment		(f) 4,420.00		
11	Store Equipment				
12	Acc. Depr.—Store Equipment		(g) 4,950.00		
13	Accounts Payable				
14	Federal Income Tax Payable		(h) 6,429.62		
28	Income Summary		(b) 4,819.00		4,819.00
38	Depr. Exp.—Office Equipment	(f) 4,420.00		4,420.00	
39	Depr. Exp.—Store Equipment	(g) 4,950.00		4,950.00	
40	Insurance Expense	(e) 9,600.00		9,600.00	
41	Miscellaneous Expense			13,184.80	
42	Payroll Taxes Expense			18,785.24	
43	Rent Expense			12,800.00	
44	Salary Expense			151,584.73	
45	Supplies Expense—Office	(c) 6,106.00		6,106.00	
46	Supplies Expense—Store	(d) 3,154.00		3,154.00	
47	Uncollectible Accounts Expense	(a) 2,215.00		2,215.00	
48	Utilities Expense			3,294.47	
49	Federal Income Tax Expense	(h) 6,429.62		46,429.62	
50		41,693.62	41,693.62	641,874.48	757,443.89
51	Net Income after Federal Income Tax			115,569.41	
52				757,443.89	757,443.89

Instructions:

1. Journalize the adjusting entries using page 18 of a general journal.
2. Post the adjusting entries.
3. Journalize the closing entries using page 19 of a general journal.
4. Post the closing entries.
5. Prepare a post-closing trial balance.

Answers to Audit Your Understanding

Chapter 1, Page 9

1. Planning, recording, analyzing, and interpreting financial information.
2. Answers will vary but should involve businesses that perform activities for a fee.
3. A business owned by one person.
4. Assets = Liabilities + Owner's Equity.

Chapter 1, Page 13

1. The right side must be increased.
2. If one account is increased, another account on the same side of the equation must be decreased by the same amount.
3. Buying items or services and paying for them at a future date.

Chapter 1, Page 17

1. Increased.
2. Increased
3. Decreased.

Chapter 2, Page 31

1. ASSETS = LIABILITIES + OWNER'S EQUITY
2. (1) Account balances increase on the normal balance side of an account. (2) Account balances decrease on the side opposite the normal balance side of an account.

Chapter 2, Page 37

1. (1) Which accounts are affected? (2) How is each account classified? (3) How is each classification changed? (4) How is each amount entered in the accounts?
2. Supplies and Cash.

Chapter 2, Page 44

1. Cash and Sales.
2. Accounts Receivable and Sales.
3. Owner's drawing account and Cash.
4. Credit, because revenue increases owner's equity.
5. Debit, because expenses decrease owner's equity.

Chapter 3, Page 62

1. By date.
2. Source documents are one way to verify the accuracy of a specific journal entry.
3. Date, debit, credit, and source document.

Chapter 3, Page 66

1. General Debit and Cash Credit.
2. General Debit and General Credit.
3. General Debit and Cash Credit.

Chapter 3, Page 72

1. Cash Debit and Sales Credit.
2. General Debit and Sales Credit.
3. General Debit and Cash Credit.
4. Cash Debit and General Credit.
5. General Debit and Cash Credit.

Chapter 3, Page 78

1. (1) Add each of the amount columns. (2) Add the debit column totals, and then add the credit column totals. (3) Verify that the total debits and total credits are equal.
2. Cash on hand at the beginning of the month, plus total cash received, less total cash paid.
3. (1) Rule a single line across all amount columns directly below the last entry to indicate that the columns are to be added. (2) On the next line, write the date in the Date column. (3) Write the word *Totals* in the Account Title column. (4) Write each column total below the single line. (5) Rule double lines below the column totals across all amount columns. The double lines mean that the totals have been verified as correct.

Chapter 4, Page 95

1. The first digit indicates in which general ledger division the account is located. The second and third digits indicate the location of the account within that division.
2. (1) Write the account title in the heading. (2) Write the account number in the heading.

Chapter 4, Page 99

1. (1) Write the date in the Date column of the account. (2) Write the journal page number in the Post. Ref. column of the account. (3) Write the amount in the Debit or Credit column. (4) Calculate and write the new account balance in the Balance Debit or Balance Credit column. (5) Write the account number in the Post. Ref. column of the journal.
2. No. Each separate amount in the General Debit and General Credit columns of a journal is posted to the account written in the Account Title column.

Chapter 4, Page 104

1. Special amount columns.
2. Whenever the debits in an account exceed the credits.
3. Whenever the credits in an account exceed the debits.

Chapter 4, Page 109

1. A journal entry made to correct an error in the ledger.
2. When a transaction has been improperly journalized and posted to the ledger.
3. To show the increase in this expense account.
4. To show the decrease in this expense account.

Chapter 5, Page 123

1. Blank endorsement, special endorsement, and restrictive endorsement.
2. (1) Write the amount of the check after the dollar sign at the top of the stub. (2) Write the date of the check on the Date line. (3) Write to whom the check is to be paid on the To line. (4) Record the purpose of the check on the For line. (5) Write the amount of the check after the words *Amt. This Check*. (6) Calculate the new checking balance and record it in the amount column on the last line of the stub.
3. (1) Write the date. (2) Write to whom the check is to be paid following the words *Pay to the order of*. (3) Write the amount in figures following the dollar sign. (4) Write the amount in words on the line with the word *Dollars*. (5) Write the purpose of the check on the line labeled For. (6) Sign the check.

Chapter 5, Page 128

1. (1) A service charge may not have been recorded in the depositor's business records. (2) Outstanding deposits may be recorded in the depositor's records but not on a bank statement. (3) Outstanding checks may be recorded in the depositor's records but not on a bank statement. (4) A depositor may have made a math or recording error.
2. An outstanding check.

Chapter 5, Page 133

1. (1) The check appears to be altered. (2) The signature on the check does not match the signature on the signature card. (3) The amounts written in figures and in words do not agree. (4) The check is postdated. (5) The person who wrote the check has stopped payment on it. (6) The account of the person who wrote the check has insufficient funds to pay the check.
2. Cash.
3. Cash.

Chapter 5, Page 137

1. For making small cash payments.
2. The check issued to replenish petty cash is a credit to Cash and does not affect Petty Cash.

Chapter 6, Page 155

1. Name of the business, name of report, and date of report.
2. All general ledger accounts are listed in the Trial Balance columns of a work sheet, even if some accounts do not have balances.

Chapter 6, Page 161

1. An expense should be reported in the same fiscal period that it is used to produce revenue.
2. (1) What is the balance of the account? (2) What should the balance be for this account? (3) What must be done to correct the account balance? (4) What adjustment is made?

Chapter 6, Page 166

1. Asset, liability, and owner's equity accounts.
2. Revenue and expense accounts.
3. Balance Sheet Credit column.
4. Balance Sheet Debit column.

Chapter 6, Page 170

1. Subtract the smaller total from the larger total to find the difference.
2. The difference between two column totals can be divided evenly by 9.
3. A slide.

Chapter 7, Page 186

1. Heading, revenue, expenses, and net income or net loss.
2. Total Expenses *divided by* Total Sales *equals* Total Expenses Component Percentage.
3. Net Income *divided by* Total Sales *equals* Net Income Component Percentage.

Chapter 7, Page 192

1. Heading, assets, liabilities, and owner's equity.
2. Capital Account Balance *plus* Net Income *minus* Drawing Account Balance *equals* Current Capital.

Chapter 8, Page 205

1. To update general ledger accounts at the end of a fiscal period.
2. Adjustments column of the work sheet.
3. Supplies Expense and Insurance Expense.

Chapter 8, Page 212

1. Beginning balances.
2. Changes in the owner's capital for a single fiscal period.
3. (1) An entry to close income statement accounts with credit balances. (2) An entry to close income statement accounts with debit balances. (3) An entry to record net income or net loss and close the income summary account. (4) An entry to close the owner's drawing account.

Chapter 8, Page 219

1. To assure a reader that a balance has not been omitted.
2. Only those with balances (permanent accounts).
3. Because they are closed and have zero balances.

Chapter 9, Page 241

1. Purchases of merchandise on account.
2. Frequently occurring transactions.
3. Because the same two accounts are always affected by purchase on account transactions.
4. Time is saved because using special amount columns eliminates writing an account title in the Account Title column.

Chapter 9, Page 247

1. To encourage early payment.
2. Cash payment transactions that do not occur often.
3. A business purchases merchandise to sell but buys supplies for use in the business. Supplies are not intended for sale.
4. Two ten means 2% of the invoice amount may be deducted if the invoice is paid within 10 days of the invoice date. Net thirty means that the total invoice amount must be paid within 30 days.

Chapter 9, Page 253

1. The titles of the accounts for which the petty cash fund was used.
2. The balance is usually a debit because the petty cash fund is more likely to be short than over.
3. (1) Rule a single line across all amount columns. (2) Write the date in the Date column. (3) Write *Totals* in the Account Title column. (4) Write each column total below the single line. (5) Rule a double line across all amount columns.

Chapter 9, Page 258

1. General journal.
2. To note that the invoice is for store supplies and not for purchases, ensuring that no mistake is made.
3. Because the single credit amount is posted to two accounts.
4. After each general journal entry is recorded.
5. A business can track the amount of purchases returns and allowances in a fiscal period if a separate account is used.
6. A purchases return is credit allowed for the purchase price of returned merchandise. A purchases allowance is credit allowed for part of the purchase price of merchandise that is not returned.
7. When the customer wants to record the transaction immediately, without waiting for written confirmation from the vendor.

Chapter 10, Page 275

1. A merchandising business sells merchandise; a service business sells services.
2. As a percentage of sales.
3. The amount of sales tax collected is a business liability until paid to the government.
4. Accounts Receivable.

Chapter 10, Page 284

1. The POS system produces a receipt that contains detailed information about the sale, including the merchandise's description and price. The cash register receipt does not include such detailed information.
2. A batch report can be detailed, showing each credit card sale, or it can provide a summary of the number and total of sales by credit card type.
3. The funds are transferred among the banks issuing the credit cards.

Chapter 10, Page 287

1. A sales return is credit allowed a customer for the sales price of returned merchandise; a sales allowance is credit allowed a customer for part of the sales price of merchandise that is not returned.
2. Credit memorandum.
3. Sales Returns and Allowances and Sales Tax Payable are debited; Accounts Receivable is credited.
4. To provide better information to quickly identify if the amount of sales returns and allowances is greater than expected.

Chapter 11, Page 306

1. A controlling account summarizes all accounts in a subsidiary ledger. The balance of a controlling account equals the total of all account balances in its related subsidiary ledger.
2. Accounts Payable Debit column.

Chapter 11, Page 314

1. Customer accounts listed in the Accounts Receivable Debit column.
2. Accounts Receivable Credit column.
3. All customer accounts that have balances.

Chapter 11, Page 319

1. Amounts in the Debit and Credit columns.
2. (1) Write the date in the Date column of the account. (2) Write the journal page number in the Post. Ref. column of the account. (3) Write the amount in the Debit or Credit column of the account. (4) Calculate and write the new account balance in the Balance Debit or Balance Credit column of the account. (5) Write the general ledger account number in the Post. Ref. column of the journal.

Chapter 11, Page 326

1. Each special amount column.
2. (1) Sales journal, (2) purchases journal, (3) general journal, (4) cash receipts journal, (5) cash payments journal.

Chapter 11, Page 329

1. Memorandum.
2. It does not affect the general ledger accounts.
3. Only a reference to the subsidiary ledger account is entered in the Post. Ref. column of the general journal.

Chapter 12, Page 344

1. The total amount earned by all employees for a pay period.
2. 3½ hours.
3. Overtime hours × the overtime rate.
4. \$506 (40 × \$11.00 + 4 × \$16.50).

Chapter 12, Page 350

1. Form W-4, Employee's Withholding Allowance Certificate.
2. Employee marital status and number of withholding allowances.
3. Both the employee and the employer.

Chapter 12, Page 355

1. The payroll register summarizes the payroll for one pay period and shows total earnings, payroll withholdings, and net pay of all employees.
2. By subtracting total deductions from total earnings.
3. Because a business must send a quarterly report to federal and state governments showing employee taxable earnings and taxes withheld from employee earnings.

Chapter 12, Page 358

1. To help protect and control payroll payments.
2. The payroll register.
3. Individual checks are not written and do not have to be distributed.

Chapter 13, Page 372

1. Salary Expense.
2. Employee Income Tax Payable.
3. Social Security Tax Payable.
4. Medicare Tax Payable.

Chapter 13, Page 377

1. Social security: 6.2% of earnings up to a maximum of $87,000.00 in each calendar year; Medicare: 1.45% of total employee earnings; federal unemployment: 0.8% on the first $7,000.00 earned by each employee; state unemployment: 5.4% on the first $7,000.00 earned by each employee.
2. The first $7,000.00.

Chapter 13, Page 382

1. By January 31.
2. Federal income tax, social security tax, and Medicare tax.

Chapter 13, Page 389

1. By the 15th day of the following month.
2. For paying payroll taxes and for paying federal unemployment tax.

Chapter 14, Page 408

1. Stockholders' Equity.
2. One account called Capital Stock.
3. Retained Earnings.
4. The board of directors declares a dividend.

Chapter 14, Page 414

1. Supplies—Office and Supplies Expense—Office.
2. Prepaid Insurance and Insurance Expense.

Chapter 14, Page 418

1. In the same order they appear in the general ledger.
2. Merchandise Inventory and Income Summary.
3. Debit Income Summary and credit Merchandise Inventory.
4. The Income Summary account is used to adjust the Merchandise Inventory account at the end of a fiscal period.

Chapter 14, Page 422

1. The loss is considered a regular expense of doing business. Revenue was earned when the sale was made. Failing to collect an account does not cancel the sale.
2. At the end of the fiscal period.
3. (1) Report a balance sheet amount for Accounts Receivable that reflects the amount the business expects to collect in the future. (2) Recognize the expense of uncollectible accounts in the same period in which the related revenue is recorded.
4. It reduces its related asset account, Accounts Receivable.
5. The difference between the balance of Accounts Receivable and its contra account, Allowance for Uncollectible Accounts.

Chapter 14, Page 426

1. Current assets and plant assets.
2. Original cost; estimated salvage value; estimated useful life.

Chapter 14, Page 436

1. Income Statement Debit or Credit column.
2. Balance Sheet Debit.
3. Trial balance amounts after adjustments are extended to the Adjusted Trial Balance columns, and the Adjusted Trial Balance columns are proved before extending amounts to the Income Statement and Balance Sheet columns.

Chapter 15, Page 454

1. The cost of merchandise sold section
2. Beginning merchandise inventory, *plus* purchases, *equals* total cost of merchandise available for sale, *less* ending merchandise inventory, *equals* cost of merchandise sold.
3. By comparing the amount calculated on the income statement with the amount on the work sheet.

Chapter 15, Page 460

1. (1) Cost of merchandise sold, (2) gross profit on sales, (3) total expenses, and (4) net income.
2. By making comparisons with prior fiscal periods as well as with industry standards that are published by industry organizations.
3. Net loss.

Chapter 15, Page 463

1. The changes in a corporation's ownership for a fiscal period.
2. Capital stock and retained earnings.
3. In the Capital Stock general ledger account.
4. In the Balance Sheet Credit column of a work sheet.

5. As a dividend.
6. In the Balance Sheet Debit column of a work sheet.

Chapter 15, Page 471

1. Current and plant assets.
2. (1) The balance of the asset account, (2) the balance of the asset's contra account, and (3) book value.
3. Mortgage payable.
4. From the statement of stockholders' equity.
5. Schedule of accounts payable and schedule of accounts receivable.

Chapter 16, Page 486

1. Because the heading *Adjusting Entries* is recorded in the Account Title column to explain all of the adjusting entries that follow.
2. Adjusting entry for merchandising inventory.
3. Federal Income Tax Payable.

Chapter 16, Page 493

1. Income Statement and Balance Sheet columns of the work sheet and the distribution of net income statement.
2. Income Summary.

Chapter 16, Page 498

1. General ledger accounts with balances.
2. To prove the equality of debits and credits in the general ledger.
3. In the same order as they appear in the general ledger.

GLOSSARY

A

Account a record summarizing all the information pertaining to a single item in the accounting equation. (p. 10)

Account balance the amount in an account. (p. 10)

Account number the number assigned to an account. (p. 92)

Account title the name given to an account. (p. 10)

Accounting planning, recording, analyzing, and interpreting financial information. (p. 6)

Accounting cycle the series of accounting activities included in recording financial information for a fiscal period. (p. 217)

Accounting equation an equation showing the relationship among assets, liabilities, and owner's equity. (p. 8)

Accounting period *see* fiscal period

Accounting records organized summaries of a business's financial activities. (p. 6)

Accounting system a planned process for providing financial information that will be useful to management. (p. 6)

Accounts payable ledger a subsidiary ledger containing only accounts for vendors from whom items are purchased or bought on account. (p. 298)

Accounts receivable ledger a subsidiary ledger containing only accounts for charge customers. (p. 298)

Accumulated depreciation the total amount of depreciation expense that has been recorded since the purchase of a plant asset. (p. 424)

Adjusting entries journal entries recorded to update general ledger accounts at the end of a fiscal period. (p. 202)

Adjustments changes recorded on a work sheet to update general ledger accounts at the end of a fiscal period. (p. 157)

Allowance method of recording losses from uncollectible accounts crediting the estimated value of uncollectible accounts to a contra account. (p. 419)

Asset anything of value that is owned. (p. 8)

B

Bad debts *see* uncollectible accounts

Balance sheet a financial statement that reports assets, liabilities, and owner's equity on a specific date. (p. 162)

Bank statement a report of deposits, withdrawals, and bank balances sent to a depositor by a bank. (p. 124)

Batch report a report of credit card sales produced by a point-of-sale terminal. (p. 278)

Batching out the process of preparing a batch report of credit card sales from a point-of-sale terminal. (p. 278)

Blank endorsement an endorsement consisting only of the endorser's signature. (p. 120)

Board of directors a group of persons elected by the stockholders to manage a corporation. (p. 406)

Book value the difference between an asset's account balance and its related contra account balance. (p. 419)

Book value of a plant asset the original cost of a plant asset minus accumulated depreciation. (p. 424)

Book value of accounts receivable the difference between the balance of Accounts Receivable and its contra account, Allowance for Uncollectible Accounts. (p. 419)

Business ethics the use of ethics in making business decisions. (p. 8)

C

Capital the account used to summarize the owner's equity in a business. (p. 10)

Capital stock total shares of ownership in a corporation. (p. 234)

Cash discount a deduction from the invoice amount, allowed by a vendor to encourage early payment. (p. 242)

Cash over a petty cash on hand amount that is more than a recorded amount. (p. 248)

Cash payments journal a special journal used to record only cash payment transactions. (p. 242)

Cash receipts journal a special journal used to record only cash receipt transactions. (p. 278)

Cash sale a sale in which cash is received for the total amount of the sale at the time of the transaction. (p. 276)

Cash short a petty cash on hand amount that is less than a recorded amount. (p. 248)

Charge sale *see* sale on account

Chart of accounts a list of accounts used by a business. (p. 32)

Check a business form ordering a bank to pay cash from a bank account. (p. 58)

Checking account a bank account from which payments can be ordered by a depositor. (p. 119)

Closing entries journal entries used to prepare temporary accounts for a new fiscal period. (p. 206)

Code of conduct a statement that guides the ethical behavior of a company and its employees. (p. 118)

Component percentage the percentage relationship between one financial statement item and the total that includes that item. (p. 184)

Contra account an account that reduces a related account on a financial statement. (p. 245)

Controlling account an account in a general ledger that summarizes all accounts in a subsidiary ledger. (p. 298)

Corporation an organization with the legal rights of a person and which may be owned by many persons. (p. 234)

Correcting entry a journal entry made to correct an error in the ledger. (p. 108)

Cost of goods sold *see* cost of merchandise sold

Cost of merchandise the price a business pays for goods it purchases to sell. (p. 236)

Cost of merchandise sold the total original price of all merchandise sold during a fiscal period. (p. 450)

Credit an amount recorded on the right side of a T account. (p. 29)

Credit card sale a sale in which a credit card is used for the total amount of the sale at the time of the transaction. (p. 276)

Credit memorandum a form prepared by the vendor showing the amount deducted for returns and allowances. (p. 285)

Current assets cash and other assets expected to be exchanged for cash or consumed within a year. (p. 423)

Current liabilities liabilities due within a short time, usually within a year. (p. 467)

Customer a person or business to whom merchandise or services are sold. (p. 270)

D

Debit an amount recorded on the left side of a T account. (p. 29)

Debit card a bank card that automatically deducts the amount of the purchase from the checking account of the cardholder. (p. 132)

Debit memorandum a form prepared by the customer showing the price deduction taken by the customer for returns and allowances. (p. 256)

Declaring a dividend action by a board of directors to distribute corporate earnings to stockholders. (p. 406)

Depreciation expense the portion of a plant asset's cost that is transferred to an expense account in each fiscal period during a plant asset's useful life. (p. 423)

Dishonored check a check that a bank refuses to pay. (p. 129)

Dividends earnings distributed to stockholders. (p. 405)

Double-entry accounting the recording of debit and credit parts of a transaction. (p. 57)

Doubtful accounts *see* uncollectible accounts

E

Earnings per share the amount of net income after federal income tax belonging to a single share of stock. (p. 459)

Electronic funds transfer a computerized cash payments system that transfers funds without the use of checks, currency, or other paper documents. (p. 131)

Employee earnings record a business form used to record details affecting payments made to an employee. (p. 353)

Endorsement a signature or stamp on the back of a check transferring ownership. (p. 120)

Endorsement in full *see* special endorsement

Entry information for each transaction recorded in a journal. (p. 57)

Equities financial rights to the assets of a business. (p. 8)

Estimated salvage value the amount an owner expects to receive when a plant asset is removed from use. (p. 423)

Ethics the principles of right and wrong that guide an individual in making decisions. (p. 8)

Exhibit *see* supporting schedule

Expense a decrease in owner's equity resulting from the operation of a business. (p. 15)

F

Federal unemployment tax a federal tax used for state and federal administrative expenses of the unemployment program. (p. 375)

File maintenance the procedure for arranging accounts in a general ledger, assigning account numbers, and keeping records current. (p. 93)

Financial ratio a comparison between two items of financial information. (p. 459)

Financial statements financial reports that summarize the financial conditions and operations of a business. (p. 6)

Fiscal period the length of time for which a business summarizes and reports financial information. (p. 152)

G

General amount column a journal amount column that is not headed with an account title. (p. 57)

General ledger a ledger that contains all accounts needed to prepare financial statements. (p. 92)

Gross earnings *see* total earnings

Gross pay *see* total earnings

Gross profit on sales the revenue remaining after cost of merchandise sold has been deducted. (p. 452)

I

Income statement a financial statement showing the revenue and expenses for a fiscal period. (p. 163)

Inventory *see* merchandise inventory

Invoice a form describing the goods or services sold, the quantity, and the price. (p. 58)

J

Journal a form for recording transactions in chronological order. (p. 56)

Journalizing recording transactions in a journal. (p. 56)

L

Ledger a group of accounts. (p. 92)

Liability an amount owed by a business. (p. 8)

List price the retail price listed in a catalog or on an Internet site. (p. 244)

Long-term liabilities liabilities owed for more than a year. (p. 467)

Lookback period the 12-month period that ends on June 30th of the prior year. (p. 383)

M

Markup the amount added to the cost of merchandise to establish the selling price. (p. 236)

Medicare tax a federal tax paid for hospital insurance. (p. 349)

Memorandum a form on which a brief message is written describing a transaction. (p. 59)

Merchandise goods that a merchandising business purchases to sell. (p. 234)

Merchandise inventory the amount of goods on hand for sale to customers. (p. 415)

Merchandising business a business that purchases and sells goods. (p. 234)

N

Net income the difference between total revenue and total expenses when total revenue is greater. (p. 164)

Net loss the difference between total revenue and total expenses when total expenses are greater. (p. 165)

Net pay the total earnings paid to an employee after payroll taxes and other deductions. (p. 352)

Net sales total sales less sales discount and sales returns and allowances. (p. 449)

Nominal account *see* temporary accounts

Normal balance the side of the account that is increased. (p. 29)

O

Opening an account writing an account title and number on the heading of an account. (p. 94)

Owner's equity the amount remaining after the value of all liabilities is subtracted from the value of all assets. (p. 8)

P

Par value a value assigned to a share of stock and printed on the stock certificate. (p. 461)

Pay period the period covered by a salary payment. (p. 340)

Payroll the total amount earned by all employees for a pay period. (p. 340)

Payroll register a business form used to record payroll information. (p. 351)

Payroll taxes taxes based on the payroll of a business. (p. 345)

Permanent accounts accounts used to accumulate information from one fiscal period to the next. (p. 206)

Petty cash an amount of cash kept on hand and used for making small payments. (p. 134)

Petty cash slip a form showing proof of a petty cash payment. (p. 135)

Plant assets assets that will be used for a number of years in the operation of a business. (p. 423)

Point-of-sale (POS) terminal a computer used to collect, store, and report all the information of a sales transaction. (p. 276)

Post-closing trial balance a trial balance prepared after the closing entries are posted. (p. 216)

Postdated check a check with a future date on it. (p. 121)

Posting transferring information from a journal entry to a ledger account. (p. 96)

Price-earnings ratio the relationship between the market value per share and earnings per share of a stock. (p. 459)

Proprietorship a business owned by one person. (p. 6)

Proving cash determining that the amount of cash agrees with the accounting records. (p. 76)

Purchase invoice an invoice used as a source document for recording a purchase on account transaction. (p. 238)

Purchase on account a transaction in which the merchandise purchased is to be paid for later. (p. 236)

Purchases allowance credit allowed for part of the purchase price of merchandise that is not returned, resulting in a decrease in the customer's accounts payable. (p. 256)

Purchases discount a cash discount on purchases taken by a customer. (p. 242)

Purchases journal a special journal used to record only purchases of merchandise on account. (p. 237)

Purchases return credit allowed for the purchase price of returned merchandise, resulting in a decrease in the customer's accounts payable. (p. 256)

R

Real accounts *see* permanent accounts

Receipt a business form giving written acknowledgement for cash received. (p. 59)

Residual value *see* estimated salvage value

Restrictive endorsement an endorsement restricting further transfer of a check's ownership. (p. 120)

Retail merchandising business a merchandising business that sells to those who use or consume the goods. (p. 234)

Retained earnings an amount earned by a corporation and not yet distributed to stockholders. (p. 405)

Revenue an increase in owner's equity resulting from the operation of a business. (p. 14)

S

Salary the money paid for employee services. (p. 340)

Sale on account a sale for which cash will be received at a later date. (p. 14)

Sales allowance credit allowed a customer for part of the sales price of merchandise that is not returned, resulting in a decrease in the vendor's accounts receivable. (p. 285)

Sales discount a cash discount on sales. (p. 278)

Sales invoice an invoice used as a source document for recording a sale on account. (p. 58)

Sales journal a special journal used to record only sales of merchandise on account. (p. 272)

Sales return credit allowed a customer for the sales price of returned merchandise, resulting in a decrease in the vendor's accounts receivable. (p. 285)

Sales slip *see* sales invoice

Sales tax a tax on a sale of merchandise or services. (p. 270)

Salvage value *see* estimated salvage value

Schedule of accounts payable a listing of vendor accounts, account balances, and total amount due all vendors. (p. 305)

Schedule of accounts receivable a listing of customer accounts, account balances, and total amount due from all customers. (p. 313)

Scrap value *see* estimated salvage value

Service business a business that performs an activity for a fee. (p. 6)

Share of stock each unit of ownership in a corporation. (p. 234)

Social security tax a federal tax paid for old-age, survivors, and disability insurance. (p. 349)

Sole proprietorship *see* proprietorship

Source document a business paper from which information is obtained for a journal entry. (p. 57)

Special amount column a journal amount column headed with an account title. (p. 57)

Special endorsement an endorsement indicating a new owner of a check. (p. 120)

Special journal a journal used to record only one kind of transaction. (p. 235)

Stakeholders any persons or groups who will be affected by an action. (p. 181)

State unemployment tax a state tax used to pay benefits to unemployed workers. (p. 375)

Statement of stockholders' equity a financial statement that shows changes in a corporation's ownership for a fiscal period. (p. 461)

Stockholder an owner of one or more shares of a corporation. (p. 234)

Straight-line method of depreciation charging an equal amount of depreciation expense for a plant asset in each year of useful life. (p. 424)

Subsidiary ledger a ledger that is summarized in a single general ledger account. (p. 298)

Supplementary report *see* supporting schedule

Supporting schedule a report prepared to give details about an item on a principal financial statement. (p. 470)

T

T account an accounting device used to analyze transactions. (p. 29)

Tax base the maximum amount of earnings on which a tax is calculated. (p. 349)

Temporary accounts accounts used to accumulate information until it is transferred to the owner's capital account. (p. 206)

Terminal summary the report that summarizes the cash and credit card sales of a point-of-sale terminal. (p. 276)

Terms of sale an agreement between a buyer and a seller about payment for merchandise. (p. 238)

Total earnings the total pay due for a pay period before deductions. (p. 343)

Trade discount a reduction in the list price granted to customers. (p. 244)

Transaction a business activity that changes assets, liabilities, or owner's equity. (p. 10)

Trial balance a proof of the equality of debits and credits in a general ledger. (p. 154)

U

Uncollectible accounts accounts receivable that cannot be collected. (p. 419)

V

Vendor a business from which merchandise is purchased or supplies or other assets are bought. (p. 236)

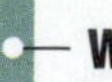

W

Wholesale merchandising business a business that buys and resells merchandise to retail merchandising businesses. (p. 234)

Withdrawals assets taken out of a business for the owner's personal use. (p. 16)

Withholding allowance a deduction from total earnings for each person legally supported by a taxpayer, including the employee. (p. 346)

Work sheet a columnar accounting form used to summarize the general ledger information needed to prepare financial statements. (p. 153)

F